W9-AYZ-829

COMMERCIAL AIR TRANSPORTATION

COMMERCIAL AIR TRANSPORTATION

By

JOHN H. FREDERICK, Ph.D.

PROFESSOR OF TRANSPORTATION AND
HEAD, DEPARTMENT OF BUSINESS ORGANIZATION
COLLEGE OF BUSINESS AND PUBLIC ADMINISTRATION
UNIVERSITY OF MARYLAND

FIFTH EDITION, 1961

RICHARD D. IRWIN, INC.
HOMEWOOD, ILLINOIS

FIFTH EDITION

Library of Congress Catalogue Card No. 61-10589

PRINTED IN THE UNITED STATES OF AMERICA

PREFACE

COMMERCIAL AIR TRANSPORTATION in the United States has arrived at its present state of development within a comparatively short period of time. Its development before World War II was so sudden that the public was hardly able to keep pace with it, or even to understand it, or to accept it fully as another means of getting from one place to another. During the war years, however, air transportation came into its own, and aeronautical progress took place at an unprecedented rate, so that at the close of hostilities we found ourselves probably fifty years further ahead in air transport techniques, in aeronautical knowledge, in the development of flying equipment and devices which could be adapted to commercial use, and in public acceptance of this new means of getting about the world than we would have been if the conflict had not taken place. This development continued at a somewhat less rapid pace for several years after the close of the war, but then came the transition to jet aircraft with consequent tremendous opportunities for expansion of commercial air transportation.

The American people, who can better afford air travel and air shipping than any other people in the world, are now using this means of transportation in large numbers; but the mass market for air travel and air shipping has barely been scratched. Because of time-saving speed, commercial air transportation has become invaluable from the standpoint of business, pleasure, and national defense. It is a young industry; yet it has made more rapid progress than has ever been made in the same period of time by any other agency of transportation. This, perhaps, is one reason why the literature on the business aspects of aviation has been somewhat limited.

The first edition of this book was published in January, 1942, in response to a demand from shippers and travelers by air, men and women in the air transportation industry or about to enter it, and students and teachers of transportation who felt the lack of study and teaching material on the commercial or business development side of this industry. Its purpose was to bring material together from many scattered sources and to analyze and interpret it so as to overcome this lack. A revised edition was published in 1946, when, with the close of hostilities, it seemed a fitting time again to examine the various aspects of commercial air transportation in order to take notice of many war-engendered developments and to bring the entire subject up to date. The third edition, published in 1951, was essentially a new book since earlier editions were entirely rewritten because of the many things influencing aeronautical development which took place after World War II. The fourth edition, published in 1955, keyed all discussions to the immediate postwar era. The commercial air transportation industry has made such strides, public interest in aviation has increased to such an extent, new uses for air transport have developed so rapidly, and the airlines have been faced with so many new problems that this fifth edition becomes necessary to present a picture of the more recent developments. Policies and regulations in this rapidly growing industry have now become somewhat solidified, so that they may be examined and certain predictions made as to future developments.

Since the appearance of the first edition, the author has been in constant contact with many people interested in developing air transportation, with various governmental regulatory agencies, and with numerous airlines, in a consulting or other capacity. Much of the firsthand information on various airline and regulatory problems thus gained is incorporated into this volume. It would, however, have been impossible to bring this material to the reader in its present form had it not been for the co-operation of many men and women in the air transportation industry, some of them former students, who have given unstintingly of their time in interviews and correspondence on various topics. It is impossible to mention each of these individually, but the author does want to express his appreciation to the airlines and others who so generously supplied illustrations. He also wishes to thank his fellow teachers who have made constructive suggestions to make this a more useful book for their purposes.

JOHN H. FREDERICK

UNIVERSITY OF MARYLAND
March, 1961

TABLE OF CONTENTS

LIST OF FIGURES

LIST OF TABLES

Chapter 1

TRANSPORT AIRCRAFT

In order to understand the steps, both technological and economic, by which air transportation has reached its present position of importance, it is necessary to review the historical development of flight.

Experiments with Lighter-than-Air Machines

Disregarding the crude attempts at human flight recorded in the early legends, histories, and literature of various peoples, the first successful experiment in air transportation took place on June 5, 1783. This was the earliest recorded modern balloon ascension, the result of experiments by the brothers Joseph and Etienne Montgolfier of France. The balloon was constructed of paper with a capacity of about 700 cubic feet. Filled with smoke and heated air, it rose to the height of 6,000 feet and traveled horizontally approximately 7,500 feet before it lost its buoyancy and sank to the ground. On November 21 of the same year, the first human ascent was made—man's first aerial voyage—when Jean-François Pilatre de Rozier and the Marquis D'Arlandes stayed aloft 23 minutes in a Montgolfier balloon.[1]

With a lifting element available, the problem now was to develop a thoroughly airtight fabric. This was important since it was becoming apparent that hydrogen would be a much more efficient lifting agent than the hot air and smoke "gas" of the Montgolfier brothers. Happily, just when the French Chemist J. A. C. Charles was experimenting with hydrogen, two brothers, A. J. and M. N. Robert discovered that it was possible to apply a coating of dissolved rubber to silk fabric and thereby secure an airtight covering. On August 20, 1783, such a balloon was filled with hydrogen and liberated. It rose to "a very great height, but because of too strong inflation it ruptured and the envelope fell to the ground."[2] In December, 1783, the chemist

[1] S. Paul Johnston, *Horizons Unlimited* (New York: Duell, Sloan and Pearce, 1941), pp. 38–41.

[2] *The Encyclopedia Americana*, Vol. 1, 1940, p. 180.

J. A. C. Charles, accompanied by one of the Roberts brothers, made an ascent from Paris which demonstrated the advantage of the hydrogen over the hot-air balloon; their flight lasted an hour and three quarters, and they traveled some 27 miles from the starting point.[3]

These flights greatly stimulated public and scientific interest in ballooning and aeronautics throughout Europe and particularly in France, where great rivalry sprang up between the Montgolfier and Charles, or "the heated air and the hydrogen, schools of ballooning."[4] Interest was also aroused in England, and in 1785 Jean Pierre Blanchard, a French aeronaut, and Dr. John Jeffries, a Boston physician who financed the project, made the first balloon flight across the English channel from Dover to a point near Calais. This trip is said to have carried the first air mail anywhere in the world.[5]

The first authenticated balloon ascent in America apparently was made at Baltimore in 1784, by Peter Carnes, who built a Montgolfier-type balloon. Before ascending, however, Carnes had a 13-year-old boy, Edward Warren, embark as a volunteer on a solo trip, so that it seems possible Warren was the first American to ascend into the air over this country.[6] A few years later, on January 9, 1793, Jean Pierre Blanchard began the first air voyage in America. Starting from Philadelphia in the presence of President George Washington and a large number of local citizens, Blanchard ascended in a hydrogen balloon, carrying a passport of introduction from Washington, which has since been considered the first air-borne letter in this country. The balloon reached a maximum altitude of 5,812 feet, traveled 15 miles in 46 minutes, and landed in the woods a little to the eastward of Woodbury, New Jersey.[7]

The first balloon constructed on anything like modern proportions was *The Great Balloon of Nassau* which, on its first ascension in 1836, was navigated from London to Weilburg, a distance of 500 miles. This balloon continued in active service for a total of some 35 years, figuring in many notable aeronautical events, "a record that has never been exceeded by any flying machine since."[8]

---

[3] S. Paul Johnston, *op. cit.*, p. 41.

[4] G. Lloyd Wilson and Leslie A. Bryan, *Air Transportation* (New York: Prentice-Hall, Inc., 1949), p. 8.

[5] *Ibid.*, p. 9.

[6] G. Lloyd Wilson and Leslie A. Bryan, *op. cit.*, p. 9.

[7] Carroll Frey, *The First Air Voyage in America* (Philadelphia: The Penn Mutual Life Insurance Co., 1933), p. 4.

[8] S. Paul Johnston, *op. cit.*, pp. 48–49.

Balloons were looked upon by many in the eighteenth and early nineteenth centuries as instruments of air navigation with almost limitless possibilities, but enthusiasts soon discovered that a craft depending solely upon the winds for its direction of flight was of no practical use in commerce. Balloons continued to be used, however, in limited ways for scientific investigation or upper air research, as new and adventurous sporting devices, as attractions at fairs and carnivals, and in World War I for observation and reconnaissance work.

The airship or dirigible was the logical technological development to follow the free balloon. This type of lighter-than-air craft contains two features not found in balloons—a rigid or semirigid structure, and motive power to give it maneuverability.[9] In 1884, Captain Charles Renard of the French War Department produced the first man-carrying airship that ever returned against the wind to its starting point, and "the first aerial vessel whose shape and dynamic adjustment even approximated the requirements of steady and swift navigation in a surrounding medium presenting various conditions of turbulence and calm."[10] The first gasoline-engine dirigible was built by a German inventor, Dr. Hans Wolfert, in 1896. His engine was about nine horsepower. Later, an Austrian inventor, David Schwartz, designed a rigid airship propelled by a benzine engine capable of attaining a speed of 17 miles per hour. The gas bag of this craft was enclosed in a thin casing of aluminum.

The greatest contributions to lighter-than-air construction and navigation were made by Captain (later Count) Ferdinand von Zeppelin. In 1900, he completed a pencil-shaped rigid airship 416 feet long, capable of attaining average speeds of 20 miles per hour. It was, however, not until 1910, after overcoming many difficulties and exhausting his financial resources, that he was able to produce his first passenger-carrying craft. "Zeppelins," as they were called, made numerous raids over England in World War I, thus proving their efficiency as long-range military weapons. In a three-year period (1910–1914), a subsidiary of the Zeppelin Company, Deutsche Luftschiffahrt Aktien-Gesellschaft, carried more than 35,000 passengers in what has been termed the first commercial common-carrier service by air transport.[11] In 1924, the United States received one of these

[9] G. Lloyd Wilson and Leslie A. Bryan, *op. cit.*, p. 12.

[10] *The Encyclopedia Americana*, *op. cit.*, p. 180.

[11] G. Lloyd Wilson and Leslie A. Bryan, *op. cit.*, p. 81.

German craft, the *Los Angeles*, which was used by the Navy for some eight years before being decommissioned. The *Graf Zeppelin* was flown on a commercial basis across the South Atlantic by the Germans for six years, completing 75 successful crossings, and in 1936, the *Hindenburg* made ten round trips over the North Atlantic before being destroyed by fire at Lakehurst, New Jersey, on May 6, 1937.

While Count von Zeppelin was constructing rigid-type airships (so-called because the external form is fixed and independent of internal gas pressure), Alberto Santos-Dumont, a Brazilian, fitted a light engine to a balloon of his own design and made successful flights. During the early 1900's Dumont built and flew 14 ships of various nonrigid and semirigid types.

In the United States, starting in 1911, the Goodyear Tire and Rubber Company of Akron, Ohio, became actively engaged in constructing and experimenting with lighter-than-air craft. In 1923, they acquired the North American patent rights of the German Zeppelin builders (Luftschiffbau-Zeppelin) and organized the Goodyear Zeppelin Corporation. This company built two large rigid airships for the Navy; the first, named the *Akron*, was delivered in 1932, and the second, the *Macon*, in 1933. Both these craft were lost in storms within a year or so after completion. The company has been more fortunate, however, with its smaller nonrigid airships, and for many years has maintained a fleet for both passenger-carrying and advertising purposes. The United States Navy has also made extensive use of the nonrigid airship, particularly for reconnaissance purposes off American coasts during World War II.[12]

Early Experiments with Heavier-than-Air Machines

In the eighteenth and nineteenth centuries, while the experiments with lighter-than-air craft were going on, similar efforts were being made with various types of machines heavier than air. The eighteenth century contributed scientific knowledge in the fields of aeronautics and aerodynamics, and progress accelerated in the nineteenth century, particularly after the discovery of steam power revealed the possibility of obtaining force enough to propel heavier-than-air craft. In 1810, Sir George Cayley, an English scientist, published a series of articles on aerial navigation in which he proposed that the surfaces (the wings of the airplane) could be made to support a given weight

[12] G. Lloyd Wilson and Leslie A. Bryan, *op. cit.*, p. 85; *The Encyclopedia Americana*, *op. cit.*, p. 181; S. Paul Johnston, *op. cit.*, pp. 73–132; P. W. Litchfield and Hugh Allen, *Why Has America No Rigid Airships?* (Cleveland: Corday and Gross, 1935).

(the weight of the entire machine) by the application of power to the resistance of air. "All successful airplanes have been constructed according to this principle."[13] In 1848, another Englishman, John Stringfellow, completed a model which was the first power-driven airplane to be flown in free flight. He was not able, however, to construct a full-sized airplane that could be flown successfully. The work of these experimenters was handicapped by the complex problems of aerodynamics and by the inability of inventors to produce engines of low weight per horsepower developed. A number of experiments followed, therefore, with gliders or engineless planes. The success of the gliding experiments carried on between 1889 and 1911—by Otto Lilenthal, a native of Pomerania, Percy S. Pilcher, an Englishman, and John J. Montgomery and Octave Chanute, Americans—developed valuable information "pertaining to the flying qualities of various types of planes and brought about a partial solution of the problems of stability."[14]

The last years of the nineteenth century and the first few years of the twentieth witnessed a race to construct and fly the first heavier-than-air, power-driven, man-carrying machine. Among those who actually built and tried such airplanes were Clement Ader, a French inventor, Sir Hiram Maxim, an Englishman, and Samuel Pierpont Langley, an American. The Ader plane was large enough to carry a man, but could not do more than make short hops along the ground. The Maxim plane, a huge affair for those times, measuring 50 feet across the wings and equipped with two 175-horsepower steam engines, proved a failure. The United States government financed Langley's construction of a tandem monoplane, but this crashed on its first launching. It remained, therefore, for the brothers Wilbur and Orville Wright to achieve finally the first powered flight of a heavier-than-air machine on December 17, 1903, at Kitty Hawk, North Carolina.[15] From this point on, the development of the airplane advanced at a phenomenal pace, with rapid strides being made in engine design, aerodynamics, and structures.

Progress after Kitty Hawk

Until about 1922, airplanes were built almost exclusively of wood, which had a high strength-weight ratio and was a natural and easy medium for experimental construction. Dr. Claude Dornier, in Ger-

---

[13] G. Lloyd Wilson and Leslie A. Bryan, *op. cit.*, p. 16.

[14] G. Lloyd Wilson and Leslie A. Bryan, *op. cit.*, pp. 18–20.

[15] Fred C. Kelly, *The Wright Brothers* (New York: Harcourt, Brace & Co., 1943).

many, was among the first to apply Duralumin to aircraft. American builders were slow to adopt metal construction, however, and it was not until 1922, when Anthony H. G. Fokker exhibited his welded steel fuselage in the United States, that metal construction became popular in this country. It was soon recognized that metal had the advantages of safety, high strength, and durability. Today both transport aircraft and smaller airplanes are made completely of aluminum alloy sheet and extruded sections.

Courtesy: Esso Export Corp. and the Smithsonian Institution

FIG. 1. The historic first flight at Kitty Hawk, N.C., on December 17, 1903. Orville Wright is the pilot while Wilbur Wright looks on. On that day four flights were made in all, two by Orville and two by Wilbur. The final one, by Wilbur, lasted for 59 seconds.

With the advent of metal construction came a new type of structure known as "semimonocuque," which has replaced the early "stick and wire" construction. In this type of structure, there is little framework other than that necessary to keep the shape, the stresses being taken by the skin or covering, reinforced by frames and stringers. The increased knowledge of the resistance of structural members exposed to the wind caused designers to "fair in" all exposed frameworks and eventually to develop cantilever wings, whose internal structure is such as to make them self-supporting without the aid of external bracing.[16]

After the Wright brothers demonstrated the practicability of heavier-than-air machines by their flights in 1903, interest in air trans-

[16] *The Encyclopedia Americana, op. cit.*, p. 182.

portation grew slowly until after 1908. Numerous types of aircraft were constructed and principles of controlled flight developed. At the start of World War I, the potentialities of the airplane as a military instrument became quickly apparent, and enormous building operations were undertaken by the belligerent governments and by private manufacturers both in this country and abroad. The development of aviation during the war years brought about improvements in airplane design and construction which otherwise would have taken many years to achieve, and at the same time broadened experience and interest in aviation.[17]

After the close of World War I, transport aircraft progressed rapidly. Small, single-engined biplanes which contained from four to ten wicker chairs, had a cruising speed of 90 miles per hour, and cost less than $10,000, soon developed into large monoplanes of two or four engines—carrying from 40 to 90 passengers plus crew, weighing up to nearly 100 tons gross, and costing from $700,000 to $1,600,000 each. The increase in size was gradual, however, and depended on parallel technical developments. Each forward step had to be based on the successful performance of a preceding one, and a successful experimental and design venture was necessary in order to obtain the new working capital for financing expansion in manufacture.

World War II telescoped into the period of a few years aircraft technical developments which normally would have taken ten. Advances ranged from a demonstration that increased wing loadings and increased landing speeds (resulting from increased gross weights for a particular type of plane) could be satisfactorily accepted when maneuverability and controllability characteristics were good; to the development of vinylite substitutes that were superior to the linoleum and rubber previously used for interior wear surfaces. There was, in fact, no part of the airplane—down to the most minute item of equipment or furnishings—that did not benefit significantly from wartime advances.

An especially important development of this period was that of practical rotary wing flight in the form of the helicopter.[18] The helicopter is the only aircraft able to gain quick and ready access to any

[17] For general discussions of the early history of air transportation, see E. P. Warner, *The Early History of Air Transportation* (Northfield, Vt.: Norwich University, 1938); E. E. Freudenthal, *The Aviation Business* (New York: The Vanguard Press, 1940); H. L. Smith, *Airways* (New York: Alfred A. Knopf, Inc., 1942).

[18] The world's first notably successful helicopter was developed by Igor Sikorsky and flown by him in 1940. Devon Francis, *The Story of the Helicopter* (New York: Coward-McCann, Inc., 1946), p. 3.

Courtesy: Braniff International Airways, Inc.

FIG. 2. The Douglas Aircraft Co. DC-3. This was the "standard plane" of the airlines until after the close of World War II. Capacity: 21 passengers and a crew of three. Speed: between 150 and 180 miles per hour. It has been called the "workhorse of air transportation" and is still in use by some airlines.

site regardless of terrain, even if the landings are at considerable altitudes. As a commercial vehicle, the helicopter's unique flying abilities have established it as a regular means of performing many functions more quickly and economically than any other medium. The Armed Forces of this country have also used helicopters to provide a degree of mobility not otherwise obtainable. Extensive operations, both military and commercial, have resulted in tremendous technical and operational advances in this type of aircraft in the last few years and have developed a substantial industry in their manufacture.

Changes in Equipment

Because of strict maintenance, commercial aircraft never really wear out. They are, however, made obsolete by newer designs which have both higher speed and useful load or are more economical to operate or offer greater passenger comfort. Several major changes have been made in air transport equipment during the last 30 years:

1. In 1931 and 1932, the old Ford and Fokker trimotored airplanes were displaced by the 18-passenger B-18 twin-engine Curtiss

Courtesy: Trans World Airlines, Inc.

FIG. 3. The Boeing 307. This was the largest type of commercial plane used for service in the United States until early in 1946. The four 1,100 horsepower engines give a cruising speed of almost 225 miles per hour. This plane carried 38 passengers and a crew of five. This TWA "Stratoliner" is in front of the Kansas City, Missouri, airport terminal, which emphasizes its size.

"Condor"; a year later these slow aircraft were displaced by the faster 15-passenger T-32 twin-engine "Condor."

2. In 1934 and 1935, the twin-engine "Condor" airplanes began to give way to the faster and more comfortable Douglas DC-2, the first twin-engine airplane really to have practical single-engine performance.

3. In 1936 and 1937, most of the airlines began dropping the DC-2 in favor of the Douglas DC-3 (Fig. 2). Even before the outbreak of World War II, the DC-3 was regarded as somewhat obsolete in design, because airplanes of larger size and substantially greater speed were being developed, thus giving lower cost of operation per passenger-seat-mile. The DC-3 was, however, used by nearly all airlines during the war because manufacturers were producing fighter and bomber planes rather than commercial models. During these years one type of four-engine airplane also was in use, the Boeing 307 (Fig. 3); but by the war's outbreak this had been put into use by only two airlines.

4. In 1945 and 1946, with the ending of World War II, the airlines were able to supplement their DC-3's with a considerable num-

ber of DC-4 aircraft obtained from the armed services and converted for commercial use (Fig. 4). This was a period in which military airplanes in use at the close of hostilities were adapted for commercial transport service until newer and more modern ones, incorporating the latest technical lessons of the war, became available. Until this time, the domestic airlines had used only two or three types of airplane (predominantly the Douglas DC-3) for all purposes. Immediately after the war, however, specially designed aircraft were developed, each suitable for the task it was to perform and the operating conditions which the individual airlines faced.

Courtesy: Douglas Aircraft Co., Inc.

FIG. 4. The DC or Douglas Commercial group including the DC-7, DC-6, DC-4, and the Super DC-3 prototype. The commercial version Super DC-3 was not produced in any quantity, and the DC-4, DC-6A (cargo version of the DC-6), DC-6B, and DC-7 are out of production although still in use.

5. In 1947–49, the airlines began to take delivery of four-engine airplanes—the Constellation ("Connie"), the DC-6, and the Boeing Stratocruiser; and of two-engine airplanes—the Consolidated Vultee ("Convair") and the Martin 2–0–2 (Figs. 5–6). During these years, several airlines retired their DC-3 and DC-4 aircraft from passenger service and began to dispose of the DC-3 even as a cargo carrier. The first airline to make this changeover was American Airlines, which on April 1, 1949, retired all its DC-3's and DC-4's from passenger service, leaving only DC-6's and Convairs. During that same

Courtesy: Northwest Airlines

FIG. 5. The Boeing Stratocruiser. This four-engine, two-deck aircraft is designed to cruise at 300 to 340 miles an hour. Completely altitude conditioned, it will fly at 15,000 to 25,000 feet altitude, with a maximum range of 4,600 miles. Seventy-five passengers and a crew of five is normal capacity, although different airlines provide varying accommodations.

year, American Airlines sold all its DC-3's. The DC-3 aircraft owned by the trunk airlines were generally sold to feeder or local service airlines, to corporations for use as private airplanes, or were disposed of in the export market. In 1949, the Douglas Aircraft Co. introduced an improved version of the DC-3 known as the "Super DC-3," but this airplane was used by only one airline. The Civil Aeronautics Administration originally set December 30, 1950, as the date the DC-3 should be retired from scheduled air carrier operation, but this date was later rescinded and the airlines using this airplane were granted an indefinite extension of time.

6. In 1950–54, the increased competition between airlines demanded more speed, seat capacities, and luxury features, and these features were soon built into various aircraft. The DC-6B (Fig. 7) and DC-7 (Fig. 4) were introduced by the Douglas Aircraft Co. The improved Super Constellation (L-1049) (Fig. 8) was put into service in 1953 by Lockheed Aircraft Corporation. In the twin-engine

Courtesy: American Airlines

FIG. 6. Consolidated Vultee—Convair-Liner (240) known as the "Convair." This aircraft carries 40 passengers and a crew of from three to four at a cruising speed of about 270 miles per hour.

field, the Glenn L. Martin Co. produced their 4–0–4 (Fig. 9) and the Consolidated Vultee Aircraft Corporation entered the market with the Convair-340. The Douglas DC-7 began operation the latter part of 1953, and in 1954 Lockheed introduced a version of the Con-

Courtesy: United Air Lines

FIG. 7. The Douglas DC-6B, which cruises at 315 miles per hour with a range of about 3,700 miles.

Courtesy: Trans World Airlines

FIG. 8. The Lockheed Super Constellation (L-1049). The "Connie," as the earlier models of this airplane were called, was the first large postwar transport to be put into actual operation on an airline. This 10,800 horsepower model carries 64 passengers at speeds of more than 300 miles an hour.

stellation equipped with the same type engine as the DC-7, the Wright Turbo Compound. Both of these airplanes operated economically at a cruising speed of about 365 miles per hour, completing coast-to-coast flights in about eight hours. These models were the last of the large transport aircraft powered with piston engines. Those of the future will be powered with turbo-prop and turbo-jet engines.[19]

In 1954, Capital Airlines placed an order with Vickers-Armstrong of England for 60 Vickers Viscount turbo-prop aircraft (Fig. 10) for delivery in 1955 and 1956. This made Capital Airlines the first

Courtesy: Eastern Air Lines

FIG. 9. The Martin 4–0–4, one of the fastest of twin-engine transports, with a normal cruising speed of 270 miles per hour and a maximum speed of 312 miles per hour. This model, known as "The Silver Falcon," carries 40 passengers.

United States carrier to operate foreign-built equipment as well as the first to operate turbo-prop-powered aircraft. Previously, Pan American World Airways ordered several British de Havilland Comet III's for international operation, but their delivery dates were to be somewhat later.[20]

[19] For a review of aircraft design developments and a broad guide to the plans which the designers of tomorrow's transports may follow, see the 16th Annual Wright Brothers' Lecture delivered by William Littlewood, excerpts from which appear in *Aviation Week*, February 9 and 16, 1953.

[20] In this connection, it is interesting to note that the Aircraft Industries Association estimates that in 1953, 90 per cent of all commercial aircraft flying in the world had been produced in the United States.

Courtesy: Capital Airlines

FIG. 10. Vickers-Armstrong, Ltd., Viscount. The first turbo-prop aircraft to be purchased by a United States airline.

Courtesy: British Overseas Airways Corp.

FIG. 11. The De Havilland Comet I. This was the first pure-jet aircraft to be placed in regular commercial service. It was capable of cruising up to 490 miles an hour with a capacity pay load, as a 36 seater, of 12,000 pounds. BOAC began operating these aircraft in 1952. None are now in service.

7. The first large-scale firm contracts for commercial jet aircraft were those placed by Pan American World Airways in 1955. Firm orders for 45 turbo-jets were divided between the Boeing Airplane Co. and Douglas Aircraft Co. The first delivery of the Boeing 707 (Fig. 12) was made in 1958, and the first trans-Atlantic flight by

Courtesy: Boeing Airplane Co.

FIG. 12. The Boeing 707, the first jet commercial-type aircraft to be built in the United States. Cruising speed 591 miles per hour. Cruising altitude 25,000–40,000 feet.

Pan American World Airways was made in October, 1958. American Airlines was the first domestic carrier to fly the turbo-jet, also the Boeing 707, starting service between New York and Los Angeles in March, 1959. Deliveries of the Douglas DC-8 began the middle of 1959.

Factors Affecting Modernization

A number of factors have entered into the rapid and continuous modernization of airline equipment. The prospect of lower unit operating costs in terms of costs per seat-mile—despite higher costs per airplane-mile in the use of the larger and newer equipment—undoubtedly exerted a major influence. Traffic demands which the airlines could not meet without additional capacity, and the optimistic belief after World War II that still greater capacity would be required, also exerted powerful pressures. Yet, important as these and other noncompetitive factors may have been, the history of equipment purchases leaves little doubt that the stimulus of competition has been the foremost factor influencing airline management in its constant search for new equipment. Thus, new equipment has usually been placed in operation first on the most competitive routes. The use of more modern aircraft by one company on such a route has been followed by a scramble on the part of competitors to introduce comparable or more advanced types; conversely, the introduction of new equipment has generally been the slowest in services where competition was not very great. Although it is probable that the largest carriers would have led the way in equipment advances even without the stimulus of competition, it is significant that these carriers operate in perhaps the most highly competitive of the major markets. It is again significant that the smaller carriers, which have trailed in the acquisition of new property, have promptly developed equipment programs when changes in route structures have placed them in competitive situations with carriers utilizing more modern equipment.[21]

As might be expected, the greatest surge in equipment purchases has come during times of optimism when there has been the prospect

---

[21] The purchase of Vickers-Viscount aircraft by Capital Airlines illustrates this situation. These foreign-built aircraft were purchased to meet the stiff competition offered by the "Big Four"—American, United, Trans World and Eastern airlines—all of which paralleled Capital to some extent and used Douglas DC-7's, Lockheed Super-Constellations, Convairs, and Martin 4–0–4's. Buying any of these aircraft would simply have matched the competitive lines. By cruising the Viscount at 335 miles per hour and introducing the novelty and improved comfort of turbo-prop operation, Capital hoped to increase its share of the traffic.

of greater passenger demand, high load factors, and over-all expansion of the industry. On the other hand, the acquisition of new equipment has not been halted by adverse economic conditions or by pessimism over the industry's prospects in the foreseeable future. What might be termed "luxury" equipment has been introduced under conditions that virtually eliminate a conclusion that economic considerations, other than competitive ones, warranted or prompted the action. It seems clear that competition, especially in the postwar period, has been sufficiently widespread and intense to play a major role in the continuous effort of each trunk-line carrier to obtain equipment superior to that of its competitors, and that the impetus afforded by this competition has largely accounted for there being made available to the public new equipment designed for the utmost in speed, comfort, and safety at the lowest possible operating cost.[22]

Motive Power[23]

Air transportation is a "service" business. Transportation is its product. Airlines must sell their product at a price the public is willing to pay. Their cost of production must be lower than their sales prices or their rates and fares, or else they will not be long in business, unless their losses can be made up in some manner such as subsidies (see Chapter 12). Transport aircraft are the productive machines of the airlines, and if the lines are to have production costs lower than sales prices, they must have efficient productive machines. These are the economic factors to be considered when a new commercial airplane is developed.

Throughout the history of air transportation, aircraft have been designed around their power plants, or engines. Over the years there has been revolutionary progress in aircraft design, but ever since the construction of the Wright brothers' machine, the performance limits of the airplane have always been established by the power plant. This is true today and will probably continue to be so.

Prior to 1950, the basic principle of the power plant developed in aircraft has been the same as the engines in automobiles, despite

---

[22] *The Role of Competition in Commercial Air Transportation, Select Committee on Small Business United States Senate* (82d Cong., 2d sess.) (1952), pp. 12–13.

[23] See a talk delivered by C. R. Smith, "The Turbine Engine and Air Transportation," and a discussion of same by Arthur D. Lewis before the Syracuse Transportation Conference, April 9, 1953. See also *The Economic Implications of the Introduction into Service of Long-Range Jet Aircraft*, International Civil Aviation Organization, Doc. 7894–C/907, 1958, pp. 13–17; "Implications of the Adoption of Commercial Jet Aircraft," a symposium edited by John H. Frederick, *Journal of Air Law and Commerce*, Spring, 1956.

their radical difference in shape; both types are piston engines. The United States has led the world in the continued development of this type of power plant. It is probable, however, that we will soon have reached the end of reasonable capacity for developing piston engines. There has been a continuing need for higher powers, both in military and civil fields, for airplanes are larger, and we expect superior performance from them. A new type of power plant, the turbine, has therefore been developed, offering better prospects for the higher powers required. That does not mean, however, that piston engines will no longer be operated. For many years after the introduction of new power plants, the majority of flights will continue to operate with the conventional type of airplane, for the piston engine is relatively efficient for operations of short and medium distance.

There are generally two types of turbine engines—one with the power plant geared to a propeller, usually called the "turbo-prop" (Fig. 10); the other without a propeller, generating "thrust" directly, called the "turbo-jet" (Fig. 12). The latter is the engine commonly meant when speaking of the pure "jet." Each type has certain advantages over the other for commercial operation.

1. *The Turbo-Prop.* An airplane equipped with the turbo-prop engine will operate more efficiently at lower altitudes and with better fuel economy than the turbo-jet. It will require shorter runways for take-off and can be fitted with reversing propellers to give better control for landing and ground operation. It will usually be faster than the airplane equipped with piston engines and slower than an airplane equipped with turbo-jet engines.

2. *The Turbo-Jet.* An airplane equipped with the turbo-jet engine is not efficient at low altitudes, giving its best performance probably at about 40,000 feet. It will accelerate slowly and will usually require longer runways for take-off. It has no propellers to be reversed, for slowing the aircraft after landing, and is less efficient for ground control. Its fuel consumption, on a relative basis, is much higher than that of a turbo-prop installation. It is capable of very high speeds.

No one can now be sure about the future of the two engines, but it is safe to predict that jet power will ultimately lead all other types for air transportation. Progress in the design and production of more efficient jet engines during the last few years has been amazing, and the trend will undoubtedly continue. Ultimately, the short-range aircraft will be equipped with the turbo-prop engine and the long-range airplane with the pure jet. The major part of the developmental work for both these engines in this country has been done for the military services. This has resulted in emphasis on the development of the pure jet, because of the military requirement for high speed.

From the point of view of economics, the essential difference between aircraft powered by turbo-prop engines and those powered by turbo-jets is that the former group fit into the general trend of development of aircraft characteristics that can be observed over the last 30 years; the latter represent a deviation from this trend in many respects. By comparison with the latest types of piston-engined aircraft, the turbo-props in service and on order exhibit no radical differences. Transport aircraft have in the past generally tended to become faster, heavier, more expensive to purchase; new types have been designed to offer greater pay load capacity, to produce less interior noise, and in some cases to be relatively cheaper to operate in terms of unit costs. The turbo-props, which as a group are slightly faster, quieter inside, and somewhat cheaper to operate than the latest piston-engined types, remain within the observed trends. For this reason the advent of the turbo-prop, although it might intensify some of the economic problems that faced the airlines, posed no serious new problems. The turbo-jets, on the other hand, display certain radical differences from piston-engined aircraft which place them outside the general trend and give rise to various problems.

There are six types of turbo-jet aircraft concerning which information is now sufficiently available to permit discussion of their economic characteristics. These are the long-range Boeing 707 and Douglas DC-8, and the medium-range Boeing 720, Convair 880, Comet 4, and Caravelle. They all, as turbo-jets, exhibit certain qualities that clearly differentiate them from piston-engined and turbo-prop types of the present or near future. They all fly faster, operate more economically at higher altitudes, are appreciably quieter and more comfortable inside, consume more fuel in relation to loads carried and distance flown, produce in varying degrees new heat, blast, and noise effects on the ground, and possess a novelty that will have an effect on their public appeal.

There are, however, additional characteristics by which the larger turbo-jets may be distinguished from the others. These are their weight, runway requirements, purchase price, and potential productive capacity. It should be pointed out here that range is in itself not a distinguishing characteristic of the long-range jets, since the maximum range of the Boeing 707 and the Douglas DC-8 is similar to that of the long-range turbo-prop Bristol Britannia and the piston-engined Lockheed L-1649A and Douglas DC-7C. The two long-range types—the Boeing 707 and the DC-8—are about 50 per cent heavier, require appreciably longer and stronger runways, and are about 50 per cent more expensive to purchase than any other aircraft now in operation.

Perhaps the characteristic by which the larger jets are most significantly set apart from other aircraft is their productivity potential. The four largest jets—the Boeing 707, Douglas DC-8, Boeing 720, and Convair 880—have a considerably greater productivity potential than any other aircraft. As a result of this high productivity potential, the capital cost of the long-range jets, although high in absolute terms, is less per unit of production than that of the latest long-range piston-engined aircraft. It is also probably safe to conclude that, on suitable trip lengths, the unit operating costs of turbine-powered aircraft per seat-mile or ton-mile of capacity offered will in general be somewhat lower than those of piston-engined types.

The turbo-jets depart from the traditional practice in commercial aircraft development. Past airline experience has been to design for long commercial life transports that can profitably be used on shorter routes of secondary importance when later models with increased power are made available. If the first aircraft is capable of economical operation only on the longer segments, it will have little economic utility as a commercial vehicle when the second-round airplane is developed. If an attempt is made to develop one airplane to straddle the operating requirements of both domestic and foreign services, the result may be a transport airplane not really suited for either, and one made rapidly obsolete by subsequent developments. This has not been a substantial problem in piston-engine use and would not likely be a major problem with a turbine-propeller airplane.

A second question of more serious concern relates to daily utilization of a turbo-jet transport. The airlines, or any given airline, may not be able to operate a small fleet of large jet airplanes at the same daily rate of utilization as a larger fleet of smaller piston-engine airplanes. The fast jet airplane will get its job done in less time than the slower piston airplane, and this will create a number of operating situations. For example, there will be less occasion to operate the jet airplane at night; intermediate ground times and turnaround time at terminal stations will comprise a higher percentage of the working day; and the ratio of aircraft undergoing operating and maintenance repairs to active aircraft may be higher.

The Helicopter

There appear to be three possible applications of the helicopter in common-carrier air transportation. These are in taxi services between airports and city centers, on suburban "commuter" routes in large metropolitan areas, and in local-schedule intercity operation. In intercity operation, the helicopter is expected to augment and perhaps eventually replace the twin-engine fixed-wing aircraft used for many years in local-scheduled operation.[24] The reasons for this are:

1. Many cities located on trunk lines today deserve air service, but are unable to afford the large airports required for fixed-wing aircraft.
2. At all distances up to 200 or 250 miles, the time required to travel from city center to city center by helicopter is less than that required in using any combination of fixed-wing aircraft plus surface vehicles to get to and from the airports.
3. The construction of superhighways to utilize the higher speed of the modern automobile may seriously affect the present local-schedule airline traffic volume.
4. Helicopter design is progressing rapidly and will continue to be accelerated by military requirements.
5. The operation of suitable helicopters will fill a definite void in our national air transportation system. This is especially true because of the relatively low capital cost requirements for landing and take-off facilities.
6. The value of the helicopter in national emergencies cannot be overestimated, particularly in cases where surface facilities have been destroyed.

The helicopter has two major advantages over fixed-wing aircraft: (*a*) it can operate from smaller terminal areas, and (*b*) it can fly at very low speeds. These are the main features which will permit air transportation to expand into fields where the airplane cannot now compete with ground transportation.

The helicopter is capable of integration into the air transport industry's local schedule requirements within the next decade if one can be developed to operate at an over-all cost no greater than those

---

[24] Air Transport Association of America, Committee on Helicopters, *Preliminary Report on the Use of Helicopters in Scheduled Airline Operations*, 1953. See also Samuel C. Williams, *Report on the Helicopter* (New York: Brundage, Story & Rose, 1955).

Courtesy: Los Angeles Airways

FIG. 13. The Sikorsky S-55 helicopter, the first to be licensed for commercial passenger operation.

involved in the use of twin-engine aircraft. This means that fares must be no higher than first-class air tariffs prevailing in recent years, adjusted to include ground transportation costs, so that the average fare to the passenger per mile will be no greater.

Successful exploitation of intercity helicopter passenger traffic will be directly related to the density of populations served, plus the distances between route cities. Where density is high and distance ranges between 40 and 175 miles, helicopter traffic will tend toward maximum passenger levels. On the other hand, if the density of population is relatively low, and the prevailing distance is within the helicopter limits mentioned above; or, if density is high and the distance is long, carrier operations are apt to be marginal. Density of population, therefore, becomes a prerequisite for successful helicopter operation. The second criterion, distance between cities, will determine the rate of foreseeable market expansion.[25]

Convertible Aircraft

The terms "convertible aircraft" and "convertiplane" refer to aircraft which duplicate the vertical flight technique of the helicopter for take-off and landing but, through various means, convert to operate essentially as conventional aircraft in horizontal flight. These aircraft have been developed since World War II in the desire to combine the most advantageous flight characteristics of both the fixed and rotary wing aircraft.[26]

One of the most successful convertiplanes was first built in Great Britain in 1947. It was known as a gyrodyne and was built by the Fairey Aviation Company, using a rotor and a shortened fixed wing for lift and standard airplane propellers for thrust. In June, 1948, the gyrodyne achieved a speed of 124 miles per hour. Since that time many types have been developed, but the type first flown in 1957, the Fairey Rotodyne (See Fig. 14), has been most successful.[27]

Convertible aircraft have a great future because they overcome some of the disadvantages of other types. Fixed-wing aircraft, for example, are designed to operate at peak efficiency only at optimum altitudes and at cruising power settings. It follows that approaches and departures from airports represent the most uneconomical portions of entire flight operations. Unfortunately, too, the conventional aircraft wing cannot be designed, aerodynamically, to make a maximum contribution to high enroute speed, because it must support the

---

[25] *Ibid.* See also, James B. Edwards, "Economic Considerations of the Transport Helicopter," a paper presented before the Institute of Aeronautical Sciences, New York, N.Y., January 29, 1954.

[26] By 1960, 24 different convertible aircraft designs had been developed. Of these, 18 had been the subject of research in the United States. The majority of the research programs were sponsored by the Department of Defense after 1950 with the expenditure of some $100 million. See C. F. Norton and J. L. Klingenhagen, "VTOL and STOL Research and Development in the Department of Defense," *The Journal of the American Helicopter Society* (January, 1959), pp. 6–7.

[27] The Kaman Aircraft Corporation has a license agreement to manufacture this aircraft in the United States. The American version will carry 48 passengers or 9,000 pounds of cargo at 185 miles per hour on a 200-mile trip; on a 400-mile trip, this aircraft is capable of carrying 34 passengers or 7,000 pounds of cargo. The manufacturer estimates direct operating costs at slightly less than five cents per passenger-mile.

aircraft at the low landing and take-off speeds. Moreover, although commercial aviation has achieved a high degree of statistical safety, it is a fact that the fixed-wing aircraft is incapable of stopping in the air. Every other form of travel is faced with the same weather contingencies that face aviation, and every other transportation mode adopts the same basic method of safe operation in bad weather; the vehicle slows down, even stops if necessary. Until aircraft can be slowed down when necessary, the very safety of air transporta-

Courtesy: Kaman Aircraft Corporation

FIG. 14. The Fairey Rotodyne.

tion hangs upon the slender thread of outside navigational aids, with the ever-present threat of mid-air accidents, crash landings, crack-ups on the runways, and fuel exhaustion while holding in "stacks" above airports.[28]

The airlines are becoming increasingly aware of the potential of convertible aircraft, particularly for short-haul and local service.[29] The increased speed of modern transport aircraft, the steady increase

---

[28] Lawrence LePage, "The Road to Air Safety," Convertible Aircraft Pioneers, *Proceedings of the Third Convertible Aircraft Congress* (Philadelphia, 1955), pp. 82–83.

[29] In 1959, New York Airways, a helicopter carrier, was planning to establish convertiplane service on its routes in the Manhattan metropolitan area by 1964.

in the minimum distance over which fixed-wing aircraft can be economically operated, and the ever-growing competition of rival transportation agencies for short-haul traffic will compel the commercial air transportation industry to pay increasing attention to convertible aircraft development.[30]

Commercial Supersonic Aircraft[31]

In order for a supersonic transport to be truly attractive for use in commercial service, it must possess characteristics and capabilities which will allow it to meet the following general requirements:

1. Its nonstop still-air range, with capacity pay load, should be at least 3,500 miles at an altitude between 11 to 15 miles above sea level. This would be high enough to prevent the unavoidable sonic boom from causing damage on the ground.
2. Its speed should be three times that of sound, or about 2,000 miles per hour.
3. At the above range, its direct operating costs per seat-mile should be comparable with those of current subsonic jet transports. The aircraft should weigh between 200,000 and 600,000 pounds and carry between 70 and 160 passengers. It may cost between $15 and $20 million.
4. The capability of operating into and out of the same airfields as the present subsonic jet transports is desirable.
5. In the attainment of high levels of safety and reliability, the supersonic transport must match or exceed the aircraft it will replace. The comfort level provided for the passengers must be adequate, commensurate with the longest flight times.

Although many difficult problems must be solved before a supersonic transport can be designed to meet the above requirements, no technological "breakthrough" is required to achieve satisfactory

---

[30] For a detailed study of the future of the convertiplane in commercial air transportation, see U.S. Air Coordinating Committee, *The Convertiplane*, A Report Prepared by the Convertiplane Working Group (Washington, 1954); William A. Rathbone, "Convertible Aircraft: The Development and Potential of a New Transportation Vehicle" (Unpublished thesis, University of Maryland, 1960).

[31] This section is based upon a paper, "Supersonic Transports—Their Economics and Timing," by E. F. Burton and V. V. Holmes, presented at the 27th Annual Meeting of the Institute of Aeronautical Sciences, New York, January, 1959. See also "Supersonic Passenger-Carrying Aircraft," a paper by B. S. Shenstone, presented before the Canadian Aeronautical Institute, November, 1956; and "Future Technical Trends in Air Transportation," a paper by G. F. Worley, presented before the Institute of Aeronautical Sciences, 1956.

solutions to all of them. It now appears that the technological state of the art will allow the development of an attractive supersonic transport in the 1965–70 time period.

Several serious problems related to the operation of supersonic transports must be solved before they can be safely operated in a near-optimum manner on the airlines of the world. Air traffic control and other related problems associated with rapid and accurate weather forecasting, long-range communications, and navigation appear to be the most serious of the operational problems. Satisfactory solutions to these operational problems involve more than technological advancements. The economic, political, and psychological aspects of solving these problems will likely delay their satisfactory solution until after the technical aspects are well in hand. Adequate and acceptable solutions to the operational problems will probably not be forthcoming until at least the 1968–72 time period.

The earliest date at which a supersonic transport can be introduced into commercial airline service is likely to be dictated by economic considerations related to the cost of development and production and the ability of the airlines to finance the initial cost of purchasing the required number of aircraft. The anticipated high cost of development for a supersonic transport will force the aircraft manufacturers to approach such a program very cautiously. The problems associated with funding and financing the development program will not be solved quickly and easily. Due to the heavy financial burdens involved in their purchase of large, subsonic jet transports such as the Boeing 707 and DC-8, as well as additional commitments they will be required to make in the next four to five years for the purchase of smaller, medium-range subsonic jet transports, the airlines will not be in a position to accept the financial burden of purchasing supersonic transports until about 1972.

It therefore appears that both the manufacturers and the airlines will approach the supersonic transport with considerable caution. The manufacturers will meticulously study the various alternate solutions to each of the design problems in order to eventually arrive at an optimum over-all design. They will closely observe and monitor the operation of subsonic jet transports over a period of years and incorporate the lessons learned from these aircraft into the supersonic design. Before the airlines will be ready to tackle the many new operational problems associated with a supersonic transport, they will want to study closely the operation of the new subsonic jets for several years until they are convinced that they have encountered and eliminated all the operational problems associated with this type. Furthermore, the airlines will want to study very carefully the profit potential of the supersonic transports, and they will want to be firmly convinced that they can operate them at a profit before they will consider purchasing them. Finally, the airlines must be in a healthy financial condition before they can accept the burden of financing the purchase of supersonic transports. They will conduct long and exhaustive studies of financing methods and sources before they will be willing to commit themselves to the purchase of fleets of supersonic transports.

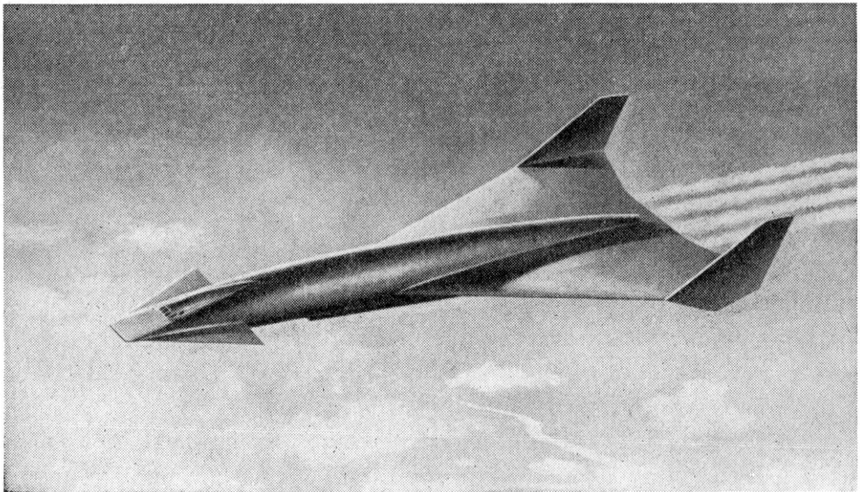

Courtesy: Convair Division of General Dynamics Corp.

FIG. 15. An artists's conception of a supersonic passenger transport to cruise at three to five times the speed of sound at 60,000 feet or higher. This is one of hundreds of configurations being studied by aircraft manufacturers.

Consideration of all the technical, operational, and economic aspects of the development of a supersonic transport, and its introduction into commercial airline service, leads to the conclusion that they will first be used by the commercial airlines in about the 1972–75 time period.

Passenger Reaction[32]

The reaction of passengers to aircraft is of great importance, particularly in planning airplanes for the future. Upon favorable pas-

---

[32] See R. D. Kelly, R. L. McBrien, and L. G. Kelso, *Evaluation Criteria for Transport Aircraft* (New York: Institute of the Aeronautical Sciences, n.d.); Ross A. McFarland, *Human Factors in Air Transport Design* (New York: McGraw-Hill Book Co., 1946);

senger reaction largely depends the ability of an airline to attract repeat business. Much still has to be done to make air travel as comfortable as it might be.

Air conditioning involving the control of temperature, ventilation, pressurization, and humidity has been receiving much attention from aircraft manufacturers. Temperatures are usually maintained between 70 and 75° F, with cabin air-heating capacity sufficient for cruising flight through atmospheric temperatures as low as —40° F. Ventilation, it is believed, should be at a rate between 30 and 40 cubic feet per minute of sea level density air per passenger, while air velocities within the passenger compartment should not exceed 40 feet per minute. The degree of pressurization required depends upon the average cruising altitude at which operations are conducted. It seems to be agreed that the cabin pressure altitude should be between 3,000 and 5,000 feet as a maximum but with most flights pressurized at the latter level. In other words, although the aircraft may be flying at 20,000 to 35,000 feet altitude, the pressure in the cabin will be as if the plane were flying at a maximum height of 5,000 feet. Humidity in the range of 25 to 40 per cent is usually provided.[a]

Rideability, while difficult to evaluate, affects comfort greatly, both on the ground and in the air. Very poor passenger reactions may be the result of disturbing movements from poor ride qualities. Hard rolling qualities, which jolt passengers during ground maneuvering, are readily noticeable even to the unseasoned traveler. Aerodynamic instabilities occasioned by rough air that create any feeling of indefiniteness of control are annoying and in some passengers aggravate tendencies toward airsickness. Interior illumination, if inadequate, is quickly detected by passengers who want to read. The direction and distribution of light are just as important as its intensity. On the whole, however, the air traveler today is not as concerned or as interested in the intimate details of aircraft design as was the more adventurous prewar air patron. All the average passenger wants today is safe, comfortable, and fast transportation to his destination. He has no desire to be part of an "adventure," or to share in the problems of an airline. He just wants to buy a service.

W. W. Davies, *Cargo Aircraft* (New York: Pitman Publishing Corp., 1946); Albert A. Arnhym, *Comfortization of Aircraft* (New York: Pitman Publishing Corp., 1944); Albert P. Elebash, "Passenger Aircraft Facilities—Design and Operation," an address before the S.A.E. National Air Transport Engineering Meeting, Chicago, 1946; *General Characteristics of Turbine-Powered Aircraft* (Washington, D.C.: Civil Aeronautics Board, 1960).

Airline Evaluation of Transport Aircraft

The airlines have been giving a great deal of thought to the type of airplane they feel most desirable. The following is a summary of the principal design criteria and operating requirements which airline engineers regard as most desirable from the operator's point of view:

1. Any transport aircraft must be planned around its passenger cabin and cargo compartment for passenger operation, or around its cargo compartments if specifically designed for freight transportation. Care must be taken in the layout of the passenger compartment to provide maximum comfort without waste of space. There should be no unnecessary frills which add to the weight; and interiors should be designed for ease of maintenance and servicing, particularly seats, floor covering, lighting fixtures, lavatories, and galleys. Baggage and cargo compartments should be readily accessible, and designed and located to permit rapid loading and unloading.
2. Transport aircraft must be made easy to maintain and service. This will probably be brought about through decentralizing controls and accessories to reduce maintenance time. It may also be achieved by providing quickly removable accessory panels and inspection doors to allow rapid change in case of failure. It should be remembered that maintenance and service costs continue throughout the life of an airplane.

In deciding the adaptability of a particular airplane to a specific type of operation, airlines usually classify the criteria used into the following groups:[33]

1. *Operating Conditions.* In deciding whether to purchase a particular airplane, a study of the type of service to be rendered by it is, of course, essential. Will the operation be primarily one of passenger transportation or freight transportation, and of what proportion of each? What lengths of route segments are involved? What volume of business is anticipated? The answers to these questions will in large part determine the general type of airplane required.

Next comes the consideration of the first cost, or purchase price, which has an all-important bearing on the size of the fleet with which

[33] Adapted from Kelley, McBrien, and Kelso, *op. cit.*

a given airline can conduct operations. A realistic allowance must also be made for the procurement of spare parts at the time of original purchase. For example, an amount equal to about 20 per cent of the purchase price of an airplane has been stated, in a number of instances, as necessary for the procurement of spare parts to start operation and carry it throughout the first year. Additional allowance also must be made for the procurement of necessary new types of ground equipment needed for servicing the airplane during maintenance stops, as well as for handling passengers and cargo at terminals. The sum of these amounts constitutes the initial investment in equipment.

The cost of introducing a fleet of new airplanes into scheduled service is very hard to predict. Airline accounting procedures have so far been inadequate to permit the development of empirical formulas by which this expense might be anticipated for new aircraft. Such expense does, however, constitute a sizable item. The education and training of ground and flight crews is in itself a time-consuming direct expense; in addition, the personnel involved in this program must be removed, for a time, from the revenue-producing operations of the airline. The period of introduction for a new airplane is usually considered to last one year from the day on which the first schedule was operated. During that time maintenance expenditures usually run appreciably higher than they do after the airplane has been in service for a longer period and the so-called "bugs" have been eliminated. Accordingly, a portion of the maintenance expense should be charged to the cost of introduction. There will also be schedule delays or flight cancellations which result in loss of revenue, both attributable to the introductory phase of operation.

Probably the most important consideration in predicting the operating economy of an airplane is an analysis of the route or routes on which it is to be used. Included in such an analysis should be the block speed and schedule time required, the maximum pay load which can be carried, the pay load limiting conditions applicable, the maximum revenue potential, the direct operating cost, and the break-even load factor.[34] Such an analysis provides the op-

[34] "Block speed" is the speed in miles per hour from airport ramp to airport ramp. The time involved includes taxi time to the end of the take-off runway, engine warm-up and check time, take-off, ascent to cruising altitude, descent from cruising altitude, and landing and taxi time to unloading ramp.

"Pay load" is the weight of revenue and nonrevenue passengers, mail, express, freight, company material, and passengers' baggage.

"Load factor" is a percentage figure arrived at by dividing the load potential of

erator with an indication of just how effectively a particular airplane can be used in his system of schedules. The segments which yield the least revenue and which must be operated at the lowest percentage of pay load available for profit are obviously the ones which should be scheduled with the lowest frequency, other things being equal.

Generally speaking, the direct operating expense is only a step in the economic analysis of an airplane. It tells only the cost per airplane-mile or per tone-mile of operation. If the airplane is to be used primarily on routes having poor traffic potential, then minimum operating expense is the primary economic criterion. For most routes it is desirable to have an airplane that provides for traffic development even though the operating cost may be proportionately higher. The equipment required on the ground for loading, unloading, and servicing aircraft should be considered along with the direct operating expense. For certain designs the initial outlay of capital for special ground equipment can be considerable. The cost of maintaining this equipment is also quite high.

The final indicator of an airline's economic success with an airplane is the annual percentage return on the initial investment in flight equipment. Flight equipment is an airline's only source of earnings. Therefore, when the purchase of a new airplane is being considered, it is of paramount importance to have an advanced indication of earning power in relation to the capital invested. If the manufacturer supplies complete cost, weight, and performance data, a route analysis can be prepared. From this and a knowledge of how the airplane will be scheduled over the airline, the anticipated earning power can be computed.

2. *Safety.* The evaluation of an airplane from the consideration of operational safety is very important, but has to be based largely on experience. An analysis of the airplane should be made from the standpoint of the personnel procedures, both normal and emergency, required to operate it. Operating procedures that require the participation of personnel, other than to direct the course or regulate the speed of flight, are usually evidence of inadequacy of design. The more complicated such procedures are, the less adequate the design. Complexity of systems, such as hydraulic, fuel, and air conditioning, must be avoided, since maintenance may be unduly ex-

---

capacity into the actual load carried. Example: a 60-passenger plane with 30 passengers aboard has a load factor of 50 per cent. Cargo load factors are figured the same way, by dividing the potential load weight into the amount actually carried.

pensive and the probability of malfunctioning may be increased. Complex systems usually require involved procedures for alternate operation in the event of irregularity. Even though an airplane may have been certified by the Federal Aviation Agency, the airline should investigate its flight characteristics thoroughly. The Civil Air Regulations under which aircraft pass tests prior to "certification" are based on minimum requirements and therefore do not necessarily represent the operator's desires. The airline must determine the degree to which the airplanes being considered measure up to regulations. For example, various characteristics may contribute to pilot fatigue or to the complexity of piloting procedures. Again, design details, particularly those of equipment and equipment installation, which influence the probability of fire occurring, should be subject to the closest scrutiny. In this connection, the possibility of passengers and crew surviving and being rescued following a crash during take-off or landing should be given full consideration. The location and simplicity of operation of escape means, the vulnerability of fuel tanks to rupture, and the incorporation of other items which will increase the probability of survival or facilitate rescue must be fully appraised.

3. *Performance.* There must be adequate separation between the minimum and maximum usable cruising speeds to insure flexibility for maintaining on-time schedule reliability in the face of varying wind conditions. The minimum speed is determined by the flight-handling characteristics of the airplane. The maximum speed is determined by the maximum power the operator deems advisable to use continuously. Usually, this power is appreciably less than the rated maximum cruising power. Differences in time for taxiing and run-up and in climb performance make the block-speed comparison of more importance than a strict comparison of cruising speeds. The operator must use experience and judgment in estimating the average time for taxi and run-up when making block-speed comparisons.

Landing aids have lessened the requirements that an airplane be able to maneuver readily and make approaches to airports under conditions of poor visibility. However, the requirement has not been eliminated, especially for the airplane designed for short-haul operation. The short-haul airplane has less chance of avoiding inclement weather and for some time yet must operate into airports not equipped with landing aids. Also, emergency conditions sometimes arise where a landing must be made without aids.

Weight restrictions imposed by performance requirements of the Civil Air Regulations must be closely scrutinized. For certain operations these restrictions may be the limiting factor, rather than the structural limits of the airplane itself. It may be entirely impractical to serve certain airports because of the restrictions imposed by the runway requirements for take-off or landing. Restrictions imposed by the required climb performance for take-off, approach, or landing configurations may also be appreciable, especially at high-elevation airports. The climb performance required en route may become restrictive for flights over high terrain.

The Commercial Transport Fleet

The fleet of aircraft operated by the domestic and international airlines of the United States consists of various types and as of the beginning of 1960 numbered 1,827, as shown in Table 1. It will be

TABLE 1

TYPES OF AIRCRAFT IN OPERATION BY UNITED STATES SCHEDULED AIR CARRIERS, DOMESTIC AND INTERNATIONAL

(As of January 1, 1960)

Type of Aircraft	*Number*	*Type of Aircraft*	*Number*
Douglas		Convair	
DC-8	18	540	1
DC-7	220	440	36
DC-6	325	340	122
DC-4	62	240	46
DC-3	305	Martin	
Viscount		404	85
V-810	15	202	19
V-745	67	Boeing	
Lockheed		707	66
188	96	377	21
1649	28	Fairchild	
1049	109	F-27	34
749–049	104	Curtiss	
Grumman		C-46	33
G-21	15	Total	1,827

Source: Federal Aviation Agency, Statistics Division.

noted that by that time only 84 turbo-jet aircraft, the DC-8 and Boeing 707, had been delivered.

The increased use of turbo-jet and turbo-prop aircraft threatened to make more than 850 piston-type commercial aircraft surplus to United States airline requirements by the end of 1961. These aircraft originally cost the airlines approximately $830 million and at the time they became surplus had an estimated book or depreciated value of $250 million.[35] This was the first time in the history of commercial aviation that such a large number of excellent used aircraft became available in such a short period of time. The problem was what to do with them.

Faced with the realization that it was virtually impossible to sell these aircraft above book value on the open markets, the airlines transferred the problem to the manufacturers of turbine aircraft by trading them in on new purchases whenever possible. The airlines also took steps to use the piston aircraft themselves by increasing their own operations for both passengers and air freight, thus removing them, at least for a time, from the surplus category. For example, new passenger services between points where it had either not been offered or had been rendered with less desirable equipment were inaugurated[36] and some of the larger aircraft, such as the DC-6, DC-7, and Lockheed L-10409, were converted for scheduled and charter air freight service although this required an additional capital outlay.

The airlines' primary financial interest was in the satisfactory disposal or utilization of DC-7 and Super Constellation type equipment, but they also had other piston-type aircraft, ranging upward from the DC-3, to dispose of. Markets for DC-3 aircraft have been available for years among the local service airlines and, more lately, for private operation by corporations. Local-service airlines were able to upgrade their equipment replacing DC-3's with Convairs; in addition, it became possible to convert at least one Convair model into a turbo-prop aircraft at a reasonable cost.

The used-aircraft disposal problem was, however, not confined to the commercial airlines of the United States, since foreign air

---

[35] See, Air Coordinating Committee, *United States Policy Concerning Disposal of Piston Transport Aircraft Replaced by Turbojet and Turboprop Equipment* (Washington, D.C., 1959); Jack Wagner, "Disposal of Surplus Aircraft," *Shell Aviation News* (January, 1960), pp. 14–18.

[36] Typical of this is what was done by United Air Lines in the latter part of 1959. In October, the first DC-7 Custom Coach service ever offered at Omaha and Milwaukee was inaugurated, and in the same month all nonstop United flights between Chicago and Cleveland began to be flown in four-engine equipment. In addition, new one-stop daytime service to Las Vagas was begun in first-class DC-7 equipment from the New York area and in DC-7 Custom Coach aircraft from Washington, D.C. DC-7 Custom Coach service was also begun overnight from Chicago to Las Vagas. Another new flight was a midday nonstop DC-7 "Red Carpet" service from Portland to Los Angeles. At the same time, the frequency of United service at Pittsburgh, flown exclusively in DC-7 aircraft, was increased 50 per cent. As one aviation analyst said at this time, "Strangely enough, it's conceivable that new piston competition may develop over routes and/or schedules not slated for the initial turbine equipment. If this occurs, the DC-7 type aircraft and the Super Constellations (Lockheed L-10409) may take on additional life."

carriers and the military services of this country were involved. By the end of 1961, the expected number of surplus airline transport-type aircraft will be as follows:

United States air carrier (556 four-engined)	843
Foreign air carriers (assuming they would retire piston type in same ratio as planned by United States airlines)	600
United States military service	250
Total	1,693

The magnitude of the used-aircraft disposal problem was recognized by the federal government as early as 1958. At that time, a policy was adopted not to release military transport aircraft to the commercial market in such a way as to depress this market and to study possibilities of sale of some aircraft in foreign markets where financial aid from this country, through the Export-Import Bank or other organization, would be necessary. The less-developed countries seem to present the best foreign market for used aircraft, but these are the ones requiring the longest credits. Moreover, preferential terms by public financing institutions for aircraft compared to other export commodities would raise such issues as: (*a*) competition with private financing, (*b*) maintenance of an orderly system of government credit terms, and (*c*) charges by foreign countries of export subsidization. In other words, sales to foreign countries, unless they can be financed through regular commercial channels, do not hold forth much hope as a means of surplus aircraft disposal when one considers the many problems and implications involved.

Up to the end of 1959, no airline had been forced to resort to a mass panic sale or unrestricted release of surplus, or about-to-become surplus, aircraft on the market. Such a situation is, however, a continuing nightmare to the industry and will be until the market for used aircraft becomes stabilized, if it ever does. To prevent any such thing from happening, an intensive research, coordination, and marketing effort has been necessary but so far has not been forthcoming even though certain disassociated approaches have been made.[37]

It has been estimated that, by 1975, the common-carrier fleet

[37] See *Prices of Used Commercial Aircraft 1959–1965* (Evanston, Ill.: The Transportation Center, Northwestern University, 1959). In 1959, the Department of Commerce and the State Department started a world-wide survey of the used-aircraft market which was not completed by the end of 1960. A partial approach to the problem was proposed by the Aircraft Exchange, organized in 1959 in New York City, whereby an analysis would be made of the potential additional uses of piston-engine aircraft in countries where transportation deficiencies currently exist.

of aircraft will total about 1,500, composed as shown in Table 2.[38] It is also expected that an additional 300 aircraft will comprise the United States international, air freight, and supplementary or nonscheduled airlines fleet.

TABLE 2

ESTIMATED COMMON-CARRIER FLEET COMPOSITION

Aircraft, Size and Type of Engine	1960–62*				1965				1975			
	No. Aircraft		Per Cent of Fleet		No. Aircraft		Per Cent of Fleet		No. Aircraft		Per Cent of Fleet	
Small, piston	331	523	23.0	36.5	254	509	20.0	41.0	131	305	9.0	21.0
Small, turbo-prop	192		13.5		255		21.0		174		12.0	
Medium, piston	474	743	33.2	52.1	109	546	8.8	44.0	53	663	3.6	45.0
Medium, turbo-prop	182		12.7		300		24.2		418		28.4	
Medium, turbo-jet	87		6.2		137		11.0		192		13.0	
Large, turbo-jet	163		11.4		184		15.0		510		34.0	
Total	1,429†		100		1,239‡		100		1,478‡		100	

* Estimated from end-1956 airline-furnished data.
† Includes international and overseas (approximately 116–250 aircraft).
‡ Domestic only.

Source: Adapted from *National Requirements for Aviation Facilities: 1965–1975*, Vol. III, Part I, p. 35.

[38] *National Requirements for Aviation Facilities: 1965–1975*, Vol. III, Part I, a report prepared by Cornell Aeronautical Laboratory for Mr. Edward P. Curtis, Special Assistant to the President for Aviation Facilities Planning, Washington, D.C., 1957. See also Albert W. Bentz, "Picture for 1957," *American Aviation* (August 12, 1957), pp. 77–78.

Chapter 2

AIRPORTS AND AIRWAYS

Aviation can progress effectively only as far as the state of its ground facilities permits. Unfortunately, the maintenance and improvement of ground facilities has, up to the present, been largely separate from the technical development of aircraft themselves. The size and speed of aircraft, the power of the engines used, and the functions and responsibilities of the air transport industry have all been pushed ahead of the ground facilities upon which they must depend. Aircraft have increased in size and speed beyond the capacities of most of the major terminal airports as well as the airways.

Until all the country's air navigation and traffic control systems, major air terminals, and related ground facilities have been improved to the point where they can adequately handle the aircraft using them, the airlines will be unable to provide absolutely safe, reliable, and efficient public service; and until they can provide such a service, the air carriers will be unable to rise much above the present plateau in their development. This means that we must begin to think ahead in airport design and construction, in methods of communication and traffic control, since these facilities are essential to both our national economy and national security.

For some time to come, the nature of air navigation and terminal facilities will be conditioned by the limitations of the human pilot. Plane size, maneuverability, and approach speeds, traffic control methods, and landing aids must all be within the grasp of human physiology and psychology. However, the time of automatic flight control is approaching; and the aids whose immediate installation is essential for use by a human intermediary should also be adapted, where possible, to integration with the "superhuman" flight era which is sure to come. Some of these aids will be outmoded when that era arrives, but there is certain to be a transition period of considerable length in which both types will be used.

The Airport System[1]

An airport may be defined as any locality adapted for the landing and taking off of aircraft and which provides facilities for their shelter, supply, and repair and for the regular reception or discharge of air passengers or cargo. Throughout the history of aviation, airports have been a problem; and the need for more or better landing and take-off facilities has been an ever-present concern to all those active in either civil or military aeronautics.

TABLE 3

AIRPORTS AND AIRFIELDS, 1926–52

Calendar Year	Total	Commercial	Municipal	CAA Intermediate	All Others	Lighted Total	Airports of Entry	
							Regular	Temporary
1926......	*	*	*	92	*	*	0	0
1927......	1,036	263	240	134	399†	*	0	0
1928......	1,364	365	368	210	421†	*	0	0
1929......	1,550	495	453	285	317†	*	10	8
1930......	1,782	564	550	354	314†	640	10	30
1931......	2,093	829	780	404	80	680	9	36
1932......	2,117	869	777	352	119	701	10	39
1933......	2,188	938	827	265	158	626	11	42
1934......	2,297	872	980	259	186	664	11	42
1935......	2,368	822	1,041	291	214	698	12	43
1936......	2,342	774	1,037	296	235	705	12	43
1937......	2,299	727	1,053	283	236	720	21	34
1938......	2,374	760	1,092	267	255	719	37	23
1939......	2,280	801	963	266	250	735	39	21
1940......	2,331	860	1,031	289	151	776	37	21
1941......	2,484	930	1,086	283	185	662	36	19
1942......	2,809	1,069	1,129	273	338	700	37	11
1943......	2,769	801	914	240	814	859	35	10
1944......	3,427	1,027	1,067	229	1,104	964	36	9
1945......	4,026	1,509	1,220	216	1,081	1,007	30	11
1946......	4,490	1,929	1,424	201	936	1,019	30	16
1947......	5,759	2,849	1,818	178	914	1,447	47	1
1948......	6,414	2,989	2,050	161	1,214	1,521	47	0
1949......	6,484	2,585	2,200	139	1,560	1,480	46	0
1950......	6,403	2,329	2,272	76	1,726	1,670	46	0
1951......	6,237	2,042	2,316	57	1,822	*	47	0
1952......	6,042	1,731	2,336	*	*	1,858	56	0

* Not available.
† Include auxiliary marked fields, later classified as to ownership, commercial or municipal.
Source: CAA, *Statistical Handbook of Civil Aviation* (Washington, D.C., 1954).

Tables 3 and 4 show the growth of the airport system of the United

[1] This section is partially adapted from John H. Frederick, *Airport Management* (Homewood, Ill.: Richard D. Irwin, Inc., 1949), chaps. i, ii, iv.

States from a total of 1,036 in 1927 to 6,426 in 1959. Official statistics are available only from 1927 because it was not until after the passage of the Air Commerce Act of 1926 that an official government agency was made responsible for airport and airway matters. An airport count was, therefore, first made in 1927 by the Bureau of Air Commerce of the United States Department of Commerce. Prior to that time, airports had, of course, been developed, often as the result of local flying interest, so that by 1912, when the first transcontinental flight was made, with many stops and delays, there

TABLE 4

AIRPORTS AND AIRFIELDS—1953–59[1]

(Data Cover Existing Airports and Airfields Recorded with FAA)

Year Ending December 31	Total	Public	Limited	Lighted Total	Airports of Entry
1953[2]	6,760	2,903	3,857	1,050	55
1954	6,977	2,783	4,194	1,108	56
1955	6,839	2,713	4,126	1,247	58
1956[3]	7,028	2,889	4,139	1,399	59
1957[3]	6,412	3,195	3,217	1,713	58
1958[3 4]	6,018	....	....	1,809	58
1959[3 4]	6,426	....	....	1,943	58

[1] Effective January 1, 1954, the type definitions of airports were revised as follows: Public-use—all airports that serve scheduled and large irregular air carriers as regular, alternate and provisional stops; all CAA intermediate landing fields; all airports having a true-light certificate to indicate a lighted airport, and all other airports which are operationally active. Limited—all airports that do not qualify as "Public-use" airports. Includes seaplane bases and heliports.

[2] As of March 1, 1954.

[3] Includes Territories and possessions.

[4] Effective April 15, 1958, type definitions of airports were revised as follows: General-use—airports serving as regular, alternate, or provisional stops for scheduled and large irregular air carriers; nonair carrier airports offering a minimum of services such as fuel and regular attendant during normal working hours; and airports operating seasonally which qualify under above definition. Limited-use—airports available to public but not equipped to offer minimum services. Restricted-use—use by general public prohibited except in case of forced landing or by previous arrangement.

Source: FAA, *Statistical Handbook of Civil Aviation* (Washington, D.C., 1960).

were about twenty recognized "landing fields," as they were then called, in the United States.

After the end of World War I, considerable interest in airport development was aroused by individuals who had purchased surplus Army planes and wanted to use them; by the Army itself, now conscious of the importance of civil landing fields to the free movement of its aircraft; and by the Post Office Department, particularly in connection with the development of a transcontinental air mail route. By 1921, therefore, the total number of airports had reached 271, of which 145 were municipal. By 1925, municipal airports had increased in number to 310, commercial fields to 225, and intermediate fields on the air mail routes to 63. The aviation boom of the late twenties was just beginning; the Air Commerce Act of 1926 was about to be passed, supplying the regulation which responsible aeronautical interests had long wanted; and scheduled air transport under private management was just getting a serious start through the letting of contracts for mail carriage. More and more cities were wanting to be included on the country's air routes, and by 1927 the number of municipally operated airports was 240 and commercial airports, 263.

An aviation boom, already well under way, was greatly accelerated by the transoceanic flights of the summer of 1927, and many new municipal fields were opened. Even more striking was the increase in the number of commercial airports. In the eager rush of a speculating public to put money into aviation, funds were provided for chains of commercial airports far in excess of any possible needs.

The first federal aid was extended to civil airports, not held primarily for the use of the federal government, through the Civil Works Administration in the fall of 1933. With the passage of the Civil Aeronautics Act of 1938, the provisions of the Air Commerce Act of 1926 forbidding the participation of the federal government in airport development were repealed. Since then the Administrator of Civil Aeronautics[2] has been empowered to make plans for the orderly development and location of landing areas and to acquire, establish, operate, and maintain such areas or facilities upon landing areas owned and maintained by others but not to acquire any airport by purchase or condemnation. The expenditure of federal funds on nonmilitary landing areas is subject to certification by the Administrator, and such landing areas must be reasonably necessary for use in air commerce or in the interest of national defense. Since 1933, federal funds have been the predominant factor in airport development. Up to 1959, it has been estimated that federal funds and property amounting to $2,681,762,412 have been contributed to civil airports, as shown in Table 5.

In the decade before World War II, the number of airports in the United States fluctuated somewhat below the 2,500 mark, but no large expansion program was undertaken. During the war, however, several hundred large airports were constructed to serve military needs. Unfortunately, many of these were located in out-of-the-way places not suited for civil airports; and because of the ban on pri-

[2] By the Federal Aviation Act of 1958 (72 stat. 731) the Civil Aeronautics Administration was made part of the Federal Aviation Agency. See Chapter 4.

vate flying during the war years, very few small airports were built. Beginning in 1945, many of the military airports (classified under "all others" in Table 3) were turned over to nearby municipalities or abandoned entirely, which partly accounts for the growth in municipal airports during 1946 and 1947. The growth in commercial airports during those same years was almost entirely due to the large amount of instructional flying caused by the various federal-aid plans for veteran education.

The end of World War II found the United States with an airport system which had not kept pace with the great expansion in civil aviation activities. The acute necessity for more airports was recog-

TABLE 5

FEDERAL CONTRIBUTION TO CIVIL AIRPORT SYSTEM

Relief Programs:		
Civil Works Agency (1933–34)	$ 15,222,372	
Federal Emergency Relief Agency (1933–38)	17,649,853	
Public Works Administration (1933–43)	28,849,672	
Works Progress Administration (1935–42)	331,584,806	
Total		$ 393,306,703
Civil Aeronautics Administration Programs (World War II):		
Development of landing area for national defense (1940–47)	$383,031,875	
Development of civil landing areas (1944–47)	9,513,995	
Total		392,545,870
Federal Airport Program		465,723,839
Emergency Landing Fields Program		10,000,000
Surplus airport property (1944–present)		1,420,186,000
Grand Total		$2,681,762,412

Source: Statement of E. R. Quesada, Administrator of the Federal Aviation Agency, presented before the Subcommittee on Aviation of the Senate Interstate and Foreign Commerce Committee, January 22, 1959.

nized by the Congress, which enacted the Federal Airport Act of 1946.[3] This law, as amended, directs the Civil Aeronautics Administration (now Federal Aviation Agency) to prepare and revise annually a national plan for the development of public airports in the United States, the Virgin Islands, and Puerto Rico and to specify the type of projects thought necessary to provide a system of public airports adequate to anticipate and meet the needs of civil aeronautics. The same act also authorized federal expenditures of $500,000,000 over a seven-year period, which were to be matched by equal sums from local public agencies known as "sponsors." Table 6 shows that up to December 31, 1958, 1,509 airports received federal aid amounting to $449,655,000.

[3] *Public Law No. 377*, 79th Cong., 2d sess. (approved May 13, 1946).

The decline in the total number of airports between 1949 and 1952 is largely accounted for by the abandonment of a number of intermediate landing fields by the Civil Aeronautics Administration and the fact that a number of smaller commercial airports, operated in connection with veteran flight-training programs, were forced out of business when this program was curtailed. The increase in the total number of airports between 1952 and 1954 is accounted for by seaplane bases and heliports. The latter had not been included in the totals before 1954.

TABLE 6

1947–60 FEDERAL-AID AIRPORT PROGRAM—NUMBER OF AIRPORTS AND FEDERAL FUNDS ALLOCATED

(As of December 31, 1959)

Service type	Air commerce airports		General aviation airports	
	Number	Federal funds (000)	Number	Federal funds (000)
Secondary[1]	14	$1, 026	683	$26, 395
Feeder	1	309	177	25, 783
Trunk	30	14, 748	427	80, 795
Express	65	57, 023	19	6, 098
Continental	37	75, 678	5	2, 344
Intercontinental	31	110, 060	------	----------
Intercontinental Express	16	108, 180	------	----------
Seaplane Facilities[1]	20	554	2	29
Heliports	0	0	1	84
TOTAL	214	367, 578	1, 314	141, 528

1 Secondary-type airports and seaplane bases in Alaska are counted as air commerce airports.

Source: FAA, *Statistical Handbook of Civil Aviation* (Washington, D.C., 1960).

By 1953, it was apparent that the federal-aid program was not achieving what had been intended, since it was not developing an integrated airport system. Much more money was being spent on Class III and larger airports, operated by municipalities and other governmental entities which were able to raise funds to match the federal funds, than on Class I and II airports, which served smaller communities unable to raise such funds. The Civil Aeronautics Administration decided, therefore, to reappraise the situation before asking Congress for additional airport aid. It was also felt that larger airport operators were now in a position to finance themselves fully if forced to do so. Some airport operators had, in fact, been refusing federal funds because of restrictions on airport development and operation which the use of such aid entailed.

Early in 1954, the Department of Commerce announced[4] a decision that some continued federal participation in financing airport development was desirable, but that such participation would be justified only if it were concentrated upon airport locations and types of construction essential to the nation's broadest interests.[5] The Department stated that it could not justify the expenditure of federal funds on projects which, though desirable, were predominantly of local rather than national importance, or on airport terminal buildings. Terminal buildings are regarded as revenue producers and, as such, have the greatest prospect for independent financing without federal aid.

The federal-aid airport program has been only moderately effective in establishing a system of airports adequate to meet the present and future needs of the foreign and domestic commerce of the United States, of the postal service, and of the national defense. The chief reason for this is that the program has never operated on anything like the dollar level originally planned. The Federal Airport Act contemplated congressional appropriations of approximately $100 million a year, whereas actual appropriations have varied from $45 million in 1947 to none at all in 1954. In the first years of the program, from 1947 to 1950, fund appropriations were held back by the inevitable complications of starting a complex national program of integrated airport development and by the requirement that local governments match the federal grants. After 1950, appropriations were successively reduced, until in 1954 not a single grant was made for new projects. In the fiscal year 1955 (beginning July 1, 1954), the program was reactivated by the appropriation of $22 million, but since 1950 the level of available funds has been far below that necessary for any extensive national program.

It has become evident that we will not obtain from all communities the matching funds needed to build an integrated system unless a way can be found to render additional financial assistance to smaller cities and less-populated counties. These have no means to

[4] Address by Robert B. Murray, Jr., Under-Secretary of Commerce for Transportation, before the Washington Chapter, National Defense Transportation Association, March 16, 1954. This was later confirmed as part of our national aviation policy in the report of the Air Coordinating Committee, *Civil Air Policy* (Washington, D.C., 1954), pp. 26–27.

[5] From statements made before the Senate Committee on Interstate and Foreign Commerce in May, 1954, it would appear that the criteria of national importance used by the Department of Commerce would be 3,000 enplaned passengers per year; or a based-aircraft population of 30; or a combination of these factors, with 100 passengers being equal to one based aircraft. As of 1954, 760 airports (accounting for 99.6 per cent of the total domestic scheduled airline traffic) met this eligibility test.

raise the funds locally, and have met with little or no success when they have applied to their state legislatures for aid. The states, for the most part, have not yet been convinced they have the same responsibility in building an integrated airport system as they do in building an integrated highway system.

The fund deficiency has been made more serious by the formula used for allocating funds among the states (half on the basis of population and half on the basis of area) and by the discretionary funds being limited to 25 per cent of the appropriation. This last provision has made it impossible to reassign sufficient funds from states not using their allocation to states needing additional amounts. The combination of low appropriations, rigid distribution formulas, and small discretionary funds has prevented granting substantial federal aid to many of the larger air terminals and local-service airports.

Granting federal assistance for airport construction seems the best way for the federal government to discharge its responsibilities in this field. Such assistance finds a precedent again in our public highway program, where federal government, like state, has played an important financial role. Federal control, designed to produce a national system of airports, is much more acceptable to local government if it is achieved through federal contributions than if it is a purely regulatory program.

Airport Classification

The airports of the United States have been classified in various ways: (1) according to their size, (2) according to the types of service they are designed to furnish, and (3) according to the nature of their ownership or control.

The size of an airport is usually indicated by the length of its landing strips and runways. The Civil Aeronautics Administration (now Federal Aviation Agency) set up minimum size standards, as shown in Table 7. One thousand feet in length of landing strips and runways is added in each case above Class V to make Classes VI, VII, and VIII. Every airport has been assigned either to one of these classes or to a sub-1 group, if its size standards do not meet even the lowest class.

Table 8 shows the Federal Aviation Agency classification of airports by types of service, together with the minimum recommended standards for runway lengths, landing strip, runway and taxiway widths, grades, and pavement loading. *Personal* airports are designed to handle light (up to 3,000 pounds) aircraft for small communities or urban areas. *Secondary* airports are for larger (2,000–15,000 pounds) aircraft in nonscheduled flying activities and will suit the needs of many smaller communities. *Feeder* airports are to serve those communities certificated for this type of scheduled local airline service. *Trunk-line* airports are designed for smaller cities on trunk airline routes. *Express* airports are designed for important cities or junction points on trunk airline routes; they accommodate the largest aircraft now in use or planned for the immediate future with a gross weight of 50,000 pounds and over. *Continental* airports are those designed to accommodate aircraft making long nonstop domestic flights. *Intercontinental* airports are designed to serve long international flights. *Intercontinental express* airports serve the highest type of transoceanic flights. The last three types are found at the major trade and industrial centers of the country, such as New York, San Francisco, Chicago, Los Angeles, Miami, San Francisco, and Boston.

TABLE 7

AIRPORT SIZE CLASSIFICATION

Recommended Minimum Standards	Class I	Class II	Class III	Class IV	Class V
Length of landing strips*....	1,800–2,700 ft.	2,700–3,700 ft.	3,700–4,700 ft.	4,700–5,700 ft.	5,700 ft. and over
Width of usable landing strips....................	300 ft.	500 ft.	500 ft.	500 ft.	500 ft.
Length of runways........	None	2,500–3,500 ft.	3,500–4,500 ft.	4,500–5,500 ft.	5,500 ft. and over
Width of runways.........	None	150 ft. (Night opr.) 100 ft. (Day opr. only)	200 ft. (Instr.) 150 ft. (Night opr.)	200 ft. (Instr.) 150 ft. (Night opr.)	200 ft. (Instr.) 150 ft. (Night opr.)

* All of the foregoing landing strip and runway lengths are based on sea-level conditions; for higher altitudes increases are necessary. One surfaced runway of dimensions shown above is recommended for each landing strip for airports in Classes II, III, IV, and V.

Source: Adapted from CAA, *Airport Design* (Washington, D.C., 1949).

Airports are also classified as in Tables 3 and 4 (pp. 39–40). A *municipal airport* is defined as one under public ownership and/or control, open to public use with aircraft services generally available. A *commercial airport* is one under nonpublic ownership and/or control, but nevertheless open to public use with aircraft services generally available. A *limited airport* is one intended for private use but allowing public use; aircraft services are limited or not available and the ownership and/or control may be public or non-public in nature. *Military airports,* as the name implies, are owned and/or controlled by a branch of the military service but open to some civil use. A *private airport* may be under public or nonpublic ownership and/or control, but is open only for uses authorized by the operators.

TABLE 8

AIRPORT SERVICE CLASSIFICATION

TYPE OF SERVICE	RUNWAY LENGTH* (FEET)	MINIMUM WIDTHS (FEET)			MAXIMUM GRADES (PER CENT)			PAVEMENT LOADING PER WHEEL (IN 1,000 LBS.)	
		Landing Strip	Runway	Taxiway	Effective†	Longitudinal‡	Transverse§	Single Wheel	Dual Wheel
Personal	1,500– 2,300	200	50‖	20‖	2	3	3	‖	‖
Secondary	2,301– 3,000	250	75‖	30‖	1½	2	2	‖	‖
Feeder	3,001– 3,500	300	100	40	1	1½	1½	15	20
Trunk line	3,501– 4,200	400	150	50	1	1½	1½	30	40
Express	4,201– 5,000	500	150	60	1	1½	1½	45	60
Continental	5,001– 5,900	500	150	75	1	1½	1½	60	80
Intercontinental	5,901– 7,000	500	200	75	1	1½	1½	75	100
Intercontinental express	7,001–10,500	500	200	100	1	1½	1½	100	125

* Designed for sea-level elevation, standard sea-level temperature of 59° F and 0 per cent effective gradient.

† Maximum effective gradient obtained by dividing the maximum difference in runway center-line elevation by the total length of the runway.

‡ When necessary, longitudinal taxiway grades may be as high as 3 per cent.

§ Percentages shown are for pavement. To improve run-off, the slopes on unpaved areas may be increased to 2 per cent, and to 5 per cent for a distance of ten feet from the edge of pavement.

‖ Pavement not required.

Source: CAA, *Airport Planning* (Washington, D.C., 1952), and FAA Office of Public Affairs.

Airport Adequacy

The adequacy of the airport system of the United States may be judged on several bases: (1) airport location in relation to the cities served, (2) airport equipment, (3) extent of protection of landing areas exclusive of the airport itself, and (4) services available for the traveling public.

1. *Location of Airports in Relation to Cities Served.* To serve a city or town to the best advantage, an airport should obviously be located as close as possible to its center. The travel time between the city center and the airport is more important to the airline user than is the distance in miles. More than half the airports serving the prin-

cipal cities of the country are a half-hour or more from their centers. Much has been done during recent years to improve airports themselves, but it has seldom been found possible to move them to points nearer city centers. In many instances, air transportation suffers because of the remoteness of airports; this is especially true where relatively short flights are involved and where the time saved over surface transportation is not substantial.

Even though it is desirable that airports lie close to the centers of the communities they serve, occasionally it proves of economic advantage for two or more neighboring communities to compromise their demands and find a location reasonably convenient to all. In such cases it is often possible to build a better airport than would be justified for any one of the towns alone.

2. *Airport Equipment and Building.* Wholly adequate airport equipment (without regard to the size of landing area) must include paved runways, taxiways, aprons, fueling facilities, hangars, and lights.

There seems to be no question about the desirability of paved runways or a hard surface of some sort, but many smaller communities seem unable to assume the financial burden even of bearing the sponsor's share of the cost for a combined federal government and local runway project. Hangars are also expensive and are lacking at many of the smaller airports. Airport lighting is of many sorts, from the rotating beacon flashing the airport code, to the boundary and high-intensity approach and runway lights; and very few airports, other than the largest, are really adequately lighted.

3. *Protecting the Vicinity of the Airport.* The landing area for aircraft is more than just the ground space required for the runways, loading and unloading ramps, and storage and servicing facilities. The air space surrounding all landing areas is of so much importance that the approaches to the ground space should be considered a part of any airport. In order to protect the approaches, tall buildings, trees, and communication and power lines must not become a hazard. The air space as well as the ground space must be protected, and some control over neighboring property is, therefore, necessary. To purchase outright enough land to make the protection complete would often require that the acreage needed for the landing area proper be multiplied by five or more. Such a purchase is usually impossible because of cost or some other reason. The remaining alternatives are to regulate the area by zoning and to acquire by purchase, lease, or condemnation the rights to unoccupied air space

above the surrounding property. The maintenance of an elevated structure near an airport has also been enjoined a nuisance by court order in cases where spite was shown to be a motive. Control of the surroundings is one of the major necessities of sound airport development; yet it seems to have been neglected in far too many cases. (See Chapter 4.)

According to the National Institute of Municipal Law Officers, there are a number of ways to protect airport approaches: (1) voluntary action by the hazard owner; (2) purchase of all land near the airport and razing of hazards located thereon; (3) purchase of air space rights over all land near the airport; (4) acquisition of air space rights over land near airports by use of the power of eminent domain in order to raze present hazards and to prevent future ones; (5) police condemnation of hazards to use of airports; (6) zoning to prevent and eliminate hazards near airports; (7) use of the commerce power by the federal government; (8) use of the war power by the federal government; and (9) use of the postal power of the federal government.[6]

About half the states have adopted laws giving cities or counties the right to purchase land and, if necessary, to acquire it by condemnation for airport purposes, either for original establishment or for later improvement and enlargement, and also to use either negotiation or condemnation to acquire the rights to the air space surrounding the airport as an assurance against its invasion by obstructions. The procedure of acquiring air rights has, however, been little used; in the event of condemnation of such rights, the courts find scanty precedent for a guide in fixing values.

The simplest solution is zoning, which eliminates separate dealings with a multitude of property holders, but little has been done with this method. While most states have airport-zoning legislation of some sort, only a few have acts considered clearly adequate by the Federal Aviation Agency. Too many leave discretion to municipal

---

[6] See National Institute of Municipal Law Officers, *Airports and Air-Plans and the Legal Problems They Create for Cities* (Washington, D.C., 1939). See also Charles S. Rhyne, *Airports and the Courts* (Washington, D.C.: National Institute of Municipal Law Officers, 1944), chap. viii; Air Transport Association of America, *Airline Airport Design Recommendations* (Washington, D.C., 1947), Part II; J. Nelson Young, *Airport Zoning* (Urbana, Ill.: University of Illinois, 1948); L. Welch Pogue and James F. Bell, "The Legal Framework of Airport Operations," *Journal of Air Law and Commerce*, Summer, 1952, pp. 253–73; Eugene A. Weibel, "Problems of Federalism in the Air Age," Part I, *Journal of Air Law and Commerce*, Spring, 1957, pp. 127–50, Part II, *Journal of Air Law and Commerce*, Summer, 1957, pp. 253–72; G. Nathan Calkins, "The Landowner and the Aircraft—1958," *Journal of Air Law and Commerce*, Autumn, 1958, pp. 373–401.

authorities and little has been done with it. An essential fact of the present status of the American airport system is that the possibility of safe and efficient use of an airport is entirely dependent on its surroundings and that few communities have so far adopted any measures to protect airports against the erection of high neighboring structures that would seriously impair their value.

4. *Services Available for the Traveling Public.* It has been well said that "the airport is the sales counter of air transportation"; but in achieving this, the objectives of the municipalities and of the airlines often conflict. One objective should be to make the airport attractive to the general public and to sight-seers, affording them parking space, an opportunity to see airport operations conducted, and a place where an inexpensive meal may be purchased. The second objective, particularly important to the airlines, is to make first-class waiting room, ticketing, and restaurant facilities available to airline passengers. Achieving the first objective develops new passengers; achieving the second is most certainly necessary to retain the passengers now using air transportation. A good airport terminal building, while it must contain all the conveniences of a good railroad station, must certainly avoid incorporating the bad features of the latter and must make provision for comfort, style, privacy, and quiet efficient service.

Public service facilities should be closely related to the passenger-handling area and should be readily accessible to each of its parts. At some large airports, decentralized public services may be necessary to: (*a*) reduce the average distance a passenger must walk to reach such services; (*b*) make more services available to more passengers; and (*c*) reduce the time interval required to reach and utilize such services. Distance between ground transportation and aircraft should be minimized.

Many airports lack provision for passengers to go aboard or deplane without getting out in the rain and walking some distance. All-weather canopies for protection against rain and snow, as well as sun, seem to be an essential part of a proper airport. Individual umbrellas and similar makeshift devices are certainly not in keeping with the standards of service that the airlines should maintain.

Viewed in the light of certain expansion, automobile parking facilities at most airports are at present wholly inadequate. In addition to outdoor parking facilities, the ideal airport should also include a garage for the use of travelers who are planning to return within a day or so and who would find storing their car at the airport a decided convenience.

Often the whole atmosphere of an otherwise well-equipped airport is destroyed through discourteous and unprepossessing municipal employees who give to the air traveler a distinctly poor impression of that community. An airport administration providing an appearance of military proficiency in the deportment of all personnel, whether airline or municipal, instills confidence in keeping with the major effort of the airlines to provide safety. This is particularly important. Nothing detracts so much from the creation of confidence as the hurrying about of many members of the personnel, the indifference of employees, or the appearance that the whole terminal operation is being conducted without precision and order.

Airport Management[7]

The commercial airports used by air carriers are generally publicly owned and managed. It has become recognized that an airport or system of airports around a city is as much a part of the transportation facilities of a metropolitan area as are its streets and boulevards, for both are designed to serve private and commercial owners of various and sundry types of vehicles.

There are several forms of airport administration:

1. By an already existing department of the city government, such as the department of public works or the park department.
2. By a new department established in the municipal government to manage the airport.
3. By an independent airport commission, which may be bipartisan and selected by the mayor or equivalent officer. The commission then selects the airport manager, who will be directly responsible to the commission rather than to any department of the city government.
4. By establishment of an airport authority, particularly where there are several airports serving a city or owned jointly by several municipalities or by a city and county.

Cities using the first method of airport administration, retaining it in one of the already existing departments, generally do so either because they do not feel the airport-management problem of sufficient importance to set up a separate department or because they could not, at least when the system was adopted, afford to employ a competent airport manager and so placed the responsibility on the shoulders of an already existing department head, where it remains for various reasons.

Any advantages which may have existed in years past from combining airport administration with other city department activities

[7] This section is adapted from Frederick, *op. cit.*, chap. viii.

have tended to disappear as the complexities of airport operation have increased; and, particularly in the larger cities, definite weaknesses of the merged form of organization have developed. These may be summarized as follows:[8] (1) Authority and responsibility are often divided among too many individuals or groups, and decisions are thus delayed. (2) The route of authority which must be followed before a decision can be reached is often too long and circuitous. (3) Airport activities are commonly subordinated to the major activities of the department in charge of the airport. (4) Despite incidental similarities between airport operation and the other activities of a certain city department, it will be found in nearly every case that the essential management requisites are basically different. For example, some cities retain control of their airport activities in the park department. They did so at the beginning chiefly because field maintenance could be conveniently carried on by that department. Before airport management and maintenance became as complicated as they now are, the chief job was grass cutting and other work similar to that already done by park employees. It has also been argued by advocates of part-department management that taxpayers will not be so prone to insist on an airport paying its way if it possesses the aura of a park and recreational facility. This is, of course, very shallow reasoning in spite of the fact that numerous city authorities contend that it is the only possible way to secure funds while an airport is in the early stages of development.

Separate airport departments have been created in many cities which realized that the problems involved and the skills required in airport administration are sufficiently unlike those of any existing department to warrant special treatment. Also, as airport operation has become more complex, the sheer volume and complexity of the problem has become an undue burden on the department which may have been entrusted with it earlier. In other cases, "the principal motivation for setting up a separate department has been the desire to emphasize and bring to closer public attention the entire problem of aviation and airports."[9] Finally, when the airport is a separate department, it is felt that a higher-type airport manager may be attracted to it. The chief disadvantage of handling the airport as a separate department is that it tends to add to the complexities of city

---

[8] See Lynn L. Bollinger, Alan Passen, and Robert E. McElfresh, *Terminal Airport Financing and Management* (Boston: Harvard Graduate School of Business Administration, 1946).

[9] *Ibid.*, p. 259.

government, thus making it still harder for the chief executive to maintain contact with all divisions.

The independent airport commission has a number of advantages which have led to its adoption in many cities. These are: (1) Individuals of a higher caliber, interested in aviation from the viewpoint of civic development rather than from a commercial one, are attracted to the nonsalaried commission. (2) Various local groups, directly interested in airports, may be represented on the commission. (3) Continuity of policy and freedom from political interference are more possible, particularly where terms of commission members overlap. Experience has, however, shown the disadvantages of the commission form of airport administration to be: (1) Commissioners are not always able to reach agreement among themselves. (2) Interposing a commission between an airport manager and the chief executive of a city sometimes results in conflict. (3) Unpaid commissioners sometimes lose interest in the airport even while continuing to serve.

The airport authority has the following advantages: (1) It is, if modeled after the Port of New York Authority, as most of them are, an independent corporate agency. Its management, its methods, and its techniques are those of a modern business organization rather than those of a state or municipality. (2) It is nonpolitical in operation, with members serving, as does the board of directors of a business corporation, usually without compensation and appointed for overlapping terms by the several political subdivisions concerned. (3) It supervises projects of a self-supporting character and relies on the revenues from these projects rather than on funds that come directly or indirectly from taxation. (4) It is adaptable to a regional approach, an aspect which makes it particularly useful in the development of interstate, joint municipal, or joint municipal and county projects.

The ability displayed by management in maintaining and improving individual airports will bear a close relationship to earnings and to the degree of public support required in the future. The best method of municipal control is difficult to evaluate because the business and profession of airport management are still, and for some time will be, in the early stages of growth. No system of management or control can yet be said to have definitely proved itself in the sense that is true in other fields of municipal management. Adequate opportunity has not yet been afforded to test fully the effects of policies thus far adopted.

Airport Income[10]

Airport charges and consequent income, or lack of it, have been the most controversial aspects of the airport problem for many years. However, as time has gone on, general principles of airport charging have gradually developed. These general principles have been based on the belief that, while airports have many of the general characteristics of public facilities, they should not be provided entirely at public expense. In other words, users of the various facilities should pay, in the form of fees, rentals, and other charges, enough to permit well-managed airports to be financially self-supporting.

The common understanding of airport charging also takes account of the fact that there are two chief parts to every airport: (*a*) the landing area, including runways, taxi strips, aprons or ramps, and their appurtenances; and (*b*) the building area. Since the landing area has many of the characteristics of what is commonly called a "public utility," it is generally agreed that charges for the use of this area should be based on cost of operation. It is not considered good airport management to try to make a profit from the landing area. It is, however, good practice to expect landing-area users, over a period of time, to bear the full costs of supplying and maintaining the facilities they need and use.[11]

The building area differs from the landing area in that here the value of the space used is a more logical base for charging than is the cost of the service rendered a tenant or holder of a concession. It is, therefore, considered good airport management to obtain as much revenue as possible from all space in the building or terminal area rather than simply to cover costs. This area, therefore, is the place where the chief profit-yielding activities of an airport may be carried on. There is, however, a complicating factor. Whereas the landing area is used only by aviation activities—the activities that "make" the airport, that encourage other activities to be carried on there, and that should be encouraged by the lowest possible charges—the building area is used by both aviation and nonaviation interests. It is again considered good management to charge aviation activities for space in the building area—such as that required for handling pas-

---

[10] This section is adapted from Frederick, *op. cit.*, chaps. x, xi.

[11] It is generally held that "costs" as here used should include an interest charge on the entire amount of capital used and also amortization of all depreciating parts of the landing area, such as runways and lights. Costs should not include any depreciation charge on the land investment, which is generally considered a nondepreciating asset.

sengers, mail and cargo, hangar use, and the like—on a cost basis or on a basis as close to cost as possible. Nonaviation activities, on the other hand, may be charged on a basis to produce maximum revenue, since it is the aviation activities of the airport that help to make possible other businesses there. It is the nonaviation activities that should produce the "profit" of any well-managed airport.

Sources of airport income may be classified as follows:

1. Landing fees from commercial operations. It is quite generally agreed that the most equitable form for such charges is on the basis of the gross weight of the aircraft using the landing area. Costs should be a basic factor in determining landing charges; and since the heavier the aircraft, the greater the expense of maintenance of runways and the greater the investment required in construction, this weight basis seems fairest to all concerned. It also makes for greater uniformity throughout the country than did previous methods based on the number of schedules operated over a given time. (It is true that weather and other considerations existing in different sections of the country will bring about slightly different operating cost figures, but the difference will be negligible.) The weight basis will also enable an airport manager to estimate the number of planes which will use his facility and their gross weight, and from this information he can easily determine what his approximate landing revenue for any future period will be.
2. Fixed base and other flying operations, such as flight instruction, aeronautical schools, flying clubs, charter and contract service, industrial services, aircraft rentals and sales, and other miscellaneous flying activities operated on a concession basis.
3. Hangar rental and other storage.
4. Gasoline and oil sales.
5. Aircraft, parts, and accessories sales.
6. Repair, overhaul, and maintenance.
7. Space rental in terminal buildings for such aviation activities as the Weather Bureau, Civil Aeronautics Administration offices, United States Post Offices, Customs and Immigration Services, airline ticket offices, airline operations offices, and the offices for aircraft service operators and others directly concerned with aviation.
8. Rental of space in terminal buildings for such nonaeronautical activities as restaurants, cocktail lounges and bars, barber shops, valet services, public stenographers, tourist bureaus, newsstands and gift shops, advertising display cases and dioramas, clubrooms, spec-

tator ramps, baggage lockers, vending machines, sleeping accommodations, and various recreational facilities.

9. Industrial area rentals on various sections of the airport for manufacturing plants, processing plants, air freight warehouses, and cold-storage plants.

10. Ground transportation franchises for the transportation of passengers between the airport and surrounding areas.

The nonaeronautical concessions provide the balance wheel in the economy of an airport. Where the flying operations might produce enough revenue to cover the costs of operation, it is the various concessions which generally determine whether the airport will operate at a profit. It is considered essential that nonaeronautical concessions be developed fully because they not only bring in added revenue but also stimulate interest in the various aeronautical activities dependent upon public support.

In this phase of airport operation, as in many of the other phases, no particular uniformity has been reached in adopting policies concerning concessions. In deciding which concessions are to be established, the principles of sound business must be followed since many concessions, which might be successful on some airports, would prove to be failures on others. Revenue from concessions depends largely upon the locality and accessibility of the airport to the community it serves, on the size and attractiveness of the airport, and on its service and its ability to produce patronage as well as other factors.

Airways

An "airway" is a path, provided with communications facilities, through the navigable air space identified by an area on the surface of the earth. In the United States, airways are designated or approved by the Federal Aviation Agency as suitable for air commerce by naming points on the earth and connecting them by straight lines. The airway extends five miles on either side of these center lines and includes all of the navigable air space above this area. Airways are designated by color and number. The colors are green, amber, red, and blue and indicate general direction. Green is main east-west, amber is main north-south, red is supplemental east-west, and blue supplemental north-south. Numbers begin at the Canadian border and Pacific Coast and work south and east. The width of the airways as shown on the map (Fig. 16) is drawn to an exaggerated scale.

In addition to the colored airways, the Federal Aviation Agency now designates "V" or Victor Airways. These are made possible with the installation of very-high-frequency, omnidirectional range equipment (VOR) on the airways. In 1958, there were 124,870 miles of Victor Airways available for use.

The airway system of the United States, as provided by the government for the use of military, commercial, and private aircraft, has constantly expanded, until today practically all the major centers of population in the country are served by fully equipped routes. The components of the system have been improved and changed as time has passed, so that the system as a whole embodies the technical advances made in electronic devices in an endeavor to meet the requirements imposed by constantly increasing traffic. Table 9 shows this growth from 1930, when there were but 15,258 miles of airways implemented by the Civil Aeronautics Administration, to 1959, when there were 176,934 miles under the jurisdiction of the Federal Aviation Agency.

Construction and operation of airways in this country, prior to 1926, was in the hands of the military and of the Post Office Department. Subsequent to that time, although certain sections of airways were constructed by two states (Pennsylvania and Michigan) and by some air carriers, the major portion of the system was constructed and operated by the federal government through the Civil Aeronautics Administration. All of the state and privately constructed airway facilities have now been acquired by the federal government, and at present the Federal Aviation Agency operates the entire federal airways system of the United States with the exception of certain military facilities operated in conjunction with military airfields. The basis for this activity of the federal government has been stated as follows:

Several important reasons seem to have determined that the Federal Government should assume the major responsibility for establishing and maintaining the airways system. Difficulties were encountered in the early developmental period in obtaining air-mail contractors for the transcontinental routes if the operators were expected to assume the costs of required aids to safe air navigation. Moreover, if private operators had installed and maintained their own aids to navigation, the use of such facilities might have been restricted largely to the owners. Under such circumstances, military, private, and charter planes would not have had full access to navigation facilities, except through complex joint-use agreements or by providing their own facilities, which would have resulted in uneconomical duplications. For these reasons, and because of the paramount public interest in safety of flying

TABLE 9

Federal Airways System, 1930–59

Year Ending December 31	Federal Airways Mileage		Radio Range Stations		Nondirectional Radio Beacons	Airways Centers	Airport Towers	Combined Station/Towers	Air Traffic Communication Stations	International Air Traffic Communication Stations	Instrument Landing Systems	Precision Approach Radar	Airport Surveillance Radar
	Low/Medium Frequency	Very-High Frequency	Low/Medium Frequency	Very-High Frequency									
1930	15,258	...	33	...	6	...	...	...	...	...	...	...	...
1931	17,152	...	47	...	46	...	...	...	...	...	...	...	...
1932	19,500	...	68	...	74	...	...	...	...	...	...	...	...
1933	18,655	...	94	...	77	...	...	...	...	...	...	...	...
1934	19,081	...	112	...	73	...	...	...	205	...	...	...	...
1935	22,012	...	137	...	57	...	...	...	206	...	...	...	...
1936	22,245	...	146	...	57	...	...	...	203	...	...	...	...
1937	22,319	...	180	...	55	8	...	...	245	...	...	...	...
1938	23,723	...	215	...	50	8	...	...	286	...	...	...	...
1939	27,074	...	244	...	44	11	...	...	321	...	...	...	...
1940	32,100	...	290	2	48*	11	...	...	365	1	1	...	...
1941	36,062	...	323	8	48*	14	...	...	413	2	1	...	...
1942	38,498	...	303	8	40*	23	61	...	430	5	1	...	...
1943	41,506	...	323	8	63*	25	101	...	408	8	8	...	...
1944	42,549	...	333	9	84*	28	104	...	439	8	9	...	...
1945	43,285	...	344	16	88*	29	107	...	438	8	9	...	...
1946	44,145	...	364	50	74	29	115	...	397	8	31	...	...
1947	47,029	...	365	100	81	31	134	...	403	15	60	4	4
1948	56,069	...	376	333	98	30	150	...	437	15	79	3	3
1949	61,392	...	378	370	120	30	162	...	464	15	94	3	3
1950	70,253	...	378	371	141	31	172	...	451	15	96	7	7
1951	74,424	...	375	385	152	31	157	19	427	15	97	10	10
1952	72,328	45,831	372	388	166	31	141	34	415	15	120	10	10
1953	72,097	54,490	368	392	181	31	115	53	395	15	143	10	17
1954	69,359	64,995	346	403	170	31	104	70	376	11	153	10	28
1955	67,770	81,209	344	424	175	31	100	75	364	11	157	10	31
1956	67,783	90,268	342	441	180	32	103	79	358	11	160	10	40
1957	64,817	104,484	332	486	185	33	110	81	350	11	165	10	42
1958	57,705	124,870	329	556	191	32	128	84	345	11	171	10	47
1959	47,302	129,632	322	661	191	33	139	83	332	11	174	11	48

* Includes VT stations. (V—Air-to-ground communication; T—Teletype.)
Source: FAA, *Statistical Handbook of Aviation* (Washington, D.C., 1960).

operations, a centralized and integrated system of control has been deemed imperative.[12]

Airway and Airport Traffic Control[13]

As air transportation grew in volume, the problem arose of preventing collision between, and expediting the movement of, aircraft flying under conditions of limited or no visibility. Around important terminals the problem became serious when aircraft on the same or converging airways were being navigated in or above clouds by means of instruments; and even under weather conditions permitting pilots to see each other's planes there was no assurance that each would make the right decision to prevent a collision. Separation of air traffic, therefore, had to be provided by a centralized agency.

As air space use by private, civil, and military aircraft increased and longer, faster, nonstop flights were inaugurated, the need for control extended further out along the airways from the principal terminals. It became apparent that a unified nation-wide control of air traffic was needed. The interstate character of the problem pointed to the federal government as the proper authority to handle the matter, and so on July 6, 1936, the Bureau of Air Commerce of the Department of Commerce took over control of air traffic through three centers which had been established by the airlines serving Newark, Cleveland, and Chicago.

The jurisdiction of the first three centers was soon expanded outward to control larger areas; and additional areas, each with its control center, were established as the need arose and funds became available. Today there are thirty-one areas covering the entire United States, in each of which all traffic on the civil airways is controlled from its airway traffic control center under the jurisdiction of the Federal Aviation Agency.

Table 10 lists the facilities provided for airway traffic control. Every airway, however, is not necessarily provided with all these components. For any specific geographic area there is a specialized

---

[12] Board of Investigation and Research, *Public Aids to Domestic Transportation* (House Doc. No. 59, 79th Cong., 1st sess.) (1944), p. 466.

[13] See Civil Aeronautics Administration, *Study of Air Traffic Control* (Washington, D.C., 1943); Glen A. Gilbert, *Air Traffic Control* (Chicago: Ziff-Davis Publishing Co., 1945); Frederick, *op. cit.*, chap. ix; Civil Aeronautics Administration, *Operation of the Air Traffic Control System* (Washington, D.C., 1953); *Aviation Facilities Planning,* a report by the President's Special Assistant (Washington, D.C., 1957); *Modernizing the National System of Aviation Facilities* (Washington, D.C.: Office of Aviation Facilities Planning, 1957); *Research and Development Program and Progress Report* (Washington, D.C.: Federal Aviation Agency, 1958); *Federal Airway Plan, 1959–1963* (Washington, D.C.: Civil Aeronautics Administration, 1958).

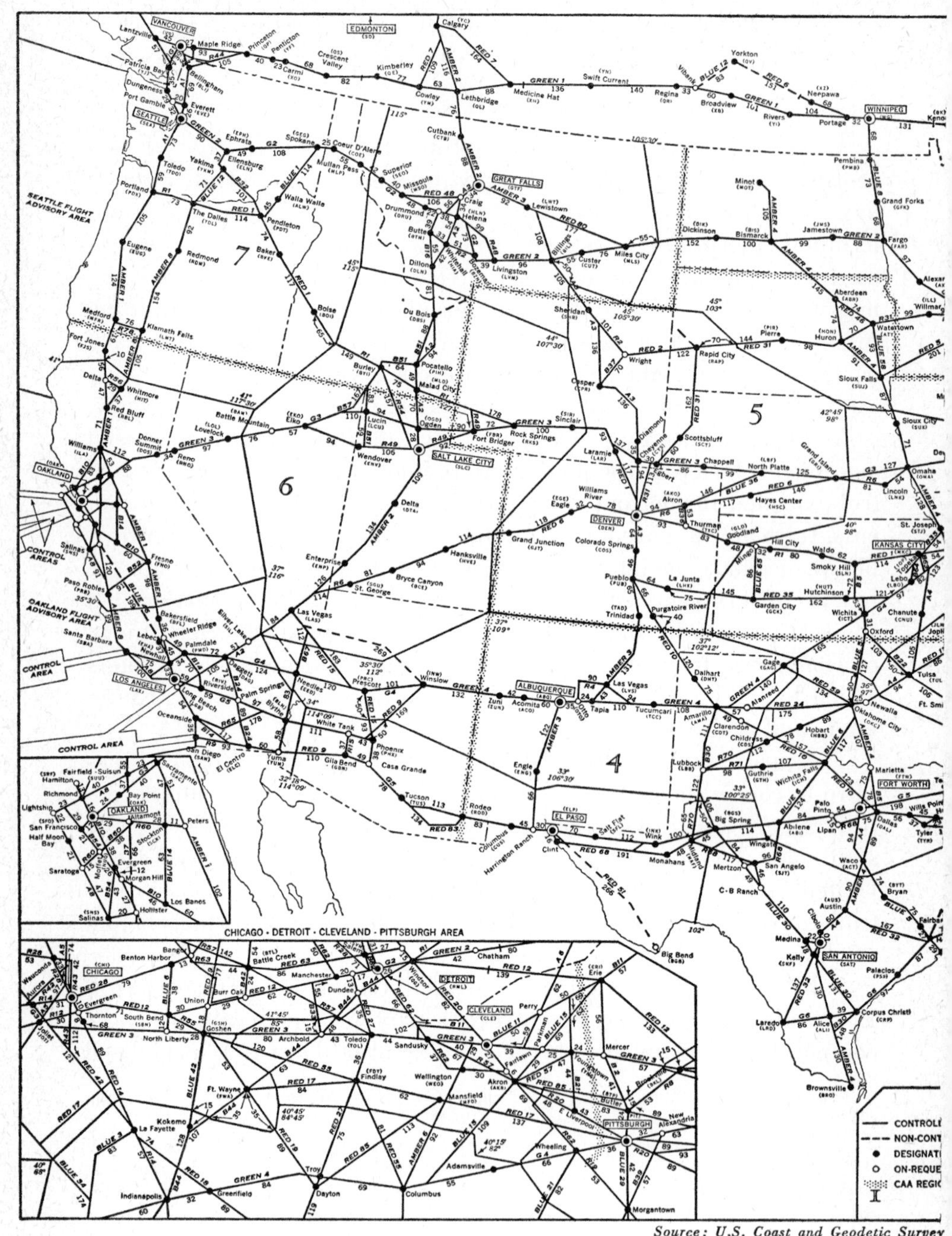

Source: U.S. Coast and Geodetic Survey

FIG. 16. Civil Airways and Mileage chart.

LEGEND
D AIRWAY
OLLED AIRWAY
D REPORTING POINT
T REPORTING POINT
NAL LIMITS
AIR ROUTE TRAFFIC CONTROL CENTER
FLIGHT ADVISORY AREA BOUNDARY
MILEAGE BETWEEN REPORTING POINTS
LOCATION IDENTIFIERS (RADIO)
MILEAGE FROM RADIO FIX TO ATC BOUNDARY WHEN OTHER THAN 25 MILES
BOSTON
NEW YORK - WASHINGTON AREA
NEW YORK OCEANIC CONTROL AREA
NEW ORLEANS OCEANIC CONTROL AREA
NEW ORLEANS FLIGHT ADVISORY AREA
JACKSONVILLE FLIGHT ADVISORY AREA
MIAMI FLIGHT ADVISORY AREA
MIAMI OCEANIC CONTROL AREA
MINNEAPOLIS
CHICAGO
DETROIT
CLEVELAND
TORONTO
MONTREAL
MONCTON
BOSTON
NEW YORK
PITTSBURGH
WASHINGTON
CINCINNATI
ST. LOUIS
MEMPHIS
ATLANTA
JACKSONVILLE
NEW ORLEANS
MIAMI

TABLE 10

FEDERALLY PROVIDED FACILITIES FOR AIRWAY TRAFFIC CONTROL

Name of Component or Facility	*Function*
Traffic control centers	An Air Route Traffic Control Center (ARTCC) is a facility providing supervision of Instrument Flight Rules (IFR) traffic within a specified control area.
Communications stations	Interstate Airways Communications Stations (INSACS) are capable of radio telephone communications with properly equipped aircraft and monitor the navigational aids along the airway. They have extensive communication links with towers and traffic control centers for relaying messages dealing with air traffic control.
Light beacons	These are rotating beacons regularly spaced along the airways supplemented by directional course lights to indicate certain specified airways; nonrotating lights for field marking, identification, hazard marking and other special purposes.
Intermediate fields	A few of these are provided along the airways for emergency use, chiefly in mountainous areas.
Fan markers	Radio location markers used as radio fixes for air traffic control reporting points.
Homing facilities	Radio beacons installed in en route areas to provide navigational guidance or used to define position reporting points for air traffic control purposes.
L/MF ranges (low and medium frequencies)	Provide courses (frequently called beams or legs) which can be followed by a properly equipped aircraft along the airway. Often arranged to serve both airways and airports. These ranges can be used for voice broadcasts and direct communication with aircraft.
VHF ranges (very-high frequencies)	Supply navigational information for aircraft en route. When located on or adjacent to an airport also provide navigational guidance to aircraft during departure or approach and let-down to the airport. These very-high-frequency omnidirectional ranges (VOR) are intended to replace the obsolescent L/MF ranges as the basic navigational guidance on the airways.
Distance measuring equipment	This component (DME) is designed to make possible in the aircraft a visual indication of the distance to an aircraft from a ground facility.

group of components which provide the federal aeronautical services to the aircraft flying or based within the area.

Airport traffic control—that is, control of traffic moving on the ground and departing and landing at airports—antedates control on the airways. The basis of airport control has heretofore been the ability of the aircraft traffic controller to see the aircraft under his control; but with the use of certain radar instruments this is no longer necessary. Airport control was established and maintained by the owners or operators of the airports; but, during World War II, this type of traffic control was taken over by the Civil Aeronautics Administration in order to centralize the control of air traffic under a single agency. It is now under the control of the Federal Aviation Agency.

Table 11 lists the facilities provided for terminal or airport traf-

TABLE 11

FEDERALLY PROVIDED FACILITIES FOR TERMINAL TRAFFIC CONTROL

Name of Component or Facility	*Function*
Control tower	Supervises, directs, and monitors air traffic within the airport control area.
Approach light lanes	Neon and high-intensity lights to aid pilot during approach and landing.
Fan markers	Used as radio fixes for air traffic control reporting points.
Instrument landing systems	Provides pilot with means for precise navigation during approach for landing.
Precision approach radar	Provides controller with precise information on the position of aircraft during approach.
Airport surveillance radar	Provides controller information on position of aircraft within the terminal area.
Homing facilities	Radio beacons used for both navigational guidance and as a radio fix for air traffic control reporting point in the terminal area.
Combined station-tower	Combines functions of both tower and interstate airways communications station.
Airport beacon	Green in color indicates lighted airport. Amber indicates seaplane base. Split beam indicates military facility.
Distance measuring equipment	A visual indication of distance from airport.

fic control, but every terminal area does not have all these components. The associated aids are added to the basic component, the control tower, as they are needed to meet operational problems peculiar to various levels of instrument weather activity or unusually high-density traffic makes necessary new facilities and procedures.

With the placing of airport traffic control under the federal government, it became possible to delegate certain responsibility for the control of air traffic under instrument conditions from an airway traffic control center to an airport traffic control tower. This is a logical extension of the functions of airport traffic control and, in effect, establishes a local "airport traffic control area" (usually an area within a three-mile radius of the control tower) within which all traffic under all weather conditions is under the jurisdiction of the control tower. The airways traffic control center co-ordinates, thru the approach control, the flow of traffic into and out of the area, over these local areas, and along the airways.

Problems of traffic control for aircraft not moving in definite, predetermined flight paths would be almost insurmountable. With their paths crossing almost anywhere, the situation would be similar to that which would arise if a hundred motorcyclists were stationed around the edges of a field and each were allowed to start for any spot on another edge at the same time with speed and direction of his own choice. Neither the drivers nor any size traffic control force could prevent collisions, even on a bright, clear day.

Traffic between terminals is therefore controlled only on the airways. It cannot be controlled like surface traffic, which is stopped by a red light. Aircraft must remain in motion at sufficient speed to maintain altitude and maneuverability. Such traffic is controlled, therefore, by advance planning. Airway traffic control anticipates and so organizes the movement of aircraft in advance that no danger of collision can arise if they proceed in accordance with instructions.

At airports there arises a combination of *surface* and *air* traffic to be kept separated. Airport traffic control provides this separation for taxiing, landing, and departing aircraft. Control of aircraft moving on the ground is particularly important, since aircraft are designed so the pilot has maximum visibility while in flight; but while on the ground the pilot's visibility is often obstructed by the motor and wings, making it quite difficult to see other aircraft and obstructions quickly enough to avoid collisions.

Providing safety, while the fundamental purpose of air traffic control, is not its only purpose. Although safety comes first, just as important a purpose, from the standpoint of air transportation, is the expeditious movement of traffic.

If commercial air transportation is to be widely used, it must maintain its advertised schedules within reasonable limits. Failure to maintain schedules has definitely hampered the development of air transportation. Delays encountered en route also cause a definitely measurable loss. Every excess minute spent in the air means just so much monetary loss for fuel, wear and tear, and other expenses.

Air traffic control must, therefore, be designed to keep traffic flowing evenly and with as little delay as possible. Only an agency having information on all traffic would be able to do this with safety. With the complete picture available, it is able to make the best possible arrangements to prevent delay along the way or in landing.

Adequacy of Airways and Traffic Control

Since World War II, the system of traffic control on the airways and airports of this country has been inadequate and has not met the requirements of its users. This has resulted in delays in air traffic during instrument weather, the saturation of traffic controller capabilities, and mid-air collisions that could have been prevented if the capacity to provide separation for a larger number of aircraft had existed in the system. Meanwhile, high-performance aircraft, operating too high or too fast to avert collision by visual means, are entering the air space and many more are on their way.

A conservative estimate for 1975 is that the total air traffic will be approximately two times what it is today, with the major proportion of aircraft flying under air traffic control. To serve these users, a tenfold increase in the capacity of the system will be needed. The major portion of the over-all demand for air traffic control will stem from the expected 400 per cent increase in general aviation. Airline movements are expected to increase about 50 per cent, while military traffic will decrease slightly. By 1975, helicopter and other short takeoff and landing aircraft flights, mostly over and around large cities, will represent about 5 per cent of the total movements.

The national system of aviation facilities includes airports, navigation aids, communications service, and a system for the controlled separation of air traffic. In modernizing this system, three objectives must be met. First, over-all safety of the system must be increased. Second, the capacity of the system must be expanded. (A tenfold increase in system capacity will be needed by 1975.) Finally, the system should cause a minimum of interference with users' operations.

As a matter of national policy, it is believed that the system must be based on the following concepts:

1. Controlled separation of all air traffic—both civil and military—in the United States must be provided by a single, integrated system of personnel, regulations, procedures, and facilities.

2. The system must support the air defense of the United States against enemy attack by providing information on friendly aircraft that is inherent in the system, and by serving as the common Army, Navy, and Air Force system of aviation facilities in time of war.

3. Conversely, the air defense system should provide the national system of aviation facilities with information that it possesses, which is useful for safe and expeditious flow of air traffic.

4. The facilities, procedures, and regulations should be designed to insure a fair priority of service for all users. This priority must give way to military necessity in times of military emergency.

5. Improvements to the system must be compatible with current procedures and equipment. Changes in system design should be evolutionary, not revolutionary.

6. The system must be flexible. It should be capable of expansion to meet unanticipated demand without major redesign and without interrupting flight operations. Similarly, it should be flexible enough to permit procedural changes to keep pace with changing conditions.

7. The cost of the system to the nation must be reasonable—compared to the over-all value of national aviation operations. For the user, the cost must be reasonable in comparison to the cost of the aircraft flown and the quality of the service desired. The system must serve the lightly equipped user effectively and without seriously increasing his operating costs.[14]

Charges for Airway Use

Airways and traffic control facilities have been supplied and operated wholly at federal expense; but there is a general belief that, since a large segment of domestic civil aviation has reached a level of economic maturity which would permit it to make a reasonable contribution toward meeting the costs of the airways system, active consideration should be given to the inauguration of a program of domestic airway user charges.

It is important, however, to approach the problem of user charges with a view to imposing an initial charge at a level that would not handicap seriously the further and continued development of the industry. Even if the other advantages to the economy of a growing air transport industry are disregarded, the sounder long-range business

[14] *Modernizing the National System of Aviation Facilities, op. cit.*

policy, from the standpoint of the government's recovering the largest part of the cost for servicing the airways, may well be to start with a low initial charge and depend upon the industry's growth for increasing government receipts for user charges. In any event, the charging method should provide for an equitable distribution of the burden of airways system costs among the various users. The alternative methods of charging fall into two broad categories—direct charges and indirect charges.

A system of direct charges for the use of specific components and services of the federal airways system would meet several of the broad requirements of an equitable program, since such charges would be directly related to both the use made of, and the benefit derived from, individual facilities and services. However, the operational and administrative problems inherent in a system of direct charges appear to make this method undesirable. By leveling a charge for each time a facility is used, the system might also discourage the use of certain services by operators trying to economize, and thus create a safety hazard. The overriding importance of safety in air transportation would appear to rule out direct charges on this count alone.

There are a number of systems of indirect charges which could be used: (1) an aviation fuel-gallonage charge applicable to all domestically operated aircraft and (2) a gross ton-mile charge on large aircraft and a graduated registration fee on light planes. Less desirable methods of determining indirect charges applicable to the large aircraft are: (1) an airplane mileage charge, (2) a revenue ton-mile charge, and (3) a gross revenue charge. Of these, the fuel-gallonage charge imposed on all aviation gasoline and jet aircraft fuel seems most desirable and is recommended as being equitable and simple to administer.

The amount of fuel consumed by an aircraft is roughly proportionate to its size and the distance it travels. Thus, assuming that on most flights an aircraft is an actual or potential user of the federal airways, the amount of gasoline consumed would be an indirect measure of both the use made of these facilities and the benefits derived from them. The major impact of this type of charge would fall on the commercial air carriers, which are both the prime users and the greatest beneficiaries of the airways system. The burden on other civil aviation would be considerably lighter. The nature of the charge would thus insure an equitable distribution among the operators of large and small aircraft.

Chapter 3

COMMERCIAL AIR CARRIERS

THE START of air transportation in the United States grew out of what has been called "the spontaneous attraction of the airplane and the Post Office for one another."[1] The carriage of passengers and cargo on a regular schedule by air had been considered for a number of years and had even taken place from time to time in an irregular fashion; but all such activities were decidedly speculative, and the idea of flying the mail seemed to meet with public acceptance more readily than the carriage of passengers.[2] Safety was not a controlling factor in mail transportation; and such service was an accepted function of the government, so that a subsidy could be obtained to carry out the developmental work. This being the case, commercial operators did not have to rely on profits at the start.

Early Post Office Activities

In 1911, the Post Office Department displayed an interest in air transportation. A few sacks of mail were carried on the first flight of mail from Nassau to Mineola, Long Island, in September of that year, and 31 such flights were made in the year following. The department made several attempts to obtain federal appropriations for air mail, beginning in 1912, but met with no success until 1916,[3] when an experimental appropriation was made. In the following year

[1] E. P. Warner, *The Early History of Air Transportation* (Northfield, Vt.: Norwich University, 1938), p. 3.

[2] The first of the early regularly scheduled passenger-carrying organizations was the St. Petersburg–Tampa Airboat Line. It was started in January, 1914, and lasted for three months. The most optimistic attempt was made in 1916, when the American Trans-Oceanic Company was formed for the purpose of flying the Atlantic Ocean on regular schedules. The most enduring early attempt at scheduled passenger operation was that of the Aero Limited Company organized on July 26, 1919. This company operated between New York City and Atlantic City in the summer and between Key West and Cuba in the winter. This company continued, until 1924, to be the outstanding carrier in the United States.

[3] Under this small appropriation, the Post Office Department advertised for bids on proposed air mail routes in Alaska and between New Bedford and Nantucket, Massachusetts; but there were no acceptable bidders. It is interesting to note that these advertisements called for service to out-of-the-way places.

another appropriation was made for experimental service and also for the purchase, operation, and maintenance of "aeroplanes." With the funds so provided, air mail service between New York and Washington was begun on May 15, 1918. The air transport part of the operation was at first conducted by the War Department, which provided airplanes and personnel; but on August 12, 1918, the Post Office Department took over the operation with its own equipment and personnel. Service was inaugurated between New York and Chicago in 1919 and was extended from Chicago to San Francisco during 1920, in which year the Chicago–St. Louis and Chicago-Minneapolis routes were also opened.

Until 1924, air mail route operation was limited to daylight flying; but, in July of that year, night service began on the portion of the transcontinental route west of Chicago and a year later between New York and Chicago, after the solution of difficult problems of airway construction through the Allegheny Mountains. The completion of a night airway system from coast to coast was one of the Post Office Department's greatest contributions to commercial air transportation.

The importance of this transcontinental night and day air mail route cannot be overemphasized. It stimulated manufacturers to build planes adapted for night flying, and the regular air mail service over so long a distance made the public realize that letters sent through the air arrived safely and promptly and that great amounts of time could be saved by using air mail. The service on this route achieved an international reputation for its regularity, comparatively few accidents, and other achievements. It brought air transportation closer to the public as a practical reality.

By 1925, the development work of the government service had reached the point where private operation of an air transport service and the retirement of the government from the operation phases of air mail transportation seemed feasible. Legislation providing for service by contract carriers accordingly was provided by the Air Mail (Kelly) Act of February 2, 1925. Some time elapsed, however, before it was possible to place the first contract service in operation, and it was not until 1926 that a number of contract routes were opened. Private carriers soon were able to demonstrate a considerable degree of operating success, and plans were therefore made for the liquidation of the government air mail transport service. The Chicago–San Francisco section of the transcontinental route was turned over to Boeing Air Transport on July 1, 1927; and the New

York–Chicago section to National Air Transport on September 1, 1927.

The Beginning of Commercial Operation

Although commercial operation of air transport services received its first impetus from the letting of air mail contracts, the passage of the Air Commerce Act of 1926 distinctly encouraged it. (See Chapter 4.) Then came the flight across the Atlantic Ocean by Charles A. Lindbergh and other spectacular flights of the year 1927, increasing the public's interest in flying and doing much to make it possible to finance the beginnings of an air transport industry in this country. Improvements in equipment and further development of auxiliary facilities also contributed to the development of the industry, so that during 1928 and 1929 a veritable air transportation boom took place. The security markets of the period were favorable to new financing; the technical progress of aviation had been demonstrated by spectacular long-distance flights; and the earlier air mail carriers with favorable routes were obtaining large profits after the reduction of postage rates in 1928 stimulated volume. Transportation companies became a new division of the aviation industry, starting under the control and patronage of the same groups that had been interested in the manufacturing companies and had waited for increased government appropriations for air mail before entering the industry.[4] There is little doubt that the intense cultivation of aviation in the 1927–29 period was due to the increasing possibilities of profits sensed by financial interests. Certainly, air transportation had not yet found an economic function that would cause the sudden interest of financiers; nor was this interest a result of the fact that financial interests had awakened to the future possibilities of air transportation, for "pioneering had always been carried on by individuals or by the government, not by the financiers."[5] Possibilities of profits arose in the form of air mail pay to air transport organizations[6] and

[4] E. E. Freudenthal, *The Aviation Business* (New York: Vanguard Press, 1940), p. 79; J. H. Hamstra, "Two Decades—Federal Aero-Regulation in Perspective," *Journal of Air Law and Commerce*, April, 1941, pp. 108–20.

[5] Freudenthal, *op. cit.*, p. 98.

[6] In the period 1927–28, many airline executives did not want to bother with passenger traffic, so that its development was entirely incidental to the real business of carrying the mail. Operators, however, were forced to recognize the demand for passenger service created by the establishment of scheduled routes, but the following is typical of airline passenger regulations of that time. "Between New York and Chicago, Passenger tickets restricted as follows: (1) One passenger per trip, provided there is no interference with mail or express to be carried. (2) At any point en route the pilot has the authority to replace a passenger with mail or express or to decline further passage based on weather data concerning the flight." See A. E. Blomquist, *Outline of Air Transport Practice* (New York: Pitman Publishing Corp., 1941), p. 17.

also from the fact that at this time huge profits could be made on stock issues. Huge holding companies were formed, controlling manufacturing and operating companies at the same time.[7]

There were also other motives which caused certain individuals and organizations to put capital into air transportation between 1927 and 1929. These may be summarized as follows: (1) There were intercity jealousies, one city wanting just as good or better air service than another; (2) control over a future competitor was desired, as, for example, when a railroad company put money into an airline; (3) wealthy individuals, who combined an enthusiasm for this new means of transportation with a desire to make their community or region a leader in air transportation, sometimes contributed capital to a new airline with the thought that if it was lost they would not miss it and if it were not they would be "in on the ground floor" with a new investment medium; (4) as airlines became more numerous and consolidations developed nation-wide operations, additional capital was sometimes made available by the companies themselves for added facilities to fend off competition; (5) new capital was made available at times to permit some of the already established through lines to add connecting links between certain points in order to strengthen their operations from a sales standpoint; (6) towns and cities which wanted to be included in an airline system appealed not only to the pride of their wealthy citizens but also to their influential politicians. This accounted for the establishment of a number of short lines, because the politicians involved persuaded others to contribute capital on the promise of a lucrative government mail contract. In the case of most of the principal lines, however, it is doubtful whether the politicians did much more than add slightly to the already powerful motives.[8]

The history of scheduled air transportation is replete with the small airlines which sprang up almost over night, operated for a few months, and then ceased, usually going into bankruptcy. There was nothing rational about the development of air transportation in this country. Investors and others believed that the industry was developing rapidly and that it would show large profits, but many of these optimists lost money.

---

[7] The chief groups dominating the whole industry, manufacturing and transportation, from 1927 to 1934 were General Motors–North American Aviation Group, Curtiss-Wright Corporation, United Aircraft and Transport Corporation, and Aviation Corporation of Delaware. For an account of their financial and other operations, see Freudenthal, *op. cit.*, chap. v.

[8] See K. T. Healy, *The Economics of Transportation in America* (New York: Ronald Press Co., 1940), pp. 124–25, for a discussion based on congressional hearings.

There were 38 airlines existing during 1929. New companies brought the total operating lines up to 43 in 1930, out of which four discontinued operations before the end of that year.

The primary reason for the passage of the Watres Act of 1930 (see Chapter 8) was to avoid unprofitable operation of mail and passenger lines, because, even with the large increase in mail poundage which came about in 1929, many mail contractors were operating at a loss. Passenger rates were too low for airlines to make money from this traffic; and whenever these rates were increased, passenger travel fell off sharply. Various passenger-carrying airlines had entered the business hoping to establish themselves and absorb their losses until they could obtain mail contracts.

Organization of Air Transport Industry, 1930–34

The Watres Act of 1930 provided that the Postmaster General unify the air transportation industry, and in the two years following he accomplished this unification among the air mail carriers. Under his direction, by awarding mail contracts without competitive bidding, which did not enable many companies to qualify, and by granting extensions many times longer than the original mail routes, the air transport system assumed the major characteristics it has today. There were three transcontinental lines organized from the mass of shorter passenger and mail carriers.[9] Several of the small passenger-carrying airlines which tried to obtain mail contracts at this time were forced into consolidation with the larger airlines.

The total number of airlines dropped from 43 in 1930 to 32 in 1932. This figure does not, however, accurately measure the extent of consolidation and abandonment of airlines, for all during this period new passenger routes were being placed into operation. Not including the carriers that changed their names during this time, there were 19 airlines which began operations in 1930, 15 in 1931, and 9 in 1932. Of the 9 carriers beginning operation in 1932, 3 discontin-

[9] United Air Lines Transport Corporation (later United Airlines) obtained the northern route through the welding together of its four operating divisions—Boeing Air Transport, Pacific Air Transport, National Air Transport, and Varney Airlines. American Airways (later American Airlines) obtained the southern transcontinental route through its operating divisions—many small airlines—which had previously gone under the names of Universal Division, Colonial Division, Southern Division, and Embry-Riddle Division. Transcontinental and Western Air, formed by a combination of some of the routes of Western Air Express and Transcontinental Air Transport–Maddux, put into operation the middle transcontinental route. Eastern Air Transport (later Eastern Air Lines) operated in the territory of the present company on the Atlantic Coast. Northwest Airways operated in the same locality as the present Northwest Airlines, and Western Air Express (later Western Air Lines) operated on the Pacific Coast and in the western states.

ued operations before December 31 of that year, and 2 more shortly after the beginning of 1933.

From 1930 to 1934, improvements and even radical changes in flying equipment and operating methods enabled more and more satisfactory service—better co-ordinated, faster, and more comfortable—and better maintenance of schedules. At the same time, there were decided developments in airways, airports, weather reporting services, and other aids to air transportation. The flying equipment itself was not, however, standardized as to type or as to utilization of specific types in specific services.[10]

The Air Transport Industry from 1934 to the Civil Aeronautics Act of 1938

In 1934, the whole air transport industry was thrown into confusion when all mail contracts were canceled by the Democratic administration, because of alleged collusion between the mail carriers and Post Office officials of the previous administration and because of other abuses under the Watres Act.[11] The Army was ordered to fly the mail.

The cancellations of the air mail contracts focused public attention on the air mail situation, but before long the attention of the country was diverted from the mail issue because of the large number of accidents occurring under Army operation of the air mail services.[12] The President was forced by these circumstances, includ-

[10] On February 19, 1934, there were 65 designs, the products of 18 different makers, in the fleets of air mail contractors. Twelve of the models had no passenger space; the remainder accommodated from two to 18 passengers each. Cruising speeds ranged from 100 to 190 miles per hour but were generally about 125 miles per hour.

[11] It was no sudden caprice on the part of the administration that caused the cancellations, but an accumulation of evidence. As early as 1932 there had been agitation for the cancellation of the contracts awarded in 1930. In February, 1933, the so-called Crane Committee of the House of Representatives reported that interlocking interests and directorates had definitely prevented the free development of aviation and had resulted in the waste of public funds. This report, commenting on the failure of the Watres Act to function properly, recommended that the rate-making powers of the Postmaster General be curbed. In the next session of Congress, the Crane Committee's report was re-enforced by the testimony before the Senate Special Committee on Investigation of Air Mail and Ocean Mail Contracts. For a detailed statement of these matters see Freudenthal, *op. cit.*, chap. viii. In July, 1941, a commissioner of the United States Court of Claims reported that there was no fraud in the air mail contracts canceled in 1934. This left the way open for the old companies, since reorganized under new names, to claim damages amounting to about $2,500,000. For a detailed discussion see Paul M. Godehn and Frank E. Quindry, "Air Mail Contract Cancellations of 1934 and Resulting Litigation," *Journal of Air Law and Commerce*, Summer, 1954.

[12] Although ten Army fliers died within a period of about four months, only four of this number were killed while actually carrying the mail, and six were in training or on the way to their mail routes.

ing unusually bad weather conditions, to order the Army to curtail its flights.[13] The Army thereafter flew the mail for several months on a restricted basis, and in the meantime the commercial airlines prepared themselves for the readjustments foreshadowed by congressional hearings prior to the passage of the Air Mail Act of 1934.[14]

By the Air Mail Act of 1934, new mail contracts were to be issued under competitive bidding for an initial period of not over one year (later increased to three years); but it was stipulated that no contract was to be awarded to any person or company even remotely involved in the former "collusion" with Post Office officials.[15] A threefold control of the industry was set up: (1) The Post Office Department awarded air mail contracts and enforced air mail regulations. (2) The Interstate Commerce Commission was to set "fair and reasonable" rates of mail pay and was directed to review rates periodically. Payments for air mail transport were to be kept within the limits of anticipated postage revenues, and no air mail carrier was to be permitted to make unwarranted profits out of its mail contract. An air mail postage rate of 6 cents per ounce or fraction thereof was set at this time. (3) The Bureau of Air Commerce in the Department of Commerce regulated the safety side of air transportation and was responsible for airway maintenance and development.

The period from 1934 to 1938 saw many changes in the organization of the air transport industry. Provisions of the Air Mail Act of

---

[13] To some, this proved the superiority of the commercial airlines and was an acknowledgment of hasty action in canceling the contracts. But to others, it pointed to the fact that there was something decidedly inadequate in the training of the Army Air Corps, and experts agreed that the Army was not trained at that time to fly across the country or in bad weather.

[14] While the Army was carrying the mail from February to June, 1934, the airlines used the interlude to reorganize in order to be eligible to bid on the new temporary certificates which it was understood would be issued. Obviously, the nuclei of the old companies would continue and, if their compliance was legally sufficient, would get the awards. This was to be expected, as the only substantial amount of money available for airline operation was in the hands of the former mail carriers. See T. P. David, *The Economics of Air Mail Transportation* (Washington, D.C.: Brookings Institution, 1934), p. 207.

[15] This stipulation was the cause of some rather ridiculous "reorganizations" among the airlines. Names were changed from "ways" to "lines": United Aircraft and Transport Corporation's transport division, United Air Lines, became United Air Lines Transport Corporation; American Airways of Aviation Corporation became American Airlines; Eastern Air Transport and Transcontinental and Western Air of the North American–General Motors Group had a good many changes involving "Inc.," "transport," and "lines" and finally became Eastern Air Lines, Western Air Express, and Transcontinental and Western Air, Inc. Besides making these name changes, the three large groups required certain black-listed officers to resign and complied with the law in diverse ways; but all of them showed a certain amount of continuity in their control and/or management. For a complete discussion of these complicated reorganizations see Freudenthal, *op. cit.*, chap. viii.

1934 intended to modify the existing relationships between the airlines and other groups interested in aviation, as well as other provisions, led to the creation of new corporate identities and caused numerous changes in the official personnel of the carriers. There were also a limited number of acquisitions or unifications of lines or routes during this period. At the end of 1933, there were 25 scheduled air carriers; at the end of 1934, there were 24; and at the end of 1938, the number had declined to 16. Competitive conditions, as evidenced by the provision in a few instances of nonmail service in a territory served by an airline holding a mail contract and by practices in connection with passenger fares, caused considerable difficulty and eventually played a part in bringing about a more comprehensive form of regulation. For another thing, the competitive bidding for air mail contracts was becoming ridiculous, since some companies bid as low as 0.0008 mills per mile on competitive routes with, of course, the expectation of later asking for, and in all probability receiving, an increase after the route had been established.

One very important difference in the whole aviation situation became apparent shortly after the period of upheaval caused by the cancellation of mail contracts came to a close. This was the separation of the aviation industry into two definite parts. From then on, transport and manufacturing were recognized as two separate industries, which they in fact are.

The volume of business done by the airlines increased in large measure during the period 1934–38, and this increase in business was accompanied by additional improvements in service. Representative speeds of about 110 miles per hour in 1934 rose to about 158 miles per hour in 1938; speeds attainable under conditions of most efficient utilization of equipment similarly rose from about 140 to 190 miles per hour. Larger and more comfortable airplanes were manufactured for airline use,[16] the effective lives of airplanes were lengthened; and costs per seat-mile noticeably declined. Increases in the size of aircraft, however, made it more difficult to utilize certain of the existing airport facilities and necessitated airport improvements. At the same time, larger airplanes gave the airlines an incentive to stress the long-haul passenger business.

From 1934 to 1938, additional capital became available to the airlines. Many of the factors attracting investors to this industry, previously discussed, were still operative; but in the later years there

[16] The increase was from an average of 8 or 9 seats on July 1, 1934, to 12.7 seats four years later, with a range in the latter year from 6 to 21 seats per airplane.

was the pressure of steadily increasing traffic which required investment in additional facilities. This probably was the major force demanding new capital, particularly after 1934, although it is hard to differentiate between it and the pressure of technical progress which forced the purchase of new aircraft but which, at the same time, was itself partially a response to the increasing traffic. A considerable proportion of the capital required by some airlines came out of earnings.[17]

It may be said that two good results came out of the air mail cancellations and resulting legislation: (1) The airlines were weaned from their complete dependence on air mail contracts and were induced to cultivate passenger and express business more intensively. (2) The separation of manufacturing and transport companies into two industries weakened, even if it did not entirely destroy, the control of the large, monopolistic holding companies.

The difficulties of the airlines, caused in part by the threefold control and other provisions of the 1934 act, were accentuated by a series of accidents in the winter of 1936–37, which undermined public confidence, and by the general business depression of early 1938. By the middle of 1938, the entire industry was in a chaotic state, with several major carriers facing bankruptcy, half the originial investment in the airlines lost forever, and new capital so backward as to be practically unobtainable.

In consequence, the air transport industry itself was sponsor for the Civil Aeronautics Act of 1938, which provided for complete federal control over every phase of interstate airline operation. (See Chapter 4.)

The Air Transport Industry from June, 1938, to December, 1941

The period between the adoption of the Civil Aeronautics Act of 1938 and the entry of the United States into World War II is one which may be characterized by the term "regulated expansion." It was also a fairly tranquil period, since for the first time commercial

[17] See Healy, *op. cit.*, p. 126. Healy points out that, in spite of the apparently general feeling of many of the original contributors to the air transport industry that profit was not the controlling reason for their investment, a few of the lines actually made rather spectacular profits. In fact, these profits were high enough to be an important source of capital for expansion of their operations or improvement of their facilities. Western Air Express, Inc., plowed back $3,000,000 of its earnings in this way, and Boeing Air Transport was able very quickly to retire the securities issued for the original $700,000 cash put up and to earn in the neighborhood of $1,000,000 a year, after deducting expenses, for the five years of its existence as an individual operator. See also *Hearings before Senate Special Committee on Air Mail and Ocean Mail Contracts* (73d Cong., 2d sess., 1935), pp. 2253, 2274–75, 2855.

and other civil aviation in the United States had the benefit of a unified and comprehensive national policy, administered by a single federal agency.

The industry got off to a good start, as under the "grandfather" clause of the Civil Aeronautics Act the 16 airlines which had been in operation were granted certificates of convenience and necessity giving them permanent rights to their particular operations as of the effective date of the act, subject only to indefinite suspension or revocation for violation of the act. Within a short time nearly all the airlines applied for new routes. This was done partly because of the monopoly value which might be attached to any route certificate acquired as well as because it appeared that air transportation had possibilities of being a profitable operation and because of the desire to consolidate and protect dominant positions in various parts of the country. Some of these routes were also apparently sought for trading purposes to aid in obtaining other routes, as well as for protection against encroachment.[18] Some new routes were also sought by entirely new companies which had never operated before but most of them could be classified as feeder or local service routes to be operated by existing airlines. In addition, there were applications pending for a number of new stops on existing routes.

The Air Transport Industry in World War II

With the entry of the United States into World War II in December, 1941, the airlines, which had felt the pressure of oncoming hostilities in many ways for months previously, definitely became a war industry. Early in the spring of 1942, 221 of the 370 transport airplanes then operated by the airlines were ordered turned over, by sale or lease, to the armed services of the United States and to others of the allied nations. Many new airplanes which the airlines had on order with aircraft manufacturers had previously been relinquished at the request of the federal government. In addition, the government stipulated that the airlines would be expected to loan equipment and

[18] If all applications for proposed airline routes as of June 30, 1940, had been granted by the Civil Aeronautics Board, the air transportation system of the United States would have been increased by at least 50 per cent. The "grandfather" certificated airlines were:

American Airlines, Inc.
Braniff Airways, Inc.
Chicago and Southern Air Lines, Inc.
Continental Air Lines, Inc.
Delta Air Corporation
Eastern Air Lines, Inc.
Inland Air Lines, Inc.
Mid-Continent Airlines, Inc.
National Airlines, Inc.
Northeast Airlines, Inc.
Northwest Airlines, Inc.
Pennsylvania-Central Airlines Corp.
Transcontinental & Western Air, Inc.
United Air Lines Transport Corp.
Western Air Express Corp.
Wilmington-Catalina Airlines, Ltd.

personnel for special military missions and to transport priority passengers and cargo on their scheduled flights. Left with less than 50 per cent of their original fleet to continue their operations under private management and as separate, independent entities, the airlines rescheduled their operations by eliminating some stops, curtailing 28 per cent of the prewar schedules, and suspending certain routes for the duration. All discounts for round trips and the 15 per cent reduction in passenger fares to credit card holders were discontinued.

The phenomenal operating achievements of the airlines during the war, accomplished through complete utilization of equipment and operating efficiency, are apparent when the traffic volume carried is compared with the number of aircraft available. There were large and impressive increases in mail, express, and passenger loads per airplane. The average passenger load factor for each plane on every flight rose from 64 per cent in 1941 to an almost full capacity load—91 per cent—in 1944. While the load factor was rising, the total number of passengers carried began diminishing in 1942 with the loss of equipment and reached the low ebb, since 1940, in 1943 with a total of 3,454,040 revenue and nonrevenue passengers for the year. These figures do not reveal the fact that some of the scheduled flights of certain airlines were approximately 100 per cent priority passengers and flew a 97 to 99 per cent capacity load every trip. Nor do they show the number of passengers turned away or removed each day for priority passengers, mail, or express.

Although the domestic airlines' operations were war-curbed by lack of equipment and suspension of a number of routes, the airlines continued to maintain their mileage near the prewar level. During 1944 the airlines' network in operation stood at 47,384 miles, compared with the 42,757 operating mileage before Pearl Harbor.

The wartime boom in airline traffic caused investors and speculators to look upon the airlines with favor. While the military contracts[19] made by the air carriers were on a cost-plus-fixed-fee basis, the airlines profited by these activities and also by their commercial transport operations. In fact, the extraordinary passenger traffic boost and the still greater expansion of air mail and air express traf-

[19] It should be realized that, at the same time the airlines were meeting the demands for wartime traffic to the best of their ability in their commercial services, almost all of them were engaged in the performance of military contracts. They ferried military aircraft; they modified, repaired, and overhauled military aircraft engines and other equipment; they trained pilots; they maintained extensive passenger and cargo transport services over most of the world; they engaged in the emergency movement of troops; they transported wounded; they built airports; and they established airways.

TABLE 12

DOMESTIC SCHEDULED OPERATORS, AIRCRAFT IN SERVICE, AVERAGE AVAILABLE SEATS, AND ROUTE MILEAGE OPERATED, 1926–59

As of December 31*	Operators	Aircraft in Service	Average Available Seats†	Route Mileage Operated
1926	13	‡	‡	‡
1927	18	‡	‡	‡
1928	34	268	‡	‡
1929	38	442	‡	‡
1930	43	497	‡	30,293
1931	39	490	‡	30,857
1932	32	456	6.61	28,956
1933	25	418	7.59	28,283
1934	24	423	8.86	28,609
1935	26	363	10.33	29,190
1936	24	280	10.67	29,797
1937	22	291	12.52	32,006
1938	16§	260§	13.91	34,879§
1939	18‖	276‖	14.66	36,654‖
1940	19	369	16.54	42,757
1941	19	370	17.54	45,163
1942	19	186	17.91	41,596
1943	19	204	18.34	42,537
1944	19	288	19.05	47,384
1945	20	421	19.68	48,516¶
1946	24	674	25.25	53,981¶
1947	28	810	29.93	62,224¶
1948	31	878	32.37	68,674¶
1949	37	913	35.03	73,955¶
1950	38	960	37.47	77,440¶
1951	38	981	39.55	78,913¶
1952	35	1,078	42.71	77,977¶
1953	32	1,139	46.07	78,384¶
1954	32	1,175	50.06	78,294¶
1955	31	1,212	51.60	78,992¶
1956	30	1,347	52.43	84,189¶
1957	30	1,494	53.99	88,325¶
1958	30	1,546	55.79	89,747¶
1959	30	1,596	59.04	96,655¶

* For the years 1938–48, route mileage operated is a weighted average for the month of December; for 1949 and subsequent years, the route mileage operated is based on the fourth quarter.

† Obtained by dividing passenger-seat-miles by revenue-miles flown in passenger service.

‡ Not available.

§ Does not include Colonial and Marine Airlines.

‖ Does not include Marine Airlines.

¶ Data subsequent to 1944 based on revised CAB procedures.

Source: FAA, *Statistical Handbook of Aviation* (Washington, D.C., 1960).

fic caused nearly all of the airlines, which had frequently been operating at a loss before the war, to show healthy net operating incomes.

The first impact of the end of the war was felt early in 1945, before the German surrender on May 8 of that year. The airlines began to receive back many of the airplanes turned over to the armed services in 1942; and as soon as possible after V-E Day, the Army started turning over other aircraft it no longer needed. Also, realizing the seriousness of the airline flight equipment shortage, the War Production Board in the latter part of April, 1945, issued a priority regulation clearing the way for immediate production of new aircraft for

TABLE 13

UNITED STATES SCHEDULED INTERNATIONAL OPERATORS, AIRCRAFT, ROUTE MILEAGE, AND LENGTH OF TRIP, 1927–59

Calendar Year*	Operators	Aircraft in Service	Route Mileage	Average Length of Passenger Trip (Miles)
1927	1	†	†	†
1928	1	57	†	†
1929	4	83	†	†
1930	3	103	19,256	464
1931	3	100	19,543	238
1932	3	108	19,574	289
1933	3	86	19,404	315
1934	2	99	22,192	351
1935	2	101	31,261	381
1936	2	94	31,990	414
1937	2	92	31,979	416
1938	2	73	34,968	487
1939	2	84	43,455	557
1940	3	68	52,322	614
1941	3	83	†	713
1942	3	68	†	880
1943	3	70	27,211	874
1944	3	70	29,708	910
1945	4	97	38,885	942
1946	9	147	66,419	1,057
1947	12	154	95,503	1,332
1948	13	175	105,853	1,376
1949	13	177	109,011	1,351
1950	12	160	106,401	1,316
1951	12	140	108,763	1,273
1952	13	149	110,465	1,277
1953	14	161	111,826	1,254
1954	15	161	112,488	1,304
1955	15	147	114,005	1,294
1956	13	196	113,694	1,298
1957	14	170	133,884	1,305
1958	15	185	135,617	1,304
1959	15	156	132,495	1,343

* Operators and aircraft in service are as of December 31 of each year. Route mileages for 1930 through 1940 are December 31 figures; for 1943 through 1948 they are averages for the month of December; for 1949 and subsequent years the route mileage operated is based on the fourth quarter.

† Not available.

Source: FAA, *Statistical Handbook of Aviation* (Washington, D.C., 1960).

the commercial airlines or for civilian transport production. Previously the War Production Board had been laboring under the impression that the airlines could secure sufficient equipment to satisfy their needs from airplanes released by the Army and the Surplus Property Board. The airlines asked for 321 planes, more than two thirds of which were four-engine equipment, delivery requested for the last quarter of 1945.

Even though some equipment was allocated to the airlines by the Surplus Property Board before the end of the war in Europe, these aircraft had to be reconverted to the needs of the airlines and to commercial standards as required by the Civil Aeronautics Board. In many instances, more man-hours were required to put an airplane back in operation than it took to build a new airplane of the same type; and costs of reconverting an airplane ran as high as $90,000 in some cases, which was almost as much as a new airplane of the same type would have cost.[20]

The worst part of the situation was, however, that the scarce mechanical and other help which was used to reconvert aircraft returned by the Army could otherwise have been used by the airlines in keeping their present airplanes in operation. Thus, the airlines' ability to operate efficiently was made more complicated by having to use their experienced personnel in reconverting surplus equipment.

A tremendous load was put on the facilities of the commercial airlines with the end of the war in Europe, because they were faced with the task of transporting military and war-important civilians to the West Coast of this country at a time when their flying equipment was still very limited. However, the consensus at that time among airline people was that, although the situation would be tight, the task of transporting military and war-important civilians to the West Coast would not be an impossible one. They were correct in these assumptions; but they were not anticipating, and therefore completely overlooked, a very important factor in their calculations. The military and the railroads had miscalculated the railway facilities that would be required to transport the troops who were being deployed from Europe to the Pacific theater of war. When the movement finally got underway, it was found that the railroads could not possibly handle all the traffic; and it was decided that the airlines would have to relieve the railroads of part of the load. This only added to the already overcrowded and confused situation on the airlines.

The demand for airline space became so acute that the airlines

---

[20] Before the war, a DC-3 cost about $125,000 new.

TABLE 14

Indicators of Growth in Traffic and Operations of the Air Carrier Industry

(Calendar Years 1949–58)

Item	1949	1950	1951	1952	1953	1954	1955	1956	1957	1958
A. Traffic in scheduled service of certificated carriers:										
1. Overall revenue ton-miles (000)	1, 133, 138	1, 359, 096	1, 689, 811	1, 970, 640	2, 246, 194	2, 511, 959	2, 981, 994	3, 386, 223	3, 762, 983	3, 799, 324
Percent change from base year	0	20	49	74	98	122	163	199	232	235
2. Cargo revenue ton-miles (freight and express) (000)	190, 334	271, 229	295, 027	330, 244	346, 323	353, 259	434, 294	504, 112	553, 789	550, 472
Percent change from base year	0	43	55	74	82	86	128	165	191	189
3. U.S.-mail ton-miles (000)	61, 669	68, 938	86, 693	92, 992	98, 161	118, 981	142, 456	152, 475	160, 675	177, 425
Percent change from base year	0	12	41	51	59	93	131	147	161	188
4. Total revenue passenger-miles (000)	8, 827, 431	10, 243, 157	13, 203, 324	15, 624, 326	18, 210, 739	20, 610, 611	24, 350, 968	27, 623, 229	31, 260, 803	31, 499, 438
Percent change from base year	0	16	50	77	106	133	176	213	254	257
5. First-class revenue passenger-miles (000)	8, 576, 141	9, 186, 796	11, 509, 461	12, 465, 842	13, 091, 719	13, 217, 929	14, 838, 208	16, 171, 815	17, 910, 721	17, 323, 104
Percent change from base year	0	7	34	45	53	54	73	89	109	102
6. Coach revenue passenger-miles (000) [1]	251, 290	1, 056, 361	1, 693, 863	3, 158, 484	5, 119, 020	7, 392, 682	9, 512, 760	11, 451, 414	13, 350, 082	14, 176, 334
Percent change from base year	0	320	574	1, 157	1, 937	2, 842	3, 686	4, 457	5, 213	5, 541
B. Traffic in nonscheduled service of certificated carriers: [2]										
7. Overall revenue ton-miles (000)	12, 157	38, 240	53, 756	32, 684	35, 818	51, 457	94, 034	199, 701	319, 410	320, 921
Percent change from base year	0	215	342	169	195	323	673	1, 543	2, 527	2, 540
8. Passenger revenue ton-miles (000)	[3] 8, 400	N.A.	24, 524	23, 618	24, 141	36, 183	36, 810	102, 718	152, 452	145, 648
Percent change from base year	0	N.A.	192	181	187	331	338	1, 123	1, 715	1, 634
9. Cargo revenue ton-miles (000)	[3] 3, 757	N.A.	29, 232	9, 066	11, 677	15, 274	57, 223	96, 983	166, 957	175, 273
Percent change from base year	0	N.A.	678	141	211	307	1, 423	2, 481	4, 344	4, 565
10. Revenue passenger-miles (000)	83, 999	N.A.	241, 449	234, 214	237, 166	362, 082	381, 533	1, 038, 015	1, 532, 299	1, 468, 275
Percent change from base year	0	N.A.	187	179	182	331	354	1, 136	1, 724	1, 648
C. Traffic of supplemental (noncertificated) carriers:										
11. Overall revenue ton-miles (000) [4]	N.A.	113, 166	187, 615	203, 881	200, 970	176, 309	214, 169	209, 040	163, 436	206, 119
Percent change from base year	N.A.	0	66	80	78	56	89	85	44	82
12. Cargo revenue ton-miles (000)	N.A.	36, 189	80, 129	78, 713	75, 279	52, 087	74, 601	108, 304	86, 708	89, 195
Percent change from base year	N.A.	0	121	117	108	44	106	199	140	146
13. Revenue passenger-miles (000)	N.A.	769, 768	1, 074, 865	1, 251, 685	1, 256, 911	1, 242, 224	1, 395, 682	1, 007, 362	767, 287	1, 169, 236
Percent change from base year	N.A.	0	40	63	63	61	81	31	0	52
D. Scope of service offered by certificated carriers:										
14. Stations served (as of June 30) [5]	583	675	699	691	692	728	708	710	705	703
Percent change from base year	0	16	20	19	19	25	21	22	21	21
15. Unduplicated route mileage operated (average over 4th quarter) [6]	181, 678	183, 841	187, 676	188, 359	190, 210	190, 782	200, 934	214, 963	238, 166	246, 177
Percent change from base year	0	1	3	4	5	5	11	18	31	36
16. Duplicated route mileage certificated (as of June 30)	323, 471	357, 199	394, 548	401, 811	411, 312	409, 614	428, 160	519, 673	554, 364	563, 844
Percent change from base year	0	10	22	24	27	27	32	61	71	74
17. Aircraft departures in scheduled service	2, 067, 327	2, 207, 960	2, 411, 577	2, 610, 364	2, 935, 793	3, 000, 713	3, 276, 386	3, 501, 652	3, 768, 861	3, 633, 348
Percent change from base year	0	7	17	26	42	45	58	69	82	76

industry:										
18. Total available seat-miles in schedules service (000)	15, 350, 493	16, 841, 573	20, 013, 727	24, 126, 154	28, 887, 433	33, 374, 457	38, 574, 201	43, 674, 463	51, 059, 269	53, 115, 173
Percent change from base year	0	10	30	57	88	117	151	185	233	246
19. Total assets (as of December 31) (000)	$714, 335	$788, 022	$882, 435	$1, 049, 217	$1, 128, 394	$1, 212, 329	$1, 371, 759	$1, 740, 857	$1, 969, 250	$2, 270, 409
Percent change from base year	0	10	24	47	58	70	92	144	176	218
20. Total capital invested (average over the year) (000)	$468, 902	$545, 231	$572, 259	$640, 900	$774, 109	$830, 127	$911, 295	$1, 104, 633	$1, 312, 059	$1, 534, 758
Percent change from base year	0	16	22	37	65	77	94	136	180	227
21. Investment in flight equipment (as of June 30) (000)	$248, 800	$257, 400	$289, 700	$370, 200	$447, 600	$524, 300	$543, 300	$648, 300	$807, 800	$993, 000
Percent change from base year	0	3	16	49	80	111	118	161	225	299
22. Number of aircraft in service (as of June 30) [7]	1, 061	1, 170	1, 207	1, 286	1, 387	1, 423	1, 448	1, 565	1, 741	1, 899
Percent change from base year	0	10	14	21	31	34	36	48	64	79
23. Number of carriers certificated (as of December 31)	70	65	63	61	59	60	58	55	54	55
Percent change from base year	0	−7	−10	−13	−16	−14	−17	−21	−23	−21
24. Number of airline employees (as of December 31)[8]	82, 315	85, 015	99, 331	107, 589	113, 207	113, 375	126, 970	136, 441	151, 681	149, 399
Percent change from base year	0	3	21	31	38	38	54	66	84	81
F. Financial and operational data of certificated carriers:										
25. Total operating revenues (including service mail pay and subsidy) (000)	$771, 261	$840, 216	$1, 024, 662	$1, 169, 683	$1, 304, 839	$1, 440, 977	$1, 640, 604	$1, 883, 497	$2, 128, 406	$2, 243, 927
Percent change from base year	0	9	33	52	69	87	113	144	176	191
26. Net income (after taxes) (000)	$17, 216	$40, 657	$56, 458	$61, 371	$60, 078	$66, 384	$79, 050	$80, 820	$44, 573	$50, 324
27. Federal subsidy accruing (fiscal year data) (000)[9]	$75, 732	$83, 512	$69, 649	$63, 536	$66, 691	$64, 309	$45, 785	$43, 791	$44, 579	$48, 311
Percent change from base year	0	10	−8	−16	−12	−15	−40	−42	−41	−36
28. Federal subsidy accruing as percent of total operating revenues (fiscal year data)	10. 1	10. 7	7. 6	5. 9	5. 4	4. 7	2. 9	2. 5	2. 2	2. 2
Percent change from base year	0	6	−25	−42	−47	−53	−71	−75	−78	−78
29. All income and other taxes paid (domestic) (000) [10]	$23, 424	$50, 252	$88, 611	$82, 901	$88, 268	$97, 317	$120, 027	$120, 627	$90, 274	N.A.
Percent change from base year	0	115	278	254	277	315	412	415	285	N.A.
30. Airmail revenues of the Post Office Department (fiscal year data) (000) [11]	$91, 081	$101, 454	$126, 057	$152, 017	$156, 610	$164, 761	$168, 655	$179, 725	$185, 308	$182, 915
Percent change from base year	0	11	38	67	72	81	85	97	104	101
31. Overall revenue ton-miles in scheduled service per airline employee	13, 766	15, 987	17, 012	18, 343	19, 599	22, 156	23, 486	24, 647	24, 809	25, 084
Percent change from base year	0	16	24	33	42	61	71	79	80	82

1 Includes economy passenger-miles. Economy service between New York, N.Y., and San Juan, P.R., was inaugurated on June 20, 1956, and between New York and Europe across the North Atlantic on April 1, 1958.

2 Data under this heading do not include figures for certain operations serving the Department of Defense for the years 1950 through 1956.

3 Estimated.

4 These figures include passenger revenue ton-miles calculated from revenue passenger-miles on the basis of 200 pounds per person.

5 Figures do not include Alaska stations.

6 Figures do not include data for routes of intra-Alaska carriers.

7 Data are from CAA (FAA 1959), *United States Aircraft Engaged in Air Transportation*; 1958 is as of January 14, 1959.

8 Data for 1949–53 do not include figures for Alaskan carriers.

9 Figures are estimates by the Rates Division, Bureau of Air Operations.

10 Not including, of course, passenger excise taxes merely collected and forwarded by the carriers.

11 Data from U.S. Post Office Department's *Cost Ascertainment Report*, 1958, Table 250, p. 106.

Note: "N.A." means "data not available."

Source: *Annual Report of the CAB, 1959* (Washington, D.C., 1960).

adopted the policy of confirming no advance reservations west of Chicago, where the conditions were worst. The carriers at that time were operating with a load factor of 90 to 95 per cent capacity west from Chicago, with priority demands taking 90 per cent of the space. The priority load became so heavy that only the highest priority passengers could expect to reach their destination on transcontinental flights either east- or west-bound. This situation was eased somewhat by the gradual release by the Army and Surplus Property procedures of 210 aircraft, which were reconverted and placed in service. These airplanes brought the airline fleet up to a total of 375 planes, more than they ever had in operation before. The Army also co-operated by releasing transport captains so that the airlines would have sufficient personnel to operate the additional equipment. Other personnel, such as co-pilots and mechanics, were also discharged but more slowly. Five airlines were assigned Army aircraft to operate transcontinental troop movements requiring 20 flights daily under contract. The original plan was to carry 25,000 men a month across the nation in the redeployment program.

After the end of the war with Japan, the airlines suddenly found themselves in the midst of plenty of available equipment as compared to the serious shortage which existed when the European war was over. Although much surplus equipment became available, the airlines in many cases did not wish to buy it from the government. Instead, they preferred to rent existing Army types until more suitable airplanes became available.

In October, 1945, the priority system was abolished, which presented the airlines with a new set of problems, since airline reservations and ticketing personnel were accustomed to the priority system, with many having worked under no other. Moreover, the abandonment of the priority system came at a time when the railroads were still very much congested. The result was a very large shifting of passenger travel to the airlines, so that the total volume of passengers to be handled was still large.

The Air Transport Industry since World War II

With the close of World War II, the expansive characteristics of early periods again became apparent with the acquisition and conversion of surplus military aircraft, the placing of orders for millions of dollars worth of more modern and faster postwar aircraft, the recruiting and training of large numbers of new personnel, and the later acquisition, testing, and introduction into service of the new, faster, and larger types of aircraft. The conversion of management and of techniques of control from the needs of the small-scale operations of the past to those of the large-scale operations which in the postwar period suddenly confronted airline managements was only one of the many and varied aspects of the expansion program. The management problems were complicated not only by the magnitude of the expansion but also by its rapidity, and they extended into all the financial and operational activities of the carriers.

One of the problems, that of re-equipment, was not limited to aircraft alone. The introduction of new types of airplanes brought with it a long series of demands for other new equipment. Overhaul shops and maintenance bases had to be equipped to handle the new airplanes and engines; new servicing facilities and loading devices were required; and spare-parts inventories had to be replaced. As a result, the replacement of the airline fleet became a major operation.

During 1946, the first full peacetime year of business since 1942, aircraft manufacturers, released from military mass production contracts, concentrated on the development of new aircraft types for the armed forces, safer and more efficient airplanes for the private owner, and larger and faster transports for commercial air transportation. The certificated airlines, free once more to acquire new and additional flight equipment, expanded their domestic aircraft fleet from a total of 378 in October, 1945 to approximately 700 in October, 1946. Internationally, American air carriers enlarged their fleet from 84 to 143. Four-engined transports were Army C-54's converted for commercial use, but many air carriers had placed orders for new and faster designs promised for 1947–48 delivery. Domestic operations were increased through amendments of existing certificates and by authorizing seven new companies to operate local feeder air services. Foreign operations of certificated United States air carriers were extended and four additional such airlines were authorized to engage in foreign air service. This action of the Civil Aeronautics Board resulted in the certification of three United States airlines to operate two round-the-world commercial air routes for the first time in history.

In collaboration with the Department of State, the Board continued efforts to secure traffic rights for United States flag carriers in foreign nations. During 1946, this resulted in the United States concluding bilateral air transport agreements with 14 countries, bringing to 32 the total of such agreements. In addition, after the ratification of the Chicago Convention in April, which established the

International Civil Aviation Organization on a permanent basis, the Board continued to participate in the formation of United States policies with reference to various economic phases of United States participation in the activities of ICAO.

The year 1947 marked the first time since the end of the war that completely new transport aircraft, larger and faster than any previously used, were placed in commercial service by the airlines. The total number of transport aircraft used by United States air carriers in domestic and foreign services increased from 843 in October, 1946 to 930 in October, 1947. During this same period, the domestic transport aircraft fleet increased from 700 to 744, while the international fleet increased from 143 to 186. Even more noticeable was the increased use of four-engined transports, in both domestic and foreign service, the number rising from 236 to 404, which included new Douglas DC-6's and Lockheed Constellations.

United States air-carrier route expansion continued. Domestically, certificated route mileage increased from 85,279 in October, 1946 to 123,846 miles by October, 1947, a new increase of 38,567 route miles. International and overseas route mileage also increased from 175,265 to 178,974, a net increase of 3,709 miles. At the same time, 13 foreign air carriers were authorized to serve the United States.

The increase in domestic route mileage, providing for the certification of new routes and the extension of existing routes, also included temporary 3-year certification of 6,321 new route miles of experimental local feeder service, bringing the total feeder-service route miles to 13,515. It was not until 1955 that Congress directed that permanent certificates of convenience and necessity be awarded to the feeder or local service airlines.

The increase in size, speed, and general complexity of air-transport aircraft and the increase in air traffic, caused a re-examination of many of the existing standards of safety, stimulated by an unprecedent series of commercial air-carrier accidents during January and May, 1947. The first of these resulted in the formation of two committees of the Congress to investigate matters of air safety, and the second of which resulted in the President appointing a Special Board of Inquiry on Air Safety.

The expansion of air-carrier routes, the gradual shift to larger and faster transport aircraft, the increase in personal aircraft from 71,000 to 83,000, the increase in private and commercial pilots from 355,000 to approximately 415,000 was indicative of the inherent vigor of American civil aviation. The unsettled economic conditions within the aviation industry, which attended the technical and operational advances of 1946, only temporarily retarded its development. By early 1948, however, the industry was faced with increasingly complex problems involving its financial and competitive position. Airline earnings during the fiscal year 1948, although somewhat improved over the preceding year, were nevertheless unsatisfactory, and it became apparent that the difficulties facing civil aviation were larger than those which could reasonably be ascribed simply to postwar adjustment.

The major task facing the carriers and the Civil Aeronautics Board at this time was the development of policies which would return the industry to a sound economic and financial basis and at the same time foster its continued growth. Moreover, both objectives had to be met at a reasonable cost to the government. The airlines were clearly incapable of continuing their operations in the face of heavy losses. On the other hand, the requirements of the postal service, the foreign and domestic commerce, and particularly the national defense, dictated the continued growth and improvement of the air transportation system. The dictates of economy and simple good sense required that the existing system and future expansion be as nearly self-supporting as possible.

Although the safety record of the airlines in 1948 was substantially improved over that of the preceding year, the fact that it was necessary to ground three of the four new postwar transport aircraft for varying periods of time, on a compulsory or voluntary basis, made more difficult the economic problems confronting the industry.

In March, 1948, the Civil Aeronautics Board issued a revised "service" mail rate for the five largest airlines, representing a substantial increase over the previously prevailing rate. It was not, however, designed to contain any element of subsidy. This was to have been a new final "service" rate, but the five carriers concerned took exception to it, and it was accordingly established as a temporary rate. The importance of the rate arose in part from the fact that the carriers to whom it applied represented, in terms of the total air transportation performed, approximately 80 per cent of the domestic industry, and in part from the importance of the concept of the "service" rate as opposed to the "need" rate.[21]

It was in 1948 that it became apparent that the previous uninterrupted growth of the airlines was becoming beset with difficulties.

[21] See Chapter 8.

The inflation in airline costs had gradually caught up with airline efficiency. The airline industry had been in a peculiarly fortunate position. In spite of postwar price inflation, the airlines acquired aircraft of improved economic performance, which together with managerial methods and controls, made it possible for airline unit costs to be steadily reduced. At the same time that wages and price levels were pushing upward, the airlines were realizing the maximum economies inherent in the larger equipment. Warning signs appeared during the latter part of 1948 however, indicating that the rising costs were beginning to outstrip airline economies. Another warning sign was a trend toward declining load factors indicating that the question of excess capacity was becoming of increasing importance. Plans and equipment programs laid immediately following the war and based on the generally favorable outlook for airline traffic were resulting in the installation of large quantities of larger and faster equipment which far exceeded the capacity of the older aircraft. It would, of course, have been unwise and unwarranted to expect the maintenance of load factors comparable to those achieved during the war period or immediately thereafter, but, at the same time, neither the airlines nor the government could long support the operation of capacity which was far in excess of a stable, or slightly diminishing, volume of traffic. The control of excess capacity appeared, therefore, to constitute a major problem for both the carriers and the Civil Aeronautics Board.

A still further difficulty concerned routes. Since the end of the war, the route pattern, both domestic and international, grew substantially. Changes in the type of equipment employed, the leveling off of passenger traffic, and the process of route consolidations made it appear that certain alterations and modifications of the existing route pattern were required.

Another important development at this time concerned a new competitive factor—the nonscheduled or irregular operator. At the close of the war, the availability of a large number of surplus transport aircraft of the C-47 and C-54 type, plus the large number of former military personnel with extensive air transport experience, led to the establishment of numerous new air-carrier ventures. The Civil Aeronautics Board, in 1947, granted an exemption from economic regulation to the so-called large irregular carriers to conduct nonscheduled, irregular operations for passengers or property domestically and for property only abroad. The basis and intent of this regulation was that these carriers would provide needed air service auxiliary to those furnished by the certificated scheduled airlines and would serve an economic function similar to that of the tramp steamer in ocean shipping. Events and developments following the issuance of this regulation demonstrated, however, that the economic opportunities for irregular operations were limited. The result was that many of these large irregular carriers suffered extensive financial reverses. Others, in an attempt to survive economically, went far beyond the letter and spirit of their exemption from economic regulation and engaged in what was in fact a scheduled service, in competition with the certificated airlines. The operations of many of these carriers were actually illegal. Most of these operations were confined to a limited number of areas in which there was a heavy flow of traffic, such as Puerto Rico to the United States, transcontinental, northwest to Alaska. The charges and the general level of service which these carriers offered were substantially below those usually furnished by the certificated trunk-line carriers, and the service was frequently referred to as "coach-type" service. In the spring and summer of 1948, the Board launched a vigorous enforcement program against those irregular carriers which appeared to be willfully and flagrantly violating the exemption provided for them. (This group constituted 25 or 30 out of a total of 110 large, irregular carriers.)

In 1949, the economic status and outlook of the air transportation industry rapidly improved with operations of the major branches of the industry conducted at a profit. To some extent, this profit was the result of bringing up-to-date rates of mail pay through retroactive adjustments and through increases in current rates. But in large measure, the profitable operations of 1949, particularly for the domestic trunk-line carriers, were the result of a substantial increase in passenger and other types of air traffic. After a decline from 1947 to 1948, passenger traffic in 1949 established a new record for domestic trunk-line carriers of 6.2 billion passenger-miles and 2 billion for our international carriers.

It was recognized, however, by the industry and by the Civil Aeronautics Board that the improvement in the situation of the airlines which had been brought about through increasing rates of mail compensation was essentially a short-run corrective designed to re-establish the industry at a point from which it could exercise its own initiative and energy in reducing its dependence on the government.

By 1953, some of the results of this initiative became apparent. One of the most important developments was the expansion of coach-type services by the certificated airlines. The first coach-type service to be offered was that of Capital Airlines, Inc., between New York and Chicago, which was inaugurated November 4, 1948. During the fiscal year 1949 several other services were started, and the expansion continued year by year so that by 1953 the domestic certificated airlines were providing 154 daily air coach schedules, serving 53 American cities with a total population of nearly 50 million. In the international field, low-fare tourist service became available to Europe, the Middle East, Central and South America, Hawaii, Alaska, and Puerto Rico, and it was anticipated that by the spring of 1954 such service would be expanded to India and Japan. Measured in terms of passenger-miles flown, low-fare air transportation services constituted about 22 per cent of the total domestic air travel market and almost 34 per cent of international passenger travel in 1953, as compared to 15 per cent and 18 per cent, respectively, in 1952. By 1958, air coach passenger traffic accounted for approximately 39 per cent of total domestic trunk-line travel and for some 68 per cent of international air passenger volume.

During the years following World War II, the public continued to benefit directly from the rate structure of the air transportation system. Although the general price level, including the rates charged by other forms of transportation, increased almost yearly, the cost per mile of air travel to the passenger actually declined. Average passenger fares per mile dropped from 5.8 cents in 1949 to 5.6 cents in 1958 for the domestic trunk carriers. In the same period, international fares declined from 7.9 cents to 6.4 cents. By decreasing the cost of air transportation despite the marked decline in the purchasing power of the dollar, the air transport industry provided one of the real bargains available to the American consumer.

During 1953, two developments of major significance occurred in mail-pay disbursement. Under the President's Reorganization Plan No. 10, the Civil Aeronautics Board was made responsible for the payment of the subsidy element in mail rates, and the Postmaster General for the payment of the compensatory or service element of the mail rates. Pursuant to this plan, the Board issued an order formally separating for the first time the compensatory and subsidy components in mail rates for all certificated mail carriers.

The second new development in this field was the establishment by the Civil Aeronautics Board of final mail rates upon petition by the Postmaster General for the carriage of first-class mail (other than air mail at the regular first-class postage rate) between Chicago, on the one hand, and Washington and Newark/New York, on the other. Such mail was to be transported on a nonpriority, space-available basis for an experimental period of one year from October 1, 1953, but was later extended indefinitely.

The year 1958 marked the twentieth anniversary of the Civil Aeronautics Act. In those twenty years, the nation witnessed a dynamic growth in aviation and air transportation. In 1938, scheduled air transportation consisted of a network of short-hop operations conducted by 23 airlines. In 1958, certificated airlines provided long- and medium-haul trunk services in domestic, overseas, and foreign operations; local services connected the smaller communities with major traffic centers; domestic, overseas and international all-cargo services; and helicopter services in and around New York, Chicago, and Los Angeles. In addition, the air transportation system of the United States consisted of 42 supplemental carriers which engaged in extensive common carrier services of a type not experienced by their predecessors, the fixed-base operators. It also comprised 72 freight forwarders and a large number of air-taxi operators. Fifty foreign air carriers had been issued foreign air-carrier permits by the Civil Aeronautics Board authorizing transportation to United States points.

In 1938, there were approximately 11,000 civil aircraft registered in the United States. By 1958, there were 67,000. In these twenty years, the number of civil pilots increased from 23,000 to 809,000. The commercial transport industry, which carried less than 1½ million passengers in 1938, carried 50 million passengers in 1958.

The growth in twenty years in size and complexity of the regulated industry can be measured, at least in part, by the following indicators:

	1938	*1958*
Domestic certificated route-miles	39,300	254,100
Foreign and territorial certificated route-miles	31,100	328,300
Domestic revenue ton-miles of certificated airlines (millions) per year	58	2,656
Domestic revenue plane-miles flown by certificated airlines (millions) per year	76	734
Scheduled revenue passenger-miles flown (millions) per year	533	29,420
Passengers (thousands) per year	1,306	50,000
Average seats per domestic trunk-line aircraft	13.9	56.2
Number of scheduled aircraft	311	1,758
Invested certificated air transport industry capital (millions)	$54	$1,307
Operating revenues per year (millions)	$57	$2,009
Operating profit (thousands) per year	−$245	$103,000

In 1958, the airlines became the nation's number one intercity common carrier, passing first the railroads and then the bus lines in passenger traffic. The next few years should bring an even greater increase in air traffic with the advent of new jet aircraft. Each of these will carry up to 165 passengers on a transcontinental trip in less than 5 hours. In 1958, a transcontinental nonstop flight with piston-engine aircraft carrying up to 85 passengers took approximately 8 hours.

In 1958, the certified airlines in the United States had 230 turbo-jet aircraft on order, all but 10 of which were scheduled for delivery by the end of 1960. In addition, 167 large turbo-prop planes were on order for delivery between 1958 and 1960, and 70 piston-engine aircraft and 7 helicopters were to be delivered by the end of 1958. This equipment program represented an investment of more than $2½ billion.

The airlines are still enjoying a dynamic growth in traffic and there are no strong indications that this development will stop. They will continue to increase their share of the common carrier market for passenger travel; great possibilities in the air-freight field are seen and aggressive efforts to develop them are underway; there is a growing possibility that all first-class mail will be transported by air whenever time can be saved; and constant technological advances in both flight and ground equipment are resulting in greater efficiency and regularity of schedules.

Types of Commercial Air Carriers

There are ten principal types of commercial air carriers comprising the air transport industry of the United States. These are based upon the scope of operations authorized or allowed by the Civil Aeronautics Board. They are:

1. *Domestic Trunk Carriers.* Those permanently certificated scheduled air carriers engaged in the transportation of mail, passengers, and property over the major airline routes of the country. These are:

American Airlines
Braniff International Airways
Continental Air Lines
Delta Air Lines
Eastern Air Lines
National Airlines
Northeast Airlines
Northwest-Orient Airlines
Trans World Airlines
United Air Lines
Western Air Lines

2. *Domestic Local-Service Carriers.* Those permanently certificated scheduled air carriers operating, in general, between smaller communities and the major traffic centers. These are:

Allegheny Airlines
Bonanza Air Lines
Central Airlines
Frontier Airlines
Lake Central Airlines
Mohawk Airlines
North Central Airlines
Ozark Air Lines
Pacific Air Lines
Piedmont Airlines
Southern Airways
Trans Texas Airways
West Coast Airlines

3. *International and Overseas United States Carriers.* This group includes all United States flag air carriers authorized to operate between the United States and foreign countries, between foreign countries, and the extension of certain domestic trunk lines into Canada, Mexico, and the Caribbean area. These are:

Alaska Airlines
American Airlines
Braniff International Airways
Caribbean-Atlantic Airlines
Delta Air Lines
Eastern Air Lines
Mackey Air Transport[22]
National Airlines
Northwest-Orient Airlines
Pacific Northern Airlines
Pan American–Grace Airways
Pan American World Airways
Samoan Air Lines[22]
South Pacific Air Lines[22]
Trans Caribbean Airways
Trans World Airlines
United Air Lines
Uraba, Medellin & Central Airways[22]
Western Air Lines

4. *Insular and Alaskan Carriers.* Certificated scheduled air carriers operating in Hawaii and Alaska or between those states and others noncontiguous. These are:

INSULAR CARRIERS

Hawaiian Airlines
Aloha Airlines

ALASKAN CARRIERS

Operating between Alaska and other noncontiguous states:

Alaska Airlines
Northwest-Orient Airlines
Pacific Northern Airlines
Pan American World Airways

Operating within Alaska:

Alaska Airlines
Alaska Coastal Airlines
Bristol Bay Airlines[23]
Cordova Airlines
Ellis Airlnes
Howard J. Mays[23]
Northern Consolidated Airlines
Pacific Northern Airlines
Pan American World Airways
Reeve Aleutian Airways
Wien Alaska Airlines

5. *Certificated All-Cargo Lines.* Operators holding temporary certificates authorizing scheduled cargo flights between designated

[22] Certificated nonmail carriers.
[23] *Ibid.*

areas in the United States and, in some cases, foreign countries. These are:

AAXICO Airlines	Riddle Airlines
Aerovias Sud Americana	Seaboard and Western Airlines
Flying Tiger Line	Slick Airways

6. *Helicopter Services.* These hold temporary certificates to operate in and around large metropolitan areas carrying mail, passengers and property. These are:

Chicago Helicopter Airways
Los Angeles Airways
New York Airways

7. *Certificated Cruise Carriers.* These operators carry passengers only in connection with escorted all-expense tours between specified areas or points. Only one is now operating:

Resort Airlines

8. *Supplemental Air Carriers.* A diversified group of operators of various types of air service authorized by the Civil Aeronautics Board through the exemption process, rather than through the requirement that a certificate of public convenience and necessity be obtained. This group changes from time to time as new companies or operators start or as others go out of business entirely, combine with others, or simply change their names. Therefore, a list of air carriers comprising this group would have little meaning. As of 1960, there were 43 operators in this group.

9. *Air-Taxi Operators.* Carriers using aircraft having a maximum certificated take-off weight not exceeding 12,500 pounds and not holding a certificate of public convenience and necessity or other economic authority from the Board. Like the subsidiary air carriers, these operators are in business through the exemption process. There are approximately two thousand air-taxi operators.

10. *Indirect Air Carriers.* This term is applied to the intermediaries between shippers and the operators of aircraft who are, nevertheless, considered to be "air carriers" under the definition contained in the Civil Aeronautics Act[24] and are regulated by the

[24] Section 1 (2) of the Civil Aeronautics Act of 1938 reads as follows: "'Air carrier' means any citizen of the United States who undertakes, whether directly or indirectly or by a lease or any orther arrangement, to engage in air transportation: *Provided,* That the Authority (now the Board) may by order relieve air carriers who are not directly engaged in the operation of aircraft in air transportation from the provisions of this Act to the extent and for such periods as may be in the public interest." See *Railway Express*

Civil Aeronautics Board. The Railway Express Agency (Air Express Division) and various freight-forwarding companies such as Emery Air Freight and the airlines' Air Cargo, Inc., come within this group of carriers.

Airline Route Pattern

The development of domestic air transportation has been largely influenced by the corporate route pattern established by the "grandfather" provisions in the Civil Aeronautics Act of 1938.[25] Future extension and development will likewise be vitally influenced by this established pattern. When that act was passed, the domestic system was made up of three roughly defined size groups: (1) the very large air carriers, commonly referred to as the "Big Four"—American Airlines, Eastern Air Lines, Transcontinental and Western Air (now Trans World Airlines), and United Air Lines; (2) the intermediate-size regional carriers, such as Northwest Airlines, Braniff Airways, Chicago and Southern Air Lines, Pennsylvania Central Airlines (later Capital Airlines), Delta Airlines, and Western Air Lines; and (3) the relatively small regional carriers, such as Inland Air Lines, Mid-Continent Airlines, and Northeast Airlines. Mergers, route sales, and new route extensions have altered the 1938 situation considerably, particularly in groups (2) and (3).[26] The inherent problems presented in the "grandfather" pattern and its development have been further emphasized by the technological progress in aviation since the close of World War II.

Many of the most difficult problems to be met in the future development of domestic air transportation will probably be the result of the conflict between the original route pattern and technological progress in aviation. The original route pattern was devised on the basis of the type of aircraft then being flown, the DC-2 and DC-3; and this flying equipment was, in general, better suited for regional operations than for long-haul operations, although by the end of the 1930's currently obtainable flying equipment had become too large for efficient operation on some of the small regional routes. Even

---

Agency, Inc., Grandfather Certificate Case, 2 CAB 531 (1941); *Universal Air Freight Corp., Investigation of Forwarding Activities Case,* 3 CAB 698 (1942); *Air Freight Forwarder Case,* 9 CAB 473 (1948); *Air Freight Forwarder Case (International),* 11 CAB 182 (1949).

[25] *Public Law No. 706,* 75th Cong., 3d sess., Sec. 401 (*a*). In 1958, this law was made a part of the Federal Aviation Act (Act of August 23, 1958, 72 Stat. 731).

[26] For current airline route maps see the latest monthly issue of *Official Airline Guide* (Chicago: American Aviation Publications).

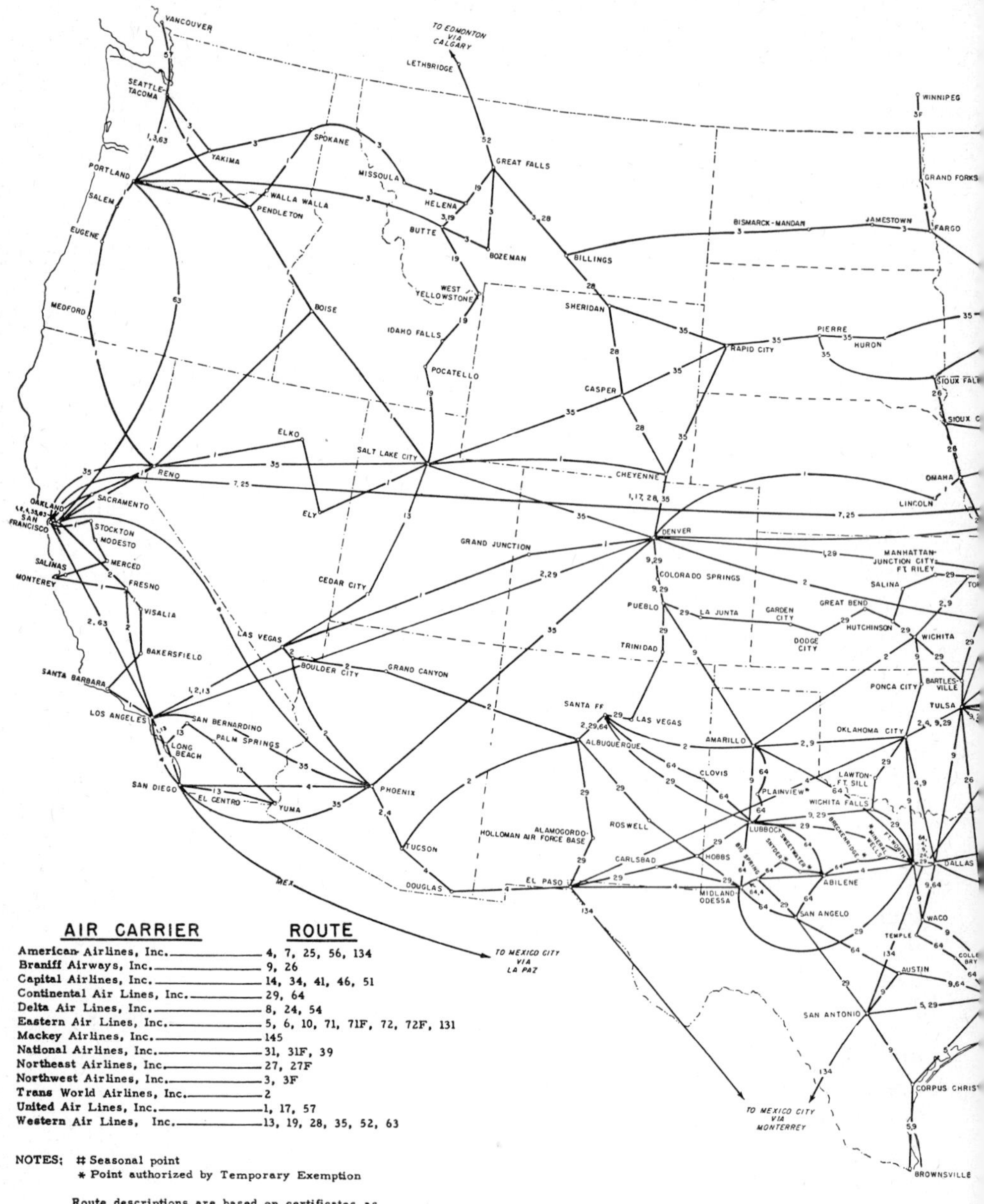

AIR CARRIER	ROUTE
American Airlines, Inc.	4, 7, 25, 56, 134
Braniff Airways, Inc.	9, 26
Capital Airlines, Inc.	14, 34, 41, 46, 51
Continental Air Lines, Inc.	29, 64
Delta Air Lines, Inc.	8, 24, 54
Eastern Air Lines, Inc.	5, 6, 10, 71, 71F, 72, 72F, 131
Mackey Airlines, Inc.	145
National Airlines, Inc.	31, 31F, 39
Northeast Airlines, Inc.	27, 27F
Northwest Airlines, Inc.	3, 3F
Trans World Airlines, Inc.	2
United Air Lines, Inc.	1, 17, 57
Western Air Lines, Inc.	13, 19, 28, 35, 52, 63

NOTES: # Seasonal point
* Point authorized by Temporary Exemption

Route descriptions are based on certificates as issued and do not purport to represent flights permissible by non-stop operations.

Certain of the points authorized to Continental, National, and Northeast are for limited periods

All points to which the holder's authority has been suspended under Section 401(g) of the Act, have been deleted from the Carrier's route description.

Source: CAB, Bureau of Air Operations, Routes Division.

FIG. 17. Routes certificated to trunk-line carriers.

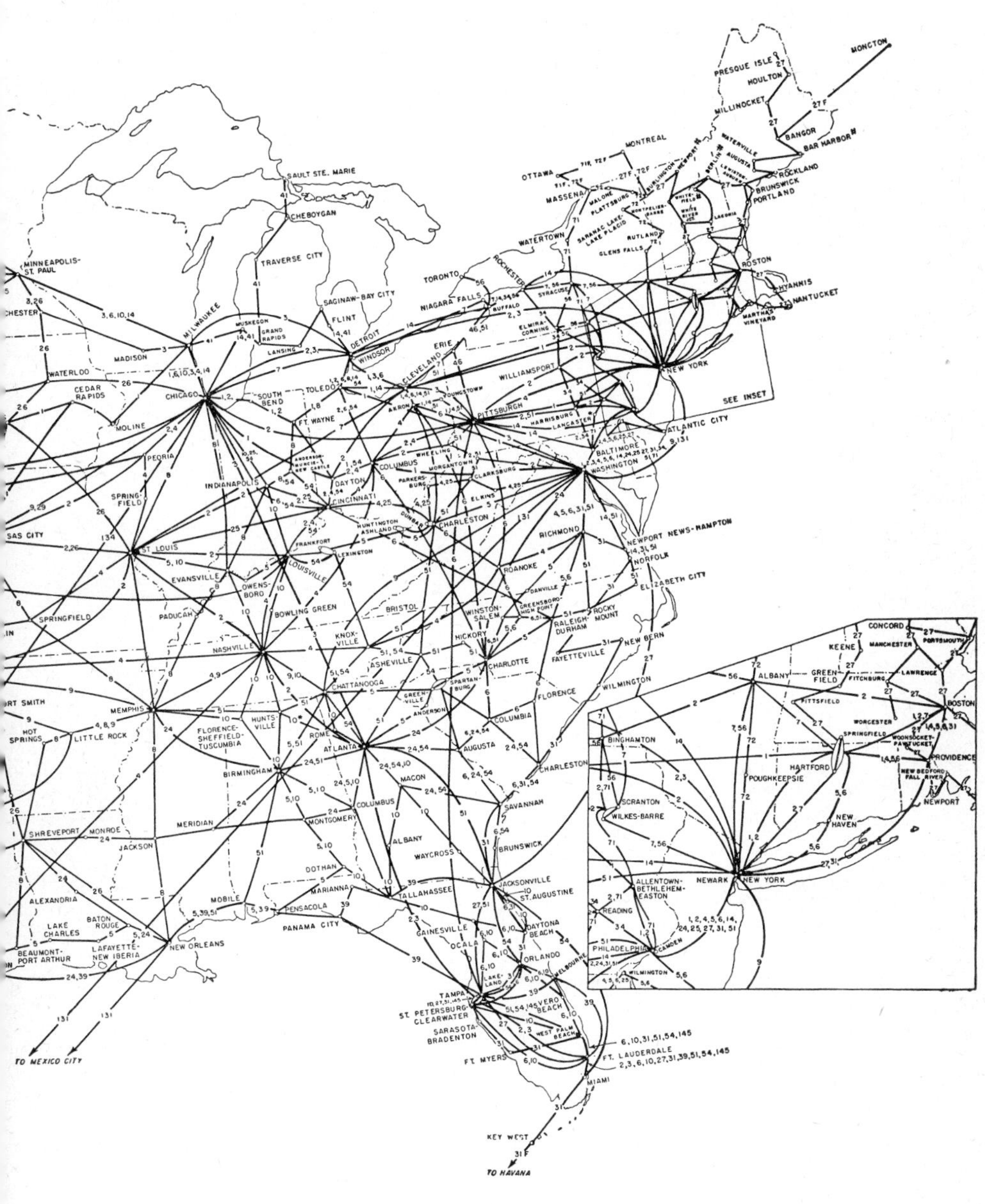
PRESQUE ISLE
MONCTON
HOULTON
MILLINOCKET
BANGOR
BAR HARBOR
MONTREAL
OTTAWA
MASSENA
ROCKLAND
BRUNSWICK
PORTLAND
SAULT STE. MARIE
CHEBOYGAN
TRAVERSE CITY
MINNEAPOLIS-ST. PAUL
WATERTOWN
RUTLAND
GLENS FALLS
BOSTON
HYANNIS
NANTUCKET
MARTHA'S VINEYARD
TORONTO
ROCHESTER
NIAGARA FALLS
BUFFALO
SYRACUSE
SAGINAW-BAY CITY
FLINT
MUSKEGON
GRAND RAPIDS
MILWAUKEE
MADISON
LANSING
DETROIT
WINDSOR
ERIE
ELMIRA-CORNING
WILLIAMSPORT
NEW YORK
SEE INSET
WATERLOO
CEDAR RAPIDS
CHICAGO
SOUTH BEND
TOLEDO
CLEVELAND
YOUNGSTOWN
AKRON
PITTSBURGH
HARRISBURG
LANCASTER
ATLANTIC CITY
MOLINE
FT. WAYNE
BALTIMORE
WASHINGTON
PEORIA
COLUMBUS
WHEELING
MORGANTOWN
CLARKSBURG
PARKERSBURG
INDIANAPOLIS
DAYTON
CINCINNATI
SPRINGFIELD
ELKINS
HUNTINGTON
ASHLAND
CHARLESTON
FRANKFORT
LEXINGTON
ST. LOUIS
LOUISVILLE
EVANSVILLE
OWENSBORO
RICHMOND
NEWPORT NEWS-HAMPTON
NORFOLK
ELIZABETH CITY
ROANOKE
DANVILLE
GREENSBORO-HIGH POINT
PADUCAH
BOWLING GREEN
BRISTOL
WINSTON-SALEM
RALEIGH-DURHAM
ROCKY MOUNT
NASHVILLE
KNOXVILLE
HICKORY
ASHEVILLE
CHARLOTTE
FAYETTEVILLE
NEW BERN
WILMINGTON
CHATTANOOGA
SPARTANBURG
GREENVILLE
ANDERSON
FLORENCE
MEMPHIS
LITTLE ROCK
HOT SPRINGS
FLORENCE-SHEFFIELD-TUSCUMBIA
HUNTSVILLE
ROME
ATLANTA
AUGUSTA
COLUMBIA
CHARLESTON
BIRMINGHAM
MACON
SAVANNAH
SHREVEPORT
MONROE
JACKSON
MERIDIAN
MONTGOMERY
COLUMBUS
ALBANY
WAYCROSS
BRUNSWICK
DOTHAN
MARIANNA
TALLAHASSEE
JACKSONVILLE
ST. AUGUSTINE
ALEXANDRIA
MOBILE
PENSACOLA
PANAMA CITY
GAINESVILLE
OCALA
DAYTONA BEACH
LAKE CHARLES
BATON ROUGE
BEAUMONT-PORT ARTHUR
LAFAYETTE-NEW IBERIA
NEW ORLEANS
ORLANDO
MELBOURNE
LAKELAND
TAMPA
ST. PETERSBURG-CLEARWATER
VERO BEACH
SARASOTA-BRADENTON
WEST PALM BEACH
FT. MYERS
FT. LAUDERDALE
MIAMI
KEY WEST
TO MEXICO CITY
TO HAVANA
CONCORD
PORTSMOUTH
KEENE
MANCHESTER
ALBANY
GREENFIELD
FITCHBURG
LAWRENCE
PITTSFIELD
WORCESTER
BINGHAMTON
SPRINGFIELD
WOONSOCKET-PAWTUCKET
PROVIDENCE
HARTFORD
POUGHKEEPSIE
NEW BEDFORD
FALL RIVER
NEWPORT
SCRANTON
WILKES-BARRE
NEW HAVEN
NEWARK
ALLENTOWN-BETHLEHEM-EASTON
READING
PHILADELPHIA
CAMDEN

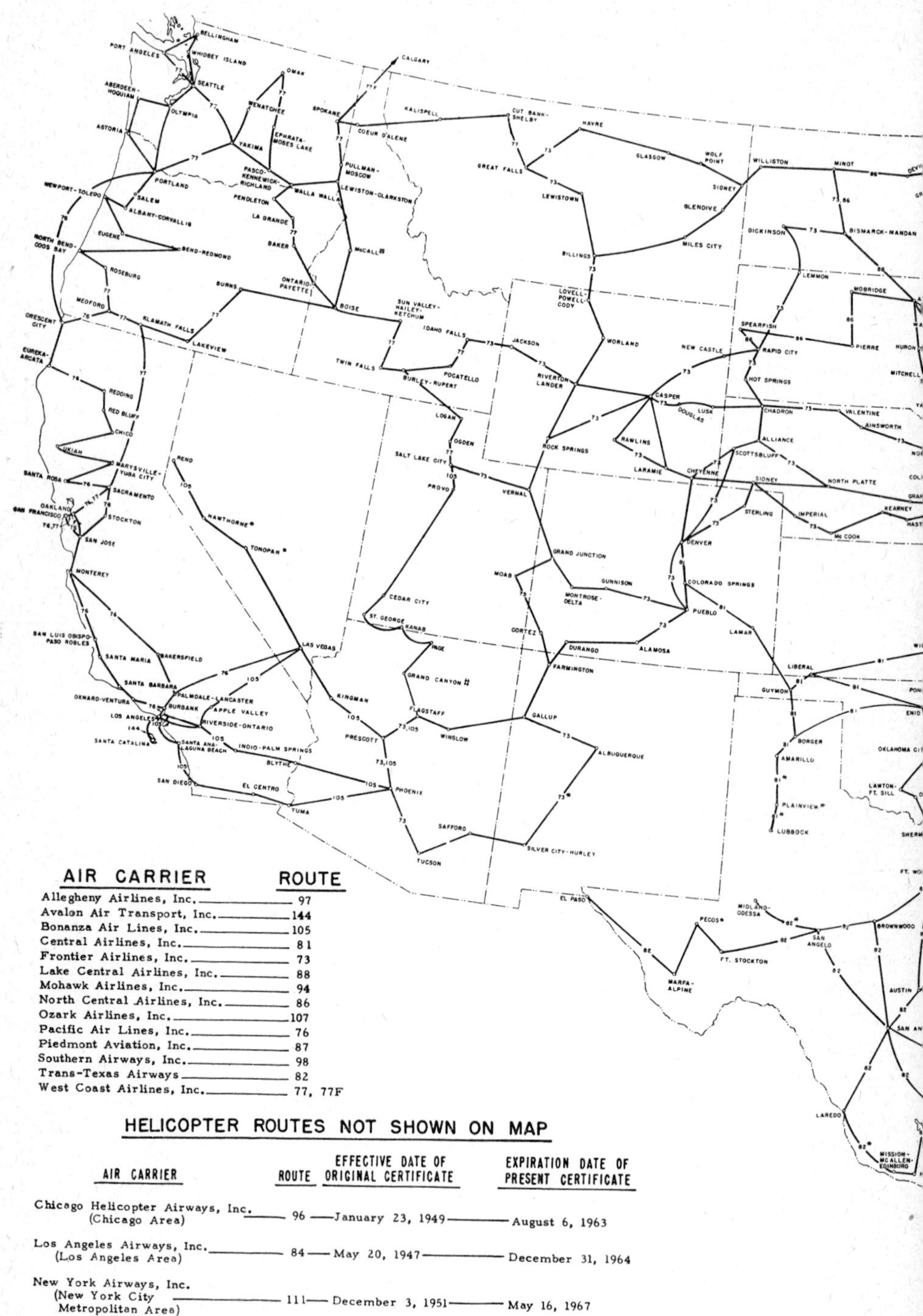

AIR CARRIER	ROUTE
Allegheny Airlines, Inc.	97
Avalon Air Transport, Inc.	144
Bonanza Air Lines, Inc.	105
Central Airlines, Inc.	81
Frontier Airlines, Inc.	73
Lake Central Airlines, Inc.	88
Mohawk Airlines, Inc.	94
North Central Airlines, Inc.	86
Ozark Airlines, Inc.	107
Pacific Air Lines, Inc.	76
Piedmont Aviation, Inc.	87
Southern Airways, Inc.	98
Trans-Texas Airways	82
West Coast Airlines, Inc.	77, 77F

HELICOPTER ROUTES NOT SHOWN ON MAP

AIR CARRIER	ROUTE	EFFECTIVE DATE OF ORIGINAL CERTIFICATE	EXPIRATION DATE OF PRESENT CERTIFICATE
Chicago Helicopter Airways, Inc. (Chicago Area)	96	January 23, 1949	August 6, 1963
Los Angeles Airways, Inc. (Los Angeles Area)	84	May 20, 1947	December 31, 1964
New York Airways, Inc. (New York City Metropolitan Area)	111	December 3, 1951	May 16, 1967

Source: CAB, Bureau of Air Operations, Routes Division.

FIG. 18. Routes certificated to local-service carriers.

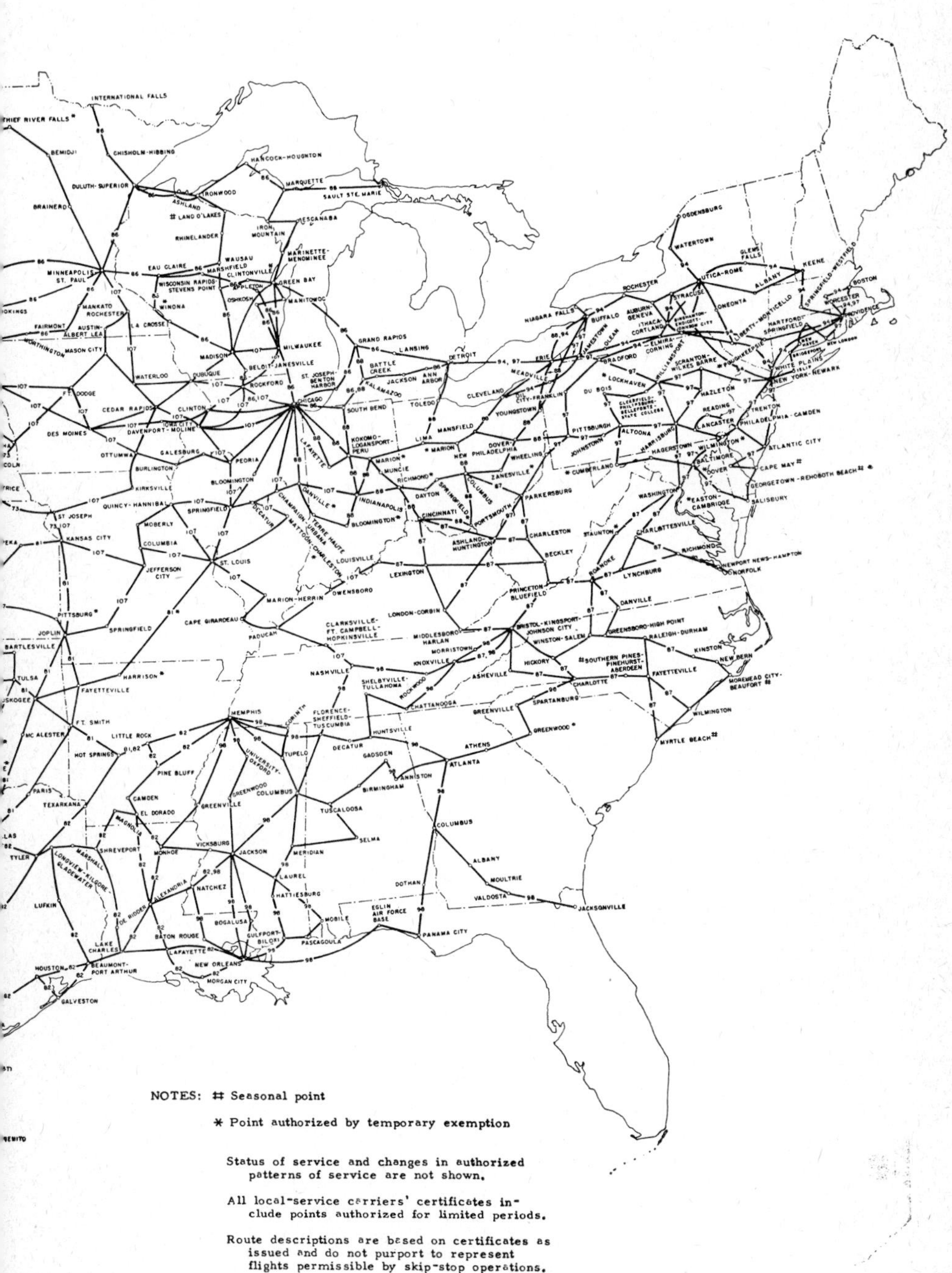

NOTES: ⌗ Seasonal point

* Point authorized by temporary exemption

Status of service and changes in authorized patterns of service are not shown.

All local-service carriers' certificates include points authorized for limited periods.

Route descriptions are based on certificates as issued and do not purport to represent flights permissible by skip-stop operations.

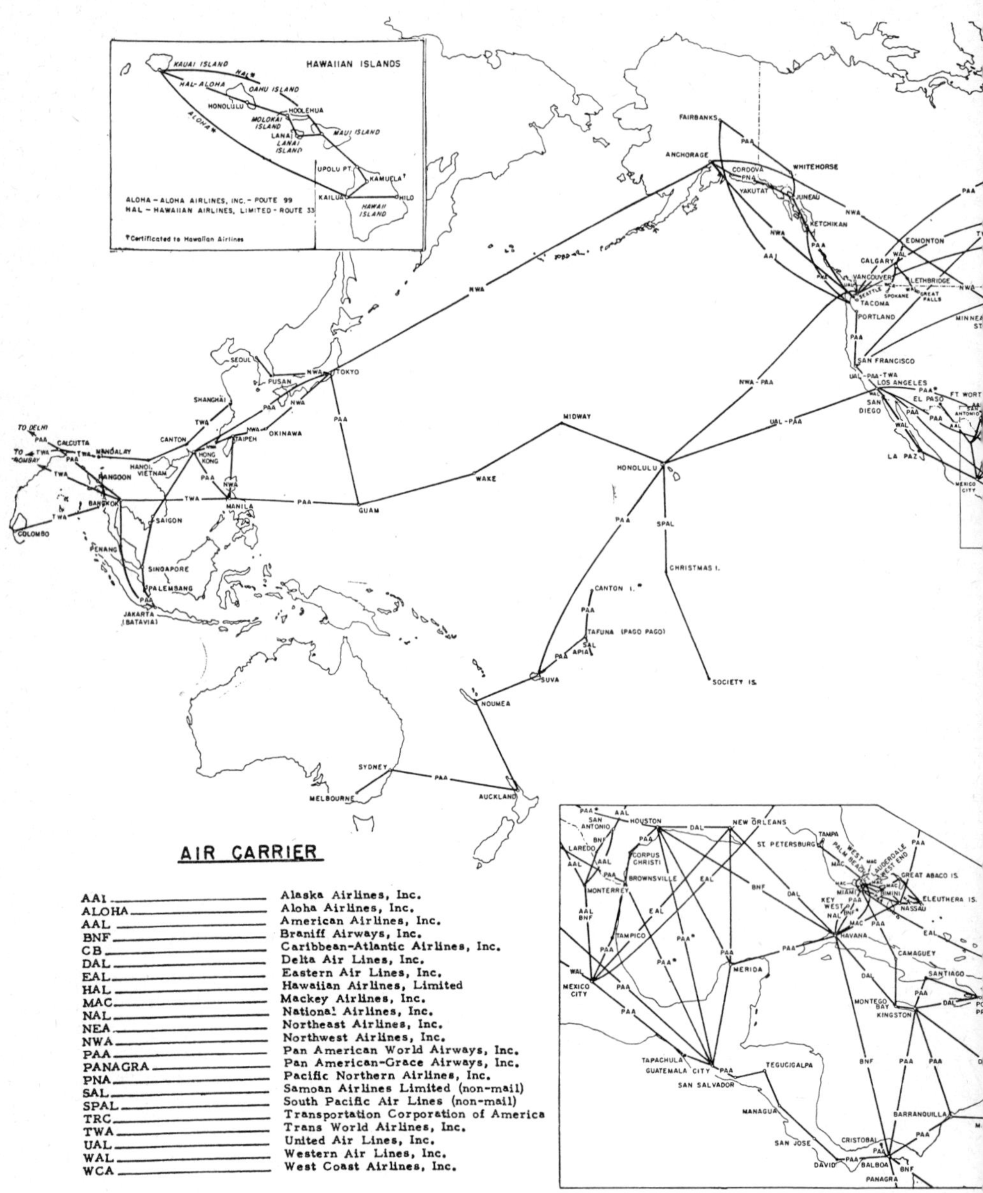

NOT SHOWN ON MAP:

Resort Airlines, Inc., certificate extended for a period of five years from September 24, 1957, to provide round-trip passenger service, in connection with all expense tours, between United States coterminals and intermediate points in Latin America and Canada.

Seaboard & Western Airlines, Inc. (See Cargo Map.)

Source: CAB, Bureau of Air Operations, Routes Division.

FIG. 19. International, overseas, Hawaiian, and Alaskan air routes of United States carriers.

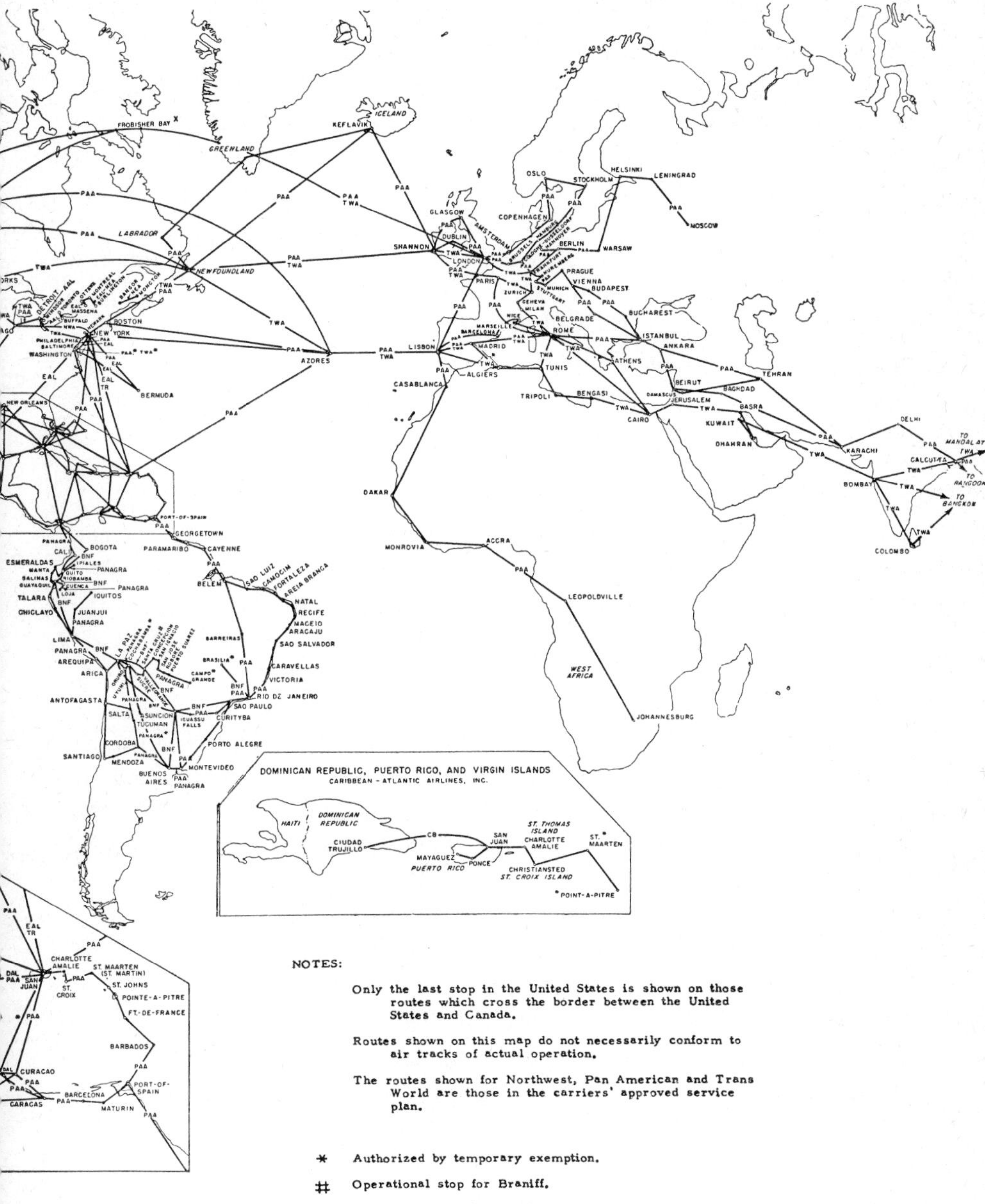

NOTES:

Only the last stop in the United States is shown on those routes which cross the border between the United States and Canada.

Routes shown on this map do not necessarily conform to air tracks of actual operation.

The routes shown for Northwest, Pan American and Trans World are those in the carriers' approved service plan.

* Authorized by temporary exemption.

Operational stop for Braniff.

• Point not presently served.

x Technical Landing

today there are no aircraft ideally suited to operations on purely regional or on local-service routes.

In contrast to domestic route development, the United States international air route pattern has (with the exception of a few overseas and transborder international routes certificated prior to 1945) been established as the result of a comprehensively planned series of proceedings before the Civil Aeronautics Board.

Competition has arisen between United States and foreign-flag carriers both from extension of our carriers into new areas and from an increase in the number and extent of foreign-flag operations. The increased foreign-flag competition between the United States and cities abroad has resulted from the reciprocal exchange of operating permits between the United States and other governments.

Prior to the passage of the Civil Aeronautics Act in 1938, international air transportation, even more than domestic, had been developed through the award of air mail contracts by the Post Office Department. During this early period Pan American Airways (now Pan American World Airways) and Pan American–Grace Airways (Panagra) were the only United States-flag carriers in the international field.

Airline route competition comes about in a number of ways: (1) by new routes and route extensions which were authorized by the Civil Aeronautics Board through the issuance of new permanent or temporary certificates of convenience and necessity or through the amendment of already existing certificates, (2) by the operations of contract carriers not subject to any economic regulation under the law, and (3) by the authorization of additional common carrier operations under blanket exemptions issued by the Civil Aeronautics Board.[27]

Even before the outbreak of World War II, there was some agreement in the industry that the public convenience and necessity required two separate types of airline service. The Civil Aeronautics Board recognized this need in 1944, when after an investigation[28] it concluded that it would be in the public interest to authorize local service to the smaller communities.

The most ideal type of service is the nonstop flight between two points. This represents the highest level of convenience to the pas-

---

[27] See Chapters 6 and 7. For a detailed study of the competitive situation see Frederick W. Gill and Gilbert L. Bates, *Airline Competition* (Cambridge, Mass.: Harvard University, 1949).

[28] *Investigation of Local, Feeder and Pick-up Air Service*, 6 CAB 1 (1944).

senger as well as profit to the carrier. Improvements in air service mean that it moves in the direction of the fast nonstop flight. There is marked difference between the requirements for equipment to perform this type of service and that required to perform a local service. Two things work constantly toward widening the gap between trunk and local service. They are: The increase in traffic and the improvements in trunk-line equipment. With the ever-increasing volume of long-haul traffic, and the ever-increasing speed and range of aircraft, nonstop service will be justified between more and more pairs of cities. With the jet-powered aircraft, the difference between equipment requirements for the trunk and local service will be more important, and it is generally agreed that the need for the two different types of service will be correspondingly increased.

When the Civil Aeronautics Act was adopted in 1938, the airline map was principally occupied by monopolies. For example, there was one carrier from New York to Miami, one from Washington to Chicago, one from New York to Boston, one from Los Angeles to San Francisco. These are some of the heaviest traffic routes in the country. Today between all these points there are at least three carriers and on some routes there are as many as seven or eight.

There is evidence that the Civil Aeronautics Board may have gone too far in authorizing parallel competition on some routes. The right number of airlines on a specific route is the number needed to provide an adequate service, with suitable competition and with a reasonable opportunity for profitable operation for each of them.

There can be too little competition, and there can be too much. There can be too few airlines on a given route, and there can be too many. If there are too many, then the total available traffic is so diluted that the loads available to each of the carriers are restricted, and often restricted below the level of reasonable opportunity for profit for an efficient operator.

The net result is that the public may pay more than it should. Competition which serves to increase the price of the product or service to the public is not economical competition; rather, it is more likely wasteful competition.

It is safe to say that we have wasteful levels of competition on some of the routes and that the cost of this excessive competition is being borne by the public, in addition to its cost to the investors in air transportation.

In the hurry of our growth we have ended up with too many airlines on some of the routes. That number cannot be continued if the airlines are to operate with profit, and to avoid return to federal subsidy. Fortunately, we can still do something about it if we take action now. There is no reason why the total trunk-line industry should not operate with profit, and without subsidy, if the right number of airlines were certificated for each of the routes.[29]

Foreign-Flag Scheduled Carriers

As of the start of 1960, the Civil Aeronautics Board had issued permits to 50 foreign-flag scheduled airlines allowing them to serve one or more points, usually on the borders of the United States or in our territories. These carriers are listed in Table 15.[30] Under their permits, the foreign airlines may carry passengers, property (cargo), and mail. They may not accept traffic between points in the United States and/or its possessions.

Air Transport Association of America

The trade association of the certificated airlines of the United States is the Air Transport Association of America, with headquarters in Washington, D.C. It has a membership of 43 companies, which pool their technical and operational knowledge as well as their airline "know-how" born of years of experience and millions of miles of flying. The funds of the association are furnished by the members on a pro rata share according to their gross receipts. Its general policies and activities are the expression of the desire for joint action and a united front from its membership.

The association's activities are carried on by the following departments or committees: operations and engineering, air navigation and traffic control, traffic or sales, economic research, governmental affairs, finance and accounting, legal, and public relations.

Military Air Transport Service

While not strictly a part of the commercial or business air transportation of this country, the Military Air Transport Service, which was established on June 1, 1948, is an important part of the total commercial aviation industry. The thousands of passengers and tons of air cargo carried are often diverted from commercial carriers and should be considered in total air transport activities.

MATS is a world-wide air route command whose primary mission is to provide scheduled and strategic airlift support to the De-

---

[29] C. R. Smith, President American Airlines, speaking before the Metropolitan Washington (D.C.) Board of Trade, April 20, 1960.

[30] See Chapter 10 for discussion of United States policy in permitting foreign-flag airlines to serve this country.

TABLE 15

FOREIGN-FLAG AIR CARRIERS HOLDING PERMITS TO OPERATE TO THE UNITED STATES, 1960

Country	*Name of Carrier*
Argentina	Aerolineas Argentina
Australia	Quantas Empire Airways Limited
Belgium	S.A. Belge d'Exploitation de la Navigation Aerienne (SABENA)
Brazil	Empresa de Transportes Aerovias Brazil, S.A. (Aerovias Brazil)
	S.A. Empresa de Viacao Rio Grandense (VARIG)
Canada	Canadian Pacific Air Lines Ltd. (CPAL)
	Pacific Western Airlines, Ltd.
	Trans Canada Air Lines (TCA)
Chile	Compana Nacional de Turismo Aereo
China (Nationalist)	China National Aviation Corporation
Colombia	Aerovias Nacionales de Colombia, S.A. (AVIANCA)
	Lineas Aereas Taca de Colombia S.A.
Costa Rica	Lineas Aereas Costarricenses, S.A. (LACSA)
Cuba	Aerovias "Q," S.A.
	Compania Cubana de Aviacion, S.A. (Cubana)
	Cuba Aeropostal, S.A.
	Expreso Aereo Inter-Americano, S.A.
Dominican Republic	Compania Dominicana de Aviacion, C. por A. (CDA)
Ecuador	Aerovias Ecuatorianas, C.A. (AREA)
El Salvador	TACA International Airlines, S.A.
	TACA, S.A.
France	Compagnie Nationale Air France (Air France)
Germany	Deutsche Lufthansa Aktiengesellschaft
Guatemala	Empresa Guatemalteca de Aviacion
Honduras	Transportes Aereos Nacionales, S.A. (TAN)
Iceland	Loftleidir H.F. (Icelandic Airlines Ltd.)
Ireland	Aerlinte Eireann Teoranta
Israel	El Al Israel Airlines Ltd. (El Al)
Italy	Alitalia-Linee Aeree Italiane, S.P.A.
Japan	Japan Air Lines Company Ltd.
Korea	Korean National Airlines
Mexico	Aeronaves de Mexico, S.A.
	Guest Aerovias Mexico, S.A.
	Compania Mexicana de Aviacion, S.A. (CMA)
	Trans Mar de Cortes, S.A.
Netherlands	Royal Dutch Airlines (KLM)
Nicaragua	Lineas Aereas de Nicaragua, S.A.
Panama	Aerovias Interamericanas de Panama, S.A.
Philippines	Philippine Air Lines, Inc.
Scandinavia	Scandinavian Airlines System (SAS)
Spain	Iberia, Lineas Aereas de Espana, S.A.
Switzerland	Swiss Air Transport Company, Ltd. (Swissair)
United Kingdom	Airwork Limited (Cargo only)
	British Caribbean Airways, Ltd.
	British Commonwealth Pacific Airlines Ltd.
	British Overseas Airways Corporation (BOAC)
	British West Indian Airways, Ltd. (BWIA)
Venezuela	Linea Aeropostal Venezolana (LAV)
	Aerovias Venezolanas, S.A.
	Rutas Aereas Nacionales, S.A.

partment of Defense. This is provided by its three transport divisions: Continental, Pacific, and Atlantic Divisions, operating in their respective geographic spheres. Another purpose of MATS is to develop a strong military air transport facility "in being" to provide logistical support or airlift capabilities to meet an emergency of a mobilization or war-readiness nature. MATS also provides technical services for the entire United States Air Force, and for other military and civil aircraft, as follows: Airways and Air Communications Service, Air Weather Service, Flight Service, Air Resupply and Communications Service, and Air Photographic and Charting Service.

The present route patterns of MATS largely parallel those of scheduled United States commercial airlines on the international and domestic routes. This becomes inevitable, in most instances, as the availability of airways and air communications services dictate that air traffic move in the same channels. Exceptions where MATS is the sole route operator are very limited and include service to such areas as Thule, Greenland, and points in Northern Canada and the Arctic regions.

MATS does not make a deliberate offer of domestic service in this country. Nevertheless, positioning its equipment for overseas operations offers lift capacity, and a substantial volume of traffic is generated directly and confined to the United States. There can be no question that in positioning aircraft by fitting them into a domestic scheduled pattern, particularly when high-class equipment is operated, considerable traffic, both passengers and freight, is generated within this country.

Chapter 4

REGULATORY LEGISLATION

THE development of a body of law regulating the use of the air as a medium of transportation was at first hampered by legal uncertainty. Those who were most interested in aviation sought a means whereby the right of flight and the regulations governing the conditions of flight might be made by the federal government, unhampered by state regulations. Another group, and by far the largest, having neither interest in nor desire to use the air as a highway, feared the effect of its use in this manner; and, remembering the historic limitations on the federal power to regulate commerce, as evident in the development of the railroads, this group actively opposed or urged caution in making any federal law on aviation.

There was also a considerable group who maintained that the air was analogous to navigable waters and that, therefore, a law controlling its use could be invoked under the admiralty powers of the federal government. A constitutional amendment was also suggested. General use of the airplane, requiring some sort of regulation, arrived before there was any unanimity of legal thought on what kind of law would be best. This confused situation resulted in a multiplicity of statutes, both state and federal.

Federal regulation of air transportation may be traced primarily to the efforts of the aircraft industry, the work of the Committee on the Law of Aeronautics of the American Bar Association, and the appointment by Congress of a number of different aircraft investigating committees and boards after the entrance of the United States into World War I. One important bill introduced in Congress, the Civil Aeronautics Bill of 1923, failed to be reported out of committee. Two of the congressional investigating committees are of special importance, for their reports were the immediate forerunners of the Air Commerce Act of 1926. The Select Committee of Inquiry into the Operations of the United States Air Services (the Lampert-Perkins Committee) was appointed in March, 1924; and the President's Aircraft Committee was appointed in September, 1925, to report upon the best means to develop and apply aircraft to national defense. The scope of inquiry by the latter committee was sufficiently broad to enable it to consider all phases of air transportation and to assist Congress in the development of a legislative program to promote civil air transportation, as well as to formulate a five-year program for developing military and naval aviation.[1]

Arguments were advanced for federal control of aviation under the constitutional powers of Congress to establish post roads and to provide for the common defense. Much of the power of the present law in establishing airways rests on the postal power. Another argument for federal control, to the virtual exclusion of state regulation, was based on the interpretation of the commerce clause of the Constitution, known as the "uniformity of regulation" theory. This theory first appeared in the case of *Cooley* v. *Port Wardens*[2] in 1851 and continued to be recognized in an unbroken line of decisions by the Supreme Court of the United States. These cases point out that a field exists in which the federal government may act under the interstate commerce power because, factually, the problems are so inherently national in character that they require uniformity of regulation affecting all the states alike.[3]

When the legal problems of flying first arose, it was not as plain as it is today that aviation, in all its phases, is inherently national in character. To have applied the uniformity of regulation theory then, Congress and the courts would have had to concede that aviation did not admit of state control. In those days Congress and the courts did not foresee the high-altitude transcontinental aircraft or even the

---

[1] See M. W. Willebrandt, "Federal Control of Air Commerce," *Journal of Air Law and Commerce,* July, 1940; O. Ryan, "Federal and State Jurisdiction over Civil Aviation," *Journal of Air Law and Commerce,* January, 1941; J. H. Hamstra, "Two Decades—Federal Aero-Regulation in Perspective," *Journal of Air Law and Commerce,* April, 1941; George W. Starr, "The Position of the State in Economic Control and Regulation of Air Commerce," *Journal of Air Law and Commerce,* Spring, 1948; Emory T. Nunneley, Jr., "Federal Aviation Legislation," *Journal of Air Law and Commerce,* Autumn, 1947; Frederick A. Ballard, "Federal Regulation of Aviation," *Harvard Law Review,* October, 1947; John C. Cooper, "State Sovereignty vs. Federal Sovereignty of Navigable Airspace," *Journal of Air Law Commerce,* Winter, 1948.

[2] 12 How. (U.S.) 299, 13 L. ed. 996. This argument was strongly advanced by Mabel W. Willebrandt, Chairman, Committee on Aeronautical Law, American Bar Association, *op. cit.*

[3] See comment note to *Kelly* v. *Washington* (302 U.S. 1), 82 L. ed. at p. 14, for other examples. *Mobile County* v. *Kimball,* 102 U.S. 691, 26 L. ed. 238 (1881) (cases involved improvement of harbors by state): "Here there can of necessity be only one system or plan of regulation, and that Congress alone can prescribe." *Missouri ex rel. Barrett* v. *Kansas Natural Gas Co.,* 265 U.S. 298, 68 L. ed. 1027 (1931): "The paramount interest [moving of natural gas from producing field] is not local but national—admitting of and requiring uniformity of regulation."

small private planes with a cruising range far wider than state lines. If, however, the question were first propounded now, there would probably be general agreement that aviation is inherently national.

The Air Commerce Act of 1926[4]

The first federal law dealing with aviation was the Air Commence Act of 1926, enacted to stabilize civil or commercial aviation so that it might attract adequate capital and to provide aviation with the assistance and legal basis necessary for its development. This law, for the first time in our history, stated the relationship of the federal government to the development of civil air transportation and provided largely for aid and encouragement rather than for regulation. The law was, in other words, intended to help civil aviation to develop rather than to regulate any existing objectionable practices.

The Air Commerce Act contained the following principal provisions:

1. All aircraft owned by United States citizens must be registered before being operated from one state to or over another state in common-carrier service or in connection with any business, including intrastate business.
2. Registered aircraft could not be operated anywhere unless properly certificated and operated by a duly certificated airman.
3. The Secretary of Commerce was authorized to establish air traffic rules, which were to govern all aircraft operating in the United States, whether or not between states and whether or not in "commerce."[5]
4. The Secretary of Commerce was authorized to establish lighted civil airways, i.e., routes "in the navigable air space designated . . . as suitable for interstate or foreign air commerce."
5. The act was to be enforced through a system of civil penalties similar to those used in enforcing the customs and water navigation laws.

No new "bureau" was established for carrying out the provisions of this act. Rather, the new work was distributed among the various existing agencies of the Department of Commerce, with only the regulatory and informational functions requiring a new subdivision. This subdivision was first known as the Aeronautics Branch; but in

---

[4] 44 Stat. 568 (1926). The best source of general information on this Act is F. P. Lee, *Legislative History of the Air Commerce Act of 1926* (1928 revision of 1923 edition of *Law Memorandum upon Civil Aeronautics*) (Washington, D.C.: U.S. Government Printing Office, 1928).

[5] The jurisdictional scope of the air traffic rules was stated in this manner in *House Report No. 1162*, 69th Cong., 1st sess. (1926), p. 2. The original air traffic rules were held applicable to intrastate flights in *Neiswonger* v. *Goodyear Tire and Rubber Co.*, 35 Fed. (2d) 761 (N.D. Ohio, 1929). The Act of 1926 was held applicable to "all types of flying" in *Sen. Report No. 185*, 75th Cong., 1st sess. (1937), p. 30.

1934 the loose organization of this branch was consolidated into a Bureau of Air Commerce, under a Director of Air Commerce.

With minor amendments in 1934,[6] primarily intended to strengthen federal authority over the airlines, the Air Commerce Act provided, until 1938, the only federal regulation of aviation. Under it, three separate agencies of the government had control over vital phases of civil aeronautics regulation: (1) The Bureau of Air Commerce of the Department of Commerce regulated safety and exercised certain promotional functions. (2) The Post Office Department, through the letting of air mail contracts, exerted substantial economic control over the airlines. (3) The Interstate Commerce Commission, through its authority to fix rates for the carriage of mail and to exercise certain regulatory functions, exerted further economic control over the airlines. The result of this divided jurisdiction over civil aeronautics was a lack of co-ordination in the efforts of the government to regulate, foster, and develop the air transportation industry and miscellaneous flying. This proved a burden upon the air carriers and private fliers and increased the work and detracted from the efficiency of the government itself in this field.

In this period, there were several laws passed, namely the Kelly Act and amendments and the Watres Act, having to do mainly with air mail (see Chapter 8).

The Civil Aeronautics Act of 1938[7]

Beginning in 1934, the air carriers themselves sought federal regulation, realizing that the history of transportation demonstrated that the absence of such regulation led to evils from which not only the public, but the industry itself, would suffer. It was in that year that the whole air transport industry was thrown into confusion when all federal mail contracts were canceled because of alleged collusion between the mail carriers and post officials and other abuses under the Watres Act (Mail Pay Act) of 1930, the Army was ordered to fly the mail. In July, 1941, a commissioner of the United States Court of Claims reported that there was no fraud in the air mail contracts canceled in 1934, leaving the way open for the airlines, whose contracts were canceled at that time, to claim damages from the government of about $2,500,000 (see Chapter 3).

---

[6] Air Mail Act of 1934, 48 Stat. 1113 (1934).

[7] 59 Stat. 977 (1938). See C. S. Rhyne, *The Civil Aeronautics Act Annotated* (Washington, D.C.: National Law Book Co., 1939): A. J. Thomas, Jr., *Economic Regulation of Scheduled Air Transport* (Buffalo, N.Y.: Dennis & Co., Inc., 1951).

Also, since the Act of 1926 had been passed before air transportation of passengers and mail had developed into a business enterprise, there was a growing sentiment that the law had become outmoded, particularly because it made no provisions for the regulation of the services, rates, and charges of common-carrier airlines. Even so, the airlines then in existence had not developed any well-defined faults to which legislation could be specifically directed. Congress, therefore, drew upon its experience in handling the problems of surface transportation, assuming that such experience furnished a reasonably sound guide for anticipating the problems of air transportation. The new act it provided came in its essentials straight from Part I of the Interstate Commerce Act of 1887 and the Motor Carrier Act of 1935.

The principal provisions of the Civil Aeronautics Act of 1938 were as follows:

1. It substituted one federal statute and agency for the several which had been regulating the industry. An administrative agency was set up consisting of three practically autonomous bodies in an attempt to draw a line of demarcation between executive, legislative, and judicial functions.

The bodies within this agency were: a five-man Authority, a three-man Air Safety Board, and an Administrator. Members of these bodies were appointed by the President with the advice and consent of the Senate. Within these groups was vested the entire regulation of civil aviation, split into three parts: (1) The five members of the authority exercised quasi-judicial and quasi-legislative functions covering economic and safety regulations. (2) The administrator exercised purely executive functions covering development, operation, etc., of air navigation facilities and general development and promotional work. (3) The air safety board was an independent body for the investigation of accidents.

The Civil Aeronautics Authority began operations in September, 1938. For the first time, all branches of the aeronautics industry were able to lay plans for the future and to adopt long-range programs based upon sound economic principles. For the first time, they found it feasible to co-operate with each other (which was in part due to the fact that the Civil Aeronautics Act of 1938 exempted the airlines from the antitrust laws) and with the federal government in the attainment of common objectives for advancing the industry on all fronts. It seemed reasonable to suppose that the airlines and others concerned would look to this one source for whatever regulation was provided by law and that this source would remain the same as long as the system worked. However, President Franklin D. Roosevelt, in April, 1940, transmitted Reorganization Plans 3 and 4 to Congress, and these became effective on June 30, 1940.[8]

Plan 3 changed the title of the Administrator of the Civil Aeronautics Authority to Administrator of Civil Aeronautics and transferred to him various administrative functions originally vested in the five members of the Authority, including the administration of safety regulation. The members of the Authority, however, were to continue to prescribe safety regulations and, after proper hearings, were to suspend or revoke certificates for airmen, aircraft, and facilities. Plan 4 placed the entire Authority within the framework of the Department of Commerce, abolished the Air Safety Board, and changed the name of the five-member Authority to Civil Aeronautics Board. The investigation of accidents, which had been performed by the Air Safety Board, was thereafter to be handled by the Bureau of Safety Regulation of the Civil Aeronautics Board. The Administrator of Civil Aeronautics was placed directly under the Secretary of Commerce; the Civil Aeronautics Board, however, while within the Department of Commerce for purposes of budgeting, personnel, and other routine management functions, was to continue its functions of rule-making, adjudication, and investigation independently.

The Civil Aeronautics Board was the independent agency of the federal government which exercised legislative, regulatory, and judicial powers over American civil aviation. On the other hand, the Civil Aeronautics Administration of the Department of Commerce was the executive agency of the federal government in civil aviation, carrying out the enforcement, operational, and promotional functions delegated to it by the Act of 1938.[9]

2. The Act of 1938 set forth a statement of policy[10] which required the Civil Aeronautics Board to regulate air transportation

[8] Plan 3 will be found in 5 Fed. Reg. 2107 (1940). Plan 4 will be found in 5 Fed. Reg. 2421 (1940). These plans were submitted by the President pursuant to the Reorganization Act of 1939 (55 Stat. 561 [1939]).

[9] See Joseph J. O'Connell, Jr., "Civil Aeronautics Board," *Air Affairs*, Autumn, 1949.

[10] Since restated in the Federal Aviation Act of 1958 (Public Law 85–726; 72 Stat. 731) which became effective on December 31, 1958. Among other things, it amended and replaced the Civil Aeronautics Act of 1938.

in the public interest, giving consideration specifically to certain objectives: (*a*) to encourage and develop an air transportation system adapted to the present and future needs of domestic and foreign commerce, the postal service, and national defense; (*b*) to regulate air transportation so as to preserve its inherent advantages, promote the highest degree of safety and sound conditions in the industry, improve relations among air transport companies, and coordinate transportation by air carriers: (*c*) to promote adequate, economical, and efficient transportation service by air carriers at reasonable charges (unjust discriminations, undue preferences or advantages, and unfair or destructive competitive practices being specifically prohibited); (*d*) to regulate the industry so as to preserve competition to the extent necessary to assure the sound development of an air transportation system for commerce, the mail service, and national defense; (*e*) to regulate the industry in such a manner as to promote the development of air commerce and to promote safety; and (*f*) to encourage and develop civil aeronautics.

3. The Act of 1938 provided for extensive regulation of the economic activities of air carriers all of which were restated in the Federal Aviation Act of 1958:

(*a*) No person or company, except as they may be exempted from the economic provisions of the act by Board order, may engage in air transportation nor may any new points be served by an air carrier,[11] without appropriate authorization by the Civil Aeronautics Board in the form of a certificate of public convenience and necessity issued to a carrier found "fit, willing and able"[12] to effectuate a

---

[11] Under the terms of the Act, the Civil Aeronautics Board has held an "air carrier" to be one who undertakes, whether directly or indirectly or by a lease or any other arrangement, to engage in the carriage by aircraft of persons or property as a common carrier for compensation or hire, or the carriage of mail by aircraft, in commerce between the geographical areas stated in section 1 (21) of the Act. Viewing this language in the light of the entire context and purpose of the Act, it seems to have the effect of dividing air carriers into two classes, one consisting of those who undertake directly to engage in the carriage by aircraft of persons, property, or mail, and the other of those who undertake, indirectly or by lease or some other arrangement, to engage in the carriage by aircraft of persons, property, or mail. Whether the undertaking be direct or indirect, the engagement must be the carriage of persons, property, or mail by aircraft as a common carrier. See CAB Orders, Serial No. 940, Docket No. 19–491 (*E*) 1. (The Board has no control over contract carriers nor over intrastate carriers.)

[12] "The Act does not define 'fit, willing and able,' but the Board has established these tests: (1) a proper organizational basis for the conduct of air transportation; (2) a plan for the conduct of the service made by competent personnel; (3) adequate financial resources" (*Braniff Airways* v. *Civil Aeronautics Board*, 147 Fed. [2d] 152, 153 [App. D.C., 1945]).

proposed operation in the public interest.[13] Under the so-called "grandfather" clause of the act, provision was made issuing certificates of convenience and necessity for routes on which carriers could show that they had supplied adequate and continuous service from May 14 to August 22, 1938, the effective date of the act. Routes once established may not be abandoned by airlines without express approval of the Authority. Air carriers must provide adequate facilities for the transportation of mail upon request of the Post Office Department.

(*b*) Foreign air carriers may not engage in transportation to or within the United States unless a permit has been issued by the Board.

(*c*) Air carriers are required to publish tariffs of rates and charges for transportation of persons or goods and to file these tariffs with the Board. No departure from these tariffs is permitted, rebating being prohibited. Changes may not be made in airline tariffs upon less than thirty days' notice, unless specifically permitted by the Board. The division of joint rates and fares to which air carriers are parties must also be filed with the Board if required by that body.

In regulating the rates of air carriers, the Board is required to take into consideration, among other factors: (1) the effect of the rates upon the movement of traffic; (2) the need in the public interest of adequate air transport service at the lowest rates consistent with such service; (3) the standards of air transport service prescribed by law; (4) the inherent advantages of transportation by aircraft; and (5) the need of each air carrier for revenue sufficient to enable such carrier under honest, economical, and efficient management to provide adequate and efficient air-carrier service.

(*d*) The Board has complete jurisdiction over awarding and terminating air mail contracts for domestic and foreign air mail services, and over the air mail schedules, maximum mail loads, and fair and reasonable compensation for air mail services.[14]

---

[13] An analysis of the Board's decisions on applications to operate competing services or new routes (other than local or feeder line services) indicates that the Board has consistently weighed three primary factors in determining the paramount public necessity or interest in each fact situation presented. These are: (1) the benefit to the public from the new services, (2) the financial and economic interest of the air carriers involved, and (3) the desirability of competition. It seems well established that the Board is the sole arbiter of the paramount public interest in domestic cases (*United Air Lines* v. *Civil Aeronautics Board,* 155 Fed. [2d] 169 [CCA D.C., 1946]). In international cases the Board is the sole arbiter as the President's adviser (*Pan American Airways, Inc.* v. *Civil Aeronautics Board,* 121 Fed. [2d] 810 [CCA 2d 1944]).

[14] "In determining the rate (for the carriage of air mail) in each case the Board shall take into consideration . . . the need of each such carrier for compensation for the trans-

(*e*) Air carriers are required to submit accounts, records, and reports to the Board annually. True copies of all contracts to which air carriers are parties must also be filed.

(*f*) The Board has jurisdiction over the consolidation or merger of control of air carriers in connection with other air carriers or other aeronautical businesses. Interlocking directorates and other communities of interest are forbidden except upon express approval. Pooling arrangements to which air carriers are parties must be submitted to the Board for approval and may be approved only if shown not to be adverse to the public interest or in violation of the Civil Aeronautics Act.

The Federal Aviation Act of 1958[15]

On August 23, 1958, Congress adopted an act chiefly directed toward continuing the Civil Aeronautics Board as an agency of the United States government, creating a Federal Aviation Agency, providing for the regulation and promotion of civil aviation in such manner as to best foster its development and safety, and providing for the safe and efficient use of the air space by both civil and military aircraft. This act replaced the Civil Aeronautics Act of 1938 as the basic legislation governing aviation activities, both civil and military, and repealed all conflicting legislation.

The Act of 1958, however, made no substantive change whatsoever in the provisions of the Act of 1938 governing air carrier economic regulation.[16] The Civil Aeronautics Board remains the economic regulatory agency of the air transportation industry as well as retaining its function of investigating aircraft accidents. The only change affecting the Board was the transfer of its safety rules writing to the newly created Federal Aviation Agency.

The chief purpose of the Act of 1958 was to correct two fundamental deficiencies which had become apparent in the exercise of the federal government's responsibility for aviation matters. These were:

1. Diffusion of authority for the general regulation of civil aeronautics together with a subordination of aviation interests within the government.

---

portation of mail sufficient to insure the performance of such service, and, together with all other revenues of the air carrier, to enable such air carrier under honest, economical, and efficient management, to maintain and continue the development of air transportation . . ."

[15] Public Law 85–726; 72 Stat. 731.

[16] *Report* to accompany S. 3880, U.S. Senate, 85th Cong., 2d. sess., Report No. 1811.

2. Lack of clear statutory authority for centralized air space management and essentially related activities.

The most important provision of the Federal Aviation Act of 1958 was, therefore, the establishment of an independent Federal Aviation Agency reporting directly to the President. This agency would absorb the Civil Aeronautics Administration and all its functions as well as the Airways Modernization Board. The Administrator of the Federal Aviation Agency has powers to:

1. Regulate the use of navigable air space of the United States; acquire, establish, operate, and improve air navigation facilities; prescribe air traffic rules for all aircraft; conduct related research and development activities.
2. Rule on the location of substantial alteration of any military or civilian airport, rocket or missile site involving the expenditure of federal funds. (This provision extends to military airports the identical review of airport locations which had been practiced by the Civil Aeronautics Administration with reference to nonmilitary airports since 1938.)
3. Make all safety rules—an authority formerly vested in the Civil Aeronautics Board.
4. Carry on the Civil Aeronautics Administration's former responsibility for issuing airman, aircraft, and airline operating certificates and for inspecting and rating air agencies and facilities. The new law retains and strengthens the right of an airman to appeal the Administrator's denial on nonrenewal of a certificate to the Civil Aeronautics Board.

The Civil Aeronautics Board remains an independent federal regulatory agency with the fundamental responsibility of promoting, encouraging, and developing civil aviation and "an air transportation system properly adapted to the present and future needs of the foreign and domestic commerce of the United States, of the Postal Service, and of the national defense . . ."

Basically, the major activities of the Board are:

1. The regulation of fares and rates for the carriage of persons and property.
2. The fixing of subsidy and service mail rates.
3. The guarantee of loans to certain classes of carriers for the purchase of flight equipment.

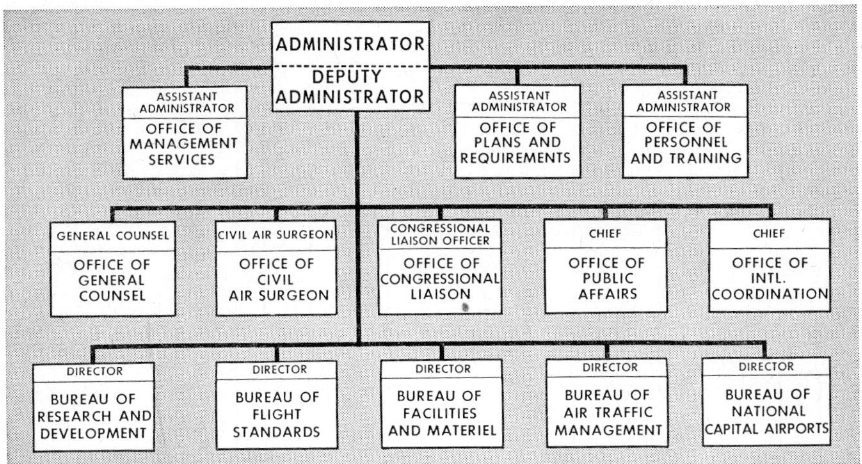

FIG. 20. Organization of the Federal Aviation Agency.

4. The enforcement of the economic provisions of the law.

5. The approval or disapproval of mergers and control and interlocking relationships and of intercarrier agreements affecting air transportation.

6. The regulation of air carrier accounting practices and the development of air carrier reporting systems.

7. The maintenance of public records of tariffs, schedules, and other material required to be filed by air carriers.

8. The licensing of domestic air routes and, with approval of the President, of international air routes operated by United States and foreign air carriers.

9. Participation in the negotiation of air agreements between the United States and other governments covering the exchange of air rights.

10. Authorization of the navigation of foreign civil aircraft in the United States.

11. Assuring protection of the public by (*a*) requiring the performance of safe and adequate air-carrier service, and (*b*) eliminating rate discriminations and unfair competition or unfair and deceptive practices in air transportation.

12. Investigation and determination of probable causes of civil aircraft accidents.

13. Adjudication of appeals from safety enforcement decisions of the Administrator of the Federal Aviation Agency, and participation when appropriate in safety rulemaking proceedings of the Administrator.

Role of the States and Municipalities in Regulation[17]

The federal government has, since 1926, virtually pre-empted the field of regulating aviation safety; but, in the realm of economic

[17] See Oswald Ryan, "Economic Regulation of Air Commerce by the States," *Virginia Law Review*, March, 1945; P. L. Waterman, *The Role of the States in Postwar Aviation*

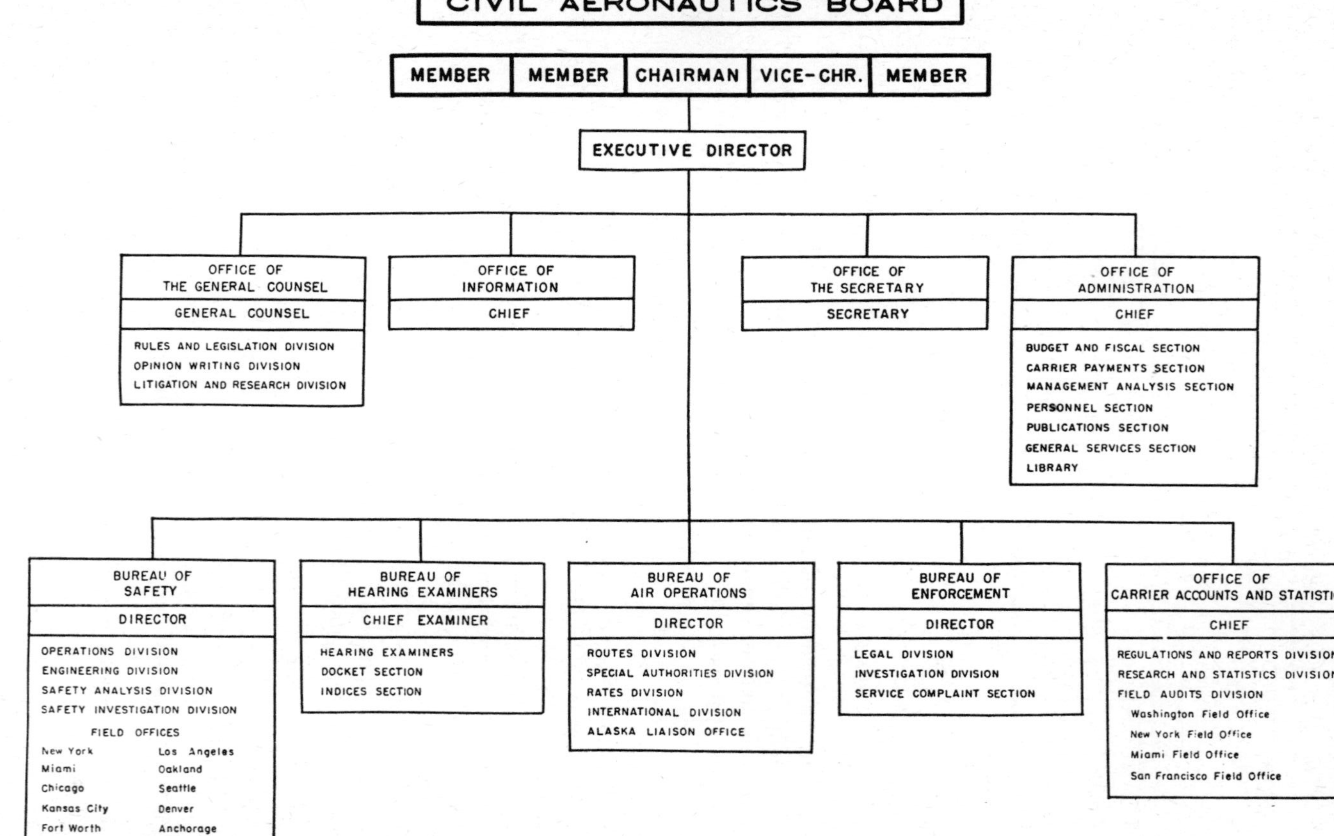

FIG. 21. Organization of the Civil Aeronautics Board.

regulation, a different situation prevails, since Title IV of the Civil Aeronautics Act of 1938 and the Federal Aviation Act of 1958 (dealing with air-carrier economic regulations) cover interstate carriers only. States may, therefore, empower a state authority to promulgate regulations; and even if the actual law remains uniform with other states, there is no way whereby the regulations can be so kept. Moreover, as the industry has become more of a paying proposition in all its branches, particularly in local operations, the creation of state regulatory bodies, often largely honorary in character, is an invitation to such bodies to assume powers, particularly in the field of economic regulation, which may not be in the best interests of the whole scheme of air transportation. Air transportation, like all other public service industries, must operate within the framework of public policy; and whether it attains or fails to attain its full capacity for public service is in large part dependent upon the soundness or unsoundness of that policy. We must not forget that aviation's ability to overcome the physical barriers of land and water gives no assurance of a similar ability to surmount political and economic barriers that may be unwisely or unwittingly erected against its progress.

State participation in safety regulation has largely been coincident with and concerned with the same aspects of air transportation as federal regulation, but in the field of economic regulation an important issue has been raised which is believed to have grave implications for the future of air transportation in this country. This issue is whether air transportation in the future is to develop under the regulatory control of the national government, as in the past, or whether it is to be subjected to the multiple and possibly conflicting control of 48 regulatory bodies in addition to the federal agency. No sound answer to this problem can be reached without taking account of the inherently interstate and national character of air transportation.

In view of the need for uniformity in aeronautical regulations, the

---

(Berkeley: University of California, Bureau of Public Administration, 1945); John H. Frederick, "State Legislation Needs for Airports," *Southern Flight*, September, 1944; Charles S. Rhyne, *Airports and the Courts* (Washington, D.C.: National Institute of Municipal Law Officers, 1944); Charles S. Rhyne, "Airport Legislation and Court Decisions," *Journal of Air Law and Commerce*, Summer, 1947; Herzel H. E. Plaine, "State Aviation Legislation," *Journal of Air Law and Commerce*, Summer, 1947; Cooper, *op. cit.;* Madeline C. Dinu, "State Aviation Officials—Some of Their Duties, Responsibilities and Activities," *Journal of Air Law and Commerce*, Summer, 1947.

Air Coordinating Committee in its report on civil air policy[18] made the following statement:

> The legislative action by the Congress, together with the implementing regulations of the responsible agencies of the Federal Government, have regulated air safety to such an extent as to constitute pre-emption of the field. Therefore, under the present statutory and regulatory structure, neither the states nor their political subdivisions may constitutionally promulgate air safety regulations.

The need for state assistance in the enforcement of violations involving the operation of small private aircraft was recognized in 1951 by a working agreement made between the federal agencies and the National Association of State Aviation Officials. Under this agreement, it was expected that the states would enforce the Federal Air Safety Regulations in such cases by using their own personnel and applying their own local laws. In this connection, the Air Coordinating Committee stated:

> The Federal Government continues to encourage state safety enforcement action in the area of violations arising out of the actual piloting or navigation of small private aircraft where quick local action is most effective. Such enforcement action should be based on local statutes prohibiting the careless and reckless operation of such aircraft, and directing the courts to consider the Federal Regulations in determining what is careless and reckless operation. State assistance in Federal prosecution of violations is also encouraged.

The nature of the air transportation business is such that the trunkline carriers perform the greater part of their services in interstate, rather than intrastate, commerce. Air transportation is long-distance transportation. The fact that the main airline selling point is speed, and that to make speed count service must generally be performed over substantial distances, inevitably means a preponderance of interstate business. Thus, from its beginning, this form of air transportation has been more definitely a matter of federal concern than any other form of transportation. Only since the close of World War II has there been any development of intrastate air transportation, which first started in Texas in 1946 and later in California. By the middle of 1949, the California operators, particularly between Los Angeles and San Francisco, had become a serious problem from the standpoint of competition with the interstate operators certifi-

[18] The President's Air Coordinating Committee, *Civil Air Policy* (Washington, D.C.), 1954. Recommendations in this report will be discussed in the appropriate chapters of this volume.

cated by the Civil Aeronautics Board to operate over the same routes. It is still an open question whether the economics of this method of transport will permit the survival of purely local operations that do not involve the carriage of passengers and property moving in interstate commerce.

Perhaps the primary threat of state economic regulation lies in its potential effect upon the national policy of regulated competition, which is discussed in Chapters 6 and 7. If each of the 50 states should exercise the right to grant certificates of public convenience and necessity to local intrastate airlines, many of which would be operating in competition with the intrastate segments of our interstate airlines, the result would probably be the economic impairment of our air transport system and an obstruction to its future growth. The interstate and intrastate activities of an airline are so intermingled that uniformity of regulatory action is an absolute essential to a sound and orderly economic development, and such uniformity is not practicable under a system of multiple control. Public regulation under such circumstances could become a crazy quilt of overlapping jurisdictions and inconsistent patterns which would destroy whatever regulated competitive balance has been built up under the federal policy to date.

It is only in the case of the airline whose operations neither parallel and compete with the interstate carrier nor connect with the interstate carrier in such a way as to carry interstate commerce that the state authority could regulate through the issuance or denial of certificates without the danger of seriously disrupting the national aviation program. It may be questioned whether many such local operations will exist. Many will doubtless be started from time to time; but, except under most unusual circumstances, few will survive in such a restricted area, since the economics of the market for air transport services will normally require the local operator to adjust his operations to a market which extends beyond the border of a single state.

Another illustration of the probable effect of imposing state economic regulation upon our scheduled airlines that carry intrastate, as well as interstate, commerce may be seen when we apply state control to the intrastate rates of our interstate airlines. Air carriers that operate across state lines, especially where their operations cross ten or twenty states, as some now do, are not likely to be effectively regulated by the action of the many states through which they pass. The various state regulatory bodies in such a case are not likely ever to be in possession of all the facts with respect to the costs of a far-flung airline. Only an agency with jurisdiction over the entire operations of such a carrier would be in a position to determine effectively the reasonableness of the over-all costs and the propriety of the cost allocations among the different classes of traffic. State regulation under such circumstances presents such complex problems that it is to be hoped that, if the states do exert jurisdiction over the economic activities of air carriers, they will at least exempt the interstate airlines from such multiple state control.[19]

Finally, there is the financial burden which compliance with multiple regulation would place upon the airlines. In the years immediately ahead, it will be necessary for air transportation to drive steadily and successfully toward lower cost levels if the industry is to serve a mass transportation market and attain economic stability and security. In this respect, air transportation differs significantly from surface transportation, both rail and highway. There are differences in the volume of operations, differences in the operating margins, a difference in the proportion which local business bears to interstate business, and differences in the number of separate jurisdictions to which air carriers would be subject; all these combine to disprove any assumed analogy between air transportation and surface transportation as a support for the multiple regulation of air commerce.

In connection with the multiple economic regulation of air commerce, the Air Coordinating Committee stated:

> Intrastate transportation of persons and property by air wholly within the boundaries of a single state and not part of nor connected with the flow of interstate or foreign commerce is properly subject to the economic regulatory control of the state involved: provided that, where such intrastate transportation is performed by an air carrier as defined in the Civil Aero-

---

[19] In *Western Air Lines* v. *Public Utilities Commission of California,* 342 U.S. 908 (1954), the Supreme Court of the United States rendered ineffective an attack by a scheduled airline on state regulation of interstate air carriers. On March 1, 1951, Western Air Lines had increased its air coach fares between Los Angeles and San Francisco with the approval of the Civil Aeronautics Board. On March 6, 1951, the Public Utilities Commission of California ordered an investigation into Western's fares in California. On April 24, 1951, the Public Utilities Commission of California issued an order effective May 7, 1951, purportedly authorizing the air carrier to increase its air coach fares to the level in the tariff previously approved by the CAB, but requiring Western to refund the excessive fares collected in the interim. Western petitioned the California Supreme Court to review the order of the California Public Utilities Commission. This petition was denied without opinion, and Western sought relief in the United States Supreme Court. This Court dismissed the appeal for want of a substantial federal question, with Mr. Justice Black and Mr. Justice Burton being of the opinion that probable jurisdiction should be noted.

nautics Act, the rates, fares, charges and practices for such transportation should be subject to the exclusive control of the Federal Government.

Exercise of Control over Air Space[20]

The ever-expanding extent in the United States of aeronautical activity, both civil and military, has brought into sharp focus the need for a greater understanding of the rights, duties, authority, and interests in air space. The problem is twofold. On the one hand, it involves a question of federal-state relations under the Constitution with respect to the power and duty to control the air space. On the other hand, it involves the relationship between the users of the air space for purposes of flight and the owners of surface interests below.

The United States as a nation has a strong national interest in the air space for at least three reasons: (*a*) It is a highway for interstate commerce; (*b*) it is a zone vital to the defense of the country; and (*c*) it is necessary to the postal service. Congress, as early as 1926, affirmed this paramount national interest and the definition of its nature and scope by adopting the Air Commerce Act of 1926, which has been previously discussed.[20] Furthermore, the legislative history of the Air Commerce Act of 1926 shows that in enacting it, Congress relied on the commerce power, the war powers, and the postal power in combination.

The Air Commerce Act of 1926 and the Civil Aeronautics Act of 1938 have thus formally recognized and asserted federal jurisdiction in the air space for all purposes necessary to control, preserve, and protect air navigation in the broadest sense. Notwithstanding this plenary power for these specified purposes in the air space above the several states, existing jurisdiction in the local governments for other purposes has not been affected. The Air Coordinating Committee therefore concluded:

> The Federal Government should continue, as it now does, to exercise exclusive control of the airspace over the United States, its territories and possessions, for the purposes of controlling, preserving, and protecting air navigation in the broadest sense. Beyond that, existing jurisdiction of the states and their political subdivisions for other purposes in the airspace above their territories should continue.

---

[20] This section is adapted from The President's Air Coordinating Committee, *Civil Air Policy*, *supra*, pp. 46–48. See also John C. Cooper, "State Sovereignty vs. Federal Sovereignty of Navigable Airspace," *Journal of Air Law and Commerce*, Winter, 1948.

[21] That act, as amended by the Civil Aeronautics Act of 1938, provides that "the United States of America is hereby declared to possess and exercise complete and exclusive national sovereignty in the airspace above the United States . . ." (49 U.S.C. 176).

The power of the federal government under the commerce clause of the United States Constitution extends not only to the instrumentalities of interstate commerce but to the medium through which they operate. Thus, the jurisdiction of the federal government extends to all air space navigable in fact in which aircraft operate while engaged in or directly affecting interstate commerce. In the enactment of the Civil Aeronautics Act of 1938, the Congress expressly exercised its regulatory power in the air space navigable in fact. Thus, the Civil Aeronautics Board was directed to adopt rules for safe altitudes of flight and for prevention of collisions between aircraft or between aircraft and land or water vehicles.

However, because the term "navigable air space" in the Civil Aeronautics Act is defined as the air space above the minimum altitudes of flight prescribed by regulations issued by the Board under the Act, and because of certain language used by the Board in these regulations, some confusion has arisen on this point. There is some doubt whether the existing federal regulations are phrased to make this provision operative throughout the take-off and landing operations of aircraft. While this doubt is hardly justified, resolution of the matter seems desirable, and the Air Coordinating Committee has recommended that:

> Existing Federal regulations relating to minimum altitudes of flight should be re-examined by the appropriate agencies to determine whether revision of such regulations is necessary or desirable in order to dispel any possible inference that the Federal Government has not exercised its regulatory jurisdiction over the entire flight of an aircraft in the airspace above the United States navigable in fact.

Instances may arise where flights over private land are so low, so frequent, and so injurious to the surface, that, if performed by the federal government, they would amount to taking private property, against which protection is afforded under the Constitution. Such instances have been rare. Whether flights by private operators through the navigable air space, as expressed by Congress in the Civil Aeronautics Act and otherwise in conformity with federal regulations, may create a valid claim in the landowner is a question the courts may still have to decide, since the air space is a highway protected by the commerce clause of the Constitution.

It is recognized that low flight may create a problem of noise and disturbance. This is primarily a social problem, to which the application of doctrines of real property law cannot afford an appropriate solution. The erection of a barrier to flight, unconnected with the safety of air operations, may aggravate the problem by causing the air traffic to engage in additional maneuvers. For this reason local ordinances and legislative enactments, which are intended to protect communities against the noise and disturbance, are not valid or proper cures. The true solution lies in improved procedures around airports, taking into account all aspects of the problem and the continuing technological improvement in aircraft performance. The Air Coordinating Committee recommendation was that:

> The Federal Government should continue to use its best efforts to devise means, methods, and improved procedures and techniques to minimize noise and disturbance caused by aircraft landing and taking off. Industry should be encouraged to do likewise. Additionally, the Federal Government should continue to watch closely any litigation which may arise in this area and where necessary participate therein to the end that the courts may be fully advised on the governmental nature of this problem.

Airspace in the vicinity of airports and airways must be protected against the erection of structures which would interfere with air navigation. The Congress has primary authority to prevent interference with air navigation, analogous in part to the authority it possesses to prevent obstructions in the navigable waters. An example of the exercise of this power is contained in the Communications Act of 1934, as amended, which includes the power of federal control over the erection of radio transmitter towers within the navigable air space which interfere with its public use. However, the provision of this Act are not adequate to cope with all hazards to air navigation, so that the Air Coordinating Committee suggested that:

> The power of the Federal Government to control the erection of structures within airspace for the purpose of controlling and protecting air navigation should be further strengthened by legislation.

Chapter 5

ECONOMICS OF COMMERCIAL AIR TRANSPORTATION

FIRMS in the commercial air transport industry have certain characteristics which influence economic adjustments in the industry. These are discussed in detail in later chapters, but may be briefly summarized here as follows:

1. The industry is considered to be "affected with the public interest," just as are other carriers and public utilities. It is therefore subject to government regulation. For the same reason, considerable government financial support has been provided for certain types of airlines, a policy that will probably continue for some time.
2. Airlines are not "natural monopolies" in the usual sense of the term, and substantial competition could develop in the industry were it not for federal regulatory policies preventing it.
3. Fixed charges are lower, for a given volume of business, than in many other forms of transportation, because of the relatively small capital investment. Thus successful airline management is more dependent on efficient control of nonfixed expenses.
4. Technological progress has been relatively rapid in the air transportation industry and has in some cases made equipment obsolete long before it has become physically worn out.

The "Public Interest" Characteristics of Air Carriers

Important questions can be raised about the attitude of governments toward the airlines. Are the companies regarded as strictly "private" business, free of government control, and operated solely in the interests of the management and the investors? Or are they regarded as public utilities analogous to electric power and telephone companies? Likewise, to what extent are the airlines regarded as instruments of national policy—economic, diplomatic, and military?

While commercial air transportation has some characteristics of a public utility, the airlines are not monopolistic in character as they are subject to very substantial competition from: (*a*) other forms of transportation; (*b*) other existing airlines or competition from within the industry; and (*c*) unpredictable future changes in route pattern under regulation. In addition, the airline industry differs markedly from regulated utilities such as electric, gas, telephone, water, and railroad, in the following major respects:

1. The airlines operate with a much higher ratio of expenses to revenues, and with a high labor component in relation to revenues and expenses.
2. The airline industry has a substantial amount of investment in flying equipment having a relatively short life due to both physical deterioration and obsolescence. This is one of the factors resulting in a net property rate base which, comparatively, is much smaller than that of the ordinary regulated utilities in relation to operating revenues.
3. The airlines are affected to an exceptional degree by continuous technological developments and radical changes in basic operating equipment.
4. Utility services such as electric, gas, water, and telephone are used daily by practically every connected customer. However, airline travel is not in the same constant, essential public use category, and probably will be much more vulnerable to diminished patronage in times of economic stress than the utility services mentioned. In the use of the regular utility services, no major consumer decision is involved; the decision to use is automatic. In the use of air transportation, however, at least three major decisions are usually involved: Is this trip necessary? Shall I go by air, car, or train? Shall I fly Eastern or National or some other airline?

Under the Act of 1938, competition was to be permitted to the extent necessary to assure the sound development of an air transport system properly adapted to needs of commerce, the postal service, and national defense. Routes were to be granted by the Board only on a showing of public convenience and necessity, and by implication, the Board was not to grant them when unnecessary competition would result. It was the intent of the act that the companies be allowed to earn a "fair" return on their investment, to the extent permitted by cost and demand conditions.

These features—regulation of rates and service, control of the entry of new firms, limitation of profit to a "fair return" figure, and the obligation to perform particular services whether profitable or not—are characteristic of regulations applied to public utilities.

The Act of 1938 also showed the congressional intent to make the airlines instruments of national policy—economic, diplomatic, and military. They were to be "adapted to the present and future needs of the foreign and domestic commerce of the United States, of the

Postal Service, and of the national defense." These are national objectives designed for the interests of the common welfare.

In respect to the question of "fair return," the government policies extend farther in the direction of attempting to insure such a return than is the case with other regulated industries. Rapid communication by the carriage of passengers and mail requires that the airlines serve many points which may offer insufficient business to make operations to them profitable. In order to make such operation possible, the Civil Aeronautics Act contains the requirement that the Board allows sufficient mail pay and/or subsidy payment to an honestly and efficiently managed airline, in conjunction with its other revenues, to permit it to cover costs of operation and, in addition, to earn a fair return on its investment. The airline, in turn, must maintain and continue the development of its system to the extent necessary to furnish satisfactory service, to set reasonable nondiscriminatory rates, to perform the required postal service, and to maintain preparedness of assistance in national defense.

Thus, in summary, the airlines, although financed by private capital and managed by private enterprises, are subject to regulation as public utilities, provided government financial assistance, and regarded as government instrumentalities in the interest of national welfare.

Airline Revenues

Table 16 shows the revenues of the scheduled airlines from various sources for selected years. Passenger revenue has accounted for a greater portion of the total than all other revenues combined. Mail revenue has been declining in relative importance, and revenue from express and freight increasing.

Airline Expenses

Table 17 shows the expenses of the airlines. *Flying operations* include the direct costs of plane operations, chiefly for wages and fuel. *Depreciation and amortization* is an important item of expense, because the rapid rate of obsolescence of aircraft due to technological developments causes the companies to depreciate such equipment over a very short period. Most airlines depreciate their newer aircraft over a period of seven years. (See Chapter 12.)

Maintenance covers the costs of periodic inspection, service, and overhaul occurring after definite periods of flying time have elapsed. Standards of equipment maintenance are extremely high.

TABLE 16: United States Scheduled Airline Operating Revenues for Selected Years (In Thousands of Dollars)

	Passenger	U. S. Mail Priority	U. S. Mail Non-Priority	Public Service Revenue [1]	Express	Freight	Other [2]	Total
Domestic Trunk Airlines								
1950	430,098	46,311	—	—	12,569	21,698	13,433	524,109
1955	1,021,855	24,230	2,708	3,192	19,405	39,605	22,353	1,133,348
1956	1,142,197	28,937	2,654	2,609	18,101	42,173	26,160	1,262,831
1957	1,287,172	31,002	2,760	1,182	14,667	49,870	32,961	1,419,614
1958	1,362,992	33,039	3,076	2,386	16,140	57,351	38,265	1,513,249
1959p	1,632,131	37,138	3,415	—	19,124	67,026	39,202	1,798,036
Local Service Airlines								
1950	10,303	16,581	—	—	230	212	544	27,870
1955	32,840	1,084	101	20,923	665	556	1,281	57,450
1956	40,166	1,004	102	23,211	775	750	1,704	67,712
1957	47,464	1,108	103	29,651	725	1,049	2,039	82,139
1958	56,488	1,273	90	32,746	809	1,183	2,364	94,953
1959p	72,989	1,467	155	41,916	985	1,735	3,174	122,421
Intra-Hawaiian Airlines								
1950	4,105	285	—	—	125	288	410	5,213
1955	5,686	48	—	291	—	752 [3]	337	7,114
1956	6,042	51	1	288	—	782	266	7,430
1957	6,975	51	2	72	—	781	479	8,360
1958	7,063	54	—	109	—	776	1,391	9,393
1959p	9,476	61	1	168	—	832	1,061	11,599
Helicopter Airlines								
1950	—	791	—	—	—	—	7	798
1955	208	250	—	2,710	100	23	64	3,355
1956	438	234	—	2,833	115	28	63	3,711
1957	968	237	—	3,567	101	36	123	5,032
1958	1,459	214	—	4,369	101	31	115	6,289
1959p	2,310	225	—	2,722	123	39	2,335	7,754
International and Overseas Airlines								
1950	160,673	55,689	—	—	15,783	5,881	22,105	260,131
1955	294,828	25,639	—	1,583	77	31,853	30,324	384,304
1956	342,553	26,926	—	8,308	82	36,683	38,113	452,665
1957	377,655	28,365	—	555	80	41,475	39,818	487,948
1958	385,999	32,655	—	—	145	43,802	43,939	506,540
1959p	432,742	35,146	7	—	93	55,536	41,532	565,056
Alaskan Airlines								
1950	2,758	2,939	—	—	—	639 [3]	3,102	9,438
1955	8,162	2,333	—	5,618	—	2,464	3,747	22,324
1956	10,200	2,477	—	6,241	—	2,754	7,680	29,352
1957	11,263	2,662	—	6,369	—	2,651	4,063	27,008
1958	12,530	2,915	—	6,839	—	2,659	3,981	28,924
1959p	14,638	3,266	2	7,473	—	2,833	5,441	33,653
All-Cargo Airlines								
1950	—	—	—	—	—	8,850	3,511	12,361
1955	—	60	—	—	—	18,640	8,335	27,035
1956	—	144	220	—	447	25,564	26,485	52,860
1957	—	189	263	—	545	29,281	55,050	85,328
1958	—	1,048	128	—	300	23,349	52,026	76,851
1959p	—	2,457	23	—	356	35,958	30,531	69,325
CONSOLIDATED INDUSTRY								
1950	**607,937**	**122,596**	—	—	**28,707**	**37,568 [3]**	**43,112**	**839,920**
1955	**1,363,579**	**53,644**	**2,809**	**34,317**	**20,247**	**93,893**	**66,441**	**1,634,930**
1956	**1,541,596**	**59,773**	**2,977**	**43,490**	**19,520**	**108,734**	**100,471**	**1,876,561**
1957	**1,731,497**	**63,614**	**3,128**	**41,396**	**16,118**	**125,143**	**134,533**	**2,115,429**
1958	**1,826,531**	**71,198**	**3,294**	**46,449**	**17,495**	**129,151**	**142,081**	**2,236,199**
1959p	**2,164,286**	**79,760**	**3,603**	**52,279**	**20,681**	**163,959**	**123,276**	**2,607,844**

p Preliminary. [1] Prior to October 1, 1953, Public Service Revenues were not reported separately. This term refers to federal subsidy payments. [2] Other revenues include revenues from excess baggage, foreign mail and charter operations, and incidental revenues. [3] Express and freight combined. Source: *Facts and Figures About Air Transportation, 1960* (Washington, D.C.: Air Transport Association, 1960).

General Services and Administration accounts for the administrative functions of air transportation production.

The analysis of airline expenses has always been a difficult problem. The difficulty stems primarily from the fact that there has been insufficient data for normal periods over a substantial length of time to determine the effect which the various operating characteristics have on costs. For example, prior to the establishment of the Uniform System of Airline Accounts by the Board, no truly consistent compilation of cost statistics was available; and since the establishment of that system, the World War II period and its aftermath, with its abnormal economic characteristics, have severely affected the available data.

It is clear, however, that two airlines having the same characteristics of size, volume of traffic, and operations, but having a different number of stations, will experience different cost levels. The one having the larger number of stations should experience higher costs, other things being comparable. This results from a number of factors. In the first place, more stations must be manned. Always associated with any station are certain expenses which are relatively the same regardless of the volume of business handled; thus total station cost is primarily dependent upon the number of stations operated. In the second place, the larger the number of stations for a given route length, the shorter will be the average flight over that route. Similarly, the shorter will be the average trip of the passengers flying over the route.

Shorter individual flights result in a larger percentage of ground time in taxiing and warming up. Furthermore, a larger number of take-offs and landings occur, and all these factors necessarily lead to a higher operating expense than would be encountered by an airline having a smaller proportion of such ground time and fewer take-offs and landings. Such elements make themselves felt very directly in maintenance expenses since they markedly affect the wear and tear upon the various parts of the aircraft, particularly the frame and engine.

Another effect which springs directly from the larger number of stations is a lower average block-to-block speed. Thus the covering of a certain number of revenue-miles of operation requires more flight time, with correspondingly higher direct expense both in terms of flying expense and maintenance, on the one hand, and depreciation of flight equipment, on the other, the latter by reason of the lower effective utilization in miles flown per day per aircraft.

TABLE 17: United States Scheduled Airline Operating Expenses for Selected Years (In Thousands of Dollars)

	Flying Operations	Maintenance	General Services & Administration: Passenger Service	Aircraft & Traffic Servicing	Promotion & Sales	Administrative	Total G. S. & A.	Depreciation & Amortization	Total Operating Expenses
Domestic Trunk Airlines									
1950	132,060	87,400	30,870	68,541	62,645	33,651	195,707	46,371	461,538
1955	302,591	196,320	72,996	133,274	134,706	68,473	409,449	101,709	1,010,069
1956	340,670	239,530	83,953	152,928	159,366	79,462	475,709	106,321	1,162,230
1957	434,842	270,328	95,505	217,208	157,561	55,164	525,438	146,968	1,377,576
1958	437,515	286,126	101,223	231,109	165,944	56,949	555,226	139,256	1,418,123
1959[p]	504,848	346,422	130,730	275,169	198,318	65,583	669,800	171,729	1,692,799
Local Service Airlines									
1950	8,330	5,256	1,090	4,969	3,241	2,484	11,784	1,836	27,206
1955	18,080	10,384	2,687	9,563	9,287	4,485	26,022	2,278	56,764
1956	21,616	12,610	3,385	11,187	11,399	5,382	31,353	2,714	68,293
1957	26,509	16,418	4,028	21,160	6,089	4,938	36,215	3,758	82,900
1958	29,267	18,572	4,528	24,047	7,026	5,544	41,146	4,351	93,336
1959[p]	36,746	24,924	6,074	31,153	9,281	6,808	53,316	6,839	121,825
Intra-Hawaiian Airlines									
1950	1,221	942	190	906	832	743	2,671	452	5,286
1955	1,942	1,278	245	1,258	1,045	964	3,512	603	7,335
1956	2,033	1,259	252	1,317	1,182	848	3,599	416	7,307
1957	2,212	1,422	278	1,521	1,265	868	3,932	515	8,081
1958	2,504	1,698	413	1,671	1,283	1,022	4,393	661	9,256
1959[p]	3,076	1,933	456	1,948	1,726	1,223	5,353	909	11,271
Helicopter Airlines									
1950	205	182	....	98	2	112	212	133	732
1955	614	871	21	425	180	393	1,019	451	2,955
1956	697	981	21	544	312	496	1,373	605	3,656
1957	1,108	1,381	....	....	....	....	1,765[1]	911	5,164
1958	1,416	1,618	....	....	....	....	1,982[1]	946	5,962
1959[p]	1,686	2,027	....	....	....	....	2,358[1]	1,041	7,112
International & Overseas Airlines									
1950	70,980	43,440	14,589	31,618	36,514	22,170	104,891	29,012	248,323
1955	108,501	58,975	26,773	46,990	61,980	31,291	167,034	31,094	365,604
1956	125,613	72,069	31,053	51,583	70,822	33,808	187,266	34,593	419,541
1957	142,944	72,326	32,519	67,187	70,902	24,631	195,239[2]	50,359	460,868
1958	155,060	79,892	35,516	72,716	75,759	24,412	210,695[2]	50,824	496,471
1959[p]	161,157	89,555	42,762	80,503	85,866	27,617	238,127[2]	58,213	547,052
Alaskan Airlines									
1950	3,020	2,365	358	966	634	1,332	3,290	1,028	9,703
1955	7,191	5,273	773	2,701	1,593	1,519	6,586	1,120	21,706[2]
1956	9,959	5,744	964	3,702	1,831	1,894	8,391	1,364	27,166[2]
1957	8,669	6,215	854	2,779	1,042	853	10,065[2]	1,646	26,595
1958	8,998	6,228	920	3,321	1,068	1,195	10,678[2]	1,920	27,824
1959[p]	10,516	7,756	1,226	3,641	1,311	1,340	12,351[2]	2,749	33,372
All-Cargo Airlines									
1950	4,633	1,769	....	1,033	1,979	1,047	4,059	329	10,790
1955	10,635	5,287	267	3,896	2,081	2,103	8,347	2,074	26,343
1956	21,677	11,662	1,614	6,353	3,883	3,454	15,304	3,155	53,879[2]
1957	36,563	18,969	3,618	12,450	4,064	4,395	25,203[2]	8,998	89,734
1958	31,929	17,903	2,503	8,878	2,612	4,388	19,145[2]	9,172	78,149
1959[p]	29,968	17,644	1,504	8,510	2,590	4,470	17,843[2]	7,464	72,919
CONSOLIDATED INDUSTRY									
1950	220,449	141,354	47,097	108,131	105,847	61,539	322,614	79,161	763,578
1955	449,554	278,388	103,762	198,107	210,872	109,228	621,969	139,329	1,490,776[2]
1956	522,265	343,855	121,242	227,614	248,795	125,344	722,995	149,168	1,742,072[2]
1957	652,847	387,060	136,802	322,305	240,923	90,848	797,855[2]	213,156	2,050,918
1958	666,689	412,037	145,103	341,742	253,692	93,510	843,265[2]	207,130	2,129,121
1959[p]	747,997	490,261	182,752	400,924	299,092	107,041	999,148[2]	248,944	2,486,350

[p] Preliminary. [1] Detailed expense data not reported. [2] Total is greater than sum of individual expense categories since segregation of expenses is not reported by all carriers. Source: *Facts and Figures About Air Transportation, 1960* (Washington, D.C.: Air Transport Association, 1960).

The manner in which the above factors affect direct expense is quite clear. However, these same factors are also responsible for higher indirect expense. Consider, for example, the effect on costs of ground operations. Such operations involve dispatching, communications, and other factors which are primarily related to the time the aircraft spends between departure and arrival. It is obvious that, since communications must be maintained with the aircraft during all the time it is engaged in a flight, the load on such communications personnel and equipment will increase with any increase in the number of hours required to cover a given number of miles of operation.

Similarly, in the category of traffic and sales, the shorter the average haul of the passengers carried by the airline, the larger the number of tickets which must be sold for a given number of passenger-miles carried by the system for any given period of time. The mere issuance of a ticket requires the expenditure of funds in cost which are to a large extent independent of the length of the trip of that passenger. It is obvious that the sales personnel must be larger when a larger number of tickets are sold by the airline during a given period. Only a few examples of these effects have been mentioned; however, these same indirect costs noted above also cause still additional indirect costs. For example, a larger sales force requires more office space, with the correspondingly higher rental charges and other associated expenses. This is true for any function requiring a larger number of personnel. As a result of the increased load due to the nature of operations and traffic, greater expenses are involved in the general and administrative category. Accounting expenses must necessarily increase, and the general supervision of all functions becomes more burdensome as the over-all personnel, equipment, and load increase.

The nature of many airline routes is seasonal. High seasonal factors result in higher unit expenses in any type of business. This is so because the organization must be set up to handle, in some manner, the peak loads imposed upon the system; yet during periods of low activity only the more direct types of expenses may be reduced in accordance with the reduced volume of operations. For the operating staff of an airline there is required a group of people having experience and training for the specialized tasks. Such a staff cannot be varied from month to month without seriously impairing the efficiency and thus increasing the costs of operation. Such a procedure would result in excessive training expenses, together with a lower effectiveness of all personnel involved. It is common in any industry that the majority of functions cannot be reduced and increased to fully compensate for the seasonal elements.

All airlines experience serious operating problems from the standpoint of weather. Safe airline operation cannot always be conducted with the present technological status of the industry. The effect is reflected directly in the operating factor and the percentage of scheduled flights completed. Since an airline organization must be set up to handle the expected scheduled operations, any period of inactivity caused by bad weather means that the organization cannot be effectively utilized. It is clear that the organization must be geared to the scheduled operations since the bad-weather periods occur in essentially unpredictable frequency from the long-range standpoint. In other words, full scheduled operations do occur often for extended periods but are then rudely interrupted by periods of relative inactivity. Thus the low operating factor, which in some periods of the year is primarily the reflection of bad weather, also causes substantially higher unit costs, both direct and indirect.

The Relation of Airline Expenses to the Volume of Traffic

As previously indicated, airlines have relatively low fixed charges, particularly when compared to the railroads, since their airways cost them little and their airport facilities are generally provided at low cost by governmental agencies. Also, the high speed of aircraft lessens the amount of capital equipment required per passenger- or ton-mile over what would otherwise be necessary.

However, a substantial portion of airline costs are *constant* costs, in the sense that they do not vary in proportion to changes in the volume of business handled. Some of these are true fixed costs (but not fixed charges) in the sense that they would continue whether the firm operated flights or not; salaries of higher officials and some depreciation charges are examples. These will continue so long as the firm continues to exist, even if it suspends actual operations. But the bulk of the constant costs are not fixed costs but are the constant (as compared to the direct) type of variable cost—that is, one which will cease if the firm suspends operations but which will not vary directly in proportion to output. As suggested above, many of the station expenses are not adjustable to the volume of business; the same is true of those for supervisory, administrative, and clerical personnel. Many of these costs are not even closely dependent upon the number of flights.

In addition, with a given number of flights, up to the limit of plane capacity, the plane operating costs—fuel, wages, maintenance, etc.—are almost completely independent of the volume of passenger, freight, and other traffic handled. Just as a railroad requires about the same expenditures for fuel, wages of operating personnel, and maintenance of equipment whether a train carries five passengers or fifty and requires only a few additional ones if it carries five hundred, so an airline will pay out almost the same amounts for plane operation and maintenance regardless of the loads handled, with a given number of flights. These plane operating costs will, of course, increase if traffic rises to the point at which additional flights must be added.

Thus, with a given number of flights, the only actual *direct* variable costs—those changing more or less in direct proportion to changes in volume of business—are those resulting from the selling of additional tickets, serving of more meals, use of some additional fuel because of the greater weight, etc. And so the *marginal cost*—the addition to total cost from the handling of the additional units of business—is extremely small. As the average load carried per flight rises, the average cost per ton—or passenger-mile drops very sharply, since the total of the constant costs is being spread over more units. As business is expanded to the extent that additional flights are necessary, the plane operating costs will rise, in total, more or less in proportion to the additional business. But the other constant costs—those not directly dependent upon the number of flights—will not increase in proportion, and average cost will continue to decline. Likewise, over a longer period, as an airline continues to expand, it may be able to realize some economies of large-scale production, especially the use of larger-capacity planes and the introduction of increased specialization in management. Thus it may obtain still further reductions in average cost per ton- or passenger-mile.

Common and Separable Costs

When airlines handle more than one type of traffic—passenger, mail, express, freight—as they usually do, a portion of their costs are *common*[1] among the various types, since no one of the types of

[1] The term "common costs" is used rather than "joint costs" because the latter term is usually applied to costs incurred in the production of two or more commodities so related that an increase in the output of one is necessarily accompanied by an increase in the output of the other. In general, airline costs are not joint in this sense, to any extent. The handling of more passengers does not necessarily involve the handling of more freight also.

traffic is responsible for any particular part of these costs. For example, if particular flights handle freight, passengers, and express, the costs of the plane operation are common among the three. No one of the three is responsible for any particular part of the wages of the pilot or the fuel costs, except to the extent that the latter are increased from the greater weight resulting from the carrying of the particular type of business.

Not all airline costs are common, however. The wage of the stewardess, for example, is a *separable* cost for which the passenger service alone is responsible. The costs of selling tickets or of soliciting freight and the costs of handling the freight and express are separable costs.

Within each general category of service, likewise, some of the costs may be common. If a number of different types of freight are handled, a portion of the costs separable to the freight as a whole will be common among the various products. This is true likewise if separate aircraft are maintained for freight operation alone; all the operating costs of these aircraft are chargeable to freight, but many are common among the various types of commodities handled.

Much confusion has arisen over the relationship of the concept of marginal cost, so widely used in economic analysis today, and separable cost per unit of traffic, or *out-of-pocket cost,* the latter term generally being employed in transportation industries. Marginal cost consists of the addition to total cost resulting from the production of an additional unit of output—the carrying of an additional passenger, for example. On the other hand, out-of-pocket cost per unit of business consists of the total separable cost for which the type of traffic is responsible, divided by the number of units of the traffic handled. Frequently, in reference to a relatively short period of time, only those separable costs which are variable costs are included in calculating out-of-pocket cost.

In any type of business, there is no necessary way in which the total common costs must be allocated among the various products or types of traffic. Frequently, business firms will make allocations for various purposes; but these are, of necessity, arbitrary.

The portion of total airline costs consisting of common costs appears to be very high, under typical operations. Evidence submitted by United Airlines in the *Air Freight Rate Investigation*[2] indicated that 61.4 per cent of the company's total costs were incurred not directly for any particular service but for all forms of traffic to-

[2] 9 CAB 340 (1948).

gether. A similar computation by American Airlines indicated that 76 per cent of that carrier's total costs consisted of common costs.

The Theory of Rate Making for Air Transportation

To present a simple theory of rate making for the air transport industry is not an easy task. Many of the problems are comparable to those relating to other carriers, around which controversy has centered for many years. Only a brief summary statement is possible.

In general, airline managements seek to attain the maximum profit possible. The intent of regulatory policy is that actual profit earned should not exceed a "normal" or "fair" rate of return on capital investment, comparable to the profit which can typically be earned in competitive industries. So long as the maximum profit which the airlines can make under existing conditions is less than a normal return, as has probably been the typical situation in the industry, there is no general conflict between the aims of regulatory policy and those of the companies, although disagreements may arise over relative rates for different services; and those services which would provide maximum contribution toward profit may sometimes be considered contrary to public welfare. If situations permit the airlines to earn an excess return, however, a real conflict arises, since regulatory agencies will attempt to hold the general rate level below that desired by the companies.

The principle has generally been accepted that, both from the standpoint of the airlines themselves and the public interest, rates should never be allowed to fall below the out-of-pocket cost on the particular traffic.[3] This rule has generally been followed in the regulation of railroad rates and to some extent in the case of motor carriers.[4] If for example, rates on air express were set so low that the

---

[3] The high percentage of total cost, which consists of common cost, in the air transport industry makes the use of out-of-pocket costs as a minimum particularly justifiable.

[4] In the case of motor carriers, and especially the truck lines, the great bulk of all costs are direct, varying closely with the volume of traffic, since the relationship between truck capacities and available business is usually such that near-capacity operation can be attained, except on very light density runs. Additional traffic handled therefore raises total cost more or less in proportion to the increase in traffic, and thus the out-of-pocket cost of additional traffic is not substantially less than the "full" or average cost of handling all traffic. Thus, more attention has been given in rate making to full cost and less to out-of-pocket cost, since the spread between the two is slight. It is sometimes argued that the airline industry is comparable to the trucking industry in respect to cost behavior; but this statement is not borne out by the facts.

total revenue received from express was less than the separable cost for which express service is responsible—that is, the amount of reduction in total cost possible if express service were eliminated—the carriers would be better off without the traffic at all. Express traffic would drain revenue away from other services and lead to higher rates on the latter or leave the companies unable to cover all costs. This rule, that rates should not fall below out-of-pocket cost, is applicable to all types of airline service. Ordinarily, of course, a company itself will not knowingly set rates at lower levels. But forces of competition may sometimes lead them to do so, especially when they have high constant costs and are anxious to maintain volume. Continuous rate reductions to meet those of competitors may pull the rates below the out-of-pocket figures before the airlines realize it, or the companies may deliberately set rates at such levels in an attempt to drive competitors out of business. Such reductions should be prevented by regulatory action.

As indicated above, the maximum over-all level, with sound regulatory policies, is one which will allow the air carriers to earn an average rate of return on their investment. Only with such a return can they continue to operate satisfactorily. Return in excess of this figure represents an unnecessary burden on the users and restricts the use of the services below optimum economic levels.

It is entirely possible, however, that, even if the airlines are allowed to set maximum-profit rates, they will not be able to earn excess profits or, perhaps, even an average rate of return. As indicated above, this has been the typical situation in the air transport field in the past. Under such circumstances, the rates on each type of service should—from the standpoint of both the companies and the public welfare—be set at levels which will maximize the contribution of the service to the profits of the firm. In recent years, however, some economists have questioned this principle and argued that the rates on each service should be set at the level equal to marginal cost. This question is discussed below. Just as with any product, two considerations determine the optimum profit rate level. The first is cost; the second is demand for the product, or "value of service."

As shown previously, at least over a substantial range of traffic, total cost does not increase as rapidly as traffic; thus average cost per unit of business handled falls. In general, this behavior of cost is due to better utilization of equipment and personnel as business increases; it is impossible to adapt this principle to small volumes of business at all exactly. Over a longer period, likewise, larger business allows utilization of better types of equipment and increased specialization. It is very important to note that the extent to which cost per unit of business falls as traffic increases is much greater up to the limit of existing flight capacities, when the latter are not fully utilized, than when additional flights are required to handle the added business. In other words, the marginal cost of additional units of business is relatively low, especially up to the capacity of existing flights and even, though to a lesser extent, beyond this, compared to the average cost per unit of handling the business. Because of the nature of the cost behavior, the airlines have particular incentive to gain additional business by all possible means, especially in order to increase the average load factor on their flights. This situation is an incentive toward lower rate levels than might be desirable if total costs increased in proportion to business handled.

But cost alone cannot be used as a basis for setting rates; both the airlines and the regulatory agencies[5] must take into consideration the demand for the service—the "value of the service" to the user. This demand is not a fixed quantity, but rather a schedule of the quantities of the service which users will employ at various possible rate levels. In general, as rates for airline service of any type are reduced, the volume of business will increase. Travelers will shift from other forms of transportation to the airlines; some persons may decide to travel who would not have otherwise done so at all. Likewise, as rates are reduced on air freight, increased amounts of traffic will shift from the surface carriers to the airlines. No data is available on the exact elasticity of demand—the relative extent to which the volume of business changes as rates are changed—for airline service; but there is reason to believe that the elasticity is relatively high, because of the existence of substitute forms of transportation. The actual quantities of service which customers will obtain at particular rates depend upon a number of considerations: the nature and quality of competing services, the quality of the airline service, its reliability and freedom from accidents, the impor-

[5] The Civil Aeronautics Board is required by law to consider in the fixing of rates "the effect of such rates upon the movement of traffic" (Civil Aeronautics Act, sec. 1002[*e*]). The same problem confronts the railroads; in one of its earliest cases the Interstate Commerce Commission said: "The value of the service is generally regarded as the most important factor in fixing rates" (*Imperial Coal Co.* v. *Pittsburgh and L.E.R. Co.*, 2 ICC 436 (1889).

As stated by D. Philip Locklin (*Economics of Transportation* [Homewood, Ill.: Richard D. Irwin, Inc., 1960], p. 151), ". . . nothing could be more unscientific than an attempt to base rates on cost in disregard of conditions of demand,"

tance which the customers attach to greater speed, the rates charged by the competing carriers, the sales activities of the airlines, etc.

Thus, in setting rates on particular types of service, the airlines must seek to estimate the costs with various quantities of traffic and the schedule of amounts of service which customers will obtain at various possible rate levels. Then, by considering the relationship of these two schedules, they can select the rate figure which will maximize the profit from the particular service. In terms of technical economic analysis, they must select the rates on each commodity which will allow equality of marginal cost and marginal revenue.

It is, of course, difficult for the airlines or the regulatory agencies to estimate either cost or demand schedules with any high degree of accuracy, but they must base their actions upon the best estimate which they can make. The same rule applies to all services provided and to particular types of the individual services, with the exception of mail. No estimates of value of mail service are possible (other than the postal charge and consumer use of it), since there is a single buyer—the government itself. At the present time, of course, legislation provides other means for setting mail rates. But apart from this legislation, some special basis must be set up, involving an allocation of common cost to mail service on some basis consistent with general welfare, because the government is the sole user and postage rates are set by act of Congress.

When rates set on the basis indicated yield no more than an average over-all rate of profit, ordinarily no readjustment of rates by regulatory agencies will be necessary. There are some exceptions, however. Optimum-profit policies may result in setting rates regarded as discriminatory. On some types of business, competition may be much more severe than on others and may lead to substantially lower rates on the former than on the latter, with resulting discrimination between the customers of the two services. For example, suppose that an airline operated routes out of Chicago to two cities each 500 miles away. On one route, railroad freight service was excellent; on the other, it was very slow. The airline, in order to obtain air freight business on the former route, would have to set lower rates than on the latter, despite the fact that distances were comparable. Shippers in the city served by the second route would, of course, argue that they were discriminated against. Discrimination cases are very difficult to decide; there is probably a limit, however, beyond which discrimination is contrary to the best interests of the economy.

When the rates set yield an excess rate of profit, regulatory agencies must, of course, compel rate reductions in the interest of the economy. But such reductions need not be uniform on all services; the decisions as to relative reductions must be based upon considerations of national policy.

Once rate levels have been set on the bases indicated, the various services are likely to yield substantially different relative contributions to common costs. The actual contribution in each case depends largely upon the "value of the service," as reflected in the demand for it. If a service cannot cover its out-of-pocket costs regardless of the rate set, it should be abandoned, unless continued operation is essential to the general welfare. Passenger service in thinly populated areas might be so regarded. So long as a service covers more than out-of-pocket cost, continued operation is clearly desirable, even if its contribution toward the covering of common cost is relatively small. In the railroad industry, for example, passenger traffic as a whole contributes relatively little to common cost; it cannot cover its share of the latter allocated on any usual basis. And yet, so long as it more than covers the out-of-pocket cost for which it is responsible—as it presumably does—it yields something toward covering common costs; and discontinuance would lessen the total profit earned by the railroads. The Interstate Commerce Commission, by arbitrarily allocating a share of common cost to railroad passenger service, makes the latter appear to result in a loss, for almost all railroads. Such procedure is misleading, as the railroads would be worse off, in all likelihood, if they abandoned all passenger operations.

In the case of the airlines, it is very likely that the freight service will contribute relatively less to common cost than the passenger and other services. Speed is probably less important, on the average, to the shipper than to the traveler; choice of type of carrier is based more closely on relative costs in the case of freight shipments by business firms. However, so long as air freight yields more than its out-of-pocket cost, the airlines are better off providing such service than discontinuing it.

In recent years some economists have questioned the principle that utility rates should be set at levels designed to insure an average rate of return. Instead, they have argued that optimum organization of production, from the standpoint of public welfare, requires that rates for each type of service be adjusted so that the rate is equal to the marginal cost of the service.[6] However, in many cases such a policy would result in continuing losses for the companies; the government would be compelled either to take over operations or to continue subsidizing the private operations. Either policy would be accompanied by obvious disadvantages; the collection of taxes necessary to cover the deficits or subsidies might produce serious adverse effects on the economy and more than offset such gains as might be obtainable from theoretically improved utilization of resources.

As indicated earlier, airline costs are substantially higher, per ton-mile, than those of surface carriers. As a consequence, airline rates have typically been higher. Because of the advantages of speed, of course, substantial business has been gained by the airlines despite the rate differential. But the rate of growth of the air transport industry would, without question, have been much faster had lower costs and rates been possible. The gap between air and surface fares and rates has been narrowing for a number of years. However, further reductions are desirable only insofar as they actually result in increased profit and reduction in government subsidy. Decreases designed merely to increase the volume of business and resulting in increased losses and greater government subsidy are contrary to the best interests of the carriers themselves, the government, and the economy as a whole. Whether future reductions in fares and rates are possible depends upon the ability of the airlines to maintain a downward trend in capacity costs (costs per available ton-mile) and at the same time hold steady or force upward the traffic capacity relationship (load factor).[7]

---

[6] This point of view was stressed by H. Hotelling, "The General Welfare in Relation to the Problems of Taxation and of Railway and Utility Rates," *Econometrica*, July, 1938. For an extended discussion see E. Troxel, *Economics of Public Utilities* (New York: Rinehart & Co., 1947), chap. xx.

[7] For an analysis of the variables which affect airline costs: (*a*) capacity of the plane; (*b*) length of the flight; (*c*) ton-mile load factor; (*d*) number of hours per day planes are utilized; (*e*) metropolitan population served; (*f*) average speed of planes; and (*g*) net assets of each firm see Jesse W. Proctor and Julius S. Duncan, "A Regression Analysis of Airline Costs," *Journal of Air Law and Commerce*, Summer, 1954.

Chapter 6

CIVIL AERONAUTICS BOARD POLICY—COMPETITION[1]

PROVIDED with the means for regulating air transportation by the Civil Aeronautics Act of 1938, the Civil Aeronautics Board was faced with the problem of operating within the limts of the inherent economic characteristics of this new industry and, in so doing, soon discovered that it could make little use of analogy to other fields of public utility regulation. (See Chapter 5.)

A limited air traffic potential and the relative ease with which, at the time, new concerns could enter the industry produced the competition and economic instability among the smaller operators that characterized the industry in the years just prior to the passage of the

---

[1] See Neil G. Molone, "Controlled Competition: Three Years of the Civil Aeronautics Act," *Journal of Air Law and Commerce*, July, 1941; J. Howard Hamstra, "Two Decades—Federal Aero-Regulation in Perspective," *Journal of Air Law and Commerce*, April, 1941; Howard C. Westwood, "Choice of the Air Carrier for New Air Transport Routes," *George Washington Law Review*, December, 1947, and February, 1948; Frederick A. Ballard, "Federal Regulation of Aviation," *Harvard Law Review*, October, 1947; James M. Landis, "Air Routes under the Civil Aeronautics Act," *Journal of Air Law and Commerce*, Summer, 1948; Joseph L. O'Connell, Jr., "Legal Problems in Revising the Air Route Pattern," *Journal of Air Law and Commerce*, Autumn, 1948; Louis E. Black, Jr., "Realignment of the Domestic Airline Route Pattern," *Journal of Air Law and Commerce*, Autumn, 1948, and Winter, 1949; "Civil Aeronautics Board Policy—An Evaluation," *Yale Law Journal*, April, 1948; Edward C. Sweeney, "Policy Formation by the Civil Aeronautics Board," *Journal of Air Law and Commerce*, Spring, 1949; F. W. Gill and G. L. Bates, *Airline Competition* (Boston: Harvard Graduate School of Business Administration, 1949); David W. Bluestone, "The Problem of Competition Among Trunk Airlines," *Journal of Air Law and Commerce*, Autumn, 1953, and Winter, 1954; Stuart G. Tipton and Stanley Gewirtz, "The Effect of Regulated Competition on the Air Transport Industry," *Journal of Air Law and Commerce*, Spring, 1955; Gilbert L. Bates, "Current Changes in Trunkline Competition," *Journal of Air Law and Commerce*, Autumn, 1955; Civil Aeronautics Board, *Materials Relative to Competition in the Regulated Civil Aviation Industry, 1956*, Select Committee on Small Business, U.S. Senate, 84th Cong. 2d sess. (Washington, D.C.) 1956; Aaron J. Gellman, "The Regulation of Competition in U.S. Domestic Air Transportation," *Journal of Air Law and Commerce*, Part I, Autumn, 1957, Part II, Spring, 1958; Samuel B. Richmond, "Creating Competition Among Airlines," *Journal of Air Law and Commerce*, Autumn, 1957; Edward J. Taaffe, "A Map Analysis of U.S. Airline Competition," *Journal of Air Law and Commerce*, Part I, Spring, 1958, Part II, Autumn, 1958.

Act of 1938. At the same time, the operational advantages of large aircraft and the importance of a high utilization of available plane space were creating an ever-tightening core of oligopoly within the industry.[2] That is, only a small number of airlines were doing the greater part of the business between the chief traffic-generating cities. Such a development was advocated by the major lines as the cure for the ills of destructive rivalry. This cure was, however, but another illness, for in it lay the germs of monopolistic inefficiency, lessened emphasis on improved technology and reduced cost, and the maintenance of inflexible rate schedules. To cope with this abnormal situation—the existence of cutthroat competition and oligopoly in the same industry—the type of regulation introduced by the Act of 1938 seemed imperative if air transportation was to develop and become an important part of our national transportation system.

Competition

The Civil Aeronautics Act, which in 1958 became the Federal Aviation Act, provides that before a new or additional air transport service can be authorized the Civil Aeronautics Board must find that such service is required by the "public convenience and necessity." Under the so-called "grandfather" clause,[3] carriers already operating at the time the act was passed were granted certificates for routes which they had served in continuous operations as air carriers from May 14 to August 22, 1938, unless the service was inadequate or inefficient. New trunk-line routes authorized since 1938 have been largely improvements in, or additions to, this basic statutory grandfather-route pattern.

Except for the routes covered by the grandfather clause, authorizations for service between the United States and foreign countries, whether granted to foreign-flag carriers by "permit" or to American-flag carriers by "certificate," have become effective only if approved by the President of the United States as well as the Board. During the period in which the foreign air services have been in the process of authorization, the State Department has been negotiating with many foreign governments for appropriate intergovernmental agreements under which these services could be conducted. Agreements providing for the exchange of commercial operating rights on a reciprocal

---

[2] The members of this oligopoly were American Airlines, United Air Lines, Transcontinental and Western Air (now Trans World Airlines), and Eastern Air Lines.

[3] Civil Aeronautics Act, sec. 401 (*e*) (1). See also sec. 401 Federal Aviation Act, 1958.

basis have been concluded with most of the countries to which United States-flag lines are certificated. (See Chapter 10.)

The principal factors which the Board is directed to consider in determining public convenience and necessity are set forth in the declaration of policy incorporated in the act.[4] This declaration of policy makes the present and future needs of United States commerce, the postal service, and the national defense the primary criteria by which the Board determines whether a particular proposal meets public convenience and necessity. Among the other general policy intentions of Congress set forth in the act is the explicit declaration in favor of competition to the extent necessary for assuring the sound development of an air transportation system adequate to our national needs.

In its first new route case[5] the Board, after reciting the declaration of policy contained in the act, discussed the position it was taking with respect to the authorization of new or additional service in the following language:

> Obviously, in the light of these standards, it was not the congressional intent that the air transportation system of the country should be "frozen" to its present pattern. On the other hand, it is equally apparent that Congress intended the Authority to exercise a firm control over the expansion of air transportation routes in order to prevent the scramble for routes which might occur under a "laissez faire" policy. Congress, in defining the problem, clearly intended to avoid the duplication of transportation facilities and services, the wasteful competitive practices, such as the opening of nonproductive routes, and other uneconomic results which characterized the development of other modes of transportation prior to the time of their governmental regulation.

In this case, together with the opinions in two other early route proceedings,[6] the Board outlined some of the fundamental considerations which govern the disposition of new route applications, as follows: (*a*) whether the new service will serve a useful public purpose, responsive to a public need; (*b*) whether this purpose can and will be served as well by existing lines or carriers; (*c*) whether it can be served by the applicant without impairing the operations of existing carriers contrary to the public interest; and (*d*) whether the cost of the proposed service to the government will be outweighed by the benefit which will accrue to the public from the new service.

---

[4] Civil Aeronautics Act, sec. 2. See also sec. 102, Federal Aviation Act, 1958.

[5] *Duluth–Twin Cities Operation,* 1 CAA 573 (1940).

[6] *Red Bluff Operation,* 1 CAA 778 (1940); *St. Louis–Nashville–Muscle Shoals Operation,* 1 CAA 792 (1940).

In what is perhaps the leading case on the subject of competition,[7] the Board further elaborated its statement of general policy on competition. After stating that competition was not mandatory in relation to any particular route or service and that it lay in the Board's discretion to decide the issue in accordance with the peculiar circumstances of each case, the opinion outlined specific considerations for ending Pan American Airways' monopoly in the trans-Atlantic service. Among other things, it pointed out that there was sufficient available traffic at that time for two successful operators in the trans-Atlantic field, that competition not only would result in improved service but would also act as a stimulus to the development of better equipment and operating methods, and that the national defense would benefit from such competition since the research and development by foreign competitors would not be available to the national defense of this country.

Increased competition in the air transport industry is created by various Board actions: (*a*) the extension of existing carriers into territory already served by other carriers; these may be authorized either to improve a long-distance service or to provide competition; (*b*) the certification of new carriers; (*c*) changes in operations arising from route consolidations and one-stop authorizations, these being granted primarily to take advantage of technological developments; and (*d*) the permission of operations by certain carriers who have been exempted from the provisions of the act. There has also been a considerable increase in the amount of foreign competition our carriers meet on international routes. This is the result of our government's granting reciprocal rights in order to obtain operating rights for our carriers from foreign countries.

Soon after its establishment, the Board evolved a policy[8] on competition which seemed to be predicated on a stratification of the airlines into categories based on common economic characteristics, with the object of maintaining "balanced competition," as opposed to undue rivalry, within each of these classifications, and of gradually strengthening the smaller carriers by the addition of new routes and the extension of existing ones.[9] Apparently the Board thought that such a policy

---

[7] *American Export Case,* 2 CAB 16 (1940).

[8] This policy was first stated in *United Air Lines Transport Corp., Acquisition of Western Air Express,* 1 CAA 739 (1940).

[9] See *Mid-Continent Airlines, Kansas City–New Orleans,* 6 CAB 253 (1945), to strengthen Mid-Continent; *Colonial Airlines, Washington-Ottawa-Montreal,* 6 CAB 481 (1945), to strengthen Colonial; *Colonial Airlines, Atlantic Seaboard Operations,* 4 CAB

would place the smaller airlines on a sounder basis to compete with the paralleling sections of the larger systems. This theory would also imply that there should be no "super-carrier" or "chosen instrument" exploitation of any specific market[10] for air transportation. Presumably the Board's aim has been to allow the development of an air transport system composed of relatively self-sufficient units, without too much difference in economic power and able to exist with a more or less common level of rates. This aim is, of course, a Utopian one, and the history of other forms of transportation points out the difficulties of its attainment. With the certification of new local-service lines and cargo carriers, existing difficulties are multiplied. Any increase in the number of airlines, or in air service rendered by other operators, complicates the problem of achieving anything like "balanced competition." The easiest and surest way to create such a competitive situation is the reduction of the number of operators through consolidation.[11] But, unless consolidations are forced, the likelihood of progress along that path is at best doubtful. The reason for this is that consolidations of the type most likely to occur voluntarily and most likely to result in strong new airlines—those between very large and very small carriers—have been and continue to be those which encounter the most opposition from competitors and from the Board itself.[12]

Unfortunately, airline routes authorized pursuant to the Act of 1938, like the services established prior thereto, were not consciously

---

552 (1944), strengthening National Airlines to compete between New York City and Miami, Florida, with Eastern Air Lines; *Milwaukee–Chicago–New York Restriction Case,* 11 CAB 310 (1950), strengthening Capital Airlines by permitting additional nonstop service between New York, Chicago, Detroit, and Cleveland. In this case see particularly the dissenting opinion of member Jones for a discussion of Board policy as to "conviction that weak carriers must be strengthened by taking away from the stronger" and "competition for competition's sake."

10 "The question whether as a matter of policy United States international air transportation shall be rendered by a single company or by a 'chosen instrument' . . . was settled by Congress in the Civil Aeronautics Act of 1938 when . . . Congress provided that this Board in its decisions in new route cases, both domestic and international, should consider as being in the public interest . . . 'competition to the extent necessary. . . .'" (*Northeast Airlines, North Atlantic Routes,* 6 CAB 319 [1945]). Pan American Airways' claim to "chosen instrument" status has always been opposed by all domestic carriers except United Air Lines, which has based its position on the alleged insufficiency of transocean traffic to warrant competition.

11 It was this very goal which Congress sought to achieve for rail transportation through the encouragement of railroad consolidations under a plan provided for in the Transportation Act of 1920, to be set forth by the Interstate Commerce Commission.

12 See *Acquisition of Western Air Express by United Air Lines,* 1 CAA 739 (1940); *American Airlines, Acquisition of Control of Mid-Continent Airlines,* 7 CAB 365 (1946); *Eastern-Colonial, Acquisition of Assets,* 18 CAB 453 (1954); *National-Colonial Integration Investigation,* 18 CAB 453 (1954).

planned on an over-all route basis. They were awarded almost always as applied for by interested carriers. That is not to say, however, that the carriers failed in all or most cases to apply for routes and services they considered best for the public, as well as their own private interests; but a planned pattern, promoted by the Civil Aeronautics Board or a disinterested nongovernmental agency, would have provided some guidance to the carriers in applying for new or additional services and have helped to set a standard, in terms of costs and expectable traffic, by which additions to the "grandfather" network could be economically made. Certainly it would have helped to limit the strong competitive scramble for new route certifications near the end and after the close of World War II.

Not until 1949 did the Board order route-pattern studies which might serve as guides to both the Board and the industry in their joint endeavor to develop the most desirable kind of an air transport system.[13] Obviously, it would have been easier to follow a planned pattern when the need for certification of new or additional air routes arose after the organization of the Board in 1939 than it will be now to revise or reduce, as may be necessary, the vast network of routes already authorized.

It is imperative to note that the traffic used to determine whether competition is in the public interest is the total traffic available to a system, rather than the volume available on particular route segments. In measuring the need for competition in local or intraregional services for a limited area, attention must likewise be paid to the total traffic which the area may be expected to generate, rather than to the travel segments which, standing alone, may or may not generate enough traffic to warrant duplication. In other words, it is necessary to determine whether such an area is likely to produce enough total traffic to support more than one local or regional carrier, even though it is physically and operationally possible to authorize service to multiple carriers, each serving separate portions of the area, without direct or paralleling competition for identical routes.

It is all too easy to draw the analogy between the corner grocery

---

[13] Civil Aeronautics Board, *Economic Program for 1949, Statement of Policy,* issued February 21, 1949. In part, these studies were undertaken in response to findings of the President's Air Policy Commission and the Congressional Aviation Policy Board of the 80th Congress. See *Survival in the Air Age, A Report by the President's Air Policy Commission,* January 1, 1948, pp. 110–16; *National Aviation Policy* (Sen. Report No. 949, 80th Cong., 2d sess.) (Washington, D.C., 1948), p. 25. Basic to these findings was the unsatisfactory financial status of several air carriers and their mounting requirements for government financial aid.

and an air carrier and to conclude, as indeed some of the permanently certificated carriers have done in their struggle for additional routes, that, since two or more neighborhood grocery stores may better serve the public, both pricewise and servicewise, than only one, competition in air transportation will be similarly beneficial. While air transportation is more subject to competitive development than a street railway or a gas or electric company, it is, like the latter services, basically a public utility, with many of the attributes of the regulated public utility industries. Investment in plant (aircraft, spare engines, and the like) and equipment (hangers, repair shops, and service facilities), although less than with other types of carriers, is still substantial. Direct duplication of such investment can be justified only where both the new and existing carriers may be expected to develop a sufficient volume of business to avoid an unreasonable increase in total operating costs. Moreover, the certificated carrier is obligated to perform the services for which it receives authorization, often without regard to their profitability.

The provision of local or intraregional services by more than one carrier involves readily recognizable costs (or so-called "wastes" of competition) in the duplication of overhead organizations, ticket offices, etc. On the other hand, the industry and the Board have long acknowledged the costs or wastes of monopoly or noncompetitive service. The latter, of course, are much more difficult to identify. They are to be found in lack of care and economy in operating expenditures for the want of comparative yardsticks and in failure to provide adequate service and develop new markets.[14] But it takes no great understanding of air transport economics to appreciate that competition can develop greater wastes than the lost opportunities of single-company service where lack of traffic or inherent difficulties of operation make duplication uneconomical.

---

[14] "It is generally recognized that economic regulation alone cannot be relied upon to take the place of the stimulus which competition provides in the advancement of technique and service in air transportation. Competition invites comparison as to equipment, cost, personnel, organization, methods of operation, solicitation and handling of traffic, and the like, all of which tend to insure the development of an air transportation system as contemplated by the Act. That the domestic air transportation system of this country has reached its present position of pre-eminence is in large part due to the competitive spirit which has existed throughout its development. The continued maintenance of that position as well as the further development of the industry demands the encouragement of free initiative and enterprise subject only to the condition that the competitive services shall not be wasteful" (*Colonial Airlines et al., Atlantic Seaboard Operation,* 4 CAB 552, 555 [1944]). These or like virtues of competition have been urged upon the Board by proponent carriers seeking to duplicate or parallel existing services in almost every major new route proceeding before the Board in recent years.

The choice in all new route proceedings under the act is not the simple one between "competition" and "monopoly" as such. The act makes it clear that the question is whether such competition—or additional competition—as is proposed is *necessary* to assure the sound development of the industry. Competition is not an end in itself. It should foster sound economic conditions in the industry. Obviously, too much competition can be as much or more of an evil than too little.[15]

Entry into Air Transportation

The Board was called upon early in its experience to formulate a policy for dealing with the new companies proposing to engage in air transportation. Soon after the Act of 1938 became effective, great numbers of applicants, attracted by the apparently limitless prospects for air commerce as well as by the opportunity for obtaining air mail pay, began to request certificates of convenience and necessity. These requests were both to serve new territories and to compete with existing airlines between cities already certificated. The first action of the Board on the question of entry of new companies into air transportation was encouraging to those hoping to become airline operators. A certificate of convenience and necessity was granted to a new firm, American Export Airlines, to operate trans-Atlantic service in competition with the so-called "benevolent" monopoly of Pan American Airways;[16] and a bit later the Board issued another certificate to a newly organized company, All American Aviation, to operate a pick-up device for air mail carriage which eliminated the necessity of a landing.[17] These Board actions seemed to establish the principle

---

[15] The Board's own investigations of New York–Detroit, Chicago-Washington, Twin Cities–Washington, and Detroit-Washington services instigated in 1949, the study by Frederick W. Gill and Gilbert L. Bates, *Airline Competition* (Boston: Harvard School of Business Administration, 1949), and the Report of the Congressional Aviation Policy Board, *National Aviation Policy* (Sen. Report No. 949, 80th Cong., 2d sess.) (Washington, D.C., 1948) all show beyond question that excessive competition and extensive new route certifications are among the primary causes of economic instability in the air transportation industry. See also, Russell B. Adams, "The Air Route Pattern Problem," *Journal of Air Law and Commerce*, Spring, 1950; M. George Goodrick, "The Air Route Problem in the United States," *Journal of Air Law and Commerce*, Summer, 1951; Hardy K. Maclay and William C. Burt, "Entry of New Carriers into Domestic Trunkline Air Transportation," *Journal of Air Law and Commerce*, Spring, 1955.

[16] *American Export Airlines, Certificate of Public Convenience and Necessity*, 2 CAB 16 (1940).

[17] *All American Aviation, Certificate of Public Convenience and Necessity*, 2 CAB 133 (1940). In this decision the Board was unequivocal in its statement that "any such theory as advocated by the interveners (Transcontinental and Western Air and Eastern Air Lines), which would result in reserving solely for existing airlines the privilege of pro-

that the existing air carriers, who had all received permanent certificates under the "grandfather" provisions of the Civil Aeronautics Act,[18] were not to be given preference in the development of new services. Only six months after the decision in the All American case, however, the Board laid down a rule of exclusion which for some time dominated its policy on certificating new operators. The Board held to the opinion that the "present" number of carriers in air transportation was sufficient to protect against monopoly and that any future expansion of the industry would best be accomplished by the certification of presently operating air carriers except under "peculiar circumstances."[19] This ruling froze the air transportation industry of the United States in the hands of the carriers existing at the time the Civil Aeronautics Act of 1938 was passed. It was practically a denial that one of the act's purposes had been to introduce new ventures and virtually held that, unless there was a definite reason for refusing to certificate an existing carrier for a given new route, the existing carrier would be preferred over a new company.

Since the close of World War II, the Board has taken a more liberal attitude and has found several instances where the "peculiar circumstances" would warrant issuing temporary or experimental certificates[20] of convenience and necessity to new companies. The best

viding all additions to the present air-transportation system of the United States, is untenable. Our adoption of such a policy would certainly not be consistent with a sound development of air transportation, and would not be conducive to the best interests of the foreign and domestic commerce of the United States, the Postal Service, and the national defense."

[18] Civil Aeronautics Act, sec. 401 (*e*). See also sec. 401, Federal Aviation Act, 1958.

[19] *Delta Air Corporation et al.*, 2 CAB 447 (1941). In this decision the Board stated that "the number of air carriers now operating appears sufficient to insure against monopoly in respect to the average new route case, and we believe that the present domestic air transportation system can by proper supervision be integrated and expanded in a manner that will in general afford the competition necessary for the development of that system in the manner contemplated by the act. In the absence of peculiar circumstances presenting an affirmative reason for a new carrier there appears to be no inherent desirability of increasing the present number of carriers merely for the purpose of numerically enlarging the industry." In view of this later decision, it appears that the Board considered the American Export and All American decisions in the category of "peculiar circumstances." Competent new concerns had to be certificated in these instances since existing airlines were not then in a position to oppose Pan American Airways, in the one instance, or to develop new devices and techniques similar to the pickup mechanism, in the other case.

[20] Temporary certificates have usually been issued for from three to five years, and some of them have already been extended and doubtless will continue to be extended until the time when they are made permanent. The longer a temporary certificate stays in effect, the greater the chances that vested interests in the operation concerned will eventually prevail upon the Board to obtain permanent certification. See, for example, *Pioneer Air Lines Amendment*, 7 CAB 469 (1946); *Pioneer Certificate Renewal Case*, CAB Docket No. 3719 *et al.* (1950); *Trans-Texas Certificate Renewal Case*, CAB Docket

publicized of these instances was the certification of what were then known as "feeder" airlines but have since become known as "local-service" airlines. The limited traffic potentialities at most of the points on such routes, the Board felt, required an unusual effort in business development. It also thought that a greater effort in traffic development and exercise of managerial ingenuity might be expected from an independent local operator, whose continuation in the air transportation business would depend on the successful development of such traffic and the operation of his routes on a different basis than the usual trunk airline operation.[21] In most of the local-service cases, although existing airlines sought feeder routes in nearly every one, new operators were selected.[22] The Board said of its feeder experi-

---

No. 3720 *et al.* (1951); *Central Renewal Proceeding,* 16 CAB 843 (1953); *Ozark Renewal Proceedings,* 19 CAB 95 (1954).

[21] *Rocky Mountain States Air Service,* 6 CAB 695 (1946); "in view of the limited traffic potentialities of the points on the new system, an unusual effort will be required to develop the maximum traffic. Greater effort and the exercise of managerial ingenuity may be expected from an independent local operator whose continuation in the air transportation business will depend upon the successful development of traffic on the routes and the operation of the service on an adequate and economical basis." *Florida Case,* 6 CAB 765 (1946); here the Board took notice of the skepticism of an established carrier seeking the local-service route as to the success of the experiment. *West Coast Case,* 6 CAB 961 (1946); here the Board pointed out that the luxuries of the conventional-type service must be avoided if local-service routes are to succeed. *New England Case,* 7 CAB 27 (1946); in this case, although the application of the established carrier for some local-service routes was denied on the basis of the reasoning in the Rocky Mountain Case, the Board found reasons to grant that same carrier a number of small points, service to and from which would hardly be distinguishable from local-carrier service. *Texas-Oklahoma Case,* 7 CAB 481 (1946); in this case several of the new companies applying for local-service routes were "sponsored" by one of the established carriers operating in the area; and, in denying their applications, that fact was mentioned, the Board holding that a local-service operation by a trunk carrier might interfere with the trunk service. *South-eastern States Case,* 7 CAB 863 (1947); in this case a member of the Board dissented from the refusal to certificate local-service routes to established carriers, arguing that the local-service experiment should include one where the service was provided by established carriers.

[22] In the *Great Lakes Area Case,* 8 CAB 360 (1947), Transcontinental and Western Air was authorized to serve, for three years, a large number of relatively small points, relatively close together, and United Air Lines was permitted to add one relatively small point to one of its routes for a similar length of time. The Board said, of TWA, that this will afford an opportunity to "experiment with short-haul services by one of the existing trunk carriers." It likewise held of the certification of United that it was for the same reason and that, therefore, no local-service carrier would be certificated in the particular region involved and that after the experimental period the results could be assessed along with the feeder experiment. Two members of the Board insisted, however, that the certification of TWA was not at all an experiment in having a trunk carrier provide short-haul service but amounted to simply putting "local" points on a trunk route, which has often been done. In any case, it seems ridiculous to term certification of one point to United as a part of the feeder experiment, and the Board made no special provision of cost reporting or otherwise as a means of assessing the alleged experiment. Nor was TWA or United prevented from serving the points in question just as they would serve any other point; in other words, service was not required to be "local" or "feeder" in nature. In the

ment that it "was definitely convinced that such services, if they are to be provided at all, would require specialized planning, specialized equipment, and specialized operators focusing on the development of the local transport market."[23] The first departure from this policy was not until 1954, when the Board permitted Continental Air Lines to merge with a local-service carrier, Pioneer Air Lines.

In several less publicized instances, the Board also granted temporary certificates to new companies. One involved suburban commuting service between New York City and nearby cities without authority to carry mail; in this case the new company was the only applicant.[24] Another involved an experimental helicopter service within the Los Angeles area proposed by two applicants, one of whom was not engaged in air transportation but the other of whom had recently been granted a certificate for a feeder service. The application of the one not already certificated for air transport service was granted.[25] Still another instance involved an application by two new companies to operate all-expense conducted air tours, carrying passengers and their belongings only, between a large number of cities and many points of tourist attraction within and beyond the continental limits of the United States. The Board first denied both applications but later, upon instructions of the President of the United States,[26] certificated one applicant, Resort Airlines, to engage in for-

Parks Investigation Case, 11 CAB 779 (1950), involving the distribution of various routes of a certificated local-service line which had not yet begun to operate, the Board granted one route to Mid-Continent Airlines. The Board was "reluctant" to extend one of the local-service applicants for this route to the west of Chicago and this "coupled with the urgent requirements of the public interest for prompt inauguration of service" resulted in "an unusual situation and special circumstances that, in this particular instance, override the Board's policy against operation of feeder routes by trunk lines. . . ."

[23] Statement of the Civil Aeronautics Board before the President's Air Policy Commission, October 27, 1947, *Survival in the Air Age* (Washington, D.C.: U.S. Government Printing Office, 1948). For examples of the Board's reasoning in awarding a local-service route to a trunk line, see *Parks Investigation Case,* 11 CAB 779 (1950).

[24] *Air Commuting, New York City Area Service,* 8 CAB 1 (1947). The Board said: "It is of considerable public interest that new types of scheduled air transportation be fostered when circumstances portend economic success." Of course, an existing company *could* provide a new type of service.

[25] *Los Angeles Helicopter Case,* 8 CAB 92 (1947). The Board said that the fact that one applicant was already a certificated carrier was "not a controlling factor in its favor" because of the great difference between its feeder operations and the proposed helicopter service, which would be very complex. It was felt that two such different and important experiments as a feeder service and a helicopter service would not be developed to the maximum if undertaken by one management and that the new company would specialize on the helicopter service "with undivided attention."

[26] The Civil Aeronautics Act, sec. 801, provides that the issuance or amendment of a certificate involving foreign or overseas routes shall be subject to the approval of the President.

eign and overseas air transportation for an experimental period of five years only.[27]

Another important approval of new air transport operators came in 1949, when the Board certificated four new companies to engage in the transportation of air cargo only for a period of five years.[28] The background of this case is significant, since it shows how the Board was placed, by a combination of its own prior actions and other circumstances, in a position where it was forced into a liberalization of its attitude toward the entry of new companies into air transportation.

At the time the Civil Aeronautics Act was adopted, there were a number of operators who had engaged in transporting passengers on a charter basis, not over fixed routes but usually from a fixed base. There was doubt at that time whether these operators were common carriers. Therefore, shortly after the passage of the act the Board sought to avoid the issue, or at least to postpone it, by exempting persons engaged exclusively in nonscheduled operations from the economic regulating provisions.[29] This was a perfectly logical thing to do because, in 1938, it would have been more trouble than it was worth to have attempted to distinguish between those nonscheduled operators who were common carriers and those who were not. (See Chapter 3.)

With the close of World War II, a different situation developed than had ever existed before in air transportation. During 1945 and 1946, hundreds of operators of aircraft sprang up. This was due partly to overenthusiasm in the belief that the air age "had arrived" and partly to the stimulating effect of the combination of relatively cheap surplus aircraft and the many trained pilots and others who had been associated with aviation during the war. At this time, also, the established air carriers were unable to handle all the passengers or cargo traffic offered them because of their still curtailed capacity. The Board's early nonscheduled exemption from the economic regulations imposed by the act became, therefore, the excuse for hundreds of new air transport ventures.

The situation finally got so far out of hand that the Board took ac-

---

[27] *Skycruise Case*, 10 CAB 393 (1949). The Board limited Resort's operations strictly as follows: (*a*) "the holder shall offer, sell or furnish the aforesaid transportation only as a part of an all-expense escorted tour including cost of hotel and other accommodations, meals, and local side trips; no authority is hereby granted to offer, sell or furnish said transportation alone." (*b*) "the holder shall offer and sell only round-trip authorization, and shall accept traffic for transportation only at co-terminal points."

[28] *Air Freight Case*, 10 CAB 572 (1949).

[29] Civil Aeronautics Act, sec. 416(b). See also sec. 416, Federal Aviation Act, 1958.

tion and issued orders to "cease and desist" in several cases where the nonscheduled nature of the operations was nominal rather than real.[30] In the meantime, however, certain operators had developed a considerable business on an exclusive cargo basis. The Board took no action against any all-cargo operators, even though, in a number of cases, it is difficult to see how their operations could have been classified as nonscheduled or how they could have been regarded solely as contract operators, who were not subject to economic regulation under the Civil Aeronautics Act of 1938. In at least one case where an operator of all-cargo planes also did a passenger business, the Board issued an order requiring the operator to cease and desist in its passenger service and its combination passenger and cargo service, but deferred any decision on its all-cargo service.[31]

Most of the air cargo operators had made application for certificates of convenience and necessity, which had been consolidated into one case, the Air Freight Case, heard in 1946; but, pending decision, the Board permitted these operators to continue on a full-fledged scheduled basis[32] for about three years. Then in 1949 the Board certificated, for a temporary period of five years, four of the new companies: The Flying Tiger Line, Slick Airways, U.S. Airlines, and Airnews, all of which had previously been operating at one time or another, first under the Board exemption as nonscheduled carriers and then under the special exemption mentioned above. In 1950, another carrier, Riddle Aviation Company was granted a certificate for service between New York, Miami, and international points, chiefly Puerto Rico. In 1951, the Airnews certificate was suspended for noncompliance with its provisions.

In issuing these temporary certificates, the Board for the first time characterized such an action as "promotional," in accordance with the responsibility vested in it by Congress to encourage and develop a national system of air transportation.[33] It also pointed out that the

---

[30] See, for example, *Page Airways Investigation*, 6 CAB 1061 (1946); *Trans-Marine Airlines Investigation*, 6 CAB 1071 (1946); *Investigation of Nonscheduled Air Services*, 6 CAB 1049 (1946). See Chapter 3.

[31] *Willis Air Service, Non-certificated Operations*, CAB Docket No. 2639 (1947).

[32] CAB Economic Regulations, sec. 292.5.

[33] "In view of the contention which has been advanced that the factual evidence of record is not sufficiently substantial to justify the certification of any all-cargo carriers, it is essential in disposing of the present case that we keep in mind the nature of the basic issue involved. That issue is primarily promotional in character and relates to developmental rather than purely regulatory purposes. This characteristic of the statutory scheme serves to distinguish the Civil Aeronautics Board from judicial tribunals and even from many regulatory bodies. Thus the Civil Aeronautics Board, in addition to regulatory

authorization of all-cargo carriers would not, in their opinion, adversely affect the competitive balance existing between all-cargo carriers and the then-certificated airlines; but, on the other hand, it said that the cargo carriers would provide a valuable yardstick for measuring the alertness and efficiency of other carriers of cargo.[34]

Restrictions of entry into the air transportation industry must be handled with great care, for some of the same factors that encourage new concerns to enter the business also tend, if these new entrants are denied, to check the effective development of the existing market potential by the airlines already in operation. Future efforts to expand domestic air traffic of both passengers and cargo must be directed toward reducing the difference in rates between air and surface carriers through reduced costs of producing air transportation. Without the competitive force provided by new entrants, existing airlines are less likely to develop their present routes to the fullest extent.

Most airline costs, as those for labor, equipment, and many airport charges, are the same for all operators. Unions have standardized rates of pay, except where regional differences are important. Modern aircraft, necessary for the best of service, are available to all airlines; airports have been made freely accessible at reasonable fees in order to attract air carriers and to stimulate business. Insulated against outside stimulus, competitive forces within the industry are diverted to the level of furnishing "service."

More new entrants into the air transportation industry could have

---

functions which are concerned with the protection of the users of a public service, has been entrusted by Congress with a major promotional and developmental responsibility—the encouragement and development of a national system of air transportation . . . Throughout the text of the Civil Aeronautics Act runs the unmistakable thread of this developmental objective. The Board is directed 'to consider as being in the public interest and in accordance with public convenience and necessity the encouragement and development' of the national (air) transportation system. . . . It is to fix mail rates, not in accordance with the orthodox standards of fair and reasonable compensation for service performed, but with due regard to the financial need of the carrier . . . Thus the Civil Aeronautics Act is not designed wholly as a code for the adjustment of conflicting private rights through adjudications, but expresses the desire of Congress, through administrative control, to encourage and guide the development of a dynamic industry vitally related to the national interest" (*Air Freight Case,* 10 CAB 572 [1949]).

[34] "The certification of unsubsidized all-cargo carriers will require such carriers to bend all their efforts and to direct their abilities and skill to the full development of the air freight potential. Such carriers will not be able to rely on passenger operations or mail payments to furnish the greater portion of their revenues. They will live and prosper only through their ability to develop an economic business and to constant search for new techniques, new business and new equipment. To the extent that they succeed in their endeavors they will, by their example, benefit the presently certificated carriers and air transportation as a whole . . . Thus, the cargo carriers will provide a valuable yardstick for measuring the alertness and efficiency of other carriers of cargo." (*Ibid.*)

supplied the competitive incentive which the Board has seemed so anxious to achieve. Until recently, however, Board policy has been to restrict entry and to rely on the airlines already operating to supply the necessary competitive incentive. Air mail subsidies have been employed to counteract the unfavorable economic trend of the industry; and the result has been a reduced emphasis on control of the sizable variable costs, which would have been the most direct approach to lower rates. Thus, while publicly stating that economic regulation alone is incapable[35] of supplying the incentive required for the development of air transportation, the Board has been forced by its own policy of restricted entry to rely on administrative techniques in an effort to achieve the goal of better service at lower rates.

Entry of Surface Carriers into Air Transportation

The Board has followed the policy of prohibiting the entry of railroads, motor carriers, and steamship operators into air transportation. In so doing it has made use of a very rigid construction of a provision of the Act of 1938 which prohibits a surface carrier from "merging with or acquiring" an existing air carrier unless such surface carrier "could employ aircraft to public advantage in its operation."[36]

Relying on a supposed intent of Congress to maintain independence between the various modes of transportation,[37] the Board has interpreted section 408(*b*) of the Civil Aeronautics Act to mean that a surface carrier could only acquire an air carrier whose operations were "incidental to the surface operations."[38] Although the prohibition in the statute was concerned with mergers and sales, the Board

[35] "Thus, economic regulation alone may not be relied on to take the place of the stimulus which competition provides to the advancement of technique and service in air transportation. Competition invites comparisons as to equipment, costs, personnel, methods of operation, solicitation of traffic, . . . all of which tend to assure the development of" the desired system. See *American Export Airlines, Trans-Atlantic Service*, 2 CAB 16 (1940).

[36] Civil Aeronautics Act, sec. 408(*b*). The Board itself has characterized its interpretation as "rigid." See *American Export Lines, Control American Export Airlines*, 4 CAB 104 (1943).

[37] This interpretation is based on a review of a series of Congressional enactments. The Board contends that as early as 1912 Congress announced a policy of independence of water carriers from railroads in the Panama Canal Act of that year. In 1935 there was incorporated into the Motor Carrier Act a similar restrictive provision in section 213 which was the basis for section 408(*b*) of the Civil Aeronautics Act. Further, Congress affirmed this policy by incorporating into the Transportation Act of 1940 the provisions of the Panama Canal Act and of section 213 of the Motor Carrier Act. See "Civil Aeronautics Board Policy—An Evaluation," *Yale Law Journal*, April, 1948.

[38] *American Export Lines, Control American Export Airlines*, 3 CAB 619 (1942), 4 CAB 104 (1943); *Acquisition of TACA, S.A. by American Export Airlines*, 3 CAB 216 (1941).

has extended this additional "incidental" criterion to restrict surface carriers seeking to enter air transportation either directly by applying for a certificate or indirectly by organizing a subsidiary.[39] The Board has voiced the opinion that this is a valid interpretation of legislative intent; but in all cases so far, when actually faced with a surface carrier's application, it has usually denied the application on the less controversial ground that some other applicant is better fitted to service the particular route or that the particular air transportation is not warranted by the public interest.[40]

The basis of the Board's specialized treatment of surface carriers was subjected to re-examination under pressure from the steamship companies in 1947, in hearings on several bills which were introduced in the first session of the 80th Congress and intended to amend and clarify the Civil Aeronautics Act on this point, and likewise in testimony before the President's Air Policy Commission.[41] Altering its position slightly, the Board conceded that Congress, while not making mandatory the application of the "incidental to surface operation" test in a situation where the surface carrier was requesting a certificate directly or indirectly, had at least enunciated the criterion as an additional guide to be considered in an evaluation of the "public interest" in the proposed operation. Despite this rather dubious distinction, it

---

[39] The Board's original view was that the statutory prohibition was solely against acquisition of an operating airline by a surface carrier and did not prevent a surface carrier from organizing a subsidiary to become an air carrier (*American Export Airlines, Inc., Certificate,* 2 CAB 16 [1940]). Pan American, as an intervenor, however, carried the case to the federal courts, where the Circuit Court of Appeals for the Second Circuit *in dictum* stated that the Civil Aeronautics Board should consider the prohibition even in granting new certificates (*Pan American* v. *Civil Aeronautics Board,* 121 Fed. [2d] 810 [CCA 2d, 1941]). Thereupon, the Board required the American Export Steamship Line to divest itself of control of the air carrier which had been granted a certificate as a subsidiary of the steamship company (*American Export Airlines,* 3 CAB 619 [1942], 4 CAB 104 [1943]).

[40] See *Braniff Airways, Kansas City–New Orleans Service,* 2 CAB 727 (1941); *Northeast Airlines, North Atlantic Routes,* 6 CAB 319 (1945); *Rocky Mountain Air Service,* 6 CAB 695 (1946); *Latin American Air Service,* 6 CAB 657 (1946); *Hawaiian Case,* 7 CAB 83 (1946). In *Great Lakes Area Case,* 8 CAB 360 (1947), a surface motor carrier running a limousine taxi service in Cleveland, Ohio, was authorized to conduct an experimental helicopter service, which never went into operation, between the Cleveland airport and points in the municipal area, without mail pay, for three years. It was the only applicant for the service. This decision is of such limited significance and rests on such peculiar circumstances that it is hardly an exception to the Board's policy.

[41] See *Hearings before Committee on Interstate and Foreign Commerce on Bills Relating to Overseas Air Transportation* (80th Cong., 1st sess.) (Washington, D.C.: U.S. Government Printing Office, 1947). The President's Air Policy Commission stated that surface carriers "should not be automatically prevented from such action (control of air carriers) simply on the grounds that they are surface carriers—as now appears from the record to be the case" (*Survival in the Air Age* [Washington, D.C.: U.S. Government Printing Office, 1948]).

seems clear that the Board will continue to consider the "incidental" test as determinative. The result is virtually a total ban on surface-carrier entry into air transportation, although legislative history does not necessarily dictate such a stand.[42] It would seem to be a sounder course for the Board to disregard the "incidental" test as now applied and to consider each individual application on its merits, treating the fact that an applicant is a surface carrier merely as one element of convenience and necessity in a particular case. Protection would be provided against any prospective monopoly by recourse to the "competition to the extent necessary" provision of the act involved in a consideration of the public interest. Certainly the Board by pursuing its arbitrary policy has barred a whole segment of trained capital from possible entry into air transportation and to this extent has restricted competitive forces. Needless to say, the certificated carriers agree with the Board's stand.

Entry of Freight Forwarders

Another phase of the problem of new companies entering air transportation in connection with air freight is the Board's policy toward freight forwarders, who have long been recognized by ground carriers as valuable middlemen between shippers and carriers. In 1942, the Board held that a forwarder shipping by air is an "indirect" air carrier within the meaning of the Civil Aeronautics Act,[43] even though he operates no aircraft and does not carry anything. Rather, forwarders arrange transportation of goods for other people who are the individuals interested in getting shipments to destination. Only one indirect carrier of the forwarder type was then permitted to operate, the Railway Express Agency, but was not required to obtain a certificate.[44] Because of their characterization, in 1942, as "indirect air car-

---

[42] The legislative history is exhaustively reviewed in the concurring opinion of James M. Landis, then Chairman of the Board, in *American President Lines, Ltd.*, 7 CAB 799 (1947). See also *Hearings before Committee on Interstate and Foreign Commerce on Bills Relating to Overseas Air Transportation* (80th Cong., 1st sess.) (1947).

[43] Civil Aeronautics Act and Federal Aviation Act, sec. 1 (3): "'Air carrier' means any citizen of the United States who undertakes, whether directly or indirectly or by a lease or any other arrangements, to engage in air transportation." Section 296.1 of the Board's Economic Regulations defines an air freight forwarder as "any person . . . which in the ordinary and usual course of his undertaking, (*a*) assembles and consolidates or provides for assembling and consolidating . . . and performs or provides for the performance of breakbulk and distributing operations . . . (*b*) assumes responsibility for the transportation of such property . . . and (*c*) utilizes . . . the services of a direct air carrier. . . ."

[44] *Railway Express Agency, Inc., Certificate of Public Convenience and Necessity*, 2 CAB 531 (1941). The Board held that the Railway Express Agency was an "air carrier" and thereby required to obtain a certificate prior to operation but that it was not entitled

riers," forwarders have sometimes claimed preferential treatment as carriers from the airlines—the "direct air carriers." The Board has, however, clearly indicated that so far as the direct air carriers are concerned, the forwarder has the status of a shipper.[45]

After the close of World War II and the start of air freight operations by the irregular or noncertificated carriers, the Board received many applications from concerns anxious to enter the field of air freight forwarding. After some five years, during which the Board investigated the whole subject of indirect air services in the transportation of property, it permitted air freight forwarders to enter domestic air transportation on a temporary five-year basis in August, 1949. Then, in September, 1949, the Board permitted freight forwarders to engage in overseas and foreign air transportation in the same manner, as they were already a part of domestic air transportation.[46] The reasons the Board gave in authorizing the air freight-forwarder operations were to make possible improved service to the shipping public and to generate additional freight traffic for the direct air carriers.

No limit was set by the Board as to the number of forwarders who might engage in handling air freight. They were exempted from the necessity of obtaining certificates of convenience and necessity, and there was no limit to the number of points an individual forwarder

---

to a "grandfather" certificate since that provision (Civil Aeronautics Act, section 4 [*e*]) only pertained to those concerns that physically operated aircraft. By this decision the Board secured control over forwarders in air transportation without committing itself to a definite stand on the status of the Railway Express Agency; and any attempt by the Interstate Commerce Commission to extend its jurisdiction over air forwarding because of the railroad ownership of Railway Express Agency was forestalled. The Board then exempted the Railway Express Agency from the necessity of obtaining a certificate. In 1942, another concern contended it was a shipper, utilizing the services of Railway Express Agency, and not an "air carrier." The Board answered this claim in the negative; refused an exemption similar to that accorded Railway Express Agency; and issued a cease and desist order (*Universal Air Freight Corp., Investigation of Forwarding Activities*, 3 CAB 698 [1942]).

45 *Air Freight Forwarder Case*, 9 CAB 473 (1948). The Supreme Court upheld this as in regard to surface forwarders in *Interstate Commerce Commission* v. *Delaware, Lackawanna and Western Ry.*, 220 U.S. 235 (1911); *United States* v. *Trucking Co.*, 310 U.S. 344 (1940); *Chicago, Milwaukee, St. Paul & Pacific R. Co.*, v. *Acme Fast Freight*, 336 U.S. 465 (1949). In the latter case the Court considered whether passage of the Freight Forwarder Act in 1942 had changed the traditional relationship between a forwarder and a railroad from that of shipper and carrier, and the decision of the court was that it had not. This decision has not been changed by a 1950 amendment to sec. 402 (*a*) (5) of the Interstate Commerce Act, which added to the definition of a freight forwarder the concept of common carriage. There is nothing inconsistent between a freight forwarder being held to the obligations of a common carrier as regards its shippers and being classified as a shipper as regards the direct carrier.

46 *Air Freight Forwarder Case* (*International*), 11 CAB 182 (1949).

might serve. All that was required was for a forwarder already in existence or one desiring to enter the business to file an application for a letter of registration along with a tariff setting forth all points between which, and the rates at which, air freight would be transported. Since many forwarders contemplating the handling of air freight were already in the business of handling shipments by surface transportation, the question arose as to whether their authorization would be in conflict with the Board policy of keeping air and ground transportation strictly separated. The Board decided that the conduct of freight-forwarding operations by air by the same companies that handled surface shipments would not be contrary to previous policy or inconsistent with the public interest except in the case of those forwarders controlled by railroads, where it was felt that such control might create a conflict of interest between the air and rail operations of the parent company which would prove detrimental to the full development of the air service. All applications by railroad-controlled organizations for registration as air freight forwarders were therefore denied.[47]

The authorization of air freight forwarders was unanimously opposed by the airlines engaged in carrying passengers, mail, express, and freight. It was favored by those companies engaged solely in air cargo operations. The combination carriers, operating only a few all-cargo aircraft and faced with the necessity of continuing to handle relatively small-sized shipments in most of their aircraft, contended that the operations of forwarders would slow down air freight transportation and thus tend to destroy its greatest advantage—speed. This would be made so by the very nature of the forwarding business, which is dependent upon holding small shipments for consolidation into larger ones. It was also claimed that such consolidations would limit the utility of cargo space on airline passenger schedules; reduce carrier revenues without materially reducing costs; and make it more difficult to reduce freight rates, particularly on large-quantity shipments, because of the forwarders' desire to have the spread between small- and large-shipment rates maintained, which is the basis on which their income depends. The strictly air cargo operators, working without the traffic solicitation organization of the established airlines, were greatly in favor of the forwarders, since they offered such

---

[47] *Air Freight Forwarder Case*, 9 CAB 473 (1948). The principles which motivated the Board in excluding railroad controlled forwarders from air freight forwarding were upheld in *National Air Freight Forwarding Corp.* v. *Civil Aeronautics Board*, 197 F. 2d 384 (1952).

operators a ready-made sales force as well as a source of traffic in airplane loads which they could well handle in their exclusive cargo aircraft.

In deciding the freight forwarder question as it did, the Board ignored an opportunity to profit from the experience in other fields of transportation. Freight forwarders, who have become important middlemen in the surface transportation field, developed only because the railroads failed to provide a satisfactory service for handling less-than-carload shipments.[48] The railroads never seemed willing to do this despite numerous recommendations that they do so, with the result that the forwarders grew powerful, and it became necessary to provide for their regulation in the passage of Part IV of the Interstate Commerce Act in 1940. The lack of interest by the railroads in handling small shipments themselves is understandable, since such shipments amount to about 2 per cent of their business and have never been considered profitable by most railroads.

Early in 1953, the Board instituted a proceeding[49] to determine future policy in regard to air freight forwarders. The occasion for this was the impending expiration of all the letters of registration issued under Part 296 of the Board's Economic Regulations, under which they had been operating since 1948. In the light of developments since 1948, particularly the entry of shippers' associations into air transportation (see Chapter 7), the scope of the investigation was expanded to include a general investigation of all indirect carriers of property, including the Railway Express Agency. As a result, the operating authority of domestic air freight forwarders was extended indefinitely. In 1958, the Board took similar action on international air freight forwarders.[50]

Freight forwarding by air has not developed to the extent hoped for in 1949. Almost none of the conditions making forwarding by rail such an important business have been present in air transportation. Less-than-plane-load traffic accounts for nearly all the air freight business and airlines have been both willing and anxious to handle the business without the use of middlemen. They have, in fact, been successful in securing the approval in their tariffs of "assembly"

---

48 In *Freight Forwarding Investigation,* 229 ICC 201 (1938), the Interstate Commerce Commission found that there was no need for forwarder services if the railroads would organize for the purpose of setting up an efficient system to take care of less-than-carload business.

49 *Air Freight Forwarder Investigation,* 21 CAB 536 (1955).

50 *International Air Freight Forwarder Investigation,* CAB Docket 7132 (1958).

rules, which permit the consolidation of small shipments over a period of time for movement to a single consignee at one destination, as well as "distribution" rules, which permit a shipment consisting of parts ultimately destined to be delivered as part shipments, to move as a unit to destination and there be broken for distribution of the several parts. (See Chapter 9.) There have been several other reasons why air freight forwarding has not become as important as many expected it would: (*a*) The airlines have not furnished the necessary aircraft to develop volume, since it has been more profitable to carry passengers than freight, and freight planes have in some instances been transformed to passenger aircraft; (*b*) the military need for aircraft in the Korean air-contact service took many from the airlines which might otherwise, in the several years of that conflict, have been made available to forwarders in this country; (*c*) freight forwarders themselves have not been able to develop the volume of domestic traffic anticipated, though they have been quite successful in foreign trade; and (*d*) freight forwarding has not been profitable since the spread between large and small shipments, upon which forwarders operate in other fields of transportation, has not been great.[51]

The future seems to promise some improvement in the conditions which have handicapped the development of air freight forwarding. For one thing, additional all-freight equipment is under purchase by the transcontinental and international carriers. Secondly, the larger aircraft coming into service in 1958–60 offer a much expanded freight capacity. Increased volume is expected to result from the requirements of an expanding economy for air freight service, diversion of traffic now moving by ship, rail express, and motor truck, extension of air freight service to additional communities, improvement in the competitive status of air freight if surface rates continue to rise faster than air, improvement in ground handling techniques, the creation of a certain amount of new traffic by extension of market areas, increased selling effort on the part of the air carriers, and improvements in the packaging and handling of commodities requiring controlled temperatures. (See Chapters 15 and 16.)

[51] A rate spread may be defined loosely as the difference between the rate charged by the forwarder and the rate which it pays the direct air carrier. This spread can be increased either by an increase in the forwarder rate or a decrease in the direct carrier rate. The rate charged by the direct air carrier is not within the control of the forwarder. The forwarder is, therefore, left with no alternative other than to operate under the spread which it creates when it establishes its own rates.

Chapter 7

CIVIL AERONAUTICS BOARD POLICY—COMPETITION (Continued)

THE Civil Aeronautics Board has for the most part followed its "balanced competition" theory as new routes and extensions to old routes have been certificated. The authority to award certificates of convenience and necessity for new service and to extend existing routes provided the Board with the means for altering the "grandfather" route pattern in the interests of efficient service and also for developing competition within the industry so as to approach the avowed goal of strengthening the smaller airlines.

Awarding New Routes

As indicated in the previous chapter, the Board at first maintained that competition between airlines was not made mandatory by the Civil Aeronautics Act but, on the other hand, was a matter of administrative discretion dependent on the facts of any particular case.[1] It therefore permitted the then-existing carriers to compete between major air terminals—first, over different intermediate routes and, later, on a point-to-point basis. Ultimately, the Board took action to develop competition on all routes which, in its opinion, exhibited two-carrier traffic potential, unless it could be shown that the service of the second airline could not be integrated into an economically self-sustaining system or that there would be undue diversion of revenue from existing carriers.[2] The Board today holds this competi-

---

[1] *American Export Airlines, Trans-Atlantic Service,* 2 CAB 16 (1940).

[2] The Board possesses wide authority under the provisions of the act (sec. 2[b] providing for "competition to the extent necessary" to prescribe the amount of competition according to its own ideas. In various cases it has shown: (1) the incentive of competition is necessary to assure the full development of air transportation; (2) it is immaterial that a carrier can, or will, render adequate service; (3) a carrier's failure to provide adequate service is evidence of a need for competition; and (4) there is a presumption in favor of competition on any route having sufficient traffic to support competing services without unreasonable increase in operating costs. See *Transcontinental and Western Air, Additional North-South California Services, Supplemental Opinion,* 4 CAB 373 (1943); *Atlan-*

tion justifiable on the grounds that it assures incentive to the carriers; it does not depend on the inability or unwillingness of any existing carrier to furnish additional service in any particular case.

As a result of its new route policy, Board action has enlarged the original "grandfather" route systems. Additional certification has multiplied route mileage, the award usually being based on a study of numerous criteria indicating possible national or local need for a particular service.[3] Further, the Board has adjusted routes in accordance with technological progress in airline operating performance when, because of the long-range flight potentialities of modern aircraft, it has granted permission to consolidate routes and to fly nonstop schedules over the resultant single route,[4] even where this has resulted in a diversion of traffic from other airlines. Effective action in supervising the over-all route pattern has, however, been handicapped by a lack of authority to revoke or order a transfer of the certificate or routes of any airline which holds permanent certificates of public convenience and necessity for such routes, even though the Board may consider such a revocation or transfer to be in the public interest.[5]

---

tic Seaboard Operation, Supplemental Opinion, 4 CAB 55 (1944); *West Coast Case,* 6 CAB 961 (1946); *Northeast Airlines, Boston Service,* 4 CAB 686 (1944); *Northeast Airlines, North Atlantic Route Case,* 6 CAB 319 (1945); *Trans-Pacific Airlines, Ltd.,* 12 CAB 900 (1951). *New York–Chicago Service Case,* 22 CAB 973 (1955); *Denver Service Case,* 22 CAB 1178 (1955); *Southwest-Northeast Service Case,* 22 CAB 52 (1955); *New York–San Francisco Nonstop Service Case,* CAB Docket No. 9214 *et al.* (1959).

[3] See "Certificates of Public Convenience and Necessity," *Aereports,* September, 1947; *Northwest Airlines, Duluth–Twin Cities Operation,* 1 CAA 573 (1940); *Transcontinental and Western Air, North-South California,* 4 CAB 254 (1943). The Board publishes the results of many surveys of market data. See CAB, *Origin and Destination of Airline Traffic* (1940); CAB, *Annual Statistics Domestic Carriers;* CAB, *Airline Traffic Survey,* for various years; CAB, *Economic Characteristics of Urban Points Not Certificated for Air Service as of April, 1945* (1946).

[4] *American Airlines, Nonstop Services,* 7 CAB 13 (1946); *American Airlines, Consolidation of Routes,* 7 CAB 337 (1946); *Northwest Airlines, Consolidation of Routes,* 7 CAB 199 (1946). The routes over which the trunk airlines were certificated in the original "grandfather" cases stemmed from the air mail contract routes originally awarded by the Post Office Department and followed the civil airways between designated points. These routes were predicated upon the use of twin-engined aircraft with an economic range of about 400 miles. The economic range of the four-engined aircraft which came into use in 1946 was at least 1,000 miles. Accordingly, it became operationally feasible to meet the demand for faster service by gradually obliterating the arbitrary course of the original routes, so as to permit direct flights between important points. The airline map, therefore, must now be read along with airline timetables in order to understand the actual flight pattern.

[5] Civil Aeronautics Act, sec. 401 (*h*), empowers the Board to "alter, amend, modify or suspend" a certificate "if public convenience and necessity require"; but it specifically limits revocation to cases of ". . . intentional failure to comply with any provision of Title IV of the Act . . . or any order, rule or regulation issued thereunder, or any term,

The Board's power to revoke permanent route certificates has never been tested; but it is certain that considerable legal wrangling will accompany any attempt to revise the airline route structure in this manner, with the final adjudication determined by the courts or ultimately resolved by the Congress.

Smaller airlines have been strengthened by route additions and extensions, but at the same time the major carriers have also been enlarged through the granting of certificates which permit them to round out strong long-range domestic routes and to engage in trans-Pacific and trans-Atlantic service.[6]

---

condition or limitation of such certificates." If there were any doubt as to the Board's inability to revoke a certificate, that doubt would be dispelled by the decision of the Supreme Court in *United States* v. *Seatrain Lines*, 329 U.S. 424 (1946), which held that certificates of public convenience and necessity cannot be revoked in the absence of statutory authority. See also *Smith Brothers, Revocation of Certificate*, 33 MCC 465, wherein the Interstate Commerce Commission held to the same opinion in dealing with a statutory provision substantially identical to sec. 401(*h*) of the Civil Aeronautics Act.

In 1947 the Board started investigations of several airlines to appraise their routes and to attempt to discover the cause of the financial crisis which each faced at that time. *Investigation of Chicago and Southern Air Lines, Inc.*, 9 CAB 827 (1947); *Investigation of Northeast Airlines, Inc.*, CAB Docket No. 2853 (1947); *Investigation of Western Air Lines, Inc.*, CAB Docket No. 2911 (1947); *Investigation of Colonial Airlines, Inc.*, 9 CAB 379 (1947); *Investigation of Capital Air Lines, Inc.*, 11 CAB 307 (1947). These inquiries were conducted under authority of sec. 205(*a*), 407(*a*), 415 and 1002(*b*) of the Civil Aeronautics Act of 1938.

In the latter part of 1948 and early part of 1949, the industry was disturbed by the issuance of what were termed "dismemberment" orders by the Board, under which it undertook to study National Airlines, Western Air Lines, and Northeast Airlines to discover whether some of their routes should not be transferred to other carriers or abandoned entirely. At the same time, the subject of mergers with other carriers, purchases, modifications, or interchange agreements were to be studied. See particularly *National Route Investigation*, 10 CAB 8 (1949) and *National Route Investigation*, CAB Docket No. 3500 *et al.* (1951). It was contended by the airlines that the Board had no authority to order any such transfers even if they should be found in the public interest. Such a contention has merit, particularly since the Board itself has stated "we know of no direct or indirect means available under existing law by which an air carrier can be forced against its will to transfer its property, business and certificate to another air carrier" (*United Air Lines, Inc., Acquisition of Air Carrier Property*, 8 CAB 298 [1947]).

By an order dated May 29, 1950, the Board found no further purpose in continuing the investigations of the finances, routes, and operations of Capital Airlines and Colonial Airlines. A report had already been submitted to the Board on Chicago and Southern Air Lines by the committee appointed to make the field study in 1947. The Northeast and Western cases were continued. (*Investigations of Finances, Routes and Operations of Capital Airlines, Inc., et al.*, 11 CAB 307 [1950]).

[6] See *Northeast Airlines, North Atlantic Routes*, 6 CAB 319 (1945). Transcontinental airlines, possessing strong financial resources and profitable domestic routes, were apparently preferred for this overseas business because of Board concern over prospective severe competition from foreign government-controlled air carriers. In less lucrative markets, such as the Caribbean, smaller domestic airlines were permitted to share along with the major airlines if the additional service could be integrated into the existing system. See *Latin American Air Service*, 6 CAB 857 (1946). See also *New York–Chicago Case, Denver Service Case*, and *Southwest-Northeast Service Case, supra.*

Operational efficiency could not have been the determining factor in the awarding of the prime overseas routes to the larger airlines, since airlines with less domestic route mileage exhibit the same operating results as the major airlines when both employ the same type of aircraft. Because of this Board policy, the major airlines have been increased to a size more than large enough to utilize modern and efficient aircraft, whereas the small lines operate systems that in most instances are incapable of efficiently employing long-range aircraft, unless the lines are permitted to expand.

The impact of technological progress has added to the ill effects of the Board's regulatory policy in route awards. The ability to realize the economies of the new aircraft rests mainly with the major carriers, who possess sufficient capital resources and have the long-haul routes between important population centers with a traffic potential that will assure adequate loads. Increased flying range further strengthens the bargaining position of the larger airlines, since they alone can supply one-plane and one-carrier service between the important cities with a minimum of inconvenient connections. As a result, the smaller airlines, unless they can arrange interchange services, suffer a further loss of traffic and revenue from the connecting service, which they formerly furnished.

An obvious fault in the Board's new route policy is a procedural one which has resulted from its not taking the initiative in planning the airline route pattern. Rather, it has simply decided cases as they have come up, as carriers have filed applications for new routes or extensions, and, as a general rule, applications are handled in the order of their priority of filing.[7] Furthermore, when the Board has

[7] In the first case where the Board had to make a choice between carriers, it was met with the argument that the carrier first applying for a route should be preferred. This argument was dealt with in these words: "To award a certificate covering a particular route upon the basis of priority of application might result in an operation entirely contrary to the public interest" (*Continental Air Lines, Mandatory Route*, 1 CAA 88 [1939]). A little later the same argument met with this treatment: ". . . we believe that in no case can priority of application be conclusive unless all other considerations are equal" (*Braniff Airways, Houston-Memphis-Louisville Route*, 2 CAB 353 [1940]). But in the next new route case, where apparently the reasons for the choice of carrier were difficult for the Board to state, prior display of interest in the route in question seems to have had some weight (*Western Air Express, Great Lakes–Lethbridge Operation*, 2 CAB 425 [1940]). Finally, the Board chose between two applicants solely on the basis of priority of applications, saying: ". . . While priority of filing does not in itself constitute a basis for selecting one carrier over another, it is a factor which must be given weight when other considerations are equal, especially as in this case where interval between filings is almost 5 years" (*Rocky Mountain States Air Service*, 6 CAB 695 [1946]). Even so, the Board has been known to deny a given application on the ground that other applications for a similar service are pending, even though some of those were not filed until after the hearing on the denied application and though none of the pending applications had yet

reached application X filed by airline A, airline B can file application Y and secure its consolidation for hearing with X. Airline B may be motivated by purely defensive considerations, or its application may be presented years before it would normally be filed because of the sudden opportunity to get a hearing. Finally, in acting upon each case, the Board is confined to the record of that case, must decide it upon its own facts, and theoretically is unable to take action which will take into account what may have to be done later in other new route cases involving, perhaps, the same airlines and related routes.

Under such a system there can be no long-range program of expansion for individual airlines or for the air transport system as a whole. Each case is presented as though the question were "Does the public immediately affected need this particular route?" This question does not present any adequate means for solving the problem of "What extensions of airline A are necessary to make it strong?" or "What extensions, if any, are desirable from the standpoint of the entire air transportation system?"

This difficulty is increased by the fact that the Board, in most cases, acts only upon evidence and arguments presented by the airlines. Public bodies, such as cities, also participate in some cases; but their viewpoint is restricted to their particular local interests. Thus, there is no national or over-all point of view presented to develop the relation of a particular case to the ultimate aim of a sound system of air transportation. The Board, however, created the function of the Public Counsel relatively early in its administration. Through him the over-all points of view presumably are to be presented in each new route case. But the end sought has not been effectively achieved, and the Public Counsel's participation in new route cases has become sharply curtailed to the point where he "is of no significance."[8]

Moreover, no statement of goals, supported by economic analysis taking the whole picture into account, prepares the Board to accomplish its task. Board action is not fitted into a plan. The destiny of a particular airline, presumably needing strength, is not defined in advance in relation to similar definitions of the destinies of other air-

---

reached the stage of active consideration (*Texas-Oklahoma Case*, 7 CAB 481 [1946]). Also, it is not unusual for the Board to defer decision on a given application pending the presentation for decision of some other case, already heard, which includes related applications (*North Central Case*, 7 CAB 639 [1946]). Such deferments, it is said, prevent mere priority of filing or of hearing from being a determining factor (*New England Case, Supplemental Opinion*, 7 CAB 439 [1946]).

[8] Howard C. Westwood, "Choice of the Air Carrier for New Air Transport Routes," *George Washington Law Review*, December, 1947, n. 312, p. 99.

lines, to guide decision. As a result, situations like the following have been created:

1. The Board certificated a relatively weak airline along a route already served, perhaps inadequately, by a strong carrier. Faced with new competition, a stable volume of traffic, and excess capacity, the stronger of the two serves the competitive route with so many schedules that it is virtually impossible for the small carrier to operate enough schedules to attract traffic and at the same time have adequate load factors.

2. The Board extended a small airline over a short but dense route segment. This was done with the expectation that it would strengthen the carrier and make it more nearly self-sufficient. Actually, the short-haul nature of the operation virtually precluded a profitable operation for the weak carrier with its available equipment and with heavy terminal costs. If the small airline was not faced with heavy competition, it might conceivably have broken even on the route. If it was involved in heavy competition, it probably lost heavily.

3. An airline applied for and was awarded too many intermediate points on a route that was weak in terminal-to-terminal traffic. (This type of situation arose usually out of the desire of intermediate points for service. They brought pressure on the airline, which in turn vigorously pressed its application.) The total traffic on the route was not sufficient to warrant both nonstop service, which was required to attract traffic moving between the terminal, and local service, which would give adequate service to the intermediate points.

These are only a few examples, but they show how the Board's policy on route certification has resulted in the evolution of at least two weaknesses in our air transportation system: inherently weak routes and the integration of routes into weak systems. This, of course, is contrary to the intent of the Civil Aeronautics Act, which was designed to avoid such situations. The country had been through the same sort of development with the railroads, and these carriers are still handicapped by this problem. The powers given to the Board were, therefore, conferred with the aim of preventing in air transportation the very situation which has developed.

A partial cause of the Board's failure to prevent what has taken place is, of course, the fact that it did not have a clean slate to start with. The existing airlines were given "grandfather" rights under the act and became permanently entitled to fly the routes they had pioneered; but the recognition of "grandfather" rights was not, by itself, too serious a handicap to the development of an adequate air transportation system.

The real handicap has been inherent in the act itself, particularly in the authority granted the Board to fix air mail rates in accordance with the "need" of individual airlines.[9] It was recognized by Congress that some subsidy was essential for the development of air transportation; but the approach of the Civil Aeronautics Act was new. The act has been interpreted by the Board as if it were authorized to guarantee in perpetuity mail pay sufficient to provide a fair return on any airline system considered desirable to fly, limited only by the Board's conception of public convenience and necessity. There are, of course, a few other limitations, but these have not been significant. There is the limit implied in the act by the words "under honest, economical and efficient management" (sec. 406[*b*], implying that the Congress does not obligate itself to reimburse management for corruption and stupidity; but this limitation has been most difficult to apply in practice. There is also the limitation inherent in the concept of public convenience and necessity, namely, that public desirability must be weighed against public cost; but this concept seems to have had no influence at all on Board action.[10]

No provision is made in the act for a budget, in the light of which the cost of present operations and contemplated expenditures needs to be measured. There is no limitation to the effect that mail pay will be available only on those routes that the Post Office wants to have flown.[11] There is not even the limitation that air mail pay authorized for the holder of a certificate of convenience and necessity can ever be effectively stopped, despite whatever original misjudgment may have occurred in its issuance or whatever changed factors may now characterize the operation.[12] Another handicap imposed by the act is that its provisions concerning certificates of convenience and necessity are modeled after those of the Interstate Commerce Act which deal with the extension and abandonment of railroads. This forgets the fact that in the railroad industry the driving force was private initiative and

---

[9] Civil Aeronautics Act and Federal Aviation Act, sec. 406(*b*).

[10] See James M. Landis, "Air Routes under the Civil Aeronautics Act," *Journal of Air Law and Commerce*, Summer, 1948.

[11] Under section 405 of the Civil Aeronautics Act, the Post Office Department can be required to meet the costs of flying both routes and schedules that it deems utterly useless for postal requirements. See also Federal Aviation Act, 1958.

[12] See Oswald Ryan, "The Revocation of an Airline Certificate of Public Convenience and Necessity," *Journal of Air Law and Commerce*, Autumn, 1948.

the willingness of private groups to take a chance on profits and absorb losses, while in air transportation, under the provisions of the act and as it was administered by the Board (at least prior to the separation of air mail pay from subsidy payments in 1953) there were to be no losses—just subsidy. (See Chapter 8.)

Criticism of the air route system as it has developed to date is frequently directed at the result, rather than at the process which has made this result almost inevitable. A portion of the air transport industry alleges too much competition has been introduced. This is true. Another portion criticizes the Board for introducing too little competition. This also is true. These are, of course, patent self-serving declarations by various air carriers. They point to certain facts but produce no answers. Nor has an answer to this problem yet been forthcoming. Indeed, the remarkable thing is that the process has worked as well as it has. From the standpoint of public need both nationally and internationally, there are few gaps in our route pattern. But as a system the pattern has its outstanding weaknesses, too often having been traded rather than engineered. The real difficulty is statutory, resting largely in the mail-pay provisions of the Civil Aeronautics Act of 1938.[13]

Local-Service Airlines

The certificated local-service carriers (or, as they have frequently been called, "feeder" airlines), occupy a unique position in the air transportation system and present competitive considerations quite different from those associated with the other domestic carriers.[14] A

[13] Much criticism has been levied against the Civil Aeronautics Board for its failure to develop an over-all domestic air transport pattern. Perhaps the two most important of such critical statements have been those of the President's Air Policy Commission and the Congressional Aviation Policy Board. The former holds that there was "widespread confusion as to the principles which guide the CAB in its route determinations" and that there was need for a "comprehensive survey of the present situation and the development of a more cohesive philosophy" for the development of a national route pattern (*Survival in the Air Age* [Washington, D.C., 1948], p. 110). The latter similarly criticized the Board and recommended that a "disinterested non-governmental agency" assist the Board in making a study of the foreign and domestic air transport systems in order to present a basic route plan which may be used as a guide for future revisions or extensions of the present route pattern (Report of the Congressional Aviation Policy Board, *National Aviation Policy*, Recommendation 33 [Washington, D.C., 1948]). The Board has so far shown little real enthusiasm for, or fundamental appreciation of, the need for making the studies recommended, stressing the difficulty in separating over-all planning of route development from its other functions.

[14] This discussion is adapted from *The Role of Competition in Commercial Air Transportation, Select Committee on Small Business, United States Senate* (82d Cong., 2d sess.) (1952).

number of considerations, based largely on the inherent characteristics of local air services, have determined the Board's policy and shaped its thinking on the role of competition in such operations. Even at the time of the Board's first over-all consideration of local service,[15] it was clear that with the extensive airline coverage of the country already in existence, any general extension of air service to communities not already served by the trunk-line carriers would require operations to cities much smaller, on the average, than the points previously certificated.

The extent to which the Board's expectations were justified has been demonstrated by studies made in connection with its initial consideration of whether certain of the early local certificates should be extended for an additional period of time. These studies revealed that the 187 points then receiving only local air service had a total population of approximately 2,535,000, or an average per station of 13,500. Had all the points then certificated to these carriers actually been served, the average population figure for points limited to local service alone would have increased to only 18,500. The inclusion of every point then certificated for feeder service, whether served exclusively by local carriers or also by trunk-line operators, would have given an average population per point of not over 85,000, despite the addition of such metropolitan centers as New York and Los Angeles. This meant that local-service airlines would be required to tap a market not already using air transportation to any great extent and having only a limited traffic potential under existing conditions. It was also clear that local services by their very nature would be relatively short-haul operations involving numerous stops, with resulting higher costs per plane-mile than those for the long-haul operations. For example, regardless of the operator's size, the flight costs of landing and taking off the DC-3 airplane generally used in local-service operations range upward from $10, whether the distance between landings averages 50 or 200 miles. A substantial part of the ground and indirect costs also remains fixed, without respect to the length of flight per departure. Poor equipment utilization is another characteristic of short-haul service.

Translated into costs, therefore, the combination of short-haul traffic with frequent stops, low traffic density, and limited volume of service can add up to only one thing—a high-cost operation. The real

[15] *Local, Feeder, and Pick-Up Air Service Case,* 6 CAB 1 (1944).

problem, therefore, is not to insure competition, but rather to avoid diluting the limited traffic available and creating still higher costs, which might call for prohibitive amounts of government subsidy.

Under these circumstances, the Board, from the outset of its local-service authorizations, tried to avoid establishing routes that were competitive with those of other local carriers or of trunk-line operators. Moreover, in order to make certain that the carriers did not stray from their assigned tasks of providing local service and enter into the trunk-line field, the Board included in the local-service certificates restrictions against nonstop and skip-stop operations.[16]

The avoidance of competitive services was not universal. In some instances local-service routes were competitive with other services over certain segments. This situation arose not from any belief that the competition was desirable, but from the knowledge that in many regions sound local-route systems could not be established without including certain points already served by other carriers under their outstanding certificates.[17]

In all local-service renewal cases, an effort has been made to readjust routes in a manner calculated to strengthen the local operators and bring about a steady lessening of the difference between their commercial revenues and expenses, meaning a subsequent reduction in the subsidy outlay of the government. In the application of this

[16] Perhaps the most emphatic pronouncement of the Board with respect to this policy was in connection with its decision in the *Bonanza-TWA Route Transfer Case,* 10 CAB 893 (1949): "We would like to emphasize again that we have neither the disposition nor the intention to permit local air carriers to metamorphose into trunk lines competitive with the permanently certificated trunk lines. The local-service carriers were certificated by us as an experimental effort to bring useful air transportation services into the smaller communities and the isolated or sparsely populated areas of this country and to feed connecting traffic to long-haul carriers. We recognize that some competition between local-service carriers and trunk lines is inevitable but we intend not only to minimize such competition but to prevent its development to the greatest feasible extent."

[17] "From the information now before the Board we are of the general opinion that feeder service should seldom if ever be competitive. The traffic potential is so limited in most feeder territory that duplicate operations by two or more carriers can seldom if ever be economical. We have reached the conclusion that in general where a feeder carrier's route is duplicated by a trunk-line carrier and such route is not necessary to the trunk-line carrier's operation, then such route should be served by the feeder carrier alone. Conversely, where a route is a necessary and integral part of a trunk-line carrier's system and essential to its economical operation, then such a route should not be served by a feeder carrier. Where two feeder carriers substantially duplicate service between certain communities, then the feeder routes should be adjusted to avoid such duplication. Of course, these general objectives cannot be achieved immediately in many cases and may not be possible to fulfill in particular situations, but they represent salutary principles which are of importance in working out the appropriate relationship between our feeder carriers and the other certificated carriers." (*Southwest Airways Co., Pioneer Airlines, Inc., and Trans-Texas Airways Show Cause Order,* CAB Order Serial No. E-2680, dated April 4, 1949.

policy, submarginal stations, even where their only air service came from local operators, have been dropped from the local-service routes; the services of trunk-line carriers have been suspended at points served solely by them and at such points as were added to the route of the local operator; and, in the case of points which could not support two services, but were certificated to both a trunk-line and local carrier, one of the carriers has been suspended.[18]

In only one respect has the Board's policy of reducing uneconomical competition among the local-service carriers, and between them and the trunk airlines, called for action that might conceivably increase competition. In an effort to bring about greater traffic density and lower costs, the Board in a number of instances has relaxed the requirement that local-service carriers on each flight stop at every point. This condition was originally imposed to make certain that the carriers concentrated on developing the local services for which they were certificated, rather than on attempting to compete in the trunk-line field. Many of the more recent local-service certificates have substituted for the older restriction the requirement that on each segment the carrier stop at a minimum number of points, but less than the total number included on the segment. It is clear that in doing this the Board has carefully restricted the freedom of the carrier in order to avoid its conversion from a local to a trunk-line operator and to prevent any undue increase in competition. The limited extent to which competition may have been increased by this course of action has been an unavoidable by-product of the more basic objective.[19]

The Board's policy on competition for the local-service carriers does not represent any change in its basic philosophy of competition

---

[18] For example, in the *West Coast Case*, 11 CAB 999 (1949), the Board proposed to suspend Salem, Ore., and Bellingham, Wash., from United Air Line's route and transfer these points to West Coast Airlines. In the *Southwest Renewal Case*, CAB Order No. E-2680 (1949), the Board proposed to transfer Eureka, Red Bluff, Monterey, and Santa Barbara, Cal., from United Air Lines to Southwest Airways. In the *Piedmont Renewal Case*, CAB Order No. E-4876 dated November 27, 1950, the Board proposed to transfer Hickory, N.C. from Capital Airlines to Piedmont Airlines. See also *Central Renewal Proceeding*, 16 CAB 843 (1953); *North Central Route Investigation Case*, 14 CAB 1027 (1951); *Ozark Certificate Renewal Case*, 19 CAB 95 (1954); *Bonanza Renewal Case*, 21 CAB 843 (1955); *Southwest Airways Renewal Case*, 21 CAB 843 (1955); *Southwest Airways Co. Permanent Certificate Case*, 21 CAB 830 (1955); *Ozark Certificate Renewal Case*, 21 CAB 86 (1955).

[19] See, for example, *Pioneer Air Lines, Inc., Amendment*, 7 CAB 469 (1946); *Southwest Airways*, 9 CAB 67 (1948); *Florida Case, Perry and Leesburg*, 9 CAB 1 (1948); *Southwest Airways, Additional California-Nevada Service Case*, 10 CAB 405 (1949); *Feederline Certificate Renewal Case*, CAB Docket No. 3718 *et al.* (1949); *Trans-Texas Airways*, CAB Docket Nos. 6442 and 6505 (1954); *Ozark Certificate Renewal Case.* 19 CAB 95 (1954).

or in its belief that sound and economical competition has been and can be a powerful force in stimulating the development of a strong air transportation system. Nor does it mean that the local-service carriers lack the incentive which competition supplies. Competitive situations between the local operators and other air carriers still exist and will continue to do so in a number of areas. For example, in an effort to obtain traffic from the trunk-line carriers, many of the local-service operators have established competitive fares between competitive terminal points, with the result that system fares, in terms of cents-per-mile, are sometimes lower for the local carriers than for the trunk-line carriers. Furthermore, there is no question but that the competition of surface transportation exercises a substantial influence on the local air carriers, though it is difficult to measure the extent precisely. It is important to remember that because of the nature and characteristics of local air transportation at its present stage of development, there are only very limited areas in which competition can economically be justified. Under these circumstances, the entire experiment would have been threatened with destruction if the Board's local-service policy had been to promote competition.

The basic problem of the local-service industry is low traffic density and passenger-load factors coupled with the high unit cost of a short-haul operation. These factors do not produce high profit margins. The Board is entirely aware of this and has attempted to overcome some of the basic handicaps by route adjustments and liberalizing operating authority.

There are definite limits to greater route flexibility in that there should be a minimum of direct competition between local-service carriers and trunk carriers. Moreover, there should not be such a degree of flexibility that the local-service carriers would tend to concentrate on the terminal-to-terminal nonstop service to the detriment of the intermediate points.

The Board has, nevertheless, granted liberalized skip-stop authority and continues to grant it where warranted. As a general rule, the Board's policy is that carriers operating new routes should have authority, after a minimum volume of two daily round trips have been scheduled to intermediate points, to provide nonstop service between noncompetitive terminals but to make at least one stop between competitive terminals. Skip-stop service results in increased length of haul, operational flexibility, and better service, at lower cost.

The Board has also adopted such measures as the suspension of trunk-line service at points served by local-service carriers, the transfer of local service authorizations of trunk lines to local-service carriers, the addition of points and routes expected to strengthen the earning potential of local carriers, and the elimination from local-service certificates of low-volume points. It is commonly conceded that low-volume communities generally gain a superior service when the service is provided by a local-service carrier.

The Board's so-called "use-it-or-lose-it policy," announced in the *Seven States Areas Case,*[20] was designed to help the local-service industry. It is a liberalized policy of affording communities of marginal traffic potentialities a chance to demonstrate whether they can support local air service. The Board announced that it would review the traffic experience of the newly certificated points and routes from time to time and on the basis of traffic results would determine whether or not to institute formal proceedings to suspend or terminate the service. The decision set forth the specific community traffic standard —five enplaned passengers daily to be achieved by the end of the first 18 months of operation.

Nonstop Operations and Route Consolidations

The Civil Aeronautics Act provides that certificates of convenience and necessity issued to air carriers shall specify the terminal points and intermediate points, if any, between which the carrier is authorized to serve the public.[21] Any change in a certificate with respect to points served on junctions of routes must be approved by the Civil Aeronautics Board. Therefore, shortly after the passage of the act, when confronted with applications from holders of "grandfather" certificates to eliminate some points on certain routes so they could fly nonstop between principal traffic-generating points, the Board adopted the policy that such nonstop services could be inaugurated upon compliance with certain stipulations:

1. Service between two points on two different routes had to be operated via a junction point between the two routes, and nonstops between two such points could not be inaugurated without an amendment to the applicant's certificate.

2. Nonstop flights between two points on the same route involving a "substantial departure" from the route outlined in the Applicant's

[20] CAB Docket No. 7454 *et al.* (1958). See also *Great Lakes Local Service Investigation,* CAB Docket No. 4251 *et al.* (1960).

[21] Civil Aeronautics Act and Federal Aviation Act, sec. 401(*e*).

certificate could be inaugurated only after the Board had found at a public hearing that the public interest was not adversely affected.

In the years between 1938 and the outbreak of World War II, a large number of nonstop applications were authorized, many of them over the protest of competing airlines or cities bypassed by such services.[22] During the war years the airlines did not have enough equipment to operate many nonstop routes and at the same time maintain adequate service to intermediate certificated route points. Nor were DC-3 aircraft practically adaptable to nonstop operations. With the end of the war, however, and the advent of four-engined transports, the airlines again began to request nonstop authorizations.[23]

Some of the postwar applications were opposed by other airlines on the grounds that granting such authorizations would, in effect, create a new route for which public convenience and necessity would have to be proved. The Board, however, adopted a liberal policy; this, together with the postwar acquisition by the airlines of greater numbers of high-speed, long-range aircraft, accounted for a large number of nonstop authorizations being granted.

Nonstop authorizations, however, did not permit the airlines to make full use of the greater flying range of their new aircraft, for, according to their route certificates, they still had to stop at junction points between points on two or more different routes. The logical way to circumvent this long-standing restriction, provided the Board would approve, was to consolidate certain routes so that the points wanting to be served with nonstop flights would then be on the same route.[24] To bring about route consolidations, the Board developed the policy of amending airline certificates so as to change the status of route junction points from that of a common terminal point on separate routes to that of an intermediate point on a single route.

By eliminating the necessity of stopping all flights at junction

[22] See, for example, *American Airlines, Non-stop Operation between Washington, D.C., and Chicago, Ill.,* 1 CAA 210 (1939); *Eastern Air Lines, Birmingham–New Orleans Non-stop Service,* 2 CAB 596 (1941); *United Air Lines, Fresno-Sacramento Non-stop Service,* 3 CAB 1 (1941).

[23] See, for example, *National Airlines, Jacksonville-Miami Non-stop Service,* 6 CAB 313 (1945); *Transcontinental and Western Air, Detroit–St. Louis Non-stop Service,* 6 CAB 471 (1945); *Northeast Airlines, Consolidation of Routes Nos. 27, 65 and 70,* 6 CAB 541 (1945).

[24] See, for example, *Northeast Airlines, Consolidation of Routes Nos. 27, 65 and 70,* 6 CAB 541 (1945); *American Airlines, Consolidation of Routes Nos. 7, 21 and 23,* 6 CAB 279 (1945); *American Airlines et al., Consolidation of Routes,* 7 CAB 337 (1946); *Transcontinental and Western Air et al., Consolidation of Routes,* 8 CAB 28 (1947); *Eastern Air Lines et al., Consolidation of Routes,* 8 CAB 580 (1947).

points, the airlines were placed in the position of being able to offer various improved services to the public. Substantial time and mileage savings were made in most instances by the more direct routings and by taking full advantage of the operational characteristics of large, fast aircraft. However, amendment of airline certificates to consolidate routes entailed considerably more than the usual aspects of operational economies and administrative savings. It caused changes to be made in service patterns, some of which were noncompetitive and of benefit to a substantial number of passengers, but many of which involved diversion from one carrier to another and had a serious competitive effect. A considerable number of the nonstop flights made possible through route consolidations brought about exact duplication, and in some instances triplication, of services.

In approaching the issue of nonstop flights, one must, of course, recognize that the network of airlines has now been built up to the point where the domestic route pattern serves nearly all important areas and centers of population. It is virtually impossible, therefore, to authorize any new service which does not affect an existing operation to some extent. The introduction of larger and faster aircraft has intensified the situation, since their greatest utility lies in long-haul services between large traffic-generating points, and these services tend to cut across existing route patterns. Increased capacity and speed mean that the amount of traffic which might have supported duplicating operations with prewar equipment will not necessarily support such operations with postwar equipment.

Authorization by the Board of all possible nonstop operations would, in effect, result in superimposing upon the present route pattern a second network of air transportation with considerable variation from that now established. Depending on the availability of traffic and mail pay, the through-service features would lead to the entry of many airlines into traffic centers or gateways which they do not presently serve and to the authorization of extensive new and additional operations over major segments, resulting in more direct competition in the future.

The Board has applied certain standards of public convenience and necessity in numerous opinions involving the establishment of new competitive relationships.[25] A major consideration is whether the pro-

---

[25] *American Export Airlines, Transcontinental Service,* 2 CAB 16 (1940); *American Airlines et al., East-West California,* 4 CAB 297 (1943); *Transcontinental and Western Air, North-South California,* 4 CAB 373 (1943); *Colonial Airlines et al., Atlantic Seaboard Operation,* 4 CAB 552 (1944); *Western Air Lines et al., Denver–Los Angeles Serv-*

posed duplication would be productive of substantial benefits to the public. The amount of diversion which any proposed duplicating services would inflict upon other carriers is also an important element. Another significant principle followed in formulating Board policy is whether the proposed duplicating services would usefully serve a public need which cannot and will not be adequately served by existing authorizations.

In passing upon route-consolidation applications, the Board has recognized the special problems confronting the carriers and has permitted them appropriate leeway in order to meet operating problems that arise from day to day and are best left to managerial discretion. However, the Board cannot overlook its regulatory function of surveilance over any potentially competitive nonstop operations which would depart from the sphere of a carrier's present service and are not now justified. Moreover, the granting of unlimited nonstop authority would be even more speculative than the usual route authorization, at the time of decision, by reason of future developments which might show that the stability of other routes would be affected and that the traffic could be better served by another carrier. Any nonstop operations which would upset competitive relationships, would result in substantial diversion from another carrier, would not serve a public need, and would not be logical in developing the route pattern of the applicant's system should not be permitted under route consolidations.

Interchange of Equipment

Until after World War II, the air transport industry had relatively little experience with the interchange of equipment between connecting carriers. Before that time Western Air Express (operating between Los Angeles and Salt Lake City) and United Air Lines (operating between Salt Lake City and cities to the east thereof) entered into an interchange agreement which provided for through sleeper-plane service between Los Angeles and various eastern points,[26] but this

ice, 6 CAB 199 (1944); *Northwest Airlines et al., Chicago–Milwaukee–New York*, 6 CAB 217 (1944); *Eastern Air Lines et al., Great Lakes–Florida*, 6 CAB 429 (1945); *West Coast Case*, 6 CAB 961 (1946); *Hawaiian Case*, 7 CAB 83 (1947); *Mississippi Valley Case*, 8 CAB 726 (1947); *Milwaukee-Chicago–New York Restriction Case*, 11 CAB 310 (1950); *T.W.A. Route Consolidation Case*, CAB Docket No. 2581 *et al.* (1950); *Reopened Southern Service to the West Case*, 18 CAB 234 (1954).

[26] *United-Western Interchange Case*, 1 CAA 723 (1940). See, Robert J. Keefer, "Airline Interchange Agreements," *Journal of Air Law and Commerce*, Winter, 1958.

operation was terminated during the war. After the close of the war the Board became interested in the possible need for similar arrangements between airlines. These would make it possible, without authorizing additional routes or route extensions, to eliminate the necessity of traffic being transferred at connecting points. With this in mind, the Board approved a number of through-service interchange operations.[27]

Most of the interchange operations were voluntarily proposed by the airlines concerned. The Board, however, took the position that it had the authority not only to provide the terms and conditions of such operations, but also to compel single-plane service by means of interchange whenever this seemed in the public interest.[28] The Board has also denied a number of interchange applications deemed not in the public interest on grounds that they would create uneconomic competition.[29]

In dealing with the subject of through service by means of interchange agreements, the Board has laid down certain principles to guide its judgment:

> It would appear to be fundamental that the interchanges which would best satisfy the public interest would be those which would cause the minimum interference with the existing route pattern and this, of course, save in exceptional cases, would favor interchanges that were not dependent upon new route extensions with their attendant cost and competitive implications to implement them. It would also seem to be a basic requirement that sound interchanges would provide an improved through service over reasonably direct routes. And finally, it should be considered that the interchange arrangement which would be most consistent with the public interest would be one which

---

[27] The Board has held that through-service arrangements are in the public interest and do not violate the provisions of the Civil Aeronautics Act, whether they contemplate that the crews change at the interchange point. (*United-Western Interchange Case,* 1 CAA 723 [1940] and *TWA-Delta Interchange Case,* 8 CAB 857 [1947] or that crews go through with the planes (*Pan American–Panagra Agreement,* 8 CAB 50 [1947] and *Capital-National Interchange Case,* 10 CAB 231 [1949]). The Civil Aeronautics Act and Federal Aviation Act, secs. 404(a) and 1002(i), give the Board the power to require interchange service to be instituted or continued, with the same power over the adequacy of such service as it has over the adequacy of service provided by a carrier on its own routes. See also *Eastern Air Lines et al., Great Lakes–Florida,* 6 CAB 429 (1944); *Northwest Airlines et al., Chicago–Milwaukee–New York,* 6 CAB 217 (1944); *Detroit-Washington Case,* 8 CAB 487 (1947); *Southern Service to the West Coast Case,* 15 CAB 94 (1952).

[28] *Through Service Proceedings and Kansas City–Memphis Florida Case,* 12 CAB 260 (1950); *Southern Service to the West Case,* 12 CAB 518 (1951).

[29] *National Route Investigation,* 12 CAB 798 (1951); *National Airlines, Inc., Pan American–Grace Airways, Inc., Interchange Agreement,* 14 CAB 320 (1951); *Chicago & Southern Air Lines, Inc., Pan American World Airways, Inc., Interchange Agreement,* 15 CAB 686 (1952); *Reopened Southern Service to the West Case,* 18 CAB 234 (1953).

would leave substantially undisturbed the historical participation of the various existing carriers in the traffic movement to be served, and which would not cause undue diversion.[30]

Experience with interchange of equipment was not satisfactory either to the airlines or to the traveling public, so that by 1960, one of the chief needs developed by the examiner in the *Southern Transcontinental Service Case*[31] was discontinuance of such arrangements in the Southwest, an area where the Board had been the most liberal in granting, encouraging, and requiring such arrangements. In fact, each of the interchange services previously granted[32] was attacked by user witnesses with a thoroughness and bitterness heretofore virtually unprecedented in a new route proceeding. The criticisms concerning the deficiencies of each of the interchanges ran the whole gamut of possible attack on faulty existing route operations, including grievances, among others, regarding poor scheduling, excessive stops, lack of space, difficulties of confirming reservations at junction points, lack of sufficient tourist service, undesirable timing of schedules, excessive elapsed time on both regional and transcontinental routings, and the general lack of dependability.

There is no doubt that interchange services, because of multiple managements, are more susceptible to errors, inconveniences, and mistakes in reservations and the clearance of space than through one-carrier services. Even more serious, however, has been the failure of the multiple managements to agree on the provision of additional capacity for particular interchange routes, even after a clear demonstration that existing interchange schedules were unable to accommodate a considerable number of passengers.

The Board has recognized in several decisions that interchanges are an unsatisfactory substitute for single-carrier service. For example, in the *Denver Service Case,*[33] the Board made the following statement:

---

[30] *Southern Service to the West Case,* 12 CAB 518 (1951).

[31] CAB Docket 7984, Examiner's initial decision June 20, 1960.

[32] Between Continental and American, under which services were operated between Houston, El Paso, and the West Coast; between National, Delta, and American, under which operations were conducted between Miami, New Orleans. Dallas or Fort Worth. and the West Coast; between Delta and American under which operations were conducted between Atlanta, Dallas or Fort Worth, and the West Coast; and between Braniff and TWA, under which operations were authorized between Houston, Amarillo, and the West Coast. *Southern Service to the West Case,* 12 CAB 518 (1951) ; 14 CAB 310 (1951) ; and 15 CAB 94 (1952) ; *Southern Service to the West Case, Reopened,* 18 CAB 234 (1953) ; 18 CAB 790 (1954) ; Order E-10082, March 9, 1956, Order E-10083, March 9, 1956; and Order E-11130, March 14, 1957.

[33] 22 CAB 1178 (1955).

As compared with single-carriers, single-plane service, an interchange service is more limited in its flexibility and does not as readily permit the frequent modifications in service necessary to meet the changing needs of air transportation. This arises chiefly from the fact that where two airline managements must agree on each schedule change, the alteration of scheduling often becomes a laborious process.

Further, in the *Florida-Texas Service Case,*[34] after citing with approval the foregoing comment from the *Denver Service Case,* the Board stated:

Where, as here, a one-carrier service can be provided economically without substantial adverse economic impact upon other carriers, such a service is to be preferred over that of an interchange. The operation of single-carrier, single-plane service is more conducive to a fuller exploitation of the traffic potential.

It is unlikely that interchange agreements will be entered into in the future despite any advantages, such as the following, which may be more apparent than real: (*a*) Costs of operations are much lower than in extending a route of a carrier; (*b*) it may be a means of strengthening a short-haul or regional carrier which ordinarily would not receive the benefits of traffic moving beyond its terminal; and (*c*) it may eliminate what is now branded excessive competition between points, since an interchange avoids the necessity of duplicating or extending routes but at the same time should offer substantially the same service to the public.

Supplemental Air Carriers

Shortly after the effective date of the Civil Aeronautics Act, the Board took action in connection with what were then termed "nonscheduled operations." Such services were authorized without compelling the operators to comply with the economic and safety requirements of the act, and this Board action has become one of the most highly controversial economic regulations in our air transport history.[35] Nonscheduled operations were defined as follows:

---

[34] 24 CAB 308 (1956).

[35] Economic Regulation 292.1, effective August 22, 1938. The first safety regulations governing nonscheduled carriers became effective August 1, 1946, and were entitled "Nonscheduled Air Carrier Certification and Operation Rules." See John P. Moore and K. Robert Hahn, "Regulation of Irregular Air Carriers," *Cornell Law Quarterly,* Fall, 1949; Victor S. Netterville, "The Regulation of Irregular Air Carriers: A History," *Journal of Air Law and Commerce,* Autumn, 1949; Charles R. Cherington, "The Essential Role of Large Irregular Air Carriers," *Journal of Air Law and Commerce,* Autumn, 1952; *Report on Role of Irregular Airlines in United States Air Transportation Industry, Select Committee on Small Business, United States Senate* (82d Cong. 1st sess.) (1951); *Future of*

Within the meaning of this regulation any operation shall be deemed to be nonscheduled if the air carrier does not hold out to the public by advertisement or otherwise that it will operate one or more airplanes between any designated points regularly, or with a reasonable degree of regularity, upon which airplane or airplanes it will accept for transportation, for compensation or hire, such members of the public as may apply therefor or such express or other property as the public may offer.

During World War II it became apparent that the Board's policy toward the nonscheduled carriers might have to be changed, and an investigation of such services was launched in 1944.[36] The result was an amendment of the previous exemption making it obligatory for nonscheduled carriers to "register" with the Board, the abandonment of the term "nonscheduled," and the creation of a classification of "irregular air carriers." This revised Economic Regulation 292.1 became effective on June 10, 1947, and was in use during most of the period of postwar growth of the noncertificated air carriers.

Irregular carriers were divided by the Board into two groups, large and small, the distinction depending upon the size and take-off weight of the aircraft employed.[37] An irregular air carrier in domestic transportation was permitted to engage in both passenger and freight operations; while in the international field, the irregular operator was restricted to the movement of property. To qualify as an irregular carrier, the applicant was required merely to file a request for a letter of registration with the Board. The Board defined an irregular carrier as one which:

does not hold out to the public, expressly or by a course of conduct, that it operates one or more aircraft between designated points, or within a designated point, regularly or with a reasonable degree of regularity, upon which aircraft it accepts for transportation, for compensation or hire, such members of the public as apply therefor or such property as the public offers. No air carrier shall be deemed to be an irregular air carrier unless the air transpor-

---

Irregular Airlines, Select Committee on Small Business, United States Senate (83d Cong. 1st sess.) (1953).

[36] *Investigation of Nonscheduled Air Services,* 6 CAB 1049 (1946).

[37] Large irregular air carriers were defined as those utilizing aircraft with an allowable gross take-off weight in excess of 10,000 pounds or a number of aircraft which together had allowable gross take-off weights exceeding 25,000 pounds. Small irregular air carriers were those operators with smaller units of equipment. Later (1947), small irregular carriers were defined as those who do not use in their transport services aircraft having a maximum certificated take-off weight in excess of 12,500 pounds for any one unit, or 25,000 pounds for the total of such units. Still later (1952), the "small irregular" classification was dropped and these operators were termed "air taxi operators," those who use only aircraft units having a maximum certificated take-off weight of 12,500 pounds or less, without regard to the number of such units being used. Starting in 1954, the Board began referring to the large irregular carriers as "irregular service carriers."

tation services offered and performed by it are of such infrequency as to preclude an implication of a uniform pattern of normal consistency of operation between, or within, such designated points.

Presumably the Board felt that it had, by the above definition, circumscribed the operating authority of an irregular carrier. But despite this and even more detailed discussions of "irregularity" contained in various Board orders subsequently issued,[38] a noncertificated air transport industry developed. Some 140 of these operations, with equipment ranging from one or two to as many as twenty DC-3 or DC-4 airplanes each, provided a variety of services, including local and transcontinental "coach type" accommodations, which the certificated airlines have since adopted. In addition to their large capital investments, many were of sufficient size to employ hundreds of technical and operating personnel. In view of the complexity of the Board's formula of "irregularity," it is probably safe to assume that where doubts existed they were resolved by the operators in favor of their own activities. It also appears that the Board was either hampered in its enforcement activities by a lack of personnel or else was willing to permit the situation to develop, feeling that, by attrition and by the philosophy of the survival of the fittest, the problem of regulation would ultimately take care of itself.[39] In any event, it was not until August, 1948, that the Board announced a series of actions affecting all large irregular air carriers moving passengers and property under the then existing exemption authority. At this time the Board: (*a*) instituted a general investigation into the practices and activities of the large irregular air carriers, (*b*) froze applications for letters of registration for large irregular carriers as of August 6,

---

[38] See, for example, the consent order adopted in the matter of *Trans-Caribbean Air Cargo Lines, Inc.*, CAB Order, Serial No. E-370, Docket No. 2593 (1947), wherein the Board defined the permissive scope of irregular operations. ". . . regularly or with a reasonable degree of regularity, which regularity is reflected by the operation of a single flight per week on the same day of each week between the same two points, or is reflected by the recurrence of operations of two round-trip flights, or flights varying from two to three or more such flights, between any same two points each week in succeeding weeks, without three intervening other weeks or approximately similar periods at irregular but frequent intervals during which no such flights are operated so as thereby to result in appreciable definite breaks in service: it being intended by this subparagraph to require irregularity in service between any such points but not to preclude the operation of more than one or two such flights in any given week, nor to prescribe any specific maximum limitation upon the number of flights which may be performed in any one week, if frequency and irregularity of service is otherwise achieved through variations in numbers of flights, and intervals between flights and through frequent and extended definite breaks in service. . . ." Identical language was used by the Board in final orders in many subsequent enforcement proceedings.

[39] See Moore and Hahn, *op. cit.*

1948, and (*c*) directed its staff to re-evaluate Economic Regulation 292.1 in light of the experience gained since its original promulgation.

In the meantime, possibly in anticipation of more strict action by the Board, many of the large irregular operators filed applications for individual exemptions to secure a more liberal operating authority than they had previously been allowed.[40] In practically all instances, these applications were dismissed; and in numerous enforcement proceedings, initiated by the Board, cease and desist orders were issued or letters of registration were revoked.[41]

The general investigation initiated by the Board into activities and practices of large irregular air carriers in August, 1948, resulted in the promulgation of a new revision of section 292.1 on December 10, 1948, to become effective in May, 1949. The most important feature of the new regulation was its withdrawal of the blanket-exemption authority hitherto conferred upon large irregular carriers and its requirement that each carrier make a new application for an individual exemption order authorizing continued irregular operations. Some 96 operators filed applications pursuant to this regulation.

On May 25, 1950, the Board issued its opinion, based upon its general investigation into the operations of the large irregular carriers,[42] and announced the policies that would guide it in disposing of applications for individual exemptions. Without attempting a detailed review of all the reasoning underlying these policies, a brief summary can be given as follows:

---

[40] See exemption requests of *Seaboard and Western Airlines, Inc.*, CAB Docket No. 3304 (1948); *Trans-Caribbean Air Cargo Lines, Inc.*, CAB Docket No. 2123 (1948); *Air America*, CAB Docket No. 3491 (1948); *American Air Transport, Inc.*, CAB Docket No. 3670 (1948); *Standard Airlines, Inc., et al., Exemption Request*, 9 CAB 583 (1948).

[41] Most enforcement proceedings were met with dogged resistance and resourceful defense tactics by the irregular operators. Standard Airlines was one of the first to take the matter into the United States District Court for the District of Columbia, seeking to restrain the Board from a cancellation of its letter of registration (*Standard Airlines, Inc.* v. *CAB*, 177 Fed. [2d] 18 [1949]). The Court ruled that "the determination of whether a carrier has forfeited the right to operate as an Irregular Carrier is a matter for the Board, in the first instance at least, to decide." See also *Transocean Air Lines, Inc., Enforcement Proceeding*, 11 CAB 350 (1950); *Viking Airliners, Noncertificated Operations*, 10 CAB 401 (1950); *Investigation of Seaboard & Western Airlines, Inc.*, 11 CAB 372 (1950); *Meteor Air Transport, Inc.*, 12 CAB 384 (1951); *Arrow Airways Enforcement Proceeding*, 12 CAB 405 (1951); *Oxnard Sky Freight Enforcement Proceeding*, 12 CAB 722 (1951); *Modern Air Transport, Inc., Exemption Application*, 14 CAB 459 (1951); *American Air Transport and Flight School, Inc., Enforcement Proceeding*, 15 CAB 218 (1952); *Air America Inc., Enforcement Proceeding*, 18 CAB 393 (1953); *North American Airlines Section 411 Proceeding*, 18 CAB 96 (1953); *Twentieth Century Air Lines, Compliance Proceeding*, 21 CAB 133 (1955).

[42] *Large Irregular Carriers, Exemptions*, 11 CAB 609 (1950).

1. Applications of irregular carriers that had been conducting route services, described by the Board as "a pattern of operations which shows a concentration of relatively frequent and regular flights between a limited number of pairs of points," were to be denied.

2. Exemptions were to be granted to those carriers which in the past had been furnishing truly irregular services.

3. The Board concluded that:

> It must be recognized that the temptation to engage in route operations will continue in the future as to those carriers which receive exemption authority. Indeed, since the number of irregular carriers utilizing large aircraft will be smaller and the competition between them lessened to that extent, the temptation will probably be greater than it has in the past. Although the carriers which will receive exemption authorization at the present time have conducted irregular services in the past, we nevertheless deem it necessary to impose further restrictions to insure that each such carrier will carry out and perform the type of service which it is our intention to authorize. Accordingly, in addition to the restrictions upon regularity which have heretofore been imposed, we shall permit only three flights in the same direction during any period of four successive calendar weeks between the following pairs of points, and only eight flights in the same direction in such period between any other pairs of cities.

The Board then listed 13 pairs of cities between which the bulk of the operations of irregular carriers had been conducted and between which operations had been characterized by frequency and regularity.[43]

4. Applications of nonoperators were to be denied. This had reference to the large number of irregular carriers which, although holding valid letters of registration, had not conducted any operations in the preceding year.

The next major step in the regulation of irregular carriers came on March 2, 1951, when the Board issued a special exemption authorizing unrestricted operations by large irregular carriers pursuant to military contracts and the establishment of joint representatives at military bases to arrange for flights of uniformed military person-

---

[43] In order to place the carriers granted individual exemptions and those still operating under the provisions of part 291 of the regulations on an equal footing, the Board followed this action with an amendment of part 291 that added the so-called "3 and 8" limitation to the regulation. The effective date of the amendment was postponed several times at the request of the Small Business Committee of the Senate and before it became effective a United States district court, in a suit brought by two large irregular carriers, held the amendment invalid as having been promulgated without observance of proper procedures. An appeal from this ruling was made by the Board but has not yet been settled.

nel traveling at their own expense to or from military bases. Also, the Board approved two organizations of irregular carriers, the Aircoach Transport Association and the Independent Military Air Transport Association, for the purpose of representing such carriers before the executive branch of the United States government and in order that the irregulars' equipment, personnel, and services might most expeditiously be utilized by the Department of Defense.

This was the situation in the regulation of large irregular carriers on September 21, 1951. On that date the Board issued an order instituting a general investigation of air services by large irregular carriers and irregular transport carriers.[44] The investigation was directed to all matters related to and concerning air transportation conducted by irregular carriers, including an inquiry into the issue of whether there is "a need for the air-transportation services now conducted by the irregular carriers in addition to and supplemental to services performed by the carriers holding certificates of public convenience and necessity." The investigation also covered many subsidiary issues, such as whether, if such supplemental services were found to be required, what type or types of service would best meet the public need and whether such services should be authorized by certificate of public convenience and necessity or by exemption.

The institution of this general investigation and the temporary suspension of any further processing of the individual exemption applications did not portend a cessation of enforcement activities against those irregular carriers which continued to ignore the provisions of the exemption regulation under which they were operating. The Board, in fact, made it plain that it could not condone violations of the act or the regulations pending disposition of the proceeding in the general investigation.[45]

---

[44] *Large Irregular Carriers and Irregular Transport Carriers*, CAB Docket No. 5132 *et al.*, Order Serial No. E-5722 (1951) and Order Serial No. E-9744 (1955).

[45] In September, 1951, the Board revoked the operating authority of Air Transport Associates, Inc. (CAB Docket No. 4265). In March, 1952, the Board suspended the operating authority of American Air Transport (CAB Docket No. 5209). In September, 1952, enforcement proceedings were instituted against Air America, Inc. (CAB Docket No. 5657) and in March, 1953, enforcement proceedings were started against North American Airlines, Trans National Airlines, Trans America Airways, Twentieth Century Airlines and Hemisphere Air Transport (CAB Docket No. 6000). In 1953 enforcement proceedings were brought against still other irregular carriers such as Peninsular Air Transport (CAB Docket No. 6124), North American Airlines (CAB Docket Nos. 5774 and 5928), and Air America, Inc. (CAB Docket No. 5766). In fact the Board was so active in connection with revocations and enforcement that some felt it was moving rapidly in the direction of eliminating the major irregular carriers long before the completion of the over-all hearing.

It took the Board over four years to conclude its investigation of the large irregular carrier situation, but on November 15, 1955, they issued the following conclusions:[46]

> The large irregular carriers and irregular transport carriers, as a class, have provided useful and necessary service in meeting fluctuating demands for air transportation, specialized services, and charter operations which have not been met by the certificated air carriers. The growth of the operations of the irregulars has not had an adverse effect upon the certificated carriers.
>
> The irregulars represent a significant part of the Nation's air transport system, and there is a continuing need for their services. They have rendered invaluable service to the military, both in the Berlin and Korean airlifts, as well as in domestic charter operations. The continued existence of their fleet is of real value in terms of the national defense, and the future ability of the irregulars to serve the military depends upon their ability to operate their planes in commercial activities when not engaged in service for the military. The Board's policy toward these carriers should be directed toward their survival and continued healthy growth, subject to the over-all objectives of the act and a proper relationship to the certificated air-carrier system.
>
> The Board, therefore, adopts a new policy with regard to the permissible operations of these carriers, which carriers will hereafter be designated as supplemental air carriers. Under this new policy these carriers will be granted authority to conduct: (1) unlimited charter operations on a planeload basis for the carriage of passengers and property in domestic overseas, and Territorial (except intra-Alaska) operations, and of property only in international operations; (2) charter operations for the carriage of passengers in international operations on an individual exemption basis similar to that which is set forth in the 1955 Transatlantic Charter Policy, E-9221, adopted May 20, 1955; and (3) individually ticketed or individually waybilled operations by each carrier not to exceed 10 trips per month in the same direction between any single pair of points in any calendar month, except as to intra-Alaska operations and except as to the carriage of passengers in international operations.
>
> The authority granted under the new policy will be supplemental and additional to the services of the certificated carriers and will not be unduly competitive with the operations of the certificated carriers.

After the issuance of the above statement of policy, the Board took approximately three years to decide which among many applicants for certificates as supplemental air carriers should be selected. In January, 1959, they officially established the new class of certified air carriers—the supplemental air carrier—and awarded temporary certificates of public convenience and necessity to twenty-three applicants as follows:

---

[46] *Large Irregular Carrier Investigation*, 22 CAB 838 (1955).

Five-Year Certificates:

- American Flyers Airline Corp.
- California Eastern Aviation, Inc.
- Capitol Airways, Inc.
- Coastal Cargo Company
- General Airways, Inc.
- Johnson Flying Service, Inc.
- Overseas National Airways, Inc.
- Southern Air Transport, Inc.
- Standard Airways
- Stewart Air Service
- Transocean Air Lines, Inc.
- World Airways, Inc.

Two-Year Certificates:

- All American Airways, Inc.
- Arctic-Pacific, Inc.
- Associated Air Transport, Inc.
- Aviation Corp. of Seattle
- Blatz Airlines, Inc.
- Conner Airlines, Inc.
- Modern Air Transport, Inc.
- Paul Mantz Air Services
- Regina Cargo Airlines, Inc.
- Sourdough Air Transport
- United States Overseas Airlines, Inc.

These carriers were permitted to operate individually ticketed passenger and waybilled-freight services in the United States on a scheduled basis, with a limit between any two points of ten round trips per airline per month. The terms of the certificates also allowed the carriers to perform scheduled domestic charter service without frequency limits, thus continuing the operating rights conferred in 1955, pending Board decision on the qualifications of the individual applicants.

This decision of the Board was immediately appealed by the trunk airlines with whom the supplementals had been in most direct competition. Grounds for appeal to the United States Court of Appeals for the District of Columbia were based on the fact that the Board had no authority to issue blanket authorization to large supplemental air carriers to operate between any two points in the United States in view of the requirements of the Federal Aviation Act of 1958 that each certificate specify the terminal points and intermediate points, if any, between which an air carrier is authorized to engage in air transportation. This contention was upheld by the Court in April, 1960.[47] The Court further held that the Board had failed to observe a provision of the Act of 1958 against restricting an air carrier's right to add or change schedules since it had limited operations of the supplemental carriers to ten flights each calendar month in the same direction between the same two points. In addition, the Court said that in many instances operations of the carriers had been small or specialized and their financial resources, adequate for these operations, were "obvi-

[47] By an opinion in No. 15025, *United Air Lines* v. *Civil Aeronautics Board et al.* See *Traffic World*, April 16, 1960, pp. 138–39. See section 401(*e*) Federal Aviation Act.

ously inadequate for operations of the scope authorized by the certificates." This action by the Court placed the future of the supplemental air carriers in doubt which could only be resolved by amending the Federal Aviation Act. This was accomplished in 1960 to permit the Board to issue limited (two-year) certificates to supplemental air carriers on the basis adopted in 1959.[48]

Even though the supplemental carriers were not originally visualized as major competitors of the scheduled lines, and whatever their place may ultimately be in the transportation of passengers by air, there is no escaping the fact that up to the present time they have been a significant force in the competitive picture. Although this competitive impact has extended to both the passenger and cargo fields and to domestic and international operations, it has not been felt uniformly in all areas. For example, it appears that in the transportation of freight the competitive influence of these carriers has been less important in the domestic than in the international field. Since the Board's exemption regulations conferred no authority to conduct passenger operations in foreign air transportation, the competitive influence on passenger services has necessarily been limited to operations within the United States and between it and its Territories.

On the whole, the supplemental carriers have concentrated their flights on the most important route segments between the heaviest traffic-producing points and have devoted an overwhelming part of their efforts to the lucrative long-haul traffic. For example, of a total of 16,189 flights (including those for the military) operated by supplemental carriers during a recent year, 52 per cent were over five route segments, and 65 per cent were over 11 segments. The remaining flights were widely scattered. Under this pattern of operation it necessarily follows that in such high-density, long-haul markets as New York–California and New York–Miami, to mention only two, services by these carriers would be highly competitive with the certificated airlines. It also follows that between a much greater number of points served by the scheduled carriers, the supplemental carriers have only a slight competitive effect, suffering from the dual drawbacks of low density and short haul.

There is no indication that their competition has exerted any important pressure toward the development of new and improved equipment. With minor exceptions, the transport equipment utilized by these carriers has consisted of surplus military aircraft, many of the

[48] Public Law 86–661, July, 1960.

type used heavily by the certificated trunk-line carriers in the early postwar era as transitional aircraft. Even today the supplementals do not operate aircraft of as advanced design as those utilized by the certificated trunk lines in the major competitive markets. Much the same situation exists in the other areas where competition as to service might occur.

As far as passenger fares go, however, the situation is different, and there the influence of the supplemental carriers has been strongly felt. From the beginning of their operations, a substantial number of them have concentrated on operating nonluxury services in the high-density markets at fares substantially below the standard fares of the certificated carriers. By operating in markets, under conditions, and at times when high-density seating could be realized and, consequently, lower fares charged, they helped to bring about the development of low-fare coach services of the type that have accounted for the largest portion of the recent growth in domestic passenger business of all air carriers. Such low-fare coach services have served as a competitive stimulus to the certificated carriers in the low-cost field, and, together with the coach services of the certificated carriers, have induced many persons to travel by air who would not have utilized air services at the higher standard fares.

The supplemental carriers have offered competition not only to the certificated carriers, but also have fought strongly among themselves for the available low-cost market. Although this latter competition has been felt somewhat by all such operators, it has had its strongest influence with respect to those relatively few of the supplemental carriers who have accounted for the bulk of the business.

The problem facing the Board under this situation has been to evaluate the beneficial and detrimental results that have in the past flowed from supplemental air-carrier operations and that may be expected to result in the future, and on the basis of that evaluation to bring about a scheme of authorizations that will promote a sound air transportation system. On the basis of the record, the Board concluded in the *Transcontinental Coach-Type Service Case*[49] that the benefits stemming from a general authorization to the noncertificated applicants to conduct unlimited transcontinental coach services were not sufficient to outweigh the detrimental effects it would have upon the air transportation system as a whole. The question of the nature and extent of any authorization to be granted these carriers to conduct sup-

---

[49] 14 CAB 720 (1951).

plementary services, falling short of the operations conducted by the certificated carriers, has been decided.

It should be pointed out, in conclusion, that, despite frequent statements to the contrary, the Board's actions have not at all been directed at restricting the scope of operations of the supplemental carriers nor have its policies resulted in economic strangulation of the industry. The military exemption previously referred to represents a substantial authorization. It has become increasingly obvious that the type of irregular operation comparable to a tramp steamer service, which was contemplated by the Board's original blanket-exemption order and which many operators started out to perform, seems to have limited economic possibilities. It is quite possible that a certain number of supplemental operators could, through a more energetic cultivation of the aircraft charter field, develop a considerable volume of business for special movements involving the charter of complete aircraft. Aside from the possibilities of certification of bona fide charter operations, the supplementals have as yet been unable to suggest a field for their activities which on a long-term basis offers much hope of economic survival.[50]

---

[50] For a detailed analysis, pro and con, of the entire subject of irregular air carrier regulation and the related subject of the feasibility of certain coach operations then being conducted chiefly by nonscheduled operators, see "Airline Industry Investigation," *Hearings before the Committee on Interstate and Foreign Commerce, U.S. Senate* (81st Cong., 1st sess.) (April and May, 1949), particularly statements by James Fishgrund, pp. 260, 823; James M. Landis, pp. 211, 295; Joseph J. O'Connell, Jr., pp. 249, 494; C. R. Smith, p. 741. See also CAB, *Statement of Action on Applications for Permission to Carry Groups on Special Transatlantic Charter Trips,* May 20, 1950; CAB, *Policy Statement on Authorization of Large Irregular Carriers,* May 26, 1950; *The Role of Competition in Commercial Air Transportation, Select Committee on Small Business, United States Senate* (82d Cong., 2d sess.) (1952), pp. 21–31; *Large Irregular Air Carrier Investigation,* CAB Docket 5132 *et al.* particularly the *Initial Decision of Examiners* served March 29, 1955.

The Air Coordinating Committee in its report to the President, *Civil Air Policy,* in 1954 made the following observations concerning nonscheduled airline operations: (1) The intent of the Civil Aeronautics Act, to establish a pattern of controlled entry with regard to common carrier air transportation, is still sound. (2) The exemption authority of section 416 of the Civil Aeronautics Act should be used only in limited and exceptional circumstances and should not be used as the basis for any significant departure from the controlled entry principle. (3) The concept of nonscheduled service does not provide a meaningful basis for exempting route-type passenger services from the normal certification requirement. In the future, there should be no general use of the exemption authority as a basis for authorizing common carrier transportation to individually ticketed passengers on large transport planes. (4) Those operations of the large irregular carriers which represent a supplementary type of service, such as bona fide charter and contract operations, should be encouraged. A new type of certificate should be developed for such operations, providing suitable flexibility in terms and areas to be served. (5) Irregular operations now conducted with small aircraft present no serious regulatory problem under their present exemption status and there appears to be no need for changing this status.

Mergers and Acquisitions

The provisions of the Civil Aeronautics Act and Federal Aviation Act dealing with mergers and acquisitions of one air carrier by another are more complex than those applying to the award of certificates, for not only must the public interest be considered but no transaction is to be approved which creates a monopoly and thereby restrains competition or jeopardizes another carrier.[51] As interpreted by the Civil Aeronautics Board, this permits the approval of arrangements that restrain competition or jeopardize another carrier so long as they do not arise from a monopoly condition.[52] It then becomes important for the Board to decide what constitutes a "monopoly." The Board has chosen to define monopoly in the economic sense of control of the market place and has rejected the antitrust definition which considers it as "restraint of competition."[53] Thus, by its findings as to the degree of control present, the Board possesses wide latitude to approve or disapprove agreements endangering competitors. In essence, the Board asserts that there may be restraint of competition without a simultaneous increase in control of the market place.

The Board has apparently regarded one of its first objectives as that of preventing the emergence of a "super carrier." In denying approval of a proposed merger which would have made the applicant the largest domestic system,[54] it was emphasized that certain routes of the contracting parties served the same population centers; and the proposal was criticized not on the size of the proposed organization

---

[51] Civil Aeronautics Act and Federal Aviation Act, sec. 408(*b*).

[52] *United Air Lines–Western Air Express, Interchange of Equipment,* 1 CAB 723 (1940). In this case, the Board approved a sleeper-plane interchange agreement between Western and United which eliminated an inconvenient connection at Salt Lake City. This transaction jeopardized another carrier, but the Board stated a principle to which it has generally adhered: "If . . . competitors are to be prevented from inaugurating improvements in service solely as a protection to a particular air carrier, the development of an adequate air transportation system in this country will be retarded rather than assured." In another case, *Northwest Airlines, Consolidation of Routes,* 7 CAB 100 (1946), Northwest was permitted to operate directly to Butte, Montana, from Portland, Oregon, since a saving of 60 minutes in travel time outweighed the ill effects of revenue diversion from United Air Lines at Portland.

[53] In *United Air Lines–Western Air Express, Interchange of Equipment,* 1 CAA 723 (1940), the Board exhaustively examined the various definitions of monopoly. The legal definition conceives a monopoly as a restraint of competition, and the antithesis as free competition; whereas to the economist, monopoly is control of the market, and its antithesis is pure competition.

[54] *Acquisition of Western Air Express by United Air Lines,* 1 CAA 739 (1940). The proposal would have merged United, one of the three transcontinental carriers at that time and the second largest of the seventeen domestic lines then certificated, with Western, a north-south regional carrier and one of the eight largest airlines then operating.

but because of the concentration of control of a particular market place that would result.

In a subsequent proceeding, the Board was confronted with a proposed acquisition of a strong regional carrier by American Airlines, already the largest domestic carrier.[55] Since the two airlines did not serve the same territory but merely crossed at one point, additional control of the same market was not involved. Classifying the two systems meeting in the one small area as impossible of "integration," the Board denied the application, thus using another reason to forestall the development of any carrier dominant either in the control of a specific market or in the matter of route size.

Another Board policy concerned with mergers, consolidations, and sales has been developed in furtherance of its declared intention to assist the small airlines. Failure of the Board's route-award policy to reduce the great difference in the size of the airlines has drawn attention to the possibility of consolidating a number of the smaller carriers; but the almost total absence of examples of voluntary mergers or consolidations among smaller lines, designed to provide competition for major air carriers, suggests that this method has only a limited possibility. The lack of success which has characterized the exercise of moral suasion to encourage private agreements on beneficial consolidations and sales has influenced some Board members to consider the use of some means of enforcing mergers of smaller units into transcontinental or multiregional airlines.[56]

---

[55] *American Airlines, Inc., Acquisition of Control of Mid-Continent Airlines,* 7 CAB 365 (1946); *North Central–Lake Central Acquisition Case,* CAB Docket 5770 (1957). The Board, however, made it clear in the American–Mid-Continent case that it made no attempt to calculate the optimum size for an air carrier, nor to express a belief that such a fixed and invariable standard exists in so dynamic a field as air transportation. The Board also stated that it did not intend to leave the impression that it felt it should strive toward an ultimate goal of parity among air carriers since factors of size and competition are relative matters and are intimately tied to the circumstances of any particular case. The Board's concern is to foster and preserve, in as realistic and practical a manner as possible, those conditions which are conducive to the creation and growth of the type of air transport system envisioned in the Civil Aeronautics and Federal Aviation Acts.

[56] See former Chairman Welch Pogue's "concurring and dissenting" opinion in *Northwest Airlines, Chicago–Milwaukee–New York,* 6 CAB 217 (1944). Former Chairman James M. Landis was of the same opinion. See *Aviation Week,* November 3, 1947, p. 51. There have, however, been a number of cases where the Board has disapproved mergers: *United Air Lines Transport Corp., Acquisition of Western Air Express Corp.,* 1 CAA 739 (1940); *American Export Airlines, Inc., Acquisition of Taca, S.A.,* 3 CAB 216 (1941); *Alaska Air Lines, Inc., et al., Service to Anchorage, Alaska,* 3 CAB 522 (1942); *Acquisition of Cordova Air Service, Inc., by Alaska Airlines, Inc.,* 4 CAB 708 (1944); *Braniff Airways, Inc., et al., Acquisition of Aerovias Braniff, S.A.,* 6 CAB 847 (1946); *National-Caribbean-Atlantic Control Case,* 6 CAB 671 (1946); *American Airlines, Inc., Acquisition of Control of Mid-Continent Airlines, Inc.,* 7 CAB 365 (1946); *Southwest–West*

At times the Board has tended to approve mergers and sales seemingly because of a dread of the supposedly evil effects of bankruptcy upon the reputation of the air transportation industry and a desire to eliminate inefficient management.[57]

The most bitterly fought merger case to come before the Board in its history involved the acquisition by Pan American World Airways of American Overseas Airlines.[58] This was at first denied by the Board but soon after permitted in compliance with a directive from the President of the United States, issued under his power to approve or disapprove matters concerning international routes of American-flag

---

Coast Merger Case, CAB Docket No. 4405 (1951); *Continental-Pioneer Acquisition Case,* CAB Docket No. 6457 *et al.* (1954).

[57] *Western-United Acquisition of Air Carrier Property,* 8 CAB 298 (1947). The Board approved a privately arranged sale by Western to United of the right to operate a specific route and permitted a purchase price that was twice the value of the tangible assets at depreciated cost. This excess amount was paid for the intangible asset, the certificate of public convenience and necessity previously granted by the Board to Western at no charge. By approving this transaction, the Board moved contrary to an express provision in the act (sec. 401[*j*]) which states that no proprietary interests are conferred on the holder of a certificate. In an earlier case, *Western Air Lines, Acquisition of Inland Air Lines,* 4 CAB 654 (1944), the sale was approved in order to eliminate Inland's inefficient management, although there was scant opportunity for integration since only 5.22 per cent of Inland's traffic traveled over Western's routes. In 1961, the Board approved the merger of Capital Airlines with United Airlines in *United–Capital Merger Case,* CAB Docket 11699, for the chief reason that without approval of the merger it was unlikely that Capital would be able to maintain operations of any kind but instead would go into bankruptcy and liquidation with the consequent disappearance of Capital's routes and services.

[58] The case history leading up to the final Board order permitting the merger (*North Atlantic Route Transfer Case,* 11 CAB 676 [1950]) is of interest: December 13, 1948—Merger proposal first announced, providing payment for American Overseas Airlines in Pan American Airways common stock. Agreement was to terminate September 13, 1949. June 24, 1949—Six weeks of hearings ended, one of the longest on record, with a transcript of testimony filling 3,873 pages. September 13, 1949—CAB proceedings not concluded; agreement between the two airlines extended to March 13, 1950, with option to June 13. The agreement was amended to provide payment of $17,500,000 cash for American Overseas Airlines instead of stock trade. December 22, 1949—The Board's examiner issued a report favoring the merger. March 1, 1950—Oral argument by Pan American Airways and American Overseas Airlines as well as intervenors, Trans World Airlines, and a group of American Overseas Airlines employees before the Board. May 17, 1950—Board disapproved sale by 3 to 2 vote. June 6, 1950—Pan American Airlines–American Overseas Airlines agreement extended to June 30, and from there on extension was a few days at a time. June 29, 1950—President Truman approved CAB decision. June 30, 1950—President Truman recalled his approval. July 10, 1950—President Truman wrote to the acting chairman of the CAB stating that he had decided to approve the sale. July 10, 1950—CAB reversed itself and issued an order approving the sale, route transfer, and consequent merger. July 11, 1950—President Truman approved the revised decision. July 12, 1950—Seaboard and Western Airlines and a group of American Overseas Airlines employees (Brian O. Sparks *et al.*) obtained a court order restraining the Board from issuing anything but its original opinion. July 13, 1950—The Department of Justice representing the CAB asked to have the restraining order dissolved. July 14, 1950—Trans World Airlines asks Board to stay issuance of second decision. July 17, 1950—Restraining order lifted, and Board issues decision approving sale after denying Trans World Airlines motion.

airlines. (See Chapter 10.) The reasons advanced for approval were: (*a*) Revival of normal transatlantic traffic had been slow following the close of World War II, and the expected volume of business did not justify three competing United States Carriers if excessive subsidies were to be avoided. (*b*) American Overseas Airlines had experienced difficulty in obtaining capital for future expansion. (*c*) Pan American World Airways operating economies expected to result from the merger would help to reverse the trend toward greater use of foreign-flag lines, which had increased their proportion of trans-Atlantic business from 24 per cent to 37 per cent in the previous year. (*d*) It was held that Pan American World Airways was operating under a competitive disadvantage over the North Atlantic since, unlike American Overseas Airlines and Trans World Airways, it lacked affiliated transcontinental routes in the United States which could feed traffic into its overseas routes.

The Board's general policy toward mergers and consolidations has been developed to the point where the following may be stated as the minimum criteria:

1. In merger cases the Board will examine the transaction to determine whether it will aid in effectuating the purposes of the Act.[59] In other words, before a merger transaction is approved, there must be a finding that it will result in tangible public benefits. The burden of proof is squarely upon the applicants to show that the merger will aid in effectuating the pruposes of the Act. A mere negative showing by the applicants that the merger is not adverse to the public interest is not sufficient.

2. The merger must help create an integrated and co-ordinated transport system properly adapted to the needs of commerce. One of the most important factors which must be determined by the Board in a merger is whether the two route systems will form an integrated pattern of air service. Although this question need not be answered in the affirmative to the exclusion of all other factors, it is nevertheless an important consideration in determining the extent of public benefits expected to result from the merger.[60]

---

[59] *American Airlines, Inc., Control of Mid-Continent Airlines, Inc.*, 7 CAB 365 (1946); *Southwest–West Coast Merger Case*, 11 CAB 999 (1950).

[60] The Board pointed out in *National Caribbean-Atlantic Control Case*, 6 CAB 671 (1946), that "a carrier's routes should be adapted to the normal flow of air traffic. If these conditions are not met, the attainment of an economically sound operation is likely to be difficult." See also *American Control of Mid-Continent Case*, 7 CAB 365 (1946).

3. The merger must result in substantial tangible benefits to the public through improved service.

4. The interests of labor must be protected.[61] Each case is carefully examined by the Board to see that justice will be done each set of employees affected by any merger of airlines. Some of the matters considered are integration of seniority lists of the merged companies; displacement allowances for employees who are not deprived of their employment as a result of a merger, but are retained in positions offering lower compensation than they received prior to the merger; dismissal allowances; traveling and moving expenses for employees who must as a result of a merger change their place of employment; and protection in real estate matters so that employees will not suffer in having to hastily dispose of their real estate interests and thus not obtain the fair market value of their property.[62]

Although there have been several mergers of domestic trunk airlines (of which Braniff/Mid-Continent; Delta–Chicago and Southern; and United-Capital are the most important) and also several local service airlines (of which Monarch-Arizona and West Coast–Empire[63] are the most important), the Board's policy on mergers and sales has been only partially successful.[64] The power to approve mergers has not been used as an affirmative weapon of Board policy, perhaps because of the Board's belief that the most effective method of overcoming the difference in size of the carriers was through the award of new route certificates. As a result of the Board's route policy, however, there may be too many systems. If so, a means must be found for their better integration. As the history of the railroads abundantly illustrates, merging or consolidation seldom takes place voluntarily. Some propulsive force from outside is necessary if real progress is to be made.

[61] In two cases the Board, in considering labor protective provisions, adopted certain provisions of what had come to be known as the "Burlington Formula" because of its use in railroad merger cases. In these decisions the Board noted, however, that while the conditions there adopted were correct for each case, it in no way intended to prejudge future cases. *United-Western, Acquisition of Air Carrier Property,* 11 CAB 701 (1950); *North Atlantic Route Transfer Case, Supplemental Opinion,* 12 CAB 124; 140 (1950).

[62] In more recent cases the Board has used what it terms the "Braniff/Mid-Continent Formula." *Braniff/Mid-Continent Merger Case,* 15 CAB 708 (1952); *Delta–Chicago and Southern Merger Case,* 16 CAB 647 (1952), *Flying Tiger–Slick Merger Case,* 18 CAB 326 (1954).

[63] *Monarch-Arizona Merger Case,* 11 CAB 246 (1950); *West Coast–Empire Case,* 15 CAB 971 (1952).

[64] See Paul D. Zook, "Recasting the Air Route Pattern by Airline Consolidations and Mergers," *Journal of Air Law and Commerce,* Summer, 1954.

Merging or consolidating airlines would appear to be much easier than merging railroads. Airlines have great flexibility, with their chief asset a certificate of convenience and necessity, a "franchise which gives them a right-of-way in the sky." There is no heavy investment by air carriers comparable to that expended by railroads in roadbed, terminals, and other fixed-property investments.

Actually, however, airline mergers have been very difficult to bring about, with each project beset by many obstacles. Once agreement at the executive level is accomplished, proposals must then obtain sanctions from the separate boards of directors and after that approval from stockholders. Dissident groups can place any compromise plan in jeopardy.[65]

[65] For an interesting and revealing discussion of some of these matters see the Report of Examiner Edward T. Stodola in *Eastern-Colonial, Acquisition of Assets,* 18 CAB 781 (1953). The following mergers have actually taken place since 1938: Western-Inland (1944); Pan American–American Overseas (1950); West Coast–Empire (1952); Braniff–Mid Continent (1952); Delta–Chicago & Southern (1952); Eastern-Colonial (1954) 1st agreement; Continental-Pioneer (1954); Eastern-Colonial (1956) 2d agreement; United-Capital (1961).

Chapter 8

CIVIL AERONAUTICS BOARD POLICY—MAIL RATES

THE exercise of its jurisdiction over rates and charges, for the transportation of mail, passengers, and property by air,[1] is one of the most important continuing responsibilities of the Civil Aeronautics Board. Airlines are required to file rate schedules for passengers and freight with the Board, which, in turn, may approve or suspend the proposed rates or may promulgate a schedule of its own choice.[2] Mail rates are not set by the airlines but by the Board itself.

Mail Rates and Subsidy Payments

The fixing of mail rates have had a fourfold significance in connection with the national policy for the development of adequate air services:

1. The rates have had to provide compensation to the carrier for the services performed in carrying the mails. When payments for transporting mail do not exceed the fully allocated costs borne by the carriers for performing the service, the mail rate is said to be a service rate.

2. The mail rates have, in certain circumstances, provided com-

[1] Civil Aeronautics Act and Federal Aviation Act, secs. 403, 404, and 406.

[2] Civil Aeronautics Act and Federal Aviation Act, sec. 403 and 1002(*d*) and (*g*). The Board possesses limited power to fix international rates to the extent necessary to correct discrimination but has frequently requested Congress to extend its powers over such rates (Civil Aeronautics Act, sec. 1002 [*f*]). In determining rates for the carriage of persons or goods, the Civil Aeronautics Board is specifically directed by the act (sec. 1002 [*e*]) to take the following factors, among others, into consideration: (*a*) The effect of such rate upon the movement of traffic. (*b*) The need in the public interest of adequate and efficient transportation of persons and property by air carrier at the lowest cost consistent with the furnishing of such service. (*c*) Such standards respecting the character and quality of service to be rendered by air carriers as may be prescribed by or pursuant to law. (*d*) The inherent advantages of transportation by aircraft. (*e*) The need for each air carrier for revenue sufficient to enable such air carrier, under honest, economical, and efficient management, to provide adequate and efficient air carrier service.

pensation to the carrier in excess of the fully allocated costs of carrying the mail. This has been in effect a payment to the carrier for providing a service required in the interests of the postal service, the commerce, and the national defense made available before and beyond what the then commercial traffic would justify the carrier in supplying. In the early years of the industry, when operations were limited in scale, it was possible to establish mail rates that would make up the deficiency in commercial revenues and provide a fair return on the investment. For most of the carriers that day is past; commercial traffic has so far outstripped mail traffic and volume has so expanded that no politically possible mail rate would suffice to guarantee a fair return on the present scale of over-all operations.

3. Mail payments may offer a device to assure efficiency and economy in management. Under the law, a carrier is entitled to reasonable compensation only so far as its operations are soundly planned and economically managed. Costs under economical and efficient management constitute the yardstick by which reasonable rates are measured.

4. Mail rates may be so administered as to further the attainment and preservation of sound competitive conditions.

It should be recognized that the term "subsidy" in connection with mail rates has generally been used by those who discuss such payments to the airlines without any exact meaning and with connotations as various as the purposes of those employing the term. Many people hold that a "subsidy" to the airlines exists in fact only if they receive mail payments which support dishonest, uneconomical, or inefficient managements or which permit the carriers to earn excessive or exorbitant profits, and that in all other cases, some party other than the carrier is the beneficiary of any "subsidy" that is paid. In other words, if the carrier develops an essential service before the commercial traffic is sufficient to justify and support that service, it is thought that the payment of some of these costs is a "subsidy" to those who benefit or use the service.[3] Similarly, if the Post Office Depart-

[3] In May, 1950, Senator Edwin Johnson, then Chairman of the Senate Committee on Interstate and Foreign Commerce, proposed a system of separation of air mail pay from subsidy under which all pay above a compensatory rate to each carrier would be earmarked as subsidy. This subsidy, on the basis of an unrevealed formula, would be reallocated as subsidy to the communities to which uneconomical airline service was being furnished. Senator Johnson found that, for the fiscal year 1949, of the $47,431,070 mail pay to the sixteen domestic trunk airlines, $24,750,286 was compensatory pay and $22,680,784 subsidy. Of this subsidy, $17,973,369 was to communities being rendered uneconomical service and $4,707,415 was to the carriers. Of the $10,365,037 in mail pay to the

ment pays more for the carriage and handling of air mail than it receives from the sale of stamps used on such mail, it is held that the "subsidy" accrues to the users of the service rather than to the carriers. However, the difference between the receipts and the estimated costs of handling the air mail by the Post Office cannot be said to measure the proper cost of the air carriage of the mail, since the difference might be greater or less than the costs of air carriage. It might also reflect an unreasonable postage rate or something less than attainable efficiency in postal operations or a questionable allocation of postal costs that placed an undue burden of general overhead on the air mail revenues. Equally inappropriate is any attempt to measure "subsidy" by the difference between the rates paid for the carriage of mail and the rates charged for other classes of traffic. Mail is relatively costly traffic to handle, since schedules may have to be adapted to the needs of the postal service; mail requires special precautions in its handling; mail does not load and unload itself; and, despite unpredicted variations in volume, mail must move promptly.

Prior to the passage of the Civil Aeronautics Act of 1938, air mail rates were based on contracts between individual carriers and the Post Office Department, with payment according to formulas varying from time to time and from carrier to carrier. For example, the Air Mail Act of 1925, known as the Kelly Act, provided that air mail postage rates be not less than 10 cents per ounce or fraction thereof and that contracts for the transportation of air mail might be made at rates not in excess of four fifths of the revenues from air mail postage. It soon became obvious that the administration of the law would require the tabulation of the postage carried by all air mail letters and its allocation among contract routes, in order to determine the compensation of the respective carriers. The Postmaster General therefore recommended that the act be amended to provide for payments to the carriers at fixed rates per pound.

During the early years of air mail transportation, the Post Office Department generally took the position that adjustments should be

---

nine feeder airlines operating throughout the fiscal year of 1949, $1,221,996 was compensatory pay and $9,143,041 subsidy. Of the subsidy, $7,105,827 was to communities and $2,037,214 to the carriers. Airline executives, who have long supported the thesis that the airlines' "need" mail pay is largely a subsidy to small towns rather than to the airlines themselves, "applauded Johnson's recognition of who really benefits from the subsidy; but pointed out that breaking down subsidy on a community-by-community basis is a monumental—if not impossible—task for a Civil Aeronautics Board which is already far behind in its work." See *Aviation Week*, May 29, 1950, p. 54.

made in individual-contract mail rates to enable the carriers to meet the costs of transporting the mails and that aid, relatively small in amount and temporary in character, should be extended to cover the deficits on the passenger service, whether such service was rendered jointly with, or apart from, mail service. Such aid was to be confined to the major routes, with the idea of giving them the incentive to continue operations until the public became educated to travel by air.

In 1930 a mail-pay formula was set up by the Watres Act passed in that year.[4] It was intended to build a rate structure capable of application to any air mail route in the United States. Instead of the direct determination of rates for particular routes upon the basis of the cost experience on such routes, differences in load and in operating conditions were compensated for by so-called "variables." Bad terrain was held to justify extra compensation of 2 cents per mile, and frequent fog, 2.5 cents. Schedules requiring night flying were to be compensated for by the payment of an additional 15 cents per mile. Radio equipment and use of multiengine planes also called for special allowances. Recognition also was given to the number of passenger seats provided, although the amounts set up were relatively unimportant. The latter variables were less important as an aid to passenger service than the indirect aid which resulted from the fact that, under the formula, a large portion of the costs of flying the planes was to be met by mail payments, whether space was reserved for 200 or 2,000 pounds of mail. The mail-load variable did not increase in proportion to the amount of mail carried, 55 cents a mile being paid for carrying 200 pounds and 95 cents for carrying 2,000 pounds.

Under the original and revised Watres Act formulas,[5] the distinction which had previously existed between compensation for mail service and payments in aid of passenger service was abandoned in practice. Air mail carriers were expected to provide passenger service on flights previously scheduled only for mail, and the transporta-

---

[4] For the legislative history see *U.S. Daily*, January 15 and 16, 1930, Vol. IV, pp. 3127 and 3138, and Vol. V, p. 3154; (71st Cong., 2d sess.), *House Report No. 9500, Sen. Doc. No. 3578, House Report No. 11704;* "Amending Air Mail Act," *Hearings before House Committee on the Post Office and Post Roads* (71st Cong., 2d sess.) (February 19, 1930), pp. 1–60; (71st Cong., 2d sess.), *House Report Nos. 966 and 1209, Sen. Report No. 524; Congressional Record,* Vol. LXXII, pp. 7372–79, 7618; *Statutes at Large,* Vol. XLVI, pp. 259–60.

[5] The original Watres Act formula was placed in effect May 1, 1930. Other formulas went into effect on April 1, 1931, January 1, 1932, November 1, 1932, July 1, 1933, and September 1, 1933. See Francis A. Spencer, *Air Mail Payment and the Government* (Washington, D.C.: Brookings Institution, 1941).

tion of mail was authorized on flights previously devoted only to passenger transportation. The mail and passenger services, which had largely been separate activities prior to the Watres Act, were thus combined into a joint mail and passenger service. The separate determination of the cost of mail service as distinguished from the cost of the joint service became difficult and was not attempted by the Post Office Department.

Up to 1932, air mail contracts, like those for ocean mail, were frankly used to subsidize companies to which these contracts were awarded. With the change in the federal administration in 1932, both types of arrangement became subject to violent attack. The chief objection to the practices which had been followed by the Post Office Department before that time was that the department had not permitted competitive bidding, and it seems to have been a fact that the Post Office Department had awarded contracts to lines which might not have received them if competition in bidding had been entirely free. This had been done by discarding offers on the ground that bidders were not responsible, by inserting terms in proposed contracts which not all operators could meet, by granting extensions to existing routes instead of asking for public bids, and by encouraging conferences between operators before bids were submitted. There were also complaints that the prices which the government had agreed to pay for mail carriage were exorbitantly high. On the other hand, critics were unable to show that conditions which had been inserted in contracts were improper. The extension of existing routes had been authorized by the law of 1930 (Watres Act); and the conferences which occurred between operators, at least so far as they were suggested by the Postmaster General, appear to have been for legitimate purposes consonant with the public interest. And finally, while the sums specified in the contested contracts for the carriage of mails had admittedly exceeded the cost of the service rendered, mail contracts had always been regarded as subsidies; and some excess of price over cost was therefore to be expected.[6]

As mentioned in earlier chapters, all air mail contracts were canceled early in 1934; but the Air Mail Act of June 12, 1934, authorized the Postmaster General to award new contracts for the transpor-

---

[6] *Hearings before a Special Committee on Investigation of Air Mail and Ocean Mail Contracts, U.S. Senate* (73d Cong., 2d sess.) (1934), testimony Wadsworth, pp. 2341–49). See also discussion in S. Daggett, *Principles of Inland Transportation* (3d ed.; New York: Harper & Bros., 1941), chap. vi, and "United States Aviation and the Air Mail," *Fortune*, May, 1934.

tation of air mail between such points as he might designate and for initial periods of not exceeding three years to the lowest responsible bidder at fixed rates per plane-mile.[7] The Interstate Commerce Commission was directed to determine and fix the fair and reasonable rates of compensation for the transportation of air mail over each air mail route, and to prescribe the method or methods—by weight, space, or some other criterion—for ascertaining such rates of compensation. These rates were to be set so as to keep the aggregate cost of the transportation of air mail within the limits of the anticipated postal revenue therefrom. In arriving at this determination, the Commission was directed to disregard losses resulting, in its opinion, from the unprofitable maintenance of nonmail schedules in those cases where the Commission might find that the gross receipts from such schedules failed to meet the additional operating expenses occasioned thereby.[8]

By the Civil Aeronautics Act of 1938, the jurisdiction of the Interstate Commerce Commission over air mail rates was transferred to the Civil Aeronautics Authority (now the Civil Aeronautics Board). In making this transfer, the whole system of contracts was abandoned; and henceforth the airlines were to notify the Post Office Department by what schedules and between what points they proposed to operate with air mail. The Postmaster General might change these schedules, subject to appeal to the Civil Aeronautics Board; but otherwise they became effective. Once the schedules were established, the Post Office Department might then tender mail for transportation on any scheduled planes. The rates to be paid for the service were to be fixed by the Civil Aeronautics Board.

The provisions in the Civil Aeronautics Act[9] requiring that all

---

[7] The act placed a limitation on the base rate which could be fixed in any contract to not more than 33½ cents per plane-mile for transporting a mail load not exceeding 300 pounds. Payment was to be at the base rate fixed in the contract for the first 300 pounds or fraction thereof plus one tenth of such base rate for each additional 100 pounds of mail or fraction thereof, computed at the end of each calendar month on the basis of the average mail load carried per mile over the route. In no case was payment to exceed 40 cents per plane-mile.

[8] The Interstate Commerce Commission considered the question of compensation to contractors for air mail carriage in a decision handed down in 1935 (206 ICC 675). The rates fixed in this decision followed those set in the Air Mail Act of 1934, using the maximum of 33⅓ cents per pound where conditions were least favorable and cutting the maximum to as little as 24 cents when conditions permitted. The Commission felt burdened by the responsibilities placed upon it and welcomed the relief which occurred in 1938, when the Civil Aeronautics Authority was created and was given jurisdiction over air mail rates.

[9] The act provides that mail rates must be "fair and reasonable." But more important than this is the requirement that the Board consider the need for compensation sufficient

other revenues of the carriers be considered in fixing mail rates have caused the Board to approach the establishment of such rates on an individual airline basis, giving consideration to the over-all revenues of each carrier and fixing a single rate for all of that carrier's operations. The single rate for the entire operations of each carrier is calculated to minimize the cost of mail payment to the government, since the profits from more lucrative routes must be used to support those less profitable before any unprofitable routes are entitled to support from mail payments.[10] The Board, however, departed from this policy in the case of several airlines operating so-called "stub end" foreign routes.[11] The action of the Board in refusing to offset domestic earnings against international losses was protested by the Post Office Department, which took the case to the United States Court of Appeals.[12] The Court directed the Board to consider all income of an airline in determining air mail rates. In other words, if there were any profits from domestic operations, they would have to be used to offset losses from foreign operations. Actually only four airlines were affected by this decision. These were Braniff International Airways, Delta-C. & S.

---

to insure performance of such service and, together with all other revenue of the air carrier, to enable such carrier under honest, economical, and efficient management to maintain and continue the development of air transportation to the extent and of the character and quality required for the commerce of the United States, the postal service, and the national defense. The Board has held that ". . . the use of the mail payments is a statutory device for the accomplishment of national objectives that transcend the interests of the postal service. Those objectives . . . encompass the maintenance and continued development of air transportation to the extent and of the character and quality required for the commerce of the United States, the postal service, and the national defense. The 'compensation' which the carrier receives thus becomes compensation not only for carrying the mail but for the building up of a system of air transportation which will service the nation's commerce and security as well. . . ." (*Pan American Airways Co., Mail Rates,* 1 CAA 220 [1939]). See also *Western Air Lines, Inc., and Inland Air Lines, Inc. Mail Rates,* 11 CAB 300 (1950).

[10] An airline operates as a system, not as a singly controlled group of independent routes; and one of the primary reasons for the success of some operators has been their skill in welding the various routes into an integrated system. All airlines freely interchange their planes among their several routes. Schedules originating on one route frequently terminate on another. Operations, traffic, advertising, and sales departments function as units for the benefit of the whole system interdependent upon each other. Few, if any, of the activities or expenses of an airline, except those which are definitely localized by fixed ground facilities, can be considered as pertaining to any single route. Many of the expenses of operation and a minor part of revenues are of such nature and are received or incurred under such circumstances that it is impossible to assign them directly to the route involved. Approximately 48 per cent of the operating expenses of a typical well-managed airline must be divided and allocated to the various routes operated by it, by arbitrary process of division, because of the circumstances under which they are incurred.

[11] See, for example, *National Airlines, Inc.,* 15 CAB 558 (1952).

[12] *Summerfield* v. *Civil Aeronautics Board,* 347 U.S. 67 (1953).

Air Lines, Northwest Orient Airlines and Trans World Airlines, all of which are engaged in both domestic and international operations, heretofore classified by the Board as separate units for rate-making purposes. Pan American World Airways, the only United States–flag international operator without any domestic operations, was not affected. The most drastic result of the court decision would be the possible necessity of dropping international routes of all the combined domestic-international airlines. This would leave Pan American World Airways as the only international United States–flag operator.

Maximum operating efficiency by the airlines and the fullest development of air transportation is achieved by placing and retaining carriers on final mail rates, under which they either reap the benefits or stand the losses from future operations. Where those rates are class-service rates, as they are now for domestic operations, there is the additional advantage that airlines are forced to compete domestically with other carriers of their class in securing revenue and in reducing or controlling costs. Under these circumstances the air transportation system will benefit from fixing final rates for domestic divisions in advance of the international (where both are operated by one airline), rather than retaining the entire air carrier systems on a temporary or cost-plus basis during the lengthy period necessary for fixing a final system rate, or for simultaneous fixing of division rates. Moreover, even if the entire air carrier systems are used as the rate-making units, present domestic earnings will not support international operations, and it may be expected that the carriers will simply become subsidized on a system, rather than a division, basis. This would carry no long-range attendant benefits, and merely serve to destroy the benefits which have been flowing from the Board's classification and rate-making policies. In addition, domestic earnings would no longer be available for providing improved domestic services and for reducing domestic rates. Treating the entire airline system as the rate-making unit for those engaged in international operations would, moreover, discriminate between carriers, since those engaged in only domestic operations will be permitted to retain their profits, whereas those engaged in both types of operations will be required to use their domestic profits to support their losing international operations. Under these circumstances the airlines involved may attempt to withdraw from international operations, and the Board may find it necessary to approve such withdrawals. A reluctant operator can hardly be said to serve the best interests of the United States in the international field.[13]

The mail rates applied by the Civil Aeronautics Board have been arbitrarily classified by that body as "service" mail rates or "need" mail rates, depending upon whether the mail payment reflects only compensation for the service of mail transportation alone or contains additional amounts representing federal aid needed by the carrier to maintain and continue the development of air transportation.[14] This results in considerable differences between airlines in the amount of mail pay received per ton-mile of mail carried.

Service mail rates are applied to ton-miles or pound-miles of mail volume. Such a rate takes into account the fact that there are fixed costs in providing the minimum capacity requirements of the mail service as well as cost economies incident to increased density of mail traffic. To reflect fixed costs, a capacity factor equivalent to an average daily load of 500 pounds for a specified mileage may be used in computing minimum mail payments. To reflect economies incident to increased mail volume, a rate of, for example, 80 cents per ton-mile is applied to the volume equivalent to 400 pounds carried over one schedule per day and a lower rate of 70 cents per ton-mile for volume in excess of this amount.[15]

Need mail rates have generally been stated as an amount per plane-mile flown. Such plane-mile rates are made subject to an automatic adjustment provision which reduces the mail rate per plane-mile as the average daily designated mail mileage is increased over

---

[13] See "Court Ruling Seen as Threat to Flag Routes," *Aviation Week*, February 15, 1954.

[14] The "service" rate was at first computed by separating the cost of carrying the mail from other expenses and then fixing a rate, based on anticipated mileage, which would return this cost plus a reasonable return on the allocated investment necessary for the mail service. "Investment" is calculated on original, rather than reproduction, cost (*Eastern Air Lines*, 3 CAB 733 [1942]; *American Airlines*, 3 CAB 770 [1942]). Accurate apportionment of expenses and investment was difficult; and the Board later concluded that it would not be required, at least during the so-called "transitional" period (*Eastern Air Lines*, 6 CAB 551 [1945]). In a decision involving a "need" carrier in the feeder category, the Board fixed a sliding-scale rate geared to passenger loads in such a manner as to provide substantial incentive to the carrier to develop passenger business (*Pioneer Air Lines, Inc.*, 8 CAB 175 [1947]). In other cases, temporary increases in air mail rates have been permitted carriers on the basis of a system of assumed, or "false," mail loads, without changing the carriers' basic rate itself (*Western Airlines Mail Rates*, CAB Docket No. 1374 [1947]).

[15] See, for example, *Pennsylvania-Central Airlines Corp.*, 8 CAB 980 (1947); *Transcontinental and Western Air*, CAB Docket No. 2849 (1947); CAB Show Cause Orders, Serial Nos. E-1351, E-1352, E-1353, E-1354, E-1355 (March 29, 1948); *American Airlines*, 9 CAB 926 (1948); *United Air Lines*, 9 CAB 930 (1948); *Caribbean-Atlantic Airlines, Inc.*, 11 CAB 1074 (1949).

a specified base mileage. The effect of this formula is to provide approximately the same monthly amount of mail payments, notwithstanding increases in mail mileages flown. When the mileage operated decreases below the base mileage, however, mail payments are decreased correspondingly.

For local-service airlines, the Board has adopted various formulas in order to set the need rate on a sliding-scale incentive basis. One of these methods makes mail pay vary with the passenger load factor, the maximum mail rate being made effective when the minimum passenger load factor is realized and the mail rate declining as the passenger load factor increases, so prescribed that the rate allows a progressive increase in the profit earned. Another method makes mail pay vary with the number of round trips flown daily over each route segment of the particular airline, declining as the carrier becomes older and in all probability, more self-sufficient. The idea behind such formulas is to create a method in each case to meet the demonstrated "need" of the carrier but at the same time to operate in such a way as to reduce mail payments as the carrier further develops its nonmail traffic.[16]

The provision in the Civil Aeronautics Act that the Board must consider economy and efficiency of management in setting mail rates is important. It poses to the Board and to the carriers the necessity of determining the characteristics of economic and efficient management in air transportation. Thus far such efforts have not met with much success, however, even though in two cases the Board went to the length of denying extra subsidy in order that a carrier might switch from one type of aircraft to another.[17] This is probably because there are numerous difficulties in the way of determining economy and efficiency of management in the airline industry. In ordinary business, economy and efficiency can be gauged, in large part, by the amount, or at least the rate, of profit which individual companies make. While a yardstick is applicable to air transportation, the act clearly recognizes that the profit criterion cannot be used in the same

---

[16] See, for example, *Piedmont Aviation, Inc.*, 11 CAB 1054 (1949); *Midwest Airlines, Inc.*, 11 CAB 1047 (1949); *Turner Airlines, Inc.*, 11 CAB 1078 (1950); *Central Airlines, Inc.*, 11 CAB 1048 (1949).

[17] In both cases the local-service airlines concerned were refused permission to switch from DC-3's to Martin 2-0-2's on the grounds that underwriting the cost of this experiment would not assist in introducing into service a new aircraft type or an aircraft primarily suited to local air service, and that the need for subsidy would be unduly increased. See *Pioneer Air Lines, Inc., Mail Rate*, 17 CAB 499 (1953); *Southwest Airways Co., Mail Rates*, 17 CAB 301 (1953).

sense that it is used elsewhere in business. In fact, the act authorizes the Board to set different mail rates for different air carriers or classes of air carriers. It need scarcely be pointed out that air routes vary widely in such characteristics as traffic density, length of haul, operational difficulties, and many other factors. The airline manager, unlike the average businessman, is not free to make changes in service or routes at will and frequently must continue to give at least minimum service even though such service is unprofitable to him.

There have been at least two basic defects in the system of air mail and subsidy payment as it has developed: (*a*) As the act was administered, air transportation became essentially a "cost plus" operation for a high proportion of the industry. Such a development was not contemplated when the Civil Aeronautics Act was passed by Congress. (*b*) There were no standards which provided for the payment of identical compensation for rendering identical service.

It was the intent of Congress, when it provided the "need" section of the Civil Aeronautics Act,[18] that the Civil Aeronautics Board should be equipped and empowered to "aid" the air carriers, if and when facts and circumstances justified such action in the national interest. There is no language in the act and no clear statement of congressional intent which would "guarantee" the solvency and the continued operation of individual air carriers. There is, therefore, no justification in the act for a policy of "cost plus" operation. The lack of standards other than an airline's "need" for payment in the transportation of mail represented a discouraging situation to the efficient operator between 1938 and 1953. One company transported mail between two terminal points, using modern equipment and adequate schedules. Another company operated along the same route, serving the same terminal points, but providing a mail service of substantially less utility than the first. But the second of the operators received two to ten times as much as the first operator for transporting a pound or ton of mail between the two identical points. Furthermore, if the first operator found a way of reducing his cost, he was likely to have his rate reduced. He might, at the same time, find the rate of his competitor increased by reason of greater "need" for additional mail compensation. It is difficult to conceive of a system doing more to discourage incentive and a high degree of managerial ability. Often, rather than offering an incentive to do their best, such a system of mail payment offered the airlines a reward for lack of results. Civil

---

[18] Civil Aeronautics Act and Federal Aviation Act, sec. 406(*b*).

Aeronautics Board action to overcome this situation is discussed later in this chapter.

To obtain mail pay, an airline first petitions the Board for some specified amount. Such petitions set forth estimates of operating revenues and expenses, and the carrier's reported operating results. These figures are analyzed for an annual period to determine the carrier's "need." At this point, the carrier's petition may be set down for formal hearing before an examiner of the Board. This process requires that the carrier supply exhibits and data to support his position, and involves procedural steps of an Examiner's Report and a final decision by the Board. Another, and usually accepted procedure, is to have informal conferences between airline representatives and members of the Board's staff to determine the amount of mail pay required for the individual operation. This latter procedure is usually more expeditious because of its informality.

The total amount of mail pay determined for a particular carrier is generally based on a compromise between the estimates of the airline and the estimates of the Board staff, after a review of the factors and information produced in the informal conference or at the hearing. The carrier may appeal to the Board if it does not agree with the staff recommendations, but where the informal procedure has been used, such appeals are rare because of the time and expense involved.

When a new carrier, such as a local-service airline, begins operations, it is granted temporary mail pay to provide it with some subsidy and service income, pending the accumulation of operating experience sufficient to determine a final total mail pay rate. The temporary rates do not allow for profit. Such rates theoretically are supposed to cover the carrier's operating costs, but so many items of expense are usually disallowed or deferred for future consideration that the carriers operating on temporary rates are almost certain to take a loss. Company directors frequently must make expenditures which they regard as essential, in spite of knowing they may be disallowed. Prior to determination of a final rate, the temporary rate is subject to adjustments.

A final rate supersedes a temporary rate and includes provision for taxes and profits. It is set when an airline's operations have stabilized sufficiently that its commercial revenues and total expenses may be projected and thus, its mail pay need determined. Because of the backlog of cases before the Board, and the great length of time involved in setting a final mail rate, such rates usually include a "past" period of operations (which really amounts to a retroactive increase in mail pay) as well as a rate for a "future" period, which may be higher or lower than the past period rate. Once a final rate is set, there are no retroactive readjustments. A final rate remains in effect until the carrier petitions for an increase, or until the Board itself issues a "show cause order" asking for evidence why the rate should not be reduced. In either case, the final rate automatically reverts into temporary status. If airlines are going through a period of expansion, as they have in recent years, and therefore cannot predict revenues and costs with reasonable accuracy, they take the safest course by petitioning for a new mail rate as soon as a final rate is set, thus avoiding substantial elements of risk.[19]

A final mail rate, in combination with all other operating income, is generally intended to yield the carrier from 7 to 8 per cent return on its investment, after taxes. This is really more a target rather than a guarantee, even to the carriers whose honesty, economy, and efficiency have not been questioned. As a practical matter, an airline seldom, if ever, earns anything like that figure. In special cases, such as those in which a carrier's capital was exceptionally small or had been wiped out by losses, the Board has occasionally awarded a carrier a specified profit per mile flown, since a return based on the amount of invested capital would clearly have provided inadequate compensation for services rendered.

The Service Mail Rate

All the methods devised prior to 1951 for the payment of air mail compensation had one important defect. None provided for a separation of those amounts paid out for the service of carrying the mail and those paid out as subsidy to the carriers. Nothing in the Civil Aeronautics Act of 1938 changed this situation. The Board was primarily concerned in the immediate prewar years with determining fair and reasonable mail compensation for the carriers and with adjudicating new route cases. During the war itself, the situation was so completely abnormal that the Board did not attempt to establish a mail rate formula that would provide a measure of division between service rates and subsidy rates.

Following the end of World War II, however, the Board became

[19] In the case of final rates, the Board's cost allowances, while more liberal than in the case of temporary rates, are sometimes arbitrary and often unpredictable. An example of the former is the practice of not recognizing as a proper expense executive salaries in excess of $15,000, which figure was recently increased from $12,000. Another is the Board's "rule of thumb" that working capital in excess of three months' cash requirements is excessive and therefore not entitled to a return.

keenly aware of the need to separate service payments and subsidy payments from the whole mail payment. Various formulas for determining the subsidy separation cropped up all over the air transport industry. In the meantime, Congress had instituted a preliminary study, by a private management consulting firm, to prepare for legislation effecting a separation of service and subsidy payment in mail to the carriers.[20]

At the same time, the Board had been proceeding with a long-pending mail rate case, involving the Big Four airlines,[21] which it had initiated on February 21, 1949, hoping to establish a rate that would contain no element of subsidy. After lengthy meetings and discussions between the staffs of the various carriers and the Board, general conclusions were reached, and on August 7, 1951, the Board announced a mail payment rate for the Big Four of 45 cents per ton-mile, beginning January 1, 1951, and projected into the future. Each of the Big Four had been receiving higher mail compensation on a temporary basis, pending this final determination. The Board's decision, therefore, resulted in the Big Four carriers repaying the United States government about $5 million. The Board held the 45 cent rate to be strictly a "service" rate and entirely free of any subsidy to these carriers.[22]

During the course of the Board's study of what should be paid as a service rate, there were some who urged that little or no attempt should be made to arrive at the *cost* of mail service and that the rate should be set on the *value* of the service. This alternative had been frequently suggested in other rate cases, particularly before the Interstate Commerce Commission, as a way of avoiding the inaccuracies and uncertainties of arriving at the cost of services common to various types of traffic. The Board however stated:

> We are not aware that this method offers greater accuracy and certainty. We rather feel as did the Interstate Commerce Commission on the occasion when it said that: ". . . As between the two cardinal principles of rate making—the cost of service and the value of the service—the first is decidedly more capable of exact determination and mathematical expression than the latter. If, as some would have us believe, no measure has yet been discovered

---

[20] This study was made by the accounting firm of Ernst and Ernst. See *Hearings on Departments of Commerce, etc. Appropriations for 1951, Subcommittee of the Senate Committee on Appropriations* (81st Cong., 2d sess.) ; Edwin C. Johnson, "Proposed Senate Action on Air Mail Subsidies," *Journal of Air Law and Commerce*, Summer, 1950.

[21] American Airlines, Inc.; Eastern Air Lines, Inc.; Trans World Airlines, Inc.; United Air Lines, Inc.

[22] *American Airlines, Inc., et al., Mail Rates,* 14 CAB 558.

for ascertaining the cost of the service, what measure is there suggesting anything definite and tangible and sufficiently practical in its application to carry conviction which can be applied to the value of the service?"[23]

The Board realized, of course, that the value-of-service concept has been employed in various degrees in fixing some commercial rates. Such products as coal and gravel are regarded as moving at railway rates below fully allocatable costs. (It should be pointed out in this connection, however, that the recent development of more refined accounting methods, together with comprehensive gathering of specific data, have substantially narrowed what was once considered large bodies of "fixed" costs in certain common-product industries, with the result that the value-of-service concept has been employed less and less, at least in the sense of "what the traffic will bear.") The inappropriateness of applying the value-of-service concept to air mail rates primarily stems from the fact that the government is the only purchaser of the mail service, and its ability to buy is limited only by its policies and financial resources. Under these circumstances application of the value-of-service concept might result in mail rates high enough to give the carriers whatever amounts are needed to enable them to perform the service, including amounts to cover losses on passenger and freight services, and render futile all effort to separate subsidy from mail payments. Nor do the rates charged by the Post Office Department for air mail provide an independent test of the value of the mail service, since they are determined by Congress as part of a broad policy which gives effect to considerations of well-being different from the objectives and tests of sound commercial practice. Furthermore, the Post Office—as the contractor for, and seller of, mail service—has costs of its own and performs classes of service other than air mail. It is entitled to apportion its costs and profits in the light of its own aims and policies, as defined for it by Congress.

Accordingly, the future service rate for the period on and after January 1, 1951, was based upon the cost of mail transportation of the Big Four carriers for the year 1950, with due consideration being given to major factors likely to influence the trend in mail cost. This cost and the proper service mail rate were, moreover, based on the cost of transporting the mail in the regular combination service (that is, in aircraft carrying first-class passengers, express, freight, and mail).

---

[23] *Boileau* v. *P. & L. E. R. R. Co.*, XXII I.C.C. Rep., 652 (1911–12).

The Board held that the Big Four constituted a homogeneous group for rate-making purposes and that, accordingly, it was appropriate to establish a group rate for them. The desirability of a uniform service mail rate had been clearly set forth by the Board in a previous mail rate case in which it stated the following:[24]

> Moreover, it is not our intention, nor do we believe it would be in the public interest, to fix the service mail rate on a cost-plus basis by extending to all carriers a uniform or fixed rate of profit on the required investment irrespective of the level of the operating costs. Except for cost differences which are inherent in the type or character of service or in the area served and where therefore are applicable alike to all carriers of comparable size, there would appear to be little justification for variations in the service mail rate because of differences in carrier operating costs. The "service" as opposed to the "need" mail rate is not designed to meet the financial need of the individual carrier but rather it is intended to be fair and reasonable in terms of both the quality of the service and the reasonable and necessary costs under conditions of economical and efficient management. Also, a uniform service mail rate provides added incentive for increased operating efficiency by competitive performance as measured by the relation of its costs to the costs of other carriers rather than upon an allowable rate of return on the investment of each individual carrier.

In the latter part of November, 1953, the Post Office Department indicated it felt that in some instances it was paying a premium for air mail transportation service via one carrier when similar service was obtainable by another carrier at lower costs. This situation arose particularly between those points served by the airlines on a 45 cent per ton-mile mail rate and those receiving 53 cents per ton-mile, both on a service rate basis. Different air transportation charges also were assessed between the same cities because of differences in mileage. The Post Office Department determined to establish a policy that, when air mail service would not be impaired, it would use the carrier assessing the lowest air transportation charges authorized by the Civil Aeronautics Board for air mail transportation. The affected carriers[25] accordingly petitioned the Board[26] for a reduction in rate as between the pairs of cities served by them and by a member or members of the Big Four to whom the lower mail ton-mile rate was applicable. The Board permitted the adjustment asked for in order to prevent the pos-

---

[24] *American Airlines, Inc., Mail Rates,* 6 CAB 567, 571 (1945).

[25] Capital Airlines, National Airlines, and Western Air Lines over their entire systems; Braniff Airways, Delta Air Lines and Northwest Airlines over their routes within the Continental United States.

[26] CAB Docket Nos. 6462, 6465, 6474, 6475, 6473, 6466 (1953).

sible diversion of important mail revenue from Braniff, Capital, Delta, and Western.[27]

On September 30, 1954, the Civil Aeronautics Board proposed a new formula, retroactive to April 1, 1954, for setting service mail rate payments for the 13 domestic trunk airlines. The objective was to develop a service mail rate structure which would produce a uniform rate for all air carriers serving any given pair of communities and thus overcome the defects of the system discussed above.[28] The new formula would utilize a so-called standard mileage basis on which to compute mail ton-miles. These standard mileages would be predicated on the shortest mileage flown in scheduled service by the short-line carrier between each pair of points. It was further proposed that the new service mail rate for each of the thirteen domestic carriers to be a two-part rate consisting of a line-haul charge of 30.17 cents per mail ton-mile and a terminal charge per pound of mail enplaned, varying according to the class of station involved. The line-haul charge would be applied to the mail ton-miles transported, computed on the basis of standard mileages. The terminal charge, which is the rate applicable at the originating station, would be applied to the pounds of mail enplaned at each station as follows:

Class of Station	*Charge per Pound*	*Station Classification Based on Total Revenue Tons or All Traffic Enplaned per Year*
A	3.32¢	7,000 and over
B	6.64	750–6,999
C	9.96	60–749
D	33.21	59 or less

This uniform two-part, or multielement rate, which produces like payment for like services, results in an average yield of 37.63¢ per mail ton-mile for the thirteen trunklines. Subsequently, the Board applied a similar multielement rate to the local-service carriers resulting in an average ton-mile rate of 93.91¢ per mail ton-mile.

Separating Mail Pay from Subsidy

Early in 1949, John F. Kennedy, a representative in Congress from Massachusetts, introduced a bill[29] providing for the separation of subsidy from air mail pay. Other similar bills were introduced in the

[27] CAB Order No. E-8146, March 2, 1954, Docket Nos. 6462, 6474, 6475, 6473.

[28] *American Airlines, Inc., et al., Domestic Trunklines, Service Mail Rates,* 21 CAB 8 (1955).

[29] House Resolution 2908, February 21, 1949.

Senate and the House, and extensive hearings were held.[30] A separation of subsidy payments from payments for carrying air mail was felt to be a pressing need. The first, and perhaps most fundamental, objective of such a separation would be to obtain some measurement of the commercial self-sufficiency in the air transportation system and of the various component parts of the system or, conversely, to obtain a reasonably accurate judgment of the amount and location of necessary government support for airline operations. Such a gauge seemed necessary in order that taxpayers might appraise the public cost of the air transportation system; in order that the airline industry might know which segments and services were not yet self-sufficient and better assess the progress these were making toward self-sufficiency; and in order that the Civil Aeronautics Board might appraise the commercial results so far achieved (as well as those they might fairly expect to be achieved) and determine whether certain marginal carriers should or should not be continued in operation.

The second fundamental objective of separation was to attain a more rational system of government accounting. The Post Office Department had for some years taken the position that it should not bear the full cost of developing air transportation. So long as subsidy was blanketed into the Post Office accounts and appropriations, neither the Department nor any other branch of the government, either legislative or executive, was able to distinguish the amounts which were properly chargeable to the mail service from amounts properly chargeable to other purposes, including the promotion of commerce and the national defense. Furthermore, the inability to measure airline subsidy, inherent in the system of payment which had so far been used, made it impossible for the government to measure the total cost of supporting aviation development.

The first subsidy separation bill proposed two things. Any subsidy which was included in payments to the airlines for transporting mail was to be stated separately so that the amount of the subsidy would be known. Second, responsibility for paying the subsidy, and securing the appropriations for it from Congress, was to be transferred from

---

30 "Air-Mail Subsidies," *Hearings before a Subcommittee of the Committee on Interstate and Foreign Commerce, House of Representatives* (81st Cong., 2d sess.) (1950); "Separation of Air Mail Pay from Subsidy," *Hearings before the Committee on Interstate and Foreign Commerce, United States Senate* (82d Cong., 1st sess.) (1951); "Air Mail Subsidies," *Hearings before the Committee on Interstate and Foreign Commerce, House of Representatives* (82d Cong., 2d sess.) (1952); "Reorganization Plan No. 10 of 1953," *Hearing before a Special Committee of the Committee on Government Operations, House of Representatives* (83d Cong., 1st sess.) (1953).

the Post Office Department to the Civil Aeronautics Board. Soon after the original bill was introduced, however, various conditions and riders were added to the proposal and other bills were introduced so that it was not long before the basic proposal, which had been generally favored, was virtually buried under an accumulation of complicated and controversial provisions, none of them essential, and many only remotely related to subsidy separation. Controversy over the fringe provisions delayed and eventually defeated efforts to enact subsidy separation legislation in 1950, 1951, and 1952.

The next step was taken on June 1, 1953, when President Dwight D. Eisenhower submitted Reorganization Plan No. 10 of 1953 to Congress under the provisions of the Reorganization Act of 1949, as amended.[31] The plan went back to the fundamental problem and provided for the separate payment of airline subsidies, in order to place responsibility for such payment in the agency which determines them, the Civil Aeronautics Board, and to enable Congress and the President to maintain effective review of the subsidy program. Reorganization Plan No. 10 was adopted by Congress and became effective October 1, 1953. It transferred from the Postmaster General to the Civil Aeronautics Board responsibility for that portion of air mail payment related to subsidy assistance.

The plan for air mail payment now in effect does not alter the basic national policy of promoting the sound development of air transportation through federal aid. Nor does it, of itself, change the total amount of revenue for which any airline is eligible. It recognizes, too, that continued subsidy support will be necessary for some time if certain segments of the industry are to achieve the full measure of growth required by the public interest. In accordance with existing policy standards of the Civil Aeronautics Act of 1938, the Civil Aeronautics Board continues to determine the over-all level of payments to be made to the airlines for carrying mail, but the Post Office Department is responsible for paying only that portion which compensates for carrying the mail on the basis of fair and reasonable rates, determined by the Board without regard to the need for federal aid. The Board itself is responsible for paying any amounts in excess of such compensation, this excess being the subsidy element of the total federal payment.

Pursuant to Reorganization Plan No. 10, the Board in September, 1953, issued an order establishing the service mail rates to be paid

[31] House Resolution 264, H. Doc. 160, 83d Cong., 1st sess.

by the Postmaster General to all certificated air mail carriers, effective October 1, 1953.[32] This order represented the first formal separation of the compensatory and subsidy components in the mail rates for all of the certificated air mail carriers. In addition, in September, 1953, the Board released the annual revision of its "administrative report," separating service mail pay from subsidy and reflecting all final mail rates established by the Board since the release of its first report on the subject.[33] It may be considered as typical of all such reports and is used in this chapter for illustrative purposes. This report contained estimates for fiscal years 1954–55 and actual data for 1951–53 and is summarized in Table 26.

In approaching the problem of administrative separation, it was necessary for the Board to determine a sound basis for determining rates to be paid the various air carriers for their service in carrying the mail. A service rate, as has been explained before, is one which compensates the air carriers for carrying the mail, reimbursing them for the related costs, including a fair return on the investment which is used in the mail service.

As previously noted, the Civil Aeronautics Board in 1951 established a service rate of 45 cents per mail ton-mile for the Big Four (American, Eastern, TWA, and United), based upon a detailed study of the costs of the mail service. This was the first service rate established by the Board during the postwar period and is the only service rate which has been fixed as the result of a comprehensive cost study.

In order to develop the service mail rates for the other domestic air carriers, it was necessary to adopt one of two courses of action: (*a*) to determine such rates on the basis of a detailed costing of the mail service for each carrier, or (*b*) to determine such rates by the use of an over-all statistical approach, without costing the mail service for each carrier.

The Board concluded that the statistical approach would permit the expeditious completion of a satisfactory study for administrative separation of mail pay. The detailed costing of the mail service for each carrier, on the other hand, would have required a large staff and an extended period of time.

Study over a period of years has shown that the unit costs of an air carrier respond directly to the following primary operating fac-

[32] CAB Order No. E-7721. The 1955 budget estimate for the Civil Aeronautics Board totaled $76,777,000, of which $3,777,000 was for expenses of the Board and the balance of $73,000,000 for subsidy payments.

[33] The CAB has issued administrative separation studies annually since 1951.

tors: (*a*) length of traffic haul and average distance between stops; (*b*) density of traffic; and (*c*) volume of operations.[34] The Board determined, after extensive analysis, that revenue ton-miles per station was the most representative single measure which would reflect the combined impact of these operating factors on attainable cost levels. Revenue ton-miles per station were obtained for each carrier by dividing the revenue ton-miles flown during the fiscal year 1951 by the average number of stations served during this period. While there are other measures which may reflect particular operating characteristics with varying degrees of accuracy, the studies of the Board's staff have indicated that revenue ton-miles per station is the best available composite measure. It does not necessarily follow, however, that air carriers transporting the same ton-miles per station will have identical operating costs in any given year, since costs are affected directly by such factors as management efficiency, types of aircraft utilized, and various short-run factors, such as adverse weather, strikes, accidents, and groundings. Since the preponderance of air carrier costs is common to all classes of traffic, the cost of carrying the mail will tend to parallel the cost of all traffic combined.

The Board rejected the individual carrier approach in favor of carrier groups, because such grouping permits the averaging of costs and thus tends to minimize deviations between the reported costs of the carriers. In addition, the establishment of groups is desirable from the standpoint of simple presentation. Accordingly, ten airline groups were set up, as shown in Tables 18 and 19.

It is expected that the level of subsidy support for international operations of United States air carriers will tend to increase over the next several years, for the following reasons: (*a*) The competition of foreign-flag air carriers is constantly increasing[35] and the need to meet growing competition requires the United States international carriers to replace their existing aircraft with those having the latest technological improvements. (*b*) Although there has been an increase in the total international operations of all United States–flag airlines, this increase has been accompanied generally by a proportionate increase in operating costs. This differs from the domestic air carrier industry,

---

[34] For example, an air carrier which is required to stop every 50 miles to pick up ten pounds of mail and express and three passengers will have a much higher unit cost than an air carrier which stops every 300 miles and, at each such stop, picks up 150 pounds of mail and express and ten passengers.

[35] For example, in the calendar years 1949–51, the percentage of total North Atlantic area passengers carried by United States–flag airlines was: 1949, 67.6 per cent; 1950, 62.8 per cent; 1951, 57.4 per cent.

where the increase in operating volume has been accompanied generally by a decline in unit operating costs. (*c*) The national interests of the United States, including both the foreign commerce and national defense, result in the operation of some foreign routes for other than purely economic considerations. The aircraft and crews of the international carriers play a prominent part in current defense planning.

Alaska is a major beneficiary of the subsidy program[36] and will continue to need increasing funds, because of the impact of inflation and the necessity for modernizing equipment and facilities. Without this subsidy air transportation, in some areas the only means of transport within the state, would virtually cease.

As with the domestic airlines, the Board believed that the most reasonable means of separating service mail pay from subsidy for the international lines was to base this separation upon the cost of carrying the mail, including a fair return on the investment which is used in the mail service. The Board further believed that the techniques of separation should be basically the same for both international and domestic air carriers, and that there was no sound principle for differentiating between them. It was recognized that carriers engaged in international air transportation are faced with many unusual problems not confronting domestic carriers, but the combined impact of these unusual problems is reflected in the international carriers' operating costs. The steps followed in establishing the service rates for international air carriers were:

1. The carriers were grouped by geographic areas to allow for variations in political-economic conditions and operational differences.
2. The so-called "stub end"[37] operations of domestic carriers were treated as extensions of the domestic system and, therefore, were assigned the same service rate as those systems.
3. Within geographic areas, carriers (except the intra-Alaskan carriers) were grouped on the basis of revenue ton-miles per station, following the same principles applied to the domestic airlines.
4. Due to the prevalence of flag-stop and "bush" operations, stations other than a few major points could not be clearly defined for intra-Alaskan carriers, and consequently these carriers were grouped by total revenue ton-miles rather than revenue ton-miles per station.
5. The cost per revenue ton-mile for each carrier was determined from its

[36] In 1960, for example, air carriers operating within Alaska and between other states and Alaska required subsidy support in excess of $8 million.

[37] The "stub ends" are the operations of American Airlines to Mexico; Colonial Airlines to Bermuda; Eastern Air Lines to Puerto Rico; National Airlines to Cuba; and United Air Lines to Hawaii. Trans-border operations terminating in Canada were included in the domestic subsidy separation study.

TABLE 18

COMPARATIVE SUMMARY OF MAIL TON-MILES, SERVICE MAIL PAY, AND SUBSIDY ESTIMATES

Fiscal Years 1951–61 (In Thousands)

Name of Carrier	1951	1952	1953	1954
Mail Ton-Miles				
Domestic trunks 1/	54,066	67,804	68,945	76,577
Local service 1/	665	833	919	1,044
Helicopters	70	69	99	125
Mail-Cargo carriers 1/	-	-	-	-
States-Alaska 1/	456	763	1,093	1,358
Intra-Alaska	817	991	1,161	1,148
Hawaiian 1/	50	49	54	57
Transatlantic	9,001	10,100	10,324	13,571
Transpacific	8,336	6,691	6,854	8,994
Latin American	3,926	4,808	4,961	5,385
Total	77,387	92,108	94,410	108,259
Service Mail Pay				
Domestic trunks 1/	$ 25,432	$ 31,769	$ 32,307	$ 32,446
Local service 1/	1,151	1,139	1,136	1,242
Helicopters	907	891	1,814	323
Mail-Cargo carriers 1/	-	-	-	-
States-Alaska 1/	214	359	515	667
Intra-Alaska	1,226	1,489	1,728	1,593
Hawaiian 1/	41	39	44	46
Transatlantic	7,651	8,585	8,776	10,313
Transpacific	5,594	4,490	4,438	5,055
Latin American	2,436	3,013	3,121	3,078
Total	$ 44,652	$ 51,774	$ 53,879	$ 54,763
Subsidy				
Domestic trunks	$ 17,612	$ 6,411	$ 3,527	$ 3,880
Local service	17,310	18,990	21,850	24,299
Helicopters	-	-	-	2,574
Mail-Cargo carriers	-	-	-	-
States-Alaska	792	2,075	3,226	3,561
Intra-Alaska	2,484	3,356	4,639	4,742
Hawaiian	48	715	871	689
Transatlantic	10,382	5,837	4,182	1,625
Tranpacific	10,776	11,641	12,173	6,803
Latin American	9,272	13,516	16,349	15,827
Total	$ 68,676	$ 62,541	$ 66,817	$ 64,000
Total Service Mail Pay and Subsidy				
Domestic trunks	$ 43,044	$ 38,180	$ 35,834	$ 36,326
Local service	18,461	20,129	22,986	25,541
Helicopters	907	891	1,814	2,897
Mail-Cargo carriers	-	-	-	-
States-Alaska	1,006	2,434	3,741	4,228
Intra-Alaska	3,710	4,845	6,367	6,335
Hawaiian	89	754	915	735
Transatlantic	18,033	14,422	12,958	11,938
Transpacific	16,370	16,131	16,611	11,858
Latin American	11,708	16,529	19,470	18,905
Total	$113,328	$114,315	$120,696	$118,763

1 Includes nonpriority mail.

2 Reflects final system rate for Pan American effective January 1, 1955. Although all divisions of the company were affected, only in the Pacific Division a negative amount of subsidy resulted.

3 Includes the $2,500,000 additional subsidy estimated for the local service group of carriers.

Source: CAB, *Service Mail Pay and Subsidy for United States Certificated Air Carriers* (Washington, D.C., 1960).

	1955	1956	1957	1958	1959	1960	1961
	83,053	87,292	94,554	99,666	109,303	115,879	126,578
	1,345	1,482	1,545	1,522	1,884	2,190	2,573
	107	91	93	88	84	87	91
	-	835	1,913	1,295	873	987	1,131
	1,300	1,374	1,583	1,607	1,842	2,117	2,636
	1,199	1,303	1,394	1,582	1,917	2,286	2,855
	57	62	67	66	73	77	85
	16,829	21,106	23,093	24,876	32,189	33,609	35,289
	22,018	25,666	24,850	26,988	35,376	36,731	39,510
	5,628	6,082	6,726	7,107	7,341	6,954	7,290
	131,536	145,293	155,818	164,797	190,882	200,917	218,038
	$ 29,655	$ 30,880	$ 32,767	$ 34,447	$ 38,149	$ 41,442	$ 45,402
	1,372	1,149	1,249	1,258	1,505	1,779	2,116
	277	235	240	226	217	224	234
	-	184	497	367	289	319	374
	630	635	710	755	847	988	1,235
	1,721	1,957	2,085	2,161	2,457	2,959	3,696
	46	50	52	53	58	62	69
	9,220	11,414	12,371	13,291	17,123	18,074	18,985
	10,733	11,582	11,721	12,238	16,133	17,088	18,341
	2,797	2,960	3,310	3,468	3,547	3,487	3,656
	$ 56,451	$ 61,046	$ 65,002	$ 68,264	$ 80,325	$ 86,422	$ 94,108
	$ 3,054	$ 1,857	$ 1,586	$ 2,282	$ 1,201	-	-
	22,570	24,442	28,777	33,246	37,493	$ 49,571	$ 56,534 3/
	2,656	2,735	3,770	4,419	4,860	4,859	4,760
	-	-	-	-	-	-	-
	3,593	4,232	2,871	2,377	2,717	2,584	2,382
	4,311	3,389	3,607	4,418	5,131	6,138	5,575
	293	290	216	115	387	-	-
	232	488	437	-	-	-	-
	-1,065 2/	351	262	-	-	-	-
	9,066	5,799	2,542	27	-	-	-
	$ 44,710	$ 43,583	$ 44,068	$ 46,884	$ 51,789	$ 63,152	$ 69,251 3/
	$ 32,709	$ 32,737	$ 34,353	$ 36,729	$ 39,350	$ 41,442	$ 45,402
	23,942	25,591	30,026	34,504	38,998	51,350	58,650 3/
	2,933	2,970	4,010	4,645	5,077	5,083	4,994
	-	184	497	367	289	319	374
	4,223	4,867	3,581	3,132	3,564	3,572	3,617
	6,032	5,346	5,692	6,579	7,588	9,097	9,271
	339	340	268	168	445	62	69
	9,452	11,902	12,808	13,291	17,123	18,074	18,985
	9,668	11,933	11,983	12,238	16,133	17,088	18,341
	11,863	8,759	5,852	3,495	3,547	3,487	3,656
	$101,161	$104,629	$109,070	$115,148	$132,114	$149,574	$163,359 3/

TABLE 19

Estimated Subsidy Accruing—By Carrier
Fiscal Years 1954–61 (In Thousands)

Name of Carrier	1954	1955	1956	1957	1958	1959	1960	1961
DOMESTIC TRUNKLINES								
American	-	-	-	-	-	-	-	-
Braniff	$ 733	$ 674	-	-	-	-	-	-
Capital	-	-	-	-	-	-	-	-
Colonial	518	409	$ 368		Merged with Eastern June 1, 1956			
Continental	761	187	-	-	-	-	-	-
Delta	-	-	-	-	-	-	-	-
Eastern	-	-	-	-	-	-	-	-
National	-	-	-	-	-	-	-	-
Northeast	1,868	1,784	1,489	$ 1,586	$ 2,282	$ 1,201	-	-
Northwest	-	-	-	-	-	-	-	-
Trans World	-	-	-	-	-	-	-	-
United	-	-	-	-	-	-	-	-
Western	-	-	-	-	-	-	-	-
Total	$ 3,880	$ 3,054	$ 1,857	$ 1,586	$ 2,282	$ 1,201	-	-
LOCAL SERVICE CARRIERS								
Allegheny	$ 1,718	$ 1,854	$ 2,300	$ 2,632	$ 3,278	$ 3,424	$ 3,826	$ 4,392
Bonanza	922	815	1,182	1,179	1,933	2,308	3,451	3,693
Central	1,709	1,919	2,191	2,380	2,705	2,798	3,193	3,072
Frontier	2,780	2,555	2,478	2,533	2,636	4,053	6,752	7,176
Lake Central	1,507	1,422	1,361	1,493	1,889	1,548	1,728	1,813
Mohawk	1,021	675	1,138	1,966	2,803	1,980	2,237	2,815
North Central	2,294	1,770	1,375	2,101	3,327	4,501	7,018	7,307
Ozark	1,882	1,734	2,248	2,712	2,623	2,672	3,455	3,675
Pacific (Southwest)	1,102	975	1,340	2,061	2,147	2,315	2,793	3,162
Piedmont	2,011	1,848	1,676	2,482	2,476	3,068	4,612	4,788
Continental (Pioneer)	1,295	1,234	1,154	405	Consolidated with trunkline			
Southern	1,901	1,706	1,721	2,024	2,188	2,342	3,222	4,146
Trans-Texas	2,636	2,468	2,471	2,881	2,954	2,939	2,995	3,317
West Coast	1,498	1,595	1,807	1,928	2,287	3,545	4,289	4,678
Wiggins	23	-	-	-	-	-	-	-
Unallocated-new routes	-	-	-	-	-	-	-	2,500
Total	$24,299	$22,570	$24,442	$28,777	$33,246	$37,493	$49,571	$56,534 2,

HELICOPTERS								
Chicago	$ 432	$ 424	$ 445	$ 909	$ 1,425	$ 1,644	$ 1,749	$ 1,747
Los Angeles	684	816	848	941	942	935	930	925
New York	1,458	1,416	1,442	1,920	2,052	2,281	2,180	2,088
Total	$ 2,574	$ 2,656	$ 2,735	$ 3,770	$ 4,419	$ 4,860	$ 4,859	$ 4,760
MAIL-CARGO CARRIERS								
Aaxico	-	-	-	-	-	-	-	-
Flying Tiger	-	-	-	-	-	-	-	-
Riddle	-	-	-	-	-	-	-	-
Slick	-	-	-	-	-	-	-	-
Total	-	-	-	-	-	-	-	-
STATES-ALASKA OPERATIONS								
Alaska Airlines	$ 1,165	$ 979	$ 821	$ 798	$ 872	$ 1,267	$ 1,230	$ 1,177
Pacific Northern	1,029	1,243	2,075	1,741	1,505	1,450	1,354	1,205
Pan American-Alaska	1,367	1,371	1,336	332	-	-	-	-
Total	$ 3,561	$ 3,593	$ 4,232	$ 2,871	$ 2,377	$ 2,717	$ 2,584	$ 2,382
INTRA-ALASKA OPERATIONS								
Alaska Airlines	$ 1,063	$ 900	$ 748	$ 616	$ 975	$ 874	$ 765	$ 617
Alaska Coastal	342	336	339	354	357	619	795	813
Byers	56	54	50		Merged with Wien July 9, 1956			
Cordova	348	351	279	264	401	467	440	407
Ellis	270	254	239	254	372	426	415	397
Northern Consolidated	1,137	944	715	607	659	735	1,195	1,070
Pacific Northern	279	340	294	770	633	614	534	434
Reeve	91	57	35	25	-	-	-	-
Wien	1,156	1,075	690	717	1,021	1,396	1,994	1,837
Total	$ 4,742	$ 4,311	$ 3,389	$ 3,607	$ 4,418	$ 5,131	$ 6,138	$ 5,575
HAWAIIAN OPERATIONS								
Aloha (Trans-Pacific)	$ 241	$ 51	$ 50	$ 37	$ 30	$ 84	-	-
Hawaiian	448	242	240	179	85	303	-	-
Total	$ 689	$ 293	$ 290	$ 216	$ 115	$ 387	-	-

Continued on next page

TABLE 19—*Continued*

TRANSATLANTIC OPERATIONS								
Pan American-Atlantic	$ 1,625	$ 232	$ 488	$ 437	-	-	-	-
Seaboard and Western	-	-	-	-	-	-	-	-
Trans World	-	-	-	-	-	-	-	-
Total	$ 1,625	$ 232	$ 488	$ 437	-	-	-	-
TRANSPACIFIC OPERATIONS								
Northwest	$ 2,249	-	-	-	-	-	-	-
Pan American-Pacific	4,554	$-1,065 1/	$ 351	$ 262	-	-	-	-
United (Hawaiian)	-	-	-	-	-	-	-	-
Total	$ 6,803	$-1,065	$ 351	$ 262	-	-	-	-
LATIN AMERICAN OPERATIONS								
American	-	-	-	-	-	-	-	-
Braniff	$ 2,009	$ 1,261	$ 867	$ 1,042	$ 27	-	-	-
Caribbean-Atlantic	93	93	-	-	-	-	-	-
Colonial	41	-	5		Merged with Eastern June 1, 1956			
Delta	-	-	-	-	-	-	-	-
Eastern	-	-	-	-	-	-	-	-
National	-	-	-	-	-	-	-	-
Panagra	2,182	1,100	-	-	-	-	-	-
Pan American-LAD	11,502	6,612	4,927	1,500	-	-	-	-
Western	-	-	-	-	-	-	-	-
Total	$15,827	$ 9,066	$ 5,799	$ 2,542	$ 27	-	-	-
Total Domestic	$30,753	$28,280	$29,034	$34,133	$39,947	$43,554	$54,430	$61,294 2/
Total All Other	$33,247	$16,430	$14,549	$ 9,935	$ 6,937	$ 8,235	$ 8,722	$ 7,957
Total All Carriers	$64,000	$44,710	$43,583	$44,068	$46,884	$51,789	$63,152	$69,251 2/

1 Reflects final system rate for Pan American effective January 1, 1955. Although all divisions of the company were affected, only in the Pacific Division a negative amount of subsidy resulted.

2 Includes the $2,500,000 additional subsidy estimated for the local service group of carriers.

Source: CAB, *Service Mail Pay and Subsidy for the United States Certificated Air Carriers* (Washington, D.C., 1960).

reports to the CAB, after eliminating costs of nonmail functions (passenger service, traffic and sales, and advertising and publicity). Flight equipment depreciation allowances were based on standard rates and uniform amounts for each equipment type.

6. The average revenue ton-mile cost was computed for each group.
7. The cost per revenue ton-mile did not include return on investment, provision for income taxes, or any of the special cost aspects of the mail service such as priority considerations. To allow for these elements, the service rate was derived for each group as follows:
   a) The percentage relationship of the average cost for each group to the average cost of 34.20 cents for the Big Four domestic carriers was computed.
   b) The service rate for each group was determined by applying the percentage relationship for each group to the 45-cent service rate established for the Big Four.[38]
8. In basing the service rate for international carriers on the ratio of their costs to the Big Four, the Board followed the procedure adopted for making the administrative separation of subsidy from total mail payments for domestic carriers.
9. For a particular fiscal year the amount of service mail pay was computed for each carrier by multiplying the applicable group service rate by the reported mail ton-miles carried during the fiscal year. The subsidy was computed by deducting the service mail pay from the total mail pay for each carrier.

The air carriers with the highest per cent of subsidy to total mail pay are the local-service airlines. This will probably continue to be the case, since these airlines suffer a number of cost handicaps implicit in the nature of such operations and making the attainment of self-support very difficult. These are: (*a*) very light average loads; (*b*) relatively short hauls, with a substantial part of the ground and indirect costs remaining fixed with respect to the length of flight per departure so that costs per plane-mile are high; (*c*) variability of the traffic carried, with sharp changes in traffic volumes daily as between schedules, directionally and seasonally; (*d*) competitive diversion of traffic, particularly to the private automobile, over short distances.

Experimental Rates

On September 8, 1953, the Postmaster General filed petitions with the Civil Aeronautics Board requesting it to fix rates for the transpor-

[38] In arriving at the 45-cent service rate in the Big Four mail rate proceeding, the Board included an 8 per cent return on the investment devoted to the mail service, including an allowance for related federal income taxes. In addition, freight and express were treated as by-products in order to recognize the priority nature of mail. It should be noted that the cost of 34.20 cents for the Big Four is an average operating cost for mail, passenger, express, and traffic combined, and does not reflect the return element nor the treatment of freight and express as by-products.

tation of first class and other preferential mail between Washington and Chicago at 20.04 cents per mail ton-mile and between New York/ Newark and Chicago at 18.66 cents per mail ton-mile on an "experimental basis" subject to the following terms and conditions:

(1) The movement by air of such mail shall be subject to the prior movement of all air mail, passengers and air express required to be transported by the carrier. In the event that any or all of such mail has not been dispatched by the carrier within such time period as may be established by the Post Office Department, the carrier shall notify the Department, and if the carrier or the Department so elects, such mail shall be returned by the carrier to the custody of the postal service at the place where the initial delivery was made, without penalty to the carrier.

(2) Any air carrier authorized to transport such mail at the aforesaid rates may decline to inaugurate service at such rates, or, after inaugurating service, may, upon 30 days' notice in writing to the Post Office Department, decline to carry such mail at such rates on and after the expiration of the 30 day period, in which event the air carrier shall be under no obligation in connection with the transportation of such mail at such rates.

(3) The Post Office Department may at any time, upon 30 days' notice in writing to the carrier or carriers involved, discontinue completely the offering of such mail for movement by air between Washington and Chicago or New York/Newark and Chicago. Except as may be required in the interest of the expeditious movement of the mail, the Department shall not discontinue offering said mail to any one or more authorized carriers which are willing to transport it at the said rate, unless the Department discontinues completely the offering of any such mail to all such authorized carriers.

(4) Such rate shall terminate one year from the inauguration of the service to which it is applicable.[39]

The Post Office Department considered the rates proposed to be reasonable since: (*a*) the air carriers would not be obligated to transport the special classes of mail specified at said rates; (*b*) the rates were applicable to traffic which would not otherwise be available to the air carriers; (*c*) the Post Office Department would be able to achieve greater efficiency and economy in its operations and this, in turn, would improve the mail service to the public; and (*d*) the air carriers would be able to utilize whatever unused capacity was available to their economic advantage and thereby improve their financial position.

All carriers authorized to transport mail by air before this time had

---

[39] The following airlines were affected: United, American, Trans World, Capital. See, for example, *United Air Lines, Inc., et al. Mail Rates for First Class and Other Preferential Mail (Other Than Airmail and Air Parcel Post)*, 17 CAB 933 (1953). For a complete discussion of the experimental rate problem see, "Air Transportation for Other Than Airmail," *Hearing before the Subcommittee on Post Office of the Committee on Post Office and Civil Service, U.S. Senate* (86th Cong., 1st sess.) (1959).

operated under rates fixed pursuant to section 406 of the Civil Aeronautics Act on the basis of a service which they were obligated to render at the request of the Postmaster General and which they had to accord highest priority. There was no intention on the part of the Post Office or the airlines to now open, or in any manner place in issue, the rates so fixed. It was simply requested that a separate order of limited duration be entered fixing rates for the transportation by air, on a space-available basis, of a class or category of mail which the carriers would be under no obligation whatever to transport unless they voluntarily inaugurated service, and which they could terminate by giving 30 days' notice. Furthermore, this proposed class of service would, in effect, have only such priority as the carriers wished to give it, the only limitation being that the Postmaster General must have returned to him any mail not dispatched within the time specified by him.

United Air Lines and American Airlines informed the Board that they were willing to start the experiment as soon as possible. The Board accordingly authorized the proposed mail rates to go into effect but made them applicable to all authorized carriers willing to provide the service between the points named, thus bringing Trans World Airlines and Capital Airlines into the operation. The Board stated:

> Obviously, a class of mail service that does not enjoy the advantages of mail bearing air mail postage, which is transported under absolute obligation on the part of the carriers and under the highest priority, is entitled to a lower rate, but exactly how much lower is practically impossible to determine in the absence of any specific experience with that type of service. We can gather some indication of the proper rate from the assignment of costs we made to compensate for the type of air mail service now in effect and paid for under outstanding orders, and we get some aid from a consideration of the rates now in effect for property and passenger services. The cost of surface transportation of such mail submitted by the Postmaster General is also of help. While all of these considerations are not as sufficient as we would normally require, we find that in view of the relatively small impact upon the total operations of the carriers that might be involved in this limited experiment, the impossibility of securing adequate data before the experiment has progressed, the fact that United and American have indicated their willingness to go along, the substantial public interest to be served in the proper development of the new service, and the fact that the Postmaster General has reached an advanced stage of preparation for conducting the experiment, the rate proposed for this new class of mail service should be fixed as the fair and reasonable rate.[40]

[40] CAB Docket No. 6599 *et al.* (1954).

On December 11, 1953, 14 local-service airlines requested the Board to fix a fair and reasonable rate of compensation of 30 cents per mail ton-mile for the transportation of preferential mails (first class, newspapers, and special handling and special delivery parcel post) and other classes of mail (other than air mail and air parcel post) over their routes on an experimental space-available, voluntary, and nonpriority basis[41] during the holiday season. The local-service carriers held that this rate would be economically advantageous and would be fair and reasonable compared with the revenue per ton-mile being received by the local-service airlines then handling air freight in volume. They also argued that it would permit the local-service airlines to utilize available and unused capacity and that the revenue derived from this lift would reduce their subsidy requirements. The main support for the requested rate of 30 cents per ton-mile was the fact that the local-service airline transporting the largest volume of freight had on file a cargo tariff providing for approximately the same revenue yield. No other cost data was submitted to support the level of the rate proposed.

The Board approved the 30-cent rate to be effective only through January 11, 1954, and stated:

> Since this is a novel service which appears at present to be of limited duration, there seem to be little, if any, readily usable cost data that can be relied upon. However, it is obvious that the rate to be established here should be lower than the rate fixed for the transportation of priority air mail, which carriers are under compulsion to carry if tendered. Normally, the Board could not possibly establish fair and reasonable rates in response to petitions so meagerly supported. Nevertheless, we are dealing with an atypical situation where permission is requested to perform a service for a very limited period of time in order to expedite the delivery of Holiday mail; and the rate proposed herein is intended to do no more than meet the special situation before us. The granting of the carriers' petitions will have several beneficial purposes. It will (1) make available to the Postmaster General the facilities of the local service airlines for the transportation of Holiday mail; and (2) result in additional revenues which should reduce the carriers' subsidy requirements.[42]

On January 11, 1954, the 14 local-service airlines asked the Board to continue the experimental rate of 30 cents per mail ton-mile until the end of the year, in order to enable the Post Office Department to:

---

[41] *Mail Rates for Preferential Mails and Other Classes of Mail (Other Than Airmail and Air Parcel Post)*, 18 CAB 419 (1954).

[42] As in the case of the service mail pay established by Order No. E-7721, issued pursuant to Reorganization Plan No. 10, the service mail compensation established is also payable in its entirety by the Postmaster General, whereas the Board is responsible for

(*a*) Experiment from time to time with the transportation of preferential and other classes of mail (other than air mail and air parcel post) over selected segments of the local-service carriers' routes; (*b*) permit the local-service carriers to transport such classes of mail where conditions of an emergency nature arise; and (*c*) allow immediate use of the facilities of the local-service carriers in situations where the Post Office Department determines that the classes of mail involved can be transported more economically through the use of such facilities. The Board permitted the requested extension and later extended all experimental mail rates for trunk-line and local-service carriers to September 30, 1955.

The next move of the Post Office Department in the "experimental rate" program was taken on February 5, 1954, when it requested the Board to make a 20.04 cent mail ton-mile rate applicable to first-class and other preferential mail (other than air mail and air parcel post) to be transported between (1) Washington and Jacksonville, Tampa, and Miami, and (2) Chicago and Jacksonville, Tampa, and Miami. It was also requested that a rate of 18.66 cents per ton-mile be made applicable to the same type of mail to be transported between New York/Newark and Jacksonville, Tampa, and Miami.[43] The Board put these rates into effect until September 30, 1954 (later extended to September 30, 1955) with the following statement:

> The aforesaid rates shall be applicable only to the transportation of first class and other preferential mail (other than air mail and air parcel post) by aircraft under the terms and conditions set forth above and shall not in any manner alter, modify, amend, revise, or place in issue the mail rates that have been established by prior orders of the Board or by subsequent orders applicable to air mail and air parcel post transported under absolute obligation and highest priority.

In the meantime, various air carriers who were not certificated to transport mail requested that they be exempted from the provisions of Title IV of the Civil Aeronautics Act to the extent necessary for them to participate in the so-called "one-year experiment" being conducted by the Postmaster General in shipping surface mail by air on a space-available basis between Washington and Chicago and New

payment of that portion of the mail compensation, payable pursuant to section 406 of the Act, which is in excess of the service mail payments. Accordingly the rate proposed does not increase the total compensation payable to each carrier under section 406 of the Act.

[43] The airlines affected were Delta, Eastern, National. The rates referred to were those in effect between Washington and Chicago and Newark/New York and Chicago under Board Orders Nos. E-7737 and E-7736 dated September 21, 1953. *Delta Air Lines, Inc., et al., First-Class and Other Preferential Mail Rates,* 18 CAB 730 (1954).

York and Chicago, and other like experiments that might be inaugurated. Thus far, only the carriers certificated for mail between these cities were participating in the experiment under the substantially lower rates previously discussed.[44] The Board ruled that it was empowered by section 416(*b*) of the Act[45] to authorize by exemption the transportation of mail by air carriers not holding certificates of public convenience and necessity. Furthermore, the Board found that it had the power to authorize by exemption the transportation of mail by such air carriers and to fix the compensatory rates for such services. The Board stated:

> It becomes difficult to perceive why the Board's authority to exempt with respect to mail traffic should be so different from and more limited than it is with respect to non-mail traffic. The Act which we administer has been described as being as comprehensive a piece of legislation as exists in the public utility field. Viewed in this light we must critically examine a construction which would deny to the biggest single customer of the airlines, the Postmaster General, any opportunity to have the subsidy-free supplemental services of non-certificated air carriers that may be made available to the most infrequent traveler or shipper.[46]

Despite this contention of its rights to exempt, the Board decided that none of the carriers who did not already hold a certificate of convenience and necessity authorizing the transportation of mail were needed at this time to insure the success of the Post Office experiment. Subsequently, in May, 1955, the Board modified its position and permitted the temporarily certificated all-cargo airlines, Slick Airways, the Flying Tiger Line, and Riddle Airlines, exemptions to participate in the surface mail experiment to the extent of their respective route authorizations.[47]

---

[44] 17 CAB 933, 18 CAB 419, *supra.*

[45] Section 416(*b*) in pertinent part provides that, "The Authority from time to time and to the extent necessary, may . . . exempt from the requirements of this title or any provision thereof, or any, rule, regulation, term, condition, or limitation prescribed thereunder, any air carrier or class of air carriers, if it finds that the enforcement of this title or such provision, or such rule, regulation, term, condition, or limitation is or would be an undue burden on such air carrier or class of air carriers and is not in the public interest."

[46] In a strongly worded dissenting opinion two members of the Board, Chairman Ryan and Member Gurney, expressed the position that "the Board's power to fix *any* rate for the carriage of mail, whether it is purely compensatory or subsidy mail pay is, by the language of section 406, expressly limited to those cases in which the recipient of the mail pay qualifies as a 'holder of a certificate authorizing the transportation of mail by aircraft.'" The dissenters expressed the opinion that those words in Section 406 which empower and direct the Board to fix mail rates only for mail certificate holders "constitute an express limitation on the Board's rate-making powers—a limitation which the Board cannot exempt from the Act and which it is without power to disregard or alter." *Supra.*

[47] *Applications of Various Air Carriers to Carry First Class and Other Preferential Surface Mail by Air on a Nonpriority Basis for the Post Office Department,* 18 CAB 201 (1953); *Surface-Mail-by-Air Exemptions,* 20 CAB 658 (1955).

On October 6, 1954, another move in the "experiment" was made when the Postmaster General requested the Board to fix a fair and reasonable service rate for the transportation of certain first-class and other preferential mail (other than air mail and air parcel post) by aircraft in a large geographical area embracing major terminals and smaller points on the West Coast.[48] The Post Office Department stated that this additional type of experience would be helpful in reaching conclusions as to the success of their experimental air transportation of so-called "surface" mail.[49] A rate of 18.98 cents per ton-mile was proposed and shorlty thereafter was approved by the Board.[50] The Board's approval was subject to the terms and conditions specified in the rate orders issued in connection with the experiments on the East Coast,[51] which have been outlined previously.

The various "experiments" in carrying surface mail had from their start been viewed suspiciously by the railroads and motor carriers, although the rail carriers had waived their objection to the continuation of the experimental services started before that on the West Coast.[52] Now, however, certain common carrier railroads petitioned to intervene, contending that the effect of continuing the experiment would be substantial revenue losses which might require the removal of certain schedules from passenger service and possibly cause loss of employment to railroad workers. This intervention was denied by the Board with respect to the temporary mail rate, but was to be permitted when the final rate came under consideration.[53]

In the meantime, on November 20, 1954, the directly affected railroads filed a complaint for declaratory judgment and injunctive relief in the United States District Court for the District of Columbia.[54] They requested that the Court find and declare the institution and conduct of the proposed air mail transportation service by the Postmaster General unlawful and beyond the authority granted to him by law, and that the Court enjoin him from instituting or conducting the proposed

---

[48] The points involved were: Seattle, Washington; Portland, Salem, Bend, Redmond, Eugene, Medford, and Klamath Falls, Oregon; San Francisco, Oakland, Sacramento, Stockton, Modesto, Merced, Salinas, Fresno, Visalia, Bakersfield, Los Angeles, and San Diego, California.

[49] *Preferential-Mail Rates, West Coast Trunkline Points,* 19 CAB 855 (1954).

[50] *Ibid.*

[51] 17 CAB 933, 18 CAB 419, *supra.*

[52] Waiver was filed by railroads on September 21, 1954.

[53] CAB Order No. E-8792 (1954).

[54] *The Atchison, Topeka and Sante Fe Railroad Co., Great Northern Railway Co., Northern Pacific Railway Co., Southern Pacific Railway Co. and Union Pacific Railroad Co.* v. *Arthur E. Summerfield,* Civil Action No. 4858–54.

service.[55] On December 13, 1954, the injunction was denied, but the legal questions involved in the suit were still to be answered. On January 28, 1955, the Court ruled that while the Postmaster General had a right to make the experiment, it "shall not be unduly prolonged." This raises the question of how long an experimental period may be and it might end by Congress making the decision.

In 1956, the Board prescribed rates for the carriage of first-class and other preferential mail between certain specified points on the East Coast and West Coast to be 19 cents a ton-mile for the domestic trunklines, 30 cents a ton-mile for the local-service and intra-Hawaii carriers, and 18 cents a ton-mile for Alaskan carriers. In this same opinion, the Board found:[56]

(1) that "first-class mail by air" service is an unique and unprecedented one and is part of an experiment being conducted by the Post Office Department to gather information as to relative merits of this transportation medium in the expedition of mail delivery; (2) the simplification of handling procedures and the proffering of mail to the carriers on a voluntary basis only to fill space that would otherwise be unused in no way interferes with other traffic, and thus places a minimum burden on the air carriers concerned; (3) that the additional cost of carrying mail is admittedly minimal—well below the 14 cents per ton-mile figure the Hearing Examiner used as a minimum in his range of costs; (4) that the direct cost of handling first-class mail is somewhat less than the cost of handling freight—in fact less than the cost of handling any particular kind of freight, and it would be reasonable to anticipate a rate for nonpriority mail at a level as low as or lower than freight rates; (5) that the data submitted by an all-cargo carrier indicate operating costs including a return element below the rates prescribed; (6) that to assign a full share of costs to a service designated and offered to reduce the cost burden imposed upon the primary services would be to ignore entirely the essential differences between a priority and a space-available service; (7) that, where, within the range below allocated costs but above added costs, the rates should fall is largely a matter of judgment to be exercised in the light of the peculiar circumstances of these cases; and (8) that the rates on newspapers, magazines, and other periodicals corroborate the reasonableness of the rates fixed for first-class mail.

---

[55] The railroad contention that the transportation of ordinary, three-cent, first-class mail by air is unlawful is based upon their interpretation of *Title 39* of the *United States Code—The Postal Service*, 43 Stat. 805, 39 USC 462, 462*a* and 463*a*. "Read in conjunction Sections 462*a* and 463*a* expressly provide that the 'rate of postage on all' 'mailable matter being transported as mail by air within the continental United States' 'shall . . . be 6 cents for each ounce or fraction thereof.' Section 463*a* fixes the rate of 'postage on all domestic air mail' at '6 cents for each ounce or fraction thereof' and Section 462*a* defines domestic air mail 'to embrace all mailable matter being transported as mail by air within the continental United States.' "

[56] *East Coast* and *West Coast* cases, CAB Order No. E-10426 (1956).

In October, 1959, the Board prescribed new rates determined on the same rates as those used for the transportation of regular air mail established in 1955 and previously discussed, but at half the amount.[57] As with regular air mail, the compensation for each carrier is computed by adding line-haul charges and terminal charges influenced by the number of miles involved in the haul and the size of the station of origin. Each airline, regardless of whether it is a trunk-line, local-service or offshore carrier, will receive a line-haul rate of 15.085 cents per mail ton-mile for first-class mail. This is approximately half the rate received per mail ton-mile for air mail, but is in line with the minimum air freight rate for standard service.[58] This multiplied by the number of miles, will determine the line-haul charge.

The terminal charge for each shipment of mail will be determined by the number of pounds involved multiplied by the rate prescribed for the station of origin. For Class A or largest stations, the terminal rate per pound is set at 1.66 cents as compared with 6.64 cents for air mail. Class C is 4.98 as compared with 9.96 cents. For Class B, the smallest station designation, the rate is 16.6 cents as compared with 33.21 cents for air mail.

Over long distances, this formula would increase the total cost of moving the mail a ton-mile only slightly above the set line-haul rate of 15.085 cents a ton-mile, since terminal charges would be spread a greater number of miles. On shorter hauls, however, the cost of moving the mail a ton-mile would be considerably higher than the line-haul rate due to the small number of miles over which to spread terminal charges.

---

[57] CAB Docket No. 10920, Order No. E-14559 (1959); *Rates for the Transportation by Air of Nonpriority Mail,* CAB Docket 11090 (1960).

[58] For the haul from Los Angeles to New York, a distance of 2,471 miles, the formula would give a yield of 16.43 cents per mail ton-mile, as compared with 19.28 cents as the minimum freight rate for a 1,000-pound shipment for standard service, 11.57 cents for an eastbound movement and 10.60 cents for deferred service. For the haul from Cincinnati to Nashville, a distance of 232 miles, the rate for the same 1,000-pound shipment would be 29.40 cents per ton-mile, under the proposed mail rate, as compared with 20 cents under the minimum freight rate for standard service and 11 cents for deferred service (see Chapter 9). Many people think that the airlines should be glad to carry the mail at rates approximating those for freight, pointing to the fact that there is less expense in handling mail than in handling freight. There are two arguments against this. First, the cost of handling small shipments the size of mail sacks is estimated at some 20 per cent higher than average cost of handling freight. More important, however, is that air freight rates, particularly the substandard service rates, are set as low as possible to develop traffic. These rates frequently do not cover fully allocated costs, and the hope is that they bring in enough revenue to do a little more than cover the added costs. This approach is reasonable and necessary in the still developmental stages of the air freight business, but these rates should not control the rates for handling mail. See Henry Beekin, "All First-Class Mail by Air," *Journal of Air Law and Commerce,* Autumn, 1954.

The airlines, of course, favor the continuance of the experimental flying of first-class mail, despite the danger that doing so at reduced rates may well undermine the straight air mail rates as previously established by the Civil Aeronautics Board. These carriers hope that eventually there will be but one first-class rate of postage with all first-class mail going by air whenever time may be saved. So far the Post Office policy, from the day of the stagecoach on down, has effectively developed for this country one of the world's finest public services. The fact that we have such an excellent system of handling the many classes of mail, including both priority and non-priority, is no reason why the Department should not experiment further in expediting the mail, just as they are constantly working to facilitate its assembly and distribution. The fact that the current two-class priority mail has been developed over many years and has become our established policy does not mean that further change and improvement is precluded. It may be that the experiments in flying so-called "surface" mail will show that the savings and over-all increase in expedition are not sufficient to justify a change at this time, but that is for the Post Office Department to decide. It should not be barred from obtaining the needed data on which to make the decision.

Mail Rate Problem

The more recent actions of the Post Office Department, the airlines, and the Board point to the need for a formal investigation of mail rates, including a careful survey of the level as well as the structure of compensating mail rates for all domestic trunk carriers in particular. Some of the recent Board orders, previously discussed, have been in the nature of "piecemeal" and "makeshift" methods of dealing with the mail rate problem.

It is true that the mail rate structure based solely on costs served reasonably well as long as the Post Office Department was charged with the responsibility of making the subsidy mail payments to the airlines, but now that the Post Office Department is required to find the most economical method of getting air mail delivered, it seems apparent that the classified rate structure should be abandoned and a new one established in its place.

A conflict has resulted under Reorganization Plan No. 10 between the self-interest of the Post Office Department and the Board's classified rate-making policy. The Post Office's interest can be protected only by selecting the carrier with the lowest rates for the service it requires. If the Post Office is successful in protecting its self-interest, the air carriers have no choice but to meet the lowest rates on all competitive routes, with the result that a uniform rate will prevail for similar service performed. This is an economic aspect of rate making that cannot be eliminated by a cost approach which, in fact, reflects only the producer's point of view. It follows that it is not possible to impose upon a user, free to make its own economic decisions, different prices for service by different producers simply because the cost of producers differ.

The Post Office Department cannot change the law under which it must operate. The Board, however, can change its policy of rate making, and it appears that this will best be accomplished by abandoning the classified rate structure, based solely upon cost, and adopting a uniform rate structure, as previously discussed. It is hoped that this will establish the same price for the same service throughout the airline industry. Under the present system as it has developed, the basic ton-mile rate alone is either too high for the long-haul carriers or too low for the short-haul carriers. The Board, therefore, in an effort to adjust this difference has given the short-haul carriers higher ton-mile rates than the long-haul carriers, with the result that we have a number of different rates based upon the differences in the route systems of the carriers rather than upon the differences in service performed. There is such a wide variance between the route systems of the different carriers that even a classified rate structure is not entirely satisfactory as a fair basis for payment, since the extremes in any classified group must accept rates which are slightly less equitable to them than to those carriers in the same group with more nearly average route systems.

The intention of Congress with respect to rate making for the transportation of mail by air is reasonably clear. In order to prevent the Post Office Department from using its great volume of traffic to force the rates of the carriers to uneconomic levels, and in order to force the carriers to transport the mail at a fair price to the government, a quasi-judicial agency was given full power to make the rates which the carriers should charge and the government pay. The Civil Aeronautics Board's role in this process is not greatly different from that of a district court which fixes the fair value of a piece of land that the government wishes to condemn. It is not regarded as proper for the government to use extralegal methods to compel settlement of such a case at a low figure, nor is it proper for the government to put such pressures on a carrier that it is forced to petition the Civil Aeronautics Board for a rate reduction.

Chapter 9

CIVIL AERONAUTICS BOARD POLICY—FREIGHT RATES AND PASSENGER FARES

WHILE a very large part of the time and effort of the Civil Aeronautics Board has been devoted to the consideration of air mail rates, it has also had to adopt certain policies concerning the other sources of airline revenue—freight and passenger traffic.

Freight Rates[1]

Prior to 1944, no air freight rates had been published by the airlines. Property rates were all published by the Railway Express Agency under its contracts with individual airlines, by which they carried any "air express" provided them by that organization. The Civil Aeronautics Board, while it approves rate agreements between the Railway Express Agency and the airlines and requires the filing of air express tariffs, has never taken formal action on nor adopted a policy concerning air express rates although it has from time to time considered the relations between the Railway Express Agency and the airlines (see Chapter 15). In the latter part of 1944, however, American Airlines, acting independently of the other carriers, established for its own routes a new, lower-cost service which it designated as "air freight," thus marking the first use of the term "freight" in connection with the transportation of property by air. Shipments moving under this service had a "deferred" status, with air express receiving preference in the event of fully loaded airplanes. Whereas air express rates at that time averaged 70 cents per ton-mile, rates under the first air

[1] See Harold W. Torgerson, "History of Air Freight Tariffs," *Journal of Air Law and Commerce,* Winter, 1948; John H. Frederick, "American Air Cargo Development," *Air Affairs,* Autumn, 1947.

freight tariff averaged approximately 44 cents per ton-mile, door to door, with a deduction made where the shipper or receiver provided his own pickup and/or delivery service. For some time, probably because the plans of most airlines to inaugurate freight services were postponed by the demands made upon them by World War II, American Airlines was the only carrier offering freight service at such low rates.

The tariffs filed by American Airlines established a system of class and specific commodity rates applicable within mileage blocks. These tariffs set a pattern which was largely followed by other airlines, such as Transcontinental and Western Air and Braniff Airways, when they inaugurated freight services in the latter part of 1945.[2] There was, however, one important departure from the American Airlines pattern in the Transcontinental and Western Air tariff. While American's tariff rates included pickup and delivery service, TWA's rates were on an airport-to-airport basis, with pickup and delivery charges quoted in a separate section of the tariff, a practice which has now become general. The Braniff Airways tariff was also similar to American's except that it introduced a more refined mileage block system which all of the certificated carriers adopted in the following months.

Early in 1946, United Air Lines filed its first freight tariff,[3] establishing a single-class air cargo rate at a level of approximately 26½ cents per ton-mile, airport to airport,[4] under which all items acceptable for air transportation were grouped in a single commodity class to which the rates named were applicable. The elimination of various classes of commodities was a considerable simplification over previous air freight tariffs, and this method subsequently became standard among the certificated airlines. Another important departure from previous tariffs was that on shipments weighing over 499 pounds the rate per 100 pounds decreased. As an illustration, graduated rates quoted by United Air Lines effective February 1, 1946, were:

---

[2] American's tariffs were Air Freight Classification No. 1, CAB No. AF-1, and Air Freight Tariff No. 1, CAB No. AF-2, both effective October 15, 1944. TWA's tariff was Air Freight Tariff No. 1, CAB No. AF-1. Baniff's tariff was Air Freight Tariff No. 2, CAB No. AF-2, effective December 1, 1945.

[3] Air Freight Tariff No. 1, CAB No. AF-1, effective February 1, 1946.

[4] There is no clear indication of the reasons for the abandonment of a classified rate structure in favor of a single rate. Presumably this represents, in part, the attitude that there was too little experience available at this early stage of the industry's development upon which to base a rate classification.

Weight Group (Lbs.)	Rate Basis per Ton-Mile	Percentage of 100-Lb. Rate
100–499	26.5¢	...
500–999	25.6	96.6
1,000–1,999	24.7	93.2
2,000–2,999	23.0	86.8
3,000 and over	21.2	80.0

The idea behind this move was to stimulate volume shipments and to make the air freight forwarder business attractive, with the result that a considerable number of companies entered this field almost at once.

Pennsylvania-Central Airlines (later Capital Airlines) filed its first freight tariffs in July, 1946, departing from the established pattern in several respects.[5] The major difference was in a decrease in the size of mileage blocks to which rates applies, so that this company had a rate advantage over the other airlines, particularly between the principal freight traffic-generating points within its territory.[6] Pennsylvania-Central also increased the reductions offered on quantity shipments weighing between 500 and 3,000 pounds, with the result that, with minor exceptions, all of its rates on quantity shipments were lower than those of competitors.

While the major airlines were launching their air freight services, a large number of new noncertificated carriers were organized and began to compete in the cargo field (see Chapter 15). Until August 1, 1947, these carriers were not required to file tariffs with the Civil Aeronautics Board, and so they were free to negotiate terms with individual shippers. There was considerable experimentation with rates; but very little of this experimentation was planned, most of it being dictated by force of circumstances—chiefly competition. There was no uniformity either among these newer cargo carriers or among one carrier and its shippers. Many rates were made as a result of bargaining between carrier and shipper and were dictated, more frequently than not, by the competition of the one-plane veteran operators who were consistently carrying loads at whatever the traffic would bear. For example, the average revenue per ton-mile flown by Slick Airways, one of the most important of the new operators, in the months of March, April, May, and June, 1947, was 20.1, 16.1, 17.5, and 13.6

[5] Air Freight Rules Tariff No. 1, CAB No. 1; Air Freight Tariff No. 2, CAB No. 2; and Air Freight Tariff No. 3 (Terminal Area Directory), CAB No. 3, effective July 15, 1946. This company later changed its name to Capital Airlines.

[6] Chicago-Detroit, Chicago–New York, and Pittsburgh–New York.

cents, respectively.[7] The situation was chaotic but, as one looks back on it, probably inevitable.

The certificated airlines took various steps to meet competition from the noncertificated cargo carriers. In June, 1946, American Airlines established a Contract Air Freight Division, which operated independently of the common carrier freight division and at rates reported to be as low as 11 cents per ton-mile for transcontinental shipments.[8] In an effort to reduce its handicap, United Air Lines added new weight groups and new rules covering accumulation and consolidation so as to make its services increasingly attractive to large shippers and freight forwarders.[9] Pennsylvania-Central Airlines (later Capital Airlines) also liberalized its assembly and distribution service and provided for "shippers all-risk insurance," with coverage somewhat broader than that usually assumed by a common carrier.[10]

The next major development was the cancellation by the certificated airlines of their individually issued and outstanding general commodity tariffs and the filing with the Board of three consolidated tariffs, concurred in by all of them, to become effective August 1, 1947.[11] The consolidated tariff provided an average rate of 20 cents a ton-mile, with a spread ranging from 33 cents a ton-mile for small packages moving short distances to 14 cents for planeloads of 16,000 pounds. The freight forwarders suffered from these new charges, which were set up so as to prevent the forwarders from profitably using the services of the certificated airlines by consolidating small shipments into larger lots, thus taking advantage of the rate differentials contained in previous individual airline tariffs.

When, in May, 1947, the Civil Aeronautics Board permitted the noncertificated cargo carriers to operate on a scheduled basis[12] as common carriers rather than to operate only upon an irregular or noncommon carrier basis, such operators were required to file tariffs and reports. The basic principle apparently underlying the cargo

---

[7] Economic Exhibit of Slick Airways, Inc., submitted to Civil Aeronautics Board in Docket No. 810 *et al.* (*Air Freight Case*), p. SA 354, 9 CAB 340 (1948).

[8] *American Aviation*, June 15, 1946, p. 24.

[9] Supplements Nos. 1 and 2 to Air Freight Rules Tariff No. 1-A, CAB No. 4, effective 1946.

[10] Supplements No. 1 and 2 to Air Freight Rules Tariff No. 1-A, CAB No. 4, effective February 15, 1947.

[11] Official Air Freight Rules Tariff No. 1, CAB No. 1; Official Air Freight Pickup and Delivery Tariff No. 1, CAB No. 3; Official Air Freight Tariff No. 1, CAB No. 2.

[12] See Chapter 6.

tariffs filed by the noncertificated operators in the summer and early fall of 1947 was that their rates should, in order to develop traffic, and could, because of savings in operating and other costs, offer air cargo service at substantially less than the certificated airlines could afford to charge.

Some of the certificated airlines maintained that these tariffs represented an "undercutting" or a rate-war "salvo" by the cargo operators, since the tariffs presented rates below those then current in the airline tariffs. Whether this was so, the fact remains that the all-cargo operators proceeded from the outset of their enterprises in the belief that they could "out operate" the certificated airlines on cargo since the latter were still primarily concerned with the problems incident to their growing passenger traffic. The air cargo operators were convinced, from their studies of airline costs, that efficient air cargo lines which concentrated on low-cost, highly efficient, all-cargo operations could provide the public with air cargo service at rates not only lower than any of the passenger-carrying airlines had offered so far, but probably lower than they could charge on a basis of costs involved. It is true that the air cargo operators were probably prepared to have a few of the airlines meet their rates, on a basis of pure competition; but it is also true that none of them believed that the certificated airlines could or would be permitted to undercut the strictly air cargo operators' rates.

Shortly after the first of September, 1947, American Airlines, Pennsylvania-Central Airlines (later Capital Airlines), and United Air Lines, all in active competition with the noncertificated operators, proposed rates of approximately 12 cents a ton-mile on many of the chief commodities carried by air; on those constituting the major portion of the traffic of the all-cargo carriers,[13] and between the most important cities served by both groups of carriers. These specific commodity tariffs provided rates generally lower than those of noncertificated operators and hurt the interests of freight forwarders, since the 100-pound rates of the certificated airlines were made equal to the rates in the 1,000–2,999-pound bracket of the leading all-cargo

[13] The tariffs were American Airlines, Inc., Air Freight Tariff No. 22, CAB No. 31; Pennsylvania-Central Airlines Air Freight Tariff No. 4, CAB No. 1; and United Air Lines, Inc., Air Freight Tariff No. 3, CAB No. 8. The application was to 100 pounds and heavier shipments of the following commodities to be transported between designated cities: agricultural and horticultural products (except cut flowers), aircraft and automobile parts and accessories, wearing apparel, drugs, dry goods, electrical appliances or parts, films, fresh fruit or vegetables, radios or radio parts, machines or machine parts, and telephone or telegraph instruments, parts, or supplies. The cities between which the new rates applied included Chicago, Detroit, Los Angeles, Newark, and New York.

operators. The airline commodity tariffs did not reduce rates between points where no substantial cargo-operator competition existed, but were directed rather to the long-haul transcontinental routes. It was on these routes that the strictly cargo operators had been concentrating since the issuance of the Board's order exempting them from the need for certification as common carriers, pending decision on their applications for certificates of convenience and necessity.

It is not surprising that the freight forwarders and cargo operators raised the cry of "rate war" and requested the Board to suspend the specific commodity tariffs filed by American, Pennsylvania-Central, and United. This the Board refused to do on the grounds that the cargo operators had asked to be permitted to compete as common carriers with the certificated airlines and that the airlines were simply meeting competition by their latest rates; but, at the same time, it ordered an investigation of the tariffs of both certificated and uncertificated carriers. The goal of this investigation was "to attempt to develop some rational principles for tariff-making in air transportation as well as to inquire into the validity of the tariffs that have been filed."[14]

The Board was faced with the realization that the investigation would probably take some time; that in the meantime the low rates proposed by the commodity tariffs then on file, and others proposed by the rest of the certificated airlines during the month of October, 1947, would be in effect; and that the noncertificated carriers would therefore be rapidly forced out of business, since their rates had already reached the point where they couldn't hope to cover operating costs. The Board was really placed in a dilemma since it permitted mail rates averaging, for the larger carriers, between 45 and 60 cents a ton-mile and passenger rates averaging 50 cents a ton-mile. The question naturally arose as to whether such high mail rates and passenger fares were justified if the airlines could carry cargo at 12 cents a ton-mile. In other words, were the airlines being subsidized by air mail payments so as to enable them to force independent air cargo operators out of business? The Board, therefore, halted all rate reductions pending the investigation already ordered and suspended the tariffs in question.[15]

---

[14] *Motions of Air Freight Forwarder Association et al.*, CAB Order, Serial Nos. E-852, E-853 (October 2, 1947), 8 CAB 469 (1947).

[15] By an order (Serial No. E-1016) dated November 20, 1947, the Board consolidated this and certain other investigations into one proceeding (Docket No. 1705 *et al.*) known as the Air Freight Rate Investigation. Hearings on this docket were begun February 2, 1948, and it was decided on April 21, 1948. The reason for such unusually rapid action on the part of the Board was that the Civil Aeronautics Act (sec. 1002 [g]) does not per-

The noncertificated cargo carriers asked the Board to do two things: (*a*) to adopt a regulatory scheme for air freight rates which would make it impossible for the passenger lines arbitrarily, and without reference to their costs of providing air freight service, to charge rates which were lower than those of strictly air freight carriers; and (*b*) to permit the air cargo operators to file new tariffs in the near future containing rates sufficiently higher than those presently offered in order to meet their increasing costs of service.

As the Board's investigation went on, the chief issue turned out to be the proper method of calculating the costs of a multiple-service (passenger, mail, and property) operator in rendering air cargo service. Everyone seemed to agree that, as a general proposition, air cargo rates should bear a "reasonable relation" to the cost of providing the service. Serious differences of opinion, however, existed between the air cargo operators and the scheduled airlines as to what formula would most nearly determine the "costs" to which airline cargo rates should bear a "reasonable relation."

The air cargo operators claimed that, in their case, no problem arose—their costs of providing service were the total costs of their business, since (with some exceptions) their sole business was air cargo service. They also contended, and rightly so, that their rates had to be sufficiently high to cover their costs of operation and to provide a reasonable margin of profit. The certificated airlines, on the other hand, were not entirely unanimous in their attitude toward computing their air cargo costs; but most of them took the position that their cargo costs were properly to be computed on an "additive cost" or "by-product" theory of accounting. They also pointed out that, if this theory was adopted, their air cargo costs were not only substantially below the rates published in any of their tariffs but generally below any that the air cargo operators could immediately hope to achieve.

The certificated airlines asked the Board not to be "diverted by false issues concerning the need of protection by the noncertificated cargo carriers," but to adopt a long-range approach to the development of cargo transportation by air and, above all, to reject any system of minimum rates because of the "hampering restrictions" which would thus be imposed on their operations. They also requested that the suspended tariffs be permitted to go into effect.

Table 20 shows the trends of freight rates for various types of air

mit tariffs to be kept under suspension for longer than 180 days beyond the date they were originally intended to go into effect. See *Air Freight Rate Investigation*, 9 CAB 340 (1948).

carriers from 1955 through 1959. All-cargo carrier rates have consistently remained below those of the combination, domestic trunk, airlines although both groups of rates increased during this five-year period.

Setting Minimum Freight Rates

In its investigation of air freight rates the Board found that an unsound competitive condition existed in the cargo phase of air transportation in this country. This was particularly true in the transportation of freight between the large cities, where a number of the air-

TABLE 20

FREIGHT-RATE TRENDS, 1955–59

Average freight-rate yield per ton-mile for all commodities by carrier group (cents)

Period	Domestic trunk operations	Domestic all-cargo carriers	Local-service and helicopter carriers	Intra-Alaska carriers [1]	Intra-Hawaii carriers	International and territorial operations [1]
Fiscal years ended June 30—						
1955	23.00	17.10	43.78	63.63	44.28	35.55
1956	22.56	16.37	44.89	70.24	48.25	34.13
1957	21.87	17.69	49.71	63.86	53.38	33.73
1958	23.71	17.61	53.61	64.58	48.97	33.52
1959	23.74	19.00	55.01	60.55	50.19	33.22
Index (1955=100)						
1955	100.0	100.0	100.0	100.0	100.0	100.0
1956	98.1	95.7	102.5	110.4	109.0	96.0
1957	95.1	103.5	113.5	100.4	120.6	94.9
1958	103.1	103.0	122.5	101.5	110.6	94.3
1959	103.2	111.1	125.7	95.2	113.3	93.4

[1] The intra-Alaska operations of Alaska Airlines and Pacific Northern Airlines, not identified in reporting of system data after 1957, are included in "international and territorial operations" for all periods.
Source: CAB *Annual Report,* 1959.

lines, as well as the cargo operators, had established rates that were unjustified economically with the result that some of the carriers were incurring substantial operating losses. In the judgment of the Board, therefore, the situation required promulgation of a general minimum-rate order, applicable to the entire industry, setting a floor below which no freight rate might go without approval of the Board. The following rates were therefore set: (*a*) a minimum rate of 16 cents per ton-mile covering the first 1,000 freight ton-miles of any shipment and (*b*) a minimum rate of 13 cents per ton-mile covering the ton-miles in excess of 1,000 for any shipment.[16]

[16] *Air Freight Rate Case,* 9 CAB 340 (1948).

In fixing general minimum rates, the Board avoided prescribing, establishing, or determining particular rates, rate structures, or levels of rates. It was felt that not only was the information gained as a result of the Board investigation inadequate for such purposes but also that, at the present state of development of air freight, the prescription of actual rates by regulatory action might well be so restrictive as to be extremely unwise. Of course, the fixing of general minimum rates, by its very nature, cannot assure profitable operation or guarantee the continued sound development of air freight. It does, however, do what the Board thought absolutely necessary at that time—prevent unlimited rate cutting on a purely competitive basis.

Some in the industry questioned the Board's wisdom in setting minimum rates so far below what appeared to be industry cost levels, but it must be borne in mind that the Board's rates represented the *minimum* and not the *actual* rates and gave recognition to the developmental character of the service.

The Board stated that it was not its intention to freeze rates in the early developmental period or to outlaw competitive rates, but merely to "prevent the financial stability of the industry from being imperiled by unrestricted competitive pressures which drive the rate structure generally to unremunerative levels." To provide for the possibility of developmental rates and to permit flexibility and experimentation, the Board stated that it would be "receptive" to petitions for exemptions from the minimum rates in particular instances where such exemptions are necessary to the proper development of air cargo to remove inequities or disparities within the rate structure.[17]

It is a truism in transportation that a regulated minimum rate in most cases becomes a maximum rate where route competition exists. Although the Board suggested that carriers set their rates above the minima prescribed, the direct competitive situation which exists on all major cargo routes provides a perfect set of circumstances for this rule again to prove itself. Certainly the Board's order and the circumstances surrounding its promulgation make clear that, at that time, air

---

[17] On February 21, 1949, the Board instituted its Class Rate Investigation, Docket No. 3665, to determine whether it "should determine and prescribe just and reasonable class rates for the interstate transportation of freight by air carriers as the lawful rates, and if so, what class rates (or maximum or minimum, or the maximum and minimum thereof) should be demanded, charged, collected or received as the lawful rates." As of the end of 1960, this investigation had not been completed.

On August 26, 1960, the Board instituted an investigation to determine whether existing minimum freight rate orders should be modified or revoked and, if modified, in what manner. CAB Order E-15672 in Docket No. 11728, *Domestic Air Freight Investigation.*

cargo rates were passing through a critical formative period, that the most intense competition prevailed among the carriers, and that the experience required to develop accurate cost determination methods had not yet been developed by either the Board, the certificated airlines, or the then noncertificated cargo carriers.

Since the minimum-rate order has been in operation, the all-cargo operators have continued to confine their activities to moving large shipments for long distances. Even after temporary certificates were granted them, they operated on even less than the proverbial "shoestring" and had to follow only the most profitable courses. On the other hand, the airlines continued to encourage small, short-haul shipments in their combination equipment but with an increasing interest in the volume traffic which can be obtained, they hope, directly from shippers without forwarder intervention (see Chapters 15 and 16).

On August 20, 1953, Slick Airways, Inc., filed a petition with the Board asking that minimum rates for air freight be increased by 25 per cent. The other most important all-cargo carrier, Flying Tiger Line, Inc., concurred in this request. The Board granted this increase, to become effective October 1, 1953.[18] The grounds for the cargo carrying airlines' request were that the costs of carrying freight on all-cargo aircraft had risen sharply since 1948, when minimum rates were first set by the Board. Table 21 shows total cost including all ground and indirect expenses for the all-cargo carriers. It also shows the flight costs, direct maintenance, depreciation of flight equipment, and ground and indirect maintenance costs allocated to aircraft types on the basis of direct labor charges for the latter, incurred in all-cargo operations by the three so-called "combination" airlines in direct, transcontinental competition with Slick and Flying Tiger. The fact that operating expenses in mid-1953 for all-cargo carriers were so close to the minimum rates previously set by the Board indicates that such minimums were probably no longer effective in preventing competition from holding rates below the cost of carriage in all-cargo planes.[19] The action of the Board in granting the increases requested, over the objections of at least one of the "combination" airlines,

[18] *Air Freight Rate Case,* 16 CAB 254 (1953). The Board called attention to the fact that a 25 per cent increase in minimum rates did not mean that there would be a like increase in actual rates charged. At the time the order was issued most rates were at least 10 per cent above the minimum rates, and many exceeded the minimums by even greater amounts. Accordingly, the requested 25 per cent increase in minimum rates would seldom force an effective rate increase exceeding 12 per cent, and in many cases the required increase would be less.

[19] Financial reports of the two major all-cargo carriers submitted to the Board along with the petition of Slick Airways in August, 1953, indicated that Flying Tiger was barely

American Airlines,[20] was unprecedented in the annals of rate regulation since the overriding and, indeed, only immediate considerations were that two of the experimental cargo carriers were conducting marginal operations and that Slick, in particular, had urgent need for prompt rate relief. The Board gave no consideration to such statutory rate-making factors as the effect of rates upon the movement of traffic, the public interest in having adequate and efficient transportation at the lowest cost consistent with furnishing such service, and the efficiency of carrier operations.

TABLE 21

COST OF "ALL-CARGO" OPERATIONS, 1952–53
(In cents per available ton-mile, 12 months ended June 30, 1953)

Carrier	Type Aircraft	Total Operating Expense
Flying Tiger Line	C-46	*13.09¢
Slick Airways	C-46	*14.58¢
Slick Airways	DC-6A	*17.52¢
American Airlines	DC-4	†12.13¢
Trans-World Airlines	DC-4	†14.15¢
United Air Lines	DC-4	†15.76¢

* Total operating expense.

† No attempt has been made to allocate scheduled combination carrier's overhead costs to the all-cargo service.

Source: CAB Docket 1705 *et al.* (1953).

As time goes on, competition for large shipments probably will tend to be more on the basis of service to the shipper than on rates. Transportation history shows that "service" competition may employ measures which are just as destructive as those in "rate" competition and which become infinitely more difficult to control.

breaking even on their scheduled flight operations, while Slick appeared to be suffering substantial losses.

[20] American Airlines agreed that the costs of carrying air freight had risen sharply but took the position that since, in 1952, it was able to maintain a 68.3 per cent load factor in its all-cargo operations, yet carry 68.5 per cent of its cargo traffic in aircraft along with passengers, mail and express, it could, in using such aircraft, carry freight cheaper than the all-cargo carriers. Under such circumstances it argued that the Board should consider this factor in fixing minimum rates, thus being consistent with the position maintained by the combination airlines in all-cargo rate cases to date. American also pointed out that air freight was in a critical developmental stage with a critical need for volume growth; that volume had developed to a lesser extent than anticipated in 1948; that it was adding substantially to its all-cargo fleet; and that the increase in minimum rates proposed would not be consistent with the objective of developing the air freight volume required by the new capacity.

Setting Directional Freight Rates

An example of the Board's flexible treatment of the minimum freight rates set in 1948 is its handling of carrier requests for decreases to encourage the development of directional or backhaul traffic. Between July 21, 1948, when the Board issued its minimum-rate order, and April 10, 1950, five supplemental rate orders modifying the minimum rates were issued. Some of these provided rates as low as 8 cents per ton-mile for quantity shipments. The order of April 10, 1950, was the most important, providing reductions for eastbound and northbound traffic, with the exception of certain commodities, as follows: Shipments in an easterly direction, not exceeding 650 miles, to take rates 100 per cent of the minima prescribed in July, 1948 (16 cents per ton-mile for the first 1,000 ton-miles and 13 cents per ton-mile for those in excess of 1,000 for any shipment); but shipments carried between 650 and 1,300 miles to take rates decreasing gradually from 100 per cent to 60 per cent of the present minima. For shipments moving 1,300 miles or more, the directional minima were to be 60 per cent of the present minimum rates. In recognition of the shorter distances from south to north as compared to those from west to east, the breaking points for the northerly routes were set at 550 and 1,100 miles, respectively.[21]

Air cargo carriers have a very serious backhaul problem. This is so because a much greater amount of freight is carried from east to west and from north to south than in the opposite directions. This unbalanced movement of freight results in a substantial amount of unused freight space on return flights from the West Coast to the East Coast and from the south to north. The variation between westbound and eastbound loads is largely because the average length of haul of westbound traffic is substantially greater than that of the eastbound haul. For example, during a typical month, freight tonnage leaving California moved on the average of 1,738 miles, whereas the movement of such tonnage destined for California averaged 2,220 miles. Also, the off-loading of eastward traffic at intermediate points without the enplaning of comparable loads, together with the failure to originate as much traffic from California as is unloaded there, results in low loads in the backhaul direction. The Texas and Florida backhaul problems are similar to that of the West Coast. For Texas, the backhauls

[21] *Air Freight Rate Investigation* (*Directional Rates*), 11 CAB 228 (1950).

are westward from that state to California and northbound to the northeast and central areas. The directional disparity for Florida exists northbound from Florida to the northeast and central areas.

The directional problem has been further complicated by the fact that a large portion of the traffic in the off direction goes to intermediate points rather than to coastal terminal points. Lower directional rates were at first permitted by the Board on an experimental basis but later were placed on a permanent basis.[22] Such rates help to meet the problem in two ways: (*a*) They stimulate the growth of long-haul traffic; and (*b*) they develop directional traffic at intermediate points, since, with increasing volume, the scheduling problem which limits the servicing of intermediate points by all-cargo aircraft is lessened.

The existence of unused space in the backhaul direction has a restrictive effect on the proper development of air freight in two important respects: (*a*) Substantial revenue is lost from empty space in the backhaul direction, and (*b*) carriers restrict their operations in the heavy or going direction because of the backhaul problem in the reverse direction. The concentration of effort, in other words, is in trying to develop eastbound long-haul traffic. Were this same effort expended in the development of westbound traffic, a substantial increase in volume of that traffic would doubtless be experienced. Thus the problem results not only in the loss of revenue caused by excessive available space on return trips but in a loss in revenue from the nonrealization of the full freight potential at the rates then current in the predominant direction.

If air freight transportation is to become a self-sustaining business, it is essential that the revenue from its carriage in both directions be sufficient to cover the total cost of so doing. If traffic were carried in the forward direction at the minimum rates as prescribed in 1948 and in the off direction at lower than minimum rates, it seemed to the Board that it would not be possible to meet total costs. It was for this reason that the Board, in setting the original minima, stated that they were to be regarded as a "floor under which no rate should go" and that it "expected carriers to establish rates for most commodities above that floor in order to make the operation profitable." Instead, as already has been discussed, the carriers tended to establish rates for all commodities at or near the minimum levels. This will almost

---

[22] *Air Freight Rate Investigation (Directional Rates)*, 16 CAB 254 (1952).

surely again be the case, and directional minima will tend to become the maximum rates.[23]

In hearings prior to the issuance of its directional-rate order, the Board was advised by the combination passenger and cargo carriers that it would be best to do nothing ratewise, as a thorough sales effort on the West Coast would largely correct any unbalance. The Board, however, felt that the results of intensified sales efforts so far did not indicate that promotional programs alone could correct the existing unbalance and that, therefore, the most logical solution, offering the most reasonable prospects of success, was for the carriers to at least experiment with lower rates in the off direction.[24] The Board stated its belief, however, that rates in the backhaul direction should not be permitted to go below the minima based on out-of-pocket costs,[25] plus some contribution to other operating expenses but not necessarily assuming the fully allocated cost of handling the traffic.[26] This theory is apparently based on the facts that: (*a*) Since the movement of aircraft westbound makes available space in an eastbound direction, the round-trip movement must be regarded as an indivisible unit of opera-

[23] The Board excluded the following commodities from the application of backhaul minimum rates since they had already moved in considerable quantities at prevailing rates: art works, cut flowers, gold coins and bullion, household goods, human remains, ladies' hats, live animals, negotiable securities, paper currency, personal effects, platinum and precious metals, and wearing apparel on racks or hangers.

[24] Another logically possible solution was to reduce the forward haul by increasing forward haul rates. The Board felt, however, that a general increase in westbound rates to equalize traffic movement would hamper the developmet of the full air freight potential and seriously limit operations. In addition, such an increase would be economically unsound since the burden of the costs would be increased to the remaining traffic. *Air Freight Rate Investigation* (*Directional Rates*), 11 CAB 228 (1950).

It should be noted that there is no rule of law which requires that rates be the same in both directions. There is justification for the establishment of directional rates where transportation conditions are substantially different. An examination of the cases decided by the Interstate Commerce Commission reveals that the carriers have been permitted to establish reduced rates to encourage business where the preponderance of freight was so large in one direction that the supply of empty cars exceeded the demand for return loads at full rates. *Boileau* v. *P. & L. E. R. Co.*, 24 ICC 129 (1912); *F. Schumacher Milling Co.* v. *C. R. I. & P. Ry. Co.*, 6 ICC 61 (1893); *James and Abbott* v. *Tenn., Va. and Ga. R. Co. et al.*, 3 ICC 225 (1889).

[25] Here defined by the Board "as the additional cost of carrying the traffic in question over and above the costs which would be incurred if it were not carried."

[26] The Board was consistent here, as it had previously stated: "We are of the opinion that economic considerations do not demand that at all times the rates for any class of traffic or type of service must cover the fully allocated cost of carrying that traffic or providing that service; rather that rates must at all times be reasonably related to costs. The test of reasonableness must include recognition of variations in the ability of traffic to carry a full share of costs at different stages in the development of that traffic, the effect of low rates in generating new traffic and the resultant effect of increased volume on reductions in unit costs" (*Air Freight Rate Investigation*, 9 CAB 340 [1948]).

tion, the costs of which must be compensated for by the charges for cargo moved in both directions, and that (*b*) to whatever extent there is available empty space, the increased burden of covering the costs of the round-trip operation should fall upon the freight that is moving. Therefore, the carriage of any freight that will yield additional revenues will contribute to the net revenue of the round-trip operation, and there is an inherent cost advantage in the availability of the space which can be used at little added cost. It is the Board's opinion that to prohibit ratewise the use of such space would not only impair the sound economic development of air cargo but require higher rates in the predominant direction. Thus lower directional rates, by permitting a fuller utilization of space, would aid the shippers not only in the backhaul but in the predominant direction.

Accumulation, Assembly, and Distribution Rules

Almost since the beginning of air freight transportation, airline tariffs have contained rules providing for accumulation, assembly, or distribution services. The purpose of the assembly and accumulation rules has been to permit the consolidation of small shipments over a period of time for movement to a single consignee at one destination. The purpose of the distribution rules has been to permit a shipment consisting of parts ultimately destined to be delivered as part shipments to move as a unit to destination and there be broken for distribution of the several parts. In connection with these rules, the effect has been to permit the aggregation of a total weight subject to a lower rate than would apply to each component part if shipped individually.

The Civil Aeronautics Board investigated these practices of the airlines in 1949 because it was felt that they might affect the cargo rate minima which the airlines had established in 1948.[27] A Board order setting forth the assembly and distribution service rules was issued in September, 1950.[28]

Pursuant to accumulation rules, all parts of a shipment received by a carrier within a given period (which varies with different airlines from twenty-four hours to one calendar week), from one consignor at one address for transportation on one air waybill to one consignee at one destination address, can move at the volume rate which applies to the total weight, just as if the individual parts had been tendered at

---

[27] CAB Order, Serial No. E-1639, June 2, 1948.

[28] *Investigation of Accumulation, Assembly and Distribution Rules*, 12 CAB 337 (1950).

one time, provided the aggregate weight of all the parts equals or exceeds a specified minimum weight. This minimum weight also varies from airline to airline, being as low as 1,000 pounds in some instances and as high as 16,000 pounds in others. There is usually no charge for accumulation service in addition to the line-haul service, and the usual practice is for the carriers to forward individual parts of the accumulated shipment as received, rather than to hold them until the entire shipment has been placed in their hands.

Assembly rules vary considerably, but in general they provide a service similar to that provided under accumulation rules. However, assembly and accumulation rules differ in three important respects: (*a*) The provision of accumulation service is dependent upon the aggregate weight, being equal to or greater than a minimum specified, while assembly service will be provided on any shipment, regardless of the aggregate weight; (*b*) there is no charge for the performance of accumulation service, but there is for assembly service; (*c*) accumulation rules do not specify or limit the persons who may request the service nor those for whom the service might be provided, whereas assembly rules usually provide for services thereunder to be performed on the instructions, and for the account of, the consignor or owner.

Rules and practices of the carriers are also different for distribution services. The rules usually provided that, upon prior instructions from the consignee or owner, the carrier will break a shipment at destination and distribute the individual parts for the account of the consignee or owner. This rule is not always observed, however, since carriers perform distribution service at the request of the consignor for multiple consignees and this might involve delivery of parts of a shipment at more than one destination.

Charges vary for both assembly and distribution services, with the predominant charge being 25 cents per part, minimum $1.00 per shipment. Some carriers charge only for each addressee in addition to the first. If delivery service is provided, each part is assessed a delivery charge based upon the weight of the individual part in accordance with applicable pickup and delivery tariff provisions; these charges are in addition to that for the distribution service. Some carriers require prepayment of charges on distributed shipments, whereas others permit charges to be either prepaid or collect.

Proponents of the accumulation, assembly, and distribution rules argue that such services make air freight more attractive to shippers and consignees, and enable certificated direct air carriers to compete ratewise with forwarders and irregular air carriers. Opponents of the rules urge that their use reduces cargo rates below the minimum level of reasonableness, and afford an unfair competitive tool which would enable direct carriers to acquire business which otherwise would go via forwarders.

The Board has held that the performance of accumulation, assembly, and distribution services by the direct air carriers is not unreasonable nor unjustly discriminatory, unduly preferential, nor unduly prejudicial and that, therefore, they should be permitted to continue. It is true that the revenue per ton-mile obtained by the carrier is less on shipments receiving any of the three services than would have been realized if the component parts had moved as separate shipments, but that difference is justifiable insofar as such shipments retain some of the characteristics of large volume shipments for which the Board has previously found reduced rates to be lawful.

The Board's rules for assembly (or accumulation) do not provide that such shipments must be transported as a whole. In other words, there is nothing to prevent an airline from transporting some of the parts of a shipment before all of them have been received by the carrier or from transporting a shipment in different aircraft. By so doing, the carrier is prevented, of course, from moving all the parts of a shipment as one unit, one of the factors justifying varying rates with variations in the size of shipment.[29] This, however, is logical for air transportation, where the major difference between large and small shipments is in ground costs. Also, any minor differences in transportation costs between small and large shipments may well be offset by the advantage to the carrier of being able to ship the parts of an assembled or accumulated shipment at the time most convenient from an operational standpoint, without waiting for the receipt of the last part of any particular shipment. However, if carriers were permitted to ship parts of an assembled or accumulated shipment as received and to deliver them at destination as the parts arrived, there would arise an unjust discrimination against shippers of single shipments. For this reason, the Board has ruled that all parts of an assembled or accumulated shipment must be delivered at destination at one time as

[29] In the case of surface transportation, the practice of moving part of a shipment under assembly or accumulation rules prior to receipt of the entire shipment has been found unjustly discriminatory. See *Southern Pacific Company's Ownership of Atlantic Steamship Lines,* 43 ICC 168 (1917). See also *Aggregating Express Shipments,* 192 ICC 301 (1933); *The Providence Coal Company* v. *The Providence and Worcester Railroad Co.,* 1 ICC (1887); and *Forwarder Rates Conditioned upon Aggregates of Tonnage,* 264 ICC 225 (1945).

a single unit, except in those cases where a part or parts have been misplaced. Under such provisions, carriers are afforded maximum flexibility of operations without causing undue discrimination against shippers of single parcels.

Deferred Air Freight

In April, 1956, the Board authorized the airlines to introduce a deferred air freight service on an experimental basis for a one-year period.[30] This was later extended for an indefinite period.[31]

Traffic carried on the deferred air freight rates is accepted on a space-available basis. It is not released to consignees at destination airports prior to 7:00 P.M. the second day after it arrives, where the movement is under 2,100 miles, and not before 7:00 P.M. the third day where the movement is 2,100 miles or over. This delayed delivery is supposed to preserve the distinction between deferred and regular service. Rates are set at a minimum of 55 per cent of the published minimum rates for ordinary air freight.

American Airlines was the originator of the deferred rate method and the first to put it into effect. Basic reasons for such a service, from the airline point of view, are:

1. Aircraft carrying passengers, mail, and express and ordinary freight have a considerable amount of unused space on nearly every flight so this "wasted cargo capacity" might as well be used to expand the development of air freight.
2. The use of already existing unused space on aircraft would involve no additional direct aircraft operating costs, nor would ground handling costs be increased since staff and space at airports are already available.

When the Board was considering American's proposal, which was also supported by the Flying Tiger Line and Trans World Airlines, strong opposition came from the Railway Express Agency with some support from Slick Airways, Northwest Orient, and United Airlines. Opponents' arguments were:

1. A deferred air freight service would be uneconomic since it would divert a substantial volume of traffic from the regular freight service.
2. Under the rates proposed, the deferred system would heighten existing directional unbalance of freight traffic if heavier discounts from regular rates should be allowed on westbound than on eastbound shipments.

---

[30] *Petition of American Airlines, Inc., to Modify the Minimum Rate Order*, CAB Order No. E-10203 (1956), Supplemental Opinion and Order on Reconsideration, CAB Order No. E-10373, June 14, 1956. The Board's order was affirmed in *Railway Express Agency* v. *Civil Aeronautics Board*, 243 F. 2d 422 (D.C. Cir. 1957).

[31] *Deferred Air Freight Renewal Case*, CAB Docket No. 1705–9 (1958).

3. The rates proposed were unreasonably low and noncompensatory.
4. The complexity of handling the deferred air freight would result in higher costs than for regular air freight.
5. There would be unavoidable shipper and consignee pressures on the airlines using such rates to release shipments early resulting in the eventual shortening of the mandatory delay period.
6. Administrative difficulties involved in segregating, checking, billing, and collecting for the preferred traffic would be too great to justify the service.
7. So much rail express traffic might be diverted to the new service that the Railway Express Agency might be unable to continue its air express service, depending, as it does, on the ground service devoted primarily to rail traffic.

Deferred air freight tariffs provide that such traffic is to be received only pursuant to written instructions from the shippers or the consignees directing that such shipments be moved as deferred air freight. They also provide that the shipper's copy of the airway bill clearly show that the property would be transported on space-available basis and set forth the earliest permissable time of release of the property. The Board imposed a requirement that deferred freight tariffs prevent the carriers from charging for storage or reducing their liability to that of a warehouseman prior to 24 hours after notification to the consignee of arrival of the shipment or termination of the mandatory holding period, whichever was later.

The action of the Board in permitting a deferred air freight service took other forms of transportation by surprise, and its true significance is not even now realized. It seems obvious that, even with rigid tariff compliance, there will be shipper and consignee pressure for a gradual reduction in the time of holding at destination, and for a continuing expansion of the deferred freight experiment, thus tending to break down the distinction between the two classes of air freight service leading toward the eventual undermining of the entire rate structure.[32]

The theory upon which the air carriers have supplied a deferred service is simple but dangerous. They argue that their aircraft will

[32] In its order of November 6, 1958, the Board reduced the holding time by five hours, advancing it from 12:01 A.M. of the third day to 7:00 P.M. of the second day in one case and from 12:01 A.M. of the fourth day to 7:00 P.M. of the third day in the other. The Board also permitted a combination of deferred and regular air freight service subject to the requirement that the carrier makes it clear that: (1) The shipment is not transported in deferred air freight service until it arrives at the point where it actually enters such service; (2) the shipment enters deferred air freight service on a space-available basis only; and (3) the permissable release time is computed from the time the shipment actually enters the deferred air freight service.

operate anyhow; that the added expense of taking more traffic will be comparatively little or nonexistent; that if they can obtain some of the traffic now going by ground carriers (chiefly rail express) at some margin over any "added" or "out-of-pocket" expense it will help them just that much. The danger of this theory is twofold. In the first place, the airlines have always had an imperfect knowledge of what this "added" expense might be. In the second place, the theory places the chief burden of sustaining the profits and credit of the air carriers upon the traffic which under no circumstances would want to move on the deferred basis or on the traffic which would be noncompetitive with the ground carriers. Such a burden is likely to increase progressively. Gradually the traffic moving on the low rates ceases to be mere "added" traffic and the "out-of-pocket" expense swells in volume as does the burden on the noncompetitive traffic.

It must be realized that a dual rate scale cannot be confined to one type of carrier. Until now the competitive impact of the deferred air freight service has been greatest on the Railway Express Agency. However, the airlines anticipate substantial economies from the use of jet aircraft and consequent lower air freight rates thus bringing a similar impact to the railroads, motor carriers, and freight forwarders. Many transportation people feel that from an over-all commercial or rate standpoint there can be no justification for establishing such an inherently discriminatory practice as that typified by the present deferred air freight service. The only excuse for it is that certain carriers can thus increase their revenues, but this can only be done at the risk of disrupting the established rate patterns and the commercial community built upon them.

From the point of view of regulation, the deferred air freight service is impractical. Whenever an individual carrier can offer two levels of service depending upon availability of space, the way is wide open for discrimination. What shipper would complain if his "deferred freight" arrived on the fast schedule? What shipper would be foolish enough to pay the normal rate on regular freight which had the same transit time as the deferred service due to operating difficulties? It seems as if it may not be long before all air freight will move in the differential service at the differential rates not only because, due to operational difficulties, the two services were occasionally comparable; but for the further reason that the shipper at regular rates could not long compete economically with a shipper who used the deferred rates. The difference in cost will compel all competitors to use the deferred rates with the result that much of the freight that is now moving in regular service at regular rates will be diverted to the new service.

The deferred air freight service is based on availability of space. Looking at it realistically, it can be seen that the question might often arise as to whose freight was to be moved on a given day. Will it be the freight which first arrived at the airport, or will it be the freight of some shipper especially favored by the traffic solicitors? The whipsawing would first favor one and then the other. The question confronting the employees at the airport would be, Whose traffic goes first? There is sure to be constant conflict between shippers moving goods at the lower rate and those granted unusual services at ordinary rates.

Consolidated Freight Tariffs

As soon as they began handling air freight, the airlines realized that they should, if possible, avoid the development of an unwieldy and complicated rate structure. Therefore, as a step toward simplification and ease of working with tariffs, they decided to issue consolidated rules, regulations, and tariffs.[33] All the certificated airlines agreed to take part in such a move, although the agreements, being subject to the approval or disapproval of the Civil Aeronautics Board, were on a temporary basis until the Board could look into the entire matter of tariff publication. This investigation took approximately four years, after which time the Board issued a qualified approval of the airline action.[34]

The objective of the consolidated air freight tariff agreement is to provide reasonable through service, establish reasonable and just rates by the participating air carriers, and eliminate unnecessary variance in classification, rules, regulations, practices, and services in connection with the transportation of air freight. These are very practical objectives. From the point of view of the carrier, relatively simple and uniform rules add to the attractiveness of the service offered and tend toward elimination of confusion for the user. They also help speed the movement of interline shipments and aid in developing a smooth-working transportation system.

The Board approved the efforts of the airlines to achieve uniformity of rules and regulations, particularly since the carriers emphasized their intention not to follow a program of uniformity at

[33] CAB Order No. E-179 (December 12, 1946); CAB Order No. E-755 (August 15, 1947).

[34] *Air Freight Tariff Agreement Case*, 14 CAB 424 (1951).

all costs, but rather to provide for a considerable amount of flexibility which would eliminate stagnation, sometimes the price of uniformity. The Board also approved the publication of consolidated air freight tariffs and the designation of an agent to file and publish such tariffs. It was recognized that such publication offers many advantages: the shipper is provided with one tariff instead of 20 or 30, making it much easier to check rates and other tariff provisions affecting him; a shipper has complete information concerning the services of participating carriers; and the airlines save expenses of tariff publication and distribution. Against these obvious advantages is the disadvantage that consolidated tariffs tend to eliminate competition in the field of rates. The Board held that this would not be in the public interest, since is would make it more difficult to pass on to the public, in the form of lower rates, any lower costs which development of air freight transportation might bring. However, after balancing this tendency against the demonstrated advantages of a consolidated tariff, the Board concluded that by and large the public interest would not be injured by generally approving such a tariff for air freight.

The Board denied the airlines the right to permit competing carriers to meet one another's tariff changes, at the time they became effective, by having advance notice of the changes. This would bring about uniformity of rates as well as rules and regulations. Here the Board deviated from provisions of the Reed-Bulwinkle Act, where the Interstate Commerce Commission held that rates charged for transportation, if clearly not beyond the bounds of reason, were of "inferior importance to obtaining rates that, among other things, are as steady as the nature of things is practicable."

Whatever might be the state of rail freight transportation and factors determining rail rate-making procedures, the Board said:

> We are not presently prepared to accept the proposition that the level of air freight rates is of little importance compared to the maintenance of uniformity in such rates. Compulsory filing of advance notices of proposed tariff revisions would tend to eliminate individual incentives in this area as it would deprive a carrier of the opportunity of obtaining a competitive advantage from such initiative. . . . Elimination of the opportunity would mean the removal of almost the last vestige of competition in the air freight field, since the other parts of the agreement already discussed provide for uniform rules, regulations, service, and practices.

With these limitations, intended to maintain rate competition among the carriers, the airlines received Board approval for their consolidated tariffs.

Passenger Fares[35]

The airlines have so far enjoyed more latitude in setting passenger fares than in making freight rates; nevertheless, the Board has had to take strong action from time to time. During World War II, the profit position of the airlines was greatly improved by peak loads and high aircraft utilization, so that the Board considered a rate reduction appropriate. Therefore, in February, 1943, it instituted its first proceeding to investigate the lawfulness of passenger fares and issued an order requiring eleven of the sixteen carriers then operating to show cause why air passenger fares should not be reduced 10 per cent.[36] This investigation was never pushed to its conclusion, being dropped after five airlines had complied by reducing rates 6 to 10 per cent. Again, in January, 1945, in connection with the setting of the 45 cents per ton-mile mail rate for the "Big Four" carriers, a general reduction in passenger fares took place, resulting in passenger fares and mail rates being the same on a ton-mile basis for American Airlines, United Air Lines, Trans World Airlines, and Eastern Air Lines.[37] When larger airlines reduced their fares to 4.5 cents per mile, the smaller carriers were forced to follow; and these rates remained in effect until 1947. Passenger fare yields from 1955 through 1959 are shown in Table 22.

The failure of anticipated traffic volume to materialize at the low rates, coupled with the increasing general price level, caused two increases of 10 per cent each in fares for most of the carriers during 1947. These were requested by the airlines concerned. The passenger fare level then was about 5.5 cents per passenger-mile. Financial difficulties continued to harass certificated airline operators, however, so that, in 1948, fares were increased to approximately a 6.5-cent level. What began as a rate increase, not ordered by the Board but at least given its "blessing," turned out to be a rate-cutting fight among the larger carriers. Various "promotional" tariffs were filed with the Board as experimental and temporary.

The experimental fares and tariffs filed by various airlines during the latter part of 1948 and early part of 1949 fell into two general groups: (1) coach fares and (2) family fare plans.

---

[35] See Lucile Sheppard Keyes, "Passenger Fare Policies of the Civil Aeronautics Board," *Journal of Air Law and Commerce*, Winter, 1951; Paul W. Cherington, *Airline Price Policy* (Boston: Harvard University Press, 1958).

[36] CAB Docket No. 850 (1943).

[37] Each passenger, including free baggage, was figured on the basis of 200 pounds, and so ten passengers equalled one ton, which at 4.5 cents per mile per passenger figured out to 45 cents per ton-mile.

1. *Coach-Type Fares.* These fares were typically at a level of approximately 4 cents a passenger-mile for specific "coach" flights, operating generally during off-peak periods and offering less luxurious standards of service than was usually provided by the airlines.

The Board found that, under certain conditions, coach tariffs generated a substantial quantity of new air travel which could profitably be carried by the certificated carriers. The special conditions which seemed to require consideration in evaluating air coach operations were first listed as: (*a*) that the operation be conducted over routes

TABLE 22

PASSENGER FARE YIELDS, 1955–59

Average yield per passenger-mile, by carrier group (cents)

Period	Domestic trunk operations	Local-service and helicopter carriers	Intra-Alaska carriers [1]	Intra-Hawaii carriers	International and territorial operations [1]
Fiscal years ended June 30—					
1955	5.35	6.24	12.97	7.29	6.71
1956	5.29	6.86	12.60	7.25	6.66
1957	5.28	6.42	12.58	7.39	6.59
1958	5.38	6.70	13.21	8.17	6.57
1959	5.72	7.19	13.18	8.63	6.34

Passenger-fare yields of domestic trunklines, by type of fare (in cents per passenger-mile)

Period	First-class [2]	Coach
Fiscal years ended June 30—		
1955	6.02	4.35
1956	5.85	4.31
1957	5.88	4.27
1958	6.05	4.36
1959	6.55	4.59

1 The intra-Alaska operations of Alaska Airlines and Pacific Northern Airlines, not identified in reporting of system data after 1957, are included in "international and territorial operations" for all periods.
2 Includes family-plan travel after December, 1955.
Source: CAB *Annual Report,* 1959.

having a heavy flow of traffic; (*b*) that high-density equipment (equipment having more than the average number of seats) be used in most cases; (*c*) that the service be scheduled so as to minimize the diversion of traffic from regular flights; and (*d*) that all nonessential services to the passenger, such as meals, extra stewardesses, full reservations procedures, etc., be eliminated.

After coach operations by the trunk airlines had been in operation for about a year, the Board changed its requirements as follows: (*a*) permitted the abandonment of the off-peak scheduling requirement, at least for transcontinental operations; (*b*) relaxed the requirement of using less speedy, nonluxury equipment; (*c*) permitted the making of tentative coach reservations by telephone; and (*d*) granted regular first-class baggage allowances to coach passengers.

On October 5, 1953, the Board issued a "Coach Policy Statement" which indefinitely extended existing services of this type at fares no higher than those then in effect, approximately 4.5 cents per passenger-mile. The Board's decision was based on the facts that such operations had been profitable, had contributed significantly to growth in total air traffic, and had apparently caused little net diversion from other services. The Board stated that fares for new coach services would not be subject to specific cents-per-mile ceilings, but to the general requirement that a proposed fare shall not disrupt the coach-fare structure in the area concerned and shall conform to the statutory standards applicable to fares. The only specific requirement applying to a fare for a new coach service is that it must not exceed 75 per cent of the corresponding first-class fare. The Board indicated its belief that a 25 per cent differential is the minimum that will reflect adequately the cost difference between the services, maintain an adequate fare distinction, and provide the incentive to generate additional traffic which is necessary for an economically sound service. The Board also retained restrictions for distinguishing coach from first-class services as follows:[38] (*a*) limitation of hours of departure for off-peak (night) coaches; (*b*) a minimum seating density, reasonably related to the safe carrying capacity of the aircraft, for coach service not restricted as to hours of departure;[39] (*c*) no free food service except for coffee or similar beverages on all coach service flights.

2. *Family Fare Plan.* By the middle of 1950, all but one of the domestic air carriers had established a so-called family fare plan under which members of a family might travel at a reduction (usually 50 per cent of the regular first-class fare) if traveling with the head of the family on certain off-peak days of the week, such as Monday, Tuesday, or Wednesday. This plan has been successful in building up traffic for the carriers during the periods of the week when traffic is usually light. The success of the plan in generating new traffic, as opposed to simply diverting traffic from a peak to an off-peak period of the week, is still not entirely clear; but the indications from the material which has been submitted to the Board, from time to time, by

---

[38] CAB, *Coach Policy for the Certificated Domestic Carriers,* statement of October 5, 1953.

[39] Minimum seating densities for coach aircraft used in coach services were set as follows: DC-4, 64; DC-6, 72; DC-6B, 76; Constellation 049 to 749, 79; Constellation 1049 88.

the carriers are that a considerable proportion of family fare traffic is newly generated.

In all the years of regulatory control by the Civil Aeronautics Board, no general passenger fare investigation was even proposed until 1952.[40] In that year, however, the airlines became concerned with the falling off of the Korean War activities, rising costs, and surplus equipment resulting in lower load factors as well as the decline of profits. The leading carriers, therefore, filed new tariffs with the Board to: (a) increase the cost of all tickets by one dollar; (b) eliminate the 5 per cent round-trip discount. The Board permitted the one-dollar increase to go into effect, thus giving the industry for the first time a "tapering" fare recognition of the greater terminal cost of short-haul business,[41] but denied the elimination of the 5 per cent discount and at the same time announced the fare investigation. Soon thereafter airline earnings improved, and the request was made to dismiss the general passenger fare investigation. The airlines contended that they would be put to considerable expense in preparing their cases and that the issues involved were vague. Some airlines at this time also urged the substitution of an operating-ratio approach for the rate-of-return concept as a measure for the reasonableness of earnings (see Chapter 5).

After much discussion and with sharp differences of opinion, the majority of the Board dismissed the proposed fare investigation. This action was considered unfortunate since no study of the facts had ever been made in a formal proceeding; thus no reliable information was available from which to establish a policy and reach a conclusion as to fairness and reasonableness of rates.[42]

Early in 1956, pressure on the Board from several sources[43] forced

---

[40] *The General Passenger Fare Investigation*, CAB Docket No. 5509, Order No. E-6305, April 2, 1952. The CAB has conducted a number of investigations and heard complaints concerning various passenger fare matters despite its lack of an over-all study. Typical of these are: *Eastern Air Lines Rerouting Rule Case*, 11 CAB 278 (1950); *Summer Excursion Fares Case*, 11 CAB 218 (1950); *The Free and Reduced Rate Transportation Case*, 14 CAB 481 (1951); *Tour Basing Fares*, 14 CAB 257 (1951); *North Atlantic Tourist Commissions Case*, 16 CAB 225 (1952); *Pacific Northwest–Alaska Tariff Investigation*, 17 CAB 903 (1953); *Pan American Ferry Flight Case*, 18 CAB 214 (1953); *The 1955 Transatlantic Charter Policy*, 20 CAB 782 (1955).

[41] See Paul W. Cherington, *Airline Price Policy*, *op. cit.*, chap. 3; Paul L. Howell, "The Rate of Return in Air Transport," *Law and Contemporary Problems; Transportation*, Part II, Autumn, 1959.

[42] See dissenting opinion of CAB Member Adams in *General Passenger Fare Investigation*, 17 CAB 230 (1953).

[43] Two of these sources were reports submitted to Congress by the Comptroller General late in 1955 which were critical of methods used in determining airline subsidies and rates for the hauling of mail: Joseph Campbell, *Audit Report to Congress re The Civil*

it to take action on passenger fares, and three major proceedings were begun.[44] The passenger fare investigation was begun following a period of six years during which the trunk airlines had enjoyed the highest level of profits in their history. Based on the level of earnings reported by most of the airlines, it appeared to the Board that there was a possibility that the public was being subjected to excessive charges, over all, for passenger transportation. This possibility was naturally denied by the airlines and their opposition to any passenger fare investigation continued.

The two main purposes of the 1956 general fare investigation, were: (*a*) to develop appropriate and well-defined standards respecting the earnings required by the domestic trunk airlines for proper development consistent with the public interest; and (*b*) based on such standards, to require or permit such over-all decreases or increases in domestic fares as the facts may warrant.

Within eight months after the start of the 1956 fare investigation, the airlines changed from an attitude of opposition to one of anxiety and support, alleging that earnings were by then entirely inadequate and urging that matters be expedited. It was contended that earnings had fallen precipitously, that increased fares were needed for emergency relief, and that these could not wait for the determination of broader issues. In line with this contention, the trunk airlines in January, 1957, filed tariffs for increased rates, averaging 6 per cent, which the Board immediately suspended.[45] At the same time, the Board set a hearing taking precedence over the general passenger fare investigation, which was recessed. In September, 1957, the Board, regarding the then-current low earnings as a temporary situation, rejected the applications for increased rates and in January, 1958, rejected petitions for reconsideration because the airlines had "failed to establish that relief requested is warranted." In this connection, it is well to note the Board's statement of policy previously made:[46]

Aeronautics Board (Washington, D.C., 1955) and the hearings of the House Antitrust Subcommittee on competition in the airlines and reasonableness of rates held early in 1956: *Hearings Before the Antitrust Subcommittee of the House Committee of the Judiciary on Monopoly Problems in Regulated Industries* (84th Cong., 2d sess.), Part I, Vols. 1–4 (Washington, D.C., 1956).

[44] *General Passenger Fare Investigation,* CAB Docket No. 8008, Order No. E-10279, May 10, 1956; *Rate of Return of Local Service Carriers,* CAB Docket No. 8404, Order No. E-10843, Dec. 10, 1956; *Capital Gains Proceeding,* CAB Docket No. 7902, Order No. E-12855, Aug. 1, 1958.

[45] *Suspended Passenger Fare Increase,* CAB Docket No. 8613, Order E-11812, September 25, 1957.

[46] *General Passenger Fare Investigation,* 17 CAB 230 (1953).

It is our intent to examine any future fare or mail rate proposals, not only in the light of conditions prevailing at the time they are advanced but with full consideration of the abnormal earnings of prior years and the excess earnings which may be expected in the future, as indicated by such experience. In short, should earnings fall markedly in the future the carriers will be expected to absorb such losses without resort to fare or mail rate adjustments unless it can be demonstrated that such earnings are below the level necessary to provide a fair return over a reasonable extended period which includes the good years as well as the bad.

Just four weeks later, the Board changed its opinion and increased passenger fares by 4 per cent plus a dollar a ticket, on the basis of recently prepared staff memoranda[47] and earnings reports especially requested from the carriers. This increase amounted to a 6.6 per cent increase on the average.

In October, 1958, still without any decision in the over-all investigation, the Board permitted the carriers to eliminate stopover privileges, withdraw round-trip discounts, and reduce family fare discounts, which action increased rates another 4 per cent.[48]

The Board's next move in the general passenger fare investigation came the latter part of April, 1960,[49] when it voted that the measure of fair trunk-airline earnings should be based on rate of return on investment and not on operating ratio, thus settling an argument in which the airlines had been engaged for over a year. The Board concluded that on the basis of the record in the investigation thus far the fair over-all rate of return for the domestic trunk-line industry was to be approximately 10.5 per cent, based on a somewhat lower return for the Big Four carriers and a higher rate for the remaining eight trunk-line carriers. The rate of return would be computed on an investment base including equipment purchase deposits but excluding reserves for deferred income taxes and certain minor items. The Board held that this rate of return reflected the general level of earnings which it anticipated the industry should have an opportunity to attain over an extended period, but it did not necessarily prescribe or guarantee the precise level that any given carriers or the industry might realize at a given time. About the middle of August, 1960,[50] the Board announced a "determination" to increase the rate of return to be allowed

[47] See *General Passenger Fare Investigation,* CAB Docket 8008, Bureau Counsel Exhibit No. 120, *A Fair and Reasonable Rate of Return for Domestic Trunkline Air Carriers,* prepared by Paul Howell Associates, CAB (Washington, D.C., 1957).

[48] *Withdrawal of Round Trip Discounts and Related Matters,* CAB Docket No. 9931, Order No. E-13066, October 14, 1958.

[49] CAB Press Release, April 29, 1960, in Docket 8008.

[50] *Rate of Return—Local Service Carriers Investigation,* CAB Docket 8404 (1960).

local-service airlines in subsidy determinations to 12.75 per cent on investment, but in no case less than three cents per plane-mile, based on the cost of obtaining capital by these airlines rather than on the basis of "operating margin" as had been proposed by a number of carriers.

After the Board's announcement on rate of return, all trunklines filed tariffs proposing varying increases in passenger fares. These were suspended by the Board in the interest of uniformity, and on June 17, 1960, it permitted a general increase of approximately 5 per cent, achieved by raising passenger fares by 2½ per cent plus $1.00 per one-way ticket effective July 1, 1960.[51] At the same time, the Board approved jet aircraft surcharge or extra fares which, together with the $1.00 per ticket increase were to expire on June 30, 1961. The 2½ per cent increase was to remain in effect indefinitely. These increases together with 10 per cent approved in 1958 were expected to afford the industry the rate of return on investment of at least 10.5 per cent during a reasonably extended period into the future. Moreover, the Board considered that it had provided sufficient financial latitude to enable the carriers to experiment with promotional fares in view of the increases in seat capacity resulting from the introduction of new equipment.[52] This decision was concerned directly with trunkline fare levels, but local-service airlines were also permitted to increase fares.

The fare increases were not a final decision in the general passenger fare investigation, and no date was set for determining whether overall fare levels would now be reasonable or not. Since the new fare increases are in addition to interim fare increases granted in 1958, the Board may delay any final decision in order to study the effect of the latest action.

General Rate Policy

The airline rate policy, or, as it is sometimes called, its "price policy," is an increasingly important problem facing the industry. This is to be expected since the industry is moving out of the novelty or luxury class, and, therefore, pricing and price or rate competition

---

[51] CAB Press Release, June 17, 1960, in Docket 8008. This increase amounted to about 5 per cent and was estimated to increase the trunklines' revenues by approximately $84 million annually. See *General Passenger Fare Investigation*, CAB Docket 8008 *et al.* (1960).

[52] It is interesting to note that a return of 10.5 per cent is the highest in the history of regulation in the United States. No major rate-of-return allowance has exceeded 8 per cent and during the past twenty-five years none has exceeded 7 per cent. See Arthur Andersen & Co., *Return Allowed in Public Utility Rate Cases* (New York, 1958).

become of more importance. As air transportation comes more and more into direct price competition with surface carriers, which have traditionally charged rates and fares materially below the air carriers, and as air passengers are drawn from an increasingly price-conscious market, sound rate policies become mandatory for the future development of the industry. No gift of prophecy is necessary to forecast that on the future rate policies of this industry will depend to a major extent the future volume of traffic, both passenger and freight.

As has been discussed previously in this chapter, we have already seen some important changes in airline rate-making and an awakening of price-consciousness on the part of the industry, the traveling and shipping public, and the Board. After the close of World War II and until late in 1948, airline pricing was basically simple, particularly as long as these carriers were primarily passenger conscious. One took the air route distance between two points and multiplied by a standard fare level of a certain number of cents per passenger-mile. There were, of course, a considerable number of exceptions within such a general structure, reflecting competitive routings, through routes, regional differences in the fare level, and the like. There were also surcharges for luxury equipment and even a scattering of special promotional fares. But although the fare level moved down and then up several times in the postwar period, it moved within the same simple framework and without much thought of pricing as a promotional or regulatory instrument.

Beginning in the fall of 1948 and extending through 1949 and 1950, the industry became increasingly aware of air transportation pricing. This fare-consciousness was reflected in the coach fares and other types of promotional rates already discussed in this chapter. These coach and other pricing experiments were approved by the Board with considerable caution. Even so, the Board was accused by some members of the industry of adopting policies which would "result in bringing the entire airline price structure of the industry crashing down about our ears." On the other hand, others accused the Board with equal vigor of being too timid, of lacking enthusiasm for an experiment which it helped to start. The Board was, however, feeling its way. The danger that the limited promotional fares and services could quickly give way to violent fare cutting was not to be ignored.[53]

This attitude of the Board was wise, since the industry was not

[53] See Joseph J. O'Connell, Jr., "The Price Tag for Air Travel," an address before the American Association of Airport Executives, April 19, 1950.

then, or is it now, ready for rate reductions on an across-the-board basis. Despite increased traffic, it still needs a general fare level between $5\frac{1}{2}$ and 6 cents a passenger-mile. The airlines are not ready financially for a general 4-cent-per-mile domestic passenger rate. To make broad and deep fare cuts would inevitably, at least during the last few years, invite either financial disaster or else enormously increased subsidization. In the immediate future, therefore, a continuation of promotional pricing on a restricted and highly selective basis seems to be the course of wisdom. This does not mean, however, that both the industry and the Board should not start preparing answers to some of the price policy or rate problems which are bound to arise sooner than some perhaps think.

The Board's policy, in effect since 1949–50, of selective promotional pricing appears to have been successful, both as to passengers and freight, in assisting the airlines out of a bad financial period and at the same time bringing to the traveling and shipping public the advantages and opportunities of air transportation at reduced fares and rates. Nevertheless, there are obvious limitations to this policy in terms of the long-range development of air transportation.

The general criteria and objectives of a sound long-range rate and fare policy have been summed up as follows:

1. The further encouragement and development of air transportation.
2. Reasonable simplicity of the fare and rate structure.
3. A close relationship between the level and structure of rates of fares and cost to the carriers of performing various types of services so that the various classes and types of traffic each bears as nearly as possible its fair share of costs.
4. A fare and rate structure and level which, at least in sum, will be fully compensatory to an increasingly wide area of the industry so that the carriers can operate without being a burden on the general taxpayer through subsidy support.[54]

These are the criteria which probably will determine the Board's general rate policy in the immediate future. Some of them are conflicting, at least in part, but so are the objectives set forth in the Civil Aeronautics Act of 1938 and the Federal Aviation Act of 1958, as, for example, the requirement that the Board foster sound economic conditions in air transportation at the same time that it is developing a system adapted to the present and *future* needs of the commerce, postal service, and the national defense. Obviously, there must be a balancing and weighing of objectives. This means that, domestically,

---

[54] *Ibid.*

more and more airline traffic should pay its own way and that subsidy should be increasingly restricted to special, experimental operations and to providing smaller communities with assistance during their initial period as airline stations. It should not be used as a tool to build up air traffic in general. There is simply not enough subsidy to do that effectively.

The fact that the industry is now in a period when it seems desirable to hold down the general fare and rate line, while at the same time experimenting with selective promotional pricing, gives the Board and the airlines a unique opportunity to start thinking and studying the long-range future of rate policy. If it is correct that rate policy will continue to grow in importance in the affairs of air transportation and that air fares and freight rates should meet, at least in broad outline, the objectives which are stated above, the change in emphasis may well result in a basically new regulatory approach by the Board and a basically new approach to the problems of air transportation by the industry.

Pricing problems are becoming more important as the area in which air transportation is self-sufficient expands. This, in and of itself, requires a reorientation of thinking on the part of the Board. Until very lately, the chief concern has been with problems involving the route pattern, "need" carriers, and subsidy. There must, of course, continue to be shifts and improvements in the route pattern; and, to the extent that these can be intelligently and promptly made, the area of self-sufficiency for air transportation should be increased. There is also every indication that mail-pay and subsidy questions will continue to claim a great deal of the Board's attention for some time to come. But, as the area of self-sufficiency expands, the Board will be less concerned with subsidy questions and more and more concerned with developing a sound commercial fare and rate policy. In short, although the basic objective of the Civil Aeronautics Act of 1938 and the Federal Aviation Act of 1958—that is, the rapid development of air transportation to its proper and economic place in the transportation system of the United States—will continue, the regulatory tools by which this promotional policy is carried out may be changed.

It is to be hoped, for example, that the Board can be less concerned with minute scrutiny of the efficiency and internal workings of airline management and instead devote more attention to the somewhat broader economic questions of rate making or "transportation pricing," not only within the airline industry itself, but as between air transportation and surface transportation. There should be nothing alarming, either for the Board or for the industry, about any such shift in emphasis; this is particularly true if the period of experimental promotional pricing is utilized to make a basic study of longer-range pricing problems. If the Board and industry do an intelligent and skillful job in the years immediately ahead, they should be able to avoid many of the pitfalls into which surface transportation has fallen, particularly some of the least justified complications which have crept into surface transportation rate and fare structures. Intelligent rate or pricing policies for passengers and freight can prove of much greater significance and assistance to the future development of air transportation than can any amount of government subsidy.

Chapter 10

INTERNATIONAL AIR TRANSPORTATION POLICY OF THE UNITED STATES[1]

In the years before World War II the United States really had no international air transportation policy other than to encourage the development of American-flag operations through mail payments. Virtually all of our international air operations were conducted by Pan American Airways (now Pan American World Airways) or by its associate company, Pan American–Grace Airways (known as Panagra). Although our laws made no provision for the concentration of international aviation in a single company, the administrative policy of the Post Office Department and even the actions of Congress encouraged that result.

Pan American's monopoly was largely the result of the corporate policy of Pan American itself. Once having achieved a dominant po-

[1] See Oliver J. Lissitzyn, *International Air Transport and National Policy* (New York: Council on Foreign Relations, 1942) ; Burnet Hershey, *The Air Future* (New York: Duell, Sloan & Pearce, 1943) ; J. Parker Van Zandt, *The Geography of World Air Transport* (Washington, D.C.: Brookings Institution, 1944) ; J. Parker Van Zandt, *Civil Aviation and Peace* (Washington, D.C.: Brookings Institution, 1944) ; Osborne Mance, *International Air Transport* (London: Oxford University Press, 1944) ; Matthew Josephson, *Empire of the Air* (New York: Harcourt, Brace & Co., 1944) ; Alberta Worthington, *International Airways* (New York: H. W. Wilson Co., 1945) ; Lucien Zacharoff, *Vital Problems of Air Commerce* (New York: Duell, Sloan & Pearce, 1946) ; Lucien Zacharoff, *The World's Wings* (New York: Duell, Sloan & Pearce, 1946) ; John C. Cooper, *The Right to Fly* (New York: Henry Holt & Co., 1947) ; Burr W. Leyson, *Wings around the World* (New York: E. P. Dutton & Co., 1948) ; Oliver La Farge, *The Eagle and the Egg* (Boston: Houghton Mifflin Co., 1949) ; *International Air Transport Policy* (House Doc. No. 142, 79th Cong., 1st sess.) (Washington, D.C.: U.S. Government Printing Office, 1945) ; *International Commercial Aviation* (Sen. Doc. No. 173, 79th Cong. 2d sess.) (Washington, D.C.: U.S. Government Printing Office, 1946) ; *International Civil Aviation, 1945–1948* and *1948–1949* reports of the representative of the United States to the International Civil Aviation Organization (Washington, D.C.: U.S. Government Printing Office, 1948, 1949) ; Department of State, *Aspects of United States Participation in International Civil Aviation* (Washington, D.C., 1949) ; *IATA: The First Three Decades* (Montreal: International Air Transport Association, 1949) ; John C. Cooper, *Summary and Background Material on International Ownership and Operation of World Air Transport Services* (Princeton: Princeton University, 1949) ; Henry L. Smith, *Airways Abroad* (Madison: University of Wisconsin Press, 1950).

sition and having secured the requisite operating rights, Pan American always seemed in the position of being the carrier best qualified to receive the air mail contracts, which were the foundation of prewar commercial aviation. The award of air mail contracts to Pan American rather than to other American companies gave Pan American the indispensable economic basis for survival and expansion. Other companies were not so fortunate. For example, it is reported that the Postmaster General refused to advertise for air mail contract bids until Pan American and the New York, Rio, and Buenos Aires Airline (NYRBA) merged, a decision which enabled Pan American in September, 1930, to acquire a strong potential competitor.[2]

Soon after its establishment, the Civil Aeronautics Board moved to encourage competition in the international field. In this respect, the Board has consistently held that the development of a sound air transportation system properly adapted to the national needs, as outlined in the Civil Aeronautics Act, demands that more than one international air carrier be certificated under the American flag. The Board has stated:

> We recognize that competition from foreign air carrier services will develop on important routes. Such foreign competition, however, is not an adequate reason for abandoning the present statutory policy of this Government. The greatest gain from competition whether actual or potential is the stimulus to devise and experiment with new operating techniques and new equipment, to develop new means of acquiring and promoting business, including the rendering of better service to the customer and to the country, and to afford the Government comparative yardsticks by which the performance of United States operators can be measured. No matter how many foreign competitors may be in the field their research and development will not be fully available to our industry. The technical advancement of aircraft that may be stimulated by competition, together with progressive and competitive engineering and research associated therewith, will contribute to the peace-time advancement and maintenance of the aircraft manufacturing industry.[3]

But the Board's decisions supporting such a state of affairs were not made really effective until after the close of World War II. For example, the refusal of Congress to vote an air mail appropriation for American Export Airlines, after the Civil Aeronautics Board had resolved the issue of steamship ownership by granting a certificate of convenience and necessity for a trans-Atlantic operation, has been interpreted as indicating that a majority in the Senate was favorable to

---

[2] See Lissitzyn, *op. cit.*

[3] *American Export Air, Trans-Atlantic Service*, 2 CAB 16 (1940); *Northeast Airlines, Inc., et al., North Atlantic Route Case*, 6 CAB 319 (1945).

a single-company policy at that time. With respect to the issue of steamship ownership, Pan American successfully challenged the order of the Board,[4] and thereafter, in conformity with the court's ruling, the Board entered an order requiring American Export Lines to divest itself of its ownership of American Export Airlines.

Without any change in the public policy provided for in the Civil Aeronautics Act of 1938, the Board in the international route cases heard since the close of World War II has found that the public interest requires the operation of more than one United States international air carrier. It has sought to develop the strongest possible system in international air service, providing competition only where it has been considered to be justified by the actual and potential traffic. For example, in the so-called North Atlantic Route Case,[5] the Board certificated American Export Airlines and Transcontinental and Western Air (now Trans World Airlines), in addition to Pan American, to provide service to London and to Paris and beyond to other points in Europe, the Near East, and Asia. Before the war, both Pan American and Panagra had extensive routes in Latin America. The Latin American Decision[6] granted new routes in the Caribbean, Central America, and South America to several other United States-flag carriers. Braniff Airways was certificated to operate to Mexico, Cuba, the Canal Zone, and South America; Chicago and Southern Airlines to Caracas, Venezuela, San Juan, and other points in the Caribbean; Western Airlines to Mexico City; Eastern Air Lines to Mexico City and San Juan; National Airlines to Havana; Colonial Airlines to Bermuda; and American Airlines' temporary extension to Mexico City was made permanent. A number of additional services were also granted both Pan American and Panagra.

Pan American was also operating across the Pacific before the war. In the Hawaiian Case,[7] United Air Lines was authorized to operate between Honolulu and San Francisco. In the Pacific Case,[8] Northwest Airlines (now Northwest-Orient Airlines) was certificated to operate to Alaska and the Orient from the terminal points of New York and Chicago via the intermediate points of Twin Cities and Edmonton, Canada, and from the terminal points of Seattle. In the same proceeding, Pan American was authorized to extend its Central Pacific

---

[4] *Pan American Airways Co.* v. *Civil Aeronautics Board,* 121 Fed. (2d) 810.

[5] 6 CAB 319 (1945).

[6] 6 CAB 857 (1946).

[7] 7 CAB 83 (1946).

[8] 7 CAB 209 (1946).

route from Midway to Tokyo, Shanghai, and Hongkong and from Manila to Saigon, Singapore, and Batavia; this route was further extended from Hongkong to Indo-China and India to connect with Pan American's North Atlantic route. Pan American thus became the only carrier to operate around the world. Pan American's South Pacific route was extended from New Caledonia to Australia. In addition to the new round-the-world route of Pan American, the Board extended Transcontinental and Western Air's (now Trans World Airlines) North Atlantic route from India to Shanghai to connect with newly authorized Pacific routes, thus establishing, in effect, a second United States-flag round-the-world service. New services between the United States and Africa resulted from an authorization issued to Pan American in the South Atlantic Case[9] to operate between New York and the co-terminal points of Johannesburg and Capetown via the Azores, Dakar, Monrovia, and Leopoldsville. In addition, Pan American's present route to Brazil was extended beyond Natal to Ascension Island and Johannesburg and Capetown.

The development of Pan American Airways was inevitably influenced by the necessity of coming to terms with the several governments through whose territories operating rights were sought. In general, the influence of the foreign governments was directed toward obtaining as much service as possible; and, fortunately, political considerations were not of great importance.

In the prewar years, American international aviation by and large was able to develop without regard to the policies pursued by other air-minded nations. Throughout Latin America the problem was largely one of meeting subsidized European operations. Inasmuch as the two American airlines were willing to serve on a commercial basis and the service was welcomed throughout Latin America, Pan American Airways and Pan American–Grace Airways were able to obtain, sometimes with the assistance of our diplomatic representatives, the necessary franchises to permit the development of economically sound and comprehensive air operations.[10]

Similarly, Pan American Airways was able to extend its operations across the Pacific, using islands under United States sovereignty as stepping stones all the way to the Asiatic mainland. However, China was at that time unwilling to permit any foreign-flag operations to en-

[9] 7 CAB 285 (1946).

[10] A willingness to assist in the promotion and development of national companies in Central and South America doubtless facilitated the development of its international network by Pan American Airways. See Josephson, *op. cit.*, chap. v.

ter the country, a prohibition directed against Japan. Hence, the trans-Pacific line terminated at Portuguese Macao and at Hongkong, where the British granted landing rights after Pan American had secured landing rights at the nearby Portuguese island. In 1941, Pan American extended its operations southward from Manila to Singapore, which required the company to negotiate operating agreements with other countries. Franchises were procured for a line running from Honolulu through Canton Island and Noumea (New Caledonia) to Auckland, New Zealand.

The establishment of trans-Atlantic operations, however, necessitated the active participation of the United States government. Although Pan American Airways and Imperial Airways, the British company, were successful in their negotiations with Portugal for landing rights at Lisbon and Horta, negotiations through diplomatic channels were necessary in concluding the agreements with the governments of the United Kingdom (for England, Bermuda, and Newfoundland), Canada, and Eire. These formal governmental negotiations provided for the issuance of reciprocal operating rights by the governments concerned to the American and British companies. In like manner, reciprocal operating rights were issued for the service to France.

In prewar Europe the historical development was not very different. Air policy was made largely by the airlines themselves, working through pools and other cartel arrangements. While the several European states sought to foster their respective airlines for reasons of political policy, the airlines were successful in using the political power of the different countries to bolster and support the program of cartel co-operation which the various operators had worked out. Commercial aviation, therefore, developed according to a co-operative, rather than a competitive, pattern. Most European airlines, whether operated by government corporations or private companies, were supported by liberal subsidies of one kind or another.[11] The airlines of the several countries pooled their operations, with some agreements providing for a pooling of revenues. Expenses were not pooled, but operations were so allocated that each company became responsible for operating specific parts of the joint service at its own expense. For example, the flight from Stockholm via Copenhagen to Amsterdam might be conducted as a pool operation with three airlines participating; but, if the route could support only three flights daily,

---

[11] For a discussion of these various subsidies, see Lissitzyn, *op. cit.*, chap. viii.

the three participants would alternate in flying the route so that each would bear its share of the cost.

Objectives for United States Air Policy

During World War II the potential of international air transportation for the United States became fully apparent because of the remarkable combined performances of the Armed Forces and the airlines, the latter operating under contracts with the government. With the close of hostilities, it was realized that the objectives of the United States international air policy should be examined from two points of view: what policy would promote the best interests of the national economy, and what policy would encourage the maximum development of air transport.

Air transportation had become an indispensable instrument for the promotion of international trade and foreign investment. The availability of air mail to effect a quick interchange of intelligence—documents, legal papers, technical reports, and the like—supplied a service which could not be performed by the cable, radio, and telephone services. The availability of air transport made it possible for firms having foreign connections to maintain frequent personal contacts with foreign representatives or branch offices, to arrange for personal meetings with customers, and to call together executives from distant points for quick conferences.

Beyond its contribution to the advance of American business and industry abroad, the fullest development of air transportation was important to the people generally and to the security of the nation. The military importance of air transport in peace, as well as in war, gave an urgency to all policies which would encourage the intensive development of an extensive air transport industry. It was felt, moreover, that such an industry would serve to maintain manufacturing capacity, to train air personnel and ground forces, and to provide a flexible means of quick transport which might be of crucial importance in a military emergency.

It was decided that the first objective of United States international air policy must, therefore, be the maximum development of this mode of transport. This meant that the immediate concern of national policy should be the creation of the political and economic frameworks that would permit air transportation to achieve its full potential development.

At the same time, it was evident that it would not be good policy for the United States to seem to dominate air transportation either in the Western Hemisphere or on a world basis. In fact, it was well understood that such a policy would create international antagonisms harmful to the whole industry. Within the limits dictated by essential national interests, it was decided, therefore, that our policy would be not to exclude any foreign-flag airline from seeking an opportunity to take part in the industry. The United States took a leading position in fostering the development of international air law along channels to facilitate the maximum growth and utilization of commercial aviation. Everyone understood that, in the interests of national defense, restrictions might have to be imposed upon the use of our air space and certain landing areas; but it was made clear that neither the United States nor any other nation should seek to use its sovereignty of the air or its control over airports to handicap foreign-flag operations in the interest of giving improper advantage to its own airlines. Even though political means may have to be used at times to prevent discrimination against a nation's airlines by other countries, a sound economic framework is indispensable to a sound air transport industry. The international policy under which commercial aviation operates should assure that no company will be discriminated against by reason of its nationality or size. The policy should assure that an airline's chances of survival and success will depend upon efficiency and economy, not upon political manipulations or privileged position.

In summary, the nation's policy[12] was to seek to assure (*a*) that United States aviation would continue to be progressive in the development and adoption of the newest types of equipment and the best operating procedures, (*b*) that adequate incentives would compel efficiency in operation, (*c*) that the full economic potentialities of air transport would be realized by a constant widening of the market through reductions in costs and rates, (*d*) that healthy financial conditions would assure the inflow of adequate capital, and (*e*) that United States airlines would carry a volume of world traffic commensurate with the importance of the United States as a market for air transport services.

Air transportation is a national asset, an implement to promote international trade and investment. However, it must be recognized that an extensive international trade is necessary to support an intensive air transport industry. The best guarantee that United States international aviation will find a large sphere for service will be the encour-

[12] See *International Air Transport Policy* (House Doc. No. 142, 79th Cong., 1st sess.) (Washington, D.C.: U.S. Government Printing Office, 1945).

agement and expansion of American trade and investment in all parts of the world in order to develop business travel and shipping; otherwise air transport can have only an insecure economic base in the foreign travel of American tourists.

No problem can be solved on its own level alone. The national policy with respect to air transportation cannot be framed simply with reference to the commercial interests of air transportation. The relationship of air transportation to other modes of transport, to the development of the national economy, to the preservation of healthy competitive conditions at home and abroad, and above all to the military security of the nation indicates that commercial aviation must always be the servant, not the master. Therefore, a discussion of national policy must proceed with an awareness of the limitations and requirements of all the public interests which impinge upon this form of transportation.

International Legal Framework

The legal constitution under which international aviation has operated is a product of developments over a period of years. Like most social institutions, the system of legal principles governing air transportation has lagged behind the technical and commercial growth of the industry. The tremendous technical advances that occurred under the stimulus of war necessity made the institutional lag in the growth of legal principles a serious obstacle to the resumption of world-wide aviation after the war.

International aviation has been carried on under the principles established by a series of international conventions. The most important of these was the International Convention for Air Navigation (C.I.N.A.), concluded at Paris in 1919. This convention was ratified by twenty-six countries and served as the constitution for international aviation outside of the Western Hemisphere. This convention was not ratified by the United States because it was associated with the League of Nations to which this country did not belong. The C.I.N.A. Convention asserted the principle of national sovereignty of the air; and, as finally interpreted and amended, it required that explicit authority be secured from each country before commercial air services might be operated over that country. The C.I.N.A. was never able to deal with international aviation on a world-wide basis since its membership consisted chiefly of European countries.

The Pan American Convention on Commercial Aviation, signed at Havana, Cuba, on February 20, 1928, also recognized that each country had complete and exclusive sovereignty of the air over its own territory and territorial waters. This convention was signed by twenty-one countries, including the United States. By its terms, the convention extended "freedom of innocent passage" to aircraft engaged in air transportation; but, in practice, the air carriers of one signatory power have been required to obtain special permission to establish scheduled operations over the territory of other parties. Thus, international aviation in the Western Hemisphere developed under legal principles substantially similar to those embodied in the C.I.N.A. Convention.

During World War II, the United States policy for a bilateral approach[13] to the matter of securing landing rights for our airlines was formally announced in a joint statement by the Department of State and Civil Aeronautics Board.[14] This provided that the Department of State was to conduct negotiations with foreign governments for any new or additional landing rights which might be determined desirable through collaboration between the Board and the State Department. It was expected that the rights acquired in this manner would be in general terms, not mentioning any specific carrier or carriers until the Board could determine the fitness and ability of applicants for certificates of convenience and necessity. This statement also provided that foreign air carriers applying to the Board under section 402 of the act for permits to operate into the United States should forward such applications through diplomatic channels for transmission to the Board. The Board, however, stated that, while landing rights were to be secured through intergovernmental negotiations as a general procedure, this practice was not to be considered arbitrary or inflexible and that, therefore, an air carrier might present any unusual or compelling reasons which it thought would justify it to conduct independent negotiations with a foreign nation.

This joint statement of policy for acquiring foreign landing rights on the bilateral basis was inaugurated by the United States for the following principal reasons: (*a*) the desire to avoid confusing and perhaps embarrassing situations resulting from several carriers competing with each other in negotiations with foreign governments or foreign carriers, (*b*) the desire to avoid a situation whereby a carrier

[13] The terms used in this discussion to denote method of international agreement may be briefly defined as follows: *unilateral*—between a company and a nation, but the company (air carrier in these instances) cannot bind the country of which it is a citizen; *bilateral*—between two nations; *multilateral*—between more than two nations.

[14] Memorandum issued by the Civil Aeronautics Board, December 2, 1943, addressed to "all holders of and applicants for certificates of convenience and necessity."

which had successfully concluded such foreign negotiations was later denied a certificate by the Civil Aeronautics Board on the grounds that convenience and necessity did not justify the operation contemplated, and (*c*) the desire to avoid the possibility of any exclusive arrangement being negotiated by an individual carrier which would be designed to restrict the Civil Aeronautic Board's power to select operating carriers. In the interest of equity to all United States air carriers, the Board could not be influenced in the final selection of a carrier by consideration of special or private arrangements previously concluded by that carrier on its own initiative.

The discussion of a postwar legal framework for international aviation at first centered on proposals to achieve a greater measure of freedom for international aviation through a multilateral agreement signed by all interested nations. The necessity of negotiating bilateral agreements between countries or unilateral agreements between the air carrier of one country and the country over which it proposed to operate, both to fly over the country and to engage in air commerce to and from the country, operated in prewar years as a serious restriction upon the establishment of the most economical air routes. Countries denied such operating rights to foreign-flag airlines in order to promote their own airlines or for reasons of political hostility. In other instances, operating rights were granted subject to restrictive conditions which prevented or retarded the development of the best service. It was realized that in the future it might be anticipated that the continuance of the old practice of individual negotiation with respect to each air operation would constitute an even more serious obstacle to international aviation. More countries were interested in promoting their own international services, and they were more disposed to be insistent on securing reciprocal rights for their own air carriers or prescribing conditions designed to improve the competitive position of their own airlines. All these facts led to the conclusion that international aviation must have a more liberal legal framework if it was to develop on sound lines.

Realizing that a postwar international organization was needed not only to set up air navigation standards and practices for the whole world but also to deal with the economic problems of international air transport, the United States took the lead by inviting most of the nations of the world to attend an international conference on civil aviation to be held in Chicago in the latter part of 1944. Representatives of fifty-four nations attended. The only major nonemeny or nonenemy-occupied countries which did not participate were Argentina, which was not invited, and the Union of Soviet Socialist Republics, which did not attend. Argentina, in June, 1946, agreed to the convention resulting from the Chicago conference, but Russia never took any action.

So far as civil aviation was concerned, the movement for international collaboration developed into three separate projects at this international civil aviation conference.[15] The first proposal, made by the representatives from New Zealand and Australia, was that international civil aviation should be truly international in character, carried on by a single international corporation in which every nation should participate. This is a noble conception, but manifestly impractical and impossible of becoming a reality until all nations are prepared to pool their interests.

The second proposal was advanced by the British. It began by suggesting the establishment of an international board which should do for the world substantially what the Civil Aeronautics Board has done for the United States. Carriers which wished to fly international routes should apply for a license, and it would be granted or refused on an economic showing of international convenience and necessity. It was also proposed that such a board might even do things which the Civil Aeronautics Board cannot do and has never done, such as regulate the number of flights each company might make, determine the percentage of traffic which each country's lines might carry in any region, and allocate certain routes to certain countries to the exclusion of others.

The third plan of co-operation was proposed by the Canadians, who saw that merely assigning power to any international body, as proposed by the British, answered no questions. In consequence, beginning with the idea of an international Civil Aeronautics Board, they endeavored to analyze the job it would have to do. In their analysis they split the work of international air commerce into five elements, which have come to be known as the "Five Freedoms":

1. The right of transit or freedom for peaceful commercial aircraft to fly through the air of another country. This involves the right to use the airspaces of any nation for nonstop flight. The importance of the right lies in the fact that its denial may prevent an air service from following the most economical route. Although it is technically possible for United States airlines to reach all continents without

[15] See *Blueprint for World Civil Aviation*, Department of State Publication No. 2348 (Washington, D.C., 1945).

passing over the territory of other countries, the shortest routes between the United States and either Europe or Asia pass over the territory of other countries. For example, the shortest route to northern Europe passes over or close to Canada, Greenland, and Iceland. Any operation to the interior of Europe would involve not only passing over foreign territory in this hemisphere but also passing over one or more of the countries of western Europe. It is of substantial advantage to the United States and to other air-minded nations if their airplanes enjoy the general right of passage over all countries.

2. The right to land for technical reasons, refueling, repairs, or other services, but not to take on or discharge commerce. This is of great practical importance. While it would be possible with airplanes now available to operate nonstop between United States airports and the principal traffic centers of the world, it would be highly uneconomical to conduct all international aviation in that fashion. The most efficient service can probably be rendered if planes stop at intervals of 1,500 to 2,000 miles for refueling, since flights in excess of these distances necessitate replacing valuable payload capacity with additional fuel.

It would, therefore, be in the interest of the United States to have the right of transit and the right to land established as a universal principle for international aviation. Any arrangement less than a universal and world-wide arrangement respecting the right to land would be of limited importance for the United States. For example, a reciprocal exchange of landing rights with Great Britian, including the Crown colonies but not the dominions, would give the British valuable rights and would give the United States almost nothing.

The advantages accruing from a world-wide interchange of landing rights would be greatly in excess of any loss to any individual country that might result from granting such general rights with respect to territory under its sovereignty. For the United States, landing rights are most important in Canada, Newfoundland, Siberia, India, and on some of the islands of the Atlantic and the South Pacific. Insofar as the Continental United States is concerned, such rights of transit and landing would be of principal advantage to Canada in establishing service to Bermuda and British Caribbean possessions and to Canada and Australia or New Zealand in operating service between North America and Australia. Landing rights in Hawaii and Alaska are essential for any airline seeking to operate either of the two main routes between Asia and North America.

3. The right of commercial entry or freedom to carry traffic from

a plane's country of origin to any other country. This would mean freedom for all commercial airlines (and other nonmilitary planes) to traverse the airspaces of any country without the necessity of securing prior permission from the authorities of that country, to land at any public airport, and to engage in air commerce, all subject to compliance with the applicable air traffic rules. This would mean free competition between national and foreign airlines.

4. The right to pick up traffic in other countries destined for the plane's homeland. Under this freedom, an American aircraft returning from Paris to New York could accept passengers bound only for the United States at Paris and at any other airport, such as Shannon, it might touch on the homeward journey. But it could not, unless the fifth freedom were agreed upon, carry a passenger who only wanted to go from Paris to Shannon.

5. The right for a foreign aircraft to carry traffic between countries outside its own. Thus, an American aircraft homeward bound from Paris could take on and drop off passengers and cargo moving between Paris and Shannon or between any other two countries along its route. This "fifth freedom" is of particular importance to nations like the United States that operate long-range, trunkline international air services. Long-haul carriers seek fifth-freedom rights in order to keep their aircraft full over long international routes. The regional carriers of the different countries over which a long route might fly have difficulty in competing with the type of equipment and service which the large airlines offer on such routes. Governments are, therefore, inclined to request concessions in negotiating for flying rights in order to protect their national interests in their own airlines.

If all five freedoms are added up, commercial aircraft would have about the same rights in the air that ships have long had on the sea.

The Chicago conference resulted in the adoption of the following:

1. General principles for international air navigation and provision for the establishment first of a "provisional" and then of a "permanent" international aviation organization. By June 26, 1945, enough countries had signed the so-called "interim agreement" to set up the Provisional International Civil Aviation Organization (PICAO), which established offices in Montreal, Canada. This was later, on April 4, 1947, converted into the permanent International Civil Aviation Organization (ICAO), with offices at the same place.

2. An international air services transit agreement, incorporating

the right to fly over sovereign territory and the right to land for non-commercial purposes.

3. An international air transport agreement incorporating various commercial air rights which were to be considered as the start of an attempt to handle the economic problems of international air transport through reciprocal granting of privileges on a multilateral basis.

4. Technical agreements which would eventually result in international standardization of air navigation procedures.

It was the third of the above agreements which proved the stumbling block. It was signed by the United States and a number of other countries, thus providing, as far as they were concerned, for real freedom of the air; but Great Britain refused to sign. As a consequence, a number of nations withdrew; and the United States was finally forced to take a step backward and abandon the international aviation principles for which this country had stood at the Chicago conference and withdraw from the International Air Transport (Five Freedom) Agreement conceived at that meeting. Circumstances, therefore, forced the United States to adopt a policy of bilateralism. Between the years 1944 and 1954, bilateral air transport agreements have been entered into with 45 countries, based largely on what has come to be known as the "Bermuda Agreement" entered into between representatives of the United States and the United Kingdom at Bermuda in 1946.[16]

The Bermuda Agreement[17]

The Bermuda Air Agreement paved the way for the development of international air transport operations by United States airlines after World War II. Practically all the bilateral agreements since entered into by the United States follow the pattern adopted therein. This pattern established a number of important steps in the negotiation of an agreement.

1. Routes have to be exchanged. In drawing up this exchange, the carriage of traffic, not only between the United States and a foreign

[16] *Air Service Agreement—United States and United Kingdom* (signed at Bermuda, February 11, 1946), Department of State Publication No. 2565, Treaties and Other International Acts, Series 1507.

[17] *International Air Agreements,* Report of the Committee on Interstate and Foreign Commerce, U.S. Senate, 84th Cong. 2d sess. (Washington, D.C., 1956); P. Adriani, "The Bermuda Capacity Clauses," *Journal of Air Law and Commerce,* Autumn, 1955; Albert W. Stoffel, "American Bilateral Air Transport Agreements on the Threshold of the Jet Transport Age," *Journal of Air Law and Commerce,* Spring, 1959; L. L. Doty "Bilateral Issues Threaten Route Growth," *Aviation Week,* June 20, 1960.

country, but also between that foreign country and third countries by the foreign country, must be negotiated. This latter third-country traffic is the fill-up business essential to the economical operation of aircraft.

2. General standards for governing the amount of capacity to be operated must be agreed upon.

3. A procedure must be established to deal with the problem of rates to be charged and for the service.

The Bermuda Agreement capacity provisions laid down the principles governing the amount of service which may be operated over the routes exchanged. The basis of this principle was that the services provided shall retain, as their primary objective, the provision of capacity adequate to meet the traffic demands between the country of which an airline is a national and the countries of ultimate destination of the traffic. Thus, the backbone of United States air carrier traffic must be that between the United States and countries of ultimate destination of the traffic. Similarly, in the United Kingdom, the backbone of its traffic had to be that between the United Kingdom and countries of ultimate destination of the traffic. In this manner, an effective brake was put upon the operation of services primarily for the carriage of third-country traffic. After this test of primary objective was met, then the right existed to pick up third-country traffic subject to general rules of a qualitative nature which, while not providing for any mathematical formula, have been generally recognized as sound principles to guide the day-to-day determination of capacity offered in international air transportation. These rules are as follows:

> The air services made available to the public by the airlines operating under this Agreement shall bear a close relationship to the requirements of the public for such services.
>
> It is the understanding of both contracting parties that services provided by a designated airline under the present Agreement shall retain as their primary objective the provision of capacity adequate to the traffic demands between the country of which an airline is a national and the countries of ultimate destination of the traffic. The right to embark or disembark on such services international traffic destined for and coming from third countries at a point or points on the routes specified in this Agreement shall be applied in accordance with the general principles or orderly development to which both contracting parties subscribe and shall be subject to the general principle that capacity should be related—
>
> (*a*) to traffic requirements between the country of origin and the countries of ultimate destination of the traffic;
>
> (*b*) to the requirements of through airline operations; and

(*c*) to the traffic requirements of the area through which the airline passes after taking account of local and regional services.

The capacity clauses in the Bermuda Agreement establish a firm relationship between the capacity provided by a carrier and the traffic requirements of the routes served by that carrier. These clauses open a "fair and equal opportunity" to each contracting party by permitting both carriers to promote new traffic by offering adequate service, yet preventing one carrier from absorbing a quantity of traffic that would be detrimental to the other carrier.

Although it is not specifically spelled out in the clauses, it is possible for either country to ask for a review of traffic activities at at any time to determine whether capacity offered is in line with the Bermuda principles.

In effect, the capacity clauses can be interpreted to permit wide freedom of operation in open competition or tight control of operations to protect national interests. This permits each country to adjust schedules according to existing conditions through consultation. Because of this flexibility, the Bermuda Agreement is likely to hold its position as the standard blueprint for all bilaterals in the foreseeable future.

The fact remains, however, that this wide gap in interpretations sets sharply defined battle lines in negotiations. Since the two diverse views represent two virtually incompatible philosophies, stalemates are inevitable if a compromise can't be reached.

In exchanging air transport rights, the United States might well be governed by the following policies:

1. In determining the services which may be justified under Bermuda-type bilaterals, the affirmative principles of such agreements should be considered as well as those which relate to the limitation of capacity to be operated. The affirmative principles recognize the advantages to the "common welfare of both countries" in the widest possible distribution of the benefits of air travel. In applying the principles in such agreements relating to the capacity to be operated, no rigid formula should be applied to all types of routes. For example, "capacity adequate to the traffic demand" between two countries may very well mean daily service regardless of the relative volume of third- and fourth-freedom traffic compared with fifth-freedom traffic carried on that route. For that reason it has been suggested:

(*a*) The volume of the service to be allowed on low-density routes should be based on the *frequency* (not seat capacity) needed by postal, commercial, and national interests for speedy communications. In only rare cases should services of less than one a day be prohibited.

(*b*) The volume of service to be allowed on heavy traffic routes should be based on the economy of the operation; services that cannot be economically justified should be curtailed, but no others.

2. When the United States government negotiates for air transport rights, it should utilize all its bargaining powers, even though they all may not relate to aviation matters. It is a mistake to regard the welfare of our country as neatly divided into "aviation," "shipping," "taxation," "foreign trade," and so on, and to deal with each category separately. To do so inevitably places our country at a disadvantage. We freely permit foreign countries to carry most of our traffic moving by sea and then offer only the weakest resistance when the foreign countries propose to restrict our carriers by air. It makes no sense to limit our aviation bargaining to aviation matters since we necessarily ask for much and have relatively little to offer in return.

3. Where our government representatives meet with severe opposition to our established policies, the issues should not be conceded but should be handled at top policy levels with officials in foreign governments interested in the welfare of their country as a whole, not with the local officials responsible solely for aeronautics. Many of the existing bilaterals were secured only by top representation on our part meeting with the top officials in foreign governments. Top-level handling is essential to prevent the complete deterioration of United States airlines' position around the world.

The Character of Intergovernmental Agreements

The intergovernmental agreements to which the United States is a party are the most important part of the legal framework within which our international aviation must develop. Every consideration must, therefore, be given to concluding such intergovernmental agreements as will be conducive to the creation of a sound and progressive international air service. The problems of international aviation are, however, more complex than those of domestic commercial flying, for they are tied in with the right of foreign nations to refuse landing rights or to grant such permission only under conditions which may prove objectionable to our airlines.

The government of the United States has made marked advances in securing air rights through bilateral negotiation. There is little justification for the criticism, heard from some quarters, which alleges that we have bargained away our competitive position, since in every case negotiation with other countries has required a recognition of their rights as well as our own. So far we have secured the operating rights required by our international airlines by providing for the exchange of such rights with nearly all the important nations of the world. While the pattern of these rights is stronger than those secured by unilateral (airline and country) negotiation, such a pattern still has two fundamental defects—a lack of stability and a lack of uniformity. For these reasons many feel that it is imperative that the bilateral agreements be replaced by the right kind of multilateral agreement as soon as possible.

It is relatively easy to cancel a bilateral agreement, since it involves relations with only one other nation and air transport operations with other nations can continue. While it is perfectly true that all nations desire access to United States traffic, so that any one of them will hesitate before canceling an agreement with us, still the economic and political pressures in the world today may impel one or more nations to insist upon amendments to bilateral agreements imposing restrictions on our right to commercial operation or, in the alternative, upon a cancellation of the agreements. Under a multilateral agreement, nations might cancel a separate bilateral route arrangement but would still be required to make no agreements inconsistent with the principles embodied in the multilateral agreement; consequently, they would find it impossible to bargain one by one into restrictive arrangements all the nations with whom they have bilateral agreements. Thus, it would become much more difficult, if not entirely impossible, for any nation to gain tangible advantages from the cancellation of a route arrangement. Although a nation might withdraw from the multilateral agreement entirely, there would be heavy moral pressures against doing so; moreover, little would be gained, since its relations with all the nations participating in the multilateral agreements would have to be consistent with the terms of that agreement. Thus many forces work against denunciation of a multilateral agreement but are weaker in or absent from the bilateral pattern.

The bilateral system has another serious defect in its lack of uniformity. Bilateral negotiations, which involve all the provisions of an air transport agreement, inevitably lead to bargaining over each provision which is conceived to be of special interest to one or the other of the bargaining nations. In spite of strenuous efforts, it has been impossible for the United States to avoid making minor changes in various standard provisions. When the challenges come, as they will when other nations have developed their airlines to the point where competition for traffic is keener, these "minor" variations may present operating problems of considerable magnitude. For example, there are variants in the statement of "capacity language" in the agreements with India, the Philippines, China, Argentina, Australia, and others. The Annex of the Australian agreement comes close to a rate differential. Many differences in the language affect rates and charges.

A soundly conceived multilateral agreement would provide much needed uniformity in the general rules under which international air transport operations are conducted and would serve as a bulwark against attacks upon the present relative freedom of operations. However, certain essential elements would have to be contained in a multilateral agreement before it would be desirable from the standpoint of the United States:

a) Provisions calling for separate bilateral exchanges of routes. There are in today's world powerful economic and security reasons which make an automatic multilateral exchange of routes completely undesirable.

b) Provisions which will clearly allow adequate freedom for the carriage of third-, fourth-, and fifth-freedom traffic.

c) Machinery for the handling of disputes by a method of arbitration that will assure expertness, impartiality, and some degree of continuity, rather than by resort to the Council of the International Civil Aviation Organization or some similar body. This group would operate only if negotiation failed.

Owing to the rapid development of aviation after the close of World War II, the need for international air services, and the desirability of securing the necessary air rights for United States air carriers without delay, it was determined that, as a matter of policy, bilateral air transport agreements should be negotiated as executive agreements rather than as treaties. Bilateral air transport agreements were concluded between the United States and eleven foreign governments during the fiscal year 1946 and with sixteen others during the fiscal year 1947. It is hardly possible that such a large number of agreements could have been concluded within this period had it been necessary to comply with the cumbersome treaty procedure requiring approval by the Senate. Executive agreements are subject to amendment from time to time in the light of new developments, thus affording an efficient and flexible procedure for modifying the terms of agreements. The treaty procedure, on the other hand, is not adaptable to continuous and frequent revision. In this connection it is significant that six of the forty bilateral agreements which we have concluded have already required amendment.

In section 6 (*c*) of the Air Commerce Act of 1926 and sections 2 (*a*) and (*d*) and 301 of the Civil Aeronautics Act of 1938, Congress has clearly set forth the policy of this government to foster air commerce between the United States and foreign countries. It has indicated its understanding that, in order to foster such air commerce, it is necessary to enter into agreements with foreign countries; and in section 802 of the 1938 Act, the Secretary of State is recognized as the appropriate authority to negotiate such agreements (in consultation with the Civil Aeronautics Board). In section 1102 of the act, the Board is directed to exercise and perform its powers and duties consistent with any obligation assumed by the United States in any treaty, convention, or agreement that may be in force between the United States and any foreign country or foreign countries. Thus by legislation the Congress has specifically provided for certain types of agreements with foreign countries in the field of civil aviation being made by the Executive rather than through the treaty process.

The Air Coordinating Committee, in its statement of national policy[18] governing international aviation, made the following recommendations regarding routes and rights:

1. The exchange of air transport rights will continue to be by bilateral air transport agreement until such time as it is possible to achieve a multilateral agreement which contains principles generally in accord with those of existing United States bilateral agreements.
2. The United States will adhere to the policy of negotiating for international air rights on the basis of all five freedoms.
3. In the negotiation of its agreements for the exchange of international air rights, the United States will continue to adhere to the Bermuda principles as the most satisfactory basis for relating capacity to traffic.
4. In determining the rights to be included in bilateral air transport agreements, the United States will continue its objective of establishing, insofar as possible, an equitable exchange of economic benefits.
5. The United States will seek interpretation and application of its agreements in a manner which will accord with the over-all objectives of an effective international air transport system.

Technical Facilities and Standard Operating Procedures

After a means had been developed to make it legally possible for the aircraft of one nation to operate into the airspace of others, an-

[18] Air Coordinating Committee, *Civil Air Policy* (Washington, D.C., 1954).

other group of requirements was necessary before aircraft could operate internationally. These were the technical requirements for physical equipment and rules governing operation of world airways. These needs can be grouped as follows: (*a*) Physical equipment had to be obtained and installed at specific points; (*b*) rules of the road and operating procedures had to be agreed upon; (*c*) in many of the actions under the above two requirements, it was essential that there be agreement on standards. For example, even if radio stations were to be established on a long route, it was important that the radio signals be identical and capable of receipt on one set. In addition, qualifications of personnel had to be agreed upon.

With respect to the physical equipment that had to be obtained and installed, it will be readily understood that international operation required airports with adequate runways, radio transmitters, radio receivers, and airways with navigation aids. Stations had to be established for collecting weather data and transmitting it to aircraft and to other stations on the ground. The size of this undertaking is indicated by the fact that when the plans were completed, they listed some 40,000 facilities which had to be located or services to be rendered in some manner.

The second group of requirements, namely, the rules of the road and operating procedures, presented peculiar obstacles because no other nation had anything like the United States' experience in volume commercial flying and, therefore, other nations were utterly unaware of the scope of the needs for such things as air traffic control. Americans were familiar with volume-flying into airports because in such cities as Chicago in a recent year the airline landing and take-offs numbered 266,825. This was an average of 731 per day, and that airport can handle 120 take-offs and landings per hour. But European nations had no such experience. The largest number of take-offs and landings in a given year even as late as 1953, at the busiest foreign airport, London, was only 45,501. This was the annual equivalent of the operations at Albuquerque, New Mexico, and averaged only 125 per day. Furthermore, at the start of our international operations there were no airways as we know them outside of the North American continent.

The third class of requirements was the establishment of safety standards. On some of these matters, the precise standard adopted was not so important provided it was used by all. Thus, the altitude of eastbound flights over the Atlantic could be at one level or another without catastrophe, provided that all operators followed the same practice. On the other hand, there were many areas in which the choice of the standard was of immense importance to a number of American interests, and in the choice of these standards special care was necessary. Thus, if the radio equipment prescribed as the standard equipment in aircraft or in navigation aids on the ground were of foreign design and manufacture, American equipment might become obsolete and our manufacturers would lose their place in the world markets for that equipment. Again, if aircraft designs of foreign origin become world standards, American aircraft manufacturers could lose a strategic position in the market.

The fourth area of needs related to standards for qualifications of airmen and airworthiness of aircraft. This was important because it affected several interested groups. In the United States the men who operate the airport control towers and direct the movement of American aircraft are licensed by the Civil Aeronautics Administration to give the necessary assurance of competency. Our government questioned whether, in international operations, it could be given assurance that the aircraft control tower operators in all the countries into which our aircraft would operate would be qualified for the duties they perform. Similarly, how could our government be assured that pilots licensed by foreign countries were competent to fly safely over American cities without endangering other American aircraft and American residents on the ground?

Our government maintained it was of great importance that the standards of competency be exacting enough to assure us that foreign licensed personnel could perform their functions adequately and safely. To this end, the United States urged the adoption of its personnel licensing requirements, and American standards were in the main adopted in their entirety. This was beneficial for thousands of Americans who held pilot and other airman licenses, for it meant they were qualified to fly abroad without being required to pass additional examinations.

If the airworthiness of a foreign aircraft were to be questioned by each country into which it flew, a serious delay and expense could be imposed on air lines and other operators. Recognizing this, the Chicago convention provided for agreement on standards of airworthiness which, if complied with, would permit recognition of the airworthiness certificates of individual countries and prevent duplicate examinations. Since American operators fly into as many foreign jurisdictions as the operators of any other flag, the burdens on Americans for duplicate inspection would be severe and the benefits from agreement would be enormous. Thus far it has proved impossible to develop a set of complete, comprehensive, and detailed international airworthiness specifications for the type-certification and operation of aircraft. The primary objective of international airworthiness standards has, therefore, been to define, for application by the competent national authorities, the minimum international standards by which countries should recognize certificates of airworthiness for the purpose of foreign aircraft flying into and over their territories, thereby achieving, among other things, protection of other aircraft, third persons, and property.

The task of setting up technical facilities and standard operating procedures, such as those just discussed, has belonged to the International Civil Aviation Organization. Divisional meetings, held in Montreal and elsewhere and attended by technicans from member states and international organizations, have developed recommendations for standards in each of the technical fields. The representatives of American aviation interests have been brought together through the offices of the Air Coordinating Committee to consider this problem, and a United States position has been prepared after consultation with all interested parties. A delegation representing the American point of view has attended the meetings of ICAO and sought by negotiation to reach an agreement. Although the United States has been outstandingly successful in having its views accepted, there are and will be times when contrary practices are adopted as ICAO standards. The United States may, however, refuse to accept those standards and refuse to put into effect, in this country, the requirements contained in the international standards. Such a procedure has the desirable quality of permitting each country to determine, first, whether a standard is necessary, and second, even if necessary internationally, whether it is in such conflict with domestic practice or imposes such hardships that the inconvenience it would impose far outweighs the advantages to be derived.

Procedure of the Civil Aeronautics Board[19]

Certain procedures of the Civil Aeronautics Board are geared to implement international negotiations by affording expeditious action to foreign air carriers seeking entry to the United States. They are

[19] This section is adapted from *Statement of Civil Aeronautics Board before the President's Air Policy Commission*, October 27, 1947. See also G. Nathan Calkins, Jr., "The Role of the Civil Aeronautics Board in the Grant of Operating Rights in Foreign Air Carriage," *Journal of Air Law and Commerce*, Summer, 1955.

justified since substantially the same courtesies are extended our own carriers by other nations. Other procedure, such as the requirement of presidential approval of foreign or overseas grants of routes, are necessary from the point of view of a comprehensive and uniform international policy.

The Civil Aeronautics Act of 1938 prohibits a foreign air carrier from engaging in air transportation to the United States unless it has a foreign air carrier permit issued by the Board.[20] By definition, foreign air transportation means the "carriage by aircraft of persons or property as a common carrier for compensation or hire or the carriage of mail by aircraft" in commerce between a place in the United States and any place outside thereof. Under the Civil Aeronautics Act, therefore, no authorization is required from the Board for the conduct of any services other than common carrier services. Just as for domestic air transportation, the Civil Aeronautics Act makes no distinction between scheduled and nonscheduled services in foreign air transportation.

The Air Commerce Act of 1926 provides that, if a foreign nation grants similar privileges, the Administrator of Civil Aeronautics "may authorize aircraft registered under the law of the foreign nation and not a part of the armed forces thereof to be navigated in the United States."[21] Foreign air carriers operating under foreign air carrier permits issued by the Board have, therefore, not been required by the Administrator to obtain foreign aircraft permits as required by section 6 (*c*) of the Air Commerce Act. However, the Administrator has required such permits in all other cases involving navigation in the United States of aircraft registered under the law of a foreign nation and not a part of the armed forces thereof.

It will be seen, therefore, that a clear distinction exists between operations authorized by the Civil Aeronautics Act of 1938 and operations authorized by the Air Commerce Act of 1926. The former includes all common carrier operations (scheduled or nonscheduled), and the latter includes all operations other than common carrier operations. In the administration of both acts, however, occasions frequently arise in which the exact status of proposed operations by a foreign company are difficult to classify. The difficulty of classification is increased because: (*a*) Requests for permission to operate necessarily precede actual operations and make it difficult to

---

[20] Civil Aeronautics Act and Federal Aviation Act, sec. 402.

[21] Air Commerce Act and Federal Aviation Act, sec. 6 (*c*).

determine the precise nature and characteristics of the operation, (*b*) foreign countries do not in their law distinguish between common carrier and noncommon carrier services, so that it is frequently difficult to make clear the nature of the information required, and (*c*) the barriers of distance and language frequently serve to delay and complicate the task of clearing the requests for operating permission.

By mutual arrangement between the Board and the Administrator, the latter refers for clearance by the Board's staff all requests which appear to involve common carriage or to raise substantial doubt as to their noncommon carrier status. The staff of the Board may request further information in some instances and may request the Administrator to impose appropriate conditions to assure that the noncommon carrier status of the applicant will be preserved. By this procedure it has been possible to obtain co-ordination between the agencies and uniform application and enforcement of the statutory provisions.

The procedure for the issuance of these so-called "6 (*c*) permits" serves two purposes: it permits pre-inaugural operation of a noncommon carrier nature pending the issuance of a foreign air carrier permit, and it provides for the entry of foreign nonscheduled and charter aircraft pursuant to the same type of provision extended by other countries to comparable United States operations.

The ratification of the Convention on International Civil Aviation (Chicago conference) by the United States, and its subsequently being put into effect on April 4, 1947, has changed in certain respects the application of section 6 (*c*) of the Air Commerce Act in regard to aircraft of other contracting states. Article 5 of the convention, which deals with aircraft other than those engaged in scheduled international air services, requires a contracting state to permit such aircraft of other contracting states to make flights into, and to transit nonstop across, its territories and to make stops for nontraffic purposes, all without the necessity for obtaining prior permission. Article 5 further states that such aircraft may take on or discharge passengers, cargo, or mail subject to the right of any state where such embarkation or discharge takes place to impose such regulations, conditions, or limitations as it may consider desirable. It therefore appears that Article 5 repeals the "prior permission" requirement of section 6 (*c*) to the extent that such prior permission would be required of aircraft or other contracting states operating in transit across United States territory or making stops therein for nontraffic purposes. With respect to stops for traffic purposes, however, the convention and section 6 (*c*) may be construed together as requiring prior permission for the discharge or taking on of passengers, cargo, or mail.

While it is believed that this is a proper construction of section 6 (*c*), such construction is not entirely beyond doubt. Section 6 (*c*) deals primarily with the navigation of aircraft and not with conditions for the embarkation or discharge of passengers and cargo. Through administrative interpretation, however, as indicated above, section 6 (*c*) has been used to impose conditions relating to the commercial activity of foreign aircraft being navigated within the United States. It is believed, therefore, that section 6 (*c*) can still be made applicable to this type of activity. However, since the question is not entirely clear, it is believed that the amendment of section 6 (*c*) would be desirable to indicate specifically, in the case of other contracting states under the Chicago convention, that it is designed to regulate the embarkation and discharge of passengers and cargo but not to preclude other navigation of foreign aircraft under the rights granted by the convention.[22]

A definition designed to specify the difference between scheduled and nonscheduled services has, however, been adopted by the Council of the International Civil Aviation Organization. Its importance comes from the fact that the Convention on International Civil Aviation, which each member nation of ICAO has ratified, allows any aircraft not engaged in international scheduled air service to fly into or across the territories of each ICAO member without receiving prior permission, and, under certain circumstances, to carry revenue traffic into and out of these territories. On the other hand, a scheduled international air service must have special permission or other authorization from the government of each country it flies into or across. This definition provides as follows:

---

[22] The Civil Aeronautics Board has held that: (1) The restriction contained in section 1108 of the Federal Aviation Act (formerly section 6 (*b*) of the Air Commerce Act) that no foreign civil aircraft "shall take on at any point in the United States, persons, property, or mail carried for compensation or hire and destined for another point in the United States" has application to foreign civil aircraft utilized in operations conducted under authority of a foreign air carrier permit issued under sections 402 of the Civil Aviation and Federal Aviation Act. (2) Such restriction precludes, in respect to foreign civil aircraft so utilized by a given foreign air carrier, the initial taking on by that carrier at one United States point of traffic carried for compensation or hire and destined to another United States point for final discharge by that carrier, irrespective of whether the traffic will continue to move to a foreign point by another carrier, by air, or other transportation media. (3) The term "foreign air transportation" as it appears in foreign air carrier permits does not permit the initial taking on by a foreign air carrier at one United States point of traffic carried for compensation or hire and destined to another United States point for final discharge by that carrier. *Petition of Quantas Empire Airways Ltd. for Interpretative Rule*, CAB Docket 9240 (1959).

A scheduled international air service is a series of flights that possesses all the following characteristics:

a) it passes through the airspace over the territory of more than one state;

b) it is performed by aircraft for the transport of passengers, mail or cargo for remuneration, in such a manner that each flight is open to use by members of the public;

c) it is operated, so as to serve traffic between the same two or more points, either

i) according to a published timetable, or

ii) with flights so regular or frequent that they constitute a recognizably systematic series.

One of the objectives of the bilateral agreements made between the United States and other nations is the stimulation of international air travel as a means of promoting friendly understanding and goodwill. The fundamental purpose of these agreements is, therefore, the reciprocal exchange of air rights; however, any delay by one contracting party in granting operating permits to the designated airlines of the other party in reality limits the effectiveness of such agreements to a unilateral grant of rights for the length of time that such permits are withheld. Such failure on the part of the United States or any other country to perform promptly the obligations necessary for implementing an agreement obviously creates neither friendly understanding nor goodwill and is bound to affect adversely its carriers in their relations with the other country concerned.

Our standard-form bilateral agreement provides that each of the air services described therein shall be placed in operation as soon as the contracting party to whom the air rights are granted has designated an airline for the operation of such route. It also provides that the contracting party granting the rights shall be bound to give the appropriate operating permission, provided that the designated airline may be required to qualify before aeronautical authorities of the latter party, under the laws and regulations normally applied by these authorities, before being permitted to engage in the operations contemplated by the agreement. This provision in the Bermuda Agreement and in several other United States bilaterals includes the language "without undue delay." In either case the intent is the same, and an obligation is imposed upon each contracting party to grant the necessary operating permission as expeditiously as possible.

So far as the United States is concerned, section 1102 of the Civil Aeronautics Act requires the Board to perform its duties "consistently with any obligation assumed by the United States in any treaty, convention, or agreement that may be in force between the United

States and any foreign country or countries . . ." However, the act also requires in section 402 that a foreign air carrier secure a permit through the formal process of notice and hearing—a process which is necessarily time consuming.

Prompt issuance of operating permissions by foreign governments has been of particular importance to the United States, whose airlines are usually prepared to inaugurate services immediately upon the conclusion of a bilateral agreement and frequently before the other country's airlines are prepared to operate. Other governments, having airlines capable of immediately inaugurating services, have complained of the undue delay and hardship to their airlines caused by the extensive documentation and hearings required by the Civil Aeronautics Act in reviewing applications for foreign air carrier permits. Ill feeling engendered by such difficulties has at times adversely affected the handling of applications filed by our carriers with foreign countries, particularly since few other countries impose requirements as strict as those of the United States. A specific example of this was the action of the Swedish government with respect to the application of American Overseas Airlines for a route to Stockholm. The American legation in Stockholm was informed that the application of American Overseas had been approved but that such approval would not be announced officially until the United States issued a permit to SILA, the Swedish airline. It was emphasized that it had not originally been the intention of the Swedish government to make announcement of its approval contingent upon the granting of a permit to SILA, but that Swedish officials were "quite frankly irritated" over the delay encountered by SILA in obtaining a permit from the United States.

These complaints have arisen in spite of the fact that the applications have been handled by the Board with unusual speed and in most instances without the time which is necessarily consumed when there are interveners in the proceeding. The problem is simply that even an expedited processing of an application for a foreign air carrier permit compares unfavorably with the speed with which many foreign governments are able to act in granting operating permissions to our air carriers after the conclusion of bilateral agreements.

It has been suggested that section 402 of the act, providing for issuance of permits to foreign air carriers, be amended to require a finding of "public convenience and necessity." It is, however, difficult to see how such an amendment would accomplish any beneficial purpose in promoting the sound development of either national or international air transportation; nor does it appear that such an amendment would require the Board to take into consideration any matter that is not already used in determining whether the air transportation proposed by a foreign air carrier, in seeking to obtain a permit, is or is not in the "public interest."

Under the act as it now stands, the Board is authorized to issue a foreign air carrier permit after notice and hearing if the Board finds that the applicant is fit, willing, and able to conduct the air transportation properly and to conform to the provisions of the act and the rules, regulations, and requirements of the Board thereunder. In addition, the Board must make a finding that the air transportation proposed is in the "public interest."[23] The Board has indicated, in cases involving foreign air carrier permits, that it considers the following as evidence of public interest: effectuating of international aviation agreements entered into by the United States,[24] improvement of transportation facilities,[25] promotion of the "good neighbor" pol-

---

[23] The Board stated in an early case involving an application for a foreign air carrier permit that the term "public interest" as used in the act was not a mere general reference to public welfare but had a direct relation to definite statutory objectives. The Board pointed out: "It is apparent from this section (sec. 2) that the interest to be considered is the national interest, and that the 'public' is not limited to the public within the corporate limits of the cities which the proposed application would link together. In determining whether the inauguration of the foreign air carrier service is in the public interest and will further the objectives of the act as set forth in the declaration of policy, we must consider not only the needs of the two sections to be served, but the national interest and the relationship that the proposed service bears to the development of a nationally adequate and economically sound air transportation system, as new services authorized should fit logically into the existing air transportation system" (*Trans-Canada Air Lines, Permit to Foreign Air Carrier,* 2 CAB 616 [1941]).

In another case the Board said: "We must, therefore, determine whether the public interest requires service between Montreal and New York in addition to that operated by the incorporated company pursuant to its certificate. This involves our consideration of some of the questions which we have stated in previous opinions to be essential to the disposition of applications involving the issue of public convenience and necessity in proceedings dealing with wholly domestic air transportation, namely, whether the proposed service (foreign air carrier service) will serve a useful public purpose responsive to a public need, and whether this need can and will be served adequately by existing transportation facilities" (*Canadian Colonial Airways, Ltd., Permit to Foreign Air Carrier,* 3 CAB 50 [1941]).

[24] *Airways (Atlantic), Ltd., Permit to Foreign Air Carrier,* 2 CAB 181, 187 (1940); *Trans-Canada Air Lines, Foreign Air Carrier Permit (Whitehorse-Fairbanks),* 6 CAB 529 (1945); *Swedish International Airlines, Foreign Air Carrier Permit (Stockholm–New York–Chicago),* 6 CAB 631 (1946); *Trans-Canada Air Lines, Montreal–New York Service,* 11 CAB 209 (1950).

[25] *Caribbean Investigation,* 4 CAB 199 (1943); *Trans-Canada Air Lines, Permit to Foreign Air Carrier (New York–Toronto),* 2 CAB 616, 622 (1941); *Trans-Canada Air Lines, Permit to Foreign Air Carrier (Whitehorse-Fairbanks),* 6 CAB 529 (1945).

icy,[26] alternate routing during the winter months,[27] and expediting of service and reductions of costs.[28] From these cases it appears that the Board inclines toward a broad, flexible construction of the term "public interest," and that it will be construed in such a manner as to best promote the national and international policies of the United States. It should also be noted that, unlike applications for purely domestic service, section 1102 of the act requires that an additional and important factor be taken into consideration in passing upon applications for foreign air carrier permits. That section provides that the Board in exercising and performing its powers and duties under the act shall do so consistently with any obligation assumed by the United States in any treaty, convention, or agreement that may be in force between the United States and any foreign country.[29] This has been faithfully observed by the United States.

If section 402 of the act were amended to include the term "public convenience and necessity," it would not change the requirements that foreign air carrier permits be approved by the President under section 801; nor would it accomplish any beneficial purpose or require the Board to consider an additional matter that is not now considered by it in making a determination that a proposed foreign air carrier permit is in the "public interest." In addition, the requirement of section 1102 would remain unchanged, so that the board would still be required to act within the broad policy declared in the international air transport agreements.

Presidential Power over International Routes

Under the Civil Aeronautics Act and Federal Aviation Act, the President has the power to select the routes which can be operated

---

[26] *Aero-Transportes, S.A., Temporary Foreign Air Carrier Permit,* 6 CAB 159 (1944), 6 CAB 383 (1945); *Lineas Aereas Mexicanas, S. A., Temporary Foreign Air Carrier Permit,* 6 CAB 165 (1944), 6 CAB 299 (1945).

[27] *British Overseas Airways Corporation, Temporary Amendment of Permit,* 4 CAB 57 (1942).

[28] *British Overseas Airways Corporation, Amendment to Permit,* 2 CAB 823, 825 (1941).

[29] In an opinion of the Attorney General dated June 18, 1946, in response to a request from the Secretary of State, it was stated that the statutory provisions of the act (secs. 801, 802, and 1102) made it clear that the Congress contemplated the consummation of agreements with foreign nations relating to international civil aviation and that the Attorney General concurred in the position taken by the Department of State that none of the then existing aviation executive agreements purports to waive the necessity of proceeding under section 402 of the act (*Opinions of the Attorney General,* Vol. XL, Op. No. 110 [1946]).

in foreign and overseas air transportation by United States carriers or to choose the carriers for such routes.[30] It has been suggested that this power should be eliminated entirely or limited to a veto only; that is, the President would not have power affirmatively to choose routes or carriers.

Since the Civil Aeronautics Act became effective in 1938, there have been several instances in which the President, in the exercise of his power, has not followed the Board's recommendations.[31] Even so, the Board has indicated that the present powers of the President should not be changed,[32] because its consideration of new route cases is necessarily confined to the record made before it by the parties to the proceeding and must be governed by the principles set forth in the act defining public convenience and necessity. After considering the record, the Board, as the administrative agency charged with the primary responsibility for developing a sound air transportation system, makes its recommendations in considerable detail to the President. However, the President has an additional responsibility in all matters pertaining to the proper conduct of our international relations, having under the Constitution responsibility and duty to conduct the foreign affairs of the United States. The President has access to many sources of information and to data not included in the record before the Board. Much of this data may consist of secret and confidential material which it would be improper to include in an open record. The President must also take into consideration many factors relating to the conduct of international affairs of which the Board is unaware. For this reason, many believe that the law should not be amended to remove this power from the President.

But this is not the only reason why the President's powers over international air transportation should be continued. Under the Constitution the Congress has power to regulate commerce with foreign nations, but the President has responsibility for the proper conduct of

---

30 Section 801 of the act provides in part that the "issuance, denial, transfer, amendment, . . . of . . . any certificate authorizing an air carrier to engage in overseas or foreign air transportation, or air transportation between places in the same Territory or possession, . . . shall be subject to the approval of the President."

31 See *American Airlines, Mexico City Operation,* 3 CAB 415 (1942); *Latin American Service Case,* 6 CAB 857 (1946); *Colonial Airlines, Inc., et al., Atlantic Seaboard Operations,* 4 CAB 392 (1943); *North Atlantic Route Transfer Case,* 11 CAB 676 (1950); *Eastern-Colonial, Acquisition of Assets,* 18 CAB 453 *Trans-Pacific Certificate Renewal Case,* 20 CAB 47 (1955); *West Coast–Hawaii Case,* 20 CAB 7 (1955).

32 *Statement of the Civil Aeronautics Board before the President's Air Policy Commission,* October 27, 1947.

our international relations.[33] In the handling of our international relations, the President speaks as the sole organ of our government entrusted with that function.[34] It seems clear that, where the handling of international regulations overlaps the regulation of commerce with foreign nations, the possibility of serious and even disastrous conflict and division might result if the Congress did not entrust the balancing of conflicting considerations to the President.[35]

The very nature of international cases makes it impossible for the Board's action to be final. Operating rights and privileges must be obtained from foreign countries, and these can be obtained only by bilateral or multilateral agreements and arrangements, with the President charged with the exclusive responsibility for negotiating such arrangements. A route and carrier selected by the President cannot be operated unless implemented by rights obtained from the foreign country under the President's supervision and direction. It makes good sense, therefore, to centralize the power to correlate and coordinate these actions of the government in the hands of the President.

It would be possible, of course, to amend the law so as to give only a veto power to the President, while at the same time circumscribing his present power to choose affirmatively the routes and carriers. In other words, the law could be made to spell out clearly that the President can either approve or disapprove but has no power to indicate which routes and carriers shall be selected. It would seem, however, that any attempt to circumscribe or decrease the President's powers in this manner would be either ineffectual or unwise. So long as he has power to disapprove the Board's action, the President can continue to disapprove successive solutions suggested by the Board until the Board finally comes forth with the solution which he is willing to approve. Rather than go through this ritualistic and time-consuming process, it is preferable to have the President indicate, at the first opportunity following his consideration of the Board's recommendations, the route and carrier which he will approve. On the other hand, if the law is amended so that the Board can override the President's

---

[33] Constitution of the United States, Art. I, sec. 8, and Art. II, secs. 1 and 2.

[34] *United States* v. *Belmont,* 301 U.S. 324 (1937); and *U.S.* v. *Curtiss-Wright Corp.,* 299 U.S. 304 (1936).

[35] In the absence of section 801, the act would strip the President of his ". . . very delicate, plenary, and exclusive power . . . as the policy organ of the Federal Government in the field of international relations—a power which does not require as a basis for its existence an act of Congress . . ." (*U.S.* v. *Curtiss-Wright Corp.,* 299 U.S. 304 [1936] p. 320).

veto, then obviously the conduct of international affairs may be prejudiced, and responsibility divided and weakened. Power to override the President's veto would be as unwise as complete repeal of the pertinent section, for it is the controversial cases in which the President's views should and must prevail.

It would also be possible to change the law in other respects. It could be provided, for example, that the Board's opinions be published and made subject to judicial review before they go to the President for approval. It seems that such a process would be unnecessary and time-consuming in view of the fact that the President may reach a different result.[36]

It would also be possible to amend the law so as to provide that the President's action shall be taken only upon the record compiled before the Board, that it shall be in accordance with the standards of convenience and necessity as set forth in the act, and that such action shall be subject to judicial review. This proposal, however, is subject to the same objections as the proposal to repeal the pertinent section entirely. It not only would prevent the President from taking advantage of information not in the record, but would also be ineffectual in view of his plenary power in the conduct of our international relations. For example, although the record might require the President to select carrier X for a particular route, the President in his conduct of international relations might find it necessary to reject both the route and the carrier in concluding a bilateral agreement with the foreign nation concerned. It is to be noted that international route decisions of the Civil Aeronautics Board are considered to be really orders of the President and as such not subject to judicial review.

---

[36] The United States Circuit Court of Appeals for the Second Circuit held in *Pan American Airways Co.* v. *Civil Aeronautics Board*, 121 Fed. (2d) 810 (1941), that in proceedings under section 801 of the act the Board acts as the President's adviser and that the President and not the Board is the ultimate arbiter. In other words, said that court, "orders of the Board which by the provisions of section 801, require the President's approval, are considered to be in reality orders made by the President and not by the Board. . . . Such action is not subject to judicial review and in such circumstances a serious question arises as to whether it is within the power of the Board to reopen for further argument and consideration . . . a case in which all applications had been denied by the President."

In another case Colonial Airlines contended that section 402 (*b*) of the act as controlled by section 801 was a delegation to the President of the United States of the exclusive plenary congressional power over foreign commerce without any standards, limitations, or statutory controls whatever and consequently unconstitutional. This contention was raised directly before the United States District Court for the District of Columbia, and that court upheld the constitutionality of the challenged sections of the act (*Colonial Airlines, Inc.* v. *Russell B. Adams et al.*, 87 Fed. Supp. 242 [1949]). See also *C. & S. Air Lines, Inc.* v. *Waterman S. S. Corp.*, 33 U.S. 103 (1948).

Authority to Fix International Rates

Under the Civil Aeronautics Act, the Board has jurisdiction to fix passenger and property rates between points within the United States, as well as to fix reasonable minimum and maximum rates in overseas air transportation, that is, in transportation between a place in the continental United States and a place in one of its territories or between a place in one territory and a place in another territory.[37] However, the Board lacks statutory powers to prescribe passenger and property rates for United States air carriers operating in foreign air transportation.

When the Civil Aeronautics Act was passed, there was considerable opposition to granting such power; but any argument against it has little validity today because of changed conditions. As a matter of fact, the opposition was sufficiently great and doubt as to what should be the policy so manifest that section 404 (c) of the act empowered and directed the Board to investigate and report to Congress within one year the extent to which the federal government should regulate rates in foreign air transportation. Within the year, the Board made a report recommending that further extension of control over international rates not be made at that time, largely because of the limited extent of practical experience in the field.

In 1938 and 1939 long-range international air transportation was relatively unimportant. Further, the pattern of rate determination in the slowly developing field of international air transportation seemed destined to follow that of international shipping, where carrier conferences set the rates. Most governments concerned themselves little, if at all, with the rates charged by foreign air carriers operating into their territories or by their own air carriers operating abroad. Consequently, it seemed possible that it might unduly prejudice the interests of United States air carriers who might participate in rate conferences if they alone were subject to government control; and further it seemed possible that action by the United States in this field might lead to similar action by other governments.

Since 1939 the situation has changed completely. Every important nation of the world is participating extensively in international air transportation. The result has been a great increase in competition among air carriers throughout the world. Since nearly all air carriers

---

[37] Civil Aeronautics Act and Federal Aviation Act, secs. 403 and 404.

are subsidized to a greater or lesser extent by their governments, it is natural that the increasing competition has led most nations to assert control over rates charged by air carriers operating into their territories.

This development has occurred even though the air carriers who are members of the International Air Transport Association (IATA) have created rate-fixing machinery. Under this machinery, rates for international air travel are considered at regular intervals at regional or joint rate conferences by the scheduled international airlines which are members of IATA. Rate agreements unanimously adopted by the conferences are binding on the individual airline members, subject, however, to approval by the respective governments. If the members of a conference do not reach unanimous agreement or if a rate resolution adopted by a conference is not approved by all the governments whose airlines are members of the conference, an "open rate" results; and the member carriers are free competitively to quote individual tariffs until another "closed conference rate" is agreed upon by all and approved. An open-rate situation exists continuously in certain areas, such as South America, where some carriers are not members of IATA; consequently it is impractical for the IATA members to bind themselves not to meet the rate competition of non–IATA carriers.

Since some areas of the world have been continuously in an open-rate situation and since one negative vote by a participating air carrier can create an open-rate situation in any area, the only recourse for a government wishing to protect its own air carriers from the dire consequences of a rate war in a subsidized industry is to assert its own power to approve or disapprove rates in international air transportation. This is, however, really more of a problem for foreigners than it is for Americans, as United States carriers have much more subsidy strength available.

This determination of foreign governments to retain control over international rates has been intensified by the position of the United States. The advanced state of our aircraft industry, the great experience and technical proficiency of United States–flag air carriers, and the economic strength of the government which stands behind them have combined to arouse the fears of foreign governments, especially since our government exercises no direct control over the international rates charged by its air carriers.

It is true that the Board does have an indirect control over such rates, when they are established through IATA Traffic Conferences;[38] but however useful such a control may be, it does not serve to calm the fears of other governments, who recognize the possibility that a United States air carrier can by a negative vote create an open-rate situation in which the Board's indirect control is no longer possible. Whether these fears concerning United States air carriers are justified is less important than the fact that they exist. The result has been that in negotiation of many of our bilateral air transport agreements, including those with most of the countries which are leaders in international air transportation, the United States has found itself handicapped because of the Civil Aeronautics Board's lack of power to determine fair and reasonable rates for our air carriers operating abroad. These countries have insisted, as a condition for according traffic rights to our airlines within their territories, that the possibility of destructive rate wars between international carriers be made impossible through the insertion in agreements of provisions relating to the fixing of rates. It has been the contention of these foreign countries that the United States carriers could operate more efficiently and cheaply due to the advanced state of our aviation industry than their carriers, and that unrestricted competition might drive the latter from the air. This fear, whether or not well founded, has been the driving force in their insistence on rate provisions.

The objective of these rate provisions in all cases is to assure that international air carriers will not charge unfair or uneconomic rates. To accomplish this objective, three alternative tools are provided for, as follows:

1. Rate fixing, where the aeronautical authority concerned has the power to set rates. If the other country involved does not agree that the rate set is a proper one, machinery is provided for consultation and ultimate reference to the International Civil Aviation Organization for an advisory report.

2. Unanimous agreement of all airlines concerned through the IATA Air Traffic Conference machinery, subject to the approval of the respective states involved.

3. Unilateral determination and exclusion by the foreign country

---

[38] This jurisdiction stems from section 412 of the Civil Aeronautics Act and Federal Aviation Act, which provides for approval of agreements between an air carrier and other air carriers and foreign air carriers. The IATA conference machinery was originally approved by the Board on February 19, 1946, subject to the reservation that each resolution of the conference establishing agreed rates must be submitted to the Board for approval.

in cases where no rate has been fixed by the aeronautical authority of the airlines and no rate agreement is in force, with provision for consultation between the states concerned and with reference to ICAO contemplated.

While the procedures contemplated by both (1) and (2), above, call for reference to ICAO in case of dispute about what the proper rate is, it is worthy of note that, if the rate has been fixed under (1), it will continue in effect until further action is taken by the party setting the rate, which action need not be taken until after the advisory report is handed down by ICAO. On the other hand, if the paragraph (3) procedure is followed, the airline involved may be prevented from operating into the foreign territory at the disputed rate until after the report from ICAO has been handed down.

Analysis of the foregoing alternative procedures indicates that direct governmental control is the most advantageous method of handling this rate problem. The rate is set in the first instance by the government whose airline is involved, and the burden rests upon the foreign governments to challenge the rate and to show that it is unfair and uneconomic. Under the conference method of procedure, as under the procedure of paragraph (3), there is an almost absolute veto power on the part of the foreign government, and the burden rests upon the national government of the airline concerned to challenge the action thus taken. In effect, the choice is whether rates of United States international air carriers will be determined by the United States or whether they will be determined by foreign governments.

There are several important benefits that would accrue to our international air commerce from control by the Civil Aeronautics Board over international rates, in addition to the substantial advantage of having our rates given effect by foreign governments pending any intergovernmental consultation. If the Board has control over the rates of our carriers, any foreign fears of rate wars would be allayed; Board approval would be a virtual guarantee that the rates are reasonable and free from any taint of discriminatory, prejudicial, or below-cost characteristics. Disputes as to rates would be negotiated on a governmental level, not, as at present, with our carriers at a disadvantage in negotiating with aeronautical authorities of foreign governments. Indeed, the strongest argument for foreign interference with the rates of our carriers—the present absence of control by the Board—would be removed. Finally, it may be noted that the IATA machinery, on which we are now completely dependent, is susceptible to abuses. The requirement of unanimous action, a reasonable rule under present circumstances, imposes a necessity for compromise on a rate acceptable to all carriers, the low cost and the high cost; and in the absence of agreement on new rates, the tendency is to revert to the old rates in order to avoid open-rate situations.

Other countries do not hesitate to interfere with the rates of our carriers serving their cities and even to make the continuance of operations conditional on their observing acceptable rates. We are unable to exercise a similar control over foreign-flag carriers coming to this country, except by revocation of permits. The revocation of an operating right is too drastic a device to use in dealing with rate matters, as it invites retaliation against our carriers.

Thus far, emphasis has been placed on conditions in the international sphere which have led to the belief that it is necessary for the Board to exercise control over the rates charged by United States air carriers in foreign air transportation. Entirely aside from these considerations, however, is our domestic concern, which furnishes an equally strong reason. Lack of such jurisdiction may prejudice the economically sound development of this country's international air transport industry. Under the Civil Aeronautics Act the Board is required to fix rates of compensation for the carriage of mail and, in so doing, to take into account the broad policy objectives set forth in the act,[39] including the need of each air carrier; and to the extent that these rates of mail pay exceed the actual cost of transporting the mail, they contain an element of subsidy. The Board has sought to keep the air mail pay bill of the government as low as possible, consistent with carrying out the public interest objectives of the act. Insofar as domestic and territorial carriers are concerned, an element of control in this regard is provided by the Board's power to fix rates for the carriage of persons and property. The Board is empowered to influence the carriers' commercial revenues, in relation to costs, as it believes to be in the over-all public interest. The direct cost of service to

---

[39] Civil Aeronautics Act and Federal Aviation Act, sec. 406(*b*). The Air Coordinating Committee in its report on "Civil Air Policy," *supra*, made the following recommendations: (1) Full United States support, consistent with the Civil Aeronautics Act, should be given to the International Air Transport Association (IATA) as the primary instrument for establishing and maintaining a sound fare and rate structure for international air services. (2) The Civil Aeronautics Board should be empowered by Congress, through amendment of the Civil Aeronautics Act, (*a*) to control the fares, rates, rules, and practices of United States air carriers, applicable to transportation to and from the United States, to the same extent as the Board now has power to act with respect to domestic air transportation, and (*b*) to control the fares, rates and rules, and practices of foreign air carriers, applicable to transportation to and from the United States, more effectively than is now possible under the Civil Aeronautics Act.

the public is balanced against the indirect public cost involved in subsidy payments.

However, under the Board's present lack of jurisdiction over international passenger and property rates, it is unable to influence the revenues of carriers engaged in foreign air transportation through review and determination of the rates which they charge. Such carriers may establish rates at levels which give them a less favorable profit-and-loss result than would be possible if rates were fixed at a different level. The Board has no power to prevent the establishment of such rates, and the United States government may well find that a unilateral action by one of its own air carriers in a field outside of governmental control has operated to increase substantially the amount of subsidy support required.

International Aviation Organizations[40]

There are two international organizations dealing with aviation matters. The International Civil Aviation Organization (ICAO), which, as has been discussed, grew out of the Chicago convention and became a permanent organization in 1947, and the International Air Transport Association (IATA), the co-operative organization of the world's airlines.

Eighty-three nations are now members of ICAO, whose airlines operate more than 90 per cent of all international civil air transportation. A number of nations are still absent from the membership list, one of these being Russia. China, formerly a member, withdrew in 1951. Subject to the conditions laid down in the Chicago convention, all nations are welcome to become members provided only that they agree to adhere to the principles of the convention and to accept the corresponding responsibilities.

All member states of ICAO are sovereign and equal; the organization is governed by an assembly in which each state has one vote. The assembly meets annually; the first meeting took place in Montreal, Canada, in May, 1947. The assembly is the organization's legislative body. It elects a council of twenty-one members to serve as the executive body. The president of the council is elected for a term of three years.

The council, which remains in virtually continuous session, creates

---

[40] See Eugene Pepin, "I.C.A.O. and Other Agencies Dealing With Air Regulation," *Journal of Air Law and Commerce*, Spring, 1952. Leonard Bebchick, "The International Air Transport Association and the Civil Aeronautics Board," *Journal of Air Law and Commerce*, Winter, 1958.

standards for international air navigation, an important feature of ICAO's work. It may act, if requested, as a tribunal for the settlement of certain international disputes. Under the terms of the convention, it is responsible for the establishment of air navigation and air transport groups, each of which has responsibility for its own particular field of action. There are three other committees which play an important part in ICAO's functioning: the Legal Committee, the Committee on International Convention, and the Committee on Joint Support of Air Navigation Services.

The administrative functions of the organization are performed by the secretariat, the third principal organ of ICAO. It is headed by the Secretary-General. Secretariat members are selected for technical competence in their specialized fields. In order that the work of the secretariat may reflect a truly international approach, technical and senior administrative personnel are recruited on a broad international basis.

The ICAO has its most easily understood and, so far, its most effective area of accomplishment in the field of standardization of technical matters, such, for example, as the standards for airworthiness of aircraft, which are of obvious importance to passengers, operators, and manufacturers. Standards are developed first in international meetings of divisions of the Air Navigation Committee at which expert delegations come from the member states. The standards they agree upon are reviewed in relation to the standards in other technical fields by the standing Air Navigation Committee. After further opportunity for study by home governments, the standards come to the council for final approval. They come into effect under the convention after compliance with further procedural requirements. It then becomes a requirement for member states to implement the standards through their respective national regulations, inspection services, and so on, or for them to announce to the world the specific extent to which they deviate from the agreed standards or practices.

Some examples of agreements that have been reached indicate the widely varied nature of the subjects dealt with—the qualifications and experience necessary for aircrew licenses, the amount of fuel that an aircraft must carry over and above that calculated to be necessary for a flight to allow for possible emergency and unforeseen contingency, standard symbols to be used on aeronautical maps and charts, and codes for the reporting of meteorological conditions.

ICAO also has certain powers of action in the field called "facilitation of international air travel and transport." Here it deals with standards and recommended practices, expediting and simplifying customs, immigration, public health, passport, visa, and other border-crossing formalities. The procedure for developing standards and putting them into effect is similar to that in the technical field, and the legal effect of the standards when once adopted is the same.

The International Air Transport Association (IATA) has some 89 members working together to knit their individual routes into an international air transport system, along whose every mile there will be the same high standards of safety, economy, efficiency, and service to the public. In a world which speaks many languages and uses many varied systems of writing, law, currency, and measurement, IATA is the airlines' answer to the imperative need for complete international understanding of all procedures, practices, and devices used in an industry in which all peoples are vitally concerned.

IATA is a voluntary association of airline companies, with headquarters in Montreal, Canada. Any company is eligible to join IATA as an active member if it operates a scheduled air service between two or more countries for the transport of passengers, mail, or cargo under the flag of a state eligible for membership in ICAO. Domestic operators of these states may join as associate members, participating to a limited extent in IATA activities and paying a lower subscription than active members.

Basic policies of the association are laid down by an annual general meeting, in which each active member company has a single vote. Direction of IATA's continuing affairs is vested in an Executive Committee, whose members are elected for terms of three years each. Its work is carried out under a Director General and other executive officers who are nominated by the Executive Committee and confirmed by the annual general meeting.

IATA is supported entirely by the dues paid by its members, who are assessed in proportion to the amount of international air traffic carried by each.

In practice, IATA is the agency through which the airlines seek to solve jointly those problems they cannot individually surmount and to do that work which can be carried out more effectively or economically by combined effort. It is active in the fields of traffic, finance, legal and technical matters, medicine, public information, and the like. In some cases, IATA acts as a central bank of information and technical knowledge for all member airlines; in others, IATA is preparing to publish tariffs and timetables; it conducts such enterprises as the IATA Clearing House; it administers committees of airline experts set up to deal with continuing problems; and it represents the airlines in their dealings with other international organizations.

The creating work of IATA is done largely by its four standing committees—Financial, Legal, Technical, and Traffic. Like the Executive Committee which nominates them, these committees and their subcommittees are made up of the best talent available in the member airlines. IATA's small secretariat administers the affairs of these committees, provides services for them, and carries forward their recommendations. Rules for the conduct of the committees are laid down, and their decisions are subject to final approval by the Executive Committee.

Chapter 11

SAFETY IN AIR TRANSPORTATION

IN DEVELOPING any new means of transportation, the problem of improving safety is important. This is not new or peculiar to air transportation, since accidents are sometimes unavoidable with any agency of transportation. It has been said that "lack of safety is the price we pay for motion." In the early years of American railroad transportation, there were many bad accidents; and although steady progress has been made in safety, until at the present time American railroads have achieved an enviable safety record, there are still accidents. A similar evolution has been, and is, taking place in air transportation. The airlines are not yet as free from danger as our railroads, and it will be some time before they are; but there have been outstanding achievements in the development of safety in air transportation.

Safety in air transportation depends on many things, among which are: (*a*) proper equipment properly maintained; (*b*) pilot skill, intelligence, and psychology; (*c*) skillful dispatching and adequate flight control; (*d*) adequate airway and airport facilities; (*e*) adequate weather forecasting and reporting; and (*f*) the promulgation and enforcement of rules designed to promote safety. Domestic scheduled airline passenger fatalities, per 100 million passenger-miles, dropped from 4.5 in 1938 to 0.7 in 1959, while the same figure for scheduled international United States carriers dropped from 13.2 in 1938 to 0.8 in 1959, as shown in Table 23.

Nature of the Air Safety Problem

It is almost impossible to relate accurately the accident rate in air carrier operation to accident rates in other fields of transport. One can, of course, use the same ratios, but it is doubtful whether these ratios have the same meaning when applied to other fields of transport. To illustrate, a comparison of passenger fatalities per 100 million passenger-miles for various classes of transportation is shown in Table 24.

TABLE 23

Comparative Safety Statistics, Scheduled Airlines, 1938–59

Scheduled Domestic Operations
(U.S. Trunk, Feeder, and Territorial Carriers)

Year	Fatal Accidents	Passenger Fatalities	Crew Fatalities	Passenger-Miles Flown per Passenger Fatality*	Passenger Fatalities per 100 Million Passenger-Miles*
1938	5	25	10	22,400,205	4.5
1939	2	9	3	83,927,533	1.2
1940	3	35	10	33,114,118	3.0
1941	4	35	9	43,063,944	2.3
1942	5	55	16	27,286,599	3.7
1943	2	22	8	75,951,578	1.3
1944	3	48	8	47,907,077	2.1
1945	7	76	11	46,746,305	2.1
1946	9	75	22	80,894,782	1.2
1947	5	199	17	31,696,899	3.2
1948	5	83	15	75,035,325	1.3
1949	4	93	11	76,032,710	1.3
1950	4	96	13	87,118,531	1.1
1951	8	142	24	77,111,993	1.3
1952	5	46	6	282,536,326	0.4
1953	4	86	15	178,346,047	0.6
1954	4	16	7	1,086,863,563	0.1
1955	7	156	21	131,736,795	0.8
1956	4	143	13	161,924,147	0.6
1957	3	31	2	846,848,161	0.1
1958	4	114	22	230,407,026	0.4
1959	11	198	35	153,512,429	0.7

Scheduled International Operations
(U.S. Carriers)

Year	Fatal Accidents	Passenger Fatalities	Crew Fatalities	Passenger-Miles Flown per Passenger Fatality*	Passenger Fatalities per 100 Million Passenger-Miles*
1938	2	7	10	7,601,860	13.2
1939	1	10	4	7,826,592	12.8
1940	0	0	0	....	0
1941	1	2	0	84,261,841	1.2
1942	0	0	0	....	0
1943	1	10	4	25,437,434	3.9
1944	1	17	0	18,737,317	5.3
1945	2	17	10	19,584,343	5.1
1946	2	40	12	28,150,765	3.6
1947	3	20	13	93,163,400	1.1
1948	1	20	10	98,089,700	1.0
1949	0	0	0	....	0
1950	2	48	8	48,713,167	2.1
1951	1	31	9	88,223,032	1.1
1952	3	94	9	33,795,043	3.0
1953	2	2	0	1,782,710,000	0.1
1954	0	0	0	....	0
1955	1	2	2	2,300,636,500	.04
1956	0	0	0	....	0
1957	1	36	8	166,162,250	0.6
1958	2	10	0	623,073,200	0.2
1959	2	59	12	124,239,220	0.8

* Includes both revenue and nonrevenue passengers and passenger-miles.
Source: FAA, *Statistical Handbook of Civil Aviation* (Washington, D.C., 1960).

Safety of the railroads as compared to scheduled air transport might perhaps better be compared by a ratio that would relate the number of fatalities to the time spent in transport rather than to miles covered or to a combination of those two. The yardstick commonly used to measure safety in transportation is passenger fatalities per 100 million passenger-miles traveled, probably because this was the method established to measure railroad safety. This is a good criterion for railroads, because in a typical railroad accident usually only a small percentage of the passengers are killed. (When a fatal accident occurs, there is still a reasonable chance of survival.) Fatal accidents involving aircraft, however, usually result in a much larger percentage of occupants being killed, and so a better yardstick here is to reckon flying safety in the same terms as might a member of the flight crew. A pilot could not accurately

TABLE 24

COMPARISON OF PASSENGER FATALITIES, 1951–58
(Number of Passenger Fatalities and Rate per 100 Million Passenger-Miles)

	1951	1952	1953	1954	1955	1956	1957	1958
Motor Buses								
Fatalities	140	120	100	60	90	80	90	120
Rate	.24	.21	.18	.11	.18	.16	.17	.24
Railroad Passenger Trains								
Fatalities	150	14	50	23	19	57	17	62
Rate	.43	.04	.16	.08	.07	.20	.07	.27
Passenger Autos and Taxis								
Fatalities	22,200	23,300	23,900	22,700	25,100	26,600	25,600	24,200
Rate	3.0	3.0	2.9	2.7	2.7	2.7	2.6	2.3

Source: Air Tranport Association of America, *Air Transport Facts and Figures* (Washington, D.C., 1960).

measure his air life expectancy on the basis of passenger-miles because he rides whether or not passengers are being carried. He should reckon his exposure to fatality on the basis of pilot fatalities per hour or miles of exposure flown or per thousand hours or miles flown. The true standard of safety should be life expectancy, which for aircraft is more nearly akin to hours or miles one has left to live while flying, rather than so many passengers traveling so many miles. On the other hand, an index of public transportation safety must show the public (passenger) stake—it must answer the question, "What are his chances of survival?" In other words, how many passenger-miles can he fly before the law of averages may involve him fatally? That is why the Index of Passenger Rate per 100 Million Passenger-Miles is accepted in this country and throughout the world for this purpose.[1]

The completely proper measurement of safety for air transportation, however, has not yet been found, and further study of the problem is desirable. But whatever yardstick is selected, its principal use will be to determine trends rather than to assess exposure to accident, inasmuch as the airlines' record for safety is within the public concept and acceptance of safety in other fields of activity. Statistics, however, fail to make much impression on public consciousness.

Dramatic accidents occur and receive considerable publicity, and for that reason the public in general feels that air travel is much more dangerous than it really is. One reason for this is that the type of plane now employed by air carriers has a passenger capacity frequently four times that commonly employed by air carriers some years ago.

Another reason for the public attitude toward air safety is that it does not distinguish between accidents on United States certificated airlines and those in nonscheduled flying, in private flying, in military flying, or even on foreign-owned airlines outside the United States, which, incidentally, were 3 to 20 times as dangerous as United States certificated airlines during the latest period for which we have figures for most countries.

Aviation, which enjoys the fruits of tremendous publicity for its constructive achievements, also receives the same widespread publicity for its difficulties. All who are concerned with the future of civil aviation should welcome such publicity, for an aroused public opinion will help bring steps to improve aviation safety. If the public did not care about air safety, progress in this field would not be nearly as rapid as has been shown possible.

Until a few years ago, the industry was flying very few passenger-miles a year, so that the element of chance affected the figures for any one year enormously. An accident happening in December of one year rather than January of the next would change the unit safety record by as much as 30 to 50 per cent, and the only really

---

[1] For a discussion of the statistical approach to the subject of air safety see Ben W. Ashmead, "The Statistical Trends in Air Safety," a paper presented to the American Society of Mechanical Engineers, Los Angeles, Cal., June 28, 1953. See also Ross A. McFarland, "Health and Safety in Transportation," *Public Health Reports*, August, 1958; *Transport Airplane Accidents, Hazards and Malfunctions Scheduled Domestic and Foreign/Overseas Passenger Operations, July 1, 1947 through December 1, 1954*, CAB Bureau of Safety Investigation (Washington, D.C., 1956).

fair indication of safety progress was the average safety performance over 3 to 5 years. When the industry was flying a few billion passenger-miles a year, an accident with 20 people killed affected the safety record by a very large percentage, whereas now that airlines are flying between 30 and 40 billion passenger-miles, the element of chance does not have nearly the same effect on the year's record.

Good though the record of the certificated airlines is in relation to previous achievements, there is certainly no reason to regard it with complacency or even with satisfaction. Safety and regularity can, and must, be vastly improved if air transport is to realize its potential as a medium of mass transportation.

The speed with which safety and regularity are improved will determine to a very large degree how rapidly the United States will reap the fullest benefit from air transport and realize the fullest return from its already substantial investment in airways, airports, and other civil aviation facilities. Our present air transport safety record would have been far better had not the modernization of our airways facilities—planned to begin on a large scale in 1941—been delayed for over four years as a result of World War II and the difficulties of reconversion. The important factors which will contribute to the rapid improvement of air safety seem to be the following:

1. The efficiency and ability of our transport companies.
2. The ability of pilots.
3. The sound design of our commercial aircraft.
4. The soundness with which our system of air navigation facilities is planned.
5. The speed with which technical improvements in air navigation facilities are introduced, which depends in turn on (*a*) the rate of technical progress, to the point where large-scale service installations are justified, and (*b*) the rate at which funds are provided for such installations.
6. The intelligence with which our safety regulations are framed.
7. The efficiency with which those regulations are administered.

Regularity of service is second only to safety. Cancellations of flights or delays or diversion to other than the intended destination are exceedingly costly. It has been stated that the airlines suffer a loss of about $20 million annually due to loss of revenue from nonproductive equipment and personnel when planes are grounded, diverted, or delayed because of bad weather.

There are many factors affecting the safety of life and property in airline operation today. Inherent in the fundamental characteristics of air transportation is the indisputable truth that factors which in general would seem trivial can, with the right chain of circumstances, be the cause of a serious accident. By the very same rule, matters which seem to bulk large in the safety picture can, because of their general recognition and acceptance by all concerned, be relatively unimportant considerations in the safety of airline operation. In other words, it is the exception instead of the rule that causes the accident.

The present trend of trying to build airplane safety through restrictive regulation is not only alarming to the airline pilot but also places an unnecessary burden upon his capabilities, which could far better be expended upon a direct contribution to the safety of the flight under his command.

Under the present procedure, when an accident happens, many restrictions are often applied by the regulatory authority which have no bearing on the actual accident in question. It is a facetious saying among airline pilots that "if they want to make airplanes 100 per cent safe, why not pass a law making it illegal to take an airplane out of the hangar, and be done with it." What the airline pilots actually want is a more realistic approach to the problem. There has been, for example, too much comparison from a safety standpoint between military and naval operations and commercial operations. The control of traffic over New York in one day is forty times as complicated as flying a thousand or fifteen hundred bombers from England over Europe and back, because under wartime conditions the flow of traffic was parallel. All aircraft were either landing or taking off, and there were no take-offs while the landings were taking place. All aircraft were proceeding in one direction. In New York, there are four commercial airports with aircraft coming from all directions and, in addition, through traffic. In other words, there is a meshing of traffic, much like a seine, with a large number of arteries or patterns of traffic flow; and it is not possible to segregate the various patterns. One aircraft cannot land at the expense of another.

Federal Regulation of Air Safety

The federal agencies primarily concerned with promoting safety in civil aviation are the Civil Aeronautics Board and the Federal Aviation Agency. Other agencies which have incidental and indirect responsibilities with regard to air safety are the Weather Bureau, the Coast Guard Service, the Air Coordinating Committee, and the

National Advisory Committee for Aeronautics. Agencies such as the Air Force, Army, and Navy have also contributed greatly to the cause of air safety by making the results of their research and experience available to the civil authorities.

Until the passage of the Federal Aviation Act in 1958, the Civil Aeronautics Board had two general functions in the field of air safety. These were the promulgation of appropriate regulations governing air safety and the investigation of accidents. The Act of 1958 transferred the rule-making function to the Federal Aviation Agency, although the Board retained the duty of investigation of accidents and the issuance of reports thereon. The Federal Aviation Agency is responsible for fixing the standard for such things as the issuance of airman certificates, aircraft types, airworthiness certificates, and a number of related matters. It is also responsible for promulgating aircraft traffic rules, fixing minimum standards for the operation of all classes of air carriers, adopting such other rules and standards as may be necessary for the maintenance of safety in air commerce, enforcing these rules and standards for the development and operation of the civil airways, and for doing such research as is authorized year by year.

Investigation of Accidents

The investigation of accidents is of enormous importance, because it is by thorough investigations that we learn to correct previous errors. The reports issued after the investigation of an accident are studied with care not only in the air transport industry but also in the aircraft manufacturing industry. As a result of these investigations, improvements in design and operation often occur independently of any action that may be taken by either the Civil Aeronautics Board or the Federal Aviation Agency.

The Board cannot conceivably investigate every accident that occurs. It does, however, require the submission of complete reports on all accidents. These reports are made the subject of study and analysis by its Accident Analysis Division. The policy of the Board with regard to studying accidents is to investigate the following types:

1. Air carrier accidents which result in serious or fatal injuries or which are potentially serious.
2. Accidents where mechanical failures of the aircraft have been contributory, including fire in the air.
3. Accidents involving collision of aircraft in the air.

4. Any other accidents from which it appears that important accident-prevention knowledge may be obtained.

The Board actively investigates those accidents that have involved the scheduled air carriers and the nonscheduled air carriers using large equipment, but such accidents comprise only 5 to 10 per cent of the total. Thus between 90 to 95 per cent of the actual accident investigations are carried out by the Federal Aviation Agency personnel. These include the large bulk of the accidents which are involved in private flying operations and in small nonscheduled operations plus all other minor accidents which may involve only a slight structural damage to the aircraft itself but which are of vital importance in determining ways to improve design and obtain correction of maintenance or other difficulties in the field.

The manner in which investigations have been handled in the past should not be criticized lightly. The work has been painstakingly thorough and the results worthwhile. There are two suggestions, however, which might make possible even improved results.[2] In the first place, the attention of investigators is too frequently limited to the probable cause of an accident; this, of course, is important, but the causes of major accidents are rarely simple, nor is their correction an easy matter. Behind the final cause—usually the last circumstance that is designated as the probable cause—lies a chain of events that precipitated a situation in which it was possible for the last circumstance to occur. The investigation of an accident should not focus on the last happening, but must rather evaluate the entire situation. It must, if possible, bring forth recommendations that will not only insure against the recurrence of the particular accident, but will prevent other potential accidents which might be caused by the existing hazards that the investigation reveals. Errors are always possible in the operation of aircraft; the most important goals are lessening the chance of error and planning ways to make errors, when committed, less costly.

This approach calls for more than mere investigation. It demands a constant scrutiny of the entire field and the planning of remedies to correct whatever hazards are found to exist. This points to the second way of improving the process of accident investigation, namely, providing that the study of investigative results, as well as the planning and conduct of the investigation, be conducted always at high levels. The Board, as such, has not always been able to do this. As

[2] See *Report to the President of the United States by the President's Special Board of Inquiry on Air Safety, 1947.*

originally constituted, its prime objective has been to regulate the economic phases of air transport, and its chief energies have therefore been devoted to that task. An equally concentrated approach to the problems of air safety might produce as comprehensive and productive results as those already achieved in regulating the economic phases of the industry.

The usual steps in accident investigations are as follows:

1. *Notification of Accident or Potential Hazard.* All accidents involving serious or fatal injury, any air carrier, air collision, fire in flight, structural failure or aircraft or power plant or prop control operations.
2. *Field Investigations.* Includes investigation of the accident or review of accident reports to determine adequacy of report.
3. *Laboratory Tests of Failed Parts.* Tests of failed parts by appropriate government or commercial laboratories.
4. *Public Hearing.* Hearings held when it is in the public interest to bring out the facts.
5. *Technical Analysis and Digest of Evidence.* Technical analysis of facts, conditions, and circumstances brought out in hearing and digest of all the evidence.
6. *Public Report of Findings.* Release of public report showing facts, conditions, and circumstances including analysis, probable cause, and recommendations for corrective action.

Causes of Air Accidents

No matter what the rules and precautions, accidents will occur. The causes are many. Mechanical failures will happen, no matter how careful the inspections and tests by manufacturers and airline maintenance forces, and no matter how careful the flight crew and ground personnel. The modern aircraft contains thousands of vital parts, many of them at once intricate, delicate, and required to function under violent stresses and fantastic changes in temperature. Human error will creep in; and in nearly every case had one less error been committed, the accident probably could have been prevented. The remarkable thing is not that some accidents occur but that they occur so seldom.

Over the years, more accidents have been ascribed to failure on the part of airline personnel than to any other cause. More often than not, individual accident reports list such personnel errors as "pilot error." In fact, it may be said that pilot error runs through all the other causes, that is, terrain, weather, structural failures, or power plant failures—less in the latter than in the former. Pilot error is a very difficult thing to describe, and one must not confuse pilot blame and pilot error. All human beings are subject to human frailty, and they may fall down on the job. It is not the blame of the pilot. It means, however, that it is incumbent on the Civil Aeronautics Board and Federal Aviation Agency to see that training programs and selection requirements for pilots are the best that our techniques and knowledge up to this stage can devise.

Airline pilots, being human, naturally make mistakes occasionally, and sometimes the results are serious. However, the flat verdict "pilot error" should not be applied to any accident without first taking all extenuating circumstances into consideration and also a complete appreciation of the fact that, when an airplane departs, the pilot automatically assumes the ultimate responsibility for all mistakes made by practically everyone else in connection with the flight.

Thus, if a careless agent loads the aircraft improperly so that it is completely out of balance, the pilot must absorb this error and quite often do so on a difficult instrument procedure which could, under many circumstances, be problem enough with a properly loaded airplane.

If a mistake is made in dispatching, choosing of alternate airports, estimating the fuel necessary for a given weather condition, or many similar instances, the pilot must either catch the error at its source, which is invariably difficult and frequently impossible, or absorb the emergency created by the errors of the other departments when the situation develops.

If a mechanic makes a mistake in engine maintenance or overhaul, not only will the pilot eventually have to handle an engine out—or adopt what is known as "single-engine procedure"—but it is entirely possible that he may have to conduct the emergency in a severe frontal or squall condition that was completely missed on the weather forecast issued by the meteorology department.

The failure and malfunction of ground facilities, such as radio ranges, two-way voice communications, or airport lights, are additional burdens upon the pilot at frequent intervals.

Airline pilots have no desire whatsoever to dodge or avoid any of this final responsibility. However, they do emphatically feel that the interests of airline safety would be better served if investigating agencies would concentrate on a proper evaluation of all extenuating circumstances and contributing factors instead of coming out with the flat announcement of "pilot error," which thereby absolves the many agencies, and departments, and everyone else that has contributed to the cause of the accident.

Although structural and power plant failures are not now the major problem they were in the early days of air transportation, such mishaps do occur often enough to be significant in the "cause of accidents" summary. As new aircraft and new power plants come into use, a great deal of research is required to provide the knowledge necessary to achieve satisfactory safety standards. For example, in jet power plants there is still much to be learned before materials are completely satisfactory and integrity can be assured. New alloys for aircraft construction call for extensive study and experimentation, particularly in fatigue and corrosion resistance.[3] Studies of this type should give assurance that tomorrow's aircraft should be safer than those of today.

The occurrence of fires in the air is another item that calls for attention. Although they occur but seldom, at least in the well-proved aircraft, their effect is so terrifying and results so severe that they are a matter of prime importance.[4] The problem itself is difficult of solution because equipment must be so compact and because, in aircraft, the amount of fuel handled and the rate of energy release is so much greater per unit of volume than is any other transportation device. A better method of extinguishing fires when they occur is needed. Carbon dioxide and methyl bromide are being used, but both have serious shortcomings. A paramount need is a really satisfactory fire detector. None has yet been developed which has the desired reliability. Too frequently, fire detectors fail to operate, or they give a warning when no fire is occurring. Either situation obviously tends to detract from their effectiveness.

Considerable research has been performed on nonflammable lubricating oils, but the results thus far are not hopeful. More success has been had in developing nonflammable hydraulic fluids. Several of these bear considerable promise for utilization in the near future.

The exploration of so-called "safety" fuels is potentially fruitful but has not resulted in any phenomenal advances as yet. It must be remembered that fuel is, by definition, something that will burn; and, hence, there are certain conditions of temperature, exposure to oxygen, and any source of ignition which will make it a fire hazard. Although it is conceivable that a fuel could be developed which would burn only under conditions found inside an engine and under

---

[3] See C. C. Furnas, "Research for Aircraft Safety," *Aeronautical Engineering Review*, July, 1949.

[4] It has been estimated that about 5 per cent of air carrier accidents are caused directly or indirectly by fire in flight. *Ibid.*

no combination of conditions which could be found outside, there appears to be little real hope of complete success along this line.

Bad weather is an important cause of air accidents, and it has been made much more difficult to overcome because of the increasing requirements for all-weather operation in the air transport industry. With the present integrity of aircraft, if flying operations were confined to fair weather, the accident record would probably be of much smaller proportions. Although many airline accidents are attributed to pilot error, the bulk of these are really attributable to emergency situations, arising during poor weather conditions, which human beings cannot reasonably be expected to handle. It has been estimated that, if these emergencies based on weather were eliminated, about 40 per cent of the present accidents would never happen.[5] Probably an adequate solution lies in the various electronic devices with suitable adjuncts which will give a requisite amount of intelligence and a proper degree of communication and control (see Chapter 2).

The Content of Safety Regulation

Regulations as such cannot alone bring about conformance to safe operating procedures and standards. Indeed, an effort must be made to keep regulations at a minimum so as to avoid confusion and disorder. The prime responsibility for the observance of good operating procedures must be placed upon the air carriers themselves. The Board has consistently followed this policy, but in doing so has sought advice and suggestions from the operating personnel of the air transportation industry.

As time has gone on, two factors have evolved in connection with safety regulation. The first is that the growing knowledge of the nature of air transport permits the Board to move from rules to the writing of standards. This is a natural development that has taken place in many related fields. Portions of the Civil Air Regulations, which started off frequently as special solutions for certain situations, have already been revised, with some details being eliminated.

The second factor is the maturing of the industry itself. The air transport industry is probably more conscious of the significance of clean, safe operations than is anyone else. It is showing this consciousness in its research activities and its general organization to bring about that end. This enables the government to delegate

[5] Jerome Lederer, "Loss Prevention Programs in Civil Aviation," *Aeronautical Engineering Review*, July, 1948.

more and more of its detailed responsibilities in this connection to the industry. Examples of this are to be found in the devising of air carrier maintenance certificates and technical standard orders. This does not mean that the government should neglect or abrogate its responsibilities, but it does mean that government should be able to content itself with specifying the broad objectives that must be met and leave to industry the manner in which it will choose to meet those standards. In the fields of airworthiness standards, fire prevention, auxiliary devices, and even operations, much can be done along this line. And so long as the industry keeps its sense of responsibility, the resulting simplification will provide both safety and greater flexibility in development.

Our national policy regarding aviation safety was outlined by the Air Coordinating Committee as follows:

1. The Federal government's paramount objective in the field of aviation safety shall be to assure the highest practicable degree of safety in civil aviation. In the fulfillment of this objective, all appropriate United States government agencies shall cooperate in fostering and encouraging safety concepts and in the removal of technical, administrative and political obstacles to the safe and orderly development of domestic and international civil aviation.

2. The advancement of aviation safety shall continue to be regarded as a cooperative effort of government and industry. An effort designed to contribute both to the national welfare and to the continuing best interests of the civil aviation industry itself.

3. The government should continue the trend toward (1) safety rules and regulations which prescribe the particular objective sought rather than the means by which it is attained and (2) curtailment of the supplementary directives of a mandatory nature. Safety rules and regulations should be drawn so as to reduce to the greatest degree compatible with safety the administrative burden on both industry and government attendant upon their implementation and enforcement.

4. As a corollary to these policies, the air carriers, manufacturers and other industry organizations must assume primary responsibility for assuring adherence to safety standards within their organizations. The governmental safety authorities should hold management accountable for company-wide compliance with safety standards, rules and regulations, and should emphasize dealings with company management to secure desired improvements in safety.

5. Because of the large number and dispersion of individuals and organizations associated with general aviation, such as private flyers and other non-air-carrier operators, the Federal safety authorities must in the interest of efficiency devote their major attention in the general aviation field to those organizations and individuals that have the greatest potential effect upon safety, such as aviation schools, repair stations, other individuals and organizations the scale or character of whose activities warrants special attention,

and to the designees who have been delegated governmental examining and inspectional responsibilities. The policy of utilizing designees who are not on the federal payroll to perform the great bulk of examining, certification, and inspection work with respect to individual aircraft and airmen shall be continued.

6. The governmental safety authorities should devote increasing emphasis to singling out and attacking the really key factors and problems that have the greatest impact upon the safety of air operations. This will involve statistical and other investigations to isolate major safety and hazard-generating factors in aircraft, airmen, operations, and facilities; the solicitation of the opinions of industry and aviation organizations in the nature of such problems, and their cooperation in developing solutions; the pooling of the results of research and experience bearing upon these problems; and the open-minded exploration of fresh approaches to their solutions.[6]

Airline Liability and Insurance[7]

Certificated airlines are common carriers and as such are required to use the greatest care, vigilance, and caution consistent with the practical operation of aircraft.[8] However, passengers by air must assume all the usual and ordinary perils which are incident to that type of travel and which may exist over and above the perils which a common carrier, under its legal liability, must guard against.[9] In one case, the court held:

> In an airplane accident the limitation of responsibility may be said to consist of a plane in good mechanical condition, handled by a careful pilot, maneuvered in a careful way under conditions that, so far as can be foreseen and overcome by the use of ordinary skill, such as unfavorable weather conditions, so that the ordinary pilot could observe them as such.[10]

The general rule of proof is that the mere occurrence of an accident does not, in itself, raise a presumption of negligence on the part of a common carrier by air, despite the fact that the carrier is charged with the duty of exercising the highest degree of care in protecting its passengers and cargo.

[6] Air Coordinating Committee, *Civil Air Policy* (Washington, D.C., 1954).

[7] See G. O. and L. G. Dykstra, *The Business Law of Aviation* (New York: McGraw-Hill Book Co., 1946), Parts III and IV; Charles S. Rhyne, *Aviation Accident Law* (Washington, D.C.: Columbia Law Book Co., 1947); G. L. Wilson and L. A. Bryan, *Air Transportation* (New York: Prentice-Hall, Inc., 1949), chaps. xxi and xxiv.

[8] This theory has been upheld numerous times by the courts, which have usually distinguished between the standards required of common carriers and those imposed by law on private or contract carriers. See *Wilson* v. *Colonial Air Transport, Inc.*, 278 Mass. 420 (1932); *Foote* v. *Northwest Airways, Inc.*, 1931 U.S. Av. R. 66 (1931). In one case, however, the court held the airline liable for only ordinary care. See *Greunke* v. *North American Airways Co.*, 201 Wis. 565 (1930).

[9] *Allison* v. *Standard Air Lines, Inc.*, 1930 U.S. Av. R. 292 (1930).

[10] *Seaman* v. *Curtiss Flying Service, Inc.*, 1929 U.S. Av. R. 48 (1929).

Common carriers of goods by air are subject to the same general rules applicable to other forms of transportation. That is, they are held generally liable for loss or damage of goods while in their custody and are responsible for the safe transportation and proper delivery of the goods to consignees, except for loss or damage caused by acts of God, acts of the public enemy, or other excuses for failure to transport and deliver which are recognized by the common law or applicable statutory law. The Railway Express Agency in conducting its air express service uses an air express receipt which provides, as does the uniform express contract used in the railway express business by land and water routes, that the liability of the carrier is limited in consideration of the rate charged for the transportation service. This rate is dependent upon the value of the property and is based upon an agreed valuation not over $50 for any shipment of 100 pounds or less and not exceeding 50 cents per pound, actual weight, for any shipment in excess of 100 pounds, unless a greater value is declared and stated in the receipt. Wilson and Bryan state that, while "there is little statutory or case law in claims for damage to express and baggage as the result of aircraft accidents," the courts "are almost certain to apply the usual common law rules holding the common carriers as insurers of the goods" subject to the usual exceptions provided for other types of carriers.[11]

Rules for air carrier accident liability in international air transportation are prescribed by the Warsaw Convention adopted in 1929, to which the United States is a party. This provides, in substance, that the air carrier shall be liable for damages sustained by (*a*) death or injury to the passengers; (*b*) destruction, loss, or damage to baggage or goods; and (*c*) loss resulting from delay in the transportation of passengers, baggage, or merchandise. The Convention provides that, for passengers, liability cannot be escaped unless the carrier proves that he or his agent took all necessary measures to avoid the damage or that it was impossible to take such measures. In the case of baggage or goods, the carrier can successfully defend any claim for damage if he proves that the damage was caused by an error in piloting, in the handling of aircraft, or in navigation and that he or his agents had taken all necessary measures to avoid the damage. Wilson and Bryan point out that "there have been few court decisions under the Warsaw Convention" but that the leading American case holds that "no new substantive rights

[11] Wilson and Bryan, *op. cit.*, p. 413. See Chapter 17 for a more detailed discussion of airline liability for air cargo and insurance coverage.

were created by the Warsaw Convention, and all the rules laid down are well within the framework of the existing legal rights and remedies."[12]

In 1949 the Civil Aeronautics Board began a basic study and review of the tariff rules and airline practices relating to the liability of air carriers to the traveling and shipping public, and particularly to limitation of liability and procedures for making and collecting claims for damage and/or injury.[13]

In 1954[14] the Board clarified its economic regulations to make it unnecessary for air carriers or foreign air carriers to file rules for personal injury and death as part of their tariffs. This action was taken because of the Board's concern with the following:

(*a*) While the Board recognizes that certain advantages to the air carriers might result if a uniform federal rule of this nature were prescribed, the Board believes that in the present state of the art and the widespread public acceptance of aviation, the public interest requires a different type of uniformity—that is, uniformity of rules regulating the bringing of suits for personal injury and death within the local jurisdiction governing the claim. The traveling public and their lawyers do not tend to think of aviation in terms of special rules in respect of negligence actions which require procedures, notification of claims, and special limitations of actions differing from those applicable to other negligence actions. Weighing the relative advantages to air carriers of uniformity throughout the country against the advantages of uniformity of treatment within each local jurisdiction to the users of transportation, the Board believes that conformity with state practice is the more desirable result at the present state of development of air transportation.

(*b*) Even if federal regulation in this precise field were considered desirable, the Board does not believe that arriving at such result through the medium of tariff regulations, in the instance of these particular rules, is in the public interest, because actual notice of the rules is seldom brought home to passengers or their representatives. Legal actions against private persons in respect of personal injury or death are generally governed by statute; and passengers and general practitioners are not accustomed to thinking of such matters as being limited or otherwise adversely affected by tariff publications.

---

[12] *Ibid.*, p. 416. Also see *Wyman and Bartlett* v. *Pan American Airways, Inc.*, 1943 U.S. Av. R. 1 (1943). One of the major provisions of the 1929 Warsaw Convention sets the maximum liability an airline may have for each passenger in case of bodily injury or death during an international flight at $8,291 (U.S.). There is also a maximum of $16.58 for each kilogram of checked baggage and cargo, and $331.67 for any possessions the passenger carries with him. (This limitation of liability does not exist if the damage was caused by wilful misconduct on the part of the carrier.)

[13] CAB Order E-3183 (1949). The inquiry was broadened in 1950 by CAB Order E-4680.

[14] Economic Regulations, Amendment No. 1 to Part 221, Regulation No. E.R.-195, effective March 2, 1954.

Consequently, in the absence of positive notification of their presence and effect, these rules tend to become traps for the unwary.

Insurance is an important part of air transportation, as it is of all commercial enterprise. Airlines buy insurance to protect their investment in aircraft and other equipment against numerous and varied risks. Bankers financing the purchase of aircraft and other equipment require that it be insured. Shippers and bankers financing shipments also demand the protection of insurance for their goods while in transit. Liability insurance serves also to meet liabilities to persons suffering financial loss from personal injury and property damage inevitably resulting from accidents in the use of any medium of transportation.[15] No certificated United States airline carries insurance coverage of less than $40,000 per passenger and not less than $150,000 per accident. With respect to airline liability to persons on the ground who are not passengers, none of the certificated airlines carries less insurance coverage than $50,000 per person and $500,000 per accident. With respect to public liability for property damage on the ground for third persons, no certificated airline has insurance coverage of less than $500,000 per accident. These figures represent the least carried by a certificated airline, including the smallest. The average airline carries much higher limits; for example, one middle-sized airline carries insurance of $75,000 for each passenger and $2,000,000 for each accident, and with respect to its liability to persons on the ground it carries insurance coverage of $100,000 per person and $1,000,000 per accident. To cover its potential liabilities for damage to property on the ground, this same airline carries insurance of $1,000,000 per accident.

The group plan of underwriting has been the manner in which aviation insurance has developed in this country. The two underwriting groups which dominate the domestic aviation insurance market are Associated Aviation Underwriters and United States Aviation Underwriters, Inc. This plan, which spreads any given risk among a number of companies, was evolved in part as answer to the unfortunate financial experience of several insurance companies which undertook to write aviation insurance individually in the 1920's. Under the group plan, several insurance companies authorized to write a similar line of insurance, such as fire insurance, for example, mutually agree to divide among themselves, in speci-

[15] See Civil Aeronautics Board, *A Study of Aviation Insurance* (Washington, D.C., 1944).

fied proportions, all of their aviation insurance business. To facilitate the administration of their undertaking, the several insurance companies designate an organization to have the exclusive management of the underwriting of all aviation risks assumed by each company. Similarly, a group of insurance companies authorized to write casualty insurance agree among themselves to share all their aviation risks and designate as the exclusive underwriting manager, for their aviation business, the same organization which handles the underwriting activities for the fire insurance companies.

The underwriting groups provide a wide range of coverage for aeronautical risks, but all coverage falls broadly into two categories —airline and nonairline. The airline category includes all forms of insurance which the underwriting groups write for the scheduled airlines.[16] Coverage for the airlines is divided into hull and liability insurance. Hull insurance, which is written by fire insurance companies, is intended to cover all the hazards pertaining to the aircraft and other airline property, such as fire and lightning, wind storm, tornado and cyclone, mooring (seaplanes), theft, perils of the air, or crash and land damage. Liability insurance, which is written by the casualty companies, covers the air carriers against liability to passengers, employees, and third persons and against liability for damage to property, including such risks as public liability, passenger liability, property damage, airport and hangar keeper's liability, baggage and cargo liability, and workmen's compensation.

Nonairline insurance is chiefly of the following types: (*a*) industrial, covering the industrial enterprises owning their own aircraft to transport persons and property in connection with their business; (*b*) flying services, such as the fixed-base or aircraft service operator giving flying instruction and conducting sightseeing and other charter operations; (*c*) private pleasure, covering persons who use aircraft for pleasure and other noncommercial purposes; (*d*) manufacturers, including the producers of aircraft and aircraft parts who purchase not only liability and workmen's compensation coverage but also liability insurance (the latter covers the manufacturer against liabilities arising from handling, use, or condition of aircraft after the manufacturer has made delivery); (*e*) airport

[16] Airline and nonairline purchasers also carry insurance other than that furnished by the two groups specializing in aviation insurance. Examples of such other coverage are bonding insurance and fire and liability insurance on buildings and automobiles. For a more complete discussion of air cargo insurance see William H. Rodda, *Inland Marine and Transportation Insurance*, 2d ed. (Inglewood Cliffs, N.J.: Prentice-Hall, Inc., 1958), chap. ix.

operators who insure against liability to third persons; and (*f*) accident insurance for individuals or groups who fly as passengers or pilots.

The Economic-Safety Equation[17]

Air transportation is unique among industries in the importance of safety. On the one hand, the safety of air transportation is itself part and parcel of the product the industry sells to the public. On the other hand, because of the new dimension in airspace in which it carries on its business, there is no such thing as an acceptable risk. In most other industries, while safety is a factor affecting costs or even the reputation of the company, the product is usually saleable regardless of the safety record of the industry itself. The economic success of air transportation, on the other hand, rests primarily on public confidence in its safety record.

The relationship between economics and safety has been a basic postulate of government intervention in the air transport industry. The Civil Aeronautics Act passed in 1938 had as two of its basic assumptions, first, that the industry could not achieve a satisfactory safety record without a measure of economic stability; and conversely, that it could not achieve economic stability without improving its safety record and public confidence in the use of air transportation. These two interdependent assumptions compose the economic-safety equation. In fact, the whole scheme of promotion and regulation incorporated in the Civil Aeronautics Act was aimed at these aspects of the problem. By direct aid, the government proposed to assist the air transport industry in achieving economic stability and to provide some of the necessary tools of safe operation. At the same time, the government contemplated the achievement of continued economic stability and safety through economic control of entry, rates, and other economic practices combined with acceptable standards of safety.

It is unfortunate that, despite the importance of the economic-safety equation, it has never been fully defined or assessed. No formula or balance sheet has ever been developed to show the relationship, yet all parts of the industry concerned with making safety work are familiar with the problem in its simplest terms. In other words, how much does a particular safety device cost? How much will some safety instrument or device increase or decrease

[17] Adapted from an address by James R. Durfee, then Chairman of the Civil Aeronautics Board at the Flight Safety Symposium, Las Vegas, Nevada, April 16, 1959.

aircraft efficiency? Does the economic penalty imposed destroy the economic value of the airplane? We should, however, be concerned with broader implications which are difficult to measure but extremely important, such as: What is the impact of accidents on the development of aviation and air transportation? What is the impact of palliative safety measures or safety limitations that must be resorted to when we fail to provide an adequate basic framework for safe operations?

Chapter 12

FINANCING AIRLINES

UNTIL the close of World War II, the capital requirements of the air transport industry were met primarily through the sale of capital or common stock, generally referred to as "equity financing." The requirements of the industry for capital were small at that time, both in absolute terms and relative to the investment which has taken place since the war. Moreover, the industry was regarded as intensely speculative, and there were few fixed assets on which money could be borrowed through the issuance of such securities as mortgage bonds.

The situation changed rapidly in the first few years after the war with debt capital representing about half of the total. It is generally agreed that a 30 to 40 per cent debt ratio would not be too difficult for the airlines to handle in the immediate future.

The postwar trend to debt financing has been held by some authorities to have been far more pronounced and rapid than either necessary or desirable.[1] Some of the airlines failed to take advantage of the favorable market for their common stock which occurred during and immediately following the war; and, in 1946, the equity market, particularly for airline securities, collapsed. Unfortunately, it was approximately at this time that many of the carriers were in greatest need of new money to complete their programs of conversion to new equipment. In consequence, a number of the airlines were forced to resort to long-term borrowing to meet current needs as well as to keep abreast of aeronautical advances.

The increase in debt has serious implications not only for the immediate future but, more important, in connection with the ability of the airlines to face economic fluctuations. Obviously, if the industry and the Civil Aeronautics Board have done their job in accordance with the general requirements and responsibilities of the

[1] See statement of Joseph J. O'Connell, Jr., then Chairman of the Civil Aeronautics Board, before Senate Committee on Interstate and Foreign Commerce in "Airline Industry Investigation" (81st Cong., 1st sess.), April 11, 1949.

Civil Aeronautics Act, a substantial part of the industry should be able to weather reasonable economic fluctuations as they may occur. If, on the other hand, the financial structure of the industry is such that it endangers continued operations in the face of a general economic decline, it may be properly said that the air transportation system is not soundly financed. The danger in the present amount of long-term or funded debt is that it imposes relatively heavy fixed charges on an industry whose margin of revenue after operating expenses has fluctuated from time to time and, on the average, has been low.

The business of air transportation is highly sensitive to changes in the volume of traffic. Its operating ratio, which represents the relationship which operating expenses bear to all sources of revenue, is high. For example, the Class I railroads typically show an

COMPOSITE OPERATING RATIO DOMESTIC TRUNK AIRLINES

Year	Ratio	Year	Ratio	Year	Ratio
1946	101.5	1950	93.5	1954	95.0
1947	104.2	1951	93.0	1955	95.3
1948	100.4	1952	94.0	1956	96.5
1949	96.2	1953	95.4		

Average 1946–56 = 96.8; Average 1951–56 = 95.1.

Operating ratio-relationship of the sum of operating expenses, depreciation, and all taxes to operating revenues.

Source: General Passenger Fare Investigation, CAB Docket No. 8008 (1958), Ex. AA-901.

operating ratio of about 75 per cent. In air transportation, an operating ratio of 95 per cent, or even slightly higher, has been the average over the years. The other important consideration, apart from the ratio itself, is the extent to which costs can be promptly adjusted to changes in the volume of traffic. Even though a very large part of airline expenses are variable, others are relatively constant. For example, depreciation must be accrued regardless of whether the individual aircraft is flying. The salaries of both flight and ground personnel are the same whether 50 per cent or 75 per cent of the seats are occupied by paying passengers. Even a reduction in schedules does not result in a proportionate decrease in cost since the same number of aircraft and other facilities must usually be maintained.

The air transport industry, therefore, not only has a high operating ratio but has a large proportion of expenses which do not vary directly with the volume of business. Thus, operating income fluctuates widely as a result of even small increases or decreases in traffic. In describing this condition, one might say that the airlines have a high break-even point; this is one of the most important characteristics of the business. When an airline goes into debt, it assumes fixed charges which serve to increase even further the proportion of constant expenses. Large-scale borrowing, therefore, has the effect of raising the high break-even point to an even higher level and of accentuating the instability of earning power. This undesirable development can be avoided, however, by financing with preferred and common stocks, which do not add fixed charges.

Ideally, therefore, an airline might be capitalized entirely with common stock; but, to be more realistic, one must recognize the need for intermediate debt financing of equipment purchases. The introduction of new types of equipment in the industry means that at any time an airline may find it necessary and desirable to replace a substantial proportion of its fleet, as has happened in the transition to jet aircraft starting in 1959.

In financing the transition to jet aircraft, the airlines have typically followed a pattern of long-term financing, chiefly through loans from insurance companies, supplemented by shorter-term loans from banks to cover requirements not met by the long-term financing. Some equity financing was undertaken in 1956 and early 1957, when conditions in the equity market and carrier earnings were more favorable. None has been undertaken since. In contrast to the Big Four airlines, the medium-sized trunk lines have had less success in arranging long-term loans. Moreover, it is doubtful whether, under earning conditions in the foreseeable future, any further long-term funds will be available to medium-sized airlines except in limited amounts, at relatively high interest rates approaching 6 per cent, and under highly restrictive covenants.

To the extent that bank loans have been arranged, the insistence of the banks on loans of relatively short terms (no longer than ten years and generally less) has imposed onerous repayment requirements on the airlines concerned. In addition, the financing requirements of the various jet programs have been so large in relation to the capitalization of individual companies that debt ratios, already high for most of the carriers, are exceeding the limits considered prudent or acceptable by financial institutions. It seems clear, therefore, that additional equity financing will be required in most cases in the future as a condition precedent to the granting of bank loans.[2]

[2] For a complete discussion of the subject, see Paul W. Cherington, *The Status and Economic Significance of the Airline Equipment Investment Program*, a report prepared for the President's Special Assistant for Aviation (Washington, D.C., 1958).

Probably never before in the business history of the United States has there been an industry which has required such a huge relative capital expansion in such a short period of time as has been true of the airline industry since 1958. The intensity of need has been the product both of the amount needed and of the short time within which the need had to be met coming at a time when there was a universal shortage of funds and a great demand for capital.

Financing Equipment Purchases

Assuming that modern all-metal aircraft do not wear out because the continuous process of rebuilding is a part of airline maintenance procedure, the main interest of those asked to aid in financing equipment purchases is the question of obsolescence and the possible use of the equipment on the same or other airlines should the borrower default.

The development of an airplane requires three years or more from its conception to the earning stage. New developments are taking place continuously, but such developments do not come about at one time. Turbine and jet propulsion, for example, may revolutionize aircraft power and eventually, either in conjunction with reciprocating engines or in substitution for them, render obsolete all aircraft now in existence or in the developmental stages. But a change of so radical a nature should not jeopardize loans on equipment in the meantime, if such loans are made for a fairly short period of time. Furthermore, the reduction of such loans by regular annual payments (amortization) should be carried out while new types are being substituted for existing equipment.

The period over which an equipment loan should be paid ought to be based as far as possible upon a forecast by the airline of the actual figures and not arbitrarily made to fit some other period of time. Heretofore, loans on airline equipment have usually been made to run from three to five years. The equipment more recently bought is being amortized by the airlines over a period of seven years. In any event, the annual payments should be arranged so that 100 per cent of the loans on the equipment would be paid off within the period in which the operator writes the original book value down to the allowed nominal residual value.

The prospective lender is apt to question what disposition he would make of modern aircraft in case of default of his loans. The assumption is that such equipment would be operated for the lender by the receiver (or his modern counterpart, the trustee) of the airline and that the owner of the equipment would be in a favored position in dealing with the receiver for the airline.

If the airline is to continue in operation, the question of disposal of equipment probably will not arise. However, in case of abandonment,[3] the problem is less easy to solve. The tendency is for each airline to select its planes and other equipment to meet the specific needs of particular traffic, so that, in order to dispose of repossessed aircraft and parts without loss, it would be necessary to find another airline operating under similar conditions and needing additional equipment.

The most important factor effecting equipment loans will, no doubt, prove to be the lender's confidence in the ability of the particular airline to utilize the equipment that is being financed on a profitable basis under the conditions met with by the individual operator. Probably the resale value of the equipment would prove to be of much less importance, even though in principle its value would always be larger than the outstanding amount of the loan.

The real protection derived by the lender will be based on the position his security interest in the airline's flying equipment gives him in case of receivership, so that he can promptly work out an arrangement with the receiver for the continued operation of the equipment, predicated upon the payment of interest and amortization in accordance with his contract. Banks and other lenders seem to feel that an airline should have an equity of somewhere between 20 to 30 per cent in each airplane at the start, depending upon the type of equipment and the credit of the operator.

It has been suggested that the operator's equity in the aircraft themselves might be decreased if a lien were obtained on spare engines, propellers, and parts. When an airline purchases a new fleet of aircraft, it is essential to buy spare engines and spare parts in sufficient number to permit replacement of engines for overhaul and replacement of parts of both aircraft and engines. Also these must be purchased in adequate number to permit distribution at points along the airline's routes. These spares are absolutely essential to permit the economical and safe operation of aircraft, but they substantially increase the expense of a new fleet.

Depending upon the number and type of airplanes to be pur-

[3] It is almost inconceivable that an airline, possessing a permanent certificate of convenience and necessity issued by the Civil Aeronautics Board, would ever be entirely abandoned. The same is not true of temporarily certificated carriers, several of which have already gone out of business.

chased and the length and kind of the routes involved, it has generally been found that about 25 per cent of the cost of the aircraft themselves should be spent for spare parts. In addition, the airline should maintain the spare-part inventory in virtually its original condition through all but the final stages of the life of this particular type of aircraft. Airlines are able to give valid liens both on aircraft and on inventories of essential spare parts.

Payments on loans made to finance new aircraft usually begin three to six months after the start of the earning life of the equipment, since there is always a time when it is being used for training crews, and so forth, and has not yet started to produce any revenue. For this reason, and also because deliveries of aircraft called for by sales contracts are usually spaced at intervals of several weeks or months, the loan should, except in unusual instances, be so arranged as to apply to individual airplanes.

The fleet of each airline should be covered by insurance against crash and destruction through other causes. Although in the past, when individual aircraft cost less and hence were depreciated more quickly, it has been the policy of some airlines to self-insure, such will not generally be the case in the future. In isolated cases, airlines have followed the procedure of insuring a number of aircraft not identified, rather than each specific aircraft. It appears that no fixed rule on insurance can be laid down. Any arrangement which provides for proper protection to the lender and to the borrower would probably be satisfactory. It seems reasonable for lenders to require that adequate insurance be carried on the fleet, at least to the extent of the loans.

Airline equipment loans have been based on conditional sales contracts, equipment trusts, and chattel mortgages; and although the last form has been used most often, it has not become the definitely established form. There are probably two reasons for this situation: lack of precedent and lack of clearly defined advantages for any one type. There may also be a difference in the relative advantages of the various forms of loan instruments between equipment for use wholly within the United States and equipment for use in foreign operation.

Under equipment trust financing, a bank or group of banks lends the required money for the purchase of new equipment; but the title remains in the banks, who are the trustees of the series of certificates issued with the equipment as security. The equipment trust certificates are owned by the banks doing the financing and are held by them or sold to investors who hold them until maturity. The certificates mature serially, so many each year; and the company operating the equipment pays enough each year to retire a series of the certificates and to pay interest on those remaining in the hands of banks or investors. The virtue of this type of financing rests in the fact that, as each annual payment is made, the equity behind the remaining certificates becomes greater, since the entire lot of equipment is security for the entire issue of certificates until all are paid off.

The chief difference between equipment trust financing for railroads and airlines is that the period to final maturity for railroad equipment trusts extends over ten or fifteen years, whereas for new aircraft the term would probably be limited to ten years. The principle involved is the same, i.e., payments by the operating company will retire, during the useful life of the equipment, the entire amount of the securities issued. The historical record of railroad equipment trust certificates is such that this type of security is regarded highly by investors.

Chattel mortgages are considered more suitable for airline use than for railroads because airlines do not, as a rule, have general mortgages containing "after-acquired property" clauses. Railroads commonly have such mortgages; and if they purchased equipment and took title thereto, the equipment would fall into the "maw" of the general mortgages, and it would be impossible thereafter to give first liens by way of chattel mortgages on such equipment.[4]

Under the conditional sales contract, the seller of the equipment retains title to it as a security instrument until the entire price is paid, but the purchaser obtains possession as soon as delivery can be made. The chief difference between this method and the equipment trust system is that in the latter a trustee holds title until payment is completed, making it a three-party arrangement. The conditional sales contract is therefore simpler, provided the seller has the financial ability to carry the purchaser and the purchaser's credit is good enough to warrant such an arrangement.

In 1957, the Civil Aeronautics Board was authorized to guarantee

---

[4] It has become a custom of the railroads to finance equipment through the use of equipment trusts wherever sales of the obligations are to be made to the public and through the use of conditional sale contracts where there is a single lender or a limited number of lenders. In either case, the instrument is generally recorded in the states in which the equipment will normally be operated, and the equipment is marked as the property of the lender. The holders of equipment trust and conditonal sales obligations of railroads have additional protection under section 77j of the Bankruptcy Act, whereby in railroad reorganizations the holder of title to the equipment may secure possession of the property. Similar protection has been extended to the holders of security titles to aircraft and spare parts by an amendment to Chapter X of the Bankruptcy Act in 1957.

loans to local-service airlines for the purchase of new aircraft.[5] Thirty carriers are presently eligible for this assistance, including the mainland local-service airlines, the carriers providing local services in Alaska and Hawaii and to the Bahamas, and the three certificated metropolitan helicopter services. The law authorizes the Board to guarantee loans up to $5 million per airline with the guaranty not to exceed 90 per cent of the loan. Guaranties may be made only if the Board finds that the air carrier would not otherwise be able to obtain funds for the purchase of aircraft upon reasonable terms, and only if the aircraft purchased will improve service and efficiency. The authority of the Board to guarantee these loans will expire in 1962. As of June 30, 1959, the Board had guaranteed between $18 and $20 million under this authorization.[6]

Control over Airline Securities

The Federal Aviation Act does not provide for control over airline security issues by the Board, with the result that this body is nothing more than an interested, but largely ineffectual, bystander in airline financing. There are some who maintain that Board control over airline securities is both unnecessary and undesirable. Many of this group feel, for example, that special emphasis must be placed on having the market for airline securities free from direct intervention by the Civil Aeronautics Board because of the peculiar position which that body occupies through its control of mail pay and subsidy payments. When a railroad security is offered for sale, after its issuance has been approved by the Interstate Commerce Commission, the investor is simply assured that the proceeds will be used for legitimate purposes, that the Commission has no objection to the form of the financing as a general principle, and that the terms of sale are reasonably favorable to the railway. There is no guarantee or implication that the Commission will see to the payment of interest or dividends on the new security, because it is well known that the Commission is in no position to make good any such undertaking. It can permit rate increases, but in most cases only for the railways as a group because of the lack of noncompetitive traffic. Also, it is known that, under some circumstances at least, higher rates may produce no greater net income.

Those maintaining that airline securities should be free from Board control point out that the Board, on the other hand, has the

[5] Public Law 85–307 (1957).

[6] CAB, *Annual Report*, 1959, p. 21.

power and often the obligation to transform an individual airline's deficit into net income by increasing its subsidy under the "need" provision of the law. Unlike a general rate increase, which may drive traffic to competitors in other forms of transportation, a revision in mail rates or subsidy payments simply adds the equivalent amount of net income. Since the Board is in a position to bolster any security with earning power in this manner, approval of a new issue might be interpreted freely by investors as a rather definite assurance of safety.

It is maintained, therefore, that it is undesirable for the Board to incur even an implied responsibility for any new security issues which would in any way restrict its freedom of action in carrying out its regulatory functions. The way to avoid this and yet to give the Board a voice in the market for airline securities is to encourage free expressions of opinion about the general financial practices of the airlines. From time to time, the Board could speak for or against any particular trend in financing without passing upon specific applications. Such expressions of the Board's point of view, it is felt, would be given appropriate weight along with the opinions of airline management and their financial advisors.[7]

The Board, however, is unanimous in believing authority over airline securities to be necessary, particularly since the industry, in the last analysis, relies on the government to save it from bankruptcy. There is, of course, no implication that, should the Board have authority over airline financing, there will then be an absolute guarantee that airline financial structures will be sound or that capital will be attracted on reasonable terms. Private capital is far more concerned with the rate and route policies being pursued by the Board, since these exert a vital effect on the destinies of the individual carriers. This emphasizes the necessity of adopting a broad perspective toward the regulatory processes of the industry. Without a constructive and consistent approach toward rate making and route awards, no mere assumption of control over capital structures by the Board will provide any cure for the carrier's ailments.

The natural tendency of all industry—and the airlines are no exception—is to resist all extensions of government controls and what might be considered undue interference with private enterprise, except to the extent that control may help their activities, as

---

[7] See Roger F. Murray, "Regulation of Airline Securities," *Harvard Business Review*, May, 1950. See also *Aviation Study*, Senate Doc. No. 163, 83d Cong., 2d sess. (Washington, D.C., 1955), p. 57.

is the case, for example, with the regulation of competition. The fact remains, however, that the carriers are endowed with a public interest and enjoy a franchise which provides them with a degree of monopoly and affords a certain amount of protection against competition. Moreover, financial assistance is afforded certain parts of the industry through subsidy payments and indirectly through the flying aids sponsored by the government.[8]

The airlines will have continuing need for large new capital requirements. It is important, therefore, to avoid the mistakes which occurred in the earlier stages of technological development of other public utility enterprises. Giving the Board control over airline capital structures will not in itself solve all the industry's problems and assure it of sustained earnings. It will, however, co-ordinate the regulatory processes, center them in the one government agency expected to be best qualified to deal with such matters, and make a substantial contribution toward a sounder and better air transportation industry.

Fair Rate of Return[9]

The "fair rate of return" for a major airline should be sufficient to enable it to have and maintain at all times a modern, efficient air transport system both adequate to meet the growing public needs

[8] The need for security controls has been clearly established and accepted in other regulated industries. Under the Transportation Act of 1920 (sec. 20A), the Interstate Commerce Commission is required to approve the kind and amount of securities to be issued by railroads, as well as the price at which these securities are to be offered for sale. This power was given the Commission to protect the general public by preventing unwarranted additions to railway capitalization, to protect the investors in railroad stocks and bonds against unwise financial practices, and to protect the railroads against paying more than they should for the capital they needed. The ICC experiences with railroad financing comprise a rich background which may find constructive application in the case of the airlines. To make control over the issuance of securities effective, the ICC found it necessary to pass on the underwriting provisions and other details concerning the offering of these securities. There exist wide variations in practices which can materially affect the net proceeds obtained by an issuing corporation in underwriting of securities. For this reason, unless properly defined, the terms of underwriting agreements can preclude adequate control over the issuance of new securities.

A number of railroad receiverships, some observers believe, might have been avoided if the carriers had not developed top-heavy capital structures. Burdened with an abnormal amount of funded debt, many of the railroads were unable to service their interest requirements when their earnings evaporated with the decline in traffic and revenues. It was not until 1920, when most of the railroad financing had already been accomplished, that the ICC was empowered to act on new security issues.

See John H. Frederick, *Federal Regulation of Railway Securities under the Transportation Act of 1920* (Philadelphia: Westbrook Publishing Co., 1927); Selig Altschul, "Security Reins to CAB?" *Air Transport*, December, 1947.

[9] Adapted from Exhibit No. AA 4, *General Passenger Fare Investigation*, CAB Docket No. 8008 (1957).

for expanded service and improved equipment, and commensurate with our developing national economy and potential defense requirements.

By "fair rate of return" is meant that percentage which, when applied to the invested capital rate base, will provide the amount in dollars, after all expense, including provision for depreciation and taxes, which the enterprise should be allowed a reasonable chance to earn. The return should be adequate, under efficient and economical management, to maintain and support the company's credit and assure confidence in its financial soundness, so that the company will be able to raise the money necessary for the proper discharge of its public duties.

To achieve these ends, the return must be sufficient to provide the necessary payment for the cost of capital in the form of interest, preferred and common stock dividends, and a margin of return in excess of interest and dividend requirements to pass on to surplus. To be fair, the return must provide the common stockholder adequate compensation for the risks attached to his investment, and commensurate with returns in other enterprises having corresponding risks.

The "fair rate of return" should be computed exclusive of profits realized from the sale or disposition of equipment. Such profits should be regarded as a form of capital available for investment in new equipment. They serve to reduce proportionately the amount of capital required from other sources such as retained earnings or new security issues. These gains are relatively small in relation to a reasonable return allowance and are undependable. Thus, while the amount of such capital gains has increased in recent years, equipment sales have, at times, actually resulted in net losses for the industry. Moreover, a number of the larger trunklines have been experiencing difficulty in selling old planes in 1959–60, while the impending increase in the supply of obsolete piston-type aircraft poses problems as to the potential of this source of funds for investment in new equipment. Since such profits (or losses) are nonoperating in nature, unpredictable in amount, and variable from company to company and from time to time, they should not be included in the "fair rate of return" for a domestic trunkline.

"Cost of capital" is an important factor in the formation of any opinion as to a fair rate of return. "Cost of capital" represents the computed cost to a particular company or to a particular type of company of specific segments of the capital structure in question or of some assumed capital structure. Such separately determined cost rates are then applied to the relative proportion of each class of capital in the capital structure selected or adopted, producing a composite or over-all cost rate applicable to total capitalization.

To illustrate, let us assume that we are studying a company having a capital structure with two components: 30 per cent bonds and 70 per cent common stock and surplus. Let us further assume that the evidence indicates that the reasonable "current" cost rates are 5 per cent for the bonds and 15 per cent for common stock. The application of these two cost rates to the respective segments of total capitalization would produce an over-all annual cost of total capital of 12 per cent calculated as follows:

	Per Cent of Total Capitalization	*Rate*	*Annual Cost*
Bonds	30%	5%	1.50%
Common equity	70	15	10.50
Total	100%		
Annual cost of total capital			12.00%

At any particular time, indications of the current cost of debt securities and preferred stocks may be obtained from (1) the current yield at the current market price of already outstanding issues of the company and of generally comparable issues, after adjustment for cost of financing and for necessary underpricing or market pressures, and (2) the cost of new issues of the company or of other generally comparable companies sold at a date close to the time of the study. For such fixed income securities, the rates to be paid by the company have been established by contract.

However, at the level of common stock cost determination, judgment must be exercised, since common stock has no maturity and no contractual rate of dividends and no fixed claim on earnings. The problem is to determine what rates of earnings and dividends on common stock are necessary to induce investors to supply the necessary capital.

Evidences relating to the cost of common capital which may be computed mathematically are: (1) the earnings–market price ratio; (2) the earnings–net proceeds to company ratio on the sale of additional shares of common stock; and (3) the common earnings–common equity ratio.

The earnings–market price ratio expresses the arithmetic relationship between the earnings per share and the market price of a common stock. If a common stock had earnings equivalent to $2.50 a share in the latest year and is currently selling in the open market for \$20, the earnings–market price ratio would be 12.5 per cent, obtained by dividing the earnings by the market price per share.

The earnings–net proceeds to company ratio represents the relationship between the applicable earnings per share of common stock to the net price per share received by a company for an additional block of common stock sold directly to the public or to its stockholders through rights, after deducting all selling commissions and expenses. The earnings–common equity ratio represents the percentage relationship of earnings available for common stock to the sum of the paid-in common stock capital plus surplus.

Financial authorities believe that none of these mathematical ratios *alone* completely evidences the investor's requirement, for the primary reason that none of these ratios reflects the *future* income or capital appreciation expectations which lead the investor to supply the common stock capital. The exercise of judgment is the only way in which these mathematically computed cost ratios can be weighted properly to reflect the future expectations of investors and other appropriate factors. To assume that the recent past or current market prices usually employed in the computation of the earnings–market price ratios are the prices that investors offer for the then known earnings and the then paid dividends is contrary to sound investment judgment, because the market price of a stock is the investor's appraisal of a group of factors, of which current or past earnings is but one. Much more important factors which influence the price which an investor will pay for a common stock are concerned with *future* considerations, such as (1) the existence or nonexistence of growth for the company; (2) the prospects for investment appreciation for the investor; and (3) the future expectancies as to earnings and dividends. Past earnings are significant only to the extent that they may provide some guidance to the level or trend of future earnings.

Total capitalization represents the amount of money which investors have committed to the enterprise, and it is on this amount the company should be permitted to earn a fair return. This method of rate control is often called the prudent-investment principle and its principal advantages and objections which are sometimes raised thereto are as follows:

Advantages

1. This method is simple to administer in that the so-called rate base, being the total capitalization, is much easier to determine than a rate base

dependent on plant investment, with its problems of original cost, reproduction cost, fair value, accrued depreciation, working capital, etc.

2. This method regulates income according to the needs of the utility as measured by the amount required to pay interest on outstanding bonds, dividends on preferred stock, and to produce sufficient earnings to attract equity capital into the enterprise.

Objections

1. Capitalization may not represent the amount of money prudently invested in plant.

   No doubt this was true to some extent many years ago with respect to certain utility companies. However, since the advent of strong regulatory controls, and uniform modern accounting procedures, the so-called "watered stock" has all but disappeared. Also, there is doubt that this old bugaboo would have any particular application to the modern airlines industry.

2. A rate base equal to the total capitalization would include a substantial amount representing other assets such as cash balances, security investments, and progress payments on equipment, with the result that earnings permitted would be in excess of that applicable to a rate base of net plant plus working capital.

   This is true, but there is nothing unfair in the result. The method recognizes that the important fact from the investor's viewpoint is the amount of capital which is committed by him in the enterprise. What the investor has committed to the enterprise is capital or money, not property, and that is the amount upon which a fair and proper return allowance should be based.

It is believed that additional strong support for the use of a total capitalization rate base for the airlines is provided by: (1) the substantial progress payments required by most manufacturers on the contract price prior to delivery of aircraft and equipment to the airlines; and (2) the necessity for advance loan commitments by most airlines to reserve the capital required for acquisition of additional equipment well before the delivery date. These factors are of only minor significance in other regulated industries, but are extremely important in the airline industry because they require substantial progress payments, working capital, and cash balances—all of which are fully reflected in the total capitalization of the airlines.

In the General Passenger Fare Investigation,[10] several airlines proposed the use of the operating ratio, or its complement, the return margin, as the primary measure of fair and reasonable earnings instead of the traditional rate of return on investment. Most of the ar-

[10] CAB Docket No. 8008 (1957–60).

guments in favor of so doing rested on a conclusion that risk in the air transportation industry is related more to volume of business and capital turnover than to the amount of capital invested. As has been pointed out by one of the Civil Aeronautics Board examiners,[11] the subject of the risk in air transportation is, as in other industries, the money invested. The amount at risk is the amount which an airline may lose, and this is the amount invested. The degree of risk is the degree of probability of such loss. The degree of risk differs according to the venture involved and the circumstances affecting it. This would include capital turnover and operating ratio, which are factors to be considered along with all other relevant considerations. However, the amount at risk cannot differ according to the venture since it is solely and exclusively the amount invested.

Rate of return on investment is the only composite of the many variables which make up risk. Any other known ratio shows only a part of the whole picture. Financial authorities have long recognized that rate of return on investment is a free market's indicator of risk and that relative differences in return on investment reflect the market's evaluation of relative differences in the degree of risk of investment in various enterprises. There has been no such universal recognition of operating ratio or return margin or capital turnover as an indication or measure of risk since these measures are always subject to an "all other things being equal" qualification and are meaningless statistics when considered alone.[12] Allowance of a fair rate of return on the prudent investment is a method which assures justice to both the investors and the public. The investors will be adequately rewarded, and the shipping and traveling public will not be overcharged. No other known method is so efficient in reaching this result.

---

[11] See *General Passenger Fare Investigation, Initial Decision of Examiner Ralph L. Wiser,* served May 27, 1959, pp. 74–86. (See Chapter 9.)

[12] The Interstate Commerce Commission has relied primarily on operating ratio in regulating motor carrier revenues on the basis of its conclusion that the investment in this industry is so small in relation to total costs that the investment is not the primary factor in determining revenue needs. In the proceeding, in which the Commission discussed this problem at greatest length (*Middle West General Increases,* 48 MCC 541 [1948]), the Commission adverted to the fact that in 1946 the Class 1 motor carriers had a net investment of $22,389,500 and operating expenses of $84,691,000, or $3.78 of expenses for $1.00 of investment. The trunk air carriers in 1959 were about midway in this respect between the motor carriers and the railroads and nontransportation utilities. An 11-year average capital turnover for the airlines is 1.53. In comparison, the intercity motor carriers of property had a turnover of 4.28 and of passengers, 1.81. The railroads and nontransportation utilities (electric, gas, and telephone) had averages ranging from 0.30 to 0.58. While the airlines have a lower investment in relationship to volume of business than do the railroads and the nontransportation utilities, their investment is approximately two thirds of the annual revenues and cannot be viewed as insignificant.

Public Aid to Air Transportation[13]

In discussing the problems of airline financing, one must not lose sight of the fact that very few such carriers would be in operation today anywhere in the world were it not that they receive public aid in one form or another. Such aid is usually referred to under the broad classification of "subsidy." Much confusion exists, however, in the use of the word in connection with air transportation, chiefly because the average person does not analyze what the term subsidy includes. There has been some form of government subsidization in every air transport operating country under one or more of the following forms:

1. Direct financial payments.
2. Air mail payments exceeding the economic rate for the work done.
3. The provision of airways and other navigational facilities.
4. The provision of airport facilities.
5. The provision of aircraft.
6. Taxation concessions.
7. The financing of aeronautical research and development.

In the past, at least in some countries, government subsidies, especially "hidden" subsidies, have been granted frequently for purposes other than the direct advancement of air transport—for example, for enhancing national prestige, military training, obtaining a monopoly of certain traffic, and the like.

It is generally agreed that there is ample economic and social justification for a measure of government assistance in the early stages of the development of any transportation agency. In the early stages there is not the normal process of economic growth, in which lower costs permit lower rates and fares, which generate a greater demand leading to a further lowering of costs, and so on. Costs are high in

[13] See Richard W. Lindholm, *Public Finance of Air Transportation* (Columbus: Ohio State University, 1948); Committee on Interstate and Foreign Commerce, *National Transportation Inquiry, Public Aid to Air Transportation* (House Report No. 1612, 80th Cong., 2d sess.) (Washington, D.C., 1948); Paul T. David, *The Economics of Air Mail Transportation* (Washington, D.C.: Brookings Institution, 1934); Federal Coordinator of Transportation, *Public Aids to Transportation* (Washington, D.C., 1940); Francis A. Spencer, *Air Mail Payment and the Government* (Washington, D.C.: Brookings Institution, 1941); Board of Investigation and Research, *Public Aids to Domestic Transportation* (House Doc. No. 159, 79th Cong., 1st sess.) (Washington, D.C., 1945), pp 4, 26–30, 428–513; Report of the Special Committee on Transportation, *National Transportation Inquiry* (House Report No. 2735, 79th Cong., 2d sess.) (Washington, D.C., 1946), pp. 387–91; Oliver J. Lissitzyn, "Public Aid to Major Foreign Airlines," *Journal of Air Law and Commerce*, Autumn, 1951 and Winter, 1952; Donald W. Nyrop, "The Question of U.S. Air Mail Subsidy," *Journal of Air Law and Commerce*, Autumn, 1951; Harvey C. Bunke, "The Fetish of Separating Subsidy from Air Mail Payments," *Journal of Air Law and Commerce*, Summer, 1953.

any new agency of transportation; and this has been particularly true of air transportation, because equipment is undeveloped and relatively inefficient, and demand for the service rendered at economic prices is limited.

As far as air transportation has been concerned, public aid has been justified and may still be justified for limited periods because of the need for the initial development of new routes and the introduction of new equipment into service for the advancement of operating speeds, etc., ahead of what is immediately practical on an economic basis.

Governments have recognized the potential benefits of civil air transportation and have also recognized that the general economic and social welfare is secured by speeding up the process of development. From that standpoint and acting on behalf of the community, they have applied public funds to this end. In various ways this assistance has lowered costs and rates, thereby increasing demand and effectively stimulating the growth process. In addition to justification as a temporary aid to development, which should be discontinued as the industry gets properly under way, there is a case for government assistance in two other connections:

1. In providing services on social or international policy grounds, for which there may be no commercial demand even in the full maturity of the industry.
2. In providing facilities and services, such as navigational, meteorological, air traffic control, and search and rescue services, which are required also for aviation generally. This is similar to the provision of roads, bridges, road lighting, and traffic regulating systems for highways and marine channels, lighthouses, and other aids to shipping.

While a healthy and fully matured air transport industry may only require a minimum of assistance in the second of these connections, such a minimum would be analogous to that provided on justifiable economic and social grounds to other public utilities. It should not be regarded as abnormal or indicative of the inability of the industry eventually to be self-supporting, provided, of course, that any aid is in line with the general benefits accruing therefrom.

A transportation industry may be termed self-supporting when the assistance given justifiably as an aid to early development, as well as any excessive and misdirected assistance given from undue consideration of national economic rivalry, prestige, and strategy, has been eliminated.

Public aid to air transportation in the United States has taken the following forms:

1. Air mail payments exceeding a so-called "service" rate.
2. The provision of airways and other navigational facilities.
3. The provision of airport facilities.
4. Taxation concessions.
5. The financing of aeronautical research and development.

Insofar as any of the fundamental facilities of air transportation, such as airways and airports, are supplied to users at less than a fair and economic rate for the service rendered, to that extent may such users be regarded as government supported.

It must be borne in mind, however, in attempting to assess the progress made so far toward self-support and the future prospects of attaining the desired end, that civil air transportation as a whole covers a wide range of operations varying widely in their economic characteristics and potential profitability, under the influence of a large number of factors of technical, geographical, meteorological, and economic importance, and that, at any stage of development of the industry, individual operations or groups of operations may range from the highly profitable to the highly unprofitable. The effort of technical and economic development is to shift the whole universe of operations generally up the scale of profitability, although not necessarily preserving their relative order.

It is practically impossible to state at any given time what amount of direct and indirect assistance is being given by a particular government to air transportation. This is particularly true of international air transport. For example, in the United States, American-flag international air transport may receive government support through air mail payments to be paid in an amount or at a rate fixed by the Civil Aeronautics Board. Until lately this rate has been fixed without formal differentiation between the amount which should be paid to the air carrier as just compensation for the carriage of air mail and the amount needed by the air carrier for continued operation within the limits contemplated by the law. It has, therefore, been exceedingly difficult, if not impossible without extended cost studies over a longer period of time than that covered by our experience to date, to say how much direct subsidy has been granted to American international air carriers. To a certain degree the same facts apply in connection with domestic air carriers and the amount they have received for carrying the mail.[14]

[14] See Senate Committee on Interstate and Foreign Commerce, *Interim Report on Separation of Air-Mail Pay from Subsidy* (81st Cong., 2d sess.), May 5, 1950 (committee

National Policy on Airline Subsidies

In its report on Civil Air Policy, the Air Coordinating Committee[15] recognized the continued need for subsidy of some existing and some possible future air transport services, but at the same time held that the federal government should, at this time, move as rapidly as possible to terminate eligibility for subsidy for any segments of the industry which are now, or can readily be made, self-sufficient. The committee stated the following "basic principles for future subsidy policy":

> The national interest in promoting air transportation must take account of the parallel national interest in the adequacy and economic soundness of all forms of transportation. This principle has assumed increasing importance as air transportation itself has grown in size and competitive impact. In the long run, the public can best be assured of maximum economy and efficiency of the over-all transportation system if each form of transportation is required to compete with other forms on the basis of inherent service advantages and true economic costs.

The committee made the following recommendations relating to airline subsidies:

1. Airline subsidy policy must be properly related to over-all transportation objectives.
2. In keeping with over-all transportation objectives, airline subsidy should, so far as possible, be limited to strictly temporary aid, designed to develop needed services, which could not progress at an adequate rate without federal support.
3. It is recognized that foreign competition and other special factors will probably prolong the period during which subsidy will be required for international air transportation operations.
4. Where the public interest requires the continued maintenance of uneconomical services, increased emphasis should be placed upon the inclusion of such operations within route systems that are capable of absorbing their cost without subsidy.
5. When any carrier or group of carriers achieves the basic capability for sustained self-sufficiency, it should be removed from the protection of subsidy eligibility.

---

print). For the fiscal year 1961 subsidy payments to United States airlines were classified as follows:

Helicopter air carriers	$ 4,800,000
Local-service air carriers	56,534,000
Alaskan carriers	7,957,000
Total	$69,291,000

[15] Air Coordinating Committee, *Civil Air Policy* (Washington, D.C., 1954).

6. The existence of a route certificate should not in itself obligate the government to continue subsidizing a service, if it is determined that the cost has become disproportionate to the public benefits.

7. In the future, the government's maximum commitment for subsidizing any new or renewed route should be limited, both as to amount and duration, at the time the route authorization is granted. If it becomes impossible for a carrier, within its authorized subsidy, to provide the service for which it was certificated, it would then be necessary for such carrier to seek reconsideration of its route certificate.

8. Legislation should provide a basis for the more effective control by the President and Congress of the aggregate level of subsidy, while at the same time assuring individual carriers of reasonable stability of subsidy eligibility.

9. Schedules should immediately be established for the orderly reduction, and withdrawal where appropriate, of domestic air carrier subsidy support.

During the last few years, various proposals have been made to limit, curtail, exclude, or altogether eliminate subsidy support to the airlines. As future events unfold, the pressure on Congress to enact some form of legislation along these lines will be increased. In part, this pressure will be based to a large extent on the effects of the severe competition in the airline industry.

All who are concerned with subsidy to the airlines must recognize these inescapable facts:

1. Presuming honest, efficient, and economical management as required by law, then the volume of subsidy required is related to the amount and quality or type of service provided.

2. Reduction in subsidy total to any individual airline or group of airlines, as an aribitrary act, without compensating access to additional or offsetting commercial revenue must inevitably result in a reduction in service, a downgrading of service, outright elimination of service, or a combination of all three results. The degree to which this occurs must be related exactly to a noncompensated reduction in subsidy.[16]

---

[16] Leslie O. Barnes, "Airline Subsidies—Purpose, Cause, and Control," *Journal of Air Law and Commerce,* Autumn, 1959 and Winter, 1960.

Chapter 13

AIRLINE ORGANIZATION

AIRLINES have grown so rapidly that it is difficult to say that any one organization is typical or that the organization of one company at any particular time is the one in effect even a few months later. However, all airlines do have certain organizational traits in common. Each carries on the major management functions of:

1. Deciding on route structures, equipment, and schedules.
2. Conducting flight operations.
3. Maintaining and servicing aircraft.
4. Servicing passengers and shippers.
5. Advertising, sales promotion, and public relations.
6. Dealing with governmental and other public bodies.
7. Purchasing and inventory control.
8. Financial planning.
9. Industrial relations.

Organization, or lack of it, has often been blamed for the deficiencies of airline management, although personal administration of assigned responsibilities, rather than faults of organization, may more often be responsible.[1] The role of organization is, however, most important in all airline functions and should be considered of prime importance for proper airline management. The vigorous growth of airlines in the past has caused constant changes in basic organizational policies, and the future will probably require the solution of even greater organizational problems. Moreover, the organizational problems of airlines are unique and more complex than those of industries, outside of transportation and other public utilities, because of the twenty-four hours a day, seven days a week work schedule and the widely dispersed nature of their operations.

Principles of Organization

The chief purpose of airline organizational structure, as of all other businesses, is that of establishing efficient lines of responsibility

[1] See R. Dixon Speas, "Organizing for Airline Efficiency," *Air Transport*, June, 1944.

and authority. These so-called lines must be designed in such a manner as to:

1. *Fix responsibility for each activity important to the success of the airline.* The purpose of this principle would seem obvious, yet it has often been violated. Airline organizations have sometimes been regarded as complete even though certain functions essential to the accomplishment of their objectives have been overlooked in creating the organization plan. Not only must the major functions be assigned to large elements of the company, but it is equally important that smaller component functions be allocated to subsidiary organization elements.

2. *Clearly define responsibility, authority, and accountability for all activities.* In order to accomplish functions in the most economical manner, it is essential that each organization element understand clearly the exact nature of its responsibilities and authorities. The result of general and vague assignments of functions is to create confusion about the precise responsibilities of the organizational elements concerned and about the extent of their authority. Certainly an organizational element cannot be held responsible for accomplishing a job when it has not been told exactly what result it is expected to achieve. To assure full performance, responsibilities must be clearly and concisely stated in terms of the specific accomplishments expected.

3. *Group together those activities which have a common purpose or which require close co-ordination.* No major function should be assigned to more than one independent element of an organization. Overlapping responsibility results in nothing but confusion and delay. Specific responsibilities must be assigned to each organizational element in such a manner that the same responsibility is not performed by more than one part of the company.

4. *Recognize the distinction between system-wide activities and those which lend themselves to geographic decentralization.* For example, flight operations should be centrally controlled, while many elements of station operation can be decentralized, thus giving management in the field the freedom to concentrate on those things where greater knowledge of local needs can achieve better service and lower costs. Conversely, such a method frees those in the field of the frustration that must result from trying to carry the responsibility for activities to which, realistically, they cannot make significant contributions. However, because of the interrelationship between all

functions of an airline, it is not possible to eliminate all problems of co-ordination. The role of the superintendent of flight dispatch, who links flight with ground operations on most airlines and thus belongs wholly to neither, is an example. These fuzzy areas should, however, be reduced to a minimum.

5. *Create lines of administrative authority which are definite and clearly understood.* Each employee from the top to the bottom must know to whom he reports, and who reports to him. There should be no divided authority. No member of the organization should report to more than one supervisor, or he may violate the instructions of one in his effort to follow the instructions of the other. Of course, an individual may talk with others in higher echelons and obtain their advice and guidance, but his line of direct administrative responsibility should stem from only one supervisor.

6. *Maintain a distinction between line and staff, or between functional responsibility and authority.* The line organization should be responsible for making decisions. It has the responsibility for seeing that all assigned work is performed in accordance with established methods, procedures, and standards. It determines the need, time, and place for action. It has the authority of command and direct administrative control. The staff or functional organization should be responsible for developing plans, obtaining information, rendering advice, and performing follow-up to see whether work has been carried out in accordance with line decisions.

7. *Limit the number of subordinates that any one individual is required to supervise.* There is a definite limit to the number of persons one individual can supervise effectively, although there is no fixed formula to determine the number of subordinates that should report to any one supervisor, since circumstances and the factors involved vary so much. The greater the similarity of duties among subordinates, the larger will be the number of persons whom one supervisor can co-ordinate and direct effectively. The character of the duties has a bearing, for when duties of subordinates are of a routine nature, such as handling airline reservations, for example, the demands upon the time of a supervisor are fewer. Also, the level of management should be considered, because more time for planning and less time for details should be spent at higher levels of management.

8. *Provide a framework for the development of personnel.* The best way to develop and test managers, for example, is to create a plan of organization which as nearly as possible "puts them in busi-

ness for themselves"; which creates on a small scale a duplicate of the total organization; which enables each member of management to see readily how his function relates to the total; and which gives local management substantial authority to make decisions. In this manner, local management provides a training ground for regional management, and regional management for top management.

Organizational Characteristics and Conditions

In deciding on one or another plan of organization for an airline, consideration must be given to a number of the inherent characteristics of the industry and the conditions under which the organization must operate. All these have been discussed in detail in previous chapters.

1. *Interdependence of activities.* One of the unique characteristics of the airline business is that, to a greater extent than almost any other business, most activities are interdependent. Nearly everything from reservations through aircraft servicing and maintenance are so interrelated that when something takes place in one activity, it affects all the others. This places a high premium on the grouping together of activities which have common end purposes, such as serving passengers and servicing aircraft. It also makes it important to provide for the close co-ordination of related activities.

2. *System-wide vs. geographic activities.* Certain airline activities can best be directed by regional and local management, while others do not lend themselves to decentralization and can best be planned, administered, and controlled centrally. For example, most of the service functions such as reservations, ticketing, maintenance, and other aircraft service activities can be most efficiently managed by a field executive who has an intimate knowledge of local needs and is in a position to make on-the-spot decisions. This is a broad area of action where local management will be more realistic, economical, and adaptable than direction from headquarters or the general office. For obvious reasons, however, the over-all policies and procedures for this work must be established centrally. On the other hand, certain activities such as schedule planning, conduct of flight operations, and the like, can best be planned, administered, and controlled centrally. In fact, local interests must sometimes be disregarded in making decisions which are for the over-all good, but local opinion should, of course, be sought and local conditions given consideration in planning.

3. *Need for flexibility.* The airline industry must be operated with an extreme amount of flexibility to provide for the change and uncertainty that is an inherent condition and to make proper provision for it.

4. *Rapid obsolescence and technological change.* There is a very rapid obsolescence and high degree of technological change in the airline industry. This means that top management must be free to concentrate their attention on the development of better equipment and methods in planning for the future.

5. *Nature of costs.* Airline organization is affected by the economics of air transportation. Compared with many other industries, this is a low-profit-margin, high-risk business, with a higher proportion of payroll costs and a very large number of independent profit centers as represented by each airline's stations. The only way that costs can be effectively controlled is to give those in charge of these profit centers (stations) the responsibility and authority to make decisions involving costs and to hold them accountable for results.

Departmental Organization

As has already been mentioned, there is no typical airline organization, but certain functions of management are always provided for. Usually these are divided into the following departments:

OPERATIONS

Most airlines place a vice-president in charge of this department and make him responsible for the activities of four subdivisions, each responsible for its own part in accomplishing two things: (*a*) the successful completion of each schedule and (*b*) the constant improvement of technique, with the aim of achieving more dependable operation.

Flight Operations Division. Headed by a director of flight operations, this division is usually responsible for all matters affecting the piloting, dispatching, and controlling in flights of airline aircraft. It is also responsible for establishing and maintaining liaison with the Civil Aeronautics Administration concerning all matters pertaining to the flight operation of aircraft, pilot, and dispatcher certificates and qualifications, and the keeping of necessary records relative thereto. The director of flight operations is generally assisted by a chief pilot and chief flight dispatcher.

The chief pilot on most airlines has direct supervision over all captains and first officers, so as to develop and maintain the highest possible standards of safety and operational efficiency. He aids in selecting pilots and is responsible for their training and proficiency checks and for maintaining complete pilot records. The chief flight dispatcher plans and controls the use of flight equipment in accordance with schedules, regulations, meteorological conditions, and airport facilities.

Ground Operations Division. Headed by a director of ground operations, this division is usually responsible for the administration of stations, the servicing and maintenance of aircraft away from the base station, and the operation of ground communications equipment, such as the teletype and telephone systems. The director of ground operations also maintains liaison with the Civil Aeronautics Administration concerning all matters pertaining to air carrier facility inspections and air carrier communication coverage.

Maintenance and Engineering Division. This division is usually headed by a director of maintenance, who is responsible for maintaining flight and ground equipment in a safe and operational condition, for co-ordinating the activities within this division, and for maintaining liaison with the Civil Aeronautics Administration concerning all matters pertaining to maintenance and engineering problems. The director of this division is assisted on most airlines by the following persons:

1. Superintendent of maintenance, who is responsible for the overhaul, line service, and inspection of aircraft.
2. Superintendent of communications, who is responsible for supervising construction, installation, and maintenance of all air and ground radio, telephone, teletype, telephone and electronics equipment.
3. Chief engineer, who is responsible for supervising all engineering activities related to flight equipment, aircraft ground equipment, and operations ground equipment, including engineering and research related to new flight equipment and components.
4. Superintendent of stores, who is responsible for supervising the storage, classification, and issuance of company materials and supplies.
5. Superintendent of buildings and grounds, who is responsible for the maintenance of company-occupied buildings and grounds.
6. Supervisor of vehicle maintenance, who is responsible for the inspection, overhaul, repair, cleaning, and servicing of all company-operated automotive equipment.

Airports and Facilities Division. This division is under a director who is generally responsible for providing technical assistance in the planning and designing of construction or improvements to airline facilities on airports, buildings, offices, and related facilities; and for the assembly, verification, and distribution of airport route data and other information necessary to flight operations. On most airlines he is assisted by:

1. A civil engineer responsible for preparing necessary designs, plans, and specifications for airport and airway projects as an airline may be requested for such aid.
2. An architect responsible for developing designs, plans, and specifications for the construction of hangars, shops, terminals, offices (including ticket office), and special structures, and for supervising such construction.
3. A supervisor of flight information responsible for the assembly, verification, and distribution of flight information, including flight manuals, airport and route data, aviation charts, and emergency kits.

Traffic or Sales

The principal duty of this department is to obtain business for the airline. Thus far, it has been the practice to give one vice-president responsibility for developing passenger, freight, and mail traffic. As time goes on, the airlines will certainly follow the railroad practice of dividing freight and passenger sales activities. It is also the duty of the traffic department to make rates for both passengers and freight. All its functions bring this department into close contact with the operations department, which performs the transportation service. Under a chief traffic executive, most airlines divide the work of this department as follows:

1. General traffic and sales manager, who is responsible for planning the company's sales programs and for the development of all passenger and freight sales through regional and district offices.[2]

[2] There appears to be an increasing need to co-ordinate all aspects of customer relations or service. The airline industry has now reached a point where the expansion of the business through attracting first riders and shippers is less important competitively than building the loyalty of repeat riders and shippers to a certain airline. Most of the criticisms directed against any airline relate to some aspect of the handling of passengers or freight. Significantly, American Airlines, which has so often led the way in various aspects of airline development, announced, in 1954, the organization of a customer service department to pull together all aspects of customer relations.

2. The traffic advisory committee, which is composed of the chief personnel of the revenue auditor and the director of ground operations. Its chief function is to co-ordinate the activities of these sections with the traffic department.

3. Manager of agency, interline, and foreign sales, who is responsible for creating an organization of commission agents or travel agents and for developing interline and foreign sales programs.

4. Passenger service manager, who is responsible for all hostess and commissary activities. On some airlines, he is also responsible for passenger baggage handling, ground transportation, and the establishment of effective passenger relations.

5. Systems reservation manager, who is in charge of establishing effective reservations procedures and administering all reservations activities.

6. Manager of schedules and tariffs, who is responsible for the creation of all schedules and for co-operation with the maintenance, flight operations, and ground operations departments. He is also responsible for the making of passenger and freight tariffs and the scheduling of charter or special flights.

7. Manager of mail and freight, who is responsible for the development of freight traffic sales and for the administration and operation of the company air mail and air freight system.

8. A group of regional traffic managers, who are responsible for the administration and direction of all sales, reservations, ticketing, advertising, publicity, passenger relations, and freight activities in their respective regions.

Staff Departments

Treasury. This department is usually charged with the receipt and safeguarding of the company's passenger, mail, freight, and other revenues. It is also responsible for accounting for all receipts and disbursements. Scheduled airline accounts are kept in accordance with the uniform system established by the Civil Aeronautics Board.[3] The airlines may, however, keep additional accounts or records, provided they do not impair the integrity of the uniform accounting system or impose an undue financial burden upon the individual carriers.

---

[3] Civil Aeronautics Act, sec. 407; Civil Aeronautics Board, Economic Regulations, Part 202. The accounts are listed in Civil Aeronautics Board, *Uniform System of Accounts for Air Carriers*, as amended. This manual was originally published in 1947.

Industrial Relations. This department is responsible for procuring personnel, for labor relations, for wage and salary administration, for employee services, and for administering training programs. The director of personnel and training is assisted by the following in most airline organizations:

1. Director of industrial relations, who is usually responsible for the supervision and operation of all divisions of the department and for the company's relations with regard to labor, labor unions, and government labor laws.
2. Employment manager, who is usually responsible for the actual employment of personnel, including recruitment, interviewing, testing, selection, placement, and procedural steps relating to interdepartmental transfer of personnel in co-ordination with department, division, and section managers.
3. Supervisor of personnel records and services, who is usually in charge of the creation and maintenance of filing and record systems on current and terminated employees and the handling of promotion of company insurance programs, employee retirement plans, and other benefits to employees.
4. Health service, which is in charge of first aid to injured employees, maintenance of sanitary standards in the company commissary and elsewhere, and employee health education. Some airlines expand this activity into a regular medical program, with a physician in charge.
5. Superintendent of training, who is responsible in most organizations for the operation of the training division, covering all apprentice training programs, Civil Aeronautics Administration practical examinations, training courses for operations and traffic departments, and the like.

Public Relations. This department has the responsibility to act in an advisory capacity to management in determining company policy; to interpret and maintain an understanding of such policy among the general public, governmental officers and bodies, and company employees; and to operate the publicity and advertising departments, as well as to represent the company in directing the activities of outside advertising and publicity agencies employed by the company.

Legal. Much of the responsibility for dealing with governmental and other public bodies is frequently placed in this department, the head of which is generally called General Counsel. In most airlines, the department is charged with the following:

1. The handling of all legal corporate matters involving compliance with local, state, federal, and foreign laws wherever the company may operate.
2. The drafting of contracts required by officers and departments of the company.
3. The advising of officers and directors concerning the interpretation of laws, regulations, and contracts, and the company's rights and obligations thereunder.
4. Supervision and counsel with the company's local attorneys regarding claims and actions for or against the company.
5. The conduct of investigations and hearings, when required, under labor contracts and the rendering of decisions in connection therewith.
6. The rendering of advice and assistance in drafting instruments or documents for presentation to the Civil Aeronautics Board in connection with route cases and other matters within the jurisdiction of the Board.
7. The filing of contracts and agreements with the Civil Aeronautics Board as required by Section 412 of the Civil Aeronautics Act. In this connection, most airlines require all contracts and agreements entered into by all departments of the company to be transmitted to the legal department. The legal department then determines whether the agreement or contract comes within the intent of the act. In the event it does, the legal department will make the necessary arrangements for such filing and will then transmit the agreement or contract to the office of the secretary-treasurer of the company for filing. In the event the agreement or contract does not require filing under the act, the legal department transmits it directly to the office of the secretary-treasurer of the company.

Economic Research. The specific duties of this department usually include:

1. Conducting continuing industrial studies and research applicable to new route, mail rate, and other company proceedings before the Civil Aeronautics Board; preparing exhibits for these; and co-operating and conferring with the traffic, operations, and treasury departments in so doing.

2. Conferring and co-operating with all departments of the company in order to keep advised of their statistical and research needs, determining the usefulness and effectiveness of studies conducted on a continuing basis, and suggesting ways and means by which the department can assist other departments in increasing efficiency, economy, and control in their operations.

3. Conducting research and preparing statistics for use in traffic development and for publicity, advertising, and public relations work, including speeches, special articles, reports to stockholders, etc.

4. Maintaining effective liaison with the treasury and engineering departments to assure full and effective use of material and information available for statistical and research work, and co-ordinating research work with those departments and other departments of the company to assure a maximum of efficiency and economy.

Purchasing and Stores. Every airline has a department in charge of purchasing supplies and materials. Some practice the policy of having most supplies and materials delivered directly to the departments for which they are intended or even directly to the divisions where they are to be used; others maintain general stores from which supplies are distributed as needed. (When sent out over the line, they are sent as "company material.")

Chapter 14

AIRLINE PASSENGER TRAFFIC DEVELOPMENT

In air transportation, the technicians have done a much better job, relatively speaking, in their fields than have those responsible for traffic development. Airline executives have shown a much better understanding of how to operate their companies than of how the service they created—air transportation—should be sold. This was perhaps a natural condition in an industry where the first task had been to develop a service in which the public would have confidence, in an industry confronted at first with selling something absolutely new, and in an industry which had to perfect its service very largely out of capital and not out of earnings. For hundreds of years, people had been thinking in terms of land and water transportation, the accepted means of travel. At the start, therefore, the air transportation industry was faced with the barriers of old established travel habits. It still is faced with the problem of overcoming these same habits to a very large degree. Moreover, the air transportation industry found it necessary to perfect a service far beyond what the consumer demand warranted at the time. Probably no other service or product ever presented to the public had to be so perfect, so safe, and so reliable as did the type of transportation offered by the airlines before public acceptance could be expected.

The managers of airlines in the earlier days, and to a great degree today, devoted their time chiefly to building an organization for the purpose of manufacturing air transportation. These men made little attempt to sell this transportation in terms of what it would do for the person who used it. No particular effort was made to induce people to think in terms of how air transportation might affect them in their personal and business affairs. Yet if air transportation is to be sold, people must think that way. No matter how fine the equipment of the airlines, no matter how well they may be operated, the most important part of air transportation is the use people make of it. Reduced to the barest elements, all any agency of transportation does is bridge time and distance for travelers, mail, and freight. Air transportation does it faster than any other means. In exact ratio, as people think in terms of what air transportation makes possible, the use of the airlines will be multiplied far beyond any present conception.

From a traffic development standpoint, no one envisages a saturation point for air transportation. As people think in terms of air travel, they will continually find newer and different uses for it and more ways to benefit from it. When automobiles were invented, they did not simply move people out of horse-drawn buggies and take that same number of people on the same trips they would have taken in buggies. Automobiles greatly expanded, multiplied, and diversified travel because they made possible the use of transportation in many more and different ways. More ways for people to use air transportation advantageously is the ultimate measure of the market for the product of the airlines.

Measuring Passenger Traffic

The development of airline passenger traffic may be measured in several ways:

1. By the number of passenger seat-miles flown in succeeding years, as is shown in Table 25. This figure is often referred to as "available seat-miles" and means the miles flown per each interstation trip for the carriage of passengers (as distinguished from the rated passenger-carrying capacity of a particular aircraft). Seat-miles are usually associated with what is termed "load factor" or the ratio, expressed as a percentage, of passenger-miles to available seat-miles. The number of available seat-miles on a flight, therefore, represents the passenger-mile capacity of the flight, and the load factor represents the degree to which that capacity is utilized. In other words, load factor measures the extent to which the service produced by the airlines is being consumed.[1] A relatively high revenue-passenger load factor usually means relatively high revenue per dollar of operating costs, since such costs, in total, are not much affected by the degree to which a particular flight's passenger-carrying capacity is used. Experience seems to indicate, however, that the best load factor from the standpoint of airline operations is not far from 70 per cent, varying with circumstances for individual operators.

[1] See William L. Grossman, *Air Passenger Traffic* (Brooklyn: Chemical Publishing Co., 1947), chap. i. See also Chapter 5.

TABLE 25

PASSENGER SEAT-MILES FLOWN, PASSENGER LOAD FACTOR, AND PASSENGER FARE PER MILE, 1926–59
(Scheduled Airlines)

YEAR	DOMESTIC				INTERNATIONAL		
	Passenger Seat-Miles Flown (000 Omitted)	Passenger Load Factor (%)		Average Passenger Revenue per Passenger-Mile	Passenger Seat-Miles (000 Omitted)	Passenger Load Factor (%)	
		Revenue	Revenue and Non-revenue			Revenue and Non-revenue	Revenue
1926	*	*	*	$0.12	*	*	*
1927	*	*	*	0.106	*	*	*
1928	*	*	*	0.11	*	*	*
1929	*	*	*	0.12	*	*	*
1930	*	*	*	0.083	*	*	*
1931	*	*	*	0.067	*	*	*
1932	303,582	*	41.98	0.061	*	*	*
1933	373,762	*	46.77	0.061	*	*	*
1934	367,777	*	51.61	0.059	*	*	*
1935	577,651	*	54.76	0.057	*	*	*
1936	686,225	*	63.97	0.057	*	*	*
1937	836,151	49.22	57.54	0.056	*	*	*
1938	951,458	50.43	58.93	0.0518	116,100	46.34	45.83
1939	1,215,158	56.20	62.14	0.0510	134,399	58.24	53.46
1940	1,817,085	57.90	63.72	0.0507	175,454	59.56	56.88
1941	2,341,877	59.13	64.32	0.0504	248,331	66.83	65.57
1942	1,963,617	72.22	76.45	0.0528	313,109	76.75	75.68
1943	1,856,954	88.00	89.98	0.0527	307,513	82.72	79.42
1944	2,436,846	89.39	90.77	0.0535	391,293	82.32	79.37
1945	3,815,573	88.12	89.33	0.0495	583,440	79.22	76.78
1946	7,556,469	78.71	80.31	0.0463	1,553,691	72.74	70.85
1947	9,373,761	65.12	67.29	0.0506	2,924,375	63.96	61.90
1948	10,385,083	57.42	59.97	0.0576	3,292,319	59.59	57.38
1949	11,672,921	57.85	60.53	0.0576	3,625,673	59.83	56.67
1950	13,064,473	61.26	63.93	0.0555	3,695,447	63.21	59.71
1951	15,565,749	67.88	70.35	0.0560	4,327,656	63.18	60.08
1952	19,097,091	65.60	68.10	0.0555	4,850,893	65.39	62.28
1953	23,268,559	63.43	65.92	0.0545	5,472,481	65.03	61.87
1954	26,851,433	62.45	63.36	0.0539	6,288,491	59.56	59.53
1955	31,299,151	63.32	*	0.0535	7,037,733	65.36	62.81
1956	35,285,701	63.37	*	0.0532	8,104,662	65.49	63.25
1957	41,653,275	60.83	*	0.0530	9,076,429	65.91	63.57
1958	42,643,019	59.43	*	0.0563	10,103,161	61.67	59.31
1959	48,304,117	60.59	*	0.0555	10,528,815	68.18	65.71

* Not available.

Source: FAA, *Statistical Handbook of Aviation* (Washington, D.C., 1960).

The load factor may be too high as well as too low. An extremely high load factor, such as that experienced by the domestic carriers in 1944, may be a disadvantage since it means that many would-be passengers have been refused, with consequent inconvenience to them and loss of revenue to the airlines. Moreover, as the airlines discovered during the years of very high load factors, the unavailability of space causes certain costs to increase more than in proportion to the number of passengers or passenger-miles. For example, the handling of calls from persons who desire reservations, but who must be refused, increases the reservation expense per passenger carried.[2]

2. By the number of passenger-miles, as shown in Table 26. A passenger-mile is the transportation of one passenger for one mile and is arrived at by multiplying the miles flown on each interstation flight by the number of passengers carried on that trip. Prior to 1946, the

TABLE 26

PASSENGER-MILES FLOWN BY SCHEDULED AIRLINES, 1930–59

YEAR	DOMESTIC (ADD 000)			INTERNATIONAL (ADD 000)		
	Total	Revenue*	Non-revenue*	Total	Revenue	Non-revenue
1930	85,125	†	†	18,622	†	†
1931	106,952	†	†	14,171	†	†
1932	127,433	†	†	20,754	†	†
1933	174,820	†	†	24,956	†	†
1934	189,806	†	†	36,844	†	†
1935	316,336	†	†	46,035	†	†
1936	438,989	†	†	41,829	†	†
1937	481,116	411,545	69,571	53,742	†	†
1938	560,660	479,844	80,816	53,799	53,208	591
1939	755,118	682,904	72,214	78,271	71,845	6,426
1940	1,157,900	1,052,156	105,744	104,495	99,795	4,700
1941	1,506,303	1,384,733	121,570	165,950	162,824	3,126
1942	1,501,279	1,418,042	83,237	240,314	236,956	3,358
1943	1,670,935	1,634,135	36,800	254,374	244,229	10,145
1944	2,211,905	2,178,207	33,698	322,123	310,574	11,549
1945	3,408,290	3,362,455	45,835	462,180	447,968	14,212
1946	6,068,315	5,947,956	120,359	1,130,196	1,100,741	29,455
1947	6,307,690	6,103,878	203,812	1,863,268	1,810,045	53,223
1948	6,227,932	5,963,180	264,752	1,961,794	1,888,997	72,797
1949	7,065,199	6,752,622	312,577	2,168,799	2,053,998	114,801
1950	8,351,745	8,002,825	348,920	2,335,956	2,206,396	129,560
1951	10,949,898	10,566,182	383,716	2,734,014	2,599,847	134,167
1952	12,996,657	12,528,318	468,339	3,172,209	3,021,001	151,208
1953	15,337,760	14,760,309	577,451	3,558,509	3,385,563	172,946
1954	17,132,000	16,769,000	†	3,898,656	3,749,634	149,022
1955	19,819,000	19,819,000	†	4,600,006	4,420,166	179,840
1956	22,362,000	22,362,000	†	5,307,543	5,126,052	181,491
1957	25,340,000	25,340,000	†	5,981,831	5,769,472	212,359
1958	25,343,000	25,343,000	†	6,230,732	5,992,256	238,476
1959	29,269,033	29,269,033	†	7,178,849	6,918,839	260,010

* Not reported separately prior to May, 1936.
† Not available.
Source: FAA, *Statistical Handbook of Aviation* (Washington, D.C., 1960).

[2] *Ibid.*, p. 7.

domestic airlines reported, and the statistics derived from their reports therefore showed, passenger-miles based on course-flown distances. Since January 1 of that year, the Civil Aeronautics Board has required airline reports to be based on airport-to-airport mileage, which is considered to be the shortest distance (Great Circle track) from the point at which air mail is loaded on planes at one airport to the corresponding point at the other airport. The official airport-to-airport mileages have been determined by the Civil Aeronautics Administration and are published as *Mileage Book No. 1* (domestic) and *Mileage Book No. 2* (international) by the Civil Aeronautics Board. Airport-to-airport mileages are, on the average, about 4½ per cent shorter than course-flown mileages.[3]

3. By the number of passengers carried, as shown in Tables 27 and 28. In the current statistical publications of both the Civil Aeronautics Board and the Civil Aeronautics Administration, a person making a round trip is counted as two passengers; a person who makes a stopover becomes another passenger when he boards a plane after the stopover; a person who makes a trip over several routes by one airline is counted as one passenger; and the person who makes a trip by several airlines is counted as a separate passenger for each line. In Civil Aeronautics Board statistics for periods prior to 1942 and in Civil Aeronautics Administration statistics for periods prior to 1944, a person making a trip over several routes of one airline was counted as a number of passengers, one for each of the routes. For an airline that operated several routes, the difference between an unduplicated number of passengers and the duplicated number might be great enough to mislead anyone using one figure as if it were the other. For example, in 1943, American Airlines, operating ten routes, carried 788,990 revenue passengers by an unduplicated count and 919,958 by a duplicated count.[4]

Factors Affecting Growth

The following factors have all played a part to a greater or less degree in airline passenger traffic growth:

1. The increasing safety of air transportation, as discussed in Chapter 11.

2. New routes tapping smaller communities, new stations on existing routes, and new routes serving more pairs of cities.

[3] *Ibid.*, p. 5.

[4] *Ibid.*, pp. 3–4.

TABLE 27

SCHEDULED AIRLINE PASSENGERS CARRIED (DUPLICATED), 1926–59

Year	Domestic			International		
	Total	Revenue	Nonrevenue	Total	Revenue	Nonrevenue
1926...	5,782	*	*	*	*	*
1927...	8,679	*	*	*	*	*
1928...	48,312	*	*	1,401	*	*
1929...	161,933	*	*	11,472	*	*
1930...	384,506	*	*	32,999	*	*
1931...	472,438	*	*	59,224	*	*
1932...	476,041	*	*	71,519	*	*
1933...	502,218	*	*	74,394	*	*
1934...	475,461	*	*	96,804	*	*
1935...	762,820	678,549	84,271	111,296	*	*
1936...	1,042,042	931,683	110,359	87,723	*	*
1937...	1,130,338	985,084	145,254	112,324	*	*
1938...	1,365,706	1,197,100	168,606	*	109,265	*
1939...	1,895,793	1,704,762	161,031	136,090	129,028	7,062
1940...	3,038,619	2,802,781	235,838	170,179	162,617	7,562
1941...	4,141,748	3,848,882	292,866	235,802	228,524	7,278
1942...	3,559,369	3,370,398	188,971	276,200	269,345	6,855
1943...	3,484,203	3,387,967	96,236	292,888	279,402	13,486
1944...	4,761,313	4,675,164	86,149	356,662	341,496	15,166
1945...	7,605,856	7,494,140	111,716	493,498	475,558	17,940
1946...	13,705,360	13,453,110	252,250	1,066,414	1,041,283	25,131
1947...	†	†	†	‡	1,359,410	‡
1948...	†	†	†	‡	1,372,856	‡
1949...	†	†	†	‡	1,520,067	‡
1950...	†	†	†	‡	1,675,477	‡
1951...	†	†	†	‡	2,041,807	‡
1952...	†	†	†	‡	2,365,223	‡
1953...	†	†	†	‡	2,699,000	‡
1954...	†	†	†	‡	2,875,000	‡
1955...	†	†	†	‡	3,416,000	‡
1956...	†	†	†	‡	3,949,000	‡
1957...	†	†	†	‡	4,422,000	‡
1958...	†	†	†	‡	4,594,000	‡
1959...	†	†	†	‡	5,151,000	‡

* Not available.

† Subsequent to 1946 only the unduplicated number of passengers is reported by the domestic airlines; see Table 41.

‡ International airlines required to report only revenue passengers.

Source: FAA, *Statistical Handbook of Aviation* (Washington, D.C., 1960).

3. Expanded flight schedules, so that passengers can travel more nearly at their own convenience.

4. Better service, especially fewer flight cancellations.

5. Reduction of delays in arrival and departure brought about by improved air traffic control, as discussed in Chapter 2.

6. Reduction of "downtown-to-downtown" time through improving surface transportation facilities and thus, in effect, moving airports closer to the business centers of cities.

TABLE 28

SCHEDULED AIRLINE PASSENGERS CARRIED (UNDUPLICATED) 1942–58

Year	Total	Revenue	Nonrevenue
1942	3,225,726	3,136,755	188,971
1943	3,115,972	3,019,736	96,236
1944	4,132,114	4,045,965	86,149
1945	6,687,968	6,576,252	111,716
1946	12,465,695	12,213,445	252,250
1947	*	12,890,208	*
1948	*	13,168,095	*
1949	*	15,080,704	*
1950	*	17,343,681	*
1951	*	22,652,179	*
1952	*	25,010,000	*
1953	*	28,721,000	*
1954	*	32,343,000	*
1955	*	38,025,000	*
1956	*	41,738,000	*
1957	*	48,464,000	*
1958	*	48,130,000	*
1959	*	54,768,000	*

* Beginning with 1947 only revenue passengers carried are reported by the carriers.

Source: FAA, *Statistical Handbook of Aviation* (Washington, D.C., 1960).

7. The reduction in the winter slump in traffic. Seasonal decline has been reduced materially because of the education of the traveling public by the airlines on the subject of relative flying safety and smoothness of air in winter versus summer.

8. Growth in public acceptance. World War II accomplished a tremendous selling job for air transportation. Not only did it create, directly, millions of potential customers and enthusiasts among the men and women of the air forces and their families, but also it caused air travel to be introduced to thousands of persons, such as soldiers on furlough, government officials, businessmen, etc., who, had it not been for war-created emergencies, probably would not have had the occasion to make the trip at all or would have used surface transportation. Beyond these direct effects, the role of aviation in the war changed the whole psychology of the nation toward air transportation and particularly toward travel by air. It made aviation an accepted, almost commonplace, part not only of our transportation system but of our entire way of life. The war engendered among the youth of this country, especially, an enthusiasm for and familiarity with air transportation which has already been reflected in the growth of air travel.

Air Passenger Fares

During the time that the number of air travelers was increasing rapidly from year to year, the average passenger fare per mile or average passenger revenue per passenger-mile, as shown in Table 28, was gradually declining. In 1926 the average passenger fare per mile in domestic operations was 12 cents; by 1933 this had declined to slightly over 6 cents; by 1939, to slightly over 5 cents; and by 1946, to 4.6 cents, the low point so far. Since 1946, fares have been increased slightly, so that in 1958, they averaged 5 cents per mile for standard service.

Airlines must adapt their fares to meet the direct or indirect competition of various other passenger transportation agencies, particularly the railroads. The competition in fares between these two agencies must take into consideration the regularity of the service, dependability, comfort, speed, safety, accessibility, convenience of schedules, and other factors besides the price. The fares charged for each form of passenger transportation service react upon all other services and affect the volume of traffic obtainable at each particular rate.

Different conditions and practices make it difficult to generalize with respect to the comparative costs of ground and air journeys. But it can no longer be said that air travel is a luxury to be afforded only by the wealthy, by those who are in need of speed only, and by persons who are attracted to the novelty of the service and who pay for it as they would for any other unusual and occasional entertainment.

It has been obvious for some time that air fares would have to come down if air service for passengers is to become a major transportation activity. This could be achieved either through an across-the-board fare reduction affecting every carrier in the country or in stages by the introduction of air coach or other cut-rate devices discussed later in this chapter. The introduction of air coach fares by such an important operator as American Airlines, for example, meant that competitors had to follow. When the transcontinentals began to lower fares for a coach service, every other carrier in the country was affected. The institution of air coach by American Airlines in 1950 was, in effect, the first step in general fare reductions everywhere. Regardless of how much high-fare scheduling is retained, it seems likely that the bulk of air transport equipment will be utilized in low-fare service in due course. How fast the transition takes place is up to the Board, traffic demands, and other factors; but what began to happen in 1950 is what many in the industry expected to happen earlier. The length of time and the cost in putting postwar equipment into service, the time necessary to solve air traffic control problems at busy terminal airports, and general national inflationary trends all tended to hold off the inevitable day when the major airlines would start fighting for traffic and offering low fares.

The next few years will probably again focus attention on the weaknesses in the competitive air transport picture. It will tend to increase, instead of decrease, the problems of weaker airlines. Any development in which the fastest and latest equipment is placed into the lowest-fare market is destined to have keen significance in the economics of the industry as a whole. There will be an even sharper division between the high-unit-cost local-service airlines operating in sparse territory and the volume operators serving the big cities. There will be renewed talk about "too many airlines" and pressures for consolidations and mergers not only among the smaller but among regional carriers also (see Chapter 7).

Revenue passenger-miles should take another leap upward. The experience of air coach operators, both scheduled and nonscheduled, has given abundant evidence that a far bigger market awaits the airlines in the lower-fare brackets. Top airline managements have been fully aware of this; but time has not been ripe, costwise, equipmentwise, and operationwise, to enter this market sooner.

Penetration of Travel Markets

The progress made by the airlines in obtaining a share of the total intercity passenger traffic of the country, as compared to other carriers, is shown in Table 29. In the year 1959, the combined private and common-carrier intercity passenger market generated over 731 billions of revenue passenger-miles. Of this amount, common carriers accounted for slightly over 61 billions. In 1939, the airline proportion of the combined common carrier travel was 2.3 per cent. By 1959, this had increased to 47.4 per cent.

Selling Air Travel

Analysis of literally hundreds of reasons stated by people as to why they travel reveals not more than three fundamental conclusions:[5]

[5] As stated by Grahame H. Aldrich in "Market Analysis of Air Traffic Potential," before a joint meeting of the Radio Technical Commission for Aeronautics, The Franklin Institute Laboratories for Research and Development, The Institute of the Aeronautic Sciences (Philadelphia Section), and the Institute of Radio Engineers (Philadelphia Chapter), April 22, 1954.

TABLE 29

PASSENGER-MILES FOR VARIOUS TYPES OF INTERCITY TRANSPORTATION BY COMMON CARRIERS AND PRIVATE AUTOMOBILE

(For Selected Years, in Millions)

	1939	1949	1955	1956	1957	1958	1959
Railroad travel:[1]							
First class	7,527	9,349	6,440	6,275	5,185	4,249	3,819
Coach	11,180	20,310	17,329	17,105	16,365	14,230	13,683[5]
Air travel:[2]							
First class	654	6,454	13,025	14,202	15,736	15,180	16,847
Coach	....	251	6,716	8,074	9,510	10,076	12,304
Motor bus travel[3]	9,100	22,411	16,562	16,409	16,377	15,083	14,700[5]
Total common carriers	28,461	58,775	60,072	62,065	63,173	58,818	61,510
Airline share of total	2.3	11.4	32.9	35.9	40.0	42.9	47.4
Private automobile, intercity[4]	234,700	376,313	585,800	617,700	644,800	663,700	670,000[5]
Total common carrier and auto	263,161	435,088	645,872	679,765	707,973	722,518	731,510
Airline share of total intercity travel	0.2	1.5	3.1	3.3	3.6	3.5	4.0

1 I.C.C., Statistics of Railways in the United States, 1959, Statement M-250.

2 1939, CAB, Annual Airline Statistics; 1949, CAB, Recurrent Reports on Traffic Statistics; 1955–58, CAB, Monthly Reports on Air Carrier Traffic; 1959, Carrier Reports to CAB.

3 1939, I.C.C. Statement No. 531, Jan., 1953; 1949–57, I.C.C. Transport Economics, Jan., 1960.

4 1939, NAMBO, Bus Facts, 20th Edition; 1949–56, I.C.C. Transport Economics, May, 1956 and Dec., 1959.

5 Estimated.

1. All reasons can be assigned to either a business requirement, a personal desire, or the chance happening of a genuine emergency.

2. Rarely, during the past thirty years, has a form of common-carrier transportation, in and by itself, constituted a bona fide "reason" for travel.

3. The discovery of a "new reason" to motivate passenger travel is rare to the point of nonexistence.

Passenger decisions as to choice of conveyance are subject to a similar series of specific conclusions:

1. Business travel occurs as a combination of type of business activity plus occupation within the same activity. This combination, in nine chances out of ten, will determine the frequency and pattern of travel as well as the method of travel. In the latter selection, "value of service" (as measured by carrier schedule frequency, speed, reliability, safety and convenience) is weighed against the business evaluation which will result from the trip. If it is worth taking at all, it is worth the best. The great majority of business travel, therefore, makes use of first-class travel accommodations, and moves in definite, easy-to-follow patterns.

2. Travel which is undertaken to satisfy a personal reason is the product of individual environment, habits, and tastes, accompanied by sufficient income to translate desire or need into active want followed by decisions. The level of available personal income wholly

dominates the multiple question—"If," "when," "where," and especially, "how" shall this trip be taken? Such carrier features as speed, safety, frequency of schedule, dependability, convenience, and the like, are weighed against out-of-pocket expenditures for the purchase of tickets. Because individual habits and personal traits exhibit marked stability, and because levels of personal income tend to expand rather slowly, the choice of carrier to be used and the resultant patterns of significant passenger movement are highly static. Few repetitive trips are taken in the interest of experiment or curiosity. It follows that most personal transportation is relatively stable as to pattern and is characterized by trip lengths which are shorter than those of the business passenger.

3. Emergency travel occurs in variable quantities and patterns. When the emergency is purely a personal affair or due to an unexpected business development, the choice of carrier frequently follows the respective travel habits previously established by the business passenger or by the personal passenger. Most emergency trips are, of course, nonrepetitive. They represent a purely temporary condition. When this condition is satisfied or otherwise removed, no valid reason for additional travel remains. On the other hand, when the emergency is national in scope, such as during World War II, emergency travel becomes repetitive. Patterns of movement remain virtually constant for the duration of the emergency, but choice of carrier is apt to depend upon space availability rather than upon the price of the ticket or the caliber of carrier services.

Bearing in mind the reasons why people travel as well as the considerations affecting their choice of carrier, it will be seen that the three component parts of every sale, whether of a tangible or an intangible nature, apply to selling air transportation. These are : (1) finding the prospect or the person needing the service, (2) making the sale or turning the person who needs into a person who wants, and (3) performing the service.

It is necessary for the salesman of air transportation to know what a prospect for such service is before he can know where to find such a prospect. Although everyone is a prospect for the sale of some form of transportation, not everyone is a prospect for the sale of air transportation. Nevertheless, a prospect for air transportation may be defined broadly as "anyone who has occasion to travel a territory served by a particular airline, either by this line directly or by some means of connecting services." In accordance with this definition, airline prospects might be broadly classified as follows:

1. Those who know that airline service meets their transportation requirements. This group includes the steady users of the airlines who recognize the advantages of such a method of travel.

2. Those who think that airline service might possibly meet their transportation requirements. This group includes many of those now using the Pullman services of the railroads. It clearly includes all those who make inquiries concerning fares, airline facilities, routes, connections, times of arrivals and departures, and many other matters concerned with the transportation service they have in mind at the moment of inquiry. They know their transportation needs and voluntarily make the attempt to discover if the airlines can supply those needs. When these prospects are sold, they automatically enter the first group and become airline customers.

3. Those who are unaware of the advantages of airline service in meeting their transportation requirements. This is the largest group of all and includes a considerable number of passengers now using the Pullman services on the railroads. These prospects either have never used air transportation or have used it very seldom. Many of them have never even given a thought to the possibility of using air transportation because of custom or habit which causes them to use rail and motor services instead. They do not know what airline fares or schedules are and make no attempt to find out. This group includes excellent prospects; they are usually out of touch with recent developments in air transportation and do not know how airline services can meet their requirements or the advantages of air travel.

4. Those who deny or refuse to admit that airline service meets their transportation requirements. These travelers, either because of personal experience or because their sales resistances of fear of the unknown or ideas as to the cost of air travel have not been overcome, refuse to admit that air transportation offers any advantages to them. Sometimes their opinions are based on a misunderstanding of their own transportation requirements. These prospects offer the greatest challenge to airline salesmen.

Classifying Prospects

Even the aforementioned four groups are generally too broad for the most efficient selling of air transportation, and most airlines have found it necessary to concentrate their sales efforts on certain sources within these four groups. Arranged in the order of their importance and accessibility, in combination with the volume of business to be expected, these sources are:

1. Holders of Air Travel Card contracts, discussed later in this chapter. In a sense, an organization holding such a contract has passed out of the prospect stage into the customer stage, but salesmen must maintain regular contact with the individuals in any such organization in order that the contract will be used. These prospects are most accessible, since every airline office has an up-to-date list of Air Travel Card contract holders.

2. Companies with home offices elsewhere but with branches in the territories served by a particular airline. These prospects are disclosed either by the nature of the company or by its advertising in trade papers, in classified sections of telephone books, in trade directories, and elsewhere. The nature of a company's product or service also points it out as a prospect. For example, manufacturers of oil well supplies and equipment are prospects for the service of an airline serving petroleum-producing territories.

3. Companies distributing their products or services in the territories served by a particular airline. These prospects are discovered in much the same manner as those discussed under group 2.

4. Branches of companies whose headquarters are in the territory of a particular airline. These prospects are also discovered in much the same manner as groups 2 and 3.

5. Professional men whose practice is concentrated in the areas served by a particular airline. These prospects are somewhat hard to locate but include, for example, petroleum geologists who would be interested in travel to, from, and through the petroleum-producing regions of the country, trade association executives, lawyers, congressmen and other legislators who have occasion to travel to and from the various capitals, merchandising specialists who conduct special sales campaigns for department stores, and so on.

6. Individuals who have specific reasons for making particular trips. The local newspapers are fertile sources of leads to these prospects. Such a group includes delegates to conventions, representatives of construction companies and other contractors who have been awarded contracts in areas served by a particular airline, department store buyers who must make frequent trips to and from buying centers, members of families one or more of whom may have met with

accidents in areas served by a particular line, people planning to attend expositions and merchandise shows, football and baseball fans who like to follow the local teams to distant games, and so forth.

7. Vacationists. This group represents a large potential volume of business but is placed last in the classification of prospects because a vacationist makes one or two trips a year in contrast to ten, twenty, or thirty trips made for business reasons by members of other groups. Vacation travel can, however, be solicited along with business travel and does not require as much special sales segregation. Competition for vacation travel, however, includes not only other systems of transportation, including the private automobile, but also other airlines serving the same vacation areas as the particular airline whose services are being sold. These prospects are also less accessible than the other groups because it is difficult to acquire a source of information that will tell a salesman just when a vacation prospect is planning to take a trip. Sometimes clues may be obtained from the hobbies of prospects, as disclosed by club affiliations. For example, trapshooters are generally hunters also, and members of Isaak Walton League chapters are fishermen. Sporting goods stores are excellent sources of leads since they know their clientele, know when they are planning trips, and know those who can afford to take week-end and other special trips.

Locating the source of prospects does not constitute all there is to finding prospective airline passengers. Within the source must be located the individual prospect who does the traveling. This applies particularly to sources 1, 2, 3, and 4 discussed above. Once the individual prospect is found, the salesman must convert him into someone anxious to travel by air, and this cannot be done until something is known about him and his travel needs. The best chance of success in selling airline service is to apply the product—transportation by air—to an individual's needs.

Surrounding every prospect are key people who also are in a position to assist the salesman of air transportation. These people are the receptionists, telephone girls, and secretaries who make it easy or difficult for the prospect to be seen; yet these individuals never, or seldom, travel themselves. They should not, however, be overlooked. They should be as thoroughly sold as the man who might have occasion to travel by air. There are also those persons surrounding the actual prospect who may not have occasion to travel themselves but who definitely control the travel and travel methods used by the prospect. For example, the head of an organization may forbid his men to travel by air. In such cases, even though the individual prospect is thoroughly sold on this mode of travel, no business results because the "big boss" has said "No."

Making the Sale

Few, if any, people are going to travel by a particular airline just because it is "American," "Braniff," "United," "Eastern," or some other. Few, if any, people are going to travel by air instead of by other means just because it is flying. Traveling by air must be sold to new prospects by applying the schedules and fares of an airline or connecting lines to their particular problems and showing them the personal advantages to be gained from the use of air transportation.

Greater earning possibilities result from the additional time air travel makes available for other things; from the increased opportunities open because of the rapidity of travel to distant and otherwise inaccessible cities or territories, thus opening sales possibilities which otherwise would have to be foregone or be placed in the hands of less capable salesmen or negotiators; from the closer supervision and more frequent contacts with the sales organizations; from quicker action on servicing jobs, as when heavy machinery breaks down in the field and requires experts for repairing; from added energy because of less "travel fatigue" and more sleep in stationary beds; from more time for refreshing relaxations; and, last but by no means least, from the actual dollar value of the working hours made available by more rapid transportation. Few businessmen bother to translate into terms of salary dollars the extra working hours made available by air travel. This is the job of the air transportation salesman. The most obvious advantage of air transportation over other means is speed, which at the same time registers a negative reaction in a lot of minds. The average person's conception of speed is still "danger." In his mind is the thought that riding at 75 or 80 miles per hour in an automobile seriously jeopardizes life and limb. So instead of talking speed, the well-trained airline salesman talks of the results of speed—a saving in time—to his prospects from the standpoint of not only what air travel accomplishes for the traveler himself but what rewards are obtainable in his business and for his family.

Much air passenger traffic is noncompetitive with other carriers. A great deal of the business of the airlines is created by the speed of air transport. That is, if air transportation were not available, much of the travel on the airlines would not take place at all. For example, the businessman who makes a hurried trip from one coast to another often would not make the trip at all except for the fact that he is able to get to his destination, transact his business, and return within the space of a couple of days.[6]

Courtesy: United Air Lines

FIG. 22. A Typical airline ticket office

Moreover, the speed of air transportation is building business for other carriers in increasing amounts year by year. More and more,

[6] Surveys by various airlines reveal that 70 per cent of their total passengers are men, 60 per cent are traveling on business and 15 per cent of their travelers account for 54 per cent of the trips. Also, while the airlines have made relatively deep penetration of the business travel market, which accounts for about 38 per cent of the total market, they have only captured 14 per cent of the pleasure travel market.

modern business and sales methods depend on close personal contact between the seller and the purchaser. The speed of air transportation makes it possible for more organizations than ever before to extend their markets throughout the country because they are able, without the expense of a large number of salesmen, to use air transportation for the purpose of keeping in touch with their customers. This creates a demand for goods that in large measure are shipped by other carriers.

Sales Resistances to Be Overcome

Air transportation has attained all the technical perfection attached to a major transportation system. Before reaching a full measure of success, however, the airlines have still to overcome certain mass resistances to this mode of travel. This is probably the greatest challenge ever offered to the selling of a service, since practically the entire job of promoting air transportation to a position of mass acceptance in this country has yet to be accomplished. In a country of approximately 150,000,000 people, only an estimated 300,000 to 400,000 people normally make extensive use of air travel. Other forms of transportation have their problems, but the airlines are confronted by certain real and definite complexes on the part of the general public. Before mass acceptance becomes a fact, these will have to be overcome.

Most important of these complexes is that of fear, which may be characterized by ignorance and fear of the unknown, which itself is based on ignorance.[7] These are the psychological factors involved, and they work together. They do not exist as separate hazards to the progress of air transportation, and so they contribute equally to each of the following mass resistances which the salesman of air transportation has to overcome:

1. "I'll stay on the ground, thanks!" Fear for personal safety has been characterized as "the first protective wrapping around the blind prejudice of the person who prefers to stay on the ground." If this prospect for air travel could be educated so that he realized that he was as safe in an airplane, particularly the commercial transport plane, as in another vehicle, he would have taken the first and longest step toward becoming a steady air traveler (see Chapter 11).

[7] Many traffic surveys and market analyses have been made by the individual airlines, publishers, and others who are interested in the future of air transportation. All such surveys have had practically the same percentage of answers to the question "Why don't more people fly?" In every case, 65–70 per cent of those questioned said "fear" was the prime reason. "Cost" was second in 35–40 per cent of the answers in nearly all surveys.

2. "Flying costs too much." This is the second most popular misconception—that travel by air is extremely expensive. Various studies have contradicted this statement, particularly for business executives. For such travelers, air travel is more economical than any other. The argument is, however, still strong for other types of prospects even though for most trips it can be shown that, on a one-way first-class base, air travel costs no more than rail.

3. "I won't let my husband fly." One of the most serious problems still faced by air transportation is the opposition of women to their husbands or other relatives using the airlines.

It must be admitted that the increased use of air transportation by all classes of people during World War II did much to break down these resistances and particulary to make women realize that air travel is simply another means of getting about the world, speeding communications, and making it possible to get more places and do more in a given time. However, for airlines to feel they no longer have to overcome any resistances is too optimistic, because "fear" of getting off the ground will be with us for a long time.

Other, but less important, resistances which have to be overcome in individual cases might be classified as follows: uncertainty of weather, improved rail transportation, habit of using other forms of transportation, distance to airports, baggage restrictions, and the necessity of making definite reservations.

Plans for Increasing Air Travel

Air Travel Card Plan. Up until World War II, the efforts of airlines to increase air travel were largely confined to the development of what became known as the Air Travel Card plan, which had been originated by American Airlines in 1934. Under this plan, a subscribing company or individual made a deposit of $425 with an airline and was given one or more Air Travel Cards. On presentation of these cards at any airline ticket office, the holders received regular airline tickets, the cost of which—less 15 per cent from one-way fares—was billed to their companies or whomever had entered into the contract. In 1941 the deposit required to open an Air Travel Card account was increased to $450, but shortly thereafter again was made $425. Soon after the United States entered World War II, the 15 per cent discount feature was removed so that since that time, accounts have been charge propositions only. In 1942 and again in 1945 the Civil Aeronautics Board undertook an investigation of this plan of selling air transportation with the idea of ascertaining whether it was or was not unduly discriminatory. The conclusion of the Board was that the plan, with certain minor adjustments, could be considered as not discriminatory.[8]

The advantages of the Air Travel Card plan for the airlines and the users of air transportation may be summarized as follows:

For the Airlines—(1) Sales personnel have an easy selling approach with something definite to talk about. When all sales are for cash, wide and costly solicitation effort is necessary to find a few needful individuals. Holders of Air Travel Cards become more frequent users of air transportation and are easily reached by airline salesmen since their names are known. (2) The amount of bond and insurance required to protect cash received at ticket sales points in the course of daily business is reduced, since Air Travel Card sales are charge transactions. (3) Because the charges to a relatively small percentage of the accounts exceed $425 monthly and these accounts are generally paid promptly, the deposit system is virtually prepayment for transportation, despite the fact that the whole sum may be withdrawn without any sales.[9] (4) In the eyes of the user of air transportation, a nation-wide system of air transportation is created, owing to the ability to buy through tickets and through-trip insurance and to check baggage to destination even though several lines may be involved.

For Subscribers—(1) Time is saved in purchasing air transportation. (2) Convenience is increased in using air transportation at any time without cash. (3) A check record is made available on the individual travel habits of subscribers' personnel and their expenses.

Under the present plan, no limit is placed on the number of Air Travel Cards which may be issued to any eligible person under any contract so as to promote wider and more extensive use of air transportation by such individuals. Because of the concentrated groups of prospective air travelers represented by the card holders, among whom solicitation is fruitful in comparison with a widely scattered, though more numerous, group whose travel habits or needs are unknown, the airlines generally feel that the plan permits effective sales work with a substantially smaller sales force. Many reasons are given for this condition, among them that the plan makes accessible large

---

[8] *Universal Air Travel Plan Case,* CAB Docket No. 1939 (1946).

[9] The Air Travel Card plan generates a considerable amount of interest-free working capital for the airlines. As of Dec. 31, 1951, air travel plan deposits with fifteen certificated airlines in the United States amounted to $16,313,827, or 24 per cent of the total net working capital of the industry at that time.

numbers of potential users whose travel habits are known or can be ascertained; that the contract, when made, overcomes objections to air transportation of subordinate personnel; and that it therefore renders less difficult the salesman's task in promoting air travel.

As of 1955, seventy-seven of the world's scheduled certificated airlines were parties to the Universal Air Travel Plan, the only worldwide credit plan in operation. The plan is jointly sponsored by the Air Traffic Conference of the Air Transport Association and by the International Air Transport Association. Over half a million cards of three chief types are outstanding, any of which may be either territorial, international, or controlled: (*a*) personal air travel cards; (*b*) air travel "K" cards; (*c*) air travel "Q" cards. Any individual designated in writing by a subscriber may receive a personal or "Q" card. "K" cards are issued only to employees or members of a subscriber's family.

The holders of territorial cards are restricted as to what air travel may be charged. In the United States, this type card is known as a "North American Card" and entitles the holder to charge all tickets issued by participating carriers on the North American continent, Central America, the Bahamas, West Indies, Bermuda, and the Hawaiian Islands. The international cards are good on participating airlines throughout the world. Controlled cards are issued when the purchaser is a citizen of a country which has restrictions on the amount of air travel purchased during a given period of time. Of the 820,375 holders of Air Travel Cards in 1957, residents of the United States and Canada held 564,470, with this country having by far the largest number.

The Family Fare. This plan was initiated by American Airlines and subsequently adopted by most of the other airlines. It permits one member of a family paying full fare to be accompanied by additional members at half fare on flights originating during Monday, Tuesday, or Wednesday, when traffic is usually lighter than during the remaining four days of the week.

The family fare plan seems to put substantially more traffic on aircraft during the days on which it applies, but it is hard to say how many travelers who normally might travel on other days of the week put off their trips or move them up so as to take advantage of the plan and take wives and children along for half fares.

Installment Purchases. Starting in 1954, Pan American World Airways introduced the plan of selling foreign travel on installments. Under such a plan, a traveler may go into any ticket office of the company or to any of the 1,500 travel agencies in this country accredited by Pan American and buy a complete foreign trip including all travel, hotels, meals, etc., and arrange to pay for it in up to twenty monthly installments financed through arrangements between the airline and a personal finance organization, operating offices throughout the United States. Other airlines, particularly American Airlines and Trans World Airlines, instituted plans of their own to sell air travel on credit during 1954. The plans now in effect fall into two main categories: (*a*) One group works with the personal finance type of organization; (*b*) the second uses consumer credit departments of commercial banks.

Adherents of the first category maintain that the finance companies are better geared to handle this type of credit and can expedite transactions on satisfactory risks without undue complication and delay. The supporters of the commercial bank medium assert that interest cost for the consumer averages lower than through any other financing medium available.[10]

Extension of credit to finance consumer travel by air is not new, but it has been unsuccessful in the past because ease of arrangement and ready availability at point of sale were lacking. Further, national promotion was difficult because past plans were unavailable from coast to coast on a standard basis.

All plans require a down payment of at least 10 per cent, including the financing charges. The balance is payable in installments up to twenty months. This payment more than covers the usual commission to travel agents, where their services are involved (7½ per cent), so at the very worst, if the credit traveler defaults, the carrier will be out only the amount of its services.

The chances are that the credit volume of passenger traffic will fill up seats that otherwise might have been empty. Accordingly, the airlines can gain much in additional revenues, which may have a major impact on earnings with only a limited risk. This is true because, once operating costs are covered, virtually all additional revenue received flows through to net income.

The Air Coach[11]

The term "air coach service" has had various definitions, depending largely on who was defining it. An executive of an irregular air

[10] See Selig Altschul, "Carriers Like Pay Later Plans," *Aviation Week*, September 6, 1954.

[11] See Harold A. Jones and Frederick Davis, "The Air Coach Experiment and National Air Transport Policy," *Journal of Air Law and Commerce*, Autumn and Winter, 1950; Stanley Berge, "Regulation of Air Coach Service Standards," *Journal of Air Law and Commerce*, Winter, 1953.

carrier might describe it, for example, as a new type of service originated by noncertificated carriers and designed for the poor man's purse, lacking various "frills," and contrasting with the "luxury" air service offered by the certificated airlines.[12] An executive of a certificated airline might see the air coach as merely "low-cost service at the lowest rates consistent with sound business principles."[13] The Civil Aeronautics Board, in 1949, defined it as:

> . . . non-deluxe air transportation offered by certain of the air carriers, at a fare approximately four cents per passenger-mile, as compared with the average of about six cents per passenger-mile for regular services, with departure times from the terminals generally between ten or eleven o'clock at night and three o'clock in the morning, and eliminating the usual reservation procedures and meals featured by standard air service.[14]

Early in 1950, however, when transcontinental air coach service began to be offered by American Airlines and TWA, the Board modified its rules concerning departure times and reservations, so that departures could be made at more convenient hours and reservations made in advance. As time has gone on, therefore, air coach service has been hard to define exactly, except that lower fares are involved.

Air coach service was first introduced by certain noncertificated or irregular carriers flying between the chief traffic-generating centers, principally the transcontinental and New York City–Florida routes, under an exemption from the economic provisions of the Civil Aeronautics Act. This exemption had been granted by the Board under circumstances explained in Chapter 6.

Spurred on by the success of the irregulars, the certificated airlines, beginning with Capital Airlines in 1949, gradually began offering the coach-type service. By January, 1951, all the larger carriers had begun to offer the service, and by 1954, coach passenger-miles accounted for 31.7 per cent of the total traffic of the certificated domestic air carriers as shown in Table 30.

There is no doubt that the availability of the cheaper air coach service has promoted air travel and will continue to do so, but there is considerable risk that its expansion may have already developed uneconomic conditions. These have come about because (*a*) seating capacity has been increased, partly to equalize the effect on total revenues of the reduced fares at the very time when the industry's

[12] See *Hearings before the Committee on Interstate and Foreign Commerce on Sen. Res. 50* (81st Cong., 1st sess.) (1949), p. 260 ff.

[13] *Ibid.*, p. 1126.

[14] CAB, *Domestic Sky-Coach Survey* (Washington, D.C., 1949).

TABLE 30

AIR COACH OPERATIONS OF CERTIFICATED DOMESTIC AIR CARRIERS, 1948–59*

Year and Month	Revenue Miles	Revenue Passengers	Revenue Passenger-Miles (000)	Passenger Seat-Miles (000)	Revenue Passenger Load Factor Per Cent	Coach Passenger-Miles as Per Cent of Total
1948........	120,301	7,603	4,835	6,636	72.86	....
1949........	7,919,563	323,838	251,288	358,363	70.12	3.7
1950........	2,431,699	1,267,381	1,056,093	1,422,641	74.23	13.2
1951........	27,684,125	1,519,849	1,272,332	1,708,115	74.19	12.5
1952........	47,721,091	2,434,382	2,345,677	3,104,877	75.55	18.7
1953........	75,950,311	3,689,257	3,731,915	5,128,925	72.76	25.3
1954........	108,961,000	5,630,000	5,321,173	7,802,978	68.19	31.7
1955........	139,602,000	†	6,716,376	9,936,276	67.59	33.9
1956........	174,031,000	†	8,074,053	12,005,131	67.26	36.1
1957........	214,301,000	†	9,510,346	14,619,718	65.05	37.5
1958........	241,976,000	†	10,075,760	16,324,535	61.72	39.8
1959........	292,343,000	†	12,303,720	19,190,792	64.11	42.0

† Not available.

* These figures are included as part of the domestic scheduled air carrier operating statistics in Tables 25, 26, and 28. Domestic coach service was inaugurated November 4, 1948.

Source: FAA, *Statistical Handbook of Aviation* (Washington, D.C., 1960).

basic problem has been overexpansion and increased costs, (*b*) the prospective gain in traffic over the long run may be insufficient to allow profitable operations without serious diversion from standard service flights.

The two magic words "air coach" were supposed by some in the industry to be the open sesame to a new day of profitable volume air travel. The air coach was to create a great mass of new traffic. But coining new words has not altered the simple fact that an air coach ticket is nothing more or less than a ticket on an airplane, and whether or not it produces a profit or loss must be measured by the identical economic processes by which profit and loss are determined with regular-fare seats. The adoption of the air coach was simply applying good salesmanship to a price reduction on the basic product. By reducing the price of the product, the proponents of air coach service were trying to attract an entirely new group of travelers who would choose the airplane instead of the automobile, the railroad, or the bus.

Essentially, the provision of air coach service involves the application of the principles of discriminatory pricing to air passenger service. It represents an attempt to exploit differences in elasticity of demand in the various parts of the potential market, lower rates being offered to those customers whose demand for the service is relatively elastic. These, in general, are the persons to whom lower fares are much more significant than high quality of service. Greater speed cannot attract them to the airlines from surface carriers at the relatively high air fares, but they can be attracted at lower rates. Were the airlines to lower fares on all types of traffic in order to get these customers, they would be getting less revenue from existing passengers than they now obtain. But by holding up fares on the higher-quality service and providing low coach rates, revenues are kept at existing levels from present customers and additional revenue is obtained from the new customers.

The introduction of air coach service is profitable, of course, only if it adds more to the airlines' total revenue than it adds to their total cost. If the air coach service merely diverted passengers from the luxury service, the change would obviously be unprofitable. But if little diversion occurs and substantial new business develops, the new service is definitely advantageous from the standpoint of both the companies and the customers. Price discrimination of this type offers substantial possibilities for improved utilization of resources in the industry. However, to price such service so low that total profits are reduced is obviously unwarranted. It has been well said that "there is no sense in pricing a product below cost and there is no use trying to fool one another about catch-names like air coach."[15]

Indications are, however, that the airlines may change from their present policy of offering over 85 per cent of their services as de luxe or first-class to one of offering over 50 per cent air coach within a comparatively short time, in an effort to meet economic conditions affecting the travel markets. This will affect aircraft manufacturers as well as the airlines. To the manufacturers it means a re-evaluation of the new transport designs on their drawing boards in order to achieve every bit of pay-load capacity through quick and cheap conversion to high-density seating.[16] For the airlines it will mean mass market sales promotion and perhaps a universal adoption of the installment selling plan introduced by Pan American World Airways in the foreign field. The coach market will, however, be more sensitive to economic changes and definitely more seasonal than first-class.

Airline Public Relations

In developing passenger traffic, the conduct of public relations has played a very important part. This has involved contacts of all

[15] See "The Air Coach Dilemma," *American Aviation*, August 15, 1949.

[16] See Lee Moore, "Switch to Coach May Alter Plane Design," *Aviation Week*, November 10, 1952.

kinds in order to establish and maintain goodwill not only toward individual airlines but toward the air transportation industry as a whole. Airline public relations activities have endeavored to pave the way for favorable legislation, desirable trade relations, advantageous financial connections, and increased demand for their services.

The policies and actions of airlines seem to indicate a difference of opinion as to just who constitutes the airline public, in terms of public relations activities. Many airlines have come to recognize their employees as a very important part of their public relations program. Some companies carry out their public relations programs through representatives in different regions. These operate with the purpose of considering the local customs, tastes, and opinions of each area. It may be said that the public of any airline would include the following:

Employees
Passengers, present and prospective
Competitors (airlines and other transportation agencies)
Suppliers of planes and equipment
Communities
1. Local
2. Area surrounding and between terminal points
3. National
Newspaper profession
Readers of newspapers and magazines
Professional groups
Stockholders and prospective investors
State and federal government agencies and officials
Educators

Seemingly, the importance given to any or all of the specific groups of the public varies with different airlines. Several companies consider the establishment of the proper attitude between labor and management as the biggest job of their public relations departments. These companies are attempting to build public relations from the ground up.

Civil officials in various communities served by an airline, prominent businessmen, other airlines and other transportation agencies, legislators in states where a line operates, and governmental agencies (all of which are contacted by the traffic department of an airline) are considered important parts of the public with which most companies are concerned.

The job of building and maintaining goodwill toward individual airlines is carried on by nearly all companies, but there is no uniformity in the terminology used in designating these departments. They are known variously as departments of public relations, publicity, public information, advertising, education, and traffic. Sometimes contacts of company executives and company representatives with the various segments of an airline's public are relied on to do the complete job. In companies with the most thorough public relations systems, every member (labor and management combined) of the organization has been included in the program.

Public relations work takes many forms, including writing, lecturing, photographing, escorting tours of visitors about airports and maintenance bases, and co-operating with the press. The person who does public relations work deals with anyone who wants to ask a question about an airline. The public might be children, writers, newspaper reporters, photographers, program chairmen for fraternal, business, and women's clubs, and anyone else who is interested in air transportation. Through public relations activities, newspapers and magazines are given news and photographs which will be of interest to the public and which will bring the airlines before the public in a favorable way. Getting favorable attention in newsreels and other moving pictures, influencing famous people to fly, and attending business shows, conventions, and meetings of people who travel extensively are a few other public relations activities.

Most airlines consider it a good policy to have a general publicity or promotional program worked out for the year. In this program will be indicated the thing to be emphasized most at specific times and the kind of effort each company unit is expected to contribute.

An up-to-date calendar of events, such as festivals, sports, contests, historical events, state and national holidays, etc., prevents the overlooking of many good promotion possibilities and provides the outline for the bulk of a year's promotional plans. As each year's activity determines the worthwhile promotions and adds to the list of opportunities, the calendar becomes more important.

The newspaper and magazine are used to place paid advertisements and to get the airline news to the reading public. News items deal with such things as:

Passenger lists—Names of prominent people taking trips by plane will make news. (Prominent politically, socially, in theater, sports, foreign, or business world.) Pictures of prominent people on a plane interviewing airline officials, with some member or members of the trip crew, or enjoying some specific airline service give the public interesting news.

Traffic and volume of trade
Resort, business, and club travel
Vacation travel and vacation spots
Student travel
Airline personnel
Management activity on policy
Services—change of, new services, regular services, emergency services
Some phase of the line's operation
Spot news—presented to bring goodwill and to avert criticism of the line

Air transportation has reached a stage of development where it can consider itself grown to man's size and can therefore conduct itself as a very vital, matured, and dignified business. The circus-type ballyhoo, so often practiced in the industry's early years, will probably become less and less used and considerably subdued in public relations work. America is air-minded, and so various aspects of airline work will always be newsworthy; but news will no longer have to be "manufactured."

The public is, however, still generally ignorant of the development of commercial air transportation as a whole and of its future potentialities. Heretofore, not enough has been done to interpret the airline industry to the public in the language of people's thoughts, habits, and personal interest. This is the job of public relations men and women.

Chapter 15

AIRLINE PASSENGER HANDLING[1]

THE success or failure of an airline or any other service organization depends almost entirely upon pleasing its patrons with the service rendered. No matter how excellent a selling job is performed, failure to provide the service sold will inevitably lose the patron for future business. During an ordinary trip, a passenger contacts a very small part of the personnel of an airline; yet the passenger's opinion and future use of the services of a particular company are entirely dependent upon the treatment received from station employees, pilots, hostesses, and sales personnel.

Airline experience has shown that passenger goodwill can be maintained even in spite of inconvenience, flight cancellations, and delay if the employees handling passengers are cheerful and courteous and exhibit a friendly and understanding attitude. While it is fundamentally the job of those personally contacting passengers to build goodwill, this can be accomplished only if the employees on whom such a responsibility rests are supported from behind the scenes with prompt and accurate information concerning flight operations, prompt handling of reservation requests, and a multitude of other services provided by the respective departments of an airline.

Perhaps no single feature acts more quickly to determine an outsider's opinion of an airline than the personal appearance and conduct of its employees. Airline employees when on duty at city ticket offices or at airports should, therefore, maintain a businesslike manner and attitude, avoiding unnecessary loud talking or other boisterous conduct. Problems relating to operations should not be discussed between employees in the presence of passengers since the technical

[1] For a more detailed discussion of this subject see William L. Grossman, *Air Passenger Traffic* (New York: Chemical Publishing Co., Inc., 1947); Morris B. Baker, *Airline Traffic and Operations* (New York: McGraw-Hill Book Co., Inc., 1947); Gene Kropf, *Airline Traffic Procedures* (New York: McGraw-Hill Book Co., Inc., 1949).

terms sometimes involved may be confusing or misleading, resulting in adverse criticism. An alert and aggressive sales policy should be the objective of all airline employees, not simply that of those primarily charged with sales work.

Many of the first contacts between an airline and prospective passengers occur when the prospect makes a telephone call to the airline office. Obviously, persons sufficiently interested to inquire about airline service are potential customers, and a little well-directed effort may secure and maintain profitable traffic. A passenger's opinion of an airline may be as readily formed through telephone conversations with employees as by personal contacts. A satisfactory and pleasing impression from a phone call results if the conversation is clear and distinct. Equally important is the attitude or "tone" of a conversation. A friendly and co-operative approach is usually the determining factor in the results obtained. Regardless of the purpose of a call made to an airline, or by whom made, it should be so handled by the receiving employee in such a way as to make the person glad he called.

Reservations

Most space (seats) on airlines are reserved[2] for several reasons: (*a*) Reserved space is part of the first-class accommodation and service demanded by most airline travelers. (*b*) Airplanes have definite limitations on the amount of pay load that can be carried over varying distances. (*c*) Airlines must obtain the greatest possible use of the available seats on each airplane. At the same time, because of the limited number of seats to an airplane, the passenger must be assured of space before starting his journey. Unless fares were lower than on a reserved basis and service was frequent, very few passengers would be satisfied to go out to an airport on the mere chance that a seat might be available. (*d*) Control of available space (seats) is necessary to prevent sale of more space on one or more portions of a flight than is available on that portion. When such an "oversale" occurs, and if there are no cancellations, an airline must then deny transportation on the flight to at least one passenger who has a reservation, thus risking ill will or, possibly, legal liability.[3]

There are almost as many different types of reservation systems as there are airlines. They all have a common purpose, however,

---

[2] This applies to coach-type, as well as to regular, services on most airlines today, although at first, under CAB regulations, a coach reservation was not made without the sale of a ticket.

[3] See Grossman, *op. cit.*, chap. xi.

which is the elimination of the bottlenecks and delays which air travelers find so irksome.

The most common reservation systems are operated as follows:[4]

1. All space is controlled by one central reservations office located near the geographical center of operation of an airline. Under this system, which is sometimes called the "automatic sales procedure," airline offices out on the line, after referring to a chart indicating space availability, are able to give the passenger immediate confirmation of all on-line space desired. Then these offices record such sales with the central reservations control office. Such a system has many advantages: (*a*) It affords immediate confirmation of on-line space. (*b*) Favorable passenger reaction results from better and quicker reservations service. (*c*) There is a certain competitive sales advantage over other airlines using more cumbersome systems. (*d*) There is a decrease in telephone calls to passengers as the result of confirmation on the original call. (*e*) Company messages by teletype or otherwise are lessened. (*f*) There is elimination of what is known as "shopping for space" and keeping the prospective passenger uninformed for long periods of time. (*g*) There is better utilization of space, as it is centrally controlled by experts. (*h*) The entire reservations picture at any one time is available in one place.

2. Space is allotted to the individual stations of an airline on the basis of the normal needs of each point. If more space is needed, it has to be obtained from another station located behind the requesting station on a particular route. Under this system, there is the danger that space allotments to individual stations will not be adequate under varying traffic conditions and that stations will continue to hold space they cannot sell. Continuous traffic studies, however, enable most airlines to determine quite closely the number of seats each station should normally sell.

Within the last few years, several airlines have installed electronic reservations systems. Typical of these is the "Sabre" developed by International Business Machines which American Airlines began to install in 1961. It links 1,100 reservations sales desks in 61 cities served by this carrier. It handles all the functions and procedures associated with the sale—confirmation and control of an air travel reservation from the time a customer calls for information on a flight to the time he or she arrives at his or her final destination. It will be able to store more than 600 million characters and to handle more than 7,500 complete airline reservations in an hour.

---

[4] See Kropf, *op. cit.*, pp. 44–45.

Sabre is a completely automatic, centralized, electronic system which will provide the answer, in seconds, to virtually any problem on reservations likely to be put by any passenger, prospective or actual, to any booking agent of American Airlines anywhere in the United States.

At the New York center, the complete reservations record of every American Airlines' passenger will be electronically recorded and electronically filed. Information will include the passenger's name, itinerary, telephone number, and related data. There will also be an up-to-the-second inventory of available seats on every flight in the American Airlines system for instant reference by reservations agents throughout the country. These two basic reservations records, the passenger name record and the seat inventory, are combined in a centralized automatic file in Sabre.

Mechanization of reservations records puts the power and accuracy of the central processor at the agent's finger tips; it gives him instant and accurate second-by-second answers to his customer's questions. Immediate access to the passenger name record makes it possible for any agent to confirm, alter, or cancel all or any part of any passenger record no matter where the original reservation may have been made. The seat inventory enables agents anywhere in the United States to determine quickly the availability of seats on any of the airline's 1,200 daily flight stages.

While keeping tab on all reservations, Sabre will also perform the following operations automatically: (*a*) send teletype messages to other airlines requesting space on their flights, follow up these messages if no reply is received, and answer requests from other airlines; (*b*) quote fares for most itineraries; (*c*) maintain and process waiting lists of passengers desiring space on fully booked flights; (*d*) supply information on departure and arrival times for the current day's flights; and (*e*) notify agents when special action is required, such as calling a passenger to inform him of changes.

On any given day, American Airlines may have as many as a million passenger reservations on file. The average time needed to complete the processing of a reservations transaction under the manual system, with its complex behind-the-scenes filing procedures, is 45 minutes. Sabre, with all these reservations records in its "memory," will do the same job in an average of three seconds.[5]

In contrast to the development of automatic reservations systems, other airlines have taken steps to abandon reservations on certain

[5] Another similar electronic system is the one based on the Remington Rand Univac File Computer used by Northwest Orient Airlines and others.

flights. Typical of this activity are the "no reservation commuter-flights" of companies like Allegheny Airlines, which it has been estimated can be operated at about half the first-class indirect cost per passenger of other flights.

No system of reservations is perfect, and quite often what is known as "overbooking" occurs. This is usually unintentional, resulting from airline "free sale" and "sell and report" reservation practices permitting the sale of space by one airline on another without prior clearance, from the lag in communicating reservations to reservation departments, or from human error. Intentional overbooking, which has become more and more frequent and of which passengers rightfully complain, takes place where reservations are made in excess of capacity on particular flights, usually on heavily traveled segments such as between New York and Florida in the winter season, in the anticipation of later cancellations or "no shows." In other instances, overbooking takes place under circumstances, which may or may not be avoidable, where smaller equipment is substituted for larger on scheduled flights for one reason or another. The overbooking problem, particularly as a means of overcoming the "no show" situation on certain airlines, became so serious in 1959–60 that the Civil Aeronautics Board initiated an investigation of the practice to determine and fix regulatory policy for the future.[6]

The carriers, which from time to time have resorted to deliberate overbooking, contend that the effect of unused reservations on their load factors on certain flights has been such that the practice is forced upon them by economic necessity. Problems caused by "no shows" exist throughout the industry, although there may be variations depending upon the route and the season. It has even been alleged that under certain circumstances overbooking, adopted as a solution to the "no show" problem, produces advantages in terms of operating efficiency which far outweigh any inconvenience to passengers. From the airline standpoint this may be true, but the airlines lose sight of the very important effect on passenger relations.

Scheduling[7]

One of the most intricate and vital challenges to airline management is the scheduling of capacity over its particular route system in

---

[6] CAB Order No. E-15615 in Docket No. 11683, *Overbooking Practices of Trunkline Carriers* (1960).

[7] Adapted from *General Passenger Fare Investigation,* CAB Docket No. 8008 (1958) brief of the Air Transport Association of America.

such a relation to traffic demand that it will produce the optimum balance between (1) economy of operation and (2) service to the public. These are, in a real sense, warring objectives, since the former points toward high-load factors, and the latter toward low-load factors. The greater the percentage of seats filled, on the average flight, the less the average cost and the greater the chance of profit for each mile of passenger haul. On the other hand, the greater the percentage of seats filled, the greater the chance that some passengers will be unable to obtain space and so will have to postpone their trips, take less desired flights, or forego air travel altogether.

Nor is scheduling, as reflected in the load factor, simply a matter of compromise between economy and service. Under competitive conditions such as the domestic trunklines now face, and will increasingly face, the airline which seeks to maximize load factors (and profits) by being niggardly in scheduling is likely to lose traffic, either because space is more readily available on its competitors' services or because its competitors offer service of greater frequency or at hours more convenient to the particular market. And, quite apart from the competitive aspect, the carrier which skimps on service may create public ill will and adequacy-of-service complaints, to say nothing of certification of additional carriers over its routes to provide a "competitive spur." Thus, scheduling for profit must be well tempered by scheduling for service.

Other complicating factors arise from the dynamic nature of the airline industry. While traffic generally grows from year to year, there are no mathematical formulas for predicting how much, if any, growth will occur in a given period or for a given carrier or in a given market. Accordingly, aircraft purchased may prove too many or too few when they come on the line some two or more years after being ordered. And schedules set up in November may prove excessive or inadequate come January.

Moreover, each airline's schedules must be built up on a segment-by-segment basis, even though the ultimate financial results of the carrier's operation will reflect its system-wide operation. Thus, to take a vastly oversimplified example, an airline, in order to maintain a minimum-service pattern of two daily flights each day between the city pairs A-B and C-D, may have to accept 40 per cent load factors over these segments. In order to avoid excessive load factors on a twice-a-day schedule between E and F, it may have to add a third flight, reducing the average E-F load factor to 50 per cent. In order to get aircraft back from F to the home base, A, for overnight maintenance, it may have to accept an off-peak flight, F-A, at 30 per cent load factor. The carrier can fulfill these requirements and still achieve an over-all economic operation only to the extent it is able to schedule over other segments—say, G-H, I-J, etc.—at a sufficiently higher load factor to bring its system average up to a profitable level.[8] And no amount of emphasis on *system* load factor will enable this airline to avoid the exigencies of scheduling over segments A-B, C-D, E-F, and F-A to meet the service needs and operational requirements.

As these illustrations indicate, the extent of managerial skills in scheduling can go far to make or break an airline. Although such factors as route structure and access to developable markets are important, each trunkline has a substantial area within which the skill of management in scheduling to its own system will have a significant impact on the economy of the airline and the public service it renders. Within this area, the most important single factor is likely to be the informed judgment of the airline's management as to the schedules which will best fit the requirements of its markets, and thereby produce for it the greatest volume of traffic which can be competitively generated without plunging it into uneconomic operations.

The profit motive will almost invariably impel an airline to maximize its load factor, and thus maximize its profits. There need be little concern, on the part of the Civil Aeronautics Board, with measures to push domestic trunkline load factors up. The airlines, left alone, will likely do that themselves, to the extent they can, although the Board may find it appropriate on occasion to consider measures to deter excessive load factors, lest some airlines place economy of operation unduly ahead of public service. Moreover, the profit motive's strong stimulus toward higher load factors points directly to the conclusion that the recent two-year decline in industry load factors must be attributed to factors largely beyond management control (see Table 25). The introduction of larger aircraft will tend to depress load factors in the foreseeable future, despite the best efforts of airline management to improve this situation.

The obligation of the Board to guarantee adequate service is made clear in the law, and the fact that only a few adequacy-of-service or -scheduling orders have been issued in the past twenty years

---

[8] Note that, in order to achieve a 60 per cent system load factor, the carrier would have to operate 14 additional flights at an average 70 per cent load factor (assuming all segments are of equal length and operated with aircraft of identical seating capacity).

reflects the way in which air transportation has developed.[9] Reliance has been placed upon competition among the carriers to ensure adequacy of service. The Washington-Baltimore Adequacy-of-Service Case is, however, a major attempt on the part of the Board to regulate scheduling, but it is strongly opposed by the airlines as a move into an area that should be left to management and private competition. The Board concedes that the Federal Aviation Act does not give it specific power to regulate scheduling but that section 404(a) provides that airlines must provide "safe and adequate service, equipment, and facilities." The standard adopted by the Board in the Baltimore case provides that any "market" or route between two cities served by a trunkline, that has or can generate at least 10 passengers a day, is entitled to one round trip daily with no more than two intermediate stops. In other words, if a total of 10 passengers a day (10 one way or 5 each way on a round trip) use a flight, service is inadequate unless the service is provided daily with a maximum of two stops. The airlines claim that according to this standard, 87 per cent of the "markets" in the United States are today inadequately served and that such a standard would be especially damaging at the time when the airlines are installing larger aircraft seating from 70 to 120 persons.

It seems fundamental that the Board should have the power to compel an airline to provide adequate service over the routes it is authorized to serve. Otherwise if they chose to do so, the carriers would be able to divide the available routes and then, their individual and collective monopolies assured, to render as little service as they might wish and to skim the cream by concentrating on easy and low-cost markets, which is a great temptation with long-range jet aircraft, leaving the rest of the country inadequately served.

Another aspect of scheduling concerns on-time performance, and, in order to have some control over this, the Board has established a "standard of performance."[10] This regulation requires each airline, with the exception of helicopter operations or all-cargo flights, to complete at least 75 per cent of all flights within 15 minutes of the block-to-block time shown on its published schedules. Block-to-block

[9] See, for example, *New York–Florida Case*, 24 CAB, 94 (1956); *Toledo Adequacy of Service Investigation*, Order E-14629, November 10, 1959, and Order No. E-14725, December 9, 1959; *Flint–Grand Rapids Adequacy of Service Investigation*, Order No. E-15161; *Washington-Baltimore Adequacy of Service Investigation*, CAB Docket No. 8148 (1960); *Fort Worth Investigation*, CAB Docket No. 7382, Supplemental Opinion and Order (1960); *New York Short-haul Coach Investigation*, CAB Docket No. 9973 (1960).

[10] Part 234, CAB Economic Regulations, adopted Aug. 16, 1957.

time, as applied by the Board, is measured from the time an aircraft leaves its airport gate position at its point of origin and arrives at its gate position at the airport of its final destination. Airlines failing to meet the requirements of this regulation over any three-month period are in violation unless they are able to show justification for noncompliance caused by conditions beyond their control.

In issuing this regulation, the Board said that it was promulgated as a result of numerous complaints received of poor schedule performance so that there appeared to be a need to correct unrealistic scheduling practices, usually arising out of competition and each airline's desire to show a shorter scheduled time between points than its competitors. Such practices subjected those airlines publishing realistic time schedules to unfair competition.

In general, the airlines object to this regulation on the grounds that most delays occur regardless of the scheduled time of flights and are beyond their control. Moreover, the carriers point out that no one is more interested in on-time performance than they are since their welfare depends on the service they offer to the public. Table 31 shows reported schedule performance in a typical month.

The problem involved in the regulation of schedule performance is that of assuring the traveling public that it is being given reasonably accurate information as to the probable arrival and departure times of aircraft. The on-time operation of each flight is always at the mercy of the elements and of chance, therefore it seems unreasonable for the Board to require any flight actually to meet the time publicized in schedules. Government regulation can hardly deal with performance, but it can deal with prediction of performance, which is what the airlines do in issuing their printed schedules.

Flight Forecasts and Advisories

When a passenger buys a ticket on an airline, he expects and deserves to know whether the flight for which he is paying will operate on schedule. A passenger resents being led to believe that his flight will operate as scheduled, only to find it canceled or delayed. He also does not receive the service to which he is entitled if he is discouraged from flying in advance only to find later that the flight has operated through to completion.

To assist employees charged with the handling of passengers, scheduled flight forecasts or advisories are issued. These are designed to inform local stations and traffic offices of what may be expected in the way of flight operations for the period covered by the

TABLE 31

ON-TIME PERFORMANCE—JUNE, 1959
On-Time Dependability of Trips at Termination as Reported to CAB
Nonstop and One-Stop Flights Only

	Rank	On time to 15 min. late	On time to 5 min. late	6-15 min. late	16-30 min. late	Over 30 min. late	Total trips reported
TRUNKS							
American	3	71.7%	54.1%	17.6%	12.7%	15.6%	5,816
Braniff	1	80.1	59.6	20.5	11.0	8.9	1,696
Capital	9	55.2	30.3	24.9	23.5	21.3	4,700
Continental	5	68.2	46.6	21.6	18.7	13.1	1,022
Delta	7	63.6	34.6	29.0	21.3	15.1	1,659
Eastern	6	66.8	43.6	23.2	16.8	16.4	5,498
National	10	48.3	30.6	17.7	20.3	31.4	741
Northeast	8	55.7	35.6	20.1	17.9	26.4	2,810
Northwest	9	55.2	34.5	20.7	17.4	27.4	1,503
TWA		N.A.	N.A.	N.A.	N.A.	N.A.	N.A.
United	2	77.7	56.7	21.0	10.9	11.4	4,412
Western	4	71.5	45.0	26.5	16.6	11.9	1,068
Totals		66.3%	44.5%	21.8%	16.4%	17.3%	30,925
LOCALS							
Allegheny	11	59.1%	37.2%	21.9%	18.6%	22.3%	269
Bonanza	9	71.5	60.4	11.1	10.7	17.8	325
Central	1	92.0	82.0	10.0	7.0	1.0	100
Frontier	4	82.7	66.2	16.5	10.7	6.6	242
Lake Central	6	78.3	52.2	26.1	10.1	11.6	138
North Central		N.A.	N.A.	N.A.	N.A.	N.A.	N.A.
Mohawk	10	60.8	37.0	23.8	17.9	21.3	1,184
Ozark	3	88.3	53.3	35.0	10.6	1.1	649
Pacific	5	81.4	55.6	25.8	9.3	9.3	205
Southern	8	73.1	38.5	34.6	17.6	9.3	416
West Coast	2	89.2	78.0	11.2	5.4	5.4	242
Piedmont	7	75.8	48.2	27.6	17.3	6.9	29
Totals		73.5%	49.3%	24.2%	13.8%	12.7%	3,799
BOEING 707							
American	1	27.3%	17.0%	10.3%	20.9%	51.8%	598
Continental	2	30.1	12.5	17.6	43.7	26.2	80
TWA		N.A.	N.A.	N.A.	N.A.	N.A.	N.A.
Totals		27.7%	16.5%	11.2%	23.5%	48.8%	678
LOCKHEED ELECTRA							
American	1	79.6%	63.0%	16.6%	9.4%	11.0%	843
Eastern	2	63.0	42.3	20.7	16.7	20.3	993
National	3	33.8	14.5	19.3	25.3	40.9	83
Totals		69.1%	50.3%	18.8%	13.8%	17.1%	1,919

NA—Not available. Carriers failed to report by deadline.
Local airlines not shown failed to report by deadline.

Source: *Airlift*, September, 1959.

advisory message. On most airlines, flight forecasts are issued for twelve-hour periods and are supplemented four hours before expiration with a new advisory.

The flight advisory is not necessarily an absolute and unchangeable plan of operation, since conditions may vary quickly at times and thus change the operations proposed. However, the advisory does represent what the airline flight dispatcher anticipates and is therefore a good indication of what may be expected and what information may be given passengers concerning the operation of flights in which they may be interested. At most times, flight dispatchers, with the assistance of meteorologists, can predict the clearance of flights in advance when an analysis of the existing weather conditions and the weather maps available shows no indications of unfavorable flight conditions over the territory in question. Less frequently, flight dispatchers cannot a number of hours in advance state with any exactness what the conditions may be, and accurate information can be given only after analysis of later weather reports. This condition is neither pessimistic nor optimistic; and the flight in question may be cleared to destination, delayed, or canceled, depending on the outcome of the conditions existing at the time of clearance. The flight will be cleared if conditions permit and if the weather is above the standards prescribed for flight operations. Whenever weather reports indicate that a flight will not be able to operate, flight dispatchers usually cancel its operation as far in advance as possible. The only reason that a decision concerning the operation of a flight will be deferred is because a flight dispatcher feels that there is a possibility of safe operation but must necessarily delay his decision until favorable weather reports are received.

When describing the anticipated operation or status of flights scheduled to operate, or presently operating, three terms are commonly used:

1. *Routine.* The flight will operate without interruption on or about its published schedule.
2. *Subject.* The flight dispatcher plans to operate the flight if late weather reports are above minimum standards, although a definite decision will be made later.
3. *Cancel.* The flight will not be operated.

Special passenger-handling problems are created in the case of "subject" and "cancel" operations. In such cases, it is necessary for the station concerned to keep in touch with passengers scheduled to depart on the "subject" flight and to make tentative arrangements for either eventuality—if the flight does or does not operate. Upon receiving a "subject" forecast for a trip affecting a given station, airline employees usually begin to make the necessary arrangements for the possibility of dispatching passengers for the flight to their destination by some means of ground transportation. Generally, a flight dispatcher will qualify a "subject" forecast with the term "likely," meaning that, although the flight has not as yet been definitely cleared, its operation is considered likely or "unlikely," meaning that, although there is yet the possibility of the operation of a flight, its operation is considered unlikely. These qualifications provide additional information concerning the likelihood of operations and permit more freedom in the primary arrangements to be undertaken by station personnel. If a flight forecast indicates the possibility of cancellation at a given station, tentative arrangements are usually made in order to care for the transportation and accommodation of passengers who may be deplaned at that point either temporarily or permanently, as well as to provide for passengers arriving on connecting airlines. Probably no other phase of passenger handling calls for greater ability, experience, and tact than when operations are irregular or uncertain.

Care should be taken to avoid making any statement which may cause doubt or fear in a passenger's mind concerning the operation of a trip. Many passengers are frankly afraid or worried by what they feel is "bad" or "doubtful" weather, as well as by an apparent indecision on the part of the employee with whom they may be discussing the matter. If a passenger is told that a flight is "doubtful," or the weather is "bad around Kansas City," or "I don't know whether this flight will operate or not," this passenger may cancel his reservation when actually there is only the usual risk of doubt involved in the flight. No airline ever clears a flight unless, in the opinion of a flight dispatcher, its operation is absolutely safe.

Ticketing

All rates, fares, charges, rules, and regulations concerning the transportation of airline passengers and their baggage are published in airline passenger tariffs, on file at all stations. Except as otherwise provided in airline tariffs, tickets are valid for a period of 120 days after they are issued and expire at midnight on the date of expiration. Tickets will, however, be extended for passengers who are unable to obtain a reservation on the date of expiration due to lack of space or flight cancellation, but for a time not to exceed the first comparable schedule on which space is available.

Tickets are of various types:

One Way. A trip in one direction only between two stations.

Round Trip. A trip from one station to another and return to the station of origin when using the same airline in both directions.

Circle Trip. A trip from one station to two or more stations and return to the station of origin; for example, a trip from Dallas to Atlanta via Delta Air Lines, Atlanta to New York via Eastern Air Lines, and New York to Dallas via American Airlines.

Open Jaw. A trip from one station to two or more other stations, involving travel in both directions; for example New York to Seattle, Seattle to Los Angeles, and Los Angeles to Miami.

Open Date. A ticket issued without any definite reservation in advance.

Interline. Indicates the use of two or more airlines.

Joint Issue. The issuing of two or more tickets in connection with each other to cover one complete trip.

Passengers are permitted to carry 40 pounds of baggage free of charge in the United States and 66 pounds on foreign flights. This is the general rule to which there are some exceptions. For example, on some domestic flights, such as San Francisco to Honolulu, 66 pounds are allowed, while on some foreign flights, such as Seattle to Vancouver, only 40 pounds are allowed. There are also special rules; for example, United States-flag lines between San Francisco and Vancouver will handle only 40 pounds of baggage free, while foreign-flag airlines between those points will handle 66 pounds. This free baggage includes handbags, suitcases, brief cases, etc. Any baggage or personal belongings above the full weight allowance is charged the excess baggage rate published in airline passenger tariffs. Excess baggage charges are collected at the point of origin for the entire one-way trip to destination. If there is a stopover en route, the excess charges are made from the point of origin to the point of first stopover. Baggage is usually checked only as far as space is confirmed.

Routing

Fares quoted in airline tariffs provide for routing on a much less generous basis than do rail or bus tariffs. Airline fares are applicable only over a particular routing specified; and, if no routing is specified, the most direct route will apply. Where there is more than one applicable route, at a published fare, the passenger may specify the desired routing prior to beginning a trip. If he specifies that he desires an alternate routing, which is authorized at the same fare, his ticket is stamped "optional routing via (name of carrier of alternate routing)." When this is done, the passenger may choose any one of the alternates specified without further endorsement at any time prior to the start of the trip involving the alternate routing.

Any other rerouting which involves a change in participating carriers must be made by a signed endorsement of the ticket by a representative of the first participating carrier from which the routing is changed and may be secured by the direct request of the passenger to such representative. The fare for rerouting is computed as follows: The fare will be that which would have been charged had the revised routing been purchased at the point of origin; however, after a trip is started, a one-way ticket may not be converted to a round-trip or circle ticket at a corresponding fare reduction. Any difference between the fare of the revised routing and the original fare paid will be collected from the passenger.

The route selected by an individual passenger is usually based on one or more of the following factors: (*a*) the directness of the route; (*b*) the fare; (*c*) the combinations of attractions on one route versus another; for example, some passengers on a transcontinental journey choose the route that takes them over the Grand Canyon; (*d*) the sales effort put forth by individual airlines; (*e*) the type of equipment provided by one airline as compared to that of another; (*f*) the services of one company as compared to those of another, coupled with personal desire of a passenger to patronize one company rather than another; and (*g*) the desire to go one way and return another.

In the event of a change in routing due to flight cancellation or lack of space, an airline will (*a*) allow the passenger to retain the unused portion of the ticket for use on a later flight; or (*b*) refund the value of the unused portion of the ticket; or (*c*) endorse the unused portion of the ticket for purposes of rerouting; or (*d*) reroute the passenger to destination by air, rail, or other carrier and without collection of a higher fare, if a higher fare prevails for the routing designated, or, if a lower fare prevails, refund the difference to the passenger.

When a passenger is rerouted for a reason not within his control and where the rerouting calls for a fare differential in excess of that which the passenger has paid, the carrier failing to perform the service, or the line which has canceled its flight, retickets the passenger and absorbs the fare differential, except in cases where a joint fare exists, in which case the regular proportion of the fare will govern the proportion of the absorption. There should be no chance of confusion concerning the responsibility of the airline when a flight is canceled or when a scheduled stop is omitted; but when failure to make connection occurs, airlines agree that the responsibility is that of the line which failed to arrive at the point of connection in time for the passenger to catch the flight on which space was held. Most airlines will, therefore, absorb the additional amount of fare caused by rerouting when this rerouting is due to flight cancellation, missed connection, or omission of a scheduled stop.

If it is the passenger's desire to be rerouted, the price of the ticket is refigured on the basis of the fare that would have been charged had the revised routing been purchased at the point of origin. If a higher fare prevails on the new routing, the difference will be collected. Should a lower fare prevail, the difference will be refunded.

Ticket Refunds

Unused tickets or portions of unused tickets will be refunded by airlines upon surrender by the original purchaser, subject to the following conditions:

1. A passenger canceling of his own volition will be refunded the difference between the fare paid and the fare for the distance traveled.
2. Upon the cancellation of a flight by an airline due to weather conditions or other reasons beyond the control of the passenger, the passenger, with certain exceptions, will be refunded that part of the fare paid which is applicable to the remainder of the trip.
3. Refunds on tickets issued against government travel orders, Air Travel Cards, or one-trip air travel orders or tickets stamped "refunded only at general office" will be made only upon request to the general office of the airline.
4. Refunds which may result from voluntary cancellation by passengers or from a change in routing made at a passenger's request will be made only upon request to the general office of the airline.
5. Lost tickets will not be replaced or refunded until thirty days after the date passengers make application to the general office.

Inadequacies of Passenger Handling[11]

Despite the various passenger-handling devices discussed in this chapter, this aspect of air transportation still presents problems. Complicated and frustrating hurdles are faced by the prospective

[11] Based upon a talk by C. N. Sayen, President, Airline Pilots Association, before the Aero Club of Washington, D.C., April 26, 1960.

air traveler who would like to take a trip. Think of the poor individual who decides that he would like to make his trip by air and hasn't flown before. Assume this individual resides in a Chicago suburb. First, he must determine which airline goes where he wants to go. So, he places a toll call to the reservation office of one of the airlines. When he reaches the switchboard, the chances are pretty good that the reply will be, "Reservations are busy, will you wait please?" When he finally secures a reservations clerk, he may be able to determine which carrier goes where he wants to go. He then places another call to that airline and goes through the "reservations are busy, will you please wait" routine again. If he can secure a reservation, he is then informed that he should come into the city and pick up his ticket.

When he reports to the airport the required half hour before departure, if the trip hasn't been canceled or is not delayed without his being informed, he may stand in line for ten or fifteen minutes to have his ticket checked and his baggage checked. He may then walk from several hundred feet to a quarter of a mile to the gate where he is given another opportunity to stand in line for ten or fifteen minutes so that his ticket can be checked again. Finally, he is hurried out to the airplane and, on many occasions, he may then have another opportunity to stand in line, possibly in the rain, while the boarding pass or ticket is checked again at the door of the aircraft. Once on board the aircraft, things seem to go pretty well—except if he is hungry he will probably have to wait an hour or two while everybody has a drink. On arrival, there may be a wait of from fifteen minutes to a half hour for ramp space to park the aircraft, and possibly while his connecting flight takes off. Some airlines have improved their baggage handling considerably in the last one or two years, but on others he gets the feeling that the airline, having collected its money and carried him to his destination, has forgotten about him completely. No one says anything, nothing apparently happens. About the time he decides they have lost all the baggage (which they may have), a door opens and one or two porters slowly begin doling out bags one at a time to sixty or seventy passengers.

The foregoing is not descriptive of all airlines, but, unfortunately, it is descriptive of many, and the infrequent air traveler who does not understand everything that is going on finds it completely frustrating. Of course, the foregoing has concerned a relatively simple trip from a single departure terminal and without any connections. Unfortunately, there are multiple airports serving a single city and, even worse, separate terminal buildings for each airline at a single airport at a multiple airport city. Consider the plight of the poor first rider who tries to find his way through this maze.

Some way must be found of treating the airline passenger like an adult person who is entitled to at least some courteous treatment. It should hardly be necessary for him to purchase his ticket six or eight hours before his trip and thereafter have his ticket checked three or four times before he can board the aircraft. There must be some way around the long waits and the construction of terminals in which people must walk several thousand feet with luggage, babies, and so forth, to catch airplanes. Also, the building of separate terminals for each airline where connections must be made seems the height of absurdity.

The airlines are entering a period when they will have considerable excess capacity which must be sold in a more competitive market as a result of duplicating route awards. On international routes, foreign air carriers have proved to be hard competitors. Against this, only a small percentage of our population and business enterprises has learned to utilize air transportation. The industry faces a great challenge in coping with the increased capacity.

Several areas urgently require study and action. Improved methods of handling passengers on the ground must be found. The speed of air travel will make passengers increasingly impatient of inept reservations, ticketing, and slow, tiresome ground handling. While the income of the carriers must be improved to meet increasing costs, a flexible system of promotional air fares to encourage travel is imperative. Lower passenger and cargo rates are necessary where increased load factors can be promoted during low traffic periods or in specialized aircraft for this purpose. Costly terminal area and air traffic delays must be reduced.

Chapter 16

AIR EXPRESS AND FREIGHT DEVELOPMENT

ONE of the most interesting aspects of air transportation since the close of World War II has been the development of both air express and air freight, usually lumped together by the airlines and called "air cargo." The growth of these two types of service is shown in Table 32. In the last few years, new types of service have become available; new carriers have entered the field; rates have been markedly reduced; and the volume of service has greatly expanded. But in this period of rapid development, there has been a tendency to lose sight of the fact that air cargo is really not new, that some aspects of it are older than the present airlines themselves. There has also been considerable misunderstanding of the history of air cargo development and of the agencies most responsible for its present status. In order to understand the problems that must be resolved if air transportation is ever to develop as a major factor in intercity transportation of property, it is necessary to review the background of air cargo growth and to indicate the agencies most responsible for its development at various times.[1]

In recent years the volume of air freight has grown very rapidly while air express has remained relatively constant. Yet air freight and express combined have never accounted for as much as 1 per cent of the total intercity movement of freight traffic. Forecasts of potential air freight, in particular, usually predict further expansion as rates are progressively lowered; nevertheless, even the most optimistic predictions foresee a volume of traffic which for some time to come will, in absolute size, still be only a minor part of the total movement of commodities in the United States.[2]

[1] For a more detailed discussion, see John H. Frederick and Arthur D. Lewis, "History of Air Express," *Journal of Air Law and Commerce*, July, 1941; John H. Frederick, "American Air Cargo Development," *Air Affairs*, Autumn, 1947; Richard Malkin, *Boxcars in the Sky* (New York: Import Publications, Inc., 1951).

[2] In 1958, for example, percentage distribution of intercity freight traffic in the

TABLE 32

DEVELOPMENT OF AIR EXPRESS AND AIR FREIGHT, 1926–59

Calendar Year	Express Ton-Miles*	Freight Ton-Miles Combination Airlines*	Freight Ton-Miles All-Cargo Certificated Airlines	Freight Ton-Miles Noncertificated Carriers	Total
1926	996	....	....	....	996
1927	12,841	....	....	....	12,841
1928	58,913	....	....	....	58,913
1929	69,898	....	....	....	69,898
1930	100,666	....	....	....	100,666
1931	220,657	....	....	....	220,657
1932	289,512	....	....	....	289,512
1933	422,860	....	....	....	422,860
1934	597,293	....	....	....	597,293
1935	1,089,802	....	....	....	1,089,802
1936	1,860,809	....	....	....	1,860,809
1937	2,156,070	....	....	....	2,156,070
1938	2,173,706	....	....	....	2,173,706
1939	2,705,614	....	....	....	2,705,614
1940	3,469,485	....	....	....	3,469,485
1941	5,242,529	....	....	....	5,242,529
1942	11,691,208	....	....	....	11,691,208
1943	15,117,925	....	....	....	15,117,925
1944	17,094,029†	....	....	....	17,094,029†
1945 Jan.–June	11,926,481†	....	....	....	....
1945 July–Dec.	9,235,413	1,402,241	....	....	22,564,135‡
1946	23,788,392	14,822,325	....	25,183,610§	63,794,327
1947	28,766,659	35,911,554	....	47,409,062§	112,087,275
1948	30,092,833	71,283,727	....	48,115,218§	149,491,778
1949	27,773,669	95,227,983	10,541,146	45,000,000‖	178,542,798
1950	37,279,035	114,072,045	58,420,386	....	209,771,466
1951	41,268,219	102,356,646	80,851,306	....	224,476,171
1952	41,324,306	119,501,666	92,494,311	....	253,320,283
1953	43,470,800	134,460,726	89,902,278	....	267,833,804
1954	41,178,000	147,093,000	76,792,000	....	265,063,000
1955	51,043,000	177,029,000	107,944,000	....	336,016,000
1956	51,433,000	193,698,000	141,539,000	....	386,670,000
1957	44,426,000	222,057,000	156,762,000	....	423,245,000
1958	47,723,000	244,346,000	122,493,000	....	414,562,000
1959	55,357,000	287,227,000	142,066,000	....	484,650,000

* For domestic certificated airlines, trunk and local service.

† Includes both express and freight since there was no segregation by the Civil Aeronautics Board of freight and express statistics prior to July 1, 1945, and no airline carried freight as distinct from air express until American Airlines started doing so in 1944.

‡ Calendar year of 1945.

§ Includes the leading noncertificated carriers during those years: Air Cargo Express, California Eastern Flamingo, the Flying Tiger Line, Mutual, Riddle, Slick Airways, U.S. Airlines, and Willis.

‖ Estimated. Date for noncertificated carriers not available after 1949.

Source: FAA, *Statistical Handbook of Aviation* (Washington, D.C., 1960).

United States was reported as follows:

Railroads	44.6%
Motor vehicles	20.9%
Inland waterways	15.8%
Oil pipe lines	18.5%
Air carriers	0.03%

It is probable, therefore, that the importance of air freight in the nation's commerce will never be measurable in terms of its contribution in ton-miles to total intercity traffic. Rather, its importance to society will be measured in terms of unique benefits—chiefly arising from its speed—to certain industries in particular and to commerce in general. In many industries, the speed and other advantages which air freight offers have made possible marked improvements in production and distribution methods and in the quality of products delivered to consumers. Eventually, it is hoped that these benefits will result in a lower over-all cost to consumers. To commerce in general, air freight has already demonstrated its importance for emergency shipments of various kinds and for the new competitive influence which it represents in transportation. The importance of air freight to the airlines will, of course, be measured by the gross revenue from such traffic.

Early Air Express Development

One of the first experiments in the transportation of property by air in the United States occurred in the winter of 1919, when the American Railway Express Company, in testing the possibility of transportation of express on scheduled flights, loaded a Handley-Page bomber with 1,100 pounds for a flight from Chicago to New York. A series of accidents caused the flight to be canceled at Cleveland and the goods to be sent the rest of the way by rail. From that time until 1926, there was some minor development of air express service by fixed-base operators; but the lack of government subsidy, combined with the early stage of aeronautical efficiency, resulted in very high charges, which limited the use of the service by shippers.

During the latter part of the 1920's, the use of air for property transportation was stimulated by the transfer of the air mail service from the government to private carriers. The carriage of mail on fixed schedules, with its constant source of revenue, provided the basis for the transportation of express on scheduled flights at rates considerably lower than they had previously been, thus encouraging a wider use of the service. The way was open for the development of air express as we know it today.

In 1927, the American Railway Express Company entered into contracts with four airlines, establishing an air express service under essentially the same type of arrangement that has been followed since that time. These airlines were: National Air Transport, operating between New York, Chicago, and Dallas; Boeing Air Transport, operating between Chicago and San Francisco; Western Air Express, operating between Salt Lake City and Los Angeles; and Colonial Air Transport, Inc., operating between Boston and New York. The express company contracted to perform local pickup and delivery service, as well as any necessary surface transportation to off-airline points. It also conducted all direct relations with the public and handled accounting, claims, and other business functions. The airlines' participation consisted of the loading and unloading of aircraft and the actual line-haul transportation. (In fact, from that day to this, the American Railway Express Company and its successor, the Railway Express Agency, have been strictly ground-service organizations. They have never actually flown a pound of express.) Revenues from air express operations were divided between the express company and the respective airlines on a specified percentages basis after deduction by the express company of out-of-pocket costs resulting from its pickup and delivery service and from advertising, sales, and other such functions. Originally, 25 per cent went to the express company and 75 per cent to the airlines, but it was subsequently changed to 12½ per cent to the express agency and 87½ per cent to the airlines.

By the end of 1929, the system which the Railway Express Agency assumed after the reorganization of the American Railway Express Company included the ten most important airlines of the country, offering direct service to eighty-two cities. In that year, these airlines transported 75 per cent of the total air express of the country. In addition to the airlines under contract with the Railway Express Agency, there were numerous small mail carriers as well as passenger operators who were carrying air express.

In 1932, American Airways, Transcontinental and Western Air, Eastern Air Transport, Trans-American Airlines Corp., U.S. Airways, Pennsylvania Airlines, and Ludington Airlines jointly organized General Air Express, a subsidiary service organization managed by an interline committee, to provide a unified express service over their routes. Pickup and delivery were handled by the telegraph companies,[3] and provision was made for a uniform waybill and a single uniform charge for interline shipments. This was the first major rival of the Railway Express Agency service, and rates were

[3] The system was well adapted to the small packages then moving by air, and it associated the speed of the telegraph with air transportation in the minds of shippers and receivers.

established substantially below those of the Railway Express Agency. There followed a competitive period during which the rival organizations successively undercut each other, so that, for example, the ton-mile rate between New York and Chicago was reduced from $1.19 in December, 1931, to 87 cents in June, 1933. During the period of its operation, General Air Express handled approximately one fourth of the total air express traffic.

In 1935, all but one of the airlines belonging to General Air Express discontinued their arrangements with that organization and signed contracts with the Railway Express Agency. Transcontinental and Western Air fought such an alliance of the railroads and the airlines and for a short time tried to promote air express as an independent operator, but in 1937 it too joined the Railway Express Agency. By that time, the latter organization not only covered all the major domestic airlines but also had arrangements for rendering express service to Canada, Mexico, and other countries of the Western Hemisphere.

Several reasons were given for the abandonment of General Air Express and the consolidation under one organization: (*a*) The Railway Express Agency arrangement provided a uniform service. There would be but one waybill, one bill of lading, and one airway bill. (*b*) Shipments in many instances had become too heavy for the telegraph company messengers to handle. Trucks as provided by the Railway Express Agency would be more efficient. (*c*) It was felt that there was a decided waste in having two organizations engaged in advertising and soliciting the same traffic. Not only was there an overlapping effort in solicitation, but there was a tendency for the two to fight for each other's traffic rather than to develop new traffic. (*d*) The most economical and serviceable routing could now be employed irrespective of which airline the shipment went by. (*e*) The unification of ground auxiliary systems would reduce costs of pickup and delivery, since more traffic could be spread over the same overhead.

At this time it seemed to the airlines concerned that they had no other alternative, if they were to remain in the express business at all, than to abandon General Air Express and join the group served by Railway Express Agency with its greater traffic-generating power. It is doubtful, however, if this amalgamation would have been brought about as easily had the airlines not been in a somewhat chaotic state following the 1934 air mail contract cancellations and had they been in a stronger financial position and so able to allocate the substantial funds required for the creation of an airline-owned pickup and delivery system.

The arrangements made between the airlines and Railway Express Agency were in the form of contracts between the agency and each individual airline. Each contract was separate and distinct, with contractual relationships running between each airline and the Railway Express Agency but not among the airlines. Each contract, however, had the same terms and provisions, and all airlines were to operate in the same relationship to the Railway Express Agency. With certain modifications, the arrangement between the Railway Express Agency and the airlines remained substantially the same until 1954.[4] The revised contract which became effective August 1, 1954, contained no guarantee of 10 per cent of expense as profit for the Railway Express Agency, as formerly; reduced the former 12½ per cent of expense allowance covering administration and overhead to 9½ per cent; and changed the previous revenue split of 80 per cent to the airlines and 20 per cent to Railway Express Agency to 80.69 per cent for the airlines and 19.31 per cent for Railway Express Agency. In 1959, a further revision was made so that now certain specified costs are deducted from income and the remainder split 50–50 between Railway Express Agency and the airlines. Policy and management decisions are made jointly and tariffs are filed jointly.

The unification of the air express service that resulted after the airlines contracted with Railway Express Agency alleviated the former disadvantages arising from having two competing agencies, but the results of the single-company operation were in some ways disappointing. For example, it was thought that efficiencies brought about would permit reductions in rates and thereby stimulate traffic development. However, from 1937, when the air express service became unified under the Railway Express Agency, until well into the war period there was virtually no change in the air express rate level.

From this review of the early development of air express, it will be seen that the airlines regarded the transportation of property as an important part of their activities. In fact, the industry as a whole felt that air express would develop more rapidly than passenger traffic and centered many of its activities about that service. All this took place during the period of experimentation, and it was assumed that air express transportation would be the proving ground

[4] *Railway Express Agreements,* 4 CAB 157 (1943); *Railway Express Agency, Inc.,* CAB Dockets 5115, 5115 A1, 5115 A2 (1951–54); CAB Order No. E-9876 (1955).

of commercial flying and give the airlines experience in handling intricate and hazardous operating problems. Many early predictions of the future use of air transportation foresaw the immediate acceptance of this method of transportation; but these hopes were in vain, as developments showed.

Some of the reasons why air express transportation did not develop to the extent expected in the earlier years were: (*a*) The speed of air express, probably due to its lack of reliability, was not of sufficient importance to most shippers, then using rail express, to warrant their making the change and bearing additional transportation costs. (*b*) Lack of a nation-wide, co-ordinated air express facility retarded development. Attempts to develop traffic were carried on independently by several individual operators, with no direct connection with other transport operators. There was no general set of rules for handling, no co-ordinated scale of rates, and no general agreement on the handling of shipments between airlines. (*c*) Too much emphasis was placed on carrying goods by air, whereas the real problem was in setting up and operating adequate handling and selling facilities on the ground. (*d*) Many of the airlines organized at this time were inadequately financed to sustain the necessary developmental costs or even to carry on air express operations until the traffic, which might originate at lower rates, would be sufficient to justify the service.

A National Air Express System

The contract between the Railway Express Agency and the airlines made possible a national air express system. Experience had convinced the air carriers that the era of volume use of their services for the carriage of property had not yet arrived. The only advantage they had to offer was that of speed, and only a limited number of shippers appeared to value speed highly enough to pay the necessary rates. Recognizing their obligation to the public to offer the best service possible, but at the same time conscious of their own precarious financial standing and inability to finance a nation-wide pickup and delivery service, which was a necessary adjunct to an air express service, the airlines adopted the best alternative open to them and hired the already existing services of the Railway Express Agency. It is a fact that the carriers could not, on their own, particularly during the depression years, have established a service comparable to that offered by the Railway Express. Therefore, their action was, at the time, the most feasible way by which a national system of carriage of property by air could be developed.

The uniform and extensive nation-wide coverage provided by the combined Railway Express–airline organization, the devotion of considerable amounts of money for cargo developmental purposes by the airlines, the general improvement in the regularity of air service, and improved business conditions led to steady increases in express traffic.

In 1938 the Railway Express Agency applied for a certificate of public convenience and necessity as an air carrier under the "grandfather" clause of the Civil Aeronautics Act. It did not, however, seek authority to engage in the operation of aircraft. After some deliberation, the Civil Aeronautics Board decided, in 1941, that the Railway Express Agency should be classified as an indirect air carrier but, at the same time, exempted it from the certificate requirements of the act, thereby permitting it to continue its operations.[5]

In 1942, several of the larger airlines organized a joint research project to survey air cargo possibilities. Later, all the airlines were given an opportunity to participate in the costs of this research and to share in its results, and all of the certificated carriers availed themselves of the opportunity. The group making the study was known as Air Cargo, Inc. For a time it had an independent status, but during the war years was merged with the Air Transport Association.[6]

There is abundant evidence that, prior to our entry into World War II, the airlines were beginning to recognize the potentialities of a real air freight service, as differentiated from the air express or package service. However, before any airline plans for air freight development could be brought to fruition the United States was at war; and all energies and resources were devoted to the creation of a military, domestic, and international air transportation system and the reorganization of their own greatly reduced commercial services to handle priority passengers and property.

Wartime Developments

Although noncommercial in nature, one of the major wartime developments in the field of air freight transportation was the dramatic demonstration by the military services of the potentialities for transporting all types of commodities by air. The widespread operations of the Air Transport Command and the Naval Air Transport Serv-

[5] *Railway Express Agency, Inc., Certificate of Public Convenience and Necessity,* 2 CAB 531 (1941).

[6] The completed studies of Air Cargo, Inc., have never been made available to anyone except the subscribing airlines.

ice carried huge amounts of freight to all parts of the world, the total amounting to over 3,334 million ton-miles during the years 1942–45, or nearly 40 times the aggregate traffic carried by all of the domestic airlines from 1926 through the end of the war. In the one year 1945 alone, the military transport services carried 1,805 million ton-miles, or nearly 80 times as much cargo as did the domestic airlines during the same year.

Also, for the first time the speed of air transportation came into its own. Many items which under normal conditions would have been highly unsuited to this means of transportation were sent by air, and the nature and advantages of air shipment were, therefore, discovered for the first time by many new shippers and receivers. Between 1941 and 1945, the annual volume of scheduled air cargo (freight and express together) increased by approximately 340 per cent.

Because of the great increase in the demand for air cargo services, as represented by the tremendous amount of air express offered for shipment, the carriers, led by United Air Lines and soon followed by the other transcontinentals, inaugurated daily schedules carrying mail and express only. Of course, during this war period, it was impossible to carry out any long-range plans for air cargo development; but nonetheless the airlines continued working with certain types of shippers to develop cargo use and experimenting with various methods of handling. It became apparent that at least three basic factors were of major importance in determining whether a shipper would use air transportation for a particular shipment: (*a*) the value of the product; (*b*) whether the product was perishable or fragile; and (*c*) whether the speed of air transportation was of value because of an emergency situation, style factors, and the like.

In October, 1944, American Airlines established its "air freight" service,[7] with rates averaging approximately 44 cents per ton-mile,

[7] It has turned out to be unfortunate that at the time of the organization of General Air Express in 1932 the name "air express" was adopted. This was intended in no way to limit the size or type of property that the airlines desired to carry. The name "express" was a sales device to emphasize the speed of shipment, which was the airlines' main selling point. An effort has, however, been made by the strictly air cargo carriers in urging their applications for certificates before the Board, based upon the airlines' historic use of the word "express," to characterize the airlines' efforts in the property field as having been confined to package business. The airlines hold this to be without foundation since in the earliest days of commercial air transport a bright immediate future was seen for property transportation and any error was on the side of optimism as to the volume and mass of the business that was to be transacted. They also call attention to the fact that the equipment in use in the earlier days could hardly be considered spacious and that there were physical limitations as to what could be carried. As a matter of fact, it took many years of patient experimentation and development and the impetus of a war before passenger operations were conducted with fifty-passenger equipment; and the carriage of

door to door, with a deduction for those shippers or receivers providing their own pickup and/or delivery service. Originally, service was provided to forty-three cities, but it was expanded to fifty-eight terminal areas in which pickup and delivery service was provided by motor truck operators with whom American Airlines had contracted.

The essential characteristic of the American Airlines air freight service was a somewhat slower over-all speed than air express, for generally larger shipments, at a considerably lower cost. Shipments moving under this service had a "deferred" status, with air express receiving preference in the event of fully loaded planes. The original tariff filed for this service established a rate structure with four commodity classifications, based upon value of the commodity, bulkiness, and similar factors (see Chapter 9).

Postwar Developments

For at least a year after the end of the war, most of the scheduled airlines displayed comparatively little enthusiasm for actively promoting air freight; and not until the middle of 1946 had all of them filed tariffs with the Civil Aeronautics Board providing for such service in addition to air express (see Table 33). This delay in

TABLE 33

DATE OF ISSUANCE OF FIRST AIR FREIGHT TARIFF

Airline	*First Tariff Issued*
American	Oct., 1944
Baniff	Dec., 1945
Chicago and Southern	Aug., 1946
Continental	Jan., 1946
Delta	Aug., 1946
Eastern	Apr., 1946
Inland	June, 1946
Mid-Continent	Jan., 1947
National	Sept., 1946
Northwest	Nov., 1946
Capital (Pennsylvania-Central)	July, 1946
TWA	July, 1945
United	Feb., 1946
Western	June, 1946

developing air freight services has been generally attributed to the many problems facing the airlines in establishing their passenger

property has required similar experimentation and developmental effort. See *Testimony on Behalf of American Airlines, Inc., Intervenor,* CAB Docket No. 810 *et al.* (January 15, 1947).

business on a greatly enlarged postwar basis; but there was certainly an indication of a general feeling among airline executives that this type of traffic would not, for some time, yield any significant profit at the rate levels which would be required to promote the business. In this connection it is worth noting that, prior to World War II, the revenue from cargo traffic, chiefly express, typically represented about 3 per cent of total airline revenue. To some extent, it is understandable that this attitude should have existed and that the attention of the airlines should have successively shifted from mail to passengers and last to freight. This same order, it may be noted, applies in general to the relative importance of speed to these three classes of traffic. The value of speed for both mail and passengers is self-evident. In the case of freight, on the other hand, only a minor portion of the total market for the service is significantly and directly benefited by speed; and, even for these movements, the benefits are not always readily apparent without a considerable period of active development and experimentation.[8]

An immediate effect of the end of World War II was a tremendous increase in the number of air freight carriers. From the few airlines then quoting air freight rates, as distinguished from air express, the number increased so that there arose, within a comparatively short period of time, what amounted to a separate air transportation industry operating more large planes than were owned by all the scheduled airlines before the war.

Thousands of ex-servicemen, flyers and nonflyers alike, enthusiastic about what they had seen the Army and Navy accomplish in carrying things by air, were determined to get into the air freight business. Combined with this more or less natural desire to make some use of their wartime training was the sudden availability of transport-type planes, chiefly C-47's, the Army version of the familiar DC-3. Coupled with the men and planes was the fact that the airlines, fully occupied with their exceptional passenger and express traffic, had not developed air freight in the manner that shippers and others thought possible. A certain number of newcomers to the air freight transportation field, therefore, provided a real service; and for a short time in 1945 and 1946, while transportation facilities of other types were still congested, and for certain types of promotional shipping, these operators met with a certain amount of success.

The airlines had confidently looked forward to developing their freight services over a period of time, as equipment especially de-

[8] See U.S. Department of Commerce, *Industry Report, Domestic Transportation, June-July, 1947* (Washington, D.C., 1947), p. 18.

signed for such services became available, as costs became known, and as rates could be established. They had not expected to have to hurry about any of these matters. But developments after the close of World War II, chiefly the pioneering and promotional activities of the newcomers to air transportation which proved that freight traffic could be developed, forced the airlines to push their plans ahead, perhaps by several years, and to get into the real air freight business before they were always ready or be left out of it entirely. The results were constantly changing airline rates and methods of quoting rates and rapidly expanding airline services.[9]

No one knows exactly how many noncertificated air freight carriers went into business during 1945 and 1946;[10] but it has been estimated that there were as many as 150 carriers of air freight, in addition to the certificated airlines, operating at one time or another during 1945 and the middle of 1946. These organizations had between 400 and 500 transport-type planes in use, with an average of perhaps 10 employees per plane, or a maximum of 5,000 for the industry. At one time, nonscheduled or contract carriers of air freight were coming into existence at the rate of 40 or 50 a month when equipment was readily available. Toward the middle of 1946, however, while 10 or 20 new operators might enter the field in a month, some 20 or 30 would sell out, combine with others, or just fold up. The result was one of the greatest shaking-out processes that has ever taken place in any field of transportation and was accompanied by many personal tragedies involving the loss of veterans' savings and those of their friends and families. It was bewilderingly rapid, as were all aspects of aviation development directly after World War II. Something like what went on in aviation took place in the motor carrier industry, but it was spread over a period of years instead of months.

In June, 1947, the Civil Aeronautics Board adopted a new Eco-

---

[9] See Chapter 9. Air express rates, which had been reduced by about 12½ per cent during the war, were reduced by an additional 13 per cent as of January 1, 1946, bringing their new level to an average of about 61 cents per ton-mile. Scheduled air freight rates were reduced to a level of about 26½ cents per ton-mile in 1946 also.

[10] Figures filed with the Civil Aeronautics Board, in response to its registration requirement of 1946, confuse, rather than clarify, any attempt to measure the size of the independent air freight operations. This is so because the CAB registration statements did not differentiate between purely local operators who made occasional freight charter flights and the organizations devoting their entire time and equipment to such traffic. Some operators grew in a few months to considerable size; others shrunk; and still others went out of business during the period covered by the registration statements. The CAB registration statements, therefore, showed acquisition, sale, and leasing of equipment in such confusion that it was impossible to say just how many planes were actually in air freight service at any one time or even how many operators were in the business.

nomic Regulation permitting the operation of noncertificated cargo or freight carriers.[11] It allowed those operators who had been engaged in the air transport of property on May 5, 1947, and who had applied for certificates of convenience and necessity, to operate as common carriers until the Board had acted upon their applications. The Board handed down its decision in the Air Freight Case in 1949,[12] temporarily certificating four of these operators as common carriers and thus forcing the others, operating under the so-called "292.5 exemption," to suspend operations. The four all-freight or "air cargo airlines" certificated for a five-year period were Slick Airways, U.S. Airlines, the Flying Tiger Line, and Airnews. Later, in 1951, the Board granted Riddle Aviation a certificate to operate as an air freight carrier between New York, Miami, and Caribbean points.

In certificating these specialized carriers, even for a temporary period, the Board took the position that air freight was separate and distinct from the air express business of the airlines and should be treated as such; that the air freight business should be placed on a sound basis through the issuance of certificates of public convenience and necessity, rather than to permit operators to continue on the basis of a further exemption from economic regulation; and that the great air freight potential warranted the existence of strictly air cargo carriers alongside the "combination carriers," which are the airlines that transport passengers, mail, express, and freight generally in the same aircraft.

Development after Certification

The temporary certificates of convenience and necessity issued to the air cargo carriers as a result of the Air Freight Case were intended to initiate an experiment in the promotion and development of air freight traffic. The carriers receiving temporary certification were to have experimental status and were intended to participate in a test to be conducted under relatively stable conditions during the prescribed five-year period, at the end of which the Board would review the experience. This test period expired August 12, 1954, with only four of the carriers which had received temporary certificates surviving, and two of these in the midst of merger arrangements.[13]

[11] CAB Economic Regulations, sec. 292.5.

[12] *Air Freight Case,* 10 CAB 572 (1949).

[13] Of the carriers temporarily certificated in 1949, one, Airnews, which was to have had a restricted operation, never did get started, and their certificate was later revoked by the

During the five-year period it became clear that a strictly all-cargo operation was not an economic air transportation unit. The Board's expectations had been these:

1. That scheduled freight traffic would be developed far beyond the increase in traffic indicated by statistical projection.
2. That all-cargo carriers would be specialists in their field and would concentrate on all-cargo service.
3. That a demand type of service would best develop the air freight potential, and that service to demand points would in any event be adequate.
4. That rates would not advance and indeed might be reduced.
5. That the all-freight carriers would supply a cost yardstick, and would accumulate traffic and other data which would contribute to the sound development of air freight.

During the five years of the experimental period, none of these objectives had been achieved nor had the all-cargo carriers made a significant advance toward any of them.

Not only had the expected traffic development failed to reach the straight statistical projection contemplated by the Board as a minimum goal for the first four years of the experiment, but in that time it had reached less than 200 million ton-miles, whereas one carrier's forecast for the industry for 1953 was 1.2 billion ton-miles.

The second point anticipated that these all-cargo carriers would be specialists. The Flying Tiger's scheduled freight revenues constituted only 26.1 per cent of its total revenues in typical years, and Slick Airways freight revenue was only 47.4 per cent of its total revenue.

The thinking with respect to "demand type" service was also a failure, since for long periods not a single ton of air freight was enplaned at any demand point listed by both Slick and Flying Tiger.

The fourth expectation of the Board in granting these temporary certificates concerned rates—Slick Airways' forecast that rates would fall to 9 cents per ton-mile by 1950. Instead, this carrier's

---

Board. U.S. Airlines, running from Florida to the Northeast, operated but suffered various financial difficulties and did not develop much traffic. The Flying Tiger Line and Slick Airways, the two transcontinental air freight lines, both developed substantial common-carrier traffic, but even they did most of their business on a contract basis with various branches of the Armed Services. In 1953, the Flying Tiger Line and Slick Airways filed an application with the Civil Aeronautics Board to merge, and the Board approved this merger early in 1954. The companies held that a merger would enable them to improve service to the shipping public by consolidating low load-factor flights, to eliminate inefficient routing, and to alternate intermediate stops, thereby improving delivery time. The merger, however, was never consummated because of labor protection conditions which, the companies estimated, would have cost the surviving company several million dollars. *Flying Tiger–Slick Merger Case,* 18 CAB 326 (1954).

revenue per ton-mile moved from 12.71 cents in 1947 to 14.42 cents in 1952; and Flying Tiger revenue per ton-mile for the same years advanced from 12.84 to 16.25 cents.

In accordance with the revised minimum rate order issued by the Board on October 21, 1953 (see Chapter 9), freight rates were increased by 25 per cent. This action was taken at the request of the all-cargo carriers against the protest and objection of the combination airlines which were forced against their will to institute such rate increases.

The final point was that the all-cargo operators would supply a cost yardstick, but, on the contrary, the diverse operations of the surviving carriers served only to complicate further the problems of allocation which exist in any multiple-service operation. The different accounting methods followed by each company prevented a comparison of their operations with each other or with the combination airlines.

In 1954 and 1955, the Board considered the applications of Flying Tiger Lines, Slick Airways, U.S. Airlines, Riddle Airlines, and American Air Export and Import Company (AAXICO) for renewal of temporary certificates.[14] The result was issuance, in 1956, of new five-year certificates for all but U.S. Airlines, increasing the scope of operations of these carriers by permitting them to carry air express. They were also authorized to carry air mail on a nonsubsidy, strictly service-rate basis for a period of one year. Grounds for the renewal were the fact that the freight carriers were transporting a substantial amount of freight; that they had stimulated the growth of traffic; and that specialized freight carriers, which could not shift aircraft and equipment to the more profitable passenger fields appeared to be necessary to the development of the generally less profitable property field. There was also the fact that the combination airlines had failed to prove that their all-cargo operations were cheaper than those of the freight carriers by virtue of their passenger and mail operations; that their costs would be substantially lower if the all-freight carriers were eliminated; or that passenger aircraft were adequate for moving all types of air freight.[15]

---

[14] *Air Freight Renewal Case*, CAB Docket No. 4770 *et al.* (1955); *North-South Air Freight Renewal Case*, 22 CAB 253 (1955).

[15] Some idea of the problem of shipping certain commodities via passenger aircraft is gleaned from the fact that the combination airlines will usually not accept for carriage on its passenger aircraft the following: animals, tropical fish, birds, live lobsters, fruit, vegetables, garments on hangars, garments not boxed or crated, live plants, meats, perishables not in leakproof containers, and human remains.

From time to time, since 1956, the all-freight carriers have attempted to obtain amendments to the Civil Aeronautics Act and the Federal Aviation Act to require their permanent certification on the grounds that:

1. Their operations history gives every indication that this type of service has in fact become firmly established as a permanent part of the air transport picture. Furthermore, this growth has been accomplished without the aid of any subsidy whatever.
2. Operating under "temporary" certificates it is almost impossible for these carriers to obtain adequate long-term financing for the purchase of larger, more efficient, specially designed aircraft required for sound, economic development of the air cargo industry. For the same reason, it is also more difficult to build up firm working relationships with surface carriers whose services are an integral part of air cargo operations.
3. Cargo carriers are at a competitive disadvantage to permanently certificated lines in bidding for the services of topflight pilots and other airline personnel.
4. Lacking permanent status, cargo carriers have been faced with an almost continuous round of costly and time-consuming proceedings before the Board for certificate application and renewal. With the security offered by a permanent certificate, the money and executive talent now diverted by these proceedings could be turned toward improving airline operations and management.
5. Strengthening the all-cargo carriers' operations by placing them on a "permanent" basis would be of value to the national defense. These carriers served in both the Berlin and Korean airlifts; they now provide substantial supplementary transport services to the Armed Forces on a contract basis; and they form an important ready reserve of trained personnel and equipment in the event of a national emergency.

These efforts have been unsuccessful and opposed by the Board for the following reasons:

1. Though the growth of air freight has been substantial, it has not measured up to the Board's original expectations.
2. Profitability of all-cargo operations has been "disappointing."
3. There has not been enough experience in this field to evolve a stable route pattern or to allow the Board to fully determine what

type of permanent certificate is best suited to this class of service.[16]

Early in 1958, the all-freight airlines found themselves in trouble with one carrier, Slick Airways, discontinuing all scheduled cargo flights in February, which action was later approved by the Board.[17] At about the same time, Slick Airways, Flying Tiger, AAXICO, and Riddle Airlines asked to be placed on a subsidy basis. This was promptly denied by the Board on the grounds that "it is clear that the all-cargo carriers' certificates were issued upon the theory that the financial success of the carriers' operations would depend upon the employment of their own resources and not upon financial assistance of the Federal Government," and that, moreover, each carrier had agreed upon accepting an extension of its certificate, in 1956, that "it is only entitled to receive service mail pay for the mail service rendered and that it is not authorized to request or receive any compensation for mail service rendered or to be rendered in excess of the amount payable by the Postmaster General."[18] At the same time, the Board expressed its concern as to the financial condition of the all-cargo carriers as well as the entire course of the all-cargo "experiment," and concluded that it should institute an investigation and examination of the need for air cargo service in the United States at the present time; whether the all-freight air carriers' services should be continued; whether such services should be subsidized; whether their route authorizations should be modified, and whether the combination airlines should be authorized to provide additional all-freight services in lieu of or in addition to those provided by the all-freight carriers. This investigation was still in progress as of the start of 1961.

The difficulties of the all-freight carriers stem, as they have in the past, from the fact that all-freight operations are not economic in themselves, that the all-cargo airlines have never made any money simply from operating as common carriers of freight, that military contract and charter work have become more difficult to obtain on a profitable basis, that there is increased competition from the combination airlines with their larger jet-type aircraft and enlarged cargo capacity, and that the cargo carriers have been trying

[16] *Permanent Certification of Domestic All-Cargo Air Carriers*, Hearings before a Subcommittee of the Committee on Interstate and Foreign Commerce, United States Senate, 85th Cong., 1st sess. (Washington, D.C., 1957).

[17] *Slick Airways, Inc.*, CAB Docket No. 9287, Order No. E-12673, June 19, 1958.

[18] CAB Dockets Nos. 9376 *et al*, decided December 12, 1958. See also, *Domestic Cargo-Mail Service Case*, CAB Docket No. 10067 *et al* (1961).

to operate with inefficient aircraft with no funds for replacement.[19]

The all-cargo airlines complain bitterly about the Board's delay in deciding the Intra-Area Cargo Case (Docket No. 9258) and the fact that they have had to operate under restrictions on the carrying of traffic between points within general regions served. They also complain that they have not been able to adjust their rates to rising costs even though there were increases allowed in 1949, 1953, and 1956. They also complain that the Board has been backward in carrying out its promotional[20] responsibilities involving air cargo carriers and that it has not required the combination airlines to operate their freight services on a self-sustaining basis but has permitted these carriers to, in effect, subsidize any cargo losses they may have encountered first from mail pay and then from passenger profits. They also complain that while denying the cargo lines equal subsidy rights with the combination lines, the Board has consistently granted a steady flow of new routes and extensions to the combination airlines overlying the routes of the cargo operators and diverting or

---

19 The only United States all-cargo operator apparently in good shape in 1960 was Seaboard & Western Airlines operating solely in the international field where there is no surface transportation competition and where the combination carriers, at least during the summer, are so busy carrying passengers that they have little time for freight.

20 This claim on the part of the all-cargo operators is not well founded since from the outset of their operations the Board has given them solicitous attention. When contract operations proved unsuccessful, they were granted an unprecedented exemption to operate scheduled all-freight services. (Section 292.5 of the Board's Economic Regulations, May 5, 1947.) When noncertificated operations proved uneconomic, the Board established minimum rates for air freight based on the attainable costs of all-cargo operations. (*Air Freight Rate Investigation*, 9 CAB 340 [1948]). When noncertificated operations continued to be unsuccessful, the Board granted several all-cargo carriers five-year certificates of unprecedented scope and flexibility. (*Air Freight Case*, 10 CAB 572 [1949]). When the all-cargo operators requested reduced eastbound rates to fill empty eastbound capacity and thereby improve their revenue position, the Board granted that request. (*Directional Rate Case*, 11 CAB 228 [1950]; 16 CAB 254 [1952].) When the all-cargo operators objected to the payment of any subsidy to combination airlines to underwrite all-cargo operations, the Board prohibited any such subsidy. (*American Airlines, Inc., et al., Mail Rates*, 14 CAB 558 [1951].) When the all-cargo operators continued to suffer "substantial losses" so that "prompt rate relief is urgent," the Board granted their request to increase minimum air freight rates. (Tenth Supplemental Order, *Minimum Rate Case*, Orders Nos. E-7735, September 21, 1953, and E-7837, October 21, 1953.) When two of the all-cargo operators, Slick and Flying Tiger, proposed to merge in order to increase revenues and reduce expenses, the Board approved the merger. (*Flying Tiger–Slick Merger Case*, 18 CAB 326 [1954].) When this merger proved too costly, the Board approved termination of the merger arrangements. (*Slick-Flying Tiger Agreement*, Order Nos. E-86865, October 4, 1954, and E-8715, October 19, 1954.) When the all-cargo operators sought permission to carry first-class mail without a certificate but on a nonsubsidy basis, the Board granted such any exemption. (*Surface Mail by Air Exemptions*, 20 CAB 658 [1955].) When the all-cargo carriers' applications for renewal of their first five-year certificates were heard, the Board granted virtually everything they requested, including air express and mail authority. (*Air Freight Certificate Renewal Case*, 23 CAB 186 [1956].)

diluting their traffic. Finally, it is charged that the Board, while acknowledging that the dual rate structures maintained by the combination airlines were inequitable, had done nothing to correct the "abuse." (Under these structures, the combination airlines charge higher freight rates to noncompetitive points and use this advantage to maintain lower rates to points competitive with the cargo carriers.)

The loudest complaint of the all-cargo carriers is, however, directed toward the government-operated Military Air Transport Service and its use by the Department of Defense. Slick Airways, for example, points out that their earnings from military traffic fell off more than 50 per cent within a year when backlogs of cargo frequently accumulated at air force bases, awaiting MATS planes, while Slick or other carrier planes have stood idle. In fact, it is held that the government, despite the fact that it is the largest consumer of air transportation, has adopted policies ruinous to the civilian freight carrier. Directives of Congress calling upon the military to reduce its competition with the civilian carrier and channel specific percentages of its traffic into commercial air transportation have been ignored, it is alleged, and, at the same time, the military has set up parallel air systems transporting military freight which could as readily be carried by the all-cargo carriers.

Riddle has boldly put it up to the CAB in these words: "the Civil Aeronautics Act does not intend that the Board stand by in witness of the quiet expiration of the certified all-cargo industry, carrier by carrier . . . (the) Civil Aeronautics Board, must provide mail pay sufficient to meet the 'need' . . . it is not a matter of choice for the Board." The CAB is vulnerable here as when, in 1956, they renewed the all-cargo certificates for another five years it was said: "These (all-cargo) carriers are performing a useful public service . . . and . . . their service is required to exploit our vast untapped cargo potential in the interests of our commercial needs. . . . We would be derelict in our duty if we did not give them as much assistance and encouragement for economic survival as we can within the framework of the act."

Of course, the combination airlines have all along contended that a specialized all-cargo service was not necessary and that they were able to provide any service demanded by shippers. They will object strenuously to subsidization, and they now seem to be in an "I told you so" position. Certainly combination airline cargo business has continued to grow as the services, promotion, and sales activities have improved.

The Air Freight Potential

Despite the growth in air freight since the close of World War II, its rate of development has been disappointing to many forecasters who had seen a much more rapid increase. For example, in 1948, the Civil Aeronautics Administration predicted that, by 1955, 1,150,-000,000 ton-miles of domestic air freight would move at an average rate of 18 cents per ton-mile. In 1945, Douglas Aircraft predicted that 5 billion ton-miles would be moving by 1950 at an average rate of 9 cents per ton-mile. Reference to Table 32 will reveal that nothing like the volume predicted moved in the year indicated.[21] In 1952 the Civil Aeronautics Administration again reviewed the situation and predicted that domestic commercial air freight volume would rise gradually to an estimated 400 million ton-miles by 1955, and to 600 to 800 million ton-miles by 1960, depending on the vigor with which the air carriers developed the potential and assuming a continued high level of prosperity for the national economy and no substantial change in rates or equipment during the period fore-casted.[22]

Several factors account for the wide divergence between early air freight forecasts and actual accomplishments. Probably the most important was the fact that the transportation of air freight was a new industry at the time when most of the predictions were made, and not enough data were available on which to base any reliable projection. Thus, in each case, the forecast largely reflected the optimism or pessimism with which an individual forecaster viewed the future and his own assumptions regarding the interaction of such factors as: (*a*) the amount of existing traffic which could be diverted from surface carriers; (*b*) the amount of new traffic which air shipment could generate; (*c*) the possible future of the nonscheduled air carriers; (*d*) the rate structure which air transport would be able to operate under; (*e*) the type of commodities which tended to profit most from air shipment.[23]

---

[21] Civil Aeronautics Administration, Staff Study, *Domestic Air Cargo Forecast 1955 & 1960* (Washington, D.C., 1952).

[22] See Stanley H. Brewer, *Air Cargo—The Big Breakthrough*, University of Washington (Seattle, 1959).

[23] Civil Aeronautics Administration, Staff Study, *op. cit.*

Many of the forecasters also overestimated the rapidity with which air transportation would penetrate the assumed potential. For example, it was generally assumed that there would be a fairly rapid diversion of traffic from railway express, considered to be highly competitive with the air freight service. While railway express traffic has been the source of the largest part of air freight, this penetration has been much lower than was anticipated. Again, a large potential was estimated by certain forecasters in fresh fruit and vegetables, sea foods, and other perishables, but this potential has never fully been realized.[24]

It must be recognized in considering the volume of air freight that may move at any particular time that there will always be a certain proportion of the total property shipped by air that will be transported on a contract basis or in airplanes owned by shippers. It is also probable that contract carriers will continue to operate alongside common carriers and that these contract carriers will handle a substantial volume of freight.[25]

Abnormal economic conditions gave a considerable impetus to air freight movement in the postwar period, but actual experience has demonstrated that there is a real and continuing field for contract carriage in air transportation. Many shippers control sufficient quantity to pay them to employ an entire aircraft to take care of their traffic, or a shipper may have peculiar packing or in-transit requirements which make it advisable for him to have one special carrier do all his business because of special services a contract carrier will give him. Furthermore, the really large shippers who come to use air freight may well purchase their own aircraft and operate their own air transportation in much the same way that they have purchased trucks to meet their particular needs. The price of aircraft will certainly not be prohibitive for some volume shippers; and, if they have their own trucks to render pickup and delivery service,

---

[24] It has been held that a major factor contributing to the slow development of traffic volume in fresh produce was the tendency to neglect the marketing of airflown perishables. The airlines failed to realize the relationship between air cargo transportation and marketing. Apparently, it was felt that rate reductions alone would generate a satisfactory volume of traffic, but this was not true unless the marketing problems inherent in perishable traffic were solved. See Dwight L. Gentry, "Air Cargo Transportation and Marketing," *Journal of Marketing*, July, 1952.

[25] Carriage for contract had its origin in motor truck operation. It is an arrangement whereby the carrier transports goods under special and individual contracts with particular shippers. The equipment in which the transportation is performed is owned by the carrier and operated by personnel employed by him. The carrier is liable for the goods transported and also to the public for loss and damage arising from such an operation. See G. L. Wilson, *Motor Freight Transportation and Regulation* (Chicago: Traffic Service Corporation, 1937), p. 22.

it can be expected that some of these shippers will enter air transportation for their own account.

It must, therefore, be realized that whatever the air freight potential may be, it will not all go by common carriers, a fact which seems to have escaped the attention of many of the applicants in the Air Freight Case. Probably common carriers will, in the future, haul no more than half the total amount of air freight that may move in the United States. Moreover, if we are to have any volume of such transportation at all, the potential, whatever it may be, can only be developed by an intensive promotional campaign and educational program to convince shippers of the advantages and economies of shipping by air.

It seems apparent that air freight will not for some time compete with surface agencies on a basis of rates alone. Shippers, however, will use air wherever its speed can produce values translatable into the price consumers are, or will be, willing to pay; they will also use air transportation if their total distribution costs can be reduced in an amount greater than the difference between air rates and those charged by surface carriers. Conceivably, the shipper of any product able to fit into an airplane may, under certain conditions, find the speed of air transportation worth its extra cost.[26]

Air freight will, in many cases, offer shippers certain ways to reduce distribution or financing costs. Interest charges on the money invested in valuable articles while in transit will be lessened, as well as money invested in inventories of many types. In such cases, receivers may be willing to pay higher transportation costs to gain an advantage. Except in special instances, however, the importance of these factors becomes apparent only when the differential in speed is measured in weeks rather than in hours. For example, the differential in time for air express over rail express from New York to Los

---

[26] The greatest asset of the air carrier in competition with surface carriers is, of course, its speed. As used in transportation, speed has a number of meanings, among them: (*a*) time per mile while in motion; (*b*) time between originating and terminating stations; (*c*) time between shipment and receipt; and (*d*) "constructive time" between shipment and receipt, or time which is commercially productive to shipper or receiver. It is obvious that the last named is the most significant concept in any discussion of speed as a marketable service. Time in motion, per se, is rather meaningless. For example, if a shipper sent out an order at 6:00 P.M. because this customer needed it at the opening of business at 9:00 the next morning, it matters little whether transit time is one or twelve hours. So long as the order is on hand at the time required, all the advantages of speed have been utilized. Similarly, the carrier which is faster in motion but is delayed at way-stops may take a longer time to cover the route than the slower carrier making a nonstop haul, and the carrier that neglects to deliver its cargo promptly from the terminal to the receiver may lose all its advantages in speed entirely. See Civil Aeronautics Administration, *Domestic Air Cargo* (Washington, D.C., 1948). See also George M. Shutes, "Airfreight from a Marketing Viewpoint," *Journal of Marketing*, October, 1960.

Angeles at the present time is three days, so that at 6 per cent the interest on this time saved would represent only five mills on a hundred-dollar shipment.

Savings in weight of packing and crating may also reduce the over-all cost differential between air and surface transportation, when new packaging methods have been devised. Such a narrowing of the cost differential, however, is likely to be gradual, inasmuch as packing for air freight may require just as much strength as that for surface carriers, because of ground handling at both ends of the haul. The experience of the Army and Navy air transport services during World War II demonstrated that substantial packing economies are possible for almost all commodities flown. These economies for certain commodities reached 70 per cent of the total shipping weight, while the average reduction in shipping weight was reported as approximately 30 per cent. Any general improvements in packing would, of course, reduce expenses not only for air transportation but for other methods of transportation as well.

The possibilities of extending market areas arising from the speed of air transportation may also encourage its greater use. This factor has been particularly explored in the field of perishable commodities, because less time in transit permits products to remain in prime salable condition for a longer period after reaching distant markets.

Wider markets may well develop for such tropical and semitropical perishables as mangoes and avocados, for fresh sea foods, for baby chicks and poults, and for other commodities now closely restricted to the localities of their supply. The most important development in this field has been in fresh-cut flowers, the transportation of which has become a mainstay of the strictly air freight operators. Little has been accomplished as yet with fruits and vegetables of lower value.

The availability of air freight may make it unnecessary for a distributor to maintain any inventory at all for certain specialized products. Under such circumstances, savings and interest charges may become significant, but even more important probably will be the savings in warehouse space and the like.

Air Freight Service on an Area Basis

Experience has shown that better service is rendered shippers and receivers and more money is made by the air carriers if they confine themselves to flights between distant areas of the country and to or from all markets or producing centers in such areas without attempting to serve points between areas. In other words, it has been discovered that the passenger route pattern of airline service, as laid down for the combination carriers in their certificates of convenience and necessity, does not necessarily apply to strictly cargo operations. This fact might have been expected to emerge after air freight started to really develop because such movement does not necessarily follow the pattern of population distribution. This is especially true with perishables where many important producing points are very sparsely populated (for example, several very important perishable shipping points of California and Texas have populations of less than 10,000 each).

Several important air freight generating or consuming areas have been discovered in the United States. These are generally referred to as "air freight areas," which may be defined as sections of the country producing substantial quantities of such traffic produced outside the area. In determining the boundaries of an air freight area, one is concerned, therefore, with the volume of air traffic that may be interchanged by one area with other areas. This must be a two-way traffic consisting of considerable quantities of products susceptible of air shipment so that carriers will be able to develop relatively high load factors.

Another consideration dictating the size of an air freight area is the continuity of its production. For example, in Louisiana, a principal source of air cargo is sea food. Other air freight traffic is made up of agricultural products of a seasonal nature, such as strawberries which are only produced for three months out of the year. Obviously a three-month producing season would not permit of year-round schedules into this area, but, by combining into one air freight area the sections which produce strawberries and those producing sea food, a year-round outbound traffic from the area as a whole may be assured.

A third consideration entering into a determination of the size of an area is the flexibility of the service which can be provided for shippers. This flexibility is important in both originating and terminating flights. While New York City, for example, is a large consuming point for perishables produced in other air freight areas, the New York market may at times become glutted. The inclusion of other large cities such as Washington, Boston, and other consuming points in the same area with New York permits diversion of flights to those cities where the shipper may find more demand for his products at some particular time.

A fourth consideration limiting the size of an area is the amount of nonrevenue flying which may have to be done within it. Since usually no service within an area is contemplated, it should not be so large as to involve an undue amount of ferrying of planes.

All these considerations are important because: (1) It is axiomatic that aircraft should be operated with as high load factors as possible. In order to attain high load factors, it is necessary to determine areas where the outbound air freight traffic is roughly in proportion to the inbound traffic. (2) An area service makes possible a flexibility of operation of great importance in the transportation of many products. Shippers of fresh fruits and vegetables, for example, must have an adequate number of aircraft at the right places at the right times. Also, the destination as well as the origin of agricultural air traffic changes from time to time so that a service rendered between areas is more suited than is a service between designated points. (3) Under the area plan, shippers are offered both direct service and broad geographical coverage. Moreover, the area plan of service, by broadening the sources of traffic originated and terminated, makes possible higher load factors and hence eventually lower rates to shippers. (4) An area operation permits the operating flexibility of air transportation to be fully utilized and recognizes essential differences between the requirements of air freight and passenger transportation. It compensates for the fact that a community may originate shipments yet may not be an important delivery point and *vice versa.* Also, while making service immediately available to an entire area, allowance is made for the present status of air freight since it is still difficult to determine the total possibilities of an area and to select all the specific points which should be served now.

In developing air freight on an area basis, it is not contemplated that service between points in the same area will be rendered because the advantages of air transportation are not as great over short distances where overnight truck and rail express service are generally available and air service has less chance of competing with ground transportation. Also, service to points outside of an area is not contemplated, except to other areas, because such points do not usually produce a volume of air freight traffic equal to the consumption of such traffic and high, consistent load factors cannot, therefore, be maintained. Through service from area to area has been found to be the most profitable.

Air freight experience indicates that the westbound and southbound traffic most readily available consists largely of manufactured goods requiring prompt distribution. Eastbound and northbound, the bulk of traffic consists of perishables, flowers, and some merchandise. The westbound and southbound traffic requires close scheduling, while perishable traffic requires great flexibility. Almost all air freight shippers desire arrivals to be on schedule. In some cases, particularly for perishables, departure times can be varied to some extent to permit certain economies resulting from more flexible scheduling of equipment. In general, merchandise shipments require regular schedules daily, whereas perishable shipments fluctuate over a wide range from week to week, or month to month. This set of conditions makes it essential to provide, first, a scheduled service, and second, a flexible service. It is thought that the area type of service pattern meets these specifications.

The advantages of an area cargo operation, over service to a limited number of points, may be summarized as follows: (1) Direct long-haul service is provided to and from all points in an area, thus avoiding the time and expense of carriage to the major city in the area for transshipment. (2) By serving an entire area, the carrier can arrange schedules to "follow the crops" as well as to take care of any seasonal variations in manufactured goods, thereby maintaining higher load factors, greater plane utilization, and lower costs. (3) When an entire area is served, the carrier can draw on a greater diversity of types of shipments to maintain higher load factors and reduce rates. (4) Shippers are offered a choice of alternate markets within an area should conditions change while shipment is en route. (5) By making direct, long-haul service available to all points in an area, new production of both agricultural and industrial products may be stimulated, new distribution centers may be opened, and both buyers and sellers have a wider choice of markets. (6) Connecting entire areas by a choice of routes offers operational and dependability advantages with arrivals and departures co-ordinated to meet needs of shippers and receivers. This may be achieved through dispatching aircraft over the most feasible flying route, which is not always possible when point-to-point service is all that can be provided.

Considerations for Air Freight Development

There has now been sufficient experience with air freight to indicate the basic considerations for its successful development. These may be summarized as follows:

1. Air freight will move in the quantity foreseeable in the future only over relatively long distances, probably 500 miles or more. At the higher rates which air carriers must charge, the airplane will not be able to compete with rail and motor transport on distances where such surface carriers can provide overnight service. It follows, therefore, that the short, high-density passenger routes which have proven so profitable to the airlines, such as Boston–New York, New York–Washington, Chicago–St. Louis and the like will not be as profitable for air freight. The airplane reaches its maximum utility for freight on coast-to-coast and New York–to–Florida hauls, where its speed produces the important time savings which are its greatest contribution to efficient transportation.

2. There will always be a certain amount of seasonality in air freight transportation. Many, perhaps the majority, of the perishables which will move by air are what may be termed "ultraseasonal" in character, since it is the earliest crops, commanding the highest prices, that are likely to move. Such a crop as tomatoes, of course, may move the year round, but during the year they will be shipped to market from different places, as various crops ripen and are harvested in the varying producing regions. This creates the interesting situation that producing centers which require a high degree of regular, scheduled air transportation at the peaks of their producing seasons do not require any air transportation at all, or so little as to make it unnecessary to render them service, during the remainder of the year. Consequently, any air freight operation must be flexible enough to utilize its equipment throughout the year, perhaps flying a variable pattern of routes and schedules as demand dictates.

3. There will probably be a directional unbalance of flow for air cargo for some time, despite efforts to equalize it by rate adjustments. (See Chapter 9.) It has been found that westbound traffic exceeds eastbound traffic and that southbound traffic exceeds northbound. Unbalance in one direction is, however, nothing new, as it has long existed in the fields of rail, motor, and water transporta-

tion. Perishable air freight, for example, has a one-directional flow in every instance.

4. If the airplane is to achieve its maximum usefulness as a freight transport—and upon its doing so depends the very existence of the specialized air freight carriers—it has to go where things are and take them where people are. The oysterman in Hampton, Long Island, or the vegetable grower in Salinas, California, is not always satisfied by being told that air service is available at New York or Los Angeles. Such shippers do not want a long truck or rail haul from dock or farm to airport. If perishable products are to fly, they must fly immediately, not after hours have been spent getting them to the point of departure. Also, if the air transportation available cannot provide single-plane service to ultimate markets, shippers of perishables are not interested at all. The delays, damage, and expense involved in transferring cargo from one airplane to another almost always will offset the advantages inherent in air transportation. This means that, if we are ever to have large-scale use of air transportation for perishable shipments, interchange of equipment between presently certificated cargo carriers is desirable.[27] A soundly conceived air freight system must, therefore, be radically different from a sound passenger system, because each must be planned to accomplish an entirely different type of service.

5. "Scheduled" service for air freight will for a long time mean something very different from scheduled passenger service. To the airline passenger, hours and minutes are important. The time of departure, the time in flight, the time of arrival at destination all guide him in his selection of carrier and particular flight. To the air freight shipper, on the other hand, "scheduled service" does not mean split-second timing; it means "regularity" and "dependability" of service. The shipper in Florida has no concern with the minute that a northbound freight plane departs or arrives. If he is promised "next morning delivery" in New York, Boston, or Chicago, he has little reason to care when the airplane departs or arrives just so long as the service is otherwise satisfactory. Where the airplane goes, what route it follows, or what stops it makes are of absolutely no concern to the shipper. This means that the air freight carriers have a flexibility in their operations and a margin for irregularity

[27] While equipment interchange is certainly desirable, most perishable traffic passes through central wholesale markets, and the major markets are already served by each of the transcontinental and north-south certificated cargo carriers.

and schedule deviation that would not be possible were they transporting passengers.

6. No air freight carrier can as yet depend for livelihood on one or two types of traffic. It has been said that air transportation, in many of its characteristics, is akin to motor transportation and that, because it has been found that motor carriers may be sensibly and economically classified and restricted to the carriage of particular commodities, the same is true of the air carriers. This is not so; and, in the foreseeable future, air freight carriers must be permitted to carry a variety of traffic if their service is to be economically sound. This means that each freight carrier must have access to the sources and to the markets of the products and commodities which are most susceptible to air transportation.

7. Passenger routes sometimes furnish no clue whatsoever to the "community of interest" which might justify a freight route. This may well be one of the reasons why the airlines, certificated on a strictly passenger and mail basis, have found it so difficult at times to develop air freight business. For example, the *people* of Hartford, Connecticut, may have their greatest community of interest with New York City, and their greatest demand for transportation service may lie in that direction. Yet the *products* of Hartford may require transportation to factories in the Midwest and on the West Coast. So it is also with a fruit- and vegetable-producing area in California or Florida. The need of such an area for passenger air transportation to Detroit, Chicago, and New York may be virtually nil; yet those cities may represent the greatest markets for its produce.

8. Since air freight moves generally on long hauls and since the shipper, while he may be concerned with selecting the particular air carrier, is not interested in the routing to be followed, an air freight operator must be permitted a great deal of flexibility. The shipper of California peas or other perishables to the eastern market does not care whether his shipment reaches New York by way of Fort Worth, Kansas City, Denver, or a great circle course. Hence, an air freight operation should not be restricted to linear courses, defined by intermediate points, but should be authorized to fly between terminals over whatever airway or course offers the best flying conditions, just as do the airlines in their nonstop passenger operations between points like New York and Los Angeles. Flexibility in operations makes for economy and likewise permits greater regularity of service and prevents cancellations because of weather conditions.

Conversely, rigidity of routing serves no useful purpose in air freight operations.

9. Air freight rates will eventually have to be made on the basis of a classification of some sort (see Chapter 9). Except for a very short time at the start of air freight transportation, commodity or group, rather than class, rates have been used by the airlines and other freight carriers. At least four factors will probably govern whether a commodity is placed in a high or low class for rate-making purposes. These are:

(*a*) *Density or Weight per Cubic Foot of Space Occupied.* Unlike other carriers, aircraft cannot be loaded safely above their rated capacity, nor can their capacity be increased in any way to meet emergencies. Hanging loads are not possible in air transportation as they are for motor carriers, and trailer planes have not yet been developed. Therefore, since weight determines the carrying limitation of any airplane to a greater extent than is true of other means of transportation, it would seem logical that air freight should be classified with density or pounds per cubic foot as the chief governing factor.

Weight being the definite limitation on the amount of freight an airplane may carry, it can be seen that an airplane reaches its maximum operating efficiency when its area-cubic capacity is filled with shipments meeting the maximum weight capacity. Although there are many products that meet the requirements of both weight and area, the possibility of freight always being available to fill the area capacity and the weight capacity at the same time is unlikely.

Since rates are on a pound or ton-mile basis, it is more desirable for the carrier to attain the maximum weight capacity of an aircraft than it is to fill the cubic area. Air carriers are already figuring rates on the basis of a weight or measurement pound, whichever is the greatest, so as to reach the weight-carrying capacity from an income standpoint even though the area-carrying capacity is not fully utilized.[28]

(*b*) *Perishability.* The very essence of air transportation is speed, and perishable commodities have usually tended to use the most rapid means of transportation. Aside from the increased cost

[28] The measurement weight of a plane can be determined by dividing the area-carrying capacity by the maximum weight limit. This will give the area that can be allotted to a unit such as, for example, a pound. Air carriers have defined a measurement-pound as equaling 400 cubic inches. Of course, as progress is made in aircraft design for cargo, this figure might well vary with the different types of planes used by the air carriers.

to an air carrier of handling perishables because of special services required, there is also a definite increase in the risk of loss and damage. If a carrier accepts a shipment, it guarantees perfect delivery if at all possible. If the perishability of a commodity is high, the risk is increased. This increased risk, with the added cost of special handling facilities, would have the definite effect of increasing the costs of transporting such commodities and should be considered in any classification.

(*c*) *Fragility.* Like perishability, breakability will surely characterize many shipments by air. A commodity may be considered fragile when special care in handling or special packing is required to avoid damage under normal conditions of air transportation. In fact, the packing or crating of any shipment plays a very important part in determining its fragility from the standpoint of the carrier.

(*d*) *Value per Pound.* Value is very important in classification. The shipper of a high-priced or valuable article is much more able to pay a relatively high transportation cost than the shipper of a low-priced article. High-cost transportation is much more easily absorbed by a high-value commodity since the transportation cost is a proportionally lower part of its total cost than is the case for a low-value commodity. Therefore, any increase in price to cover the higher transportation costs has less effect on the market for a high-priced article than does a corresponding increase on a low-value commodity. Air carriers have already found it wise to require a declared value per pound above the base insurance value of all shipments, which proportionally increases the rate for more valuable shipments. This is because of the airline common carrier responsibility for loss and damage.

The number of items in an air freight classification should be kept as small as possible, and what is known as the analogous rule in ground transportation should be allowed to operate even more freely for the air carriers than it has for the others. This refers to the practice of placing articles with the same transportation characteristics into the same classes for rate making—for example, canned peas and canned pineapple or beer in glass bottles and ginger ale in glass bottles. In this way the classification will be kept relatively simple, and competitive items will automatically fall into the same categories. As an illustration, a very simple classification might make the following groupings on a volume-density basis rather than by commodities, as has been the usual practice with ground carriers:

Weight per Cubic Foot	*Class*
4–8 lbs.	A
8–12 lbs.	B
12–16 lbs.	C
Over 16 lbs.	D

If such a classification were used, a simple measuring device could be attached to the scales on which shipments were weighed and the proper classification assigned automatically.

A New Sales Approach

Despite the great growth in the air freight traffic during the past few years (see Table 32), and the fact that by 1965 an increase of as much as 670 per cent over present volume has been predicted, the airlines, both combination and all-cargo, have reached a point where, if this great volume is to be obtained, they must take a very careful look at their freight-selling techniques. In the first place, they must decide whether they really want to be in the air *freight* business or the small package business. (This, of course, applies with greatest force to the combination carriers.) The combination airlines all seem to have developed passenger traffic in much the same way, but there is a great difference between them when one looks at what they have done with air freight. Until lately, very few of the trunkline passenger airlines have displayed any great amount of interest in air cargo, and many shippers have come to the conclusion that the big airlines would rather not have this business but will handle freight if it is forced on them. There are various reasons for this attitude, but they can all be reduced to the matter of relative profitability.

Because the passenger, on the average, produces about 50 cents per ton-mile in revenue, he has been given a high priority along with his excess baggage yielding from 65 to 75 cents per ton-mile. Next has come mail with a yield of upwards of 38 cents per ton-mile, depending on the services performed by the airlines, because the cost of handling mail has been less than that of handling any particular kind of freight. Last has come many types of freight at rates ranging from as low as 12.45 cents per ton-mile to as high as 47.10 cents, but averaging around 20 cents. It is seen, therefore, that the least profitable business for the combination airlines has been the movement of freight. Even for the all-cargo carriers, aircraft charters and leasing arrangements, for their four-motored aircraft, have been more profitable than freight hauling.

As it now stands, freight is the stepchild of the passenger carriers and is not given major consideration in management thinking. This attitude is never openly mentioned, of course. The situation is quietly handled by holding back on selling freight service. As long as this attitude prevails, what do these carriers really have to sell? They have used their older equipment on their cargo schedules and will very likely continue to do so. (This downgrading is partly due to the competition between companies in the use of modern aircraft, but it is also a manifestation of the status freight traffic has in airline thinking.) They will purchase very few, if any, new aircraft for moving air freight. They will continue to carry freight in the baggage compartments of their passenger planes, thus keeping it a package business.

Much has been said about the increased cargo capacity of the new big jet aircraft. But these will be used, at least at first, in the very profitable long-haul and limited-stop operations. Passengers will be anxious to ride these modern aircraft, and so, in order to obtain maximum utilization, the airlines will cut ground time to a minimum which will simply eliminate time for loading and unloading freight. As is only natural as well as being vital to the carriers, business with the highest priority and earning power will be moved first.

Even without an increase of the present 40-pound baggage allowance to 60 pounds on domestic flights, as has been proposed, 120 passengers will require 4,800 of the 18,000-pound cargo capacity of a Boeing 707. Increased mail load when all first-class mail starts going by air, as it will eventually, plus excess baggage and express will use much of the remainder of this capacity. Loading time and package size limitations will also reduce the air freight capacity of the new jet aircraft. In fact, as the Boeing Airplane Company pointed out in a recent study, "intense competition for the cargo space in passenger airplanes is already a matter of some concern to the airlines."[29]

If the combination airlines are really interested in freight, they will begin scheduling stops and turn-around schedules for their aircraft so as to allow sufficient time for loading and unloading freight. They will eliminate practices now tending to delay freight with the

---

[29] Stanley H. Brewer, *Air Cargo—The Next Ten Years*, Boeing Airplane Co. (Renton, Wash.), 1957. The author is indebted to Professor Brewer for much of the discussion in this section.

resulting unreliability in delivery schedules. They will purchase all-cargo aircraft of the most modern design as they become available. The all-cargo carriers, on the other hand, will have to make a choice between being aircraft charterers and freight carriers.

If it is finally decided that the airlines are going to be in the air freight business, another aspect of the problem should be examined. For too long the airlines have used a passenger technique in selling freight service. This has meant an overemphasis on speed and speed alone. Such an approach has been fine for emergency traffic but will never develop the steady volume necessary for profits and the enabling of air freight to fulfill its potentialities. There is just not enough emergency traffic to spread between carriers so that everyone can make money.

Speed is really the second most important thing the airlines have to sell. Shipping by air is not only faster, but it is often the most economical way to do business, and it is this latter, less romantic aspect of the service that has to be sold to traffic executives. We all know that the airplane is the fastest means of transportation and that no surface carrier can come anywhere near it for speed, but what shippers need to be told is how this speed can be used in their business. More shippers have to be convinced that air freight is a normal, routine means of transportation.[30]

Lastly, methods of air freight pricing will have to be re-examined. Airline management has naturally been concerned with the broad problems of rate making and the adjustment of the rate level; at the same time, it has been influenced by the need for stimulating low rates to provide sufficient volume to insure operation. Too much attention has been given to making air freight rates competitive with ground rates without giving full credit to the service made available. Shippers are not as much concerned with the price of a line haul by air as they are by a complete and reliable service. Laid down, cost of one method of transportation versus another is more important when one takes all matters of inventory, insurance, packing, etc., into account.

Through past airline pricing methods and sales techniques, too many traffic managers have been trained to use air transportation

[30] It should not be thought that all airlines have neglected developmental selling based on total distribution costs as opposed to only transportation charges of a single shipment. For example, since 1955, American Airlines has been developing a program of long-range selling which proves to potential shippers that lower distribution costs, expanded markets, and improved customer service result from the use of air freight.

for freight movement only in cases of emergency. The small shipper, without a trained traffic manager, continues to place great reliance on what he considers "average rates" to determine his attitude toward one form of transport or another. He sees, for example, that average rail rates are reported to be 1.4 cents a ton-mile, truck rates slightly above 6 cents per ton-mile, and air freight rates more than 20 cents per ton-mile. But he fails to take into consideration the many factors to be examined in arriving at total transportation charges and particularly that there is very little comparison possible between air ton-mile rates and surface ton-mile rates between any pair of cities because of the differences in mileages. A big sales point for the airlines is that between the leading pairs of cities in this country air mileages average 26.36 per cent less than rail distances and 20.42 per cent less than highway distances (see Table 34).

TABLE 34

AVERAGE PER CENT OF DIFFERENCE AIRLINE MILEAGE COMPARED TO RAIL AND MOTOR DISTANCES BETWEEN SELECTED CITIES AND ELEVEN IMPORTANT SHIPPING POINTS*

City	Per Cent Difference Short-Line Rail and Air	Per Cent Difference Motor and Air
Atlanta	17.73	15.30
Boston	19.65	17.66
Dallas	25.24	21.02
Denver	25.45	20.90
Detroit	23.30	18.99
Chicago	24.43	20.87
Kansas City	21.58	16.79
Los Angeles	30.62	23.55
Miami	26.15	21.04
San Francisco	28.03	23.33
Seattle	24.01	27.01
New York	23.72	18.55
Average of Averages	26.36	20.42

* The cities were the same as those listed in the table.
Source: Compiled from Stanley H. Brewer, *Air Cargo in the Next Ten Years*, Boeing Airplane Company, 1957.

Another sales point for the airlines is that ground carrier rates, due to continued increases over the last few years, have now come quite close to air rates considering the line haul alone. Table 35 reduces average surface and air rates to an index basis to show that air freight rates have declined in relation to rail and motor carrier

TABLE 35

INDEX OF AVERAGE RAIL, TRUCK, AND AIR CARGO RATES

Year	Rail	Truck	Air Freight	Air Express
1947	100.0	100.0	100.0	100.0
1948	116.3	106.2	82.7	90.5
1949	124.4	108.1	81.9	88.6
1950	123.5	103.3	81.0	93.0
1951	124.2	106.7	88.2	98.9
1952	132.9	106.6	91.6	106.2
1953	137.4	118.4	93.7	107.0
1954	132.1	125.8	87.8	100.5
1955	127.3	134.7	95.8	105.7

Source: Stanley H. Brewer, *Air Cargo in the Next Ten Years*, Boeing Airplane Company, 1957.

charges. Indications are that the prices of all forms of transportation are coming closer together and will continue to do so.[31]

[31] See, Howard T. Lewis and Jack D. Steele, *The Role of Air Freight in Physical Distribution*, Harvard University (Cambridge, Mass., 1956); Stuart G. Tipton, *How the Businessman Can Use Air Freight in an Expanding Economy*, Air Transport Association (Washington, D.C., 1956).

Chapter 17

AIR FREIGHT HANDLING

THE airlines have found that problems involved in handling air freight are in many respects much more complicated than those encountered in handling passengers. This is due in part to the inanimate nature of all types of cargo, to the type of goods going by air, to marketing and sales conditions that help determine whether a shipper or receiver will use air transportation, to the costs involved not only in transporting freight through the air but in handling it on the ground, and to airport problems which are far different from those involving passengers.

The Pattern of Air Freight Traffic

When all property shipments by air were handled by express, the commodities then moving were those related to the speeding-up or functioning of industry rather than those for ultimate consumer use. But in 1945, when the airlines began to place some all-freight aircraft into operation, consumer goods began to be shipped by air in increasing quantities.

A shift toward consumer goods was natural as the base of air freight broadened. Consumer goods generally have lower density than producer goods. This is of extreme importance in considering the pattern, present and future, of air freight traffic. The limiting effect of the density factor on its development is obvious. According to a study by the United States Tariff Commission[1] only 3 per cent of commodities shipped in domestic freight have an average density of 6 pounds or less, only 18 per cent of 15 pounds or less, and only 27 per cent of 20 pounds or less. (Density means the weight of a commodity that can be put in a cubic foot of space.) Moreover, most of the lower-density items are concentrated in highly fabricated commodity groups—for example, in textiles and apparel products. By contrast, agricultural and fishery products, in which it is hoped that a substantial volume of air freight traffic will develop, have

[1] See Civil Aeronautics Administration, *Domestic Air Cargo* (Washington, D.C., 1948).

higher average densities than the average of all commodities studied by the Tariff Commission. Only 1 per cent of this group has an average density of 10 pounds or less, only 4 per cent of 15 pounds or less, and only 11 per cent of 20 pounds or less.

The growth of all-cargo operations since the close of World War II compelled increasing attention from the carriers to the density problem. The nonscheduled carriers, faced with the necessity of obtaining higher pay loads for their aircraft devoted exclusively to freight, specialized in the development of traffic in apparel, dry goods, cut flowers, leather products, sea foods, and meats. All these products fell within commodity groups with relatively lower density than the machinery, electrical appliances, and vehicle parts, the most important commodity groups from which the certificated carriers drew their freight traffic. Concentration on low-density items, particularly when coupled with high value, appears to be the path that promotional activity in air freight should take as offering the best possibility for steady development.

It should be borne in mind, however, that, while low-density items offer good prospects for air freight, their carriage involves extra handling costs as a rule and, when lower than the effective density of any particular airplane, means unused weight capacity. This accentuates the problem of obtaining a proper "mix" of commodities in air freight traffic for maximum efficient operation, as well as the need for radical changes in equipment design, which might substantially increase effective density.

The present pattern of air freight traffic indicates that a full pay load of consumer goods is more valuable to the carrier than a full pay load of producer goods. Promotional activity in the consumer goods field was stimulated by inauguration of all-cargo operations, which compelled consideration of the value of a full planeload of commodities as distinct from the value of commodities in a given cubic foot of space.

The Civil Aeronautics Administration has examined those basic attributes of commodities which are most relevant to measurement of their air freight potentialities. Two of these, density and price, were found to be basic commodity classification criteria for this purpose. Density and price together measure the relative value which can be put into a given amount of space. Applying their air freight susceptibility ratings to various commodity groups established by the Bureau of the Census and other governmental agencies, it has been estimated that, during the next few years, the percentage of enplaned cargo attributable to each would be as shown in Table 36.

TABLE 36

PROBABLE COMMODITY GROUP DISTRIBUTION OF AIR FREIGHT

Commodity Group	Per Cent of Enplaned Freight
Food and kindred products (processed)	6.2
Tobacco (processed)	3.6
Textile-mill products	18.0
Apparel	27.6
Lumber and timber	.3
Furniture and finished lumber	.6
Paper and allied products	.4
Printing, publishing, and allied products	1.7
Chemicals and allied products	2.2
Petroleum and coal products	.4
Rubber products	.8
Leather and leather products	2.7
Stone, clay, and glass products	.3
Iron and steel products	2.2
Nonferrous metals and products	5.4
Electrical machinery	2.7
Machinery (except electrical)	5.5
Automobiles and equipment	4.5
Transportation equipment (except automobiles)	1.5
Miscellaneous industry products	5.5
Metals (selected)	1.8
Agricultural products	4.9
Imports (selected)	1.2

There are, of course, differences within commodities in each of these groups, and these differences modify the classification which is based primarily on density and price. Some of these differences are: (*a*) geographic concentration of source of supply, (*b*) the average distance hauled as a measurement of the market area, (*c*) perishability or seasonality, and (*d*) gross margins as a measurement of the extent to which a commodity may absorb relatively high rates.

Packing for Air Freight and Express

One of the principal economies claimed for shippers in their use of air freight is that savings will be made in packing costs. Such savings, it is often stated, tend to offset the higher rates of air transportation. There are certain savings in packing costs when goods go by air, and these would be greater were it not for the fact that nearly every air shipment has to use a ground carrier at either end of the journey.[2] Many air express shipments go part of the way by rail because they are destined to off-airline points; all air express and all air freight, with some very few exceptions in the perishables field, are moved to and from airports by truck. This means that containers have to be stronger and heavier than they might otherwise be for the air journey alone.

The Railway Express Agency applies only the general rule to air express that "all property shall be so prepared or packed as to insure safe transportation with ordinary care and handling." The airlines specify the following packing and marking requirements in their Official Air Freight Rules Tariff:

(*a*) Shipments must be so prepared or packed as to insure safe transportation with ordinary care in handling.

(*b*) Any article susceptible to damage by ordinary handling must be adequately protected by proper packing and must be marked or bear appropriate labels.

(*c*) Any article susceptible of damage as a result of any condition which may be encountered in air transportation, such as high or low temperatures, high or low atmospheric pressures, or sudden changes in either, must be adequately protected by proper packing and any other necessary measures.

(*d*) Each piece must be legibly and durably marked with the name and address of the consignor and consignee.

(*e*) Pieces with a floor-bearing weight in excess of that which may be handled by the carrier must be provided with a skid or base, suitable for use in available aircraft, which will distribute the floor-bearing weight to that which the carrier may accept. Such skids or base must be furnished by the consignor and included in the gross weight of the piece.

(*f*) Magnetic material will be accepted only when marked "Magnetic Material."

It will be noted that several of the above packing requirements result from the peculiar characteristics of the airplane as a cargo carrier. Shippers have to bear in mind the effects of low temperature and reduced pressure in case an unpressurized aircraft goes to high altitudes. Cut flowers, fresh vegetables, and certain liquids

[2] A florist in Philadelphia said: "We simply put the flowers in boxes with a little ice which arrive in much better condition. Economy is packaging results from this type of shipment, compared with rail express which has to be packed in ice in boxes and braced against slipping." By use of air freight, a florist saves from 7 to 10 pounds of ice in the packing of a 45- to 50-pound box. Again, a firm in Ohio shipping electric motors for phonographs to New England stated: "Shipping costs no more than Railway Express because no crating has to be done." The traffic manager of a western aircraft manufacturer said: "Some saving is experienced in the lighter crating and packaging of spare parts, and even on the motors and propellers. On the motors we estimate that the saving in crating weight is about 65 pounds each." See John H. Frederick, "Packing for Motair Cargo," *Distribution Age*, October, 1949; M. R. Baruh, "Air Freight Packaging," a paper presented at the California Air Freight Clinic, August 19, 1950.

might then be in danger of freezing unless properly protected. Low pressures, on the other hand, may start leaks in some containers, which makes friction-top cans containing chemicals or liquids vulnerable to high altitudes. The floor of an airplane is not very strong; and so the density of individual packages is an important factor, which accounts for the rule for reducing floor-bearing weight to 100 pounds or less per square foot. This stipulation is not as restrictive as it might seem because a relatively small box with a base of 27 x 16 inches occupies a floor space of 432 square inches, or 3 square feet. This box could, therefore, have a load of 300 pounds without exceeding the 100-pound limit.

Because the airlines carry a considerable proportion of air freight in combination aircraft with comparatively small doors or other openings for loading and unloading, they provide that "pieces of unusual shape, or weighing in excess of 200 pounds, or more than 20 by 24 by 44 inches, or whose combined length and girth exceed 132 inches, will be accepted only by advance arrangement." It is also provided that shipments requiring special devices for safe handling will be accepted only when such special devices are provided and operated at the risk of consignor or consignee, and that shipments requiring special attention, protection, or care en route will be accepted only upon advance arrangement. The rule about marking magnetic material is because shipments are stowed as far as possible from the airplane's navigational instruments so as not to affect their accuracy.

Every now and then someone attempts to generalize on packing costs, comparing air with other forms of transportation. But unless these comparisons are based on the results obtained by actual experiments with specific shipments, the information is likely to be inconclusive or somewhat misleading. It is impossible to say with any accuracy that freight of a certain character, packed for shipment by rail or motor carrier, will, under all conditions, weigh a given amount more per unit or that the packing for ground carrier movement costs a definite amount per hundred pounds more or less than the same product packed for air transportation.

In some cases, goods can be shipped by air without any packing at all, if suitable pickup and delivery trucking arrangements are made at the journey's start and end. In such cases, it follows that large savings can be made from the absence of packing costs and charges for excess shipping weights. Such situations are, however, the exception rather than the rule and apply generally only to full-plane shipments.

There is comparatively little air freight moving in full plane-loads. The majority of air shipments weigh less than 200 pounds each, and few shipments exceed 500 pounds. This means that air freight traffic is loaded and mingled with other shipments, with baggage, and often with mail. It is therefore subject to all the stresses and strains incident to loading and unloading and handling at transfer points. It is also subject to a certain amount of damage from the weather, since few airports are yet adequately supplied with warehouse space for air freight sorting and holding until picked up by consignee or loaded at originating point. There is also the danger of loss from pilferage, which is sometimes increased by the lack of packing or by light, easily opened containers.

Under present air freight handling conditions, such shipments should be packed just as securely as if they were going by rail or motor carrier. In fact, as air freight traffic increases in volume, in distances hauled, and in the number of transfers between connecting carriers, packing requirements will certainly get closer and closer to those which experience has shown are desirable for shipment by ground carriers. But *secure* packing does not necessarily mean *heavy* packing, because lightweight containers, such as the corrugated box, have decided advantages.

Air freight rates are high as compared to those for ground transportation, and so it is to the shipper's advantage not to pay for any more weight in his containers than necessary. Most air freight is still loaded and unloaded from aircraft and trucks by hand, and here the lightweight container has a decided advantage in overcoming the natural inclination of all cargo handlers to "let gravity do the work." Bearing lightness in mind, therefore, standards of air freight packing are not very different from any others; and the practices of good packing, which have been in force for years on other carriers, all apply to air transportation.

Security for Air Freight

Up until very recently, air carriers have had a splendid record for low loss and damage to shipments. For example, one airline over quite a period of time paid claims for damage and loss running less than 1.5 per cent of total freight revenues. More recently, however, claims for loss and damage of air cargo have increased. Air freight and express may still be side-line business for most airlines, but where claims paid on single shipments run sometimes to several thousand dollars, the problem of greater security for air cargo becomes important whether volume or earnings from this source are large or small.

Adequate security for air freight must be considered in the light of (*a*) pickup and delivery service, (*b*) handling on the ground at airports, (*c*) stowage in aircraft, and (*d*) the air haul.

As will be explained later in this chapter, the pickup and delivery services for most air carriers are conducted in the various cities by independent truck operators under contractual arrangements with individual carriers or through Air Cargo, Inc. Security for shipments is equal to that for any motor freight movement. The ground haul at each end of the air haul is, therefore, not directly under the supervision of the air carriers. Air freight is picked up with other freight, is very often mixed with it in the local cartage operations, and is sorted at a downtown truck terminal before being taken to the airport. This means that it is handled no differently from other motor freight and should be packed as securely as any shipment going all the way by truck.

After an airplane is in the air, its cargo gets the benefit of the smoothest means of transportation available. Because of this, air freight salesmen have been able to promote the transportation of certain commodities with minimum crating and minimum packaging. Too often, however, sufficient attention has not been given to the ground-handling problem to and from the airports and at the airports themselves, where 95 per cent of the loss and damage sustained by air freight is experienced. In other words, ground-handling facilities and procedures have not kept pace with the rather optimistic packing sales talks.

It has, of course, been realized that freight-handling facilities are in many respects still only equal to those of the dark ages—lift, lug and load, unload, lug and leave; in other words, manpower. In spite of a few improvements, ground handling and aircraft loading depend almost entirely on the physical strength and dexterity of the men in the various stowing or ramp crews. Greater mechanization of airport freight handling is an absolute necessity for greater security.

The airlines have been remiss in some aspects of employee training in the freight-handling side of this business. Even with the fullest use of mechanical devices, there is still the necessity for personnel training and discipline leading to careful freight handling if the light-packing sales argument is still to hold. It should be drummed into handling personnel day after day that they have an important part in building and holding volume, that air freight security is their responsibility as much as it is that of anyone else.

Problems of air freight and express stowage have received much study, particularly from the standpoint of making the greatest use of the available space so that a given aircraft will carry the maximum load and obtain the greatest possible revenue for a given trip. Considerable study has also been given the problem of stowage, so as to protect aircraft from damage, through devising methods of tie-down. Because an airplane climbs and glides down, banks and turns, drops into air pockets, and rises over invisible bumps, something much better than the usual band iron or dunnage familiar to rail shippers is needed. A sharp downdraft, for example, can lift an entire cargo off the deck of an airplane, and the resultant upward strain may be as much as a couple of times greater than the weight of the cargo.

Less study has been given to the problem of protecting the cargo itself from damage it may receive through the tie-down methods used to eliminate slack and protect the aircraft. Ordinary ropes, pulled as tightly as possible, are still used; and their effect on the packages on the edge of piles is obvious. Rods, beams, locks, and jacks comprising various "skyloader" methods are also still used more effectively than ropes but still not without some danger to lightly packed cargo. In all-cargo aircraft and in some cargo compartments of combination aircraft, built-in or strap bins are used, offering more security to individual shipments than either of the other methods. Future tie-down facilities will probably take the form of a net or "covering" type of equipment, plus the simple single tie-down unit, such as a single web strap or cable and hook with toggle arrangement for taking care of the unusual or extremely heavy pieces which require separate and individual tie-downs. Considerable experimenting has been done with preloaded containers for cargo aircraft and with the use of pallets. Some in the industry think these latter methods will answer many of the security problems.

There is also the problem of stowing freight so that one type of shipment will not injure another, as would happen if heavy shipments were piled on fragile materials, if shipments were scraped against projections or against each other, and the like. An amusing but costly experience of one cargo carrier illustrates a careless type of stowage which could have been avoided. It seems that an ostrich, a live one, was being shipped, properly crated to avoid kicking but with its head outside. The ostrich was placed next to a pile of light containers of orchids on departure from San Francisco. By the time Kansas City was reached and the load was inspected, the ostrich had lunched off over $500 worth of orchids! (Probably the most expensive meal ever served in the air.)

Security in the air haul is a part of stowage as just mentioned, but it is also part of the whole problem of air safety. There have been a few strictly air-cargo aircraft lost, but every combination airplane that meets disaster also carries cargo. This problem is, of course, receiving the greatest attention of any, both by the carriers and by the government, as has been discussed in Chapter 11. Despite improvements, there will probably always be some air accidents, since, as has been said before, lack of safety is the price paid for motion. But these are the calculated risks of all transportation. It is the avoidable risks to air freight security which must receive immediate attention if the air carriers maintain the loss and damage record for which they have previously been noted.

Air Freight Insurance

The air bill, corresponding to the bill of lading used in other forms of transportation, now issued by all certificated airlines to shippers, contains no detailed statement of the liability of the carriers for freight beyond a reference to its value and condition at time of shipping. The Air Freight Rules Tariff, concurred in by all certificated airlines, is the basic document by which air carriers list liabilities accepted or rejected.

The Air Freight Rules Tariff also contains provisions placing responsibility on the shipper for such matters as proper packaging and marking and for the declaration of proper value to the carrier if he is uninsured and therefore wishes to collect from the carrier in the event of loss and/or damage.

Under normal circumstances, an airline's liability for loss and/or damage is limited to $50 per shipment or, if the weight of the shipment exceeds 100 pounds, to 50 cents per pound. If the shipment is more highly valued, it is the uninsured shipper's responsibility to make declaration of such value, which, on general cargo, may be done at an additional cost of 10 cents per $100. Various airlines have exceptions to this, generally applying to perishables and live animals. These exceptions usually restrict the liability of those carriers who have taken the exceptions to $10 per shipment or 10 cents per pound, whichever is the greater. In order to declare a higher value, it is necessary for the shipper to pay, in some instances, $2 per $100 of value and, in other instances, up to $5 per $100 of value, depending on the individual airline requirements.

Under the Air Freight Rules Tariff, declaration of value by a shipper implies liability of the airline up to that value, except were denied by a somewhat amplified statement of the usual carrier's exclusions of liability, since air carriers, unlike other carriers, may legally contract away all liability except for culpable negligence. The following exclusions as to airline liability are in effect for all certificated carriers:

1. Acts of God, public enemy, public authorities, strikes, riots and civil commotions, quarantine, war.
2. Perils of the air.
3. Act or default of consignor, consignee, or owner.
4. Defect or inherent vice of the shipment.
5. Authority of law.
6. Violations of any of the rules contained in the Air Freight Rules Tariff and supplements thereto by a party claiming an interest in the shipment.
7. Acts or omissions of warehousemen, customs and quarantine officials, or other persons gaining lawful or unlawful possession of the shipment.
8. Delay.

There is also a limitation in section 403 (b) of the Federal Aviation Act further limiting airline liability. This section prohibits rebates, and under it airlines are powerless to provide settlement of a claim not permitted under their Air Freight Rules Tariff. Carriers violating this provision are subject to penalty of a fine up to $5,000 for each violation thereof.

It is true, of course, that the exclusions of liability listed above are subject to legal contest; and, as has been the case with other types of carriers, legal decisions may in the future prove that liabilities now denied by the air carriers must be accepted. For example, when one considers the legal history of disputes over just what constitutes "perils of the sea" in ocean transportation, it would seem that the exclusions of "perils of the air" by an air carrier are ones lending themselves immediately to factual dispute. Again, the term "delay" is rather broad, and the carriers' rule makes no qualification as to whether it refers to physical loss or damage to perishable cargo caused by delay or whether it refers to such other loss as loss of market.

Shippers interested in protection beyond the Air Freight Rules

Tariff provisions are, of course, free to arrange for coverage to whatever degree desired through an insurance company. This type of coverage usually takes the form of "transit insurance." "Transit insurance" is a general category in the insurance business but usually refers to coverages that indemnify the shipper or owner of property for losses that may occur while his property is being carried from one point to another by a carrier and is, therefore, not under the control of the owner. In addition to providing indemnity for losses which an uninsured shipper might collect from the carrier, such insurance in broad terms (*a*) indemnifies the assured for losses for which the carrier is not liable, (*b*) indemnifies the assured for losses in excess of the liability of the carrier, and (*c*) usually makes it possible for the assured to obtain more prompt payment of loss from his insurance company and be relieved of the burden of collecting from the carrier.

Insurance indemnifies the shipper for those losses which occur despite precautions taken by himself and the carrier. It places him again in his original financial position before the destruction of or damage to the property shipped. In the sense of minimum protection, insurance finds its place in filling the breach created by the reasonable waiver of liability of the carrier for acts of God, perils of the air, and the other fortuitous occurrences mentioned previously. Broader protection, including what is termed "all-risk coverage," is available and is in fact the coverage provided in most cases.

Directly following World War II, insurance companies extended their policies to cover air freight in broader terms than those now in effect; and owing to their lack of knowledge of the perils of air transportation and the susceptibilities of cargoes shipped by air, plus the inefficiency and lack of dependability of some of the noncertificated carriers, heavy losses were suffered by these underwriters. Time and the constructive efforts of those involved in shipping and transporting by air have lessened most of the early problems, but the mark left on the insurance companies' experience unfortunately still has its effect on rates and the availability of coverage. The major transit insurance underwriters in the American insurance market are, however, studying air cargo insurance; and, in due course, types of coverage should emerge from the somewhat experimental stage in which this type of insurance now finds itself.[3]

[3] See Charles S. Rhyne, "Liability Problems of Air Cargo Carriage," *Law and Contemporary Problems*, Winter, 1950.

Air Freight Pickup and Delivery

When the airlines started to carry a volume of air freight, as distinct from air express, the problem arose as to how air and ground transportation was to be co-ordinated, because every airline haul became a ground carrier haul at either end of the journey. In other words, how was the pickup and delivery function to be performed? The airlines at first quoted all rates on an airport-to-airport basis on the theory that shippers would bring out their freight and consignees would call for it at the other end. It soon became apparent, however, that this was a dangerous policy, because shippers were slow to bring freight to the airports and consignees were inclined to take their own time about calling for it. Much of the speed of air transportation was lost because shipments were delayed at airports when they might have been delivered had facilities been available, and some users began to wonder if air transportation was worth what it cost.

The question was, therefore, whether the airlines should individually or collectively go into the trucking business to supply pickup and delivery or whether they should jointly contract with already existing motor carriers. Fortunately, an airline co-ordinating agency was already in existence, Air Cargo, Inc., which had been formed as a research organization, had practically died out, except for the name, during the war, but was now at hand with an excellent name, ready-made to fit the airlines' need of the moment.

The airlines, after much discussion and a number of attempts on the part of individual companies to provide the needed ground service themselves, decided in favor of contract operations on a nation-wide basis. In reaching this conclusion, a number of factors were regarded as determinative: (*a*) Providing the service by contract, rather than directly, would permit rapid establishment of the program on a nation-wide basis, with the opportunity always present to establish direct operation at any point where a contractual arrangement did not work out or was more costly. (*b*) Establishing a direct operation with the airline agency owning the trucks would involve the outlay of too much money, considering the financial condition of the air carriers. (*c*) The volume of air freight except at the largest airline points appeared to be insufficient to permit a sound and economical cartage operation for pickup and delivery of this traffic alone, whereas such a service could easily be integrated into the operations of many local motor truck operators. (*d*) The problem of obtaining local licenses and certificates to engage in trucking operations was avoided in those jurisdictions where intrastate shipments of air freight were involved. (*e*) Proceeding initially on a contractual, rather than a direct, basis would afford the airline agency—Air Cargo, Inc.—an opportunity to acquire information and experience on pickup and delivery which would be very valuable in forming later plans for a direct operation at points where such a service appeared warranted.

The first step was to draft a standard-form pickup and delivery contract. This was done by Air Cargo, Inc., in co-operation with the Executive Committee of the American Trucking Associations. The advantages of such a uniform contract are many: liability of the contractor, insurance coverage, services to be performed, accounting procedures, handling of C.O.D shipments, and numerous other items would be identical at all airline points. Thus an airline responsible for an interline shipment would have assurance that the delivery service, the insurance protection, and the accounting procedure for that shipment at destination would conform to those performed at points on its own line.

The standard-form service contract was an agreement between the local truck operator and Air Cargo, Inc., acting as agent for and on behalf of the airlines serving the particular point at which the contract was negotiated. Under these contracts, motor truck operators agreed to provide, among other things, pickup and delivery service, storage facilities, a city air freight terminal when requested by the airlines, and the issuance and execution of all necessary shipping documents. Special provision was made for the insurance of air freight in possession of the truck operator. Air Cargo, Inc., agreed, in consideration of a nominal reduction in the compensation otherwise due the contractor, to indemnify him against all liability arising from the loss of or damage to air freight while in the possession of the contractor. As a result of this contract, nationwide uniformity was obtained in the insurance protection for air freight while in the possession of trucking contractors, at a rate far below that which the majority of individual contractors would be able to obtain. The shipping public benefits by this program because the lower cost of insurance means not only lower rates but also a uniformity of responsibility and handling in the event of loss or damage; the air carriers benefit because loss or damage of air freight while it is in the possession of the trucking operators is now removed from the experience records of the airlines, thereby lowering their insurance premiums; and the truckers benefit because they obtain substantially greater insurance protection at a lower cost than would otherwise be possible.

The creation of a nation-wide pickup and delivery service using independent local truckers at each airline point presented numerous problems, however. The major objective of the airlines was to obtain uniformity of ground service, and the uniform contract helped greatly toward this end; but the fact remained that Air Cargo, Inc., and the airlines could not possibly exercise the same degree of control over operations provided by independent contractors that would be possible if Air Cargo, Inc., operated its own trucks. Further difficulties arose from the fact that there was considerable variation in local conditions, including the volume of traffic and the size and type of truck operators available. In order to create as much uniformity as possible, despite varying local conditions, Air Cargo, Inc., set up local cartage committees composed in each instance of local airline representatives to assist in negotiating and supervising local ground service. This has resulted in Air Cargo, Inc., utilizing the services of virtually every size and type of trucking operator, ranging from the large over-the-road motor freight operators, with a large fleet of both highway and city pickup and delivery trucks, to the owner-operator with only a single truck.

Truck operators involved in co-ordinating air and ground transportation fall within three classes, as follows:

1. Motor carriers engaged in general hauling activities where their air freight pickup and delivery are only a small part of their total business. Ordinarily, they have a fleet of vehicles considerably in excess of the demands of the air traffic, although they sometimes assign certain trucks exclusively to that work. In addition, the general nature of their business requires that these large truck operators maintain a city terminal which is available for the delivery and acceptance of air freight along with their other traffic. In cities of considerable geographical extent but relatively low air-freight-generating capacity, truckers of this type appear to be the most appropriately organized and equipped to provide the type of service required by air carriers. The fact that they are engaged in a general cartage business permits certain of the air freight services to be integrated with their other activities, thereby reducing the unit cost to the airlines; and the fact that they operate extensive fleets of ve-

hicles permits a rapid and effective coverage of a large geographical area.

2. Truck operators confining their activities to surface transportation for all types of air traffic. Some of these operators provide transportation for passengers and mail as well as air freight. They are well fitted for pickup and delivery operations in cities which are not extensive in area or which generate but little traffic. The fact that regularly scheduled trips must be made between an airport and the city in the course of the regular passenger and mail service enables these operators to provide air freight pickup and delivery at a very reasonable cost. This explains why a trucker in this class is at some cities the only motor carrier available and is prepared to quote a reasonable rate for the service required by the airlines.

3. Motor carriers working exclusively under a contract with Air Cargo, Inc. There are not many of these, and usually such an operator owns and operates his own truck. This is really an ideal situation from the point of view of airline supervision; but since pickup and delivery of air freight provides the sole source of revenue for the exclusive operator, there are not many places where the rates that can be collected from shippers will provide a fair return. The volume of traffic to be handled and the length of the average trip are important considerations in determining whether such an operator may earn a reasonable return without a subsidy being paid by the airlines or without the service to the public being reduced below the standard which Air Cargo, Inc., is trying to maintain.

The opportunity of selecting the type of motor carrier whose size and character of operation are most ideally suited to the particular type of service pattern required at each individual airline point has been an important factor in attaining uniformity in the quality of the pickup and delivery service provided under the uniform contract. Substantial variation in the types of motor carriers selected imposes a somewhat greater supervisory burden on Air Cargo, Inc., than would be the case if all the truckers were in the same category, because each type of operator has his own peculiar problems and cost considerations. The additional burden, however, is probably more than offset by the benefits to the over-all service resulting from this flexibility in selection.

Almost without exception, the services provided by the contracting truck operators under the standard service contract are considerably greater than are those which were previously provided for individual airlines. By concentrating the total volume of air freight at a particular point in the hands of one trucker, a substantially more effective and more frequent scheduling of trips to and from the airport is made possible. Where previously the general rule was one trip daily for the individual airlines, most truck operators make two, and frequently more, scheduled round trips; and, in addition, there are special trips, provided for at many points, made at any time of day or night at the request of shipper or consignee. Many truckers also provide city terminals where shippers may leave air freight or consignees pick it up.

Airport Handling of Air Freight

Air freight handling at airports is still a more or less makeshift matter. There are several reasons for this. For one thing, although special air-cargo aircraft have been developed, their use has been largely confined to the military. Hence the so-called all-cargo airplanes flown by the airlines and other operators are mostly passenger types not really designed to carry freight. The result is that the aircraft now in use are far from standardized; and their use has been handicapped because of the lack of multiple loading doors, limitations on full-end loading, nonrectangular cargo compartments, the shape and noncompartmentalization of the fuselage, and lack of synchronization between the plane-bed level and that of the truck bed. A further difficulty is that airport operators and air carriers are still uncertain about what the air freight will amount to, both as to nature and as to volume.

Another aspect of the problem is the fact that air cargo, using the term in its broadest sense, arrives at the airport by various means. Air freight is brought in by the truckers operating under contract with Air Cargo, Inc., as well as in the trucks of individual shippers. Air express comes in the trucks of the Railway Express Agency. Mail comes in the post office trucks. Passenger baggage, still regarded in the air cargo category by most airlines, comes by the various means with which everyone is familiar. Company material shipments originate at the airport but arrive at the loading point on the usual airline carts. A considerable amount of co-ordination is necessary, therefore, particularly since most air cargo is now carried with passengers in combination aircraft. This will probably be the case for some time to come.

One handling problem concerns the picking-up of the various types of air cargo destined to go on a particular flight. Freight can be assembled in one place; but, in the case of transfer from one airline to another, a pickup problem on the airport is created. Express may be placed with freight at the airport; but so far the Railway Express Agency has not favored this, since they feel their traffic is entitled to flight priority, at least in theory, and should be handled separately to avoid re-sortings. Air mail, which now includes fairly heavy parcel post shipments, must be separated from freight and express because of the security involved and the regulations of the Post Office Department. Baggage, which still creates a big problem with the continued use of combination aircraft, is assembled at still another place. To get all this cargo together without delay for a given flight is still an unsolved problem at many airports and involves the use of many different kinds of ground-handling equipment.

The airlines are beginning to realize that it is the ground time and costs of ground handling and loading that threaten to retard development of the vast unexploited air freight potential. In many instances, cost of handling air freight from the consignor into the aircraft and from the aircraft to the consignee approaches the actual expense of the air haul itself. This condition is also true of the time element.[4] While it is recognized that one of the principal selling advantages of air cargo is speed, it is not uncommon to have the time during which the freight is on the ground in pickup and delivery, waybilling and manifesting, and loading and unloading exceed the time that it is in the air. This unfortunate situation excludes a large segment of air freight of the so-called short-haul (500 to 750 miles) potential. While there is now some freight carried on the short haul, it is a very small part of the available potential which can be developed if and when the time comes that a shipper's freight is handled in the proper ratio of in-transit time—ground to air.

The various methods of airport freight handling are as follows:

Truck. A relatively low-powered truck is driven to each pickup spot. The cargo is loaded in sequence so that it can be loaded in station order after being driven to the loading area and backed as close to the airplane as possible. This is the simplest method and is sufficient at airports handling but a small amount of cargo. The

[4] R. Dixon Speas, former Assistant to the President of American Airlines, points out that in 1950 for a New York–Detroit trip, ground handling took 85 per cent of the total time the shipment was in transit from shipper to consignee and that, for the slightly longer flight to Chicago, this figure decreased only a little to 81 per cent and that, even for the long haul from New York to Los Angeles, ground time used 42 per cent of the total time consumed.

disadvantage is that the truck must go to several pickup spots for various kinds of cargo, since there is yet very little centralization in airport warehouses. There is also the danger that the truck will bump the aircraft when backing, and it restricts movement around the aircraft when loading and unloading.

Trucktrain. This is the familiar line of trailers pulled by a small tractor seen on many airports. The trailers are preloaded at each pickup spot, attached to the tractor, and pulled to the airplane. This is a good method, as the separate trailers can be placed at the best spots alongside the airplane, the small units are easy to maneuver, segregation of kinds of cargo is easy, and the tractor may be detached from the train and used for other purposes during loading and unloading. The disadvantages of this method are that, since the cargo is broken up into small units, care must be taken to prevent the loading sequence and arrangement from being disturbed and that, unless the carts are equipped with removable sides, they are not suitable for lifting by fork-lifts in loading.

With the cargo alongside the aircraft by one or a combination of the methods just described, it now has to be placed aboard. When the DC-3 was the only aircraft used to any extent by the carriers, a system of ladders, loading stands, and other similar equipment was used to enable a sort of bucket-brigade method of hand loading. But as volume of freight and express grew and other aircraft, like the DC-4, came into use after the close of World War II, the carriers found that the old lift-and-lug method was too slow. They then gave attention to the development of mechanical loading, which took the form of:

1. The belt conveyor, which has the advantage of speed, flexibility, and reasonable cost. Its chief disadvantages are that cargo must be handled as separate pieces, that large packages will not fit within side railings, and that the amount of incline sometimes limits its use.
2. The chute, considered the fastest method yet devised for unloading separate packages. The disadvantage of this piece of equipment is that high-density packages come down too fast and low-density ones too slowly. Also, after the chute has been used to unload cargo, it has to be wheeled out of the way, and either a belt conveyor or something else moved into place. This means two or more large pieces of equipment on the airport ramps, just that much more to be moved out of the way between flights and just that much more to be maintained.

3. The fork-lift truck has seemed to be the answer to many problems. This handling device has been adopted by the air carriers as a convenient, flexible system of elevating loads to any door height. Such trucks can also be used to tow carts or other containers around on the airport. Disadvantages of the fork-lift trucks are that a skilled operator is needed to get the full advantage from such equipment and that they are slow for lifting the average single package unless palletized or in a cart which can be elevated to the level of the airplane floor.

Scheduled or "Demand" Service

Every now and then, both in connection with domestic and foreign air freight services, the merits of scheduled service versus what has been termed "demand" operations of freight carriers have been under discussion.[5] The difference between the two terms as used by air freight operators to characterize existing or contemplated services may de defined less in terms of what demand service is than in terms of what it is not. In the first place, demand service is not a scheduled service, since no published schedule is involved. Secondly, it is operated only when sufficient cargo is aboard an all-cargo airplane to justify a departure. Lastly, no rigid route is involved, since operators send aircraft to specific points when freight is available and only then.

It will be seen that from the standpoint of the carrier this concept of demand service might result in very flexible operations. However, either there will be an operational problem in determining when and where each individual flight will be made or there will be a tentative schedule, no matter how flexible or how secret, within the organization of the carrier in order to allow some planning by crew members and operations personnel for departures. A plane hardly ever is waiting with a crew on board when the last needed pound of freight arrives at an airport. There has to be some planning.

From the standpoint of the shipper, demand service, as it is usually understood, means lack of public information. A shipper will never know just when a departure will take place, to what points it will go, or at what time it will arrive at any specific destination unless he is told by the carrier. The attractiveness of this kind of service to shippers will, therefore, depend somewhat on how good the verbal information is that they receive from employees of the car-

[5] See particularly *U.S.–Europe–Middle East Cargo Service,* CAB Docket Nos. 3041 and 3818 (1950).

rier. This really does not differ greatly from the freight services that shippers receive from the scheduled carriers, since with these carriers, shippers do not generally know in advance whether freight they offer will leave on any specific flight, unless space has been confirmed on a reservation basis. However, they do know that a certain number of schedules will be operated between certain points. In view of the published schedules of a certificated carrier, a shipper will have more definite information on the amount of space which will actually be operated between points and the average flight time freight is actually lifted.

From the standpoint of the carrier, nonscheduled demand service appears to be a more flexible operation offering substantial economies through the ability to attain maximum load factors. However, this apparent flexibility will be sure to be limited, particularly with respect to return flights, by the necessity of obtaining some reasonable utilization of equipment. The experience of nonscheduled operators thus far does not show high utilization. It has been maintained that it is not economical operation for a carrier to provide a scheduled amount of service, as the certificated carriers must do, day in and day out between points where there is usually no freight, only to have what may turn out to be an inadequate amount of space available at times when a demand develops. But the fact is that the so-called "scheduled" service of the certificated airlines is more flexible than it seems to the casual observer. Schedules are changed frequently to meet seasonal trends in traffic; extra sections are operated at times; and flights are occasionally canceled entirely. In essence, the nonscheduled and the certificated cargo carriers try to do the same thing, that is, to anticipate the demand for service between points and to plan on sufficient flights to carry the available traffic. An operator with no published schedules is merely able to make more minute changes in operations without public notice.

On the other hand, the operator having no published schedules is less subject to supervision by the Civil Aeronautics Board and affords shippers less opportunity for advance planning of their activities. Published schedules serve to indicate the general level of service between points without the necessity of actual contact with the carrier. Their absence requires a shipper in each instance to find out from the carrier whether any service is actually operated to certain points and, if so, within what period of time a shipment can be transported. The nonscheduled or demand type of service seems particularly unsatisfactory to the small shipper, whereas it can be modified by the carrier to fit the need of any particular large shipper. Discrimination is, therefore, almost certain to arise. Service to large shippers can be given when and where they desire in preference to the small competitor. The lack of any published schedules also handicaps the small shippers who might, through a consolidation of shipments, be able to fill an airplane in competition with a large shipper whose cargo by itself would be sufficient to determine the time of departure. The large shipper can always influence the timing of flights, but the lack of public notice of these timings may well prevent the smaller shippers from utilizing them even when less than a full planeload shipment is made by a large shipper.

The lack of published schedules may be of little consequence to shippers between points where there are frequent flights. Between these points, the experience of the shippers may well be sufficient economic compulsion to insure equal treatment. However, between points where frequencies by various carriers are limited, the public has a sufficient interest in knowing when a service is available to require some publication of the type of service rendered.

The arguments in favor of demand service are further weakened by the fact that nonscheduled carriers seem unwilling to specify any minimum of freight offered at particular points to justify service, any maximum of time which freight would be held before being returned to shippers in case the minimum amount to justify a flight did not turn up, or even any minimum amount of service between any points. What shippers want in order to make air freight more attractive from their standpoint are the very things which demand service lacks, and such a service would certainly offer no more benefits than the so-called "scheduled" service.

The Air Freight Forwarder[6]

In 1949, the Civil Aeronautics Board permitted freight forwarders to enter air transportation, as was discussed in Chapter 6. They were classified as "indirect air carriers," but the Board made it plain that their relationships with the airlines were strictly those of shippers. Freight-forwarder operations by air were regarded as "experimental" at first but have since been extended indefinitely.

---

[6] See briefs to the examiner filed by Trans World Airlines, Railway Express Agency, United Air Lines, and Bureau Counsel in the matter of the renewal of Part 296 of the Economic Regulations and an investigation of indirect carriage of property. CAB Docket No. 5947, *et al.* (1954).

The so-called "experiment" was conducted under circumstances strongly conducive to successful results. The nation as a whole was prosperous from 1949 to 1954. Business activity, already at a high level, was increasing during most of the period. The air transportation industry experienced its greatest prosperity during those years, and the air freight business (in its infancy when the period began) developed rapidly.

The situation which existed in the air freight business in 1948 made it a particularly opportune time for air freight forwarders to get a foothold. The airlines had begun developing air freight transportation and had built up a substantial amount of business which the forwarders could divert. Air freight was becoming a natural way of shipping, and the potential business appeared to be large. The habit of shipping by direct carrier had not been established in the public mind and customer-carrier relationships had not been firmly fixed. The service offered by the direct carriers was in a preliminary stage of development, and there had been many complaints about ground-handling delays. The energy and resources of the domestic trunk lines were heavily concentrated on operational freight problems and the necssity of providing additional flight equipment and other facilities for the expanding postwar market. These conditions were ideal for establishing new business ventures in the forwarding field.

Another development favorable to forwarder operations occurred in 1950. Military requirements for the Korean airlift severely reduced the number of suitable aircraft that were available to the direct carriers either from their own fleets or on the market. There can be no question but that the shortage of suitable aircraft slowed down the airlines' development of air freight. In many instances during this period, the forwarder, like any other shipper, found it difficult to get the amount of space he wanted at the time he wanted it; but the knowledge of the direct carriers' schedules, routes, and equipment—gained by the forwarder in the ordinary conduct of his business—put him in a better position than many other shippers to take advantage of whatever space was available on any of several airlines. As long as this advantage in finding space lasted, it must have been a valuable competitive asset to the forwarder who knew his business, and must have led many shippers to use forwarders' service.

Finally, the conditions under which the Board permitted the forwarders to operate were extremely favorable. No obligation to serve was imposed. The forwarder could serve where and when he pleased. He could begin, suspend, and again begin operations at any point or at all points. He could exclude commodities which were difficult to handle.

All things considered, it seems unlikely that conditions will ever be more favorable to forwarder operations than they were during this "trial period"; certainly there will be many times when conditions will be *less* favorable. Under these circumstances, it is surprising that the forwarders have not made a more impressive showing. Due to inadequate breakdown in the forwarders' reports, it is impossible to obtain an entirely accurate figure for the extent to which forwarders have participated in the air freight business, but the best approximations show that their share has been surprisingly small.

The future of the air freight forwarding business does not look particularly bright since the airlines are now in a better position to handle their own air freight business than they were during the trial period. The amount of lift is adequate, equipment and facilities are keeping pace with demand, and the freight service offered by the airlines has been improved and is improving. The integrated pickup and delivery service arranged through Air Cargo, Inc.—which at the time of the *Air Freight Forwarder Case* in 1948 had progressed little beyond the blueprint stage—has long since proved its usefulness. The air freight business today represents one of the airlines' greatest potential fields for expansion and there can be no doubt that they will develop it aggressively.

On the other hand, there is as yet no proof of the forwarders' ability to operate effectively in this field. Forwarder service as good as direct-carrier service is bound to cost as much, and better-than-direct-carrier service will cost more. Forwarders have undoubtedly diverted freight business from direct carriers by offering service at less-than-direct-carrier rates, but at present the offer of these lower rates appears to be limited for the most part to small shipments below the direct carriers' present minimum rates.

The forwarders have always claimed to be experts in the ground-handling of air freight and generally claim to give better service than the direct carriers at lower cost. Yet they frequently complain that, with their costs, the volume breaks are not large enough to permit their operating at a profit. To the suggestion that they raise their rates (which would make most forwarder rates equal to or higher than direct carrier rates), the forwarders reply that many shippers will not pay more than the present rates. This allows one of two conclusions to be drawn: Either forwarder service is not better than direct carrier service or, if it is better, shippers are nevertheless unwilling to pay extra for it.

The so-called straight or unconsolidated shipment presents another dilemma for the forwarder. If he receives a shipment to a destination for which he can get no other shipments, he cannot consolidate and therefore is obliged to handle it "straight" (that is, as a single shipment) either on the forwarder's air bill or on the direct carrier's air bill. If the forwarder's air bill is used, the forwarder presumably picks up and delivers (for which service he receives the tariff rate), but he has all the expense of handling one of his regular shipments. If, on the other hand, the direct carrier's air bill is used, the forwarder receives the tariff pickup charge and has all the expense usually incident to handling a shipment at the origin station, though he avoids handling the shipment at destination. There is enough competition in pickup and delivery services to justify the assumption that rates for these services are closely related to costs, and that only modest profits are earned. Assuming that the forwarder's pickup and delivery service provides no more than a fair return on his investment, the forwarder incurs (and loses) about half the cost of handling one shipment every time he handles a "straight" shipment at the origin station only; and he incurs (and loses) the full cost of handling such a shipment when he handles it at both the origin and destination station, because, not having consolidated the "straight" shipment with other shipments, there is no spread available to compensate him for his costs. It is true that he may help himself somewhat by consolidating the "straight" shipment to an intermediate point, and then shipping it beyond that point as a "straight" shipment, but this practice will probably delay the freight and will certainly increase his costs, for the "straight" shipment has to be shipped twice.

The forwarder's dilemma is that, although he loses money in handling "straight" shipments, he can scarcely afford to refuse them. If he does refuse a shipment, he loses all chance of making it part of a profitable consolidation. More important, he thereby throws away a competitive advantage he may have over the direct carrier—the ability to handle all the traffic of each customer. An airline can serve a shipper only to the points it serves directly or by connection; with other traffic it can only inform the shipper, as a matter of courtesy, which carriers provide the service. The forwarder can ship anywhere the airlines go, and it may be convenient for some shippers to have all their freight handled by one carrier. But this convenience will be lost if the "straight" shipments are refused and the shipper is turned back to the direct carriers for at least part of his traffic.

It is difficult to measure the burden imposed on the forwarder by the handling of "straight" shipments. Probably some forwarders have sacrificed the sales argument (of handling all traffic) to obtain relief from the burden, while others have thought it worthwhile to expand business by offering what amounts to free service.

Despite the dark picture presented by the first five-year "experimental" operation of the air freight forwarders, there is a place for such middlemen provided they can supply a better service to air freight users than the airlines do, and at a price which will yield a profit and which shippers and/or receivers can afford to pay. The most successful air freight forwarding organization to date has been Emery Air Freight, which has rendered a highly specialized, expedited, and personalized service at relatively high rates. (This company has not been regarded as a "typical" forwarder by the airlines since its rates are above airline freight rates and it regards consolidation of shipments as only an incidental part of its business.)[7] Certainly the experience of Amery Air Freight has shown that to operate successfully a forwarder must first of all promote a service; rates are of secondary importance.

Shippers' Associations[8]

The entry of shippers' associations into the air freight field is a comparatively recent development, and it appears that their activities may help develop air freight business. Such associations are able to save money for their members on the cost of air freight since they operate on a nonprofit or co-operative basis and eliminate the problem of handling the "straight" shipment. In at least some cases, they may be able to provide a more highly specialized service for the particular products they handle than can economically be offered by a carrier serving the public at large. So far these associations have been most active in shipping flowers from California.

Shippers' associations eliminate the "straight" shipment problem

[7] Between 1950 and 1953 it is reported that Emery Air Freight handled from one third to two fifths of the air freight forwarder tonnage.

[8] A co-operative shippers' association has been defined as a *bona fide* association of shippers which (*a*) in the name of the association or of the members thereof, ships by air the property of the association or of the members thereof, of a nonprofit basis, for the purpose of securing the benefits of volume rates and/or improved service; and (*b*) admits anyone to membership on a nondiscriminatory basis who can qualify under its articles of association and bylaws.

because they do not rely on volume breaks for revenue. Instead they prorate the shipping charges of the direct carriers among the shippers and make a flat charge for each shipment handled, the charge being fixed at an amount sufficient to cover expenses. Thus, if a shipper-member has freight for a destination to which there are no other shipments, he pays the direct carrier rate on the volume he ships. If there are other shipments to that destination, he pays his pro rata part of the direct carrier rate on the combined volume of all shipper members. The shippers' association receives compensation for the services it performs and takes no risks. In theory at least, it should be able to operate for less than a forwarder who is trying to make a profit and must take the risk of finding freight to consolidate in order to earn that profit. The reduced transportation costs achieved through shippers' associations may make possible the air transportation of freight which would otherwise travel by other media.

Air-Truck Service[9]

As far as air freight is concerned, the term "interstate air commerce" is defined in section 101(20) of the Federal Aviation Act as the carriage by aircraft of property for compensation in commerce between the states "whether such commerce moved wholly by aircraft or partly by aircraft and partly by other means of transportation." Identical language appears in the definition of "interstate air transportation" in section 101(21) of the Act. This quoted clause, appearing in the definitions of both "interstate air commerce" and "interstate air transportation," is a clear recognition by Congress that air transportation, by its very nature, may require partial movement by surface transportation if efficient air transportation is to be rendered to the public.

The certificate of public convenience and necessity issued to air carriers under section 401 of the Act authorizes air carriers to provide "air transportation" as that term is defined by the Act. This section, however, does not limit air carriers to provide only that portion of complete air transportation service performed by aircraft. Thus, insofar as the basic regulatory law is concerned, air carriers holding certificates of public convenience and necessity who engage in "air transportation" may themselves render such transportation "partly by aircraft and partly by other forms of transportation." This is not to imply, however, that substantial surface transportation

[9] This discussion is based upon the report of Examiner E. T. Stodola in *Flying Tiger Air-Truck Service,* CAB Docket No. 9175 (1959).

is available to air carriers for the performance of air transportation service at all times and without limit.[10]

The question has sometimes been raised as to the effect of section 302(b)(7a) of the Interstate Commerce Act (Motor Carrier Act of 1935) on this issue. At the time the Civil Aeronautics Act was enacted in 1938, Congress further implemented the right of air carriers to employ surface transportation in the course of providing "air transportation" by providing, in section 1107(j) of the Civil Aeronautics Act, an amendment to section 203(b) of the Interstate Commerce Act, exempting from economic regulation by the Interstate Commerce Commission "the transportation of persons or property by motor vehicle when incidental to transportation by aircraft." On many occasions since the enactment of subsection 7(a), the Interstate Commerce Commission has been called upon to determine whether, under particular circumstances, the motor transportation involved was "incidental" to movement by air and therefore exempt transportation under the Interstate Commerce Act. In general, these decisions of the Interstate Commerce Commission have fallen into one of three classes: (1) cases involving surface carriage by the Railway Express Agency by contract with motor carriers or with the agency's own trucks as a part of a through movement involving air express, (2) cases involving transportation of passengers to and from air terminals by limousine or other surface means as part of an air movement, and (3) cases involving motor truck freight service either prior or subsequent to movement by air usually within a terminal area of an airline. In some of these cases the decisions of the Interstate Commerce Commission appear to turn solely on the length of haul of the surface transportation by motor carrier. In other situations the Interstate Commerce Commission considers whether the motor transportation used by air carriers was employed for providing bona fide pickup and delivery service or for providing substitute service for transportation by aircraft under emergency conditions. In circumstances where the surface carriage amounts to

[10] It is true that a literal interpretation of the foregoing provisions of the Act would appear to allow air transportation by various and perhaps unlimited surface means when such transportation is in some way connected with service by aircraft. However, there are obvious limits to such a literal interpretation. There can be no question that trucking operations may be and often are a facet of interstate commerce. But not all trucking operations in interstate commerce, regardless of their nature, may be deemed to be "air transportation" even if connected in part with some movement by aircraft. Thus, in the *Cuban Colonial Air Express Case*, 24 CAB 235 (1956), the Board unequivocally held that where property was moved by truck from New York to Miami and then transshipped from Miami to Cuba by air, the New York–Miami transportation was not "air transportation."

a substitute service for impractical air carriage, it has uniformly been held to be exempt transportation under subsection 7(a). On the other hand, carriage complementary to air service has been held to be not exempt.[11] But whatever the considerations relied upon by the Interstate Commerce Commission in construing the phrase "incidental to transportation by aircraft," the decisions of the Commission under subsection 203(b) (7a) of the Interstate Commerce Act provide no basis for concluding that Congress, in its use of the particular language appearing in subsections 101(20) and 101(21) of the Federal Aviation Act intended to confine air carriers in their use of surface transportation services only to such surface transportation as was "incidental to transportation by aircraft." Subsections 1(20) to 1(21), and 1107(j) of the Civil Aeronautics Act were enacted at the same time, and the simple fact that Congress used different and broader language in subsections 1(20) and 1(21) than it used in section 1107(j) would appear to demonstrate that Congress did not intend to impose such a restrictive limitation on the air carriers in their use of surface transportation in providing a complete "air transportation" service. On the other hand, the Board, as already noted, has held that a substantial surface line haul operation is not "air transportation," notwithstanding subsequent transshipment to and movement by aircraft.

The strictly air freight carriers have, at times, been permitted to substitute motor for air service as a regular matter in order to facilitate pickup and delivery and more economical use of aircraft. The question has been raised whether such substitute service was a "combination air-truck" service within the meaning of the through service and joint rate provisions of section 1003 of the Act. The em-

[11] For cases illustrating some of the problems faced by the Interstate Commerce Commission under subsection (7a), see, *Railway Express Agency, Inc., Extension-West Warwick, R.I.* 31 M.C.C. 332 (1941); *Sky Freight Delivery Service, Inc.*, Common Carrier Application, 47 M.C.C. 229 (1947); *Teterboro Motor Transportation, Inc., Common Carrier Application,* 47 M.C.C. 247 (1947); *Graff Common Carrier Application,* 48 M.C.C. 310 (1948); and *Kenney Extension-Air Freight,* 61 M.C.C. 587 (1953). As neither the statute nor the certificates issued by the Civil Aeronautics Board define the limit of the terminal area of an airline, the Commission held that the operations of air carriers are sufficiently different from that of land carriers as to require a different consideration in the matter of terminal areas.

It found that such terminal area for an airline is the area covered by a bill of lading of the air carrier which includes, in addition to the line haul movement by air, the collection, delivery, and transfer service performed by a motor carrier under air billing.

As the area covered by transfer, collection, and delivery service under air billing is specified in the tariffs filed with the Civil Aeronautics Board, the Commission held that this sufficiently limited the exempt area. It stated that this finding is based on the assumption that the Civil Aeronautics Board would not hesitate to reject any publication which would result in an unreasonable enlargement of such an area.

ployment by an air carrier of substitute forms of transportation for the purpose of expediting the movement of its own traffic is a matter separate and distinct from that of combination service. The use of substitute transportation has arisen in situations where it has been impractical or uneconomical not to utilize surface facilities for a part of an over-all air movement or shipment. In such transportation, the air carrier is fully responsible under its tariff to the shipper for the movement from origin to destination, irrespective of the use by the air carrier of a substitute surface carrier for a part of the haul. The air carrier air bill issued to the shipper covers the entire movement, and the air carrier itself is solely responsible for selecting, paying, and absorbing the cost of the substitute carrier. For combination service, on the other hand, each participating carrier is responsible only for that portion of the total haul which it provides. Where a single through rate is involved in the combination service, a joint tariff must be filed by both carriers, and if air carriers and motor carriers are involved, the special joint Board provisions of subsection 1003 of the Act are involved.

Chapter 18

GENERAL AVIATION

PREVIOUS chapters have been almost wholly concerned with airline activities and problems. There is, however, another important part of commercial civil aviation which, in 1959, accounted for more cross-country flying hours than the revenue hours flown by all the scheduled airlines, domestic and international. More individual aircraft are used in the general aviation activities listed in Table 37 than are employed in the domestic certificated airline service of the United States. This increasingly important segment of aviation is termed "General Aviation."

General aviation includes all civil flying except that done by the certificated, supplemental and intrastate air carriers and by the Federal Aviation Agency. This represents the largest, though not spectacular nor publicized, portion of all civil flying in the United States. During 1959, approximately 66,500 aircraft engaged in this activity flew 1.6 billion miles, twice the mileage flown in the same year by the domestic scheduled airlines.

The basic uses of aircraft in general aviation—such as business transportation and commercial flying—registered encouraging gains during recent years (see Table 37). Together they accounted for 8,000,000 hours in 1959. On the other hand, instructional and pleasure flying have declined since 1955.

The outlook for the future indicates continued growth, but the volume of flying connected with business transportation, which is now the largest single component of general aviation, will undoubtedly be affected by general business conditions prevailing in any given year. It has been estimated, however, by the National Business Aircraft Association, that there are 20,000 firms in the United States which can profitably operate business aircraft, and that of this group only a very small number are now flying their own multiengine aircraft.

The 66,500 active aircraft in the general aviation fleet at the close of 1958, represented a gain of more than 2,400 over the active air-

TABLE 37

HOURS FLOWN IN GENERAL AVIATION BY TYPES, 1928–59
(Thousands of Hours)

YEAR	TOTAL HOURS	BUSINESS*		COMMERCIAL†		INSTRUCTIONAL		PLEASURE		OTHER‡	
		Hours	Per Cent	Hours	Per Cent	Hours	Per Cent	Hours	Per Cent	Hours	Per Cent
1928...	748	§	......	§	......	§	......	§	......	§	.....
1929...	1,266	§	......	§	......	§	......	§	......	§	.....
1930...	1,274	§	......	§	......	§	......	§	......	§	.....
1931...	1,083	152	14	281	26	307	28	343	32	....	.....
1932...	877	130	15	215	25	223	25	309	35	....	.....
1933...	795	129	16	200	25	198	25	268	34	....	.....
1934...	846	121	14	207	24	217	26	301	36	....	.....
1935...	954	132	14	229	24	292	31	301	31	....	.....
1936...	1,059	122	12	245	23	380	36	312	29	....	.....
1937...	1,173	156	13	227	19	432	37	358	31	....	.....
1938...	1,478	188	13	254	17	577	39	459	31	....	.....
1939...	1,922	246	13	332	17	755	39	589	31	....	.....
1940...	3,200	314	10	387	12	1,529	48	970	30	....	.....
1941...	4,460	250	6	511	11	2,816	63	883	20	....	.....
1942...	3,786	270	7	473	12	2,680	71	363	10	....	.....
1943...	‖	‖	......	‖	......	‖	......	‖	......	‖	.....
1944...	‖	‖	......	‖	......	‖	......	‖	......	‖	.....
1945...	‖	‖	......	‖	......	‖	......	‖	......	‖	.....
1946...	9,788	1,068	11	943	10	5,996	61	1,686	17	95	1
1947...	16,334	1,966	12	1,279	8	10,353	63	2,616	16	120	1
1948...	15,130	2,576	17	1,066	7	8,701	58	2,606	17	181	1
1949...	11,031	2,615	24	1,449	13	4,187	38	2,732	25	48	¶
1950...	**	**	......	**	......	**	......	**	......	**	.....
1951...	8,451	2,950	35	1,584	19	1,902	23	1,880	22	135	1
1952...	8,186	3,124	38	1,727	21	1,503	18	1,629	20	203	3
1953...	8,527	3,626	42	1,649	19	1,248	15	1,846	22	158	2
1954...	8,963	3,875	43	1,829	20	1,292	15	1,920	22	47	¶
1955...	9,500	4,300	45	1,950	21	1,275	13	1,975	21	....	.....
1956...	10,200	4,600	45	2,000	20	1,500	15	2,100	20	....	.....
1957...	10,938	4,864	45	2,013	18	1,864	17	2,109	19	88	1
1958...	11,700	5,300	45	2,200	19	2,000	17	2,200	19	....	.....
1959...	12,400	5,700	46	2,300	19	2,000	16	2,400	19	....	.....

* Includes flying for corporate or executive purposes as well as flying by individuals, including farmers and ranchers, on personal business.
† Includes contract, charter, industrial, and commercial agricultural flying.
‡ Testing, experimental, ferrying, Civil Air Patrol, etc.
§ Distribution by type of flying not available.
‖ Data for war years not available.
¶ Less than one half of 1 per cent.
** Data not available since no survey was conducted in this year.
Note: This table excludes all aircraft operated by the scheduled airlines and by the Civil Aeronautics Administration.
Source: FAA, *Statistical Handbook of Aviation*, 1960.

craft count at the end of 1957. Single-engine aircraft represented over 90 per cent of the active count. Based on the year-end counts of active aircraft, the number of one- and two-place planes declined slightly, the 4- and 5-place single-engine aircraft were 10 per cent higher, and a 7 per cent gain in multiengine planes raised that count to more than 5,300. Although the light twins are predominant among the multiengine aircraft, this segment of the general aviation fleet also includes transport aircraft of the same types used by the airlines.

Improvement in the quality of the general aviation fleet will probably result in increased flying because aircraft utilization tends to gain as aircraft size increases.

General Aviation Activities

General aviation is divided into four different activities, each of which will be discussed briefly:[1]

Business flying represents the use of aircraft as efficient vehicles in the conduct of a business, the same as trucks and automobiles are utilized. While the transportation of executives is an important part of business flying, these aircraft are being increasingly used to conserve the valuable working time of sales, engineering, and technical personnel as well. In addition to corporate-owned aircraft, the business fleet includes those operated by small business firms, professional people, and farmers and ranchers. Business flying is the most substantial segment of general aviation, accounting for a little under half the total hours and for half the aircraft-miles flown. The business fleet includes four out of every five multiengine aircraft flown in general aviation and half of the larger single-engine planes.

Commercial flying represents a group of activities which are generally performed on a "for hire" basis. This category includes contract, charter, air taxi, survey and patrol, and aerial application flying. Commercial flying usually accounts for about one fifth of the hours flown in general aviation.

The largest segment of commercial flying is the use of airplanes and helicopters to treat crops and forests with insecticides and fertilizers, to sow seeds, and to deposit chemicals which control weeds and brush or defoliate such crops as cotton to facilitate mechanical picking. The application of insecticides, in dry or liquid form, to crops, orchards, and forests is the most important activity. In recent years, it has accounted for almost two thirds of the flight time and three fourths of the acreage treated from aircraft. The characteristics of the biplane have made a place for it in aerial application flying as over half the flight time has been accumulated on these aircraft. Single-engine monoplanes accounted for most of the remaining time.

[1] See University of Illinois Institute of Aviation, *Operating Costs of a Light Aircraft Fleet* (Urbana, 1952); Howard F. Weeks, "Business Builds Airfleet," *Dun's Review*, April, 1953; John H. Frederick, "Private Planes—Management's Magic Carpet," *Distribution Age*, December, 1953; National Industrial Conference Board, *Managing Company Airplanes* (New York, 1954); "Twelve Thousand Company Planes," *Fortune*, January, 1956; Peter Noone, "New Phenomenon—The Executive Pilot," *Distribution Age*, July, 1960.

A smaller segment of commercial flying is patrol, survey, and miscellaneous work use. This represents the utilization of aircraft as an observation platform for the human eye, a camera, or electronic prospecting instruments. Over one third of the flight time in this segment has been required for the aerial patrol of pipe, power, and telephone lines. Fewer than 2,000 aircraft have been used primarily in patrol and survey flying, the bulk of these being single-engine aircraft. Almost one third of the general aviation helicopters were engaged during 1957 in patrol and survey flying.

Commercial flying also includes the use of aircraft to carry passengers and cargo for hire. Most of this flying is done by air taxi services and by fixed base operators who carry passengers or cargo on a contract or charter basis. Most of the aircraft used in this activity are the larger single-engine planes and the multiengine models smaller than the airline transport category.

Instructional flying covers flight training of civilians, both dual instruction and solo flying, under an instructor's supervision. The hours flown in this activity have advanced substantially from the postwar low in 1953 and reached the two-million-hour level in 1958. Single-engine planes are used almost exclusively in this flying, particularly the one- and two-place models.

Pleasure flying usually accounts for about one fifth of the hours flown in general aviation, ranking second to business transportation. Over 40 per cent of the general aviation fleet is used primarily for pleasure and personal business although many of these aircraft are used occasionally in other flying activities. Practically all these aircraft are single-engine planes, with substantial representation in the one- and two-place models. Included in pleasure flying are local hops, flying for sport or proficiency, and cross-country flights for purposes of vacation, air tours, and outdoor recreation. As a vehicle for personal transportation, an airplane extends the perimeter of travel far beyond the limits considered reasonable when an automobile is used.

DISCUSSION QUESTIONS[1]

CHAPTER 1

TRANSPORT AIRCRAFT

1. Outline briefly the early French experiments with lighter-than-air machines and indicate why all such aircraft lacked commercial utility.
2. Outline the early experiments with heavier-than-air machines culminating in the Wright brothers' success at Kitty Hawk.
3. Show how commercial aircraft, over the last twenty-five years have been made obsolete by the introduction of newer designs. Into what major change periods may this transition be divided?
4. Look over the last four issues of *Airlift* or *Aviation Week*, and see if you can locate any articles or news items dealing with any coming change in air transport equipment. Write a brief statement summarizing anything you may find.
5. Discuss the factors which have entered into the rapid and continuous modernization of airline equipment.
6. Differentiate clearly between the turbo-prop and turbo-jet engines.
7. What has been the general trend of development of aircraft characteristics in the last thirty years, and how do the turbo-jet powered types deviate from this trend?
8. What are the commercial possibilities of the helicopter?
9. Why can it be said that "convertible" aircraft have a great future?
10. What characteristics must "supersonic" aircraft possess to make them attractive for use in commercial service?
11. How has the problem of disposing of surplus piston-type aircraft been met?
12. Why is it that sales of surplus aircraft to foreign countries has not been the solution of the disposal problem?
13. If you have traveled by air recently, what were your own reactions to the aircraft in which you flew? Do you have anything to add to the passenger reactions discussed in the text?
14. In deciding the adaptability of a particular type of aircraft to a specific type of operation, the airlines use certain criteria. How may these be grouped? Discuss the important points under each.

---

[1] The purpose of these discussion questions for each chapter is not only to aid the student in his study of the text but also to familiarize him with the trade papers in the field as well as with the publications of the Civil Aeronautics Board and the Federal Aviation Agency.

CHAPTER 2

Airports and Airways

1. Define what is commonly called an "airport."
2. Briefly outline the historial development of airports in the United States.
3. When was federal aid first extended to civil airports not held primarily for the use of the federal government?
4. How may airports be classified according to: size, types of service which they are designed to furnish, and nature of ownership or control?
5. What criticism has been levied against the Civil Aeronautics Administration for its "service" classification and the runway specifications laid down for airports? Into what classification may the airport in your home community be placed?
6. Do you think we have an adequate system of airports in this country? On what basis do you make your judgment?
7. What are the chief problems of airport location in relation to the city it serves?
8. What means have been or may be taken to protect airport approaches?
9. What are the various forms of airport administration? What form is in use in your home community? If you do not have an airport, what type might be considered suitable and adequate?
10. What are the weaknesses of combining airport management with the functions of other city departments? Is there any good reason today for managing an airport in this way?
11. What can you say for and against the establishment of a separate airport department in a city administration?
12. List the advantages and disadvantages of an independent airport commission.
13. What are the chief sources of airport income?
14. Visit the airport nearest you at this time and report briefly on: (*a*) type of administration and management and (*b*) sources of income.
15. Define an "airway."
16. Outline the chief purposes of airway traffic control. How does it differ from airport traffic control?
17. Define: fan markers; L/MF Ranges, VHF Ranges, DME equipment.
18. Many hold that our system of airways and airport traffic control has been entirely inadequate for some years. On what is this contention based?
19. Go through the last few issues of *Airlift* and *Aviation Week* and report on any articles found dealing with improvements in airway traffic control.
20. Go through the last few issues of *Airlift* and *Aviation Week* and report on any articles concerned with airport management, airport construction, and the like which you may find.

21. Who pays for the construction and operation of : (*a*) airports and (*b*) airways?
22. What is meant by the common system of air traffic control?
23. Outline the concepts upon which any system of airways traffic control must be based in order to conform with national policy.
24. What are the two broad categories into which charges for the use of the airways might fall? Which are the best methods and why?
25. Do you feel that the scheduled airlines have reached a point in their development where they could carry the financial burden of airways user charges? Why or why not?

CHAPTER 3

Commercial Air Carriers[2]

1. Outline the various periods in the development of the airlines of this country, showing the significant developments in each.
2. What were the chief problems faced by the airlines directly after the close of World War II?
3. What difficulties did the airlines encounter in the 1947–49 period which interrupted the steady growth previously apparent?
4. Outline the developments in the mail pay system which either helped or hindered the airlines and their growth in the postwar period.
5. Into what classifications does the Civil Aeronautics Board divide certificated air carriers? Define each and give an example.
6. What was the effect of the "grandfather" clause of the Civil Aeronautics Act of 1938 upon the early development of our airline route pattern?
7. How does airline route competition come about?
8. What are the two broad types of airline service recognized by the Civil Aeronautics Board?
9. What is the Air Transport Association of America? Go through the last four issues of *Airlift* or *Aviation Week* and report briefly on any items concerned with recent activities of this group.

CHAPTER 4

Regulatory Legislation

1. Review some of the early arguments advanced for the control of aviation by the federal government rather than by the various states.
2. What were the chief provisions of the Air Commerce Act of 1926?
3. Why do you think it became necessary to adopt the Civil Aeronautics Act of 1938, and why did Congress lean so heavily upon already existing legislation dealing with ground carriers in formulating this act?

[2] A copy of *American Aviation Official Airline Guide* is useful with this chapter.

4. In what way did the Civil Aeronautics Act substitute one federal statute and agency for those which had previously been regulating the industry?
5. In what ways did Plans 3 and 4 for the reorganization of the federal government affect the Civil Aeronautics Board and Civil Aeronautics Administration?
6. Quote the "statement of policy" set forth in the Civil Aeronautics Act.
7. What economic regulation of air carriers was provided for in the Civil Aeronautics Act?
8. What tests has the Board developed in arriving at an answer as to which of two carriers is most "fit, willing and able"?
9. What three primary factors are usually weighed by the Board in any given situation in arriving at a decision as to operation of competing services?
10. What factors must the Board take into consideration in regulating air carrier rates?
11. Differentiate between "air carrier operating certificates" and "certificates of convenience and necessity."
12. What was the chief purpose of the Federal Aviation Act of 1958 and how, if at all, did it change the economic regulatory powers of the Civil Aeronautics Board?
13. What are the major activities of the Civil Aeronautics Board?
14. Since the Civil Aeronautics Act and the Federal Aviation Act (Title IV) apply to interstate carriers only, what is the temptation for states to undertake economic regulation? Should this be permitted? Why or why not?
15. What are the reasons for the strong national interest of the United States in air space?
16. What is the definition of "navigable air space" in the Civil Aeronautics Act, and what confusions have arisen in the public mind because of this definition?
17. Discuss the noise problem at airports and the importance of proper zoning around airports as a matter of "air space" rights.

CHAPTER 5

Economics of Commercial Air Transportation

1. What are the characteristics possessed in common by the commercial air carriers which influence economic adjustments in the industry?
2. What characteristics of the airlines differentiate them from what we ordinarily understand to be "public utilities"?
3. What is the chief revenue source for the airlines? Do you believe this will continue to be so? Give reasons for your answer.
4. What is included in the expense classification of "General Services and Administration"?

5. Why has the analysis of airline expenses always been a difficult problem?
6. Why will two airlines have the same characteristics as to size, volume of traffic, and operations, but having a different number of stations, experience different cost levels?
7. Explain the relation of airline expenses to the volume of traffic.
8. Distinguish between "common" and "separable" costs in the airline business.
9. Is the principle of making rates "that will move the traffic" as applicable to air carriers as it is to railroads? Explain fully.
10. Why is it that, at least over a substantial range of traffic, total airline cost does not increase as rapidly as traffic; and thus average cost per unit of business handled falls?
11. What is the place of the "value of service" concept in airline rate making?
12. Do you agree that, if a service cannot cover its out-of-pocket costs regardless of the rate set, it should be abandoned, unless continued operation is essential to the general welfare? Explain.

CHAPTER 6

Civil Aeronautics Board Policy—Competition

1. What factors give rise to competition in air transportation?
2. What have been the fundamental considerations used by the Civil Aeronautics Board in disposing of new route applications?
3. How has the Board itself increased competition in air transportation through its various actions?
4. Digest the following Civil Aeronautics Board cases (provided the necessary volumes of the Board's Economic Decisions are available in your library): 2 CAB 16 (1940), 6 CAB 319 (1945).
5. What is the total amount of traffic that should determine whether competition is in the public interest? Has the Board followed this principle? Cite any pertinent cases as shown in the footnotes of the text.
6. Trace the development of Board policy on "entry into air transportation," citing any pertinent cases as shown in the footnotes in the text.
7. Give several examples of cases where the Board has taken an attitude more liberal than its prewar attitude toward the entry of new companies into air transportation.
8. Why has the Board hesitated to certificate a feeder route, as such, to a trunkline carrier?
9. What is your opinion of the Board's policy as to entry of new carriers into air transportation?
10. Trace the development of the Board's policy on entry of surface carriers into air transportation, citing any pertinent cases shown in the footnotes of the text.

11. What reasons may be stated for permitting the certification of freight forwarders? Why was this opposed by the scheduled airlines?
12. Why may it be said that "the air freight rate and the question of certifying forwarders is now inextricably mingled"?
13. Go over the last four issues of *Airlift, Aviation Week,* or *Traffic World,* and write a brief report on any cases now under consideration or recently before the Board involving certificates of convenience and necessity.

CHAPTER 7

Civil Aeronautics Board Policy—Competition (*Continued*)

1. What is meant by the "balanced competition theory of the Board"?
2. Digest the following Civil Aeronautics Board cases (provided the necessary volumes of the Board's Economic Decisions are available in your library): 2 CAB 16 (1940), 4 CAB 373 (1943), 4 CAB 254 (1943).
3. What would you say were the chief obstacles which have prevented more effective action by the Board in the supervision of the over-all route pattern?
4. What is the "place" of the local-service airline?
5. What reasons can you give for the further certification of local-service airlines?
6. What reasons can you give against the further certification of local-service airlines and possibly for the abandonment of some already certificated?
7. What are the cost handicaps under which local air service must operate?
8. How have the certificated local airlines attempted to improve the situation brought about by their high-cost operations?
9. Explain the "use-it-or-lose-it" policy of the Civil Aeronautics Board applicable to local-service airlines.
10. How did the desirability of nonstop operations and route consolidations arise?
11. What are the advantages of interchange of equipment and the objections that have been raised thereto?
12. Trace the development of Board policy as to "supplemental air carriers," citing any pertinent cases shown in the text.
13. Outline the ways in which supplemental carriers may be said to have been a "significant force in the competitive picture."
14. In what ways are the provisions of the Civil Aeronautics Act and Federal Aviation Act dealing with mergers and acquisitions of one air carrier by another more complex than those applying to the award of certificates of convenience and necessity?
15. How does the Civil Aeronautics Board define a monopoly? (Discuss 1 CAA 723 (1940) in this connection.)

16. Digest the following Civil Aeronautics Board cases (provided the necessary volumes of the Board's Economic Decisions are available in your library): 1 CAA 739 (1940), 7 CAB 365 (1946), 6 CAB 217 (1940).
17. Check through the last few issues of *Airlift, Aviation Week,* and *Traffic World,* and report on any merger cases now pending or recently passed upon by the Board.
18. Outline what may be said to be the Board's minimum criteria in connection with mergers or consolidations.

CHAPTER 8

Civil Aeronautics Board Policy—Mail Rates

1. What is the "fourfold significance" of mail rates in connection with the national policy for the development of adequate air service?
2. What is your understanding of the term "subsidy" in connection with mail rates? If this departs from the discussion in the text, give reasons. (You need not necessarily agree with the author.)
3. Trace the development of air mail rates prior to and after the passage of the Civil Aeronautics Act in 1938.
4. What is the difference between the Board's classification of mail rates as "service" and "need"?
5. What is the importance of the provision in the Civil Aeronautics Act that the Board must consider "economy and efficiency" of management in setting mail rates?
6. What are at least two basic defects in the system of air mail and subsidy payment as it has developed?
7. Why is it important that carriers be placed on "final" mail rates as soon as possible?
8. Trace the development of the "service mail rate" principle.
9. How does the fact that the government is the only purchaser of mail service complicate the making of mail rates?
10. Trace the development of the campaign to separate mail pay from subsidy.
11. Define a "service rate" and describe the steps through which the Board "administratively" determines such rates.
12. Why is it likely that the level of subsidy support for international operations of United States air carriers will tend to increase over the next few years?
13. What was the purpose of the "experimental rates" instituted by the Post Office Department in 1953? What is their basis for payment?
14. What appears to be the current mail rate problem as it reflects the differing points of view of the Post Office Department and the Civil Aeronautics Board?

15. Go through the past four issues of *Airlift*, *Traffic World*, and *Aviation Week* and be prepared to report on any mail rate developments reported therein.

CHAPTER 9

Civil Aeronautics Board Policy—Freight Rates and Passenger Fares

1. Trace the history of air freight rates to date. Have we had a "rate war"? What evidence can you produce on either side?
2. What has been the Board's policy on setting minimum freight rates, and how do you feel about this method of controlling the rate situation?
3. Discuss the airline backhaul problem and show how directional rates can be used to overcome it at least in part.
4. Define accumulation, assembly, and distribution as set forth in airline tariffs. What is the purpose of such rules?
5. What is deferred air freight, and why did the airlines wish to inaugurate and maintain such a service?
6. What arguments may be advanced against any system of deferred air freight?
7. What is the main object of the consolidated air freight tariff?
8. What has been the attitude of the Board toward passenger fares?
9. Discuss the various experimental fares introduced by the airlines in 1948 and 1949 and indicate the success of each.
10. What were the main purposes of the 1956 General Fare Investigation?
11. Check through the last four issues of *American Aviation, Aviation Week*, and *Traffic World* and report on any items concerning airline passenger fares. (Do the same for air freight rates.)
12. Summarize the general rate policy which might seem to apply to airlines in the next few years.

CHAPTER 10

International Air Transportation Policy

1. What was the international air transportation policy of the United States prior to World War II?
2. Outline the part played by Pan American Airways in international air transportation prior to World War II.
3. Digest the following Civil Aeronautics Board cases (provided the necessary volumes of the Board's Economic Decisions are available in your library): 6 CAB 319 (1945), 6 CAB 857 (1946), 7 CAB 83 (1946), 7 CAB 209 (1946), 7 CAB 285 (1946).
4. Trace the development of Board policy for the development of competition on international routes.

5. What might be said to have been the pre–World War II policy of European countries for the development of international air transportation?
6. What objectives for United States international air policy seemed to emerge from our activities during World War II?
7. What are the chief international conventions under which air transport between the countries of the world is carried on?
8. What led the United States to take the lead in 1944 and to call the International Conference on Civil Aviation held in Chicago the latter part of that year?
9. Outline the proposals introduced by various nations at the Chicago conference. What were the results of this conference?
10. Define the "five freedoms."
11. The policy of the United States has been to obtain air rights by bilateral agreements. What criticisms have been levied at this method? Are they valid in your opinion, and what might be a better method?
12. What pattern of important steps for negotiating bilateral agreements was set by the Bermuda Air Agreement?
13. Show how the capacity clauses in the Bermuda-type agreements establish a relationship between the capacity provided by a carrier and the traffic requirements of the routes served by that carrier.
14. State at least three policies which might well govern the United States in exchanging air transport rights.
15. Distinguish between operations of foreign aircraft authorized by the Civil Aeronautics Act of 1938 and operations authorized by the Air Commerce Act of 1926.
16. What are some of the complaints that have arisen in connection with the Board's issuance of permits to operate foreign-flag airlines into the United States? Do you feel that these are valid? Explain.
17. Does the term "public interest" in connection with international air transport have the same connotation as it has in connection with domestic carriers by air? Discuss.
18. What is the power of the President of the United States over international air routes and air carriers in international service? Why did Congress give him this power?
19. What were the recommendations of the Air Coordinating Committee in its 1954 report as to international air routes and rights?
20. How can we group the needs for technical requirements for physical equipment and rules governing the operation of world airways? Give an illustration of each, and indicate how it has been handled to the advantage or disadvantage of the United States.
21. What is a possible definition of a "scheduled international air service"?
22. What authority does the Board have to fix international rates? Should this power be changed? Give reasons for or against.
23. What is ICAO? What is IATA?

24. Check the last four issues of *Airlift, Aviation Week,* and *Traffic World* and prepare a digest of any articles or news items dealing with international air transportation.

CHAPTER 11

Safety in Air Transportation

1. What may be said to be the chief factors on which safety in air transportation depends?
2. Why is it so difficult to relate the accident rate in air carrier operation to accident rates in other fields of transport?
3. What federal agencies are concerned with the promotion of safety in civil aviation?
4. Distinguish clearly between the functions of the Civil Aeronautics Board and those of the Federal Aviation Agency in connection with air safety.
5. Outline the usual steps taken in accident investigations.
6. List the chief causes of airline accidents.
7. The statement has been made that "regulations as such cannot bring about conformance to safe operating procedures and standards." Discuss what is meant here.
8. Outline the national policy on aviation safety as stated by the Air Coordinating Committee in its 1954 report.
9. Check through the last four issues of *Airlift* and *Aviation Week* and digest any articles or items dealing with safety in air transportation.
10. What is the liability of a common carrier airline for injury to persons or property in its custody? For injury to persons on the ground?
11. How do airlines protect themselves against the liabilities mentioned in question 10?
12. Explain the "group plan of underwriting."
13. What two interdependent assumptions compose the "economic-safety" equation? Explain their relationship.

CHAPTER 12

Financing Airlines

1. Review the history of airline financing, and point out why the earlier method was necessary and why there has been a trend lately to another policy.
2. How may equipment purchases be financed? What problems arise in the minds of lenders in connection with equipment loans?
3. In financing the transition to jet aircraft, what has been the typical pattern followed by the airlines?
4. Why are chattel mortgages more suitable for airline equipment financing than they are for railroads?

5. In what ways has progress recently been made toward facilitating a wider use of equipment trusts as instruments of airline financing, particularly in the international field?
6. What are the arguments pro and con for the control of airline securities by the Civil Aeronautics Board?
7. In financing airlines, what is meant by "fair rate of return"?
8. Explain why "cost of capital" is an important factor in the formation of any opinion as to a fair rate of return.
9. What are the advantages and objections voiced as to the use of total capitalization to represent the amount of money which investors have committed to an airline enterprise? Why is this a particularly good rate base for the airlines?
10. Why has the Civil Aeronautics Board opposed the use of the operating ratio as a basis of fair and reasonable earnings?
11. What forms have public aid to air transportation taken in the various countries? (Discuss this from an historical standpoint.)
12. Under what circumstances may public aid to air transportation be said to be justified?
13. What forms has public aid to air transportation taken in the United States?
14. Outline what may now be considered to be the national policy on airline subsidies.

CHAPTER 13

Airline Organization

1. What are the major management functions of any airline?
2. Discuss each of the principles of organization as they apply to airlines.
3. What inherent characteristics of the airline industry (together with conditions under which the industry must operate) must be considered in formulating an organization plan for any company?
4. Outline the main activities of each of the chief departments found in most airline organizations.
5. Trace through the last four issues of *Airlift* and *Aviation Week* and digest any articles you notice on the subject of airline organization, changes in existing organizations, and the like.

CHAPTER 14

Airline Passenger Traffic Development

1. Why were sales problems neglected by airline management in the earlier days? Is the same true today?
2. How may one measure the development of airline passenger traffic?
3. What factors have played a part in airline passenger growth?

4. Are the same factors of equal importance today?
5. Give a brief review of the historical development of air passenger fares.
6. To what extent have the airlines penetrated the travel market? Do you think this will continue to increase or will it be likely to remain at the present point or even decrease? Give reasons for your reply.
7. Into what broad groups may prospects for air travel be divided? Where do you personally fall in this grouping?
8. Classify prospects for air travel in the order of their importance and accessibility, in combination with the volume of business to be expected from each group.
9. What have been the sales resistances to be overcome in getting people to travel by air? Do you feel that any of these still continue to be strong? Discuss.
10. What were the advantages to the airlines from the adoption of the Air Travel Card method of selling air transportation? What were the advantages to the subscribers?
11. Outline the methods adopted by the airlines to increase air travel since the close of World War II.
12. Check over the last four issues of *Airlift, Aviation Week,* and *Traffic World.* Pick out any reports of effective sales efforts by airlines or airline personnel, and be ready to report on these to the class.
13. Define the term "air coach" and discuss the growth of this service.
14. What channels of publicity for airlines are used in your vicinity?
15. Classify the airline "public."
16. What forms may public relations work take?
17. Discuss the use of various media for airline public relations work.
18. Cite an example of good airline public relations and one of bad, if you have observed any such.
19. Check through the last four issues of *Airlift* or *Aviation Week,* and digest any articles or items on public relations activities of the airlines.

CHAPTER 15

Airline Passenger Handling

1. Discuss the importance of a good reservation system to an airline.
2. Report on any personal experiences you may have had reflecting good or bad reservation practices.
3. What are the principal methods of handling reservations?
4. Check over the past four issues of *Airlift* and *Aviation Week,* and report on any articles or items concerning airline reservation systems.
5. What is "overbooking" and how does it occur? Is there any justification for this practice?
6. What factors complicate airline scheduling?

7. What arguments do the airlines present against the Civil Aeronautics Board assuming scheduling responsibility? Are these arguments valid?
8. Discuss the importance of on-time performance and why the Civil Aeronautics Board has taken steps to protect users in this regard.
9. Define "reconfirmation" and discuss the benefits the airlines believe came out of the system.
10. Why are "flight advisory" reports important passenger-handling tools?
11. What is meant by "routine," "subject," and "cancel" in connection with flight advisories?
12. Define the following terms in connection with ticketing passengers: circle trip, open jaw, joint issue.
13. What factors usually govern the selection of one route over another by an individual passenger?
14. What is the airline policy as to ticket refunds?
15. Cite any personal experience showing good or poor passenger-handling technique by an airline.
16. Check over the past four issues of *Airlift* and *Aviation Week* and digest any items concerning airline passenger-handling technique.

CHAPTER 16

Air Express and Freight Development

1. Trace the early history of air express development.
2. What was "General Air Express," and what were the reasons for its abandonment?
3. Under what sort of an arrangement does the Railway Express Agency handle air express with the airlines?
4. Why was air express so slow in developing as a major part of airline activity?
5. Trace the development of air express after it became a unified system under the Railway Express Agency.
6. What was the effect of World War II on air freight development?
7. Which was the first airline to publish rates for "air freight"?
8. Trace the postwar developments in air freight transportation.
9. What were the Civil Aeronautics Board's expectations as to strictly all-cargo air carriers? Were they achieved during the first few years of operation of such carriers? Give reasons for your answer.
10. What has been the general development of all-cargo carriers since certification on temporary bases and does it merit permanent certification? Why or why not?
11. From what causes do the difficulties of the all-cargo carriers stem?
12. What is your opinion as to the air freight potential in this country? How do you measure it?

13. Why should consideration be given to development of air freight service on an area basis?
14. What are the chief advantages to shippers from the use of air freight transportation?
15. What factors must be considered in any plans for future air freight development?
16. Check through the last four issues of *Airlift, Aviation Week,* and *Traffic World* and digest any articles or items you may see concerning air freight development.
17. What three chief factors will probably be considered in placing commodities into classes for air freight rate making? Discuss each briefly.
18. What sort of new sales approach might be suggested for developing air freight?

CHAPTER 17

Air Freight Handling

1. What factors complicate the handling of air freight compared with the handling of air passengers?
2. What changes have taken place in the "pattern of air cargo" in recent years? Do you believe this trend is likely to continue? Give reasons for your answer.
3. Why has the growth of all-cargo operations in recent years forced the carriers to pay attention to what is known as "the density problem"?
4. What principles should be observed in packing for air freight shipment?
5. What factors govern consideration of "security" for air freight?
6. Trace the development of the system by which the airlines have handled the pickup and delivery problem.
7. State the functions of Air Cargo, Inc., as it operates today.
8. What types of truck operators are involved with Air Cargo, Inc., in coordinating air and ground transportation?
9. Why is airport handling of air cargo still on a more or less makeshift basis? Can you make any suggestions for improvement?
10. Trace through the last four issues of *Airlift* and *Aviation Week,* and digest any articles you notice on the subject of air cargo handling.
11. Under what circumstances do airlines consider themselves not liable for loss and/or damage to cargo?
12. How may a shipper protect himself fully against loss and/or damage to air cargo? Discuss any possible advantages from not relying wholly on carrier liability.
13. Why does airport handling of air freight continue to be a more or less makeshift affair?
14. Outline the various methods of handling air freight on airports.
15. Differentiate between "scheduled" and "demand" service for air cargo.

16. In what ways may discrimination arise under a system of "demand" air cargo service?
17. Why was the year 1948 a good time for air freight forwarding to start?
18. What appears to be the future for the air freight forwarders?
19. Discuss the problem presented to freight forwarders by the so-called "straight" shipment.
20. What is the place of the shippers' association in handling air freight?
21. How extensive is the right of air carriers to employ ground transportation in the course of providing air transportation?

CHAPTER 18

General Aviation

1. How may the term "general aviation" be defined?
2. What four types of flying are generally referred to as "general aviation activities"?
3. Do you know of any industry, personally, that makes use of aircraft in connection with its activities and which might be included in any discussion of general aviation? If so, give a brief description of such activities.
4. What might be said to be the advantages for owning and operating your own aircraft for business flying?
5. What do you see as the future for pleasure flying? For business flying?

BIBLIOGRAPHICAL NOTE

THE bibliography of commercial air transportation is mostly found in trade papers serving the air transportation industry and in the papers read by those using the services of commercial air carriers. To attempt to present a complete bibliography would, therefore, be impossible in a volume of this size. The author has, however, attempted to present a bibliography of the most important sources of information in the footnotes throughout the book. By including rather full notes on sources, the author feels that he has given credit where credit is due and, at the same time, has directed the reader to further sources of information. Thus the reader may limit his research to those subjects in which he is most interested and may be spared the necessity of having to search through a bulky bibliography at the end of the volume, as is customary in many books. In other words, the footnotes throughout this volume present a fairly complete working bibliography of commercial air transportation.

The trade papers in the field of aviation all include material on its commercial aspects, but some of them stress this subject more than others. The best papers to read for current developments are *Airlift*, published semimonthly by American Aviation Publications, Inc., Washington, D.C.; *Aviation Week*, published weekly by the McGraw-Hill Publishing Co., New York; and *Air Transportation*, published monthly at 10 Bridge St., New York. *Flight*, published monthly in Dallas, Texas, specializes in coverage of the news and problems of the local-service airlines.

Publications in the nature of "working tools" of the commercial air transportation industry are:

Traffic News, published daily by American Aviation Publications, Washington, D.C., which digests, abstracts, analyzes, and indexes all Civil Aeronautics Board economic regulatory actions and filings.

American Aviation Daily, published daily by American Aviation Publications, Washington, D.C., which is the newspaper of the industry.

Official Airline Guide, published monthly by American Aviation Publications, Chicago, which contains all airline schedules, rates, regulations for passenger and cargo transportation by commercial operators.

American Aviation Directory, published every six months by American Aviation Publications, Washington, D.C. This is a complete reference guide to administrative and operating personnel of the airlines, aircraft, and engine manufacturers, accessory and equipment manufacturers, organizations, schools, and United States and foreign aviation groups and departments.

Traffic World, published weekly and covering all fields of transportation by Traffic Service Corp., Chicago.

The most scholarly publication, appearing quarterly, is the *Journal of Air*

Law and Commerce, published by The Transportation Center at Northwestern University, Chicago.

The Aeronautics Branch of the United States Department of Commerce started publishing the *Air Commerce Bulletin* on July 15, 1929; and this was continued by the Civil Aeronautics Authority until December 15, 1939, when it assumed the title of *Civil Aeronautics Journal.* This is, of course, the primary source of much statistical material as well as information on current developments.

The Civil Aeronautics Administration, the Civil Aeronautics Authority, and the Civil Aeronautics Board have issued many studies dealing with the commercial side of air transportation. (The Federal Aviation Agency, since 1958, has taken over the CAA publications.) Lists are obtainable from the respective agencies. From time to time, either the Senate or the House has appointed committees to study various aspects of the subject of air transportation in general and commercial activities in particular. Lists of such committee reports as have been published are available from the Superintendent of Documents, United States Printing Office, Washington, D.C.

The Economic Decisions of the Civil Aeronautics Board have been published as follows:

Vol. I, from August, 1938, to July, 1940
Vol. II, from July, 1940, to August, 1941
Vol. III, from August, 1941, to December, 1942
Vol. IV, from December, 1942, to June, 1944
Vol. VI, from July, 1944, to May, 1946
Vol. VII, from June, 1946, to March, 1947
Vol. VIII, from April, 1947, to December, 1947
Vol. IX, from January, 1948, to December, 1948
Vol. X, from January to November, 1949
Vol. XI, from December, 1949, to August, 1950
Vol. XII, from September, 1950, to April, 1951
Vol. XIV, from May, 1951, to December, 1951
Vol. XV, from January, 1952, to June, 1952
Vol. XVI, from July, 1952, to February, 1953
Vol. XVII, from March, 1953, to September, 1953
Vol. XVIII, from October, 1953, to July, 1954
Vol. XIX, from August, 1954, to January, 1955
Vol. XX, from February, 1955, to May, 1955
Vol. XXI, from June, 1955, to October, 1955
Vol. XXII, from November, 1955, to December, 1955
Vol. XXIII, from January, 1956, to August, 1956
Vol. XXIV, from September, 1956, to March, 1957

There have been various bibliographies of books and publications dealing with aeronautics issued during the last few years, all of which include the chief publications on commercial air transportation. One of the best of these is issued by the Library of Congress. Another is issued by the Institute of the Aeronautical Sciences.

INDEX

This book has been set on the Linotype in 12 and 10 point Bodoni Book, leaded 1 point. Chapter numbers and titles are 18 point Spartan Medium. The size of the type page is 27 by 46½ picas.